SPAIN

SPAIN

The Centre of the World 1519–1682

ROBERT GOODWIN

BLOOMSBURY PRESS

NEW YORK · LONDON · NEW DELHI · SYDNEY

Bloomsbury Press
An imprint of Bloomsbury Publishing Plc

1385 Broadway   50 Bedford Square
New York   London
NY 10018   WC1B 3DP
USA   UK

www.bloomsbury.com

First published in Great Britain 2015
First U.S. edition published 2015

© Robert Goodwin, 2015
Maps by John Gilkes

ISBN: HB: 978-1-62040-360-0
ePub: 978-1-62040-361-7

Library of Congress Cataloging-in-Publication Data has been applied for.

2 4 6 8 10 9 7 5 3 1

Typeset by Newgen Knowledge Works (P) Ltd., Chennai, India
Printed and bound in Great Britain by CPI Group (UK) Ltd, Croydon CR0 4YY

To find out more about our authors and books visit www.bloomsbury.com.
Here you will find extracts, author interviews, details of forthcoming events and
the option to sign up for our newsletters.

Bloomsbury books may be purchased for business or promotional use.
For information on bulk purchases please contact Macmillan Corporate and
Premium Sales Department at specialmarkets@macmillan.com.

For Clare

Happy age, and happy days were those, to which the ancients gave the name of golden; not that gold, which in these our iron-times is so much esteemed, was to be acquired without trouble in that fortunate period; but because people then were ignorant of those two words MINE and THINE: in that sacred age, all things were common . . . All was then peace, all was harmony, and all was friendship.

Don Quixote[1]

Contents

Habsburg Iberia

Bay of Biscay
Corunna
Santiago de Compostella
ASTURIAS
Santander
BASQUE PROVINCES
FRANCE
Bilbao
Fuenterrabía
Pyrenees
Atlantic Ocean
GALICIA
LEON
NAVARRE
ROUSILLON
Burgos
Logroño
Ebro
Saragossa
CATALONIA
Valladolid
Duero
Barcelona
Zamora
Tordesillas
Segovia
ARAGON
Salamanca
CASTILE
Guadalajara
Avila
El Escorial
Madrid
PORTUGAL
Tagus
Toledo
MAJORCA
LA MANCHA
Belmonte
VALENCIA
Lisbon
Badajoz
Guadiana
Valencia
Evora
Sierra Morena
Cordova
Guadalquivir
Alicante
ANDALUSIA
Écija
MURCIA
Seville
GRANADA
Granada
Sierra Nevada
Sanlúcar de Barrameda
Malaga
Mediterranean Sea
Cadiz
Gibraltar

0 50 100 150 200 kilometres
0 25 50 75 100 miles

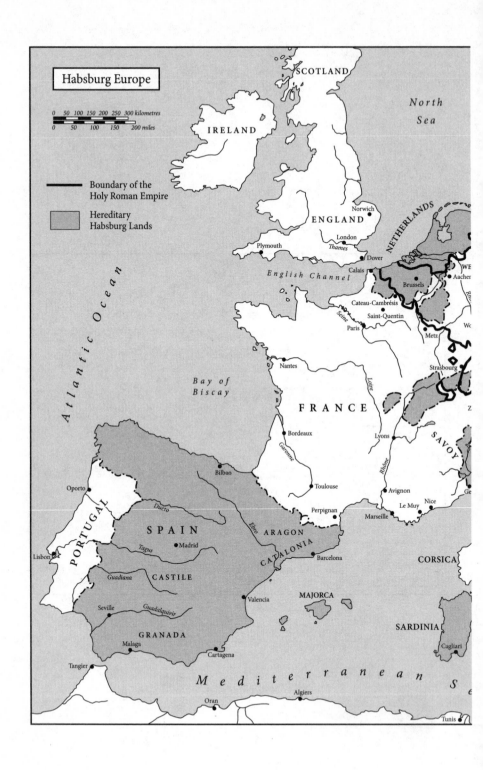

Habsburg Europe

Boundary of the
Holy Roman Empire

Hereditary
Habsburg Lands

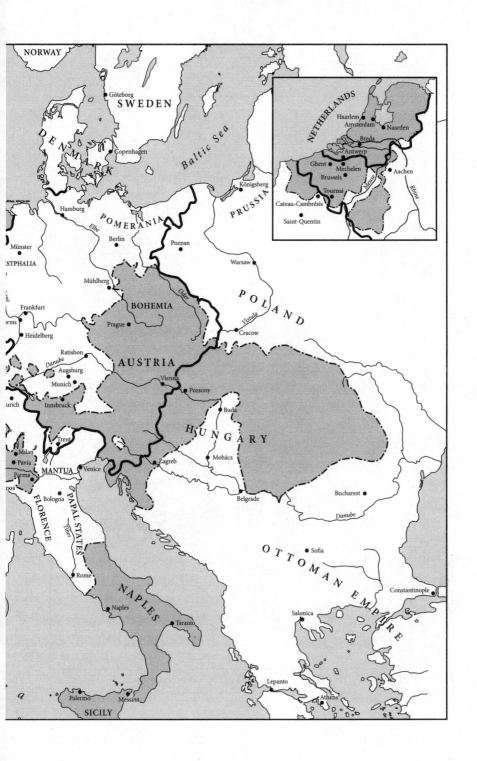

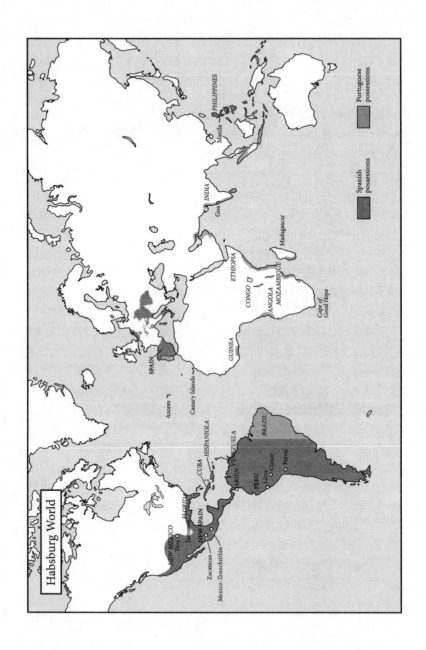

Habsburg World

Spanish possessions

Portuguese possessions

HABSBURG FAMILY TREE

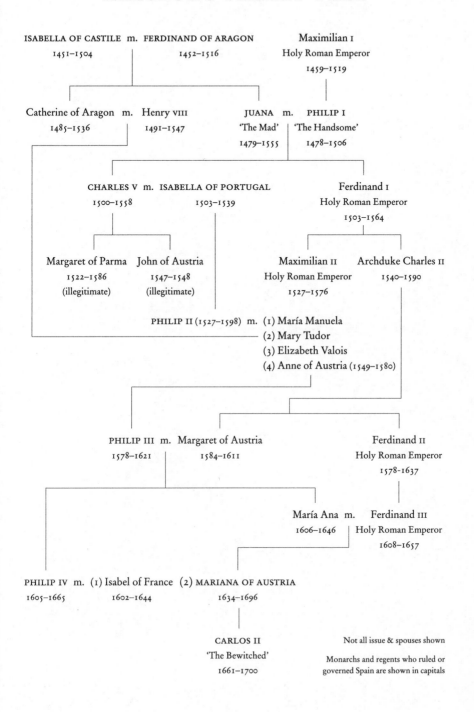

ISABELLA OF CASTILE m. FERDINAND OF ARAGON
1451–1504   1452–1516

Maximilian I
Holy Roman Emperor
1459–1519

Catherine of Aragon m. Henry VIII
1485–1536   1491–1547

JUANA m. PHILIP I
'The Mad'   'The Handsome'
1479–1555   1478–1506

CHARLES V m. ISABELLA OF PORTUGAL
1500–1558   1503–1539

Ferdinand I
Holy Roman Emperor
1503–1564

Margaret of Parma   John of Austria
1522–1586   1547–1548
(illegitimate)   (illegitimate)

Maximilian II   Archduke Charles II
Holy Roman Emperor   1540–1590
1527–1576

PHILIP II (1527–1598) m. (1) María Manuela
                           (2) Mary Tudor
                           (3) Elizabeth Valois
                           (4) Anne of Austria (1549–1580)

PHILIP III m. Margaret of Austria
1578–1621   1584–1611

Ferdinand II
Holy Roman Emperor
1578-1637

María Ana m. Ferdinand III
1606–1646   Holy Roman Emperor
               1608–1657

PHILIP IV m. (1) Isabel of France (2) MARIANA OF AUSTRIA
1605–1665   1602–1644   1634–1696

CARLOS II
'The Bewitched'
1661–1700

Not all issue & spouses shown

Monarchs and regents who ruled or
governed Spain are shown in capitals

Introduction

A t the beginning of the modern era, Spain became the centre of the western world by accident. In 1492, Columbus discovered the Americas while searching for a route to Asia across the Atlantic and claimed the New World for his Spanish sponsors. Then Charles of Ghent, born in 1500 to a Spanish mother and a Burgundian father, because of a series of marriage alliances and untimely deaths became heir to three of the most powerful royal and princely houses of Europe and a host of other lands and titles. As he grew to adulthood he inherited vast domains in the Netherlands, Burgundy, Italy, Austria and Hungary; and as the future head of the House of Habsburg he was brought up to believe in his moral right to rule the Holy Roman Empire, encompassing most of modern Germany and more. In 1517, at the age of seventeen, he left his native Flanders to claim the thrones of Castile and Aragon, the two great crowns of Spain, and with them the Kingdom of Naples and all of Spanish America. For the next century and a half, the Habsburg dynasty made Spain the economic and military centre of its world, the heart of the first global empire on earth.

In *Spain: The Centre of the World 1519–1682* I have tried to tell that epic history through the stories of two dozen emblematic Spaniards and their monarchs. Biographical anecdote, humour and moments of high drama, dudgeon and low bathos offer an intimate and familiar foreground from which to appreciate the enormity, both in time and space, of the history of Habsburg Spain. There are many 'magisterial' textbooks on the subject, as Spaniards say, but these necessarily contain almost overwhelming amounts of scholarly detail for the general reader, filled with names and dates and places and events, often

managing only occasional and fleeting moments of human contact.
So, while this piece of storytelling properly belongs alongside them,
it is not really of their ilk. This is a book for you, 'idle reader', as
the great Spanish novelist Miguel de Cervantes described you in his
introduction to his most important work, *Don Quixote*, addressing
the newly literate reading public of his age, purchasers and consumers
of the written and then printed word who forged the tradition which
you have inherited and will pass on.

In the early 700s, Muslim armies from North Africa conquered
and occupied almost all Spain. Only one chieftain held out against
the Islamic invader, Pelayo, leader of a small band of indomitable
Christians in the far north. For the next eight centuries, Iberian
history was dominated by the slow emergence of the kingdoms
of Portugal, Castile and Aragon, as the peninsula was slowly won
back by Christian crusaders and opportunist frontiersmen. By the
late fifteenth century, that Reconquista or Reconquest was almost
complete and, instead, civil war threatened to destroy Christian
Spain as the great aristocratic houses lined up their private armies
during a succession crisis in Castile. But the marriage of Ferdinand,
heir to the throne of Aragon, to Isabella, Queen of Castile, in 1476,
proved a powerful alliance, strong enough to force peace upon their
unruly subjects; and they sealed this new, fragile sense of unity by
announcing a final crusade against Granada, the last Islamic kingdom
on the Iberian Peninsula. The Spanish nobility and many foreign aristocrats from across Christendom answered that call to arms and in
January 1492 Isabella and Ferdinand, for ever to be known as the
Catholic Monarchs, marched victorious into Granada at the head of
their army; Boabdil, the last Muslim ruler in Spanish history, stopped
at a mountain pass and looked back for one final glimpse of his erstwhile paradise, and he wept; the place is still called the Moor's Sigh.
    In the euphoric aftermath of victory, the Catholic Monarchs
further embraced the current crusading spirit of religious intolerance by ordering the expulsion of all Spanish Jews. They also sent
Christopher Columbus to sail to China and India by an Atlantic
route; and his accidental discovery of the Americas enabled Spain
to become the centre of the world for almost two centuries. But,

following the death of Isabella in 1506, Ferdinand, as King of Aragon, had no right to rule in Castile; the crown should have passed to his daughter, Juana, the tragic figure always known in English as Joan the Mad, who was married to Philip the Handsome of Burgundy. Their eldest son was Charles of Ghent, their youngest was named Ferdinand after his grandfather. But when Philip died suddenly, soon after arriving in Spain to claim the throne, Ferdinand, the 'wily old Catalan', seized power, declaring Juana incapable of rule because of her insanity. The veteran monarch reigned until his death, in 1516, when the young Charles of Ghent, Lord of the Netherlands, Count Palatine of Burgundy, inherited the crowns of Castile, Aragon and Naples, and was proclaimed the King of Kings.

During the sixteenth century, the Spanish Habsburgs defended and expanded their vast Empire, which stretched from the distant east and south of Europe to Goa and the Philippines, to Chile and New Mexico. That imperial story forged the character of Spain and the Spaniards who were the heart and lifeblood of the enterprise. They went to the Americas as conquistadors and settlers, they campaigned across Europe as feared professional soldiers, they travelled as merchants and diplomats, poets and artists. Seville, the great inland southern port, became the centre of world trade, a place of foreign merchants, bankers and adventurers, all drawn to Spain by the contagious magnetism of possibility and the vast quantities of American gold and silver which poured into the kingdom. The Habsburgs and the Spaniards were, hand in hand, in the ascendant politically and militarily across half the world; at home, those fierce tensions between Crown and state, between aristocracy and urban oligarchs, between town and country, between Church, peasant and landlord, balanced one another in a dynamic equilibrium from which emerged great institutions such as universities, schools, the rule of law, banking and local government, and which fostered arts and letters, all underpinned by the severe moral authority of a newly militant Church. It was an era of great optimism and self-confidence.

Then, during the seventeenth century, Spaniards found themselves overstretched and damaged by foreign wars and ruled by decadent monarchs and their venial favourites. Slowly, the world Empire began to come apart. The Spanish Habsburgs lost control of their ancestral

lands across Europe, from Portugal to Catalonia and from Italy to the
Netherlands, and they lost important possessions overseas as well. The
Spanish Crown and its government also suffered and the Habsburgs
lost power and influence at home. Yet this period when the monarchs
and their state institutions went into sharp decline was also a time of
dazzling artistic and literary production in Spain and in many ways
Spaniards seem to have flourished in stark contrast to the decadence
of their government. The sickness of the Spanish state has, perhaps,
proved little more than a carapace which has long obscured historians'
views of the dynamic nation beneath.

The two centuries, from Columbus's discovery of America to the
death of the great playwright Pedro Calderón de la Barca have since
become known as the Spanish Golden Age, or the 'Century of Gold',
the *Siglo de Oro*. It is an aptly descriptive term that is nonetheless
confusing. First used in the mid-1700s about the poets of the sixteenth
century, it was then used in eulogy of the cultural apogee in literature
and theatre and finally art that was heralded by El Greco and then
epitomized by Cervantes and Velázquez and their contemporaries.
Yet the idea that this metaphorical Golden Age was founded on the
wealth of real gold and silver brought from the Americas gives the
terminology an irresistible allure.

Spain: The Centre of the World 1519–1682 is about the people at
the heart of that history, even as it follows this general narrative from
the rise of hard power and real wealth, as it were, to the emergence of
a soft power of cultural riches. Accordingly, the book is divided into
two parts that are different in character, reflecting the different eras
which they evoke. Part One, 'Gold', focuses on a series of key events
and individuals that together bring a strong sense of atmosphere to the
military, political and economic history, and which illustrate the rise of
key institutions during the sixteenth century. By contrast, Part Two,
'Glitter', emphasizes the most important literary and artistic figures of
the Golden Age and pays close attention to some of their most important work. Of course, there is poetry and art in Part One and plenty of
politics, economics and military history in Part Two, but, as you read,
be neither surprised nor disquieted to discover their differences, for
they are like that for good reason.

I
GOLD

Prologue

An infinite amount of gold on board, so much indeed that there was no other ballast than gold.

> Juan de Rojas y Sarmiento (astronomer and mathematician)

A lone carrack sailed into the harbour at Sanlúcar, the great Atlantic port of southern Spain. It was All Souls' Day, Halloween, of 1519. The little *Santa María* was the first ship ever to reach Europe from the newly settled shores of Mexico. Food and water were brought aboard. A handful of men went ashore. Word no doubt quickly spread through the town about the six Totonac Indian 'aristocrats' among the passengers. But there was even more excited speculation over rumours of 'an infinite amount of gold on board, so much indeed that there was no other ballast than gold'.[1] As the crew and passengers looked west across the shallow bay at the sun setting into the Atlantic like a celestial beacon of American dreams and New World nightmares, they must have experienced a turbulent mixture of exhilaration and trepidation at the reception they might receive. But they must have felt very much alive, bold but renegade adventurers come home to claim their prize.

As required by law, the ship proceeded up the olive-green River Guadalquivir that flows through the wild salt marshes, pine forests and fruit orchards of the fertile valley that was once known to medieval Arab poets as a 'paradise' on earth. On 5 November, the *Santa María* reached the provincial capital at Seville and drew up against the muddy riverbank. The port was dominated by the defensive towers and ramparts of the medieval fortifications built in the ninth century

by the Moors to repel Vikings. People came out of the cave-like wine
shops carved into the base of the great walls. Dock hands and casual
labourers crowded round. Women called out, selling wet fish or freshly
cooked foods. You can still buy fried seafood from takeaway shops in
the Arenal, the Sandy Place, as this quarter is known, and eat it in the
simple *bodegas* filled with wine casks and the mustiness of centuries,
and there is still a market here.

Royal officials representing the House of Trade, the Casa de
Contratación, which administered the Crown monopoly over
commerce with the New World, arrived at the Arenal in the flamboyant finery of their age, pushing their way through the throng. They
were welcomed aboard ship by Alonso Fernández Portocarrero and
Francisco de Montejo, soldiers of fortune who had helped to found
the first Spanish colony in Mexico under the leadership of Hernán
Cortés, that most cunning and ruthless of the conquistadors.

The royal officers must have been astonished when they gazed on
the cargo now shown them by Cortés's men. The inventory they made
there and then has survived the centuries in the archives of Seville.
It is over four folios long; each entry is brief and clear. This document describes one of the most important consignments of treasure in
history, a foretaste of the American riches that would soon subsidize
the immense cost of maintaining Spain at the epicentre of an explosive world empire. These are remarkable pages to hold in your hands
with their arabesque script, a henna-tinted *devoré* of curlicues that,
over the centuries, the alkali ink has burned into the heavy parchment-
coloured paper.[2]

The royal officers recorded 'a large gold disc with a design of a
beast in its centre surrounded by foliage motifs, which weighed 3,800
pesos de oro' and 'a large silver disc, which weighed forty-eight silver
marks'.[3] The matter-of-fact tone of the inventory only emphasizes the
marvellous objects it lists, such as 'two necklaces of gold and precious
stones, one of which has eight woven threads set with 232 red gems
and 173 green stones, with 26 gold bells hanging from the border,
in the middle of which there are four large carved gemstone figures
encrusted with gold'. Those 500-year-old words leave no doubt as to

the incredible wealth and sophistication of the Mexican world with which Cortés and his men had just made contact.

Gonzalo Fernández de Oviedo y Valdés, soon to be appointed Historian Royal of the Indies, saw the consignment at the House of Trade while on his way back to Panama. 'There was too much to take in,' he wondered, even as he praised the 'most handsome and skilfully fashioned feather-headdresses'. But Oviedo was most impressed by the 'two great discs, one of silver and one of gold, worked in half-relief', 'each nine and a half palms across and thirty palms in circumference', with which the Indians 'revered the sun and celebrated the moon'.[4] Every surviving contemporary commentary we have on this Mexican treasure begins by remarking on these two massive objects, both as tall as a sixteenth-century man and made of the most precious metals in the world. But all are equally eloquent about the brilliant craftsmanship of the many pieces of gold jewellery, the exquisite feather-work and the beauty of the weaves, the dyes and the embroidery of the almost innumerable trunk-loads of linens.

This extraordinary treasure had been sent by Cortés and his men as a present to the newly crowned King of Spain, Charles of Ghent. It must be the richest bribe ever paid to a European sovereign. The bribe was a matter of life and death for the Spanish colonists of Mexico. The Governor of Cuba had expressly forbidden Cortés to attempt to settle the mainland; but by a clever recourse to medieval Spanish legal precedent dating back to the period of the Reconquest of Spain from the Moors he attempted to formalize his independence by founding a town on the Mexican coast which he asserted should properly claim directly under the Crown, thereby circumventing the Governor's authority.[5] At the margins of the wild western Empire, possession may have been nine-tenths of the law, but at the heart of the metropolis there was no telling how the government might react: in defying the Governor of Cuba Cortés and his men had defied the authority of the Spanish Crown, so they now stood accused of treason. How would the young, untested King and his advisers respond?

The treasure was immediately impounded by the Crown officials, but for the moment that was all. Portocarrero and Montejo spent

December and January working closely with Cortés's father, Martín Cortés, arranging contracts with the leading merchants of Seville for the urgent supply of their fledgling colony despite its still uncertain legality. But the first reports of the dazzling riches that had been landed at Seville amazed Charles and his court; the tantalized King was eager to see his present for himself. So, as soon as their essential business in Seville was concluded, Cortés's envoys determined to plead their cause in person, and the three men set out for Barcelona where Charles was holding a session of the Catalan Parliament.

But as they travelled the length of Spain, they quickly saw for themselves that the kingdom was racked by plague and serious political unrest. In the towns and villages of Old Castile, the Spanish heartland, there was widespread and open dissent against the King. Charles had usurped his own mother's crown: Juana the Mad, 'la Loca', had long shown signs of disturbing eccentricity, but Charles now endorsed the diagnosis that she was insane and incapable of rule; and he ensured that she remain under house-arrest at the small town of Tordesillas, in Old Castile.

Charles had grown up in Flanders in the Low Countries of northern Europe, he spoke no Spanish, he had given the most powerful and lucrative positions to his foreign advisers; those who had seen him reported an 'ugly, sallow youth with a protruding jaw that made his mouth hang permanently open'; he was very slow of speech, even in his native French; he could not eat without drooling. To many he seemed to embody the very idiocy which he had used to discredit his own mother.[6] The Spaniards would have much preferred to have as their ruler Charles's younger brother Ferdinand, who had grown up in Spain and spoke Spanish.

THE AGE OF CHIVALRY:
CHARLES V

Realms of Gold

The King, our lord, is more of a king than any other because he has more numerous and larger kingdoms . . . he alone on this earth is King of Kings.

Pedro Ruiz de la Mota, Bishop of Badajoz

In February 1519, eight months before Cortés's men landed with their fabulous Mexican treasure, news had reached King Charles in Barcelona of the death of his grandfather, the Holy Roman Emperor, leader of a vast confederation of states and principalities in northern and central Europe from Holland in the north to parts of France in the west, parts of modern Italy in the south, most of modern Germany and parts of Austria and Hungary to the east. But the Holy Roman Empire was an uneasy alliance of provincial rulers under the centralizing stewardship of an emperor who was himself chosen by seven Electors: three bishops and three princes of the Empire and the King of Bohemia. It was a venerable confection imbued with an almost novelistic sense of chivalric medievalism and the soul of the Empire was embodied in the heavily mythologized figure of Charlemagne, crowned King of the Romans by Pope Leo III on Christmas Day, AD 800, as a reward for protecting the Papacy and crusading against Muslim Spain. That sense of history defined the spiritual mandate of the Emperor, and it would define Charles's relationship with the world.

For all that it was conferred by election, the most august title in Christendom had come to be seen by the Habsburgs as theirs by right and as the new head of the dynasty Charles asserted that sense of entitlement. But he still had to put himself up for election and a powerful rival, Francis I, King of France, stepped forward to challenge him. Defeat would be humiliating for either monarch, but especially for Charles. His agents set about canvassing and buying the support of the Electors.

On 28 June, as Cortés was first marvelling at the great discs of gold and silver on the edge of Charles's western Empire, in the historic Habsburg heartland, at Aachen, Aix-la-Chapelle in French, the Electors agreed unanimously to choose Charles as their new ruler, the Emperor Charles V. A trusted minister exclaimed: 'Sire, God has raised you above all Christian kings and princes and made you the greatest emperor and king since Charlemagne. He has set you on the path towards bringing back the whole world under a single shepherd.'[1] Those words perfectly embodied the moralizing universalism and urgent desire for religious hegemony that would bring uneasy friendship to the diverse Habsburg realms, but that was feared and resented across all the rest of Christendom. Until the Peace of Westphalia in 1648, the Habsburg lands engaged with their neighbours in a constantly fluctuating but never-ending round of conflict and diplomacy. Europe was on a permanent war footing.

News of Charles's success reached Spain only weeks before the gold and silver discs; but the election victory had come at a high price in bribes paid to the Electors: the great German banker, Jacob von Fugger, could boast that he had bought the election by personally lending Charles 543,000 of the 850,000 florins (or 360,000 ducats) that the Electors had accepted in payment for their support.[2] Cortés's treasure had arrived at a timely moment and, in 1519, a crucial relationship was established between the dazzling tangibility of American wealth and the cost to Spain of maintaining the Habsburg possessions in Europe.

Throughout 1519, as Charles negotiated for the imperial crown and grappled with Spanish hostility at home, he was repeatedly confronted with the moral imperatives of his fast-expanding and incomprehensibly distant American colonies. Two great figures in early New

World history spent the year in Barcelona complaining about the evils of conquest and lobbying loudly for support to put into practice their own personal but remarkably similar programmes of colonial settlement: Gonzalo Fernández de Oviedo y Valdés and Bartolomé de las Casas.

Oviedo is one of the most important and yet largely forgotten figures of early American history. In 1519, he was a Crown official from Panama, but in due course he would be appointed Historian Royal by Charles V, commissioned to write his massive *General History of the Indies*, the first serious history of the Americas; replete with Oviedo's own minute observation of geography, climate, agriculture and indigenous culture alongside accounts of Spanish expeditions and descriptions of the colonies, it offers a fascinating picture of the New World and even contains the earliest known drawing of a pineapple. He crossed the Atlantic seventeen times and was the author of the first novel ever written in America, an almost unreadable chivalric romance called *Claribalte*.[3] Once so influential, he and his writings have faded from our historical consciousness.

Today, the more famous of these two bitter antagonists is the firebrand Dominican friar Bartolomé de las Casas, the 'Defender of the Indians', author of the *Brief Account of the Destruction of the Indies*, a spine-wrenching diatribe filled with wildly exaggerated reports of the ghastly atrocities committed by Spanish conquistadors which he wrote in about 1542 and was first published in 1551. The unrivalled political lobbyist of his age, Las Casas was an ardent polemicist whose blood had curdled with outrage at the violence of imperialism and he had come to Spain to preach, cajole, berate and debate with Charles and his ministers, employing the relentless belligerence that characterized his every waking hour until his death in 1566.

Las Casas had been one of the earliest colonists of Santo Domingo, founded by Columbus on the island of Hispaniola, and had established an *encomienda*, a form of quasi-feudal estate of indentured Indians who paid tribute. But during Advent, 1511, he was among a crowd of colonists who listened to a famous but deeply polemical sermon preached by a Dominican friar called Antonio de

Montesinos, which denounced the *encomienda* as slavery and the Spanish settlers as savages.[4]

'I am the voice of Christ in this desert,' Montesinos had bellowed at his congregation of rugged frontiersmen, and 'this voice tells you that you now live and will die in a state of mortal sin. By what law do you hold these [Indians] in such horrible and inhuman slavery? By what authority have you waged such detestable war against people who lived peacefully and quietly? Why do you murder them in order to acquire ever more gold? Be sure,' he concluded, 'like the Moors and Turks who are without the faith of Jesus Christ, you can never save your souls!'

In a deeply faithful age, there was uproar among the colonists; but the moral message settled slowly and implacably into Las Casas's conscience. Over the following years, he decided to renounce his own *encomiendas* and sought out the spiritual wisdom of the Dominican order. He became determined to bring Christianity to America by peacefully proselytizing the Indians.

And in 1519 Las Casas brought two simple messages to Charles and his ministers: that current colonial practice in the Americas was deeply immoral and that he could offer a Christian alternative. Charles invited him to formally debate the appropriate treatment of the Indians with the recently arrived Bishop of Darien, in modern Panama, Juan de Quevedo, who was also a mortal enemy of Oviedo. Las Casas spoke at length, about the horrors of colonialism, about the 'unjust and cruel wars waged against Indians who were no danger to anyone', and about how the Spaniards had 'murdered the natural lords and leading persons', and 'enslaved their peoples by the score and by the gross', all in the service of Mammon, for 'they have been forced into the mines where in the end they all die because of the incredible toil involved in extracting the gold'. But the roots of the problem were the *encomiendas*, 'the greatest and most unjustifiable of all possible evils', worse even than the bondage imposed on the Israelites by Pharaoh.

And his argument hinged on Charles's direct moral responsibility to his subjects, 'for in over a thousand years God has not placed such an important business in the hands of any prince'. It was his sovereign duty to protect both his Indians and the souls of the Spaniards. And so, crucially, Las Casas then offered an olive branch: 'those people, mighty lord, who fill the whole of that New World with life are highly capable of accepting Christianity and virtuous ways and a reasoned understanding of doctrine'.[5] He was suggesting an alternative model of colonization that would set the Indians at liberty under the gentle tutelage of a salaried governor who would organize them into towns. He proposed creating an order of 'simple Spanish labourers who would be made knights and given habits with crosses, not unlike those of the Order of Calatrava', one of the great medieval crusading orders of knights that had emerged during the Reconquest of Spain from the Moors.[6] By their example, the Indians would soon learn that Castilian ways were fruitful and would therefore come to love the Spaniards who had taught them. Within that safe environment, the Indians would flourish and could be instructed in the True Faith; they would become farmers and might do a little service in the gold mines, paying the royal fifth, or *quinto real*, the standard tax of 20 per cent levied by the Crown since 1504 on all precious metals acquired in the Indies.

Charles and his advisers then asked Fernández de Oviedo to assess that proposal; but according to Las Casas Oviedo was a stooge appointed only to discredit him: 'a well-spoken orator [who] knew how to charm anyone; but, utterly blind to the truth, he was the greatest enemy that the Indians have ever had, perhaps because of his own great greed and ambition, the very qualities and characteristics that have destroyed these Indians'.[7]

The reality is more nuanced. Oviedo grew up an orphan, serving as a page in the household of the Crown Prince Juan, whose untimely death at nineteen made his sister Juana the Mad heir to the throne, making way for the eventual succession of her son Charles of Ghent. Oviedo then took up the life of a journeyman courtier, flitting from one aristocratic household to another in Spain and Italy; like Matisse in his decline, Oviedo enchanted his various masters and mistresses with his remarkable skill at folding paper and cutting out silhouettes. A veritable 'God of the Scissors', he was personally praised by Leonardo da Vinci for his exceptional ability to visualize a scene or design quickly and then cut it out precisely.[8]

He returned to Spain and used his noble contacts to secure a relatively lucrative position as Public Notary of Madrid, the beginning of a life devoted to serving the Crown as an administrator and a man of the pen, a soldier and adventurer in paper and ink, a man whose words would be greater deeds than his actions. He was very much a man of his time, for bureaucracy would be the making of the Spanish Empire as much as feats of arms.

In 1507, he married his first wife, Margarita, 'one of the most beautiful women in the kingdom';[9] but following her death in childbirth three years later, he accepted appointment as overseer, *veedor*, of the royal foundry at Castilla del Oro, in Darien, founded by Núñez de Balboa, who had been the first European to stare in silence with eagle eyes at the massive breakers of the Pacific Ocean while all his men looked at one another with wild surmise.[10]

Oviedo arrived in America filled with a spirit of Renaissance nobility and a strong sense of loyalty to his profession as an administrator of the Crown, but he was destined to serve under the kind of brutal governor so familiar at the edge of Empire, Pedrarias Dávila, a medieval gangster who had had Balboa beheaded because he was a threat to his authority. Pedrarias soon decided that he needed to deal with Oviedo in similarly brutal fashion. As Oviedo recalls in his *General History*, not long after he had established himself at Darien he was on his way to mass with some friends when he was accosted by the sheriff. While the two men were discussing administrative business, one of Pedrarias's thugs came up behind Oviedo 'with a very sharp knife and slashed me across the head from below my left ear down to my chin . . . and I fell to the ground and the man stabbed me again in the shoulder.'

'You traitor, why are you murdering me?' Oviedo cried and, barely able to see for the blood that was in his eyes, he drew his sword, at which the thug fled to the Cathedral, where he sought protection from the Bishop, Juan de Quevedo.[11] But Oviedo was tough, and although the surgeon marked him for a dead man and he was given confession, he recovered from the assault.

In 1519, Oviedo was in Barcelona, aggressively pursuing his case against Pedrarias, but also advocating a new model for peaceful colonization; and this was the real cause of Las Casas's unforgiving and lifelong hatred of him. Interestingly, these two intelligent and yet very different men, each with extensive experience of the problems of the American frontier, came up with essentially similar schemes for Spanish settlement and the evangelization of the Indians. Oviedo proposed maintaining the indigenous fiefdoms under their own lords or *caciques*, with each mentored by a Knight of Santiago, a soldier-monk of aristocratic birth, who would run the fief as his own *encomienda* during his lifetime, after which it would revert to the Order of Santiago. All would be under the rule of the Commander of the Order, who was to draw a salary from the Crown rather than have his own *encomienda*, but who was answerable to the democratic vote of all the Knights. 'In this way, the Indians would be very well treated and converted to the faith and the land would be well settled by honourable men of noble birth.'[12]

The only essential difference between these two visions of the Spanish future in the Americas was that, as a courtier and Crown official, Oviedo believed in the inherent nobility of aristocracy, while Las Casas, as a friar, believed in the intrinsic morality of poverty. Both men recognized that, far from the centre of royal authority, justice must necessarily depend upon the character of the men charged with exercising power.

In fact, for all Oviedo's supposed opposition, Las Casas was granted permission to establish an experimental colony in northern Venezuela. But he was unable to find the necessary fifty settlers prepared to invest 200 ducats each; ever the optimistic fantasist, he went anyway with a handful of peasants he paid for himself. By the time he reached the Caribbean, the Venezuelan Indians were at war with the Spaniards and he was forced to abandon the project altogether, taking refuge from his disappointment in the Dominican monastery at Santo Domingo. Likewise, Oviedo was offered the governorship of Santa Marta, in modern Colombia, but was refused the Knights of Santiago he claimed were essential to the success of the project. He must have known he had almost no chance of being put in charge of a hundred senior noblemen, so his purpose in asking for such a position must have been rhetorical rather than realistic. He can have had no serious intention of pursuing the proposed project; and so, needless to say, he declined the appointment; but he now had Crown support and so he returned to Darien to pursue his claim against Pedrarias, which was eventually resolved, in 1523, in the law courts of Spain.[13]

Also in 1519, one of the most charismatic figures of the age emerged on to the documentary stage of history for the first time: Garci Laso de la Vega – always now written Garcilaso – must have had truly exceptional charm and personality, for all that the reality of his life has been endlessly eclipsed by the relentlessly overblown myth-making of legion biographers caught in the dizzying Charybdis of his efferves-cent chivalric chutzpah.

Garcilaso epitomized the most noble values of the epoch into which he was born: an aristocratic younger son, he was a loyal courtier to his King, a talented musician, a gallant lover but a troubled soul; he was a brave soldier who tragically lost his life in the bathos of a pointless battle at the age of thirty-two; and, the very perfect gentle-knight, he is today best remembered as a brilliant poet, the lyrical innovator of a new kind of Renaissance Spanish verse which outshone the Italian poetry of Petrarch. He was guided in those poetical endeavours by another revered poet of the age, Joan Boscán, the leading literary courtier and private tutor to Garcilaso's close friend Fernando Álvarez de Toledo, the future third Duke of Alba. When Boscán heard that Garcilaso had been slain while high on bravado in the aftermath of a needless war that had otherwise been largely free of mortal combat, he rushed to eulogy:

> You always aimed at Goodness, Garcilaso,
> Always pursued Goodness with such power,
> Step by step you ran in Goodness' wake,
> Goodness you achieved in everything . . .[14]

It is fitting, then, sentimentally at least, that Garcilaso's superlative verse was first printed at the end of a volume of Boscán's own poetry, in 1543. This proved so popular that it ran to nineteen editions, which led to many further publications of Garcilaso's work and encouraged scholarly enthusiasm and heated debate about how his poetry should best be edited and in what order the poems should be presented. By 1569, he was widely described as the 'Prince of Castilian Poetry'. By 1588, the year of the Great Armada, his work was sufficiently well known to be included in an English anthology of poetry and rhetoric.[15] His influence remains so powerful today that he is still widely referred to as both the 'Prince' and the 'Pharaoh' of Spanish poetry.

And so Clio, that ancient and often unreliable muse of history, has established Garcilaso as an archetype of his age, a soldier with a Renaissance intellect and a poet with an instinct for chivalry; his unhappy destiny has proved a further, albeit fatal attraction. And, as if that were not enough, he has been all the more fascinating to inventive minds because he is one of those historical figures about whom we know tantalizingly much but not nearly enough. His biographers have gleefully turned to his poetry to complement our knowledge with fecund conjecture, filling his biography with further romance, notably his passion for a Portuguese beauty called Isabel Freire, whom we now know he almost certainly never met. Despite a lack of plausible evidence, this fiction was treated as irrefutable fact for over a century.[16] But then Garcilaso's sexuality has transcended the centuries to the extent that scholars have hinted that he may have been bi-curious, at least in his poetry if not in real life, a suggestion which probably has more to do with those scholars than it does with Garcilaso.[17] His fans have sculpted a deeply romantic image from the hard facts that are actually available.

In reality, Garcilaso first carved his mark into the historical record in 1519. At some point that summer, as Charles's supporters were securing his election as Holy Roman Emperor, Garcilaso was among a handful of armed noblemen, city officials and their servants who stormed into the Hospital del Nuncio, in the Castilian ecclesiastical capital of Toledo, and did sufficient mischief for four of them to be banished from the city for between one and six months. A writ of judgment survives, dated 7 September, which rusticated Garcilaso to his country estates for three months and ordered the confiscation of the arms he had been carrying at the time of the offence. There are similar writs issued against his companions. But none of these documents explains why those men violently invaded a charitable institution which was primarily a foundlings hospital dedicated to the care of abandoned infants but which also helped the insane.[18]

A note on the back of one of the writs makes reference to a dispute over the *patronato* or board of trustees of the hospital, then made up of members of the Cathedral Chapter. Since the discovery of this document in the early twentieth century, it has been assumed that the trouble was linked to the widespread discontent and turbulence then brewing among the urban population of Spain that Portocarrero, Montejo and Martín Cortés encountered as they went to meet Charles, trouble that would soon explode into a civil war with Toledo at its epicentre. But this account singularly fails to explain why a posse of upper-class teenage youths should have run riot in a building full of abandoned babies and madmen.

Recently discovered documents offer a more convincing explanation, for they show that around this time Garcilaso sired an illegitimate son by Guiomar Carrillo, the daughter of an aristocratic family from his own neighbourhood in Toledo.[19] What is more, other documents demonstrate that the child, baptized Lorenzo, was almost certainly brought up by Garcilaso's mother, Sancha de Guzmán, within her own household, where he was treated as her nephew. It seems plausible that, for the sake of Guiomar's reputation, her parents should have anonymously deposited the child in the foundlings hospital. Under such circumstances, the impetuous young Garcilaso might well have gathered together a group of friends to claim by force his own flesh and blood. Such action would certainly be more worthy of the Prince of Poets than the grubby political thuggery usually offered up as an explanation for these events.

The business of politics, however, seems to have come as naturally to Garcilaso as siring bastards; and in 1519 and 1520 Castile was undergoing a very complex power struggle indeed.

By defeating Francis I of France in the election for the imperial crown, Charles had deeply wounded the pride of a dangerous and powerful rival who would pursue a relentless policy of retribution for the rest of his life. This rift between the two great sovereigns of the age became as politically exasperating for Charles as it was bitterly personal for Francis. The Reformation has come to be interpreted as the most destructive rift of early modern Europe, but at the time Francis's hatred for Charles was more deadly still. Diplomacy, duplicity and war became the constant battlegrounds for this rivalry, and Charles was becoming concerned that France might forge an alliance with England.

Henry VIII, that caricature monarch of English history, sultanesque with his great belly, his six wives and his 'heretical' religion, is thought of today as a central figure in the Reformation, but in 1519 he was still a staunch Catholic who would soon be given the title 'Defender of the Faith' by the Pope. Christendom's diplomats knew that the powerful young English monarch was excessively influenced by his favourite, Cardinal Wolsey, one of the wiliest political figures of his age: the Vatican referred to him as 'the governor of the King of England', while Charles V's imperial Ambassador in Rome described him as making 'the King go hither and thither just as he likes'.[20]

On 8 January 1520, Charles's spies reported that Wolsey had been courting the French and that vainglorious summit between Henry and Francis which became known as the Field of the Cloth of Gold, because of the sumptuous display of tents, flags and clothing, had been arranged for 31 May 1520, in northern France. But Wolsey now began to play off Charles and Francis against each other, seeking the best deal possible for Henry. 'The result', to borrow David Starkey's memorable metaphor, 'was an extraordinary diplomatic dance between England, France and the empire,' in which Wolsey 'played the part of a coy maiden, turning now to Francis as her partner and now to Charles'.[21] Moreover, Henry was married to Charles's aunt, Catherine of Aragon, and he was eager to meet the new Emperor who would call him 'uncle'.

Already anxious to make the journey to Aachen for his coronation, Charles and his advisers immediately began to negotiate a visit to England during the voyage to the Netherlands and Germany. But, before Charles could leave Spain, he needed to persuade the Cortes, the parliament at which representatives of the main Castilian towns, the *procuradores*, debated the level of key tax revenues they would underwrite for the Crown, to vote him his travel expenses and to begin paying off the debts he had incurred in bribing the German Electors. He had already faced the Cortes in 1518 and despite bitter opposition raised 300,000 ducats; but as Portocarrero and Montejo knew, the Castilians were in riotous mood. It was a desperately inauspicious time for the unpopular young King to abandon Spain, let alone ask for more money.

Charles immediately set out to visit the two key cities of Burgos and Valladolid, in the heart of Old Castile, in an attempt to settle his subjects, but instead of convening the Cortes at one of these or the other traditional cities near by, he ordered the *procuradores* to meet in March at Santiago de Compostela, in remote Galicia in the far north-west. It was as long and arduous a journey as could be devised by his Flemish advisers, who believed that it would be easier to threaten and bribe the *procuradores* at such an immense distance from their cantankerous constituencies. But legend had it that, should the Cortes ever meet in Santiago, great calamities would befall Castile. Charles was defying yet another hallowed tradition and across the kingdom the decision was received with further fury.

The people of Toledo were especially angry because Charles's Flemish Grand Chamberlain, Guillaume de Croy, Sieur de Chièvre, had appointed his teenage nephew Archbishop of Toledo, the most important ecclesiastical position in Castile, thereby securing the income from one of the richest sees in Christendom for a member of his own family. Garcilaso de la Vega's elder brother, Pedro Laso de la Vega, addressed his fellow *regidores* in the Cabildo or Town Council. The great historian and jurist Juan Ginés de Sepúlveda reported that he was given the floor because, scion of a family of famous poets, 'he was the most eloquent among them' in a world where words were power:

> You are all well aware that when Charles arrived from the Netherlands, Castile was peaceful, prosperous and flourishing, a spirit of tranquillity reigned everywhere. Now, by contrast, how can one speak of the utter confusion brought about by the insults, liberties and greed of the Flemings without a heavy heart?... These foreigners satisfy their every

caprice without a care for our traditions. They have overlooked our most illustrious noblemen. They feel no scruples and stop at nothing: for the extent of their scruples and their conscience when it comes to appointing prelates is all too clear in the case of the archbishopric of Toledo, which has customarily and as is proper been conferred upon someone highly respectable. However, the Flemings have arranged for it to be handed over to a foreign child ignorant of our traditions so that he can govern Toledo from far-off lands through his assistants, loot our city, our great region and the richest part of Spain, taking his spoils to Flanders . . . If the king does not pay attention to our petitions, then the cities must form a common contract to take the necessary measures for the good of the kingdom and the state.[22]

It was typical of Renaissance history writing to personify a political position rhetorically by ascribing a speech to a great orator, and this was almost certainly the product of Sepúlveda's imagination. It perfectly captures the spirit with which powerful urban noblemen throughout Old Castile began to voice their discontent with Charles and to rally behind a sense of Castilian sovereignty inherent to the Crown and the kingdom.

Garci and Pedro Laso de la Vega are emblematic of the experience of Castilian aristocrats during the reign of Charles V. Their lives were inexorably linked to both the often parochial politics of Castile and the international business of the Habsburg Empire. They came from an important aristocratic family and were descended from the great medieval warrior poet the Marquis of Santillana. The family lands were entailed, held by *mayorazgo*, a form of perpetual inheritance that ensured all the property in the estate could pass to a single beneficiary, in this case Pedro, for generation after generation. The purpose was to ensure dynastic continuity by concentrating and accumulating wealth and therefore power into a single line of descent: it was an age when the bloodline was vastly more important than the individual.

It was just such a dynastic spirit of aristocratic arrogance and entitlement, his attachment to the land and memory of his forefathers, that led Pedro Laso to stand up against Charles. He spoke for others like him, but also for his people, his vassals, his tenants, his peasants, he spoke out of duty to a bond of blood and service, and his words were no mere drum of protest but plucked a chord that resonated deep and long among the angry citizenry. It was a patriotic call to arms against the colonial government of a foreign king.

During the winter of 1519 to 1520, the Castilian patriots coalesced around the recommendations of a committee of theologians appointed by the city of Salamanca who had concluded that no further taxes should be voted, that Castilian taxes should be spent in Castile and not abroad, and that the King should marry and sire an heir before leaving Spain. They also argued that the ultimate authority for the defence of Castile lay with the 'Comunidades', by which they meant the collective and representative bodies of society, such as town councils, universities and guilds. It is the first recorded use of the term and the rebellion would become widely known as the Revolt of the Comunidades, although it is now mostly referred to as the Comunero Revolt.[23] That emphasis on the Comunidades is a clear assertion of a fundamental principle that sovereignty lies with the subjects and institutions of the Crown and not in the person of the monarch. On the threshold of an age of absolute monarchies, it drew an important line in the sand for the kings of Castile.

When the royal party reached Valladolid, Charles met real Americans face to face for the first time, and for the first time he gazed in wonder at the treasures brought from his distant realms of gold. He marvelled at his good fortune and ordered that these magnificent novelties be displayed to all the ambassadors then at court.

The Totonac aristocrats also met the Pope's Ambassador, the Papal Nuncio, Archbishop of Cosenza, who described 'three men and two women, dark in colour, less black than Ethiopians . . . and of disagreeable and unprepossessing appearance. The men's bodies were pierced and scarred all over. They made a hole in the lower lip next to the chin and filled it with an ornament made of stone mosaic work, which they wear or take out at whim. They extract their front teeth in order that it should fit tightly.' The Nuncio also saw the gold and silver discs, but was appalled by the 'image of a throne' in the centre of the silver one, 'where a demon squats with a gaping mouth and bulging eyes . . . a devil they worshipped as a god'.[24]

Peter Martyr, the official court historian, an Italian humanist who first gave currency to the idea of a 'New World', also loathed the lip-plugs, but took a more enlightened view of other artefacts. 'If ever artists of this kind have touched genius,' he wrote in an open letter to Pope Leo X that was intended for widespread publication, 'then surely they are these natives. I do not admire the gold nor the precious stones so much as the skill of the artists and their workmanship, which must be worth more than the materials . . . I have never seen anything which for beauty could more delight the eye.' Across Christendom princes and their people would soon learn that the new Holy Roman Emperor was master of a western gold mine.[25]

Despite the Papal Nuncio's ambivalence towards exotic 'savages' and their religion, exaggerated rumours spread fast about the Spaniards' discovery of a great civilization in the Americas that was rich with precious metals. For Charles, it was a divinely sent solution to his current financial problems, for he could now literally point to the extraordinary wealth of his new dominions across the Ocean Sea, as the Atlantic was then known.

Henceforth, the great Habsburg Empire in Europe would depend on that promise of American money; but, in Spain, during the first months of 1520, history hung in the balance. Charles still had to hold on to Castile.

At Valladolid, the Castilian nobility pressed Charles to remain in Spain. But instead of placating them, according to Charles's own Cosmographer Royal, he lost his temper during a routine discussion about a major lawsuit and threatened to have a powerful aristocrat called Pedro Girón beheaded.[26] Young, badly advised and struggling under the burden of his vast and incoherent dominions, Charles had metaphorically lost his own head. It almost cost him Spain. Girón and other aristocrats were incandescent with rage and set off to rouse the already riotous population. Just as they were leaving the royal presence, Pedro Laso arrived at the head of a delegation from Toledo determined to have an audience with the King. But Charles was still furious and refused to give them an audience. Nature, that great play-wright of the skies, now so arranged it that a real meteorological storm should rage over Valladolid as a dramatic backdrop to the psycho-logical and political tragicomedy playing out below.

'No one could remember so much rain, nor the sky so dark,' the great Benedictine historian Friar Prudencio Sandoval wrote, 'as though it were a premonition of the evil devastation soon to rain down on Castile.' The bells were sounding in the Church of San Miguel as a signal to the populace. 'Within the hour the whole town was up in arms' to cries of 'Long live King Charles! Death to his evil counsellors!'[27]

Charles and his hated Grand Chamberlain, Chièvres, reacted quickly. They mounted the first serviceable horses they could find and set out with a limited guard for nearby Tordesillas, where Charles's mother, Juana the Mad, was kept under close guard. But as they reached the gates of the city, a handful of rioters tried to bar the way. The tiny royal party had to fight hand to hand before they were able to escape and the King and his Chamberlain could ride headlong for safety through the stormy night.[28]

Charles reached his mother's gilded prison in her palace at Tordesillas tired, soaked through, covered in mud and hungry, a humiliated fugitive monarch, chased from the de facto capital of Castile by an unruly mob. He scarcely had time to greet his mother and sister before he continued on towards Santiago. The following day, at Villapando, he finally met with Pedro Laso and the embassy from Toledo, who had been joined by the *procuradores* from Salamanca. They entreated their sovereign to remain in Spain; but, should he have to leave, they asked that the towns be represented in the government. They pleaded with him to hold the Cortes in the heart of Castile and not to try to raise further taxes. They made other petitions 'so entirely justified that just listening to them brought a doorman called Durango to tears', or so it was recorded in the chronicles.[29]

But Charles, once again surrounded by his Flemish retinue, was in an overconfident mood. With the immediate crisis averted, the court continued the slow and uncomfortable journey towards Galicia. Portocarrero, Montejo and the Mexican treasure went too.

As Castile boiled over, only the grandees, the heads of the greatest and most powerful aristocratic families of all, kept their counsel and waited, watching, every one of them a seasoned kingmaker by right of birth.

One has to wonder what the Totonac ambassadors made of Charles V's much vaunted imperial majesty and supposed royal power as they witnessed his undignified flight from Valladolid. What can they have thought as they saw the crowd of commoners armed with sticks and stones raging at the front of the royal palace while Charles escaped through the back door? Did they see his narrow escape as scuffles broke out when he reached the southern gate of the city? Did these first ambassadors to Europe from a major civilization in America go home believing that Charles was the most powerful man in the world?

Whatever they thought, Mexican culture shared with Charles V a chivalrous sense of hospitality and honour; and the Emperor-elect took good care of his guests. He had already insisted that they be given European clothes worthy of their rank. Now they were clearly suffering badly from the bitter cold of the Castilian winter, so he ordered gloves and cloaks and other clothes for them and sent them back to southern Seville. They arrived on 22 March and some time afterwards took ship for Cuba, after which they disappear from recorded history.[30] The first Mexicans to visit Spain must have returned to the Americas with a strange impression of Europeans and their affairs.

At Santiago, there was an angry mood at the Cortes as the royalist Bishop of Badajoz opened the first session with a rousing speech: 'the King, our lord, is more of a king than any other because he has more numerous and larger kingdoms, is more of a king because he alone on this earth is King of Kings, and more of a king by nature . . .' and like Trajan and Hadrian, the great Spanish emperors of Ancient Rome, he had now become 'Emperor of the World'. The Bishop eulogized this 'other New World of Gold', created by God for Charles, a world 'not yet born before our times'. Charles, he declared, 'did not accept his election as Emperor for himself, nor because he was dissatisfied with Spain and Italy and the New World of Gold, but . . . in order to battle the heathen enemies of our Holy Catholic Faith'.[31] He was trying to present Charles's international Empire to the Castilians as a glorious enterprise in which they should be proud and honoured to take part. But the only solid support for the Crown came from the royalist Andalusian cities of Granada and Seville, and from Burgos, a town which had long relied on royal protection of its monopoly over the lucrative wool trade.

The following day, Charles's Chancellor, Mercurino de Gattinara, raised the question of further taxation and then, according to an apparent eyewitness, Pedro Laso 'who had come there as the main *procurador* of Toledo responded to the King, saying that he had brought a record of the city's instructions relating to what he might do and discuss at the Cortes'. Promising to do his best by the Crown, he then admonished his sovereign, stating that 'he would rather be quartered and have His Highness order his head to be cut off than agree to any request so damaging to his city and his kingdom' as further taxation.[32] This defiance was greeted with such disorderly and rousing support from the other *procuradores* that the Cortes was suspended for three or four days.

Battling for control, Charles now banished Pedro Laso to distant Gibraltar, of which he was sheriff, but the defiant Toledan remained a few miles outside Santiago. Garcilaso now intervened, and it seems that he managed to convince his brother to abandon Santiago and at least return to the relative safety of Toledo. Without the zealous steel of Pedro Laso's leadership, the *procuradores* were slowly won over as they gave in to a bombardment of urgent threats and extensive bribery. Charles secured the all-important majority vote for further taxes and although the tax would never in fact be raised, that vote was enough to allow Charles to borrow the 400,000 ducats needed for his immediate expenses. A cycle was thus established of the Habsburgs borrowing to pay for their political and military ambitions in the rest of Europe, debt that was secured against Castilian tax revenue. It is a cycle that continued until 1648 and beyond.

With Garcilaso's help, Charles had won the battle if not the war. While Garcilaso may have been in part motivated by genuine fraternal concern when he persuaded his brother to withdraw, it is clear that he had also been won over to the royalist cause. Now he was owed his reward and on 26 April Charles made Garcilaso a salaried member of his royal household while exempting him from service when the court was abroad. We will never know for certain whether this bribe was solicited or promised, but bribes of similar value paid to men from Cuenca, Valladolid, Avila, Zamora and Segovia are well documented.[33] Whatever Garcilaso's motives, it was anyway a prudent move typical of the way powerful noble houses operated in the face of the vicissitudes of monarchy. With Garcilaso and Pedro on opposing sides, the family secured its position among the victors.[34]

At the end of April, with the desperate business of taxation temporarily settled, the Council of Castile, the close-knit heart of government in the kingdom made up of the sovereign's most trusted advisers, finally turned its attention to the question of the Mexican colonists and their insurrection. The colony was effectively put on trial in the persons of Montejo and Portocarrero. Under almost any other circumstances Cortés's men would have had little chance. They had arrived from that New World of Gold claiming to be the elected *procuradores* of their newly founded town of Villa Rica de la Vera Cruz, the Rich City of the True Cross, but they had no right to sit in the Cortes and their town was as yet unrecognized by the Crown. Yet all those in Santiago saw the stark contrast between these splendidly wealthy colonial subject citizens loyal to their sovereign and the recalcitrant Castilians. They had not simply paid Charles the *quinto real*, but claimed to be handing the Crown almost all the gold and other gifts they had received from the Mexicans, reserving for themselves only what was needed to buy provisions and arms for their colony. The Council of Castile gave them victory, albeit an incomplete one, postponing its decision on the matter indefinitely while releasing the defendants' own funds that had been impounded in Seville. An upstart captain in a distant land with a dubious claim to be an *hidalgo*, a gentleman of noble birth, had defeated the Castilian establishment by appealing directly to the beleaguered King. In due course, Cortés was rewarded with the title of Marquis of the Valley of Oaxaca, the first great aristocratic title in the Americas.

On 20 May, Charles finally sailed for England. He left his former tutor, Cardinal Adrian of Utrecht, as Governor of Spain, thus alienating further the great aristocratic families who naturally believed that the government of the kingdom should be their business.

2

Holy Roman Emperor

I cannot and will not recant anything, for to act against our conscience is neither safe for us, nor open to us. God help me, Amen.

Martin Luther

Charles's fleet was sighted off Dover on 26 May 1520; it must have made a spectacular sight with its sails and pennants beautifully decorated by a young artist called Alonso de Berruguete.[1] Wolsey rushed from Canterbury and set out with two boats to greet the Emperor, 'accompanied by many noblemen and gentlemen, richly clad in silk, and wearing massive gold chains'. They came ashore and Charles was lodged in Dover Castle. Henry VIII arrived late that night and went straight to his 'nephew's' apartment, 'where they embraced each other familiarly'.[2]

The next morning was Whit Sunday and the two monarchs rode to Canterbury, where Charles was greeted, 'outside the gates', by the sight of '60 dappled palfreys, saddled with women's pillions . . . all of cloth of gold', but every one was empty. It was an extravagant gesture typical of the Age of Chivalry, a compliment by Henry to the leading lady among his guests, Germaine de Foix, widow of Ferdinand the Catholic, rumoured to have been Charles's own lover for a while, and now married to the Marquis of Brandenburg. Inside the town, the clergy and the civic dignitaries were ready to accompany the two sovereigns to the Cathedral where the Archbishop presented Charles and then Henry with a cross to kiss as they knelt on the gorgeously embroidered golden cushions of a double prie-dieu or prayer desk. Then, together they walked solemnly beneath a golden canopy up to the high altar while a hymn was sung. Later, they attended the full Pentecost mass, to which 'six hundred lords and knights' came, 'all most sumptuously clad in cloth of gold and silver', and who 'wore massive gold chains around their necks'.

Afterwards, they retired to the Archbishop's palace where they were greeted by 'twenty-five of the handsomest and best apparelled ladies of the court'. Catherine of Aragon, Queen of England, dressed in golden cloth lined with ermine and bedecked with strings of pearls, looked on from the landing of the imposing marble staircase. It was the first time that aunt and nephew had ever met. She 'embraced him tenderly, not without tears', and the royal party went upstairs to 'a chamber where breakfast had been prepared'. And so it went on, all the public pageantry and pomp, the banqueting and the masses, the gallantry and the wooing. The four-year-old Mary Tudor, heir to the throne, played the virginal for Charles; it was a tacit offer of a tempting alliance for the unmarried Emperor.[3]

There is no record that Charles showed his Aztec treasures to Henry, Catherine and the English court. But for an Emperor now cripplingly overburdened with debt and yet faced with so many gold and silver costumes that he knew must have been originally made for Henry's meeting with the King of France, it is difficult to believe that he did not at least order the unloading of the famous discs of silver and gold in order to dazzle his English cousins. He and his advisers must have believed that the exhilarating presence of so much wealth would draw even Wolsey into its flame-like glitter, convincing him that Charles might become Emperor of the World. Whether it was Charles's Mexican gold and the amazing stories about the New World of Treasure, his charisma, his title, his aunt Catherine or the lure of power, the Emperor and his entourage won over Henry and Wolsey during that brief sojourn in Kent. Among the key points in their new alliance was the fateful promise of a marriage match between Charles and Mary Tudor, a promise he would only finally fulfil far too late, in 1554, through the proxy of his son, the future Philip II, who married the by then barren Mary. But, for the time being, Charles had outflanked Francis.

Henry and Charles kept their compact secret, to allow Henry a more friendly and revealing meeting with Francis and so as not to alarm Christendom with Charles's fearsomely rising star. But they agreed to a second meeting across the Channel at which Charles would play host, after Henry had had the measure of Francis, and once Charles had been crowned at Aachen.

At the end of August, Charles was in Brussels, where the Aztec treasure was put on public display as the gift of the powerful Emperor of the New Land of Gold to the powerful Emperor of the resurgent Ancient World of Rome. There, it was seen by Albrecht Dürer, widely regarded as the greatest artist of the northern Renaissance, who was then enjoying an extended tour of the Netherlands. Dürer kept a logbook of his two-year journey through northern Europe buying and selling works of art. This was no artist's journal, but a merchant's *Handbuch* largely concerned with money and material exchanges in which his occasional descriptions of art and architecture are generally characterized by dry brevity. However, when he sat down to record that he had seen 'the things which have been brought to the King from the new land of gold', his writing began to glow with his sense of wonder: he mentions the 'sun all of gold, a whole fathom broad' and the 'moon all of silver of the same size', and 'two rooms full of the armour of the people there, and all manner of wondrous weapons of theirs, harnesses and darts, very strange clothing, beds, and all kinds of marvellous objects of human manufacture'. 'These things were all so precious that they are valued at 100,000 guilders' (25,000 ducats), he noted, pragmatically enough, before concluding with unusual enthusiasm: 'In all the days of my life, I have seen nothing to make my heart rejoice so much as these things, for I saw amongst them wonderful works of art, and I marvelled at the subtle ingenuity of men in foreign lands. Indeed, I cannot express all I felt there.'[4]

In October, in the autumnal sunshine, Charles met the Electors outside Aachen and then entered the town with martial pomp accompanied by his Spanish grandees and members of his chivalric

Order of the Golden Fleece. That night, he took an oath to uphold the traditions and rights of the Electors and princes. He agreed that German and Latin would be the language of government, and that only Germans would be given offices. At dawn, the ceremony began in the Cathedral of Charlemagne, the 'Chapel' of Aix-la-Chapelle, to crown him King of the Romans; only the Pope in person could preside over his coronation as Holy Roman Emperor and he would have to wait for that. Charles swore to protect the Church and the Faith, and then the Archbishop of Cologne turned to the congregation and asked 'whether they would be obedient to this prince and lord, after the command of the Apostle'. And they bellowed their reply: 'Fiat! Fiat! Fiat!' Crowned by the prelate, Charles occupied the throne of Charlemagne and listened to a *Te Deum*, before the religious ceremony gave way to a day of banqueting and feasting.[5]

Charles and his advisers soon turned their attention to the forthcoming Imperial Diet or parliament which had been convened that winter at Worms. All of Christendom was anxious for Charles to clarify his position in the increasingly noisy arguments about religion and reform. In 1517, Martin Luther had ignited the debate when, according to legend, he had pinned his Ninety-Five Theses to the church door at Wittenberg and wrote to the Archbishop and Elector of Mainz criticizing the Church's sale of indulgences as putting a price on God's forgiveness. In 1518, the authorities in Rome had charged him with heresy and he had sought the protection of the Elector of Saxony, Frederick the Wise. Then, in 1520, Luther published his epistle *To the Christian Nobility of the German Nation*, which urged the aristocracy actively to support the reform of Christianity, invoking Charles himself as a beacon of hope; the first print run of 4,000 sold out in days. The debate over religious reform was becoming politicized as an issue of German nationalism; and Germans, from cobblers to knights, from peasants to burghers, rallied to the reformist cause. It was said that Luther had been born in the same year as Hernán Cortés, so that one might destroy the ancient Church while the other built a new Jerusalem in the recently conquered lands across the sea.[6]

An obdurate Papacy issued the bull *Exsurge Domine*, condemning forty-one key points raised in Luther's theses and threatening to excommunicate him if he failed to recant. Clearly in a dark mood, Luther described the Pope as the anti-Christ and likened the Church to the 'Great Harlot' described by St John the Evangelist, 'who sitteth upon many waters, with whom the kings of the earth have committed fornication'.[7]

Erasmus of Rotterdam, the most influential intellectual of the age whose 'emphasis on a cult of the spirit' would prove to be so 'especially attractive' to Spanish thinkers, had lobbied the Elector Frederick to insist Luther be given the chance to make his case before the Emperor and at the same time wrote to Luther urging caution.[8] Luther was summoned to Worms; his journey towards the Diet in the early spring of 1521 was a celebratory pilgrimage, not the progress of a condemned man to a final show trial. The churches were dangerously packed, he was greeted like a prince by the burghers of the towns he stayed in; he entered Worms to a fanfare of trumpets sounding from the tower of the Cathedral.

Charles was faced with a fearsome dilemma: on the one horn, he had sworn to defend his German subjects, now increasingly reformist; on the other, he had taken an oath to defend the Faith and the Church. He would have needed a toreador's sleight of hand to humble this dangerous beast, but he was, of course, no Spaniard.

On 18 April, Luther made his case to the Emperor in public; he spoke at length, repudiating the authority of the Pope and the Church councils and instead putting faith in the Scriptures and the word of God before concluding that 'I cannot and will not recant anything, for to act against our conscience is neither safe for us, nor open to us. God help me, Amen.'[9]

Charles's imperial role was to sit in judgment. The following day, he offered his verdict: 'I am born of the most Christian Emperors of the German Nation, of the Catholic Kings of Spain, the Archdukes of Austria, the Dukes of Burgundy, who were all to the death true sons of the Roman Church, defenders of the Catholic Faith, of the sacred customs, decrees and uses of its worship, who have bequeathed all this to me as my heritage.'

The Emperor thus began by making crystal clear that, in attacking the traditions of the Church, Luther had attacked the three great

European dynasties concentrated in Charles's person; it was an attack on the tradition by which he ruled and his raison d'être. For the Emperor, history was God's witness: 'It is certain that a single monk must err if he stands against the opinion of all Christendom, otherwise Christendom itself would have erred for more than a thousand years . . . From now on I regard Luther as a monstrous heretic.'[10]

The battle lines between Protestant Reform and Catholic orthodoxy were drawn, an antagonism that has overshadowed our perception of European history ever since.

In late May 1520, Pedro Laso had been greeted ecstatically in the streets of Toledo to shouts of 'Long live Pedro Laso, who spoke to the king man to man!'[11] A few days later, Rodrigo de Tordesillas, one of the *procuradores* who had succumbed to bribery in Galicia, presented his report to the Council of Segovia. The commoners were already in riotous mood; the day before a mob had summarily beaten and executed two unpopular royalist collaborators. Now, a gang of wool-workers stormed the Council building and dragged Tordesillas to the city jail with a noose around his neck. From there they manhandled him to the gallows, beating him and, when he was 'already half strangled by the rope, they tied him by the feet and hanged him'. Segovia now rose en masse, the populace formed a 'revolutionary committee' of patriots, and royal officials and constables had to run for their lives.[12] The following day, in Toledo, Pedro Laso's wife personally defied a bloodthirsty mob that had pursued a royal *corregidor* or chief magistrate across the threshold of the Laso home. It is a telling moment that highlights a key fault line within the Comunero movement, a division between the urban nobility and the commoners that would prove decisive within a year. Moreover, a dangerous rivalry was developing between Pedro Laso and Juan Padilla for military leadership of the patriots.[13]

Adrian of Utrecht, still Governor of Spain, was desperately isolated. The alienated grandees, who should have been natural allies of the Crown, stepped back to watch the rebellion unfold. With little money and few men, Adrian could muster only a tiny force to send to Segovia that, clearly unable to capture the city, could do no more than patrol

the hinterland to very limited effect. The royalists were now dangerously exposed to the increasingly powerful Comunero forces which
were well funded by towns and cities receiving income both from their
own tax receipts and from revenue due to the Crown.

To Pedro Laso's chagrin, Padilla was chosen to lead an army of 200
cavalry and 2,000 infantry out of Toledo to confront the royalists at
Segovia and by the time he got there his army had more than doubled
in number. But by then the royalist troops had already fled for Medina
del Campo where the royal arsenal was well stocked with artillery
and other weapons.[14] Adrian had assumed that the wealthy burghers
of royalist Medina were bound to welcome him, but instead the town
rose up against him and fought a furious running battle through the
streets, forcing the royalists to retreat. This was a very significant
victory in itself, but more important still, as the royalist soldiers abandoned the town, they set fire to many buildings, destroying the most
richly stocked warehouses in the kingdom. The wilful destruction of
property in so prized a commercial centre reduced Adrian's popularity to new lows.

Padilla's army grew quickly and he began securing the heart of Old
Castile. In a crucial move, he entered Tordesillas towards the end of
August. Charles's mother, Queen Juana the Mad, rightful ruler of
Castile, appeared on a balcony of the palace and welcomed the rebels.
Padilla knelt before her and recognized her as his sovereign. The
patriot ruling Junta now restyled itself as an emergency meeting of
the Cortes and, with Juana present, Pedro Laso spoke movingly of the
origins of Castilian resistance and led the delegates in paying homage
to their 'Queen and natural ruler'.[15]

In reply, Juana lamented the way she had been imprisoned at
Tordesillas and offered the rebels qualified support by asking them
to punish those who did evil to the kingdom.[16] Adrian had warned
Charles that if Juana signed even a single document, then he would
lose Castile; but she refused to usurp her son's throne. Instead, she
appears to have been remarkably astute in dealing with the Comuneros,
drawing them in, using them to establish control over her own household and getting them to reveal their hand. She then announced that
she wanted to meet with the Royal Council, asserting that 'since those

of the council were from the time of the Catholic king, they could not all be bad' and therefore she wanted 'to speak and communicate with them because they were experienced persons who knew the form of good government'.[17]

Juana is a deeply tragic and enigmatic character in Castilian history; disarmingly beautiful, she was psychologically fragile, ruthlessly disenfranchised and yet spirited in her rebellion against those who constrained her. Her personality has been subjected to a vast range of interpretations, from the exorcists who tried to cure her of her demons in her lifetime, through the nineteenth-century historians who imagined her as a hysterical attention seeker and the twentieth-century psychologists who have diagnosed her schizophrenia, to the feminists for whom she is the thoroughly misunderstood victim of merciless misogyny. In popular mythology she is remembered as a woman whose love for her husband, the ingrate Philip the Handsome, was disturbingly deranged, the compelling heroine of an unrequited royal romance. But recent interpretations suggest that hers was a calculated madness, a series of timely exhibitions of extreme eccentricity because that was often the only political tool available to her. Indeed, when Henry VIII met her at Windsor, he thought 'she seemed very well . . . and spoke with a good manner and countenance, without losing a point of her authority. And although her husband and those who came with him depicted her as crazy, I did not see her as other than sane.'[18]

Juana, born in 1479, was the eldest daughter of the Catholic Monarchs, Isabella of Castile and Ferdinand of Aragon, who had united the principal crowns of Spain. With his sharp eye for foreign policy, Ferdinand had married her to Philip the Handsome, Archduke of Burgundy, and sent her to the Netherlands charged with furthering Spanish interests there against the machinations of France. But he then failed to give her the resources she would need to fulfil that role. Her dowry was handed over to Philip, who proved to be unchivalrously neglectful of his bride, which crippled politically the trusted Spaniards in her household; they became demoralized and were soon muscled aside by Philip's preferred alternatives. The Spanish Ambassador reported to the Catholic Monarchs that 'if Her Highness were not so equipped with virtues, she could not bear all that she sees'; but she proved remarkably resilient, and he also observed that 'I do not think I have seen such common sense in anyone so young.'[19]

Charles was born on 24 February 1500, at Ghent. Two years later, Juana and Philip travelled overland across France to Spain so that she could receive fealty from the Castilians, although as they approached Burgos the city fathers closed the gates, mistaking their entourage for an invading army. In March 1503, while still in Spain, she gave birth to Ferdinand, who would grow up there and become a great favourite with the Spaniards. Following the death of Queen Isabella in 1504, Juana and Philip returned to Spain to be recognized as joint rulers of Castile, but Philip died almost as soon as he arrived, at the Carthusian monastery or Charterhouse of Miraflores, near Burgos. Ferdinand, wrily known as 'the Old Catalan', then began to assert his right to rule in Castile, although the crown properly should have passed to his daughter Juana; and she began to behave in a way that has seemed very strange indeed to later historians. It was said an old woman had prophesied that Philip would 'have to travel through more of Castile once dead than while he was alive', which, as one contemporary chronicler explained, 'proved true, because for many years his wife took him about with her in a coffer sealed with bitumen'.[20] Juana refused to be separated from the sarcophagus and, travelling at night, in a candlelit procession, 'accompanied by many Franciscan monks who sang masses and the Prior of Miraflores [who] came with some Carthusians', the peculiar couple went first to Burgos and then to Torquemada, where Juana gave birth to a daughter, Catherine.

In the summer of 1507, she met Ferdinand at Tórtoles, still accompanied by her husband's cadaver. They were then joined by Ferdinand's new young Queen, Germaine de Foix, and they set off again first for Santa María del Campo and then moved on to Arcos, just outside Burgos; again, Philip went with them.

Juana's insistent attachment to her husband's corpse has traditionally been interpreted as the devotion of an unhinged lover, but one royal chronicler reported that 'she never failed to show respect for her father', nor 'was she heard to babble away' like a lunatic. She clearly did not appear mad, and a more plausible explanation for this apparently eccentric behaviour is that she was determined to bury Philip in Granada, alongside Isabella, turning the royal tomb into a hugely symbolic monument to her baby Charles's right to the throne of Castile. She was fighting for her child's rightful inheritance, for if Ferdinand succeeded in siring a male heir by his new Queen, then he might well try to assert his son's right to Castile as well.

Father and daughter began to struggle for control of the corpse and the kingdom. Juana was entrenched at Arcos, but Ferdinand had taken control of her household, and had also absconded with her youngest son, Ferdinand. Her response was calculated delinquency: 'She urinates more often than ever seen in any other person. Her face and everything else, they say, lacks cleanliness. She eats on the floor' and 'many days she misses Mass', her confessor reported. This erratic behaviour forced Ferdinand's hand and he agreed to allow her to hang on to Philip's cadaver, so long as she retired to Tordesillas. When she reached the town, she took up residence in her palace-prison and kept Philip in a pretty Mudéjar chapel in the neighbouring Convent of Santa Clara, until Charles finally had his father entombed at Granada in 1527.[21]

Maligned ever since as Juana 'la Loca', this spirited, politically astute but repeatedly disempowered woman would live out her days imprisoned at Tordesillas, 'guarding her widowhood' and 'her son's inheritance'.[22] Her death in 1555 was the final catalyst to Charles's own decision to abdicate his many crowns and retire to a monastery buried deep in the Castilian forest not far from Tordesillas in order to die.

And so, from September 1520, the tiny town of Tordesillas became the seat of the only effective, albeit limited government there was in Castile because the Comunero patriots wanted the appearance of legitimacy afforded by the apparent support of Queen Juana. The Junta wrote a long letter to Charles, giving their account of the conflict and justifying their actions, which was delivered to him in Germany. By way of reply they learnt that he had imprisoned their postman.[23]

The patriots had a seemingly instinctive understanding of sovereignty and authority as rooted in the kingdom, the Crown and its
subjects, rather than in the bodily person of the monarch. Inspired by
that underlying sense of democracy, they turned their minds to codi-
fying their demands into an extraordinary document, often referred
to as a manifesto, but which embodies many of the characteristics
of both a constitution and a bill of rights. They wrote a considered
appraisal of the way the kingdom worked, suggesting how to change
and adjust the main institutions in order to make them perform better.
The work of intelligent men who knew what they were talking about,
it is a tour de force of political insight. They began by insisting that
Charles should marry a queen to be approved by the Cortes in order
to ensure 'that she will be from a friendly nation'. They were clearly
thinking of Isabella of Portugal, but the point was that they wanted a
woman they could trust to rule Castile in the Castilian interest while
Charles was abroad.[24]

They then sought to bar Flemings altogether from the government
and foreigners from the royal guard and addressed the central issues
of taxation and representation in great detail, before setting out a
comprehensive list of rules by which a whole range of social, political
and economic activities were to be controlled, from the minting of
money to the organization of government and the administration of
justice. The patriots also insisted that Seville retain its monopoly as
the clearing house for all trade with the New World, signalling their
intention to protect the Castilian Empire from Flemings and other
foreigners who might prove eager to trespass on the trade. In the
Americas, they sought to limit the *encomienda* system which 'has
caused great damage to the Royal Weal' because these Indians 'are
Christians, but have been treated like heathens and slaves', apparently
trying to prevent conquistadors and colonists from establishing the
kind of entailed seigneurial estates from which the Castilian grandees
derived their wealth and power.[25]

For a handful of intoxicatingly revolutionary weeks during late
summer and early autumn of 1520, the Comuneros seemed ready
to assume the government of their own country with Juana as their
sovereign. But that very success meant that the deep fissures within

the movement became much more significant. They were essentially an unstable coalition of self-interested individuals and groups who had been brought together in rebellion by a common sense of ethnic identity and their understandable but furious xenophobia towards Charles V and his Flemings. But once the Comuneros had the upper hand, that burning sense of patriotic nationhood fragmented into the petty localism of parish politics and class warfare. Soon, the commoners wrested control of the movement from the urban nobility and were quick to champion an aggressive and often violent policy towards the great aristocratic landowners. Many of the noble Comuneros who had at first tempered those more radical elements now lost sympathy with the Junta. In time, these urban oligarchs themselves became the targets of an increasingly lawless and blood-thirsty revolution.

More disastrous and decisive still, the rebel militias attacked towns and fortresses on land owned by the great lords, forcing these massively powerful players into identifying the Comuneros as the enemy. Meanwhile, Charles had encouraged the support of the grandees by appointing two of their number to govern alongside Adrian of Utrecht. With the King abroad and the Comuneros increasingly extreme in their attitudes, the aristocratic faction started to mobilize, and the Portuguese Crown began to lend large sums of money to the royalist cause. The endgame had commenced.

By the end of 1520, faced with this increasingly radical Junta, Pedro Laso tried to use his considerable prestige to agitate for peace and made overtures to the royalists on his own initiative. This earned him the hostility of the citizenry, even in Toledo, and the mistrust of the leading rebels. In January 1521 he was implicated in the embezzlement of patriot funds and a month later he was stripped of his office within the Junta. Pedro Laso de la Vega, who had been such a figurehead at the outset of the rebellion, began to negotiate with the royalists. After days of tense negotiation, on 21 March, Adrian of Utrecht indicated his intention to argue that the Emperor treat Pedro Laso leniently for his insurrection, and at that crucial moment of the crisis Pedro Laso turned coat; he was not alone.[26]

On 23 April 1521, threatened by the fast-growing royalist forces and feeling beleaguered in the small castle at Torrelobatón, Padilla tried to march his army of 7,000 infantry, 300 cavalry and 100 musketeers to the well-fortified city of Toro to await reinforcements. Five or six hundred royalist cavalry officers, probably with Garcilaso and Pedro Laso among them, pressed on ahead of the rest of the army and confronted the patriots; in pouring rain, Padilla lost control of his demoralized men. Twice he ordered them into formation, first in a marshy vale where the enemy horses might founder, and then a second time on high ground. But his captains disobeyed the order and pressed on towards the tiny hamlet of Villalar, hopelessly exposing the army to the enemy cavalry on a swathe of gentle farmland.[27] By the time the royalist infantry reached the battlefield, the patriot army had been routed. The following day, Padilla and a handful of other rebel leaders were summarily executed.

Although the Comunero uprising was all but finished, Toledo managed to hold out alone until February 1522 under the increasingly desperate leadership of Padilla's widow, María de Pacheco. But after Villalar, the character of the rebellion changed markedly, for, as the rebel nobility changed sides almost to a man, they left the riotous proletarian underbelly of the rebellion without the checks and balances of strong leadership. In Toledo, a rampaging mob intercepted two wealthy burghers intent on persuading María de Pacheco to sue for peace and threw them from the battlements. The many children among the deadly throng then dragged the cadavers through the streets to some nearby meadows where they tried to set fire to them. Meanwhile, a hundred or so marauders fresh from the kill were clamouring at the doors of a Trinitarian monastery, baying for the blood of Garcilaso's boyhood tutor Juan Gaitán, who escaped by the skin of his teeth.[28] As María de Pacheco resorted to paying the militias with silver raided from the Cathedral sacristy, the royalist forces surrounded the city. An army of 1,500 stalwart rebels attempted to relieve the siege, but was surprised and defeated by royalist forces at the small town of Olías. During the intense fighting, Garcilaso was wounded in the face, an injury that in due course would prove very useful when he sought to ingratiate himself further with the Emperor; he had served Charles loyally since the Cortes at Santiago and so despite his brother's treason the family survived at the heart of Castilian politics.[29]

Finally, in early February, Toledo capitulated and both Laso de la Vega brothers were among the conquering royalists who swaggered into the deserted streets of their own city. The dauntless María de Pacheco managed to escape to Portugal disguised as a peasant and carrying some geese as extra camouflage, but the Padilla family mansion was razed to the ground and Charles ordered that the lot be salted, in imitation of Julius Caesar's great general Scipio, who had rebel Carthage similarly obliterated.[30]

During the Comunero Revolt, across the Pyrenees in France, Francis I had decided to take advantage of Castilian weakness and, on 10 May 1521, a French army marched into the small frontier kingdom of Navarre and laid siege to the capital, Pamplona. Pedro Laso and other leading deserters from the Comuneros' cause seized this ideal opportunity to redeem themselves in the eyes of their Emperor and rode north to engage the enemy. But before they could relieve the town, the French assault had begun.

There was a young man among the defenders called Ignatius Loyola who took 'special delight in the military life', he would later claim. 'Led by a strong and empty desire to win for himself a great name', when 'all the other soldiers were unanimous in wishing to surrender' he persuaded the commander to defend the city. As soon as the French attack came, Ignatius exchanged confessions with a fellow nobleman and then fought with exceptional bravery until an enemy cannonball shattered one of his legs and badly injured the other.

The French took the town and Loyola spent two weeks in the care of their physicians before he was discharged and allowed to return home. But the Spanish surgeons decided that the most damaged leg should be broken once more because the bones had knitted badly, so 'he submitted to have his flesh cut again' and, he remembered grimly, bore the operation in silence, giving 'no sign of suffering save tightly clenching his fists'. But the bone was still not properly aligned, making 'the leg seem quite deformed', and so he underwent the torture of further surgery and further agonizing days spent in bed with his leg stretched.

As his life hung in the balance, the French forces abandoned Navarre, crossed the border into Castile and laid siege to Logroño, capital of the famous wine region of La Rioja. This time, they were engaged by the formidable army of newly reunited Spaniards marching north from Villalar and were easily forced back across the border into France.

As Loyola began to recover, he asked for some chivalric romances to read, for he had a special devotion to such frivolous fiction. Instead, he was given *The Life of Christ* by Rudolph the Carthusian and the *Flos sanctorum*, a collection of biographies of saints that brought about a miraculous conversion. Though he was still in great pain, that reading stimulated him to meditate on a powerful hallucination that he experienced of 'an illustrious lady' of chivalric mien. Writing his autobiography in old age, Loyola portrayed this youthful experience in terms of a series of steps, beginning with the image of a princess in a romance of chivalry, that led him to explore his inner, mystical faith through Spiritual Exercises of meditation and contemplation. Slowly, he realized that the illustrious lady must be the Madonna, the Mother of the Church, and, finally, one night, 'he plainly saw the image of the Blessed Mother of God with the Infant Jesus' and 'from that time until August 1555, when this was written, he never felt the least motion of concupiscence'.[31]

Moved to a life of spiritual piety by that emasculating trauma, contrition and reconciliation, Ignatius Loyola became one of the most driven religious figures of his age, founding the Society of Jesus. Within decades, the Jesuits would have a firm grip on education in the Catholic world, setting up schools and colleges that would do so much to formulate the knowledge and thinking of generation after generation of humble pupils who through their study would rise to occupy the ever more important, ever more influential and ever more powerful administrative offices across the Spanish Empire.

When Charles V landed at Santander on 16 July 1522, with an entourage that included 4,000 German troops lest the Comuneros show signs of revival, he in fact returned to a peaceful kingdom over which royal authority had been re-established.[32] Well aware of the economic importance of the Castilian cities to his monarchy, he was magnanimous but circumspect in victory: twenty-three rebels were executed before he signed the General Pardon, from which a further 296 individuals were excluded;[33] some had escaped, others were punished, some by confiscation of their property; all lost out financially. Pedro Laso fled to Portugal as soon as the King returned, and 'it seems that the Queen of Heaven', Oviedo wrote, 'came to his rescue, for, in truth, had he been captured, they would have celebrated his funeral just as they did with Juan de Padilla'.[34]

Meanwhile, Garcilaso's star was rising and, while Guiomar, the mother of his first child, waited patiently in Toledo for her beloved to return and marry her, he joined Charles's court at Palencia. The following summer, in 1523, at Valladolid, he was among the crowds of young noblemen who flocked to the fashionable court of Charles's sister, Eleanor, who had recently returned to Spain following the death of her first husband, Manoel I of Portugal. There, the future scions of the great aristocratic houses of Spain were getting to know one another and the dashing young Garcilaso de la Vega met Elena de Zúñiga, an aristocratic Portuguese lady-in-waiting in Eleanor's household.

3

Isabella of Portugal

A very self-assured princess . . . who seemed to look a lot like you,
Sire . . .

Alonso Enríquez de Guzmán

Charles returned to Spain with massive debts, an immensely egotis-
tical sense of his responsibilities as a Habsburg Holy Roman
Emperor and a thorough realization that he needed to make peace with
his Castilian subjects. He began to secure his power base in Castile by
negotiating with the towns, the urban elites, the lower nobility and
the growing class of new, educated men, the very social groups that
had so enthusiastically engaged with the rebellion.[1] Indeed, he began
to comply with the spirit of the patriots' demands: he remained in
Spain for the next seven years, he began to convene the Cortes with
relative frequency and, after protracted negotiations, he married the
Castilians' preferred choice of queen, Isabella of Portugal, in 1526.
Her skill at government during Charles's long absences and the fact
that she was surrounded by Castilian advisers involved, in effect, a
significant devolution of power and authority away from the person
of the monarch and on to the institution of the Crown. But, most
importantly, the Cortes was able to promote a kind of republic or state
that consolidated around key institutions: the law, the administration and especially the towns, which were significantly independent
economically and institutionally from the monarchy that coexisted
alongside them.[2]

But Charles was again at war with France, this time over the disputed succession to the Duchy of Milan; and in 1524 a French army again marched into Spain and occupied the fortress of Fuenterrabía near the Basque border. Garcilaso, freshly invested as a Knight of Santiago, answered the call to arms and during the successful campaign to retake the fortress he forged his lifelong friendship with the sixteen-year-old Fernando Álvarez de Toledo, the future third Duke of Alba, who would become the most feared general in Spanish history. Despite Fernando's age and despite his having undertaken this first military enterprise of his bellicose life without his family's permission, in the aftermath of the battle the Constable of Castile ordered him 'to take charge of the town and its fortress . . . and, although he was still young, he did so with every evidence of being a brave and spirited soldier'.[3]

But Fuenterrabía was a local aristocratic sideshow to the main events now taking place in Italy: still smarting from his defeat in the imperial election and the failure of his invasion of Navarre, Francis I determined to bolster his battered reputation and punctured pride by leading in person a French army over the Alps and into Lombardy, taking Milan, before laying siege to the city of Pavia. Charles was ready to sue for peace when Francis engaged a much weaker imperial force on a misty morning, and his luck turned. With the French in retreat but fighting a fierce rearguard action along the Ticino River valley, Francis tried to lead a squadron of his crack troops from the front, but he was unable to make them turn and face the enemy. Suddenly, he found himself alone and dangerously close to the front line. He rode hard towards a bridge over the river, desperate to reach the safety of the far bank. But an enemy harquebusier shot his horse dead beneath him and, as the animal fell, it trapped the King's leg. Almost immediately, a Basque soldier was upon him, pushing the point of his sword up against a gap in the lone Frenchman's armour, and, still unaware of his prisoner's identity, insisted he surrender. 'Upon my life,' Francis replied, 'I am the King of France and I surrender to the Emperor.' This, at least, is how Charles's chronicler reported the decisive moment at which French designs on Italy faltered.[4] The flower of the Gallic nobility were captured as well; the victory was total. It was the Emperor's birthday, 24 February 1525; he was a quarter of a century old.

Charles must have been overjoyed to hear his men had hunted down such an unexpected and important quarry, but the question of what to do with this sovereign captive was a diplomatic headache. He decided to have him brought to Spain as his prisoner, but he treated him with all the honour due to another monarch, and Francis travelled with an entourage of French noblemen and retainers and an escort of Spanish nobles.

As Francis passed through a small town called Valdaracete, he was told about a brilliant but most unusual fencing master called Esteban, famous for never having been defeated; and so the French King arranged for his most skilful swordsmen to take him on. One by one they confronted Esteban, and one by one he drew their blood first, until each had been vanquished. Such sideshow chivalry was an almost everyday pastime in that dangerously bellicose world and would normally have gone unremarked. But the astonishing thing about Esteban is that he had been baptized as a girl with the name Estefanía.

Estefanía had grown into a rumbustious tomboy, an Amazon of the Spanish plain, who was more agile, more fleet of foot and better at a whole range of sports than even the fittest young men in the town. 'It was a marvellous sight', the citizens of Valdaracete reported, 'to watch her in these games, running with her long blonde hair streaming behind.' She had begun to tour the region as a performing strong-woman, but when she reached Granada the city magistrates became suspicious and ordered qualified matrons and midwives to examine her to make sure she was really a woman; and they discovered that she was, in fact, a hermaphrodite.

It is revealing of the attitudes of the time that, rather than vilifying her as a freak, the magistrates simply ruled that she must choose the gender to which she wanted to belong. They were concerned with fitting her into an administrative structure, as much for her own benefit as their own. Interestingly, she chose to live as a man and later married, in church, becoming a head of household and acquiring all the rights of a male citizen. As far as the law was concerned, she had changed sex. But when he died, even as Esteban's widow wept beside the coffin, crying 'Ay, my husband,' Estefanía's mother was wailing 'Ay, my daughter!'[5]

Charles received Francis at the crumbling Royal Palace in Madrid and treated him as royally as possible. Years later, Charles reminded his courtiers and the world that, during this period, when the dejected French monarch fell gravely ill, he had personally attended his bedside to give him solace.[6] Of course, this was not purely altruistic, but the act of an Emperor very concerned that a king might die in his custody. That fear may have convinced him to release his troublesome enemy and, finally, in January 1526, the Treaty of Madrid was signed by the two kings. Francis agreed to restore to Charles his grandfather's Burgundian territories, annexed by France in 1477, and to give up all claims to Flanders, Artois, Tournai and Italy; in return, he would be released and allowed home to France. This new detente was sealed by his marriage to Charles's widowed sister Eleanor, but the Emperor refused to allow the French King to consummate the marriage immediately for fear he would later refuse to recognize the agreement and leave his erstwhile Spanish bride publicly dishonoured. Furthermore, Charles also required him to leave his two sons and heirs in Spain as surety against reneging on the deal. By taking the children hostage, the Emperor added to Francis's already gravely injured pride and reputation the insult of showing all too clearly that he did not trust his great rival.

In the late summer of 1525, Garcilaso de la Vega married his Portuguese lady-in-waiting, Elena de Zúñiga, at Toledo; by then, his first love Guiomar may have already taken up with the father of her second illegitimate child, a daughter who became a nun and took the name María de Jesus.[7] At the time, Toledo was basking in the sunshine of reconciliation and was finally glittering with the splendours of Charles's most cultured court, with the literary and poetic brilliance of its ambassadors, the erudition of its noblemen and the beauty of the ladies. But the court and the city were alive with the promise of a far more illustrious wedding involving a royal Portuguese match.

'Few female figures in our history have been so universally liked as Doña Isabella of Portugal,' wrote Carmen Mazarío Coleto in her now classic biography of Charles V's Empress and Queen of Castile.[8] A stunningly beautiful and brilliantly educated woman, a politically astute queen-regent in her husband's long absences abroad, a patient and loving wife, Isabella, who was his first cousin, also bore him that rarest and most precious gift, a Habsburg heir who was a capable ruler, the future Philip II. Today, we know her best from Titian's outstanding posthumous portrait of 1548, painted nine years after her death, which captures perfectly the spirit of love and reverence with which Charles remembered this most precious consort and revered political asset, whose untimely death in 1539 would leave him heartbroken.

It is an idealized image, not least because Titian had never met his subject; creating portraits from the work of others was a normal part of an artist's repertoire and Titian especially prided himself on his ability to find the defining features of his subject in the paintings he worked from. His personal motto, *Natura potentior ars*, implied, rather in the spirit of Pygmalion, that even the dead could be brought back to life by an artist.[9]

Charles had first commissioned Titian to paint Isabella's portrait in 1543 and lent him as a model a 'very lifelike' portrait 'by a painter of trifling importance'.[10] This first likeness of the Empress by Titian, destroyed by fire in 1604, showed her dressed in black with the imperial crown positioned behind her and with roses in her lap. The simplicity of the symbolism is compelling: the black in mourning for herself and their marriage, the crown recognizing her political power in that marriage, and the roses which would have been quickly understood by contemporaries as a symbol of conjugal love.[11] There can be no doubt that Charles himself had a hand in that design. But if the model had been 'very lifelike', Titian's painting seems to have been inconveniently realistic for the ageing Emperor's imperfect memory. In 1547, he made Titian repaint Isabella's nose, straightening the aquiline proboscis mentioned by contemporary chroniclers and prominent in portraits done from the life into a nose of 'improbable classical perfection', as one critic has described it.[12]

Interestingly, Titian used this earlier work, which had been subject to posthumous plastic surgery, as his model for the remarkable painting of 1548 in which he depicts Isabella as breathtakingly beautiful and which Charles is said to have adored because of its likeness. Emperor and artist had conspired to replace all memory of reality with a beautiful myth.

Isabella had been the Castilians' choice of queen, the nearest thing to a Spanish candidate: the daughter of Manoel of Portugal by his second wife, María of Aragon, Charles's aunt, she was Charles's first cousin and they needed special dispensation to marry from a reluctant Pope. Charles was able to negotiate an enormous dowry of almost a million ducats, an unheard-of sum that is testimony to the wealth pouring into Portugal from her trading colonies and possessions in Africa and the East Indies.

Charles wrote to England in pleading tones, trying to explain and justify his decision not to marry Mary Tudor, but Henry VIII was furious and Cardinal Wolsey immediately sought to renew the English friendship with France. Francis I was delighted; suddenly, he felt confident enough to refuse to ratify the Treaty of Madrid and resumed his public hostility to the Emperor. But there was an even more momentous consequence, for Henry now had to think about the English succession, for without Charles, Mary looked like a dangerously weak heir; Catherine of Aragon had failed to bear Henry the son he needed and he became so notoriously determined to be rid of her that he embraced Protestantism and effected the Reformation in England in order to make divorce possible.

In the spring of 1526, while the Emperor prepared to go to Seville to marry his bride, an astounding train of powerful aristocrats and churchmen set out from Toledo to welcome Isabella of Portugal to Castile at the border, near Badajoz, an immense festive army of gilded nobility, knights, their squires, other gentlemen and ladies, their servants, the inevitable bureaucrats and assorted hangers-on, the curious and those looking to turn a few *blancas* or *cuartos*, the basic copper currency of Castile.

On 7 February 1526, Isabella arrived on the Portuguese side of the border in a litter richly decorated with gold brocade and crimson silk, carried by a pair of fine horses. She was accompanied by two of the royal princes, her younger brothers Luis and Fernando, and eight lackeys wearing brocaded jackets and scarlet breeches, with eight more in black velvet coats over white breeches; accompanying them were four pages dressed in cloth of gold mounted on four small but handsome white horses. The contemporary historians differ as to whether it was thirty or forty or maybe fifty paces from the bridge across the river that Isabella abandoned the litter and mounted a beautiful white horse, not much bigger than a pony, with a sumptuously decorated silver saddle. Flanked by Luis and Fernando, she rode towards her destiny. The Castilian grandees advanced towards the border as well, until the two sides faced one another, barely twenty yards apart.

The Portuguese and then the Castilian aristocrats, in reverse order of rank, kissed Isabella's hand as an act of general reverence and personal homage. Fernández de Oviedo described how the Spaniards 'set their horses' hooves on the line' of the border itself, so that they could kiss their new Queen by leaning across into Portugal.[13]

According to Oviedo, the Duke of Calabria approached the Empress, his cousin, but 'she did not want to give him her hand as she had done with all the others, for all that the duke made a great fuss; but the Empress refused'. So the duke faced the Empress, with the heads of their mounts touching; the Archbishop of Toledo was on his right and the Duke of Béjar on his left. The duke's twenty-four lackeys wore scarlet from their boots to their hats, while his five mules were draped in velvets of crimson, ruby red, yellow and black. The Archbishop, dressed in crimsons and purples with sable furs, had brought an entourage of a dozen trumpeters, six horn players and three mules adorned with jingle-bells. Béjar was dressed in black satin and velvet, with his beard worn long; he came with eight trumpeters, five hornpipe players and eighteen pages, all mounted on mules or horses and dressed in vermilion and black velvet tunics embroidered in white, flying standards of white damask embroidered with his coat of arms in silver thread.[14]

Calabria then asked his secretary to read aloud the royal warrant by which Charles V had authorized him to welcome Isabella to Castile; the Castilian aristocrats removed their hats, baring their heads as though in the presence of the Emperor himself, and the secretary began to read. When he had finished it was the turn of the Portuguese Prince, Luis, whose voice resounded across the frontier: 'I surrender my lady the Empress to Your Excellency in the name of my brother and lord, the King of Portugal, as the wife of the Emperor Charles.'[15]

He then left his sister's side and Calabria approached her, with his hat in one hand; he took the reins of Isabella's horse and received her in the name of Charles. The trumpets, horns and jingle-bells sounded. Oviedo describes how fifteen or sixteen pages, all dressed in bright silks, rode forward and began to make their horses jump and dance and prance with breathtaking grace; and fifty or so of the most senior nobles present danced their mounts in a circle around the Empress, while everyone else pulled back to make room for the spectacle. As Oviedo said, it was a wondrous thing to see, not least because some of the horsemen were so young, and for almost a quarter of an hour the spectators looked on with great pleasure.[16] When the time came for the Portuguese princes to take leave of their sister there were tears on both sides, and then Isabella finally crossed into Castile.

The most desirable woman in Europe, Isabella necessarily took a keen interest in fashion, for the public image of royalty was intimately linked to the realities of power, and much of the value of her astounding dowry lay in her collection of jewellery. In an age that required monarchs and noblemen to be visually and theatrically vibrant, in an age when hierarchy and authority were communicated and reinforced through display and ritual, Isabella needed portable props with which to awe her husband's subjects.

A handful of pieces stand out even in the spectacular array of gorgeous objects listed in official royal inventories. On the basis of monetary value alone the most remarkable piece was not part of the dowry, however, but was Charles V's principal wedding present to his wife, a choker of nine large diamonds and nine pieces of gold forming the initials of Charles and Isabella, adorned with seventeen hanging pearls, valued at 23,500 ducats, a phenomenal sum for a single artefact and almost as much as all of the Mexican treasure sent to Spain by

Cortés. Then there were two gold necklaces: one, set with ten massive emeralds and seventy-two pearls, was valued at 5,500 ducats, before two further emeralds and some more pearls were added, bringing its total value to 7,500 ducats; the other, worth 3,100 ducats, was set with nine rubies and nine diamonds, each hung with a large pearl. There were also a couple of brooches, one in the form of a flower, the other worked into the form of tree roots, set with diamonds and pearls, which had a combined value of 7,800 ducats. And so the inventory continues, listing one thing after another, thousands of pieces, each of which was worth more than the average nobleman could expect to take in income in a year.[17]

Despite this truly outstanding collection of jewellery, Isabella herself was more interested in her wardrobe. She commissioned Florentine artists to design heraldic decorations for brocades that were then made in Genoa. She ordered the most expensive fabrics from across the Empire and was kept abreast of the best cloths on the market by specialist merchants and the imperial ambassadors.[18]

The basic elements of her daily dress were the *camisa*, or blouse, which was usually white, and a *mantón* or shawl, which was usually black, over which she might wear a *ropón* or long overcoat to keep out the cold. She also had a large number of silk petticoats and underskirts, including one which had belonged to Juana the Mad, made from gold brocade. She had *sayas*, or smocks, of silk or taffeta and *delanteras*, a kind of apron of white velvet decorated with gold thread. She wore *tranzados* and *cofias*, hairnets and coifs that held her hair in place. Her most prized *cofia*, woven from gold thread and holding 370 little pearls, was valued at 740 ducats. Over these, she might also wear *tocadillos* or caps of fine fabrics that were decorated with pearls and gold brocade.[19] But sleeves were probably the most important fashion item in the Age of Chivalry; they might be part of the main garment or they might be separate, attached by buttons, tapes or tassels. Made from every conceivable fabric and in every possible colour, they offered the Empress a wonderful opportunity to show off to the endless lines of courtiers, noblemen and ambassadors who daily knelt at the imperial feet and bowed to kiss her hand.

Needless to say, she was very specially and very splendidly dressed for her entry into Seville, that glittering jewel of the Andalusian south, on 3 March 1526. Amazingly, much of the dress she wore that day has survived because she bequeathed it to the Monastery of Guadalupe, where it was turned into a chasuble. By comparing this remarkable garment with Antonius Mor's famous painting of Mary Tudor and other paintings of women associated with the Habsburgs, we can see that Isabella led the way in setting a dynastic fashion for luxurious dresses made from Spanish *brocado*, a costly fabric that draped beautifully, based on a rich silk that was woven with silver and gold thread in floral arabesques.[20]

The dress she wore in Seville was almost certainly made in Granada, then the heart of the Spanish silk industry, home to the best Muslim craftsmen and seamstresses. This garment seems to have established a fashion for having a grand, stylized pomegranate on the front panel, at the waist, between the neckline and the narrowing above the hips. The pomegranate is the symbol of the city of Granada, which may have inspired the design and would certainly have meant that the embroiderers were especially experienced in elaborating the motif, but it also had huge symbolic importance because the pomegranate is also a symbol of the Virgin Mary as Mother of the Church, with the profusion of seeds characteristically bursting out of the fruit acting as an allegory for the faithful. To wear such an obvious symbol of Christian piety and fecundity across her belly was a clear reference to her roles as virgin bride, Holy Roman Empress and mother to the future of the dynasty.

Seville has long been a city famous for its fiestas, and the Portuguese chronicler Luís de Sousa commented on a reception that 'reflected the great power of that rich city and the love of her people for their princess'.[21] The Chronicler Royal, Alonso de Santa Cruz, records that when the Empress arrived at the Hospital of St Lazarus, a leper-house that was a famous landmark just outside Seville beside the great road north, she abandoned her sumptuous litter and mounted a richly adorned horse.[22] 'The Empress's face was white and her glance was honest. She spoke little and quietly. She had large eyes, a small mouth, an aquiline nose, good hands, a high and handsome throat. Honest, quiet, serious, devout, discreet, she was more retiring and deferential than she need have been.'

The Duke of Arcos kissed her hand and, accompanied by all the principal gentlemen and knights of the city, all very richly dressed, she rode into Seville by the Macarena Gate beneath a canopy of gold brocade adorned with the Emperor's coat of arms. The buildings were hung with tapestries and textiles and lit by flaming torches; opulently dressed ladies and gentlewomen watched on excitedly from the packed balconies as a sheriff and some constables forced a route through the throng, calling out to the people to bare their heads because 'her Majesty wants to get a good look at you'.[23]

At strategic points along the route, temporary but elaborate triumphal arches had been constructed, dedicated to Prudence, Strength, Clemency, Peace, Justice, the Three Graces (Faith, Hope and Charity) and the Queen of Heaven, shown with her arms outstretched towards the Emperor and his Empress. With striking symbolism, next to the arch of Strength the ever erudite Sevillians had erected a smaller span carrying an effigy of brave Horatius, the Captain of the Gate, whose legendary defence of Rome involved holding off the enemy while his companions destroyed the only bridge over the Tiber, before he survived by hurling himself into the river and swimming to safety. This bore the inscription: 'You were too strong for all the Etruscans, but Caesar is second to none and alone can take on the whole world.' Its meaning was clear: as Holy Roman Emperor, Charles could now style himself as Caesar, a Caesar who was stronger and more valiant than even Horatius had been.

The following Saturday, the Emperor arrived with the Papal Legate, a large number of prelates and many grandees of the kingdom. The Duke of Arcos and the knights of Seville and many other lords went to meet him along with the royal officials, the city sheriffs, the lieutenants, the gentlemen, the licentiates and lawyers, the professors and physicians, the public notaries, the citizens and the merchants; anyone who might claim to be anyone, locals, outsiders and foreigners alike, appears to have come to greet the Emperor. And they all came in uniform, wearing their chains or carrying their staffs of office. The documents describe them as forming into 'squadrons' according to their professional and institutional affiliations; and, interestingly, the sources record that they came armed, a timely reminder to Charles that Seville and her Andalusian hinterland were a potent ally but would likewise make a devastating enemy. He, in turn, entered Seville holding an olive branch in one hand, announcing himself as a prince of peace.[24]

Once the Emperor had attended mass, he hurried to the Royal Fortress, the Alcázar, to meet his bride. Oviedo tells us that when Charles reached the Empress's apartment and they saw each other, she immediately knelt down and begged to be allowed to kiss his hand. But the Emperor squatted down and lifted her up, hugging her. He then kissed her and, taking her by the hand, led her into the next room where they sat down. Once they had spent a quarter of an hour there surrounded by a crowd of grandees, Charles went to his own rooms.

Soon afterwards, they were married by the newly appointed Spanish Archbishop of Toledo, Alfonso de Fonseca, at a temporary altar during a very private ceremony within Isabella's apartments, with the Duke of Calabria and the Countess of Haro acting as best man and maid of honour. By now it was two in the morning and the Emperor withdrew to his own rooms to allow Isabella to prepare for her wedding night. Then, once she was in bed, he returned and consummated the marriage immediately 'like a good Catholic prince'.[25]

Charles's personal relationship with his wife is very difficult to understand at such a remove in time. They do genuinely appear to have fallen in love at first sight. In among the myriad formulaic descriptions of their marital bliss, the Count of Vimioso gives us a sense of romantic reality as well as appropriate protocol when he notes that 'it would appear that the newlyweds share a great sense of happiness . . . and when they are together they have eyes for nobody else'.[26] And, apart from her wealth, his power and the political convenience of the match, narcissism provides further credible explanation: a Spanish diplomat returning from preliminary marriage negotiations in Lisbon reported that Isabella had seemed to him to be 'a very self-assured princess . . . who seemed to look a lot like you, Sire, if I may say so'.[27]

But, for all their love, they would maintain separate households, and during his long absences from Spain Charles would have many affairs and sire some famous bastards such as the great soldier Don John of Austria and the capable Governor of the Netherlands, Margaret of Parma. They seem to have exchanged few personal letters, although it may be that their private correspondence has not survived. Isabella's repeated requests when he was abroad that he come home to Spain as soon as possible were ostensibly pleas that he deal with pressing matters of state, but such official nagging may have also been a proxy for her private emotions. At court it was clearly believed that 'she was suffering because of His Majesty's absence and that everything must be done to console her', while one of Charles's responses, written in 1536, surely betrays real emotion: explaining that he must take up arms against France, he writes in his own hand and in cipher, 'find strength in your heart to suffer God's will . . . be strong and fearless . . . I will not prolong my return over three months more than I have already promised you.'[28]

The extended programme of wedding celebrations had to be delayed because the Emperor ordered the court into mourning on hearing of the death of his sister, Isabella of Austria, the Queen Consort of Denmark. The citizens and the courtiers waited with increasingly feverish excitement until April, when the days and nights of fiestas, feasts, dances, tournaments and bullfights finally began with jousting in the main square.

In the increasingly jocular atmosphere, Garcilaso and Boscán, the latter then serving in the Duke of Alba's household as master in charge of Fernando's education, wrote a satirical poem describing how an ageing aristocrat, Luis de la Cueva, had danced the night away with a lady of dubious reputation, whom they called 'la Pájara', 'Madame Magpie'. A host of young noblemen, led by Fernando, contributed more and more verses, to the maximum amusement of everyone except poor Don Luis and companion; it is a delicious contradiction that this ditty contains the earliest known verse by Garcilaso, the prince of Castilian poets.[29]

And, as festivities continued, another royal wedding was celebrated, when Charles married Germaine de Foix (widowed first by
Ferdinand II and then by the Marquis of Brandenburg) to the Duke of
Calabria. The duke had tried desperately to evade the match because,
as a famous court jester explained, she had become enormously fat, so
obese that 'one night, while in bed with her new husband, the earth
moved, although others say it was the sound of her snoring, and she
fell out of bed with such a violent crash that the floor gave way, killing
a servant and two cooks who were asleep on the storey below'.[30] The
salacious nature of the telling surely reflects the disagreeable reality
of the marriage, but the truth is almost certainly that Calabria and
his bride had a narrow escape when their accommodation collapsed
during a major earthquake that struck while the court was summering
in Granada.[31]

In this atmosphere of festive cheer, with France seemingly
vanquished, and in lust with his wife, Charles V was in magnanimous
mood. Gonzalo Fernández de Oviedo presented him with a copy of
his recently published *Summary History of the Indies*, which at the
time was the most complete eyewitness description of the New World.
Charles was impressed by this catalogue of his American possessions
and Oviedo was soon appointed Historian Royal and sent to Santo
Domingo to begin work on his massive *General History*. Then, on
13 May 1526, following a well-timed petition by the Duke of Alba,
encouraged no doubt by Garcilaso, the Emperor lifted Pedro Laso's
banishment, allowing him to return to Spain.[32]

The following day, in the searing heat of an early Andalusian
summer, the royal couple set out across southern Spain, meeting their
subjects as they travelled to Granada by way of the baking hinterland, visiting the major southern cities of Cordova, Úbeda, Baeza and
Jáen.

Meanwhile, Garcilaso took leave of the exuberant court and went
home to Toledo. Elena was pregnant and over the summer they began
to make arrangements to set up a home for their new family. Garcilaso
had legally come of age and he and Elena signed powers of attorney,
allowing their own agents to collect various debts now due them so
they could set about finding a suitable property. For some reason,

the purchase fell through on the first group of buildings they found, early in 1527; but they eventually bought an imposing and 'important house' in the same parish as Garcilaso's family home.[33]

As the scene of Ferdinand and Isabella's decisive victory over the Moors, Granada held a bewitching symbolism for Charles, for it spoke to his dynastic destiny: as Holy Roman Emperor, he must now lead Christendom against the formidable, perhaps insurmountable threat posed by the Ottoman Turks. His conquering grandparents were entombed here in the chapel they had built for that purpose, a chapel that shone bright and new, Gothic, Christian and victorious alongside the crumbling Cathedral that, within living memory, had been the main mosque of the Muslim town. The following year, Charles would order his own father's much travelled cadaver removed from his mother's increasingly crazed custody to be buried beside them, leaving us in no doubt as to his overwhelming sense of the significance of Granada. And, as his own hopes that he might one day be buried in Burgundy alongside his ancestors began to wither, Charles came to think of Granada as his own final resting place.

For Charles, the family funerary chapel was a place of personal reverence and dynastic remembrance, but the symbolic heart of this iconic city was the great palatine citadel of the Moors, the Alhambra, which hangs like a stork's nest upon the crest of a shallow ridge, imperious above the town; at sunset on a spring evening, the haphazard arrangement of towers and bastions glows gloriously red against the great bulk of the snow-blue Sierra Nevada mountains. Across the centuries, Almoravids, Almohads and the Nasrid sultans built the Alhambra to stand sentinel over the town and market gardens of the fertile *vega*, even as they themselves addressed the cares of state from deep within the hidden pleasure-palace of columned courtyard-gardens with their pools and fountains, running with the melted mountain snow, and the mesmerizing geometric patterns of their tiles and plasterwork that, glimpsed in the dying sunbeams, hang shimmering like the kilims and carpets of an Arabian night. The al-Hambra, the 'Red Fort', is a celestial city, a paradise raised above reality so that rulers might govern in spectacular privacy. Charles V brought his Empress Isabella to honeymoon in the cool of this erstwhile Islamic Eden, there to escape the parching southern summer.

On 4 June, the royal party was greeted by the Granada oligarchs and magistrates, dressed in orange and crimson velvet. The Moriscos had built a spectacular merry-go-round with eight revolving carousels carrying groups of musicians and ululating women. There were triumphal arches designed by a young artist who had trained in Italy called Pedro Machuca and bullfights during which three men were fatally gored.[34] To the fascination of the many foreigners, many of the Moriscos were still practising Muslims who 'paid the Emperor a ducat a year to dress in their usual way and a *real* to the parish if they did not want to go to mass' and whose womenfolk wore 'baggy trousers and wrapped their heads and bodies in a single white blanket, with their faces half covered'.[35] Three years later, the exotic dress of these Spanish Moors attracted the attention of a young artist called Christoph Weiditz as he travelled through Spain: one of his watercolours shows a Morisco peasant carrying a primitive pitchfork and leading an ass on which his wife is mounted, dressed in 'Turkish trousers' and a burqa, with their small child travelling in the kind of esparto-grass saddlebag still in use today in the villages of the Alpujarras hill country.[36] It was hard to tell if these were the exotic residue of a bygone age or the heterodox survivors of an unfinished conquest.

Charles and Isabella set up their separate households within the Nasrid palaces of the Alhambra, but the Empress soon moved her entourage to a newly built Christian convent down in the main town. It is often suggested this indicates that the exotic delights of the Moorish citadel had failed to seduce her, but it seems more likely that there was friction between the Castilian courtiers and the way she managed her household. In the Portuguese tradition, her eating habits were different, she had too many chaplains and, most contentious of all, her ladies-in-waiting could come and go as they pleased in the royal household; in due course, she would agree to change these inconsistencies with Spanish practice.[37] But this domestic rupture did not prevent Charles and Isabella from conceiving their first child, the future Philip II.

The Alhambra became the preserve of Charles's dazzling international court of poet politicians, diplomat philosophers and artistic aristocrats, an intellectual elite that refracted in its every facet the brilliance of the Renaissance. Baltasar Castiglione, the Papal Nuncio, knew the continent from England to Rome and was then writing *The Book of the Courtier*, the first guide to etiquette and intrigue written especially for courtly mandarins. Andrea Navagiero, the Venetian Ambassador, was an historian, writer, poet and intimate friend of Pietro Bembo who brought Petrarch's revolutionary verses composed of classical forms written in contemporary Italian to the attention of the world. Peter Martyr was the Historian Royal who had first called America a 'New World'; Charles's Latin Secretary was the outstanding scholar Alfonso de Valdés; the Polish Ambassador Jan Dantyszek was a close friend of Erasmus. The ailing, aged Duke of Alba came, of course, with his grandson Fernando, and Juan Boscán. Garcilaso, too, appears to have joined this glittering throng amid the intoxicating romanticism of the Alhambra; how could he have kept away when so much of his family mythology was tied up with an ancestor called Garcilaso who had defeated Tafur the fearsome Moor in single combat during the conquest of Granada in 1492?

Boscán recalled that 'one day, in Granada, while discussing wit, literature and language, Andrea Navagiero begged me to try writing in Castilian the kind of sonnets and other verses being composed by the best Italian authors'.[38] Boscán implies that this was an intimate and momentary conversation the like of which may indeed have taken place among the myrtle bushes of an Alhambra courtyard. But, in typically rhetorical Renaissance fashion, he was using that vignette as a way of vividly characterizing a prolonged and developing dialogue between the Italians and Spaniards at Charles's court. They were fascinated by the way Petrarch's poetry had set the literary world of Italy afire with the virtuoso use of classical tropes and sublime metric trickery. Bembo was arguing for the imitation of Latin verse forms in Italian, retaining the style and form of original works by revered poets

of earlier generations such as Virgil and Tasso. They took obvious joy
in the laborious exploration of their models, filling their own work
with allusions and echoes evocative of phrases and images familiar
from the originals. Boscán rose to this challenge of doing the same
for Castilian Spanish with great artistry and imitative skill, but it was
Garcilaso who excelled in developing the possibilities offered up by
the passionate love triangle of Castilian resonance, Italian fashion
and classical foundations. Garcilaso became the defining influence in
Spanish poetry for the coming generations.

In an article in Fernando de Herrera's great edition of Garcilaso's
poetry, published over half a century later, in 1580, when the Habsburg
Empire was at its most powerful and extensive, the great Sevillian
scholar Francisco de Medina would argue that Garcilaso was the
Spanish Petrarch, the ideal writer of Castilian.[39] He would make the
claim that 'it has always been the natural intent of a victorious people
to spread the use of their language at least as far as the limits of their
Empire', at once likening Spain to Imperial Rome and so Spanish to
Latin.[40] Herrera's edition would be the victory shout of a handful of
brilliant scholars based in Seville, the pulsating nexus of the Empire,
who felt themselves to be at the heart of power and the very centre
of the world. But in 1526 their vision of the world was still in the
making.

That Alhambra summer of 1526 was overshadowed by news that
Francis I had announced to the world that no monarch could suffer
the indignity of a treaty agreed under the duress of prison. He pressed
the Papacy to contrive a Holy League against Charles's overbearing
might, ranging against him the independent Italian states and Henry
VIII. The ambassadors of these unnatural allies presented themselves
to Charles in public audience on 22 June, Navagiero among them. They
demanded the return of Francis's heirs, still held hostage, and insisted
that he give up all claim to Burgundy and the restitution of Milan. The
Emperor rejected each embassy in turn; he put his trust in God and
not the Pope, Francis he accused of faithlessness and his uncle Henry
of a lapse in friendship, and the Italians he threatened with war.[41] And
then in September news came from the eastern front of an Ottoman

victory at Mohács in Hungary; soon the infidel would be knocking on the door of Imperial Vienna.

For Charles, the sensuous pleasures of the Alhambra were almost over, but a German physician reported that the Emperor,

> on his last day in Granada, invited Duke Frederick to watch the Morisco girls dance in the Alhambra gardens, all wearing excellent pearls and with other precious stones hanging from their ears, their foreheads and their arms. They danced according to their custom to the sound of lutes and drums played by old women and the rough and unpleasant song of a woman who clapped along. After this, some Morisco women arrived and danced with their legs extended over a cord stretched between two walnut trees and they sang to the Emperor, 'if you live well here, you will go to heaven'.[42]

The verse was apt, for Charles was beginning to think of Granada as his tomb. And so, moved by this morbid sentiment and inspired by his Renaissance courtiers, while he was in Granada he commissioned and began to plan a very modern palace in the Italian style to be built in the heart of the Alhambra complex.

'The Alhambra is so revered among the many magnificent buildings constructed by the Moorish Kings and is still admired by all who see it for its irregular and extravagant architecture, thought to be the best in all Spain,' a contemporary chronicler explained, 'that the Emperor determined to build a new palace in competition with it and to exceed it in technique and beauty, an enterprise to the greater glory of his heroic heritage.'[43]

The tourists who nowadays congregate in the cavalry yard in front of the great west wall of Charles V's palace seem to avert their eyes as they wait impatiently for their turn to allow their romanticism free rein during their visit to the exotic centrepiece of 'Islamic Spain'. They seem offended by this stunning building, which, massive, imposing and constructed in solid stone and glistening marble, exudes an almost aristocratic sense of superiority over its surroundings, a self-confident invader among the flimsy bricks, the wood and plaster and oriental ornament of the surrounding architectural chimera. But that is a mistake because, in a sense, the artistic Golden Age of Spain began here with this unique and revolutionary edifice of the European Renaissance.

Charles placed a clever, erudite, haughty and utterly trustworthy aristocrat called Luis Hurtado de Mendoza in charge of the project. Governor of Granada, son of the Count of Tendilla, cousin to the Dukes of Infantado, he had remained resolutely loyal to Charles during the Comunero Revolt. He was almost certainly responsible for suggesting they instruct Pedro Machuca as their architect, the young artist who had designed two of the triumphal arches for Charles's entry into Granada described by Navagiero as 'ugly and clumsy'.[44] He had trained in Italy, but as a painter, and he had no experience at all of construction. Yet this novice appears slowly to have come up with an incredibly simple yet utterly revolutionary plan for the palace that must have captivated everyone who saw it.

It is clear that from the outset Charles and Mendoza had decided the palace should be a square block, two storeys tall, the epitome of contemporary Italian fashion. But it is the first Renaissance building anywhere in the world with a round courtyard set within a square ground plan. Machuca had brilliantly combined the two basic geometric forms within a three-dimensional building; but many critics have assumed that he was too inexperienced to have conceived of such a groundbreaking design. Some, over-enamoured of Italy, have suggested that Baltasar Castiglione or some other Italian must have mooted the idea first; others point out that the occasional Italian architect had drawn round courtyards into speculative plans for palaces and convents that were never commissioned and never built. It was said that Pliny the Younger's modest villa had some such arrangement in classical times; the Emperor Hadrian, who had been born in Spain, had built a villa at Tivoli with a round gallery circumscribing the garden. A more likely influence was an experienced Spanish architect, Diego de Siloe, then in Granada building the new Cathedral for which he too had adopted a revolutionary circular design for the sanctuary.[45]

But the reality is that anyone with any experience of actual construction, an architect or builder, visualizing such a building in three dimensions, would immediately perceive the almost insurmountable problem of what to do with the corners of the courtyard. In fact, in 1581 a learned Spanish architect complained that 'the royal apartments in Granada are small and truncated because the round courtyard is such a useless design when it comes to rooms and hallways'.[46] Form had indeed trumped function: this is a building designed by an artist in love with geometry not with trigonometry.

In reality, the final design of the palace that we see today came out of Machuca's inspired response to a delicately balanced negotiation between Charles's mundane functional requirements and Mendoza's educated aesthetic preferences. We are fortunate to have a number of documents that reveal the way in which this revolutionary building developed.[47]

The square block was clearly the starting point; but, very early on, someone, probably Machuca, took the axial step of suggesting that the gallery running around the courtyard should be circular, although the courtyard itself was still envisaged as being square. In early drawings made by Machuca the gallery is shown supported by a double row of columns or pillars, but this very obviously created awkward little spinneys of columns in each corner of the square courtyard where it was cut off by the gallery. The solution to the problem of what to do with these four unhappy spaces would suggest itself thanks to the accidental catalyst of Charles's own intervention.

In 1527, Charles wrote definitively delegating all further responsibility for the works to Mendoza, but insisting on two important practical points: that there should be a large audience chamber and that the octagonal chapel (in the north-east corner) should be over two levels, a standard arrangement allowing the royal family to attend mass privately from upstairs balconies or galleries while the household attended in the chapel below. The footprint of the chapel also needed to be expanded,[48] but Mendoza complained that this meant it would stick out into the courtyard and interrupt the rhythm of the colonnade below the gallery. The breakthrough came soon afterwards, when someone arrived at the entrancingly elegant solution of a round courtyard that allowed for the expanded chapel and stairwells to the second storey in each of the other corners while retaining a global sense of symmetry.

But for all the architectural ground this building broke, it was never completed; the works dragged on until, in 1637, the roofless structure became a secure store for the Alhambra complex; and work did not begin on completing the roofs until the 1950s. This most exciting of palaces became a white elephant, abandoned by the Habsburgs, overlooked by most visitors, a paradoxically modern monument too daringly alien for its medieval home.

4

Arms and Letters: Garcilaso and Alba

Who did not see his own blood on his foe's steel?

Garcilaso de la Vega, *First Elegy*

In November 1526, Garcilaso was excused from his duties at court and went home to meet his first legitimate son, also named Garcilaso, and to spend Christmas among his family. His mother remained in robust health; Pedro Laso was back in Toledo and married to a beautiful Portuguese called Beatriz de Sa. But as a *regidor* of the city, Garcilaso was soon on his way to attend the Cortes that Charles had convened for February 1527 in Valladolid. With Christendom set for turmoil, the Emperor hoped the towns would vote a special subsidy to support a campaign against the Turks.

At Valladolid, in the early hours of 21 May 1527, the Empress Isabella went into an agonizing labour that lasted for thirteen hours. Charles remained by her side throughout, and how proud he must have felt when a kindly midwife encouraged the muted, silently moaning mother to scream out and relieve her pain. 'Do not speak to me again,' his Empress replied, 'for even if I have to die, I will never scream.'[1] The Duke of Alba urged that the infant be called Ferdinand after his great-grandfather, but two weeks later he was baptized Philip after Charles's father, very much a Habsburg rather than a Spanish choice.

But even as Charles enjoyed fatherhood, rumour was rife of terrible events in Italy. In June, news officially reached Valladolid that

Charles's Imperial Army had successfully besieged Rome and run amok, committing terrible atrocities and looting the Vatican; they had even stabled their horses in Michelangelo's Sistine Chapel. As the walls were breached, the Pope had taken refuge in the Castel Sant'Angelo, where he was now confined as a prisoner.

The future Historian Royal, Juan Ginés de Sepúlveda, was then in Rome, embarking on his outstanding career as a classicist, linguist and political and legal theorist; his Latin version of Aristotle's *Politics* was still being widely praised by scholars in the nineteenth century,[2] while he would go on to become Bartolomé de las Casas's most formidable adversary, developing some of the most influential theories of just war and empire in support of Charles's aggressive imperial policies in Europe and colonialism in the Americas. He described how, when news reached the city that the Imperial Army was near at hand, 'the young men began to organize themselves according to their neighbourhoods and practise their martial skills, parading through the streets . . . shouting . . . "Rome! Rome! Rome!"' This, he remembered with fear and outrage, posed 'no little risk to the Spaniards who lived there . . . some of whom were subjected to terrible insults, while others were murdered in the dark of night'.[3]

The leaders of both sides began peace negotiations, but the Medici Pope, Clement VII, was no soldier and, ignorant of the realities of war, he placed too much confidence in the belief that the imperial generals had little intention of attacking God's city. But he had not reckoned with the men, who had long been unpaid and were used to taking plunder as reward for their service. As Sepúlveda explains, the ordinary troops were 'determined to take Rome or die trying'. The Imperial Army 'burned with resentment and hatred for the pontiff' and there was 'uproar' when the captains tried to announce a truce.[4]

The soldiers stormed the walls. When the sleeping Pope was woken by 'the thundering of the harquebus and the cannon', he got out of bed in a panic and rushed headlong for safety along the underground passageway that led from the Vatican to the Castel Sant'Angelo. Sepúlveda was also among those who sought refuge in the castle, but inside they found it barely garrisoned and poorly provisioned. By now the Spaniards had breached the walls and Rome was soon overrun by the imperial troops, who:

> looted without pause, took people prisoner, broke into people's homes ... They showed no mercy, not even to Spaniards and Germans, nor made any exception for the Italian Cardinals who had supported the Emperor ... They turned the profane and the sacred upside down, ransacking all the churches, stealing holy chalices and reliquaries containing the remains of saints; and the Lutherans especially treated such holy objects to their impiety. They even murdered the pious who took refuge at the altars and tried to defend themselves with words and prayers. And they were not satisfied with gold, silver, plate, and other loot they came across or found hidden, but they imprisoned the citizens and made them pay ransom money; and some, admittedly not many, reached such perverse extremes as to torture people to find out where they had hidden their wealth.[5]

For all that Charles may have been privately pleased at such overwhelming revenge taken against an untrustworthy Pope, he knew he had to confront an outraged world; and, as detail after terrible detail was repeated and exaggerated across Christendom in broadsides and by word of mouth, his ignominy increased in tandem with his power.

Alfonso de Valdés, his Latin Secretary, wrote the carefully considered and almost unrepentant response, damning the Pope for having brought such catastrophe upon the Papacy. Charles, he argued, had not ordered the riotous desecration of Rome, but God himself had willed it as punishment for a venal and corrupt Vatican.

The ambassadors came to chide the Emperor; but, more seriously, France invaded Italy and, with the support of the brilliant Genoese naval commander Andrea Doria and his private navy of ten warships, besieged Naples, the jewel of the Spanish possessions on the peninsula. Then, in a bizarre display of chivalric posturing, Francis challenged Charles to settle their differences in single combat. Faced with defeat in Italy, the Emperor accepted the challenge and sent his Master of Arms to France to name the powerfully symbolic town of Fuenterrabía as the duelling ground. An astonished French court

blustered and filibustered Charles's man, refusing to allow the acceptance of the challenge to be heard.[6] And then, before one of the most
improbable episodes of brinkmanship in the history of international
diplomacy could be resolved, two crucial changes in fortune saved
Naples and buried Francis's ambitions in Italy for ever.

First, the wily and silver-tongued Marquis of Vasto, who was among
the many leading Italians and Spaniards taken prisoner, managed
to persuade Andrea Doria to change sides, promising him a salary
of 60,000 ducats a year and unheard-of privileges. Doria distrusted
Francis and also concluded that only by joining Charles could he act
as kingmaker in the Mediterranean, for France was not strong enough
to defeat the Habsburgs. He was to serve the Habsburgs faithfully for
two generations, until he died well into his eighties.[7]

Second, a virulent epidemic described by contemporaries as plague
struck Naples and, even more severely, the besieging French army.
Nature's massacre forced Francis to lift the siege.

But for Garcilaso, his Emperor's victory was overshadowed by
personal sadness, for his younger brother, Hernando de Guzmán, was
a victim of the deadly disease. One of the earliest of his poems records
the pathos of that loss:

> Neither the odious weapons of the French
> That they in anger brandished at my breast,
> Nor darts and arrows, stones and all the rest,
> Hurled from the walls by guardians of the breach;
>
> Neither the dangerous fight of skirmish
> Nor the sound of thunderbolts on fire
> Manufactured for Jove to hurl in ire
> That with his artful hands did Vulcan finish,
>
> Could for a single moment, though I braved
> The risks of such cruel war, steal from me
> Neither breath nor grain of life's precious sand;
>
> But 'twas a fatal sickness come upon the breeze
> That from this world, in one short day has done for me;
> So now, far from home, I'm buried in a distant land.[8]

In that chivalric age, what could be more tragic than to go bravely to war, only to be felled by an infection brought by the breeze? But then Garcilaso's own death rivals his brother's for pathos.

For Charles, this was perhaps a time of maximum triumph: for the first time in history since the Roman emperors, a single ruler appeared truly to dominate all Christendom. He seized his moment. It was time to be crowned Holy Roman Emperor by the Pope himself.

In a powerful and self-confident speech to the Council of Castile, he claimed that the Pope was more angered by Francis's constant breaches of trust than by his imprisonment by the Imperial Army. 'For many days since I have struggled with my soul, trying to decide whether to follow my heart and go to Italy to receive the Imperial Crown . . . I have consulted with my advisers and corresponded with friends abroad, I have thought about it for long hours: I am determined to go, and no advice nor counsel will persuade me otherwise.' But then, disarmingly candid about the reasons for the Comunero Revolt, Charles promised his Castilian audience that while he had mistakenly placed his Flemish advisers in charge the last time he was absent from his Spanish kingdoms, 'this time, thanks be to God, I leave them my precious wife the Empress and my children'.[9]

Although Charles left Isabella as Queen Regent, he had made careful preparations for the real business of government to be dealt with by a handful of Spaniards with great political experience. The Council of Castile and the newly created Council of State were effectively elevated from their advisory role to a form of executive authority concentrated in the figure of Juan Talavera, President of the Council of Castile. This arrangement was overseen and thus underpinned by Talavera's close working relationship with Francisco de los Cobos, who, as Charles's most trusted secretary-confidant, travelled with the Emperor. Charles had divided his government between his Castilian advisers who were concerned to keep the peace in Spain and his own imperial party who were determined to maintain order in Christendom.[10]

Charles had designed the system to allow Isabella's acclimatization to government, and, slowly, the beautiful princess-bride learnt to rule as Empress. Meanwhile, as Charles began his preparations to visit

Italy, two other female rulers, the French Queen Mother, Louise of Savoy, and Margaret of Austria, Charles's Regent of the Netherlands, met at Cambrai, now on the Franco-Belgian border, where, over four days, they worked out a treaty that resolved Charles and Francis's constant feuding, a treaty now known as the Ladies' Peace. The key elements in the deal were that Charles would abdicate all pretensions to Burgundy and would return the French princes, while Francis would never again interfere in Italy, would pay two million ducats in ransom for his heirs and would marry Charles's sister Eleanor and treat her as his queen.

Charles was in Toledo in January 1529, preparing for his journey to Italy. Castiglione, the Papal Nuncio, must have been overjoyed to see peace at last between the Emperor and the Pope; and while the Italians must have longed for home, we can readily imagine the excitement among the Spanish courtiers eager to visit the cradle of the Renaissance. Garcilaso and Pedro Laso, now fully rehabilitated, joined Boscán in the splendid train of aristocratic travellers and their hangers-on making their way across Spain to Barcelona, where the imperial entourage would take ship for Italy. The Duke of Alba was too old and ill to sail, but went to see the Emperor embark; he took his leave, for the last time, of his brother, Pedro de Toledo, soon to be appointed Governor of Naples.

Among the innumerable and detailed logistical arrangements necessary to make the imperial voyage possible, there was one preparation that must have fundamentally changed the business of Spanish barbers: Charles decided that he would have his hair cut short and that he would grow a beard, apparently adopting a new image calculated to associate himself with the classical Roman emperors. Along with almost all the other courtiers, Boscán, Pedro Laso and Garcilaso followed this new imperial fashion, although many wept at having to cut their long, luxuriant locks.[11] But they also had graver, more personal matters on their minds. Travel was dangerous, especially a sea voyage with its threat of storms and Barbary pirates, and so Charles and everyone else made their wills. Wonderfully, Garcilaso's has survived and its detail reveals much about him as a person and a gentleman. Aside from principal clauses dealing with the distribution of his estate to his wife and children, he also remembered from the Fuenterrabía campaign that 'at a town in Navarre I owe someone called Martín an old hack which through my fault was taken by the French' and in 'Salvatierra I owe a surgeon for some food we ate in his house where I stayed after we took the town, about five or six ducats in total'. And he extended this meticulous honesty to a 'maid called Elvira to whom I am indebted for her honesty. I think she is from Torre or Almendral in Extremadura. Francisco or the Sheriff of los Arcos and his wife will know who she is. Send an honest person with a good conscience to find out if I am in her debt and if so pay her 10,000 *maravedís*, but if she is married they must be very discreet in this business.' He also made provision for the illegitimate Lorenzo so that he could study for the priesthood or to become a lawyer according to his own preference.[12] In death, Garcilaso de la Vega would remain a gentleman.

Then, on 28 July, the flower of the Spanish nobility embarked on Andrea Doria's great fleet of almost a hundred ships and sailed to Genoa, where they were met by a flotilla of 200 small boats and the deafening sound of all the guns firing in salute. Charles remained in Genoa for seventeen days, cementing his relationship with Doria and the city fathers, well aware that this port and its navy were the keys to the Mediterranean. For the first time, the two men must have discussed the possibility of a great naval campaign against Tunis or Algiers, client kingdoms of the Ottoman Sultan Suleiman the Magnificent, and the North African headquarters of the fearsome renegade pirate Barbarossa, 'Red Beard'.

But even as Charles hoped to take the war to Islam across the sea from his possessions in Spain and Italy, a massive Ottoman army had advanced into his brother's lands in the east and threatened Vienna. Comfortably and safely ensconced in his Castilian green room, as it were, Charles had clearly felt he would be omnipotent on the world stage, but now that he was actually playing his leading role, he must have recognized the insurmountable nature of the task. Even as he negotiated with the Italians and the Papacy on Italian soil, he was being urged by both Margaret of Austria and his brother Ferdinand, now governing in Austria and serving as elected king of Bohemia, to bring the weight of his authority to bear in the Netherlands and the Empire. He had very much wanted to be crowned Emperor in Rome itself, but in order to move as quickly as possible against the Lutherans and the Turks, he decided to move the ceremony to the historic university city of Bologna.

At Bologna, Charles was first crowned King of the Lombards. Two days later, he was received outside the Cathedral beneath a canopy of laurels by Clement VII and fifty-three bishops. There he was anointed with holy oil on his right arm and his sword before the Pope crowned him with the gold crown of the Empire. He prayed at the high altar and knelt to kiss the pontiff's feet before sitting on the Imperial Throne. It was his birthday, 24 February 1530.

Before leaving Italy, he spent twenty days hunting and relaxing at Mantua, in the stimulating company of the greatest art patron of Europe, Federico Gonzaga. Gonzaga introduced him to the great Venetian painter Tiziano Vecelli, always known in English as Titian. Garcilaso and Boscán must have relished the intimate world of Mantua's ducal court, with its unsurpassed collection of painting, tapestry, sculpture and literati. But Charles had already begun to reduce the size of his Spanish court in preparation for the journey north. At Mantua, he granted Garcilaso a stipend of 80,000 *maravedís* a year and absolved him from his duty of service, allowing him to return to Spain.[13]

Garcilaso was becoming an important courtier and diplomat with international experience. The Emperor had written to Isabella maintaining the fiction that Francis I, now properly married to Eleanor, 'seems determined to keep this peace and preserve our friendship'; and, appearing to address the all-important business of protocol, he explained that as he had sent his own envoy to visit the newlyweds 'if somebody has not been sent from Spain to congratulate them, it is important that some person of quality should be dispatched on a similar errand'.[14] As soon as Garcilaso reached Spain, the Empress ordered him to undertake that delicate mission. As she explained in a letter written to the Emperor in cipher, he 'will go well prepared to find out from Your Majesty's ambassadors in France what is happening there and at the same time he will look at what is going on at the border so that we are all well informed' about any possible build-up of troops or supplies.[15]

In the summer of 1531, the recently widowed Pedro Laso was seduced by the offer of an attractive double marriage alliance: he would marry his second cousin Doña Mencía de Bazán, widow of the powerful Duke of Albuquerque's brother. But that was just the icing, the cake was truly mouthwatering: his eldest son, yet another Garcilaso, then aged fifteen, was to marry Doña Mencía's eleven-year-old daughter, Isabella de la Cueva, who was heiress to the vast Albuquerque estates and the most eligible girl in all Spain. Such a match would associate the family directly with the highest rank of the aristocracy, and on 17 July Pedro Laso and Doña Mencía signed the contract.

Doña Mencía had sought out Pedro Laso and his son in a daring manoeuvre designed to stop the Duke of Albuquerque marrying Isabella to his younger brother, which would have concentrated the inheritance within the dynasty. The whole Albuquerque family appealed urgently to the Empress to prevent the match and she referred the dispute to the Emperor. But Doña Mencía was a formidable adversary; indeed she was grandmother of Admiral Álvaro de Bazán, Marquis of Santa Cruz, whose untimely death robbed the Great Armada of a commander who would have defeated England in 1588. On the eve of the Feast of the Assumption, 14 August 1531, she cunningly outflanked the aristocratic titans lining up against her. First, she asked permission to take Isabella to confession at Avila Cathedral. But, almost as soon as they reached the church, the boy-bridegroom Garcilaso appeared and soon afterwards his uncle Garcilaso de la Vega arrived. The wedding scene was set and, with a handful of servants to stand witness, a priest was pressed into carrying out the ceremony; the two children placed their right hands on a holy cross and duly exchanged their vows.

A month later, Charles's warrant arrived ordering that no marriage could go ahead without his permission. In fact, the die was not yet cast, for, as Garcilaso the nephew later claimed under interrogation, the marriage had never been consummated by 'a carnal act', a claim that seems entirely plausible given Isabella's age. But the Empress was angry and began to move against all those involved.

Charles had spent the summer of 1530 searching for some sort of reconciliation between the Protestants and the Catholic Church: he had prayed that the Diet of Augsburg would produce detente, but instead it descended into an exchange of 'bloodcurdling threats', and in early 1531 the Protestant princes of his Holy Roman Empire formally compacted politically into the Schmalkaldic League.[16] But the threat of all-out war with the Ottoman Turks on the eastern front remained a powerful Christian rallying cry and the Emperor now issued a call to arms, launching the campaigning season of 1532 at Ratisbon, by the blue waters of the Danube, which brought a temporarily united front to an ever more divided Europe.

Garcilaso and his old friend Fernando Álvarez, now the Duke of Alba following his father's death, were among the Spanish nobility who eagerly answered the Emperor's call to arms in January 1532. For Garcilaso, the journey across Europe offered welcome opportunity to escape the consequences of his role in his nephew's contentious marriage, but it was also a chance to travel in the convivial company of a man he had known since childhood. That brave Age of Chivalry blurred the boundaries between fiction and a fantastical reality: it was an age when gallant, noble knights could expect a welcome in the castles and urban palaces of Christian aristocrats, there would be challenges and damsels, banquets and tournaments, and more mundane moments of excitement on often lawless roads, where their steeds, swords and valour might be tested by brigands, outlaws and inclement weather. There would be inns and wenches and cold nights when darkness caught them in the woods and fields. The roads of France would offer them a shared sense of brotherhood and liberty.

Garcilaso met Alba at Fuenterrabía, but within days the Empress's agents had caught up with him. They tried to make him testify that the marriage had taken place. He refused, pointing out that the royal warrant did not authorize them to detain him and explaining he was on his way to serve the Emperor. The royal officers sent word to the Empress and her furious response came by return of post, leaving

Garcilaso in no doubt that he must confess; even then, he honourably refused to implicate the priest by name. But as soon as he had given his succinct and unlyrical account of the events, he was served with notice of his banishment from the court and the kingdom, and he and Alba set out across France.[17]

Garcilaso recorded their progress across Europe in a few vibrant verses within a long and fascinating eclogue or dramatic poem full of essays at changes in rhythm and rhyme. Imitating a bewildering range of classical sources, most obviously Virgil's *Aeneid*, he evoked the awesome beauty of the landscape as they crossed the mountains into France:[18]

> Through the mighty Pyrenees,   which seem to rise
> Reaching heavenward the skies,   while from high fells,
> Valleys seem the depths of hell,   all white with snow,
> Muffling brooks that scarcely flow,   springs silenced,
> Hard-frozen in the still of ice,   they make their way . . .[19]

Garcilaso's challenging rhyme scheme that requires a break in each line, known as *rima al mezzo* in Italian, is awkward, interrupting the hendecasyllabic metre, the eleven-beat lines, and the style was soon abandoned by Spanish poets. Written while he was serving Pedro de Toledo, Alba's uncle, the Viceroy of Naples, between 1533 and 1535 during his exile, it reveals Garcilaso experimenting at the very limits of what was possible in Castilian verse, having relaxed into the very Hispanicized Italian surroundings of Naples.

After allowing us to accompany the duke over the final pass and into France, the poem rushes us headlong towards Paris, where Alba is struck down by 'gaunt, jaundiced sickness'. 'Healthy in the saddle, now the duke was faint,' he becomes weak, his colour fades, until:

> Striding through wood and forest   of healing herbs
> Esculapius could be heard,   God's Physician
> Hurrying thither with healing mien   to the sickbed
> Where Fernando laid his head,   weak, pale, and wan.
> Best foot forward, the doctor's come!   Bringing his cure,
> The patient's strength to restore . . .[20]

And suddenly all is well thanks to the intervention of Esculapius, Apollo's son who had been doctor to the classical gods. Alba and Garcilaso are back on the road and crossing the Rhine and the poet 'calls to mind the hour when Latin Caesar came to the same crossing point', before the journey rattles on apace, across 'broad Germany, to where, in doubt, the Christian army lay' at Ratisbon, modern Regensburg, by the Danube.

> Wholesome love gleaming in his eyes,   Charles, our Caesar,
> Ever glorious conqueror   did then embrace
> Alba at the river gate   and the gathered
> Noblemen soldiers hollered   loud their cry
> Now certain of the victory . . .²¹

And he goes on to describe the imperial forces by imitating Herodotus' account of Xerxes' great army in his *Histories*.

Charles had amassed what one French nobleman described as 'the biggest and most beautiful army that anyone had seen in half a century', an imperial force of 150,000 infantry and 60,000 cavalry, so intimidating that Suleiman the Magnificent immediately ordered the Ottoman soldiers to retreat and there was no action.²² Aristocratic and noble adventurers, such as Alba and Garcilaso, from across Christendom swelled the ranks, while the ferocious *tercios*, squads of well-trained and professional Spanish infantrymen who were feared across Europe, had arrived en masse from their stations in Italy. The Turkish retreat left Charles's troops restless for the fight, but the victory has become legendary and the Viennese bakers are said to have baked in celebration a new, deliciously light butter pastry in the shape of the Islamic crescent moon, pastries that today we still call croissants.

But while Alba was rapturously received as the new head of one of the most powerful families in Spain, Garcilaso, in disgrace, was refused entry to Ratisbon and was instead banished to a small island in the middle of the river. Aware that he was a victim of the overbearing paternalism of monarchy and aristocracy, Garcilaso lamented that 'my body is now in the hands of one so powerful he can do with it what he will'.[23] And the all-powerful Emperor decided that he could make best use of the exile of so valuable a vassal by sending him to Naples in the service of Pedro de Toledo, whose brilliant viceregal court pulsated with a love of life and literature. With his easy social graces, Garcilaso excelled in this stimulating world of art and the intellect, and he found Naples to be the sweetest of prisons and the place where he wrote some of his greatest and most influential poetry. He became close friends with the great classicist and future Historian Royal, Juan Ginés de Sepúlveda, and dedicated a Latin ode to him. He became a regular at the Pontaniana Academy, where poets gathered to write in Latin, and exchange ideas, and met the great Pietro Bembo, who soon afterwards described Garcilaso as 'a gentleman and a brilliant gentle-poet worthy of special praise and commendation'.[24] And while in Naples he came by the copy of Castiglione's *The Courtier* from which Boscán made the first Spanish translation. He went on numerous diplomatic missions to Rome and Spain, and in 1535 he joined the great armada that Charles and Andrea Doria had gathered in the Mediterranean for a massive assault on the Ottoman redoubt of Tunis.

As he travelled back to Spain from Germany by way of Italy, Charles was forced to face a new threat. In a strategic move calculated to counteract the naval dominance of Andrea Doria, Suleiman the Magnificent had agreed terms with the famous and much feared Italian renegade pirate Barbarossa. Barbarossa's first act as a client of the Sultan was to take the city of Tunis on the North African coast, then ruled by a Muslim prince as a vassal of the Spanish Crown. Charles was determined to win it back, and for a generation of Spanish cavalier-aristocrats brought up, like Garcilaso, on Reconquest legends about their ancestors' feats of derring-do during the medieval wars against the Spanish Moors, the coming campaign in North Africa had strong historic appeal. They were excited and filled with a chivalrous hunger for battle.

Before he again left Spain in the charge of Isabella, Charles decreed that Prince Philip was now old enough, at the age of seven, to have his own household and live separately from his mother with his stewards, his majordomo, his chaplain and his schoolmasters. Special courses were prepared in grammar and reading by Dr Busto, who had translated Erasmus' *Institution of a Christian Prince* into Spanish, a work that became hugely influential among the humanists of Spain. By 1536, the Prince could say his prayers in Latin and Spanish and was beginning to read in both languages. 'Soon,' Busto reported to Charles, 'he will start to study the great writers, the first of whom will be Cato.' Philip grew up accompanied by a coterie of hand-picked aristocratic children; together, they experimented with being courtiers, organizing childish jousts and dances, learning to ride and developing a taste for hunting and fencing, martial sports at which Philip excelled.[25]

Charles mustered his army at Barcelona and, as they embarked in Doria's ships, he announced that Christ himself would be their general. They sailed for the Carthage peninsula, the site of Dido's rebel city of the Roman Empire that Scipio Africanus had razed to the ground in his final successful campaign of the Punic Wars. The imposing remains of the ancient aqueduct formed a dramatic backdrop as Charles's troops landed. But while most of his educated patrician entourage celebrated the symbolism of the newly crowned Holy Roman Emperor waging war on such historic ground, in a moving poem dedicated to Boscán, Garcilaso used it as an opportunity to question the Habsburgs' imperial pretensions.[26]

Charles himself appointed a talented Dutchman, Jan Cornelisz Vermeyen, as his war artist. Later, in commemoration of Charles's victory, Margaret of Austria commissioned from the prestigious Flanders workshop of Willem de Pannemaker a series of twelve massive and incredibly detailed tapestries based with painstaking faithfulness on Vermeyen's finely drawn sketches and cartoons.

This beautiful and vivid visual record matches closely many of the narrative descriptions of the campaign, even some moments of minor skirmishing, partly because Vermeyen used official historical material in finalizing the compositions, but also because he was actually there in person. What is more, Vermeyen himself appears in some of the images, at work, with battle raging around him, reflecting the Renaissance obsession with the notion that eyewitness accounts of history were almost incontrovertibly true. The tapestry series begins with a map-like panoramic overview of the Mediterranean, showing the movement of the individual ships which made up the fleet, with Vermeyen at a lectern to one side holding a compass in one hand as a symbol of his cartographic accuracy. We see the aristocrats passing muster outside Barcelona and there is bloodthirsty detail in the *Sack of Tunis* and the final *Departure from la Goletta*; the broad overview of the *Landing off the Cape of Carthage* has been called 'a true spec-imen-book of the ships of the period', reflecting the central role of Charles's navy in securing victory: we see great galleons in the distance, a nimble caravel and the Imperial Galley with its galley-slaves in their red breeches.[27]

These vast tapestries, eventually hung in the Great Hall of the Alcázar, the Royal Palace in Madrid, were designed to be read as a visual history, and at the bottom of each there is a poem in Latin that neatly outlines the episode it depicts. To the right side, a small 'tablet' briefly explains the geography. At the top, a longer inscription in Spanish, clearly derived from the account of the Cosmographer Royal Alonso de Santa Cruz and perhaps written by him, gives a much fuller account of the various elements shown in the tapestry. It is worth remembering that many viewers would have been involved in the action themselves and many more would have read the official histories. They would have spent hours discussing the details, with moveable scaffolds allowing the close inspection of the images from top to bottom.[28]

On the strength of his magisterial history of the campaign, *The African War*, Juan Ginés de Sepúlveda was made Historian Royal by Charles.[29] Working from an eyewitness account, he frequently throws his readers into the heat of the fray. The first major engagement took place in a sandstorm, which can just be seen in the very background of *Landing off the Cape of Carthage*, with the early blood to Barbarossa but ending in a Turkish retreat. As the skirmishing continued, a man called Juan Suárez, 'a little more arrogant than is convenient in a brave but restrained knight', Sepúlveda explains, so boasted of his bravery that Charles's secretary, Francisco de los Cobos, scolded him: 'in wartime, valour is better demonstrated through deeds than showy words'. 'The next day, as the cavalrymen of the light horse returned to camp . . . Suárez rode away from the squadron towards a group of Bedouin horsemen marauding through a nearby olive grove,' but pulled up short when they turned to face him. 'What are you tarrying for, brave knight?' his captain cried. 'Why don't you attack those enemies whom you are watching and show us your valour?' 'I'm no man to tarry,' Súarez replied and, more foolhardy than the great Don Quixote himself, he charged the foe.

Almost immediately he was surrounded and, 'because his saddle had not been properly tightened, he was knocked off his horse by the blows from the enemy lances'. The captain and two cavalry officers rushed to help, but they were greatly outnumbered by seventy Bedouin who had been quick to join the fight. With the situation looking desperate, Garcilaso de la Vega led a posse of cavalrymen to the rescue, 'fighting so bravely that fourteen men resisted eighty Bedouin'. They managed to retreat with the mortally wounded Súarez, 'who breathed his last breath on the way back to camp'. 'Garcilaso was wounded in the face and the arm,' Sepúlveda tells his readers, before embarking on an angry denunciation of such immorally suicidal behaviour.[30] Garcilaso himself, in a somewhat cryptically lyrical vein, blamed his injuries on 'ungrateful love', who had 'strengthened the hand of my enemies' so as to injure the most utilitarian body parts of a poet, his right hand and his mouth.[31]

The Emperor now sent out a detachment under the command of Luis Hurtado de Mendoza, Marquis of Mondéjar, who had done so much to influence Machuca's design of Charles's new palace at the Alhambra. According to Santa Cruz, as 'the Marquis rode in the vanguard with the cavalry, they were charged by a great multitude of Moors and because the Marquis was such a brave and powerful horseman he charged in among them'. But his men were forced to retreat, 'leaving the Marquis among the enemy. And, when the Emperor saw him . . . in such peril, he himself attacked the Moors with his lance in his hand, shouting "Santiago!" with such enthusiastic determination that he did not stop until he reached an artillery position where he ran the gunners through with his lance and captured one of the guns.'[32] According to Sepúlveda, the experienced general Hernando de Alarcón, 'no doubt using very respectful but tough language, then tried to dissuade Charles from throwing himself and his army into the fray so impetuously and thereby putting them all in great danger from the ordnance and the arrows'.[33]

Charles returned triumphant from Tunis as 'Carolus Africanus', first to Sicily and then Naples, rather than Rome, but the parallels with the triumphs of the classical Caesars were evident to all.[34] Yet amid all the bravado, Garcilaso evoked the horrors of war and the soldier's sense of anticlimax in the aftermath of battle in his *First Elegy*: 'Who did not see his blood on his foe's steel? Who did not see his life lost a thousand times only to escape by chance?' 'What comes of this? Glory? Some reward or thanks?' 'My stern Fortune would not allow Death to overcome me as I fought, run through by strong, sharp steel.'

But Garcilaso's luck was about to run out. On 19 February 1536, amid the ceaseless rejoicing and festivities in Naples, the news arrived that Francis I had again invaded Milan. Charles was incandescent with fury and, after Tunis, overconfident. Determined to crush the French, he went straight to Rome and, speaking in Castilian, he denounced Francis for over an hour in public audience with the Pope. It was clear that this time no quarter would be given; and, when the French Ambassador complained that he had not understood a word, Charles – whose mother tongue had, of course, been French – replied: 'understand that you cannot expect me to speak anything other than my Spanish tongue, which is so noble it should be learnt by every Christian'.[35]

Charles prepared to invade the South of France, first sending Garcilaso on a whirlwind mission to Genoa and Milan to discuss the most secret aspects of strategy with Doria and his generals. Garcilaso reported back to Charles and, days later, he was made Captain of Infantry with command over 3,000 men then due to arrive at Genoa at any moment on the Malaga fleet under the command of Álvaro de Bazán.[36] Bazán was brother of Isabella de la Cueva, whose clandestine marriage had led to Garcilaso's banishment; among the soldiers he was transporting was the nephew Garcilaso, the bridegroom himself, whom the Emperor immediately banned from taking part in any action.[37]

Faced with an almost undefeatable Imperial Army, Francis took refuge within the massive defensive walls of Avignon. Unable to engage the enemy in the field and unable to feed so many men, Charles was forced to retreat towards the friendly city of Nice. His vanguard arrived in the tiny town of Le Muy on 19 September 1536. According to a Cordovan soldier, 'next to the town gate there is a narrow bridge beside a well-fortified tower, where fourteen [of the enemy] were hiding'. When 'one of the Emperor's courtiers tried to climb the tower by propping a scaling-ladder against it', one of the foe 'told him not to come up and explained that they were French, that this was their land, and that they did not want to leave the tower'. 'The Emperor ordered the artillery to blow a hole' in the stonework; then Maestre de Campo Garcilaso entered with two other men, but Guillén de Moncada pleaded with them that he be allowed to lead the attack 'so that he could win a little honour for himself', as they had all won so many honours in battle while he had not as yet had the chance. And so Moncada led the way, with the others not far behind. But 'just as Garcilaso and Captain Maldonado began to climb the ladder, the Frenchmen dropped a huge stone, which fell against the ladder, smashing it, and the Maestre de Campo and the Captain fell and the Maestre de Campo bashed his head badly'.[38]

A month later, in Nice, Garcilaso died of his injuries. His death heralded the end of the Age of Chivalry when aristocratic knights aspired to be great poets and donned their armour to fight chivalrously face to face on the battlefields of Europe.

5

Rule of Law

Your Majesty is in need of a large number of judges in these kingdoms.

The Cortes to the Empress Isabella

'Your Majesty is in need of a large number of judges in these kingdoms,' the Cortes urgently advised the Empress Isabella in 1532. 'Litigation has been so much on the increase that cases are not decided with due speed, leading to such great expense and trouble for the litigants that often both parties spend much more than the case is worth and they end up completely ruined, while the advocates, solicitors and notaries get rich.'[1]

After the Comunero Revolt, fundamental social and economic change was taking place at a disorientating pace as money poured in from the Americas, trade boomed, public and private debt soared, the population grew quickly and people moved about more, migrating to new agricultural lands and the growing urban centres. So much economic activity and social upheaval led to a whole range of disputes over land, property and contracts. But, crucially, where Spaniards had once readily resorted to armed conflict in order to settle their differences, allowing the greatest aristocrats with the largest private armies to rule their estates as private fiefdoms, Castilians began to place their trust in the newly empowered Crown and instead of going into battle they went to law. Perhaps the most remarkable achievement of the ongoing negotiation between Charles and the towns following the

Comunero Revolt was the reform of the judicial system and the establishment of courts presided over by judges largely chosen on merit
and well educated in the law.[2]

Within a few years, almost all Castilian social classes began to go
to law. No one, it seems, was excluded from the system. The Crown
provided legal support to the poor, even for civil cases. So we find
the record of a slave called Marita suing for her liberty in 1551, and
a wife who sought a court order against her Town Council to ensure
'they employ someone to go and look for my husband'.[3] In 1577,
Juan Calderón, from the prosperous rural Montes region of Toledo,
sued his illegitimate brother Alonso for appropriating 100,000 *maravedís* of goods and property on the death of their father, arguing
that 'natural sons' had no right of inheritance. Alonso claimed that
the property was in lieu of 'what my father owed me for the many
years of service that I gave him', and that his brother Juan deserved
nothing 'because he did not do any work around the house but spent
all of his time learning how to read, write and count'. While we briefly
glimpse Alonso's sense of the unfairness of life, when the local court
ruled against him he proved stubbornly capable of using the law in his
own interests: first, he appealed to the senior local court, and when
that failed he took the case to one of the two great Castilian appellate courts, the Royal Audiencia and Chancellería of Valladolid. Juan
complained that 'the appeal was only meant to postpone the judgment and delay payment of what is owed'. The illiterate bastard was
working the system.[4]

The vast majority of plaintiffs and defendants were rich peasant
farmers, tradesmen, innkeepers, shopkeepers and other owners of
property, people with wealth to be recovered, but also with pride,
honour and a position to defend. El Greco, the famous Cretan
painter who settled in Spain in the 1570s, for example, seems
to have treated litigation as a normal part of his business practice,
and he won an historic action against the tax collector of Illescas
that helped establish a precedent for the exemption of painting
from royal taxation.[5]

Meanwhile, the great aristocratic families were like massive modern
corporations and, where they had once employed mercenaries, they

now retained teams of lawyers to deal with the incessant litigation in which they were involved. The dukes of Béjar, for example, had a permanent staff of nearly twenty legal advisers, while the Constable of Castile, in 1603 alone, was involved in nineteen separate suits.[6] Major cities likewise had their legal teams, with Seville's senior counsel given a budget for expenses of one million *maravedís* a year for the eighty-five cases he was overseeing in 1551.[7]

Castilian law during this period can seem entangled in an impossibly byzantine web of conflicting jurisdictions and different courts which competed with one another for litigants. A whole range of social groups claimed the right to have their cases heard in their own special courts: churchmen, soldiers, the military orders and Basques all had their own tribunals, which meant that claims and counter-claims were often brought in different courts. Moreover, these courts were presided over by judges who had remarkable leeway in their decision making: the law was not codified, nor were they required to follow precedent except in the most cursory way. Theirs was as much the wisdom of Solomon as anything else. Yet thousands of ordinary Castilians approached this Cretan Labyrinth with the same spirited and often foolhardy bravado with which the conquistadors won so much of the Americas and which made the Spanish *tercios* the most feared regiments in Europe. But even these buccaneering embracers of conflict needed the help of legal professionals to engage with such a complex system of law.

There were three categories of lawyer, the *solicitadores*, the *procuradores* and the *abogados*. The *solicitadores* were a mixed bunch of paralegal fixers who operated at the murky margins of justice. They were unregulated and mostly unqualified, except by experience, a motley parade of three or four hundred innkeepers, lackeys and other colourful characters who offered the promise of knowledge and a network of contacts to their prospective clients. They knew which officials to bribe and how much to bribe them, and they understood what the overall strategic purpose of the bribe was. The good ones were not only master magicians when it came to manipulating the system, they were also brilliant conjurors who bamboozled their adversaries with the complexities of jurisdiction, the niceties of myriad

legal instruments and their understanding of the personalities of the
lawyers, magistrates and judges. These men knew every trick in the
book: filing in the wrong court, failing to appear or deliver crucial
documents, attempting to recuse one or more of the court officials or
requesting the deposition of peasants known to be away at the harvest,
for which the court was required to allow sufficient time.

By contrast, the *procuradores* had been examined in the law and
were licensed by the courts in which they practised. In addition to
these sound foundations, most could point to years of apprenticeship
in the service of an experienced master. But the number of *procuradores* serving a particular court was limited and closely regulated;
the incumbents bought their posts and treated them as investments.
They operated a closed shop, and one gets the impression that the
unofficial ranks of *solicitadores* were growing because they were
needed to do much of the work that was supposed to be done by the
procuradores.

The *abogados* were university-trained advocates who provided
clients with an opinion on the viability of a case and, if it was deemed
worth pursuing, could argue the case on the basis of the law before
the court. They were the hired guns par excellence of the post-
medieval civic society: rhetoric-toting eloquence slingers, they brought
the drama of confrontation to the theatre of justice. But they could be
far from scrupulous: in 1554, an official inquiry at the Audiencia of
Valladolid looked into the case of *Luis de Toledo* v. *The City of Avila*
and then took to task an *abogado* called Aguiar who had 'managed
to persuade Don Luis de Toledo to pay him a salary to help him in
his case against Avila, and Avila to pay him in its case against Don
Luis, making both parties believe that he had rejected offers from the
other'.[8] The best advocates were richly rewarded, but most worked
according to official tariffs, while disgruntled clients often refused to
pay them.

The system moved slowly, sometimes excruciatingly slowly, as
litigants and their advisers used the full range of delaying tactics, a
slowness compounded by other factors such as adjournments due
to plague or epidemic and the anyway high mortality rate: it was
not unusual for a judge, lawyer or litigant to die in the middle of a

case. Most minor courts settled cases within a year, while the appeals courts could take three years or more, and there were extreme examples: *City of Toledo* v. *Counts of Belalcázar* lasted for 130 years, generating 34,000 pages of transcript, while the dispute between Columbus' descendants and the Crown over their title to lands in the New World, first filed in 1504, famously dragged on into the eighteenth century.[9]

The rate of increase in litigation in Castile during the sixteenth century is astonishing. In 1520, the Audiencia of Valladolid issued some 550 writs of judgment; in 1540 this figure had risen to over 800; and in 1580 it reached a peak of nearly 1,400. At that time it had jurisdiction over about four million people, issuing judgments at a rate of 300 per million of population. By way of comparison, in the late nineteenth century, when the state supreme courts of the United States, which served a similar purpose to jurisdictions of a similar size, were at their most active, they issued an average of about 200 opinions per million of population. More astonishing still is that, while in 1970 the US federal appellate courts docketed 11,662 cases at a time when the population was 200 million, by 1580 some 10,000 cases were being registered annually in Valladolid and at the other great Royal Audiencia and Chancellería in Granada. Intriguingly, however, these courts issued writs of judgment for only one in fifteen of those cases, suggesting that Castilians had learnt to use the threat of litigation, the issuing of claims, as part of broader strategies for resolving their disputes.[10]

Despite the many complaints about the cost and complexity, and the corruption and bribery, ordinary people trusted the system to protect them from much more powerful adversaries. Indeed, in 1543, one aristocrat complained that the courts favoured vassals over their lords. That is an exaggeration, but the independence of the Castilian judiciary can be explained by the men themselves, who mostly came from the lesser nobility and gentry and had worked hard to get where they were. They had a long history of antipathy towards the aristocracy,[11] and the records of an almighty legal battle between Juan de Cervantes, the grandfather of the great novelist, and the immensely powerful fourth Duke of Infantado offer us a story filled with twists and turns worthy of Miguel de Cervantes himself in which just such a stubbornly canny David took on a true Goliath.

The Cervantes family originated in Cordova, upriver from Seville, a city famous for its beautiful old mosque, its infernal summers, its leather goods, the broad brims of its hats and the beauty of its women-folk. For much of his life, Cordova was home to Juan de Cervantes, who in due course became a minor judge for the Inquisition. He was a typical member of the new educated middle class, neither rich nor poor, locally powerful but a pawn on the Spanish board.

In 1527, Juan took up office in Guadalajara, to the north-east of Madrid, as Sheriff of the Pastures on the seigneurial estate of the third Duke of Infantado, Diego Hurtado de Mendoza, one of a handful of the most powerful aristocrats in Spain whose decision to support the Crown had been decisive in quashing the Comuneros. But this poten-tially bountiful opportunity soon threatened to undo Juan's career and destroy his family's reputation. The Mendoza household was already controversial: in 1525, a group identifying themselves with the deeply spiritual movement much influenced by Erasmus' writings which was known as the *alumbrados*, or 'enlightened', had met regularly at the ducal palace in Guadalajara, with its Hall of the Wild Men which was decorated as a mysterious forest populated by hairy 'savages'. This particular group of *alumbrados*, many of them women, who were very obviously devoted to a deeply unorthodox and therefore suspect mysticism, were eventually tried for heresy by the Inquisition.[12]

In the spring or summer of 1529, Martín de Mendoza, the duke's bastard son by a reputedly gorgeous gypsy girl, fell madly in love with Juan Cervantes's only daughter María. Archdeacon of Guadalajara, he was destined for a career in the Church and his father had already petitioned Charles V to appoint him Archbishop of Toledo. A marriage was all but impossible. But Cervantes was a wily man of the law. No doubt recognizing both the advantages of such a relation-ship and the futility of trying to prevent it, he negotiated a lucrative marriage contract, well aware that the nuptials would never happen, but by which Martín anyway agreed to provide María with a dowry of 600,000 *maravedís* on Christmas Day 1531, a sum guaranteed by two local merchants. Cervantes ensured that she would be well paid for her concubinage.

While the aged third duke was alive, all was well, for he himself had recently married a beautiful peasant girl and was sympathetic to Cervantes's arrangement. But his prudish heir, Iñigo, was highly disapproving and on his father's death he returned from his studies in Bologna determined to restore a sense of family morality. His illegitimate brother Martín and the dowry owed to María were deeply embarrassing and he refused to release the money owed to her.

Juan Cervantes must have thought long and hard about his next move. But, on 2 April 1532, no doubt with considerable trepidation, he issued a claim on behalf of María against Martín and his guarantors for payment of the full amount. Aware that he was taking on a very powerful adversary, he immediately moved his family out of the Mendozas' seigneurial jurisdiction to the nearby university town of Alcalá de Henares, where he hoped he could rely on the fair-mindedness of the incumbent Archbishop of Toledo to protect them. An experienced litigator, Juan was preparing for war. That he was ready to do so is testimony to both his courage and his confidence in the Castilian legal system.[13]

And then the shenanigans began. The Municipal Magistrate at Guadalajara at first ordered his officers to impound from the guarantors goods or monies to the value of the debt, but his bailiff at once disappeared, soon re-emerging under the protection of the Duchess of Infantado herself. The magistrate now dissembled, caught between his duty to the law and his indebtedness to his lord. But Juan had clearly anticipated some such subterfuge, which he knew would play into his hands in the long run: seigneurial courts were famed for their flagrant bias, so inhabitants of such estates made every effort to bypass these local magistrates and appeal directly to royal justice.[14] The duke and his puppet had given Juan reasonable cause to do just that, and he now lodged a petition requesting that the magistrate recuse himself and transfer the case directly to the Council of Castile, which then functioned as the Supreme Court of Spain.

Needless to say, the now embarrassed and irate magistrate refused, but Juan must have expected that too. He now rode out to Guadalajara, where he had instructed his own lawyer to meet with the magistrate and one of the guarantors, Francisco de Ribera, outside the local prison. Juan Cervantes deliberately caused a scene, attracting a crowd of witnesses by loudly proclaiming to the magistrate: 'I do not want you to enforce the contract. It should have been done yesterday, but it wasn't. Yesterday, Francisco de Ribera had 600,000 *maravedís* of goods in his shop,' but these the sensible guarantor had in the meantime hidden. Juan added, 'I will never achieve justice in this city.'

'I'll give you justice whatever happens,' the magistrate retorted.

'I tell you, I don't want you to! Don't make me say something that will require you to imprison me; I do not want your justice, you are no magistrate.'

'What, not a magistrate? Go home now and don't leave without my permission, on pain of a fine of 200,000 *maravedís*.'

'Listen to me. You are no magistrate as far as I am concerned because I have recused you.'

Having very publicly recused the Mendozas' man, Cervantes set off back to Alcalá. He now had to turn his attention to getting another court to accept jurisdiction over the business.

Meanwhile, the Mendozas stepped up the offensive, clumsily attacking Cervantes's honour by accusing him of whoremongering. They employed the standard procedure of presenting to the court a questionnaire inviting a series of witnesses to state publicly that Martín de Mendoza 'loved and had carnal access to Doña María; and it has been public ever since that she has been his friend and lover with the knowledge and consent of Juan de Cervantes, who invited Don Martín into his home, day and night, to sleep in a bed with Doña María, and they all lunched and dined together at the same table'. They claimed that Martín had never agreed to provide María with a dowry, 'but had simply agreed to pay for the relationship'. Anyway, they argued, Martín had already given María many presents including 'jewels, gold, pearls, silks, textiles and other things worth 600,000 *maravedís*, all listed in an account' previously supplied to the court, a document that apparently bears witness to one of the most costly courtships of the sixteenth century.

By June, Juan had shifted the battleground to Valladolid, where he tried to persuade the Audiencia to accept jurisdiction over the case. The duke instructed his legal team to convince the President of the Audiencia that 'Guadalajara is not what it used to be' under the lordship of the third duke and that he himself 'was dispassionate about the whole business' and 'wished Cervantes no harm, nor wanted to frighten him'. But Juan clearly had him very worried about the new jurisdiction and the duke also told his lawyers 'not to let up until [Juan Cervantes] has been thrown out of Valladolid' and pleaded with them to 'watch out for his sleight of hand . . . Wear him down on every front,' he urged. He was especially concerned that, should Juan prevail, 'it would become public knowledge in Guadalajara that [the duke] did not carry as much weight with the magistrates in Valladolid as he did at home'. He clearly believed that he was now fighting for control over his estates. Juan had raised the stakes by appealing to a higher authority.

Then, as Juan put his appeal before the Audiencia, the duke's lawyers tried to charge him with the criminal offences of pimping his daughter and rebelling against the Guadalajara magistrate. Juan was briefly jailed, but to the duke's horror he was released within days because the prosecutors in Guadalajara could not present sufficient evidence for the Valladolid magistrates to hold him. Instead, one of the judges had praised Cervantes in public as 'very honourable and of good character', while another suggested that it would be better to pay the 600,000 *maravedís* 'so that no one can say that the Mendozas have accused him of pimping his own daughter simply so as not to pay him, which is what many people here think'. Another judge, whom the duke's beleaguered legal team had thought an ally, advised that 'if Don Martín has not paid, then he should pay, and if he has paid, then he should not pay again; and while I know him to be a sinner, I am sure that he will be relieved to unburden his conscience'.

But the course of true justice rarely runs smoothly. Finally, in December, having dismissed the criminal action, the Valladolid court refused Juan's appeal for a change of jurisdiction for the main case and sent him back to Guadalajara; but they did rule that he could appoint, at his own expense, a magistrate of his choice to sit alongside the local seigneurial officer. Cervantes named a lawyer called Segundo.

Battle was now rejoined at Guadalajara, where Don Martín and his guarantors produced a new questionnaire, citing further evidence of Cervantes's complicity in the affair. But then, for some reason left unexplained in the documents, the duke's magistrate recused himself on the grounds that he was not a qualified lawyer and appointed a replacement. He then, even more bizarrely, tried to change his mind and, although no longer on the bench, pointlessly declared that the contract had indeed been fulfilled. Whatever the reasons for the magistrate's erratic behaviour, the moment he resigned Segundo sprang into action, declaring that 'I find in this case that the defendants' opposition to the proper expropriation of their property in the sum of 600,000 *maravedís* on behalf of María de Cervantes and Juan de Cervantes, her father, is without substance, and therefore I order that the expropriation proceed and that the said property be auctioned to the highest bidder and that the remittance be paid to María de Cervantes.' And that was an end of the matter. María was paid.

Thanks to a reliable if somewhat chaotic legal system underpinned by a powerful sense of Crown authority, a clever and determined former employee had defeated at law one of the greatest and most powerful aristocratic houses in Christendom, a house to which the Emperor himself was personally greatly indebted.

So much litigation and legal thinking meant that Castilians were daily exploring the law, a spirit of inquiry that extended to their settlements and conquests among the people and places of the New World. That led leading theologians and jurists to discover the first principles of international law and to sow the seeds of the concept of human rights.

In June 1540 the 'Defender of the Indians', Bartolomé de las Casas, returned to Seville twenty years after he had left to found his colony at Cumaná. Since that disaster, he had been admitted to holy orders as a Dominican friar, and had begun writing his *History of the Indies*. He had recently 'peacefully conquered' a ferociously rebellious Indian *cacique* in Guatemala, which had greatly impressed many powerful figures in Mexico City; even his supposedly hated enemy Oviedo praised his efforts as a peacemaker. Las Casas, many people felt, had proved his point.[15]

What is more, he disembarked in an Old World beginning to embrace policies of peaceful Christian colonization: in 1537, Pope Paul III had published the crucial papal bull *Sublimus Deus*, 'From God on High'. This declared that it was the work of the devil to suggest the Indians were 'dumb brutes created for our service . . . incapable of receiving the Catholic Faith' and ruled that they must 'freely and legitimately enjoy their liberty and the possession of their property; nor should they be in any way enslaved'.[16] In Spain, a handful of influential intellectuals had begun publicly to discuss the legitimacy of the American Empire itself. The most important of these was a Dominican scholar called Francisco de Vitoria, trained in Paris and elected to the prestigious chair of theology at the University of Salamanca.

Salamanca was the oldest university in Castile at a time when universities were expanding rapidly, educating thousands of bureaucrats and professionals like Juan Cervantes, the new footsoldiers of the growing state. By the end of the sixteenth century, 25,000 students enrolled each year in Castilian universities, 7,000 of them at Salamanca.[17] Professors such as Vitoria had real political prominence and Vitoria himself attracted a coterie of outstanding students who took on the big questions of ethics, religion, society and the law; they made groundbreaking studies of ethnography and sociology and even embarked on the first tentative explorations in modern economic theory.

Vitoria himself is best remembered for developing the idea of a law of nations by examining the morality and legality of the Spanish Empire in the New World. Encouraged by *Sublimus Deus*, he set out his arguments in a series of lectures in 1538 which his students wrote up from their notes and published the following year as *On the Indians* and *On the Laws of War*. He began with the basic Christian concept of natural law, the *ius naturae*, the moral or ethical essence with which humanity had been imbued by God at the time of the Creation, and which illuminated all men with the quality of natural reason. Crucially, it embodies a morality that is universal to all people;

it is the essence of humanity and is what sets men apart from the beasts. But at the time many Europeans seriously questioned whether American Indians were truly human. While Vitoria was studying in Paris, a Scottish theologian called John Major had applied Aristotle's theory of natural slavery to the Indians. This held that humanity was divided into natural masters, who had the capacity to think rationally, and natural slaves, who had the capacity to understand reason when it was explained to them but were unable to think rationally for themselves. Aristotle included women, children and almost anyone who was not Greek in this category of amiable simpletons in need of benevolent tutelage. Major believed that the relatively simple Stone Age peoples living in the Caribbean when Columbus arrived must fit this category of natural slave and so argued that it was legitimate and even good for them to have been enslaved by Europeans.

On the one hand, Vitoria interpreted Aristotle differently, arguing that while rational men should be benevolent rulers over their more servile brethren, the institution of slavery itself was a human invention outside the scope of natural law and so its apologists needed to find some other moral or legal justification. But more importantly, on the other hand, the discovery of obviously sophisticated civilizations in Mexico and Inca Peru completely changed the debate de facto: they had rulers, laws, marriage, trade and ownership of property, and they had wars and compacts between their different states. They lived in organized societies and were therefore by definition rational men who had rights to liberty and to the ownership of property. They had also clearly occupied their lands before the arrival of the Spaniards, which meant they had *dominium* over those territories; only where the Spaniards encountered genuine wilderness, *terra nullius*, could they claim possession according to the doctrine of first discovery.[18]

Having effectively outlined the principles of sovereignty and applied them to the Americas, Vitoria ended his lectures with a discussion of how the Spaniards might legitimately claim title over the Indians and their lands. He also outlined various humanitarian principles that would allow the Spaniards to wage just war as defined by St Augustine. Most importantly, he argued that men have an obligation under natural law to wage war against tyrants who impose evil customs on their subjects, such as human sacrifice or cannibalism.[19] On the principle that under natural law 'it is considered inhuman among all nations to treat travellers badly without some special cause', he held that Spaniards must have inalienable rights to travel, trade, reside and even to preach the gospel in peace across the New World that might be enforced, if necessary, by war.[20] Modern passports reflect the endurance of this principle of free passage by asserting, to follow the British rubric, the right of 'the bearer to pass freely without let or hindrance' and to be afforded 'such assistance and protection as may be necessary'.

Vitoria established rules for colonial engagement that still appeared useful and attractive to practitioners of international law in the aftermath of the First World War.[21] The School of Salamanca established the language and the framework for all subsequent discussions of the subject.[22] When, in the eighteenth century, the biographer James Boswell offered to send the English lexicographer Samuel Johnson a postcard from Salamanca, Johnson was overwhelmed by emotion. 'I love the University of Salamanca,' he exclaimed, 'for when the Spaniards were in doubt as to the lawfulness of their conquering America, the University of Salamanca gave it as their opinion that it was not lawful.'[23]

By November 1542, a special committee of the Council of the Indies, led by Las Casas, had drafted draconian new legislation and Charles put his signature to these New Laws of Burgos, which not only declared that no Indian could be enslaved under any pretext and prohibited any new *encomiendas* of Indian vassals, but also required every Crown official, all religious foundations and anyone unable to show their legal title to their Indian vassals to release them into the custody of the Crown. At the same time, Charles ordered a whole new raft of administrative and legal institutions designed to enforce the law.[24]

But when the New Laws were promulgated across the American Empire, the colonists reacted with fury. The Viceroy of Lima was thrown out of town and later killed in battle by an army including members of the Royal Audiencia. In revolutionary mood, many leading colonists rallied behind Gonzalo Pizarro, whose brother

Francisco had conquered the Incas, and encouraged him to declare himself King of Peru and proclaim independence from Spain. In Santo Domingo, Las Casas was jeered by an angry crowd and was refused food; when he reached Mexico, he went in fear for his life. In 1545, the rebels were invoking the Comunero uprising and the forever bellicose Duke of Alba advocated sending in troops.[25] Instead, the Crown took fright and repealed the most contentious parts of the legislation. In Mexico City, a lavish bullfight was organized to celebrate the *encomenderos'* reprieve.[26]

In 1547, the battle lines were being drawn. Both Las Casas and Fernández de Oviedo were in Spain, as was a group of veteran conquistadors from Cortés's campaigns in Mexico, including Bernal Díaz del Castillo, who brought with him an early draft of his classic account of *The True History of the Conquest of New Spain*. He argued simply enough that, unlike Cortés, few of his men had become rich and most relied on their modest *encomiendas* and Indian vassals for a reasonable living. They felt that it was only right they should be allowed to leave these to their children, as just reward for their service to the Emperor. They had an influential ally in Juan Ginés de Sepúlveda, the Historian Royal, who was in Spain fighting for permission to publish his *Democrates Secundus*, 'the most virulent and uncompromising argument for the inferiority of the American Indian ever written'.[27] Cortés befriended him and Sepúlveda was a regular visitor to the intellectual salon hosted by the great conquistador in his Spanish household. Supported by the Council of Castile, Sepúlveda became the intellectual figurehead of the conquistador cause.[28]

In January 1548, Charles wrote a set of secret instructions and advice for his son, Prince Philip, clearly laying out all the major concerns of state, addressing his relations with each realm of the Empire, with foreign kings and princes, with the Pope and even with his own officials; he commented on the need for dynastic marriage, including Philip's own. And he wrote that Philip would 'need to be very circumspect' in the government of the Indies, 'and take care to find out what happens over there and to ensure that God be served there, that they be justly ruled; you must ensure you have pre-eminent

authority over the conquistadors and their estates'. Philip should be
well informed, he went on, 'about the *encomiendas* of Indians,' and
he should consult with wise men 'of good judgment who understand
things over there' to best ensure the 'common good'.[29] Vitoria had
counselled that princes should always seek the advice of 'wise men'
on matters of moral and ethical uncertainty and should always follow
that advice. This holds true, he stated, even if the advice is wrong.[30] In
1549, the Council of the Indies finally advised the Emperor to appoint
a panel of theologians and jurists to consider 'the manner in which
these conquests should be carried out' in the Americas 'in order that
they may be made justly and with security of conscience'.[31]

The stage was now set for one of the most remarkable political
debates in history: Las Casas and Sepúlveda, acting as advocates and
expert witnesses, would present their arguments and evidence to a
special committee of theologians, jurists and experienced administra-
tors under the presidency of Domingo de Soto, who had assumed the
informal leadership of the School of Salamanca following Vitoria's
death. But, before the proceedings began, on 16 April 1550, Charles
took the utterly extraordinary decision to order the suspension of all
conquests in the New World. Without American money, he could
never have survived his rivalry with Francis I, nor have defeated the
heretical German Protestants, nor have thwarted the infidel Turk.
But the most powerful man in the world now suspended the imperial expansion which generated that wealth. This is an indication of
Charles's own towering self-confidence and the self-confidence of a
Castilian society and ruling class characterized by extraordinary intellectual vigour.

The debate began in the summer of 1550, in Valladolid's influential Dominican College of St Gregory, today home to the National
Sculpture Museum. The participants came in through the main
doorway, which was gorgeously decorated in the late Gothic style
known as Plateresque for its decorative similarity to ornate silver. Its
centrepiece is the Tree of Life shown as a pomegranate rooted in the
Fountain of Eternal Youth, from which the four rivers of the earthly
paradise flow. To each side of the doorway there are Wild Men, covered
in fur, with shields and weapons, the *homines selvatici* who abided by

the law of nature, living in a state of purity beyond the realms of civi-lized nations. The idea of the Wild Man stretched back to Antiquity and beyond, but it has been suggested that another group of Wild Men higher up the façade, whose beards and headgear of woven branches make them look almost Christ-like, are a conscious representation of American Indians.[32] Las Casas, Sepúlveda and the Council of Fourteen jurists and theologians must have had their minds focused on the task in hand as they made their way daily past the sculptural coincidence of these savage guards of honour.

Sepúlveda opened the debate, addressing the wise men for three hours, summarizing the *Democrates Secundus*, a work that most of the jury must have already known.[33] He was an outsider educated in the alien intellectual world of Italy who had presented the *Democrates Secundus* as a work of literature: he dramatized the argu-ment as dialogue and dressed his prose in rhetorical flourishes. To the schoolmen of Spain, he was a humanist trespassing on their *dominium* of theology and ethics, a perspective which had led some of the Council of Fourteen to advocate (successfully) the work's suppres-sion in Spain.[34] But if his grandiloquence was a handicap, his argument was equally controversial. In the Age of Chivalry, Sepúlveda was a professional advocate for the virtues and nobility of war and that set him firmly on the other side of a long-running debate in which paci-fists such as Erasmus had argued that it was every Christian's duty to avoid military conflict.[35]

Sepúlveda engaged with Vitoria's intellectual arguments, but – aware that violence would be the emotive driving force behind the debate – he offered a relentlessly hostile representation of the Indians themselves as sub-human and bestial. He exhorted his audience to 'compare the prudence, ingenuity, magnanimous evenness of temper and humane religion' of the Spaniards with the American 'sub-men with scarcely a trace of humanity who, with their savage customs, not only lack culture but neither have writing nor conserve their history. What can we expect from people so given to every kind of passion and buggery, many of whom eat human flesh?' They are 'as inferior to the Spaniards as children to adults, women to men . . . almost . . . as monkeys are to men'.[36]

Sepúlveda knew that Las Casas's polemic would be heavily spiced with anecdotes about Spanish greed, bloodshed and cruelty, so he skilfully shifted the debate away from the atrocities themselves, by arguing that a well-intentioned ruler by whose authority a war is justly waged was not responsible for the crimes of his armies, although recognizing that 'such conquests should be entrusted to men who are not simply brave, but also just, moderate and humane'.[37] Cunningly, he appropriated Las Casas's own ideas and experience by asserting that since the arrival of Christianity and the trappings of civilization, Spanish priests had taught many to be meek and mild and as different to their primitive selves as the civilized were from barbarians.[38]

The Council of Fourteen retired for the night to await Las Casas's presentation the following day. There was almost no let-up as Las Casas, now seventy-five years old and seemingly as vigorous as he had ever been, read aloud, word by word, line by line and page by page, for five whole days, from a massive, specially prepared text, the *Apología*. When he finally came to the end of his impassioned performance, the exhausted jurors asked Domingo de Soto to draw up a manageable summary.

Las Casas began with Vitoria's model,[39] but if the driving force of his thesis was a torrential rant against the brutality of the Spaniards in which he piled example on exaggerated example of the evils of the wars of conquest and the terrible conditions in which the Indians were forced to live and labour as slaves during the peace, the real power of that thesis lay in his repeated claims to have seen these atrocities with his own eyes, because of the authority given to eyewitness testimony in the Renaissance world. And on that basis he argued from his own observation that 'it would be impossible to find a whole race, nation, region or country anywhere in the world that is so slow-witted, moronic, foolish or stupid' that it lacked 'sufficient natural knowledge and ability to rule and govern itself'.[40] If the Indians were to be classified as savages, he argued, then that must be on the basis of their actions, by which yardstick the Christian invaders were equally savage, if not more so.

As an eyewitness to American reality, Las Casas had thrown into doubt Aristotle's whole distinction between barbarians and humans that was the basis for the notion of natural slavery. Instead he had asserted the fundamental equality of all men in the eyes of both God and the law from an admixture of natural law principles and empirical observation, thus closing Vitoria's circle and expounding for the first time in modern history a basic concept of universal human rights.

Las Casas then turned his attention to Vitoria's justification of war against tyrannical rulers, arguing that 'one must refrain from war, and even tolerate the death of a few innocent infants or those we find are to be killed for sacrifice and cannibalism', if in trying to prevent such deaths one should 'move against an immense multitude of persons, including the innocent, and destroy whole kingdoms, and implant a hatred for the Christian religion in their souls'.[41] He had laid out a basic principle of intervention familiar today as the doctrine of least harm. But of course for Las Casas and the Council of Fourteen, and for Charles and the monarchy, the greater good was the conversion of these heathens to the true faith. So Las Casas asked, if we send an 'armed phalanx' of Christians 'shooting rifles and cannon' with their 'flashes of light and terrible thunder', 'if pottery shakes . . . the earth trembles, the sky is hidden in heavy darkness, the old, the young, and women are killed, homes are destroyed, and everything resounds with warlike fury . . . What will the Indians think about our religion, which those wicked tyrants claim they are teaching . . . through massacres and the force of war before the gospel is preached to them?'[42]

The limited evidence available suggests that most of the Council of Fourteen favoured Las Casas, but they were far from decisive, so both Sepúlveda and Las Casas claimed victory, while the Council of the Indies never managed to extract a formal ruling from the judges.[43] In 1552, Las Casas published his most read work, the *Brief Account of the Destruction of the Indies*, which within decades was taken up across the Protestant world as a mighty moral cudgel with which to beat the high brow of Spain. He continued to publish, preach and lobby until his death in 1566. Seven years later, in 1573, Philip II signed into law his Ordinances of Discovery, which laid down in minute detail the ways in which adventurers and settlers should approach the Indians. Most importantly, all future exploration could only be carried out under royal licence, on pain of death. Spaniards had to avoid becoming involved in any war, under any circumstances.

In the years immediately after Charles's vainglorious recapture of Tunis and the ignominiously indecisive campaign in the South of France that had cost Garcilaso his life, Charles again reached an uneasy peace with Francis I. But in Germany his relations with the Protestants deteriorated seriously and trouble was brewing in the Netherlands; he himself was anxious to lead a crusade against the Ottoman Turk. Then, on 20 April 1539, the Empress Isabella gave birth to a baby boy who died immediately; she herself fell gravely ill and, ten days later, the helpless Emperor watched her die too. Grief-stricken, he told the Duke of Gandía that he was going to retire into solitude there and then, but instead 'he retreated for a few days to the monastery of Sisla, half a league from Toledo, where he could better contemplate his tribulations', and 'so as not to have to listen to the wailing and weeping of the ladies-in-waiting'.[44] Far away in Velilla, a small village on the River Ebro, the church bells mysteriously began ringing of their own accord. It was taken to be a miraculous message from heaven. They would be heard ringing again all too soon.[45]

The burdens of international monarchy soon forced Charles to delay that longed-for retirement and he set out for the Netherlands, leaving Prince Philip, then only twelve years old, as his Regent in Spain. Charles knew the boy was as yet immature for the task, but he had little choice. The Schmalkaldic League of German Protestants was an ever more powerful threat, while Ghent had been in open revolt against the administration of his sister Mary of Hungary, who had assumed the governorship of the Netherlands on the death of Margaret of Austria in 1531. In a unique and short-lived moment of detente, Francis I now invited Charles to travel to his northern lands through France.

The most immediate threat remained Ottoman incursions into imperial territory, but at the Diet of Ratisbon, in 1541, Charles struggled with the Imperial Estates, the powerful institutions and territories with a right to send representatives to the Imperial Diet, who tried to make any support for a military campaign against the Turk conditional on the Emperor conceding freedom of worship to the Lutherans. Caught between infidels on the one hand and heretics on the other, Charles had to accept that the Estates would provide a small force to be led by his brother Ferdinand. That summer, Ferdinand set out on a campaign that failed to prevent the fall of Buda to the Turks, while Charles went south to meet the Pope.

After months of gruelling travel in the Netherlands, Germany and Italy, the Emperor sailed for the island of Majorca, where Andrea Doria was gathering the Mediterranean fleets for a major assault on Ottoman Algiers on the North African coast. The still-fresh memories of Tunis made the imperial troops overconfident and once more there was a carnivalesque atmosphere about the enterprise, which was even joined by Hernán Cortés, the conqueror of Mexico himself. Impatiently, Charles ordered the Duke of Alba to take the Spanish galleons and sit off Algiers, but as the rest of the fleet began to appear along the African coast, the weather was already deteriorating. Impetuous, the Emperor managed to land with some of his army in very rough seas, but the fleet was then blown asunder by a violent storm. On land, the skirmishing continued for days and at one point an enemy attack almost reached the Emperor's tent. When the storm temporarily abated, Charles admitted defeat and ordered a general retreat. As the hungry troops began a two-day march to reach the ships, Cortés is said to have urged Charles to turn back and take the town as he had taken Mexico, but the bedraggled soldiers continued to withdraw. No one burned their boats in the Old World, so retreat was a welcome option.

Charles returned to Spain in January 1542, humiliated, albeit sanguine about the debacle, still keenly grieving the loss of his beloved Empress. But it was to be the briefest of sojourns in Castile, the kingdom he had come to regard as his home, a place of rest where he could relax awhile and gather strength for his great peripatetic performances on the world stage. In 1543, he again departed Spain for the north, leaving the sixteen-year-old Prince Philip as Regent once more.

Charles had long argued for a great Ecumenical Council of the Church to rule on matters of religion and, finally, the delegates began to congregate at Trent, now in northern Italy, but then within the Empire, in 1545. The Emperor was beginning to regain his self-confidence and the following year he tried to force the issue of religion by holding a debate during the Diet at Ratisbon. The time was coming when he would have to take the fight to the Protestants on the battlefield. Then in 1547, on 24 February, his own birthday, his mistress gave birth to an illegitimate son whom he recognized and named Don John of Austria; it was an auspicious omen.

In the spring of that year, Charles, in person, led the Imperial Army down the left bank of the Elbe in pursuit of a German Protestant force under the Elector John Frederick. On 12 April, Frederick crossed the river, burning the bridge behind him; thinking he was protected by the Elbe, he turned back upstream towards Wittenberg. But, as Charles recalled in his memoirs, near Mühlberg he himself 'came across a young peasant riding an ass who . . . offered to guide them' to a little-known ford. In the early hours of 24 April, he ordered the advance of 'a strong body of harquebusiers' to provide covering fire. As the early-morning fog cleared, the Protestants saw the Imperial Army preparing to cross the river and they began to flee. 'The Hungarian cavalry led the way' across, while close behind them came the 'Spanish muske-teers, who swam the river with their swords between their teeth'. As his forces gathered on the far bank, Charles ordered Alba to lead the headlong pursuit of the retreating rebels, which 'went on all night and into the following day' and resulted in Frederick's capture.[46]

Alba himself, in his shining white armour, with a white ostrich feather in his helmet, and on a white Spanish mount, brought this prize captive to Charles, who sentenced him to death. The Elector's life had become a bargaining tool and in exchange for leniency the Emperor secured the surrender of Wittenberg and the appointment of his ally Maurice as Elector, ensuring the bitter hatred of the German Protestants that lingers to this day.[47]

Mary of Hungary was so puffed up by Habsburg pride that she commissioned Titian to paint portraits of the Habsburgs, their court-iers and their ministers, along with the most important Protestant prisoners, to be displayed as though in procession in a Roman Triumph, a virtual victory parade presided over by the *Equestrian Portrait of Charles V Victorious at Mühlberg*.[48] That famous image of

Charles, with lance in hand astride a prancing black charger, would be copied and adapted again and again by the Habsburg kings and princes of Spain as a symbol of the power and authority they had inherited from their ever more legendary forebear. It also sealed the close bond between the Habsburgs and Titian, who from then on became de facto court painter to the dynasty.

Charles, chronically ill and morbidly obsessed by a sense of death, now seriously turned to the complicated business of the succession. He hoped to keep his dominions concentrated in Philip's hands, but his brother Ferdinand wanted the Empire and the Netherlands for himself and his son Maximilian. Charles began the political manoeuvring in anticipation of delicate family negotiations ahead.

6

Death of the Emperor

I do not feel worthy of this great honour.

Philip II

The sixteen-year-old Prince Philip had really become a man in 1543, the year in which he assumed the regency of Spain in his own right and in which he also married his cousin María Manuela of Portugal. But two years later she died giving birth to the psychologically disturbed and physically deformed Don Carlos, who would become a tragic and terrible cross for his father to bear for the rest of the boy's life. Once again, in the small village of Velilla, on the Ebro River, the church bells rang mysteriously; and they would ring yet again.[1]

In 1548, Charles had begun preparing the way for his son's succession by sending him the secret letter filled with detailed advice about how to rule so vast an empire. But he was concerned that Philip also needed to see for himself the realms he would inherit in Italy and northern Europe, and, equally importantly, that Philip's future subjects should see the Emperor's heir. So he began planning for Philip a grand tour of Italy, Germany and the Netherlands. But first he ordered the complete reorganization of Philip's previously Castilian household according to the more lavish Burgundian tradition of the Habsburgs, which would be familiar to his northern subjects; and, in a deeply Machiavellian move, he arranged for the marriage of the Infanta María to Ferdinand's son Maximilian: this would allow Maximilian to act as Regent in Spain during Philip's absence, while simultaneously removing Maximilian from the centre of the family negotiations over the imperial succession.

The Castilians were furious on both counts. Not only was the Emperor absent himself, but now he was robbing them of their Prince Regent, and insulting their proud traditions to boot. Such was their anger that even the arch-royalist Fernández de Oviedo, then in Spain, began circulating manuscript copies of his own very detailed account of the household established by the Catholic Monarchs for Prince Juan in which Oviedo himself had been raised. It was a significant act in defiance of the Habsburg Emperor and at odds with his record of loyalty to the institution of the Crown, for it offered an alternative arrangement of impeccable Spanish provenance. Charles mollified the critics by appointing Alba as Philip's Lord High Steward, or Mayordomo Mayor, and sent him to Spain to impose the new household on the Castilians, despite Alba's own misgivings.

In the sixteenth and seventeenth centuries a royal court was partly a formal institution, with its own legal officers and jurisdiction, but it is best understood as a complex network of relationships and influence generated by the presence of the king himself.[2] This was, in a sense, the electric power that fizzed about the ruler, and that otherworldly aura was underpinned by the conscious presentation of the monarch as having a divine, almost Christ-like quality. The elaborate canopies carried over royalty during public ceremonies such as Charles's and Isabella's entries into Seville were like the canopies beneath which the Eucharist was paraded at Corpus Christi, the feast that celebrates Christ's real presence in the bread and wine following its consecration by the priest during the mass. After the introduction of the Burgundian ritual, Spanish royals attended church within a prominent 'royal box' with a curtain that could be used to hide or reveal the royal presence, an obvious allusion to the usually ornate tabernacle, the cupboard on the altar where the consecrated host is kept. Similarly, Philip mostly dined alone at a table set up at one end of the room on a dais, behind a rail, where he broke his bread in silence, like a priest before distributing communion. He was attended by noblemen, who brought him food and wine following established rituals clearly rooted in the way altar boys and acolytes attend a priest.[3]

This divine presentation, of course, required a level of reverence for the actual human form of the prince that elevated his real flesh and blood and his bodily needs above and beyond their human reality and into a sphere of spiritual and temporal isolation. A new coven-like group of courtiers quickly established themselves around the inner sanctum of the private royal apartments, known in England as the Privy Chamber.

Leading aristocrats craved these offices because they offered intimate access to the king, and most coveted of all was Groom of the Stool, who attended on the king's defecation and looked after the royal chamber pot and the 'close stool' which contained it. Self-evidently an office of enormous trust, such great physical intimacy also brought about a strong psychological and political relationship; it seems that princes would share their most secret ideas of state with the men who watched, heard and smelled them at their lavatory. In a world in which the 'king's body was seen as sacred flesh which only those of high rank are fit to touch', these courtiers were much 'more than the king's servants, they were the nearest thing he had to friends'. And, as a result, some of the awe-inspiring charisma of the monarch brushed off on them.[4]

Henry VIII's Groom of the Stool – for whom one can have nothing other than sympathy – took charge of the King's personal finances, so he eventually restyled himself as Keeper of the Privy Purse. Given the propensity for ribald humour in that age, it seems unlikely that the double-entendre was either unintended or lost on his contemporaries. In a curious linguistic parallel, the Groom of the Stool was known in Spanish as the Camarero Mayor – or Senior Chamberlain – literally the Head of the 'Cámara', a word with the primary meaning of 'Chamber' but which was also the standard early modern medical term for a 'stool'. Camarero Mayor might also be translated as 'Majordomo of the Faeces'.

Oviedo called it 'the greatest and best and most pre-eminent of all the offices in the Royal Household, in terms of both honour and benefits, for it affords the most time close to the person of the prince; and it should be occupied by someone of good bloodline, profound, naturally noble and of demonstrable virtue, for he will be the prince's secret counsel'.⁵ Oviedo's experience in the household of Prince Juan, however, implies that in his day the Chamberlain still delegated responsibility for the most menial task of removing the silver chamber pot 'on which the prince sat to perform the unavoidable' to a *mozo* or 'boy' drawn from the minor aristocracy, a boy such as Oviedo himself. Three times a day, the 'boy' had to take the chamber pot away concealed under his cloak, while at night he brought it to the royal apartment along with 'a yard of linen'. But this is as candid as the Historian Royal gets; whether the prince or his chamberlain wielded the linen remains a mystery.

Beyond the intimate orbit of the various gentlemen of the chamber was the wider courtly universe populated by ambitious courtiers and hangers-on, and in introducing the Burgundian tradition Charles also doubled the size of his son's household. This secured the support of many Spanish aristocrats, who responded enthusiastically to such an open invitation to take part in the Prince's forthcoming grand tour of Europe. It was international political strategy at its most astute. Travelling in the close-knit entourage of their Prince, the most powerful Spaniards would form a strong sense of identity and a deep loyalty to Philip; but Charles also wanted to parade the Spanish aristocracy before the rest of his subjects, for the Spaniards terrified all who saw them with their prowess at chivalric sports such as jousting and their murderous martial skills and breathtaking horsemanship.

These *nouveaux* Burgundians turned to Boscán's recent translation of Castiglione's classic handbook *The Book of the Courtier*, to find out how to navigate this strange environment: as Garcilaso explained in his introduction, 'it is most important . . . not only to behave in a manner that increases an individual's honour and worth, but even more so, to avoid doing anything that may lower one's standing'.⁶ Etiquette, in other words, was everything.

Philip and his entourage set sail from the Catalan port of Rosas on 2 November, and, despite horrifyingly stormy weather, the young Prince's letters are filled with his excitement at making this first sea voyage. At Genoa, Andrea Doria organized a memorable reception, during which the artillery salute was performed with such enthusiasm that 'the air was thick with the thundering and smoke of the guns so that the city and the hills were almost lost from view' – a timely demonstration of the Genoese admiral's military and naval might.[7]

At Milan, Duke Ferrante Gonzaga and his wife, the Princess of Mofetta, threw a spectacular New Year party. Their palace was draped with sumptuous tapestries and the courtyard was lit by a forest of burning torches 'that turned night into day'. Philip danced with Gonzaga's daughter, while Alba danced with the Princess, and no doubt Garcilaso was sorely missed. The dining room was lit by four gorgeous candelabra; the tables were adorned with tiny gilded models of all the triumphal arches that the city had built for Philip's royal entry; even the napkins had been artfully folded and decorated with gilded wax figures. The first course of elaborate salads and salmagundis was served on plates decorated with miniatures of the hunt, showing riders and their footmen pursuing all sorts of game. As the food was eaten, these hunting scenes were revealed, a witty nod in the direction of the second course of hare and game-bird terrines cooked *en croûte*. This was followed by venison, the meat of kings, and a final course of various fried foods.[8]

'The Prince', we are told, 'ate well at dinner and was in a very good mood, raising his glass to toast the Princess and her daughter and treating the ladies with such unheard-of familiarity that he allowed them to drink out of his glass.'[9] Alba must have bitten hard on his lip and kept his counsel at Philip's hopelessly laissez-faire approach. But the young Prince, who in old age would gain a reputation for a forbidding dryness of spirit, was clearly enjoying himself. When the dancing began again, he took turns with both the Princess and her daughter and then, when the fashionable 'Dance of the Candles' began, he insisted that Alba himself take the floor, which the duke 'did very well, dancing first with his candle and then inviting one of the ladies to join him, before leaving her with the candle'. On and on the musicians played until nearly dawn, when a troop of masked gentlemen appeared to a fanfare of trumpets and an army of pages served a snack of candied fruits and conserves. 'The Prince then danced some more, but at four o'clock in the morning, he bade farewell to the

Princess and her daughter and retired to rest for what little of the night remained.'¹⁰

At Milan, Philip met Titian for the first time and commissioned a portrait of himself in armour so that he could hang it in his private apartments as a companion piece for the painter's portrait of his beloved but ever-absent father. The work is a masterpiece of idealization, showing the rather slight and unprepossessing Prince as a truly majestic ruler and an apparently formidable military commander.¹¹

At Trent, the Protestant Maurice of Saxony, Charles's staunch ally at Mühlberg, joined the royal party and became Philip's closest companion. At Augsburg, they enjoyed a 'very jolly and typically German banquet at which there was plenty of drinking . . . and a beautiful Italian girl asked the prince to dance the candle'. A few days later, Philip and Alba engaged in such enthusiastic toasting that the masked ball had to be delayed while they slept off their excesses, but they both then danced with the ladies until dawn.¹² The bonhomie of the young Prince was reportedly making him friends: at Heidelberg, 'His Highness was so happy, so attentive and so sociable that it was almost as though he had learnt German; and the whole world seemed enchanted by him, especially the daughter of the Duke of Württemberg.'¹³

The Prince and the Emperor were finally reunited in Brussels on 1 April 1549, amid the most lavish displays of chivalric pageantry yet seen, which began with a spectacular tourney outside the walls, the usual entry through elaborately symbolic triumphal arches and jousting in the main square, and continued with Philip's formal reception by his aunts, Mary of Hungary and Eleanor, Queen of France, before, finally, they accompanied him to the Imperial Chamber.¹⁴

His Imperial Majesty was standing by the wall and he received His Highness's courtiers with much affection as they kissed his hands. His Highness came in, took off his hat and went towards the middle of the room; His Majesty then took three or four steps towards him, the Prince knelt; His Majesty took off his hat, bowed and kissed His Highness and gazed at [his son] a while and then turned to those present and said:

'these gentlemen will let us retire, for I have not yet welcomed you properly'.

With that, the royal family went into the Emperor's private chambers.[15] But this is as close as Charles has allowed us to get to the emotional reality of being reunited with his son after six long years apart.

At Brussels, Philip developed a crush on the pretty young Duchess of Lorraine, but Charles was eager to show his son the Netherlands, and they toured first among the southern Flemings, the Walloons, and then among the northern Dutch, where freedom of religion and Protestantism presented a growing problem for their Catholic rulers. The Prince saw at first hand just how uncohesive the Netherlands were as a political unit, a fragmented and cantankerous collection of seventeen independently minded provinces. He also began to develop a keen eye for art and saw for the first time some of the bizarre, phantasmagoric works of Hieronymus Bosch, which he went on to collect avidly.[16] At Mary of Hungary's spectacular new chateau at Binche, he saw Rogier van der Weyden's *Descent from the Cross*, which he later acquired. He was also invited to take part in an extravagant orgy of chivalric challenges, tourneys, jousting, banqueting, dancing and theatrical displays of courtly excess which included a re-enactment of scenes from *Amadis of Gaul*, a best-selling Spanish chivalric romance filled with stories of princes, princesses, knights errant, ogres, giants, love, sex and violence, which was first published by Garci Rodríguez de Montalvo in 1508. Philip was among the knights commissioned by the Queen of Destiny to test themselves against a series of challenges with names like the Isle of Adventure, the Tower of Danger and the Fortunate Crossing. Their purpose was to defeat an enemy of chivalry, an old magician or enchanter called Noraboch, who lived in a castle forever enveloped by a dark cloud. The show began with a proclamation read aloud to the Emperor: 'Oh Majestic Caesar, since time immemorial every knight and noble has been free to win honour through deeds of arms and to go in search of strange adventure, to go about at liberty in every kingdom, without hindrance of any kind, unless at the hands of highwaymen and other enemies of chivalry and virtue.'[17] That chivalric code of passage had obvious echoes in

Francisco de Vitoria's principles of free passage and liberal international trade proposed as the basis of lawful Spanish incursion into the New World.

Appropriately enough, that night, in a classic cliffhanger, 'eight well armed savages' invaded the ballroom and abducted four beautiful maidens. The following morning dawned with a multitude of spectators from the town of Binche and beyond crowding round to see what happened next. And, after an early lunch, with the royal family watching from the gallery, a group of Christian knights assaulted the ruined ramparts of the old chateau and rescued the distressed damsels from an army of determined 'savages'.[18]

As Philip and Charles travelled down the Rhine to the Imperial Diet at Augsburg in 1550, Charles began dictating his memoirs to his secretary, William van Male, yet another indication that he felt the spectre of death upon him. Then, at Augsburg, his long-trusted Imperial Chancellor died, casting Charles into even deeper melancholy. Soon afterwards, he was bitten on one of his arthritic knuckles by a mosquito and 'unable to endure it, he gently scratched himself until both his hand and his forearm became inflamed'.[19] There was a deep foreboding that the Emperor's end was nigh, and Philip commissioned the great Danish mathematician and scientist Matthias Hacus to draw up his own horoscope, a document he kept close at hand until his own death.[20]

Charles and Ferdinand now began to negotiate the imperial succession, with Mary of Hungary attempting to mediate. But with the family living cheek by jowl in the palace at Augsburg, the talks quickly broke down as the two sides began to negotiate through hastily written letters and notes.

Charles wrote to Mary of Hungary in despair: he was 'tremulous with sorrow and anxiety' and 'ready to die of the vexation'.[21] Without hope of agreement, he issued a diktat, unilaterally ruling that the imperial crown would pass first to Ferdinand, then to Philip and finally to Maximilian. It was a pragmatic solution, but it infuriated Ferdinand and Maximilian, while the Imperial Electors were quite rightly incensed at such a flagrant assumption that the Habsburg dynasty had some hereditary right over the Empire. It left Charles with so 'few friends in Germany' that even 'the Catholic towns of the south did not flock readily to his side', for they valued peace and freedom over religious imperialism. So the diktat was doomed to failure and, worse, it fomented dissent, but for the moment it did at least allow Philip to set out on the return journey to Spain. In the summer of 1551, a popular joke in Augsburg was that Charles had tried 'to buy the tears of the people for his son's departure by generously distributing Indian gold'.[22]

Philip left his father suffering from a terrible attack of gout which 'the doctors say has begun to rise to his head, which is very dangerous and may kill him at any moment. He often has asthma attacks and they also say that he has a touch of the French disease, so that he would be dead if it weren't for his strict diet' and if it weren't for the fact that 'he mixes all his medicines' with *palo santo*, a miraculous new remedy from the New World.[23]

In June 1551, Philip reached Trent, where he was able to witness sessions of the great Ecumenical Council of the Holy Catholic Church for which Charles V had agitated for so long and to meet members of the Spanish delegation, including his future confessor and the future Archbishop of Toledo, Bartolomé de Carranza. Philip took a close interest in the business of the Council, which had finally been convened by Pope Paul III in 1545.

The Emperor had hoped that the Council of Trent could heal the rift with the Reformers, and in the aftermath of Mühlberg there was still hope, for Protestant delegates sponsored by Maurice of Saxony would soon be in attendance. But in the final reckoning, that great Council, which sat intermittently for twenty-five sessions, increasingly served only to entrench the Catholic position and reject outright almost every Protestant difference as anathema. In January 1552 the Cardinal of Mainz abandoned all hope of achieving anything and left Trent complaining that the Spanish theologians 'always want to outshine and outdo everyone else'.[24]

The decrees the Council finally issued codified Catholic practice in every sphere of life, from rulings on texts that might be treated as authoritative by theologians, most importantly the Vulgate Latin Bible, to details of the liturgy and when individuals should take Holy Communion. They ruled that the miracle of transubstantiation truly took place when the priest blessed the bread and wine of communion, so that Christ's real flesh and blood were truly present in the Eucharist; they also ruled that man had free will, and insisted on the existence of Purgatory.

At the twenty-fifth session, in 1563, they even ruled on the purpose of art and images, decreeing that 'images of Christ, of the Virgin and of the other saints should be displayed in temples, and that due honour and veneration are to be given them. Not that any divinity, or virtue, is believed to be actually in them.' These were not, they explained, graven images to be worshipped on their own account as the Gentiles had done; it was simply that they should help to inspire in the faithful a sense of reverence towards the real saints they represented, so that 'when we kiss these images and uncover our head to them or prostrate ourselves before them' we are in fact 'adoring Christ and venerating the saints whose images they bear'. The bishops and clergymen were encouraged to use paintings and other representations to teach 'the histories of the mysteries of our Redemption', so 'great profit is derived from all sacred images, not only because they remind people of the benefits and gifts bestowed upon them by Christ, but also because they set the miracles which God has performed before the eyes of the faithful'. That, in turn, the theologians argued, would help them to 'live their own lives and manners in imitation of the saints and be excited to adore and love God, and to cultivate piety'.[25]

This ruling on the purpose of religious art was intended to help confound the heretical Protestant rejection of the notion that the saints might be able to intercede with God on behalf of an individual, a rejection which meant that the religious images themselves served no purpose. But this and related decrees that could be applied to literature and other kinds of artistic production became the overarching moral principle by which all artists working in the Catholic world would come to measure their work. It underpinned the great artistic flowering we now know as the Spanish Golden Age, directly influencing painters like El Greco and Velázquez and directly and indirectly influencing writers like Cervantes.

Philip himself, who would play an enduring role as the greatest patron of the arts in Spain, came to embrace that orthodoxy wholeheartedly. Indeed, he did so with quite literally monumental determination: as war flared up in Italy, he returned to his beloved Spain late in 1551, his imagination filled with plans for refurbishing the tired royal palaces and constructing his hymn to Habsburg Catholicism, his great monastery-palace complex at El Escorial.

In 1552, Maurice of Saxony abandoned the Emperor and joined the Protestant cause. He could see that Charles was dying and, having weighed up Philip at first hand, had apparently found him wanting as a successor. Entering into an alliance with France, he defeated the Imperial Army and forced Charles and his courtiers to flee Innsbruck overnight. According to Friar Prudencio Sandoval, 'while the Emperor was leaving through one gate, Maurice and his men were coming in by another' – there was not even time to save Charles's personal possessions and clothing.[26] He had escaped to fight another day and, the following winter, he besieged a French force that had occupied the city of Metz, the episcopal capital of the Empire. But Metz, built on a height above a great bend in the river, was naturally well defended, and despite his superior force Charles eventually was forced to admit defeat and raise the siege. It was an abject failure of military judgment and a political disaster.

Charles was a broken man, racked by disease, submerged by debt and short of money to spend. His strategic acumen was compromised by desperation, which surely explains why he decided to pursue his strange diplomatic dream of a durable English alliance by negotiating a marriage between Philip and the thirty-six-year-old Mary Tudor, Queen of England.[27] The wedding took place at Winchester on 25 July 1554, the Day of St James, patron saint of Spain, and the Conquest of Tunis tapestries were tactlessly displayed 'to warn English Protestants' about what Habsburgs did to infidels.[28] But Philip's Spanish entourage were very excited to visit the Castle of the Knights of the Round Table and see the putative Round Table itself, decorated at Henry VIII's instruction with the names of the knights and a portrait of Arthur; they were in the land that had inspired *Amadis of Gaul*. 'There is more to be seen in England than is written in the books [of chivalry],' one remarked glowingly; 'the dwellings in the country, the rivers, the fields, the flowered meadows, the cool springs, are all a pleasure to see.'[29]

Philip worked hard to ingratiate himself with his new quasi-subjects and brought great political insight and experience to a throne in desperate need of an intelligent incumbent. So, while he must have been greatly pleased that Catholicism again became the official religion while he was in England, he proved himself capable of pragmatic moderation even when it came to faith by taking on the Popish English radicals and convincing Parliament to prevent the Church from repossessing land sold to laymen during the Reformation. He also urged moderation in the face of Mary's famously bloody persecution of Protestants.[30] Ironically enough, concerned by England's vulnerability to invasion, he also encouraged the English to rebuild their dilapidated navy, ensuring that the island could be adequately defended against the Great Armada that he sent to conquer his erstwhile kingdom in 1588.[31] He remained in England during Mary's infamous phantom pregnancy, now thought to have been cancer of the womb; when this tragic fantasy was over, Lord North is said to have explored the possibility of pretending she had in fact given birth and substituting a common London babe.[32] Some bold cockney blood might have greatly enriched the dwindling Habsburg gene pool, but by then Philip's brief flirtation with England was all but over, and in 1554 he sailed for Brussels, where momentous business was afoot.

In 1554, Queen Juana la Loca finally died in Tordesillas. His mother's death seems to have given Charles some final, morbid impetus to abdicate all his realms and retire, as he had so often longed to do. On 25 October, frail and broken, he entered the great hall of the royal residence in Brussels, leaning on the shoulder of William of Orange, from whom the current ruling dynasty of the Netherlands descend. Much had he travelled in his realms: 'Nine times I went to Germany, six to Spain, seven to Italy, I have come to Flanders ten, been to France four, in peace and war, twice to England, and twice to Africa . . . I have made eight voyages in the Mediterranean and three in the Spanish Ocean; and now I shall make the fourth when I return there to be buried,' he explained to his tearful audience. And then Charles too began to weep as he embraced Philip as the new ruler of the Netherlands.

'I do not feel worthy of this great honour,' Philip responded, 'nor can I find the strength to bear the weight of which Your Majesty unburdens himself . . . but in obedience to Your Majesty I conform to your wishes by accepting the rule of these countries.'[33]

On 16 January the following year, Charles then transferred his Spanish crowns to his son and, in September, still Emperor, he settled the religious question at Augsburg by agreeing that the princes of the Empire could decide the religion of their subjects. He did not formally abdicate the imperial crown until May 1558, when it went to Ferdinand and, in due course, would pass to Maximilian: the Habsburg inheritance would soon be divided for ever.

But for the moment King Philip II turned to the business of defending the greatest empire in the world: on 10 August 1557, just outside the village of Saint Quentin, in northern France, Philip's armies under the command of the Duke of Savoy were attacked by the Constable of France at the head of 22,000 infantry and cavalry. The battle was short and Philip's victory was total. Savoy lost 500 men, the French 5,200; the Constable was taken prisoner, and French aristocrats were slaughtered and imprisoned by the score. Two weeks later, Philip in person led an assault on the town itself: 'we entered in strength,' he wrote, 'killing all the defenders'.[34] The place was sacked by the Germans, who refused to allow anyone else to enjoy the spoils and 'showed such cruelty as the like hath not been seen for greediness', the Earl of Bedford observed.[35]

In 1556, the Emperor Charles V retired to the humblest of Hieronymite monasteries, at Yuste, set in the beautiful woodlands of the Vera where he had hunted so often from Valladolid. He often ate with the monks and spent his days enjoying the monastery grounds and tinkering with his collection of clocks; a skilled clockmaker, he could take apart and put back together these most complex of ultra-modern technologies. But, now so fat that he could not fit between the tables of the monks' refectory, he frequently surrendered to his terrible gluttony, gorging on sausages, wild boar, ham, bacon, truffles, cherries, and strawberries and cream. He indulged his great love of fish and was sent plaice and lamprey from Lisbon, sole and oysters in *escabèche*, smoked herring and salmon, and on one occasion his physician, Dr Quijada, had to dissuade him from eating a barrel of anchovies that had putrefied in transit.[36] But, for all his bouts of a hearty appetite, Charles was a dying man and in the summer of 1558 he was taken ill in the gardens and brought to his bedroom.

> The Emperor ordered his treasurer to bring him [Titian's] portrait of the Empress, his wife. He spent a while looking at it; then he said: 'take it away and bring me the devotional painting of *Christ Praying in the Garden of Gethsemane*'. He was a long while contemplating this, seeking to find reflected there the lofty sentiments he felt in his soul. Then, he ordered them to bring the painting of the *Last Judgment*. Now he spent more time, he meditated for longer ... And then, turning to his physician with a shudder, the Emperor said: 'I feel ill.'[37]

It was 31 August. The following day, Charles began to discuss with his priest the final sacrament of extreme unction. He collapsed into an agonizing illness and was tormented by his sins and the prospect of eternal damnation. His confessor, Bartolomé de Carranza, reassured him: 'Fear not, nor allow the devil to terrorize you, and put your trust in the Lord who has already paid for your sins.'[38] Three weeks later, on 21 September, Charles died in the middle of the night while suffering terrible convulsions; at the very end he arranged to have brought to him the very same crucifix that his beloved Empress Isabella had grasped so firmly on her deathbed as he had watched on, grief-stricken. Yet again, the church bells of Velilla rang out of their own accord and the locals knew that the ailing Emperor must have died.[39]

This is how Philip II's confessor and future Prior of his great monastery-palace at El Escorial, Fray José de Sigüenza, described Charles's final illness, explaining that when the Emperor realized he was dying he surrounded himself with paintings by Titian. It is almost implausibly symbolic of Charles's place in the world that history should recall how he died at a monastery in Spain set in some of his favourite hunting forests, dreaming of his Portuguese Empress and praying to God, while he gazed upon beautiful works of art made by a brilliant Italian, which had been commissioned in Germany and paid for with money borrowed against the surety of American treasure, as his most trusted Castilian and Flemish courtiers gazed at him.

Three years earlier, on a hot June night in 1556, far away in the Caribbean, the President of the Audiencia of Santo Domingo had hurried to the fortress guarding the harbour and broken in through a side door. Inside, he had found the Sheriff and Historian Royal, Gonzalo Fernández de Oviedo y Valdés, lying on the floor, dead from old age, the keys to the fortress firmly gripped in the hand of this loyal servant of the Crown. The remarkable period of history during which Spain moved to the centre of the world was coming to an end. The time had come for consolidation.[40]

Philip was in Brussels when he first heard of his father's long-expected demise in the autumn of 1558. An ambitious soldier serving in the Emperor's own guard, Juan de Herrera, led the Cavalry of Aragon in the memorial procession through the streets of the city.[41] Soon afterwards, Mary Tudor also died. Philip was politically free and, after a brief flirtation with Elizabeth of England, the Virgin Queen, he married the beautiful and vivacious Elizabeth of Valois, with whom he would soon fall genuinely in love. On 3 April 1559, at the small village of Cateau-Cambrésis, he signed a solid and lasting peace treaty with France. At the end of that summer of detente, leaving his bastard half-sister Margaret of Parma as his Regent in the Netherlands, and with his uncle Ferdinand ruling over the Empire, Philip returned to Spain.

THE AGE OF BUREAUCRACY: PHILIP II

7

El Escorial and El Greco

Until today no detailed description of the population of these realms
has ever been made.
                    Covering letter to questionnaire in the 1570s

The monastery-palace of El Real Sitio de San Lorenzo el Escorial,
the most iconic building of the Spanish Golden Age, is best
approached along the old road from Avila that winds through the
remote pine stands of a high plain before dropping dramatically into
the bowl of a wide valley. The enormous edifice nestles in a fold of
the foothills. Seen through the trees, by a dappled light, with the
birds singing, gleaming with the evening sun on its granite walls and
slate roofs, it feels welcoming, its huge bulk dwarfed by the towering
Guadarrama Mountains. A gateway of double porticoes leads into a
desert-like expanse of granite esplanade dominated by the massive
wall of the west front. Even gilded by the evening light, that self-
assured austerity exudes a chilling air of latent potency, as though
the building and its architects are daring you to enter their realm of
power.

The Escorial is Philip II's very personal, awe-inspiring essay on
the greatness of God, the grandeur of the Habsburgs, the wonders
of Empire and the centrality of Castile, and we can still feel his regal
authority willing us to read it. It was monastery, library, art gallery,
repository for thousands of holy relics, eclectic museum and curio
collection, botanical garden filled with plants from across the world,

royal palace, personal retreat and family mausoleum, and it often functioned as the seat of government, because for Philip it was home. At the Escorial, information, knowledge and power all intersect at the spiritual heart of Philip II's Empire.

No other building has ever been so intimately connected with the personality of a great ruler as the Escorial, for no monarch can ever have taken so detailed an interest in every aspect of the planning and construction of so great a building as Philip did with his masterpiece. He used to gaze for hours at his colossal building site from a vantage point known as Philip's Seat, by the old road from Avila. The Escorial is a giant tombstone into which the most powerful monarch the world has ever known carved his epitaph to himself and the Spanish Habsburgs. No other edifice has been so studied and psychoanalysed, so much does it feel as though it must be a projection of Philip himself. As the *fin de siècle* intellectual Miguel de Unamuno once warned: 'Almost everyone who goes to see the Escorial arrives blinkered by their political and religious prejudices; and they come in search of Philip II's equally misunderstood ghost and if they do not find it, then they make it up for themselves.'[1]

On St Lawrence's Day 1557, on the battlefield at Saint Quentin, Philip supposedly vowed to build a great monastery to give thanks to the Lord for his decisive victory over the French. But his letter of foundation for the Escorial itself stated that the primary purpose of the building was as a family mausoleum where he could cherish the cadavers of a dynasty. He was determined that his brothers, his aunts and his own first wife, María Manuela, should be interred alongside his parents, Charles and Isabella. In due course, he himself would join them.[2]

He chose as his architect a Spaniard called Juan Bautista de Toledo who had worked closely with Michelangelo on St Peter's in Rome before developing a formidable reputation in Naples as Royal Master of Works for the Viceroy, Pedro de Toledo.[3] By the end of 1561, Philip had chosen a site near the miserable hamlet of El Escorial that was within easy striking distance of Madrid for royal messengers, but was a long and uncomfortable ride for unwelcome courtiers and pestering diplomats. The land was cleared and on 23 April 1563 the foundation stone was laid.

Philip worked his architect intensively, developing ideas, seeking advice from other architects, from builders and from the Hieronymite friars, making changes, always wondering. Slowly, a coherent plan emerged. This search for perfection put Toledo under such pressure that the King grew worried: 'I don't know if I have shocked him with my demands for the building.'[4] Then, in November 1563, the tragic news reached Spain that Toledo's wife and children, sailing from Naples to be with him, had been captured by Turkish corsairs.[5] The architect escaped his grief by plunging into the maelstrom of his awful workload, setting out plans that defined the principal characteristics of the building we know today. But as these were corrected and adapted in the course of construction, his behaviour became erratic and he constantly quarrelled with his assistants. At the same time, Philip also had him working to refurbish the Alcázar in Madrid and devising the hydraulic engineering needed to water the stunning gardens he was landscaping and planting at the royal palace south of Madrid at Aranjuez. In 1567 the stress, it seems, finally killed him.

In the months leading up to Toledo's death, his chief draughtsman, the young page-turned-guardsman Juan de Herrera, who had led the Aragonese cavalry in procession through the streets of Brussels when Charles V died, 'was continually seen in the company of the king'.[6] According to tradition, Herrera now became the chief architect of El Escorial, although the extent of his executive authority has been sensibly questioned by modern scholars. Whatever his precise role, he certainly played a crucial part: we know from an extensive claim for pay and expenses that he had reduced construction costs by over a million ducats, redesigning the Flemish-style roofs that Philip had requested, devising a revolutionary series of cranes for lifting building materials, and arranging the manufacture of nails on site.[7] We also know that he designed the tabernacle for the basilica and massively reworked the great staircase, the first known example of an Imperial Staircase, a type of stairway that came to dominate grand Baroque projects in the seventeenth and eighteen centuries across Europe.[8] However, he was never actually appointed chief architect; instead,

Philip placed him at the heart of his own household as *aposentador mayor*, or Royal Steward. He found in Herrera the perfect partner and servant, an able administrator and intelligent counsellor. A clever and ambitious man of humble origins, Herrera was typical of the brilliant bureaucrats who were entrusted with the everyday running of Spain and her Empire, the formulation of policy ideas and negotiating the relationship between monarchy and sovereignty.

In reality Philip himself seems to have taken overall charge of building the Escorial, working from Toledo's basic plans, while relying heavily on Herrera's exceptional skill as a draughtsman to represent his ideas in drawings from which the master masons could create the building.[9] Contemporaries marvelled at this collaboration between monarch and servant: an awed Flemish courtier said simply that 'this whole building is so excellently finished and complete and so resplendent in its perfection that it must be the most wonderful in all the world'. The first Prior of the monastery, José de Sigüenza, extolled its 'grandeur and majesty ... harmonious of form and materials, each chosen purely for its purpose or function, without unnecessary pretension; the parts so unified and related to the whole that not one of them is out of place. As a result, the whole structure has such great beauty that as we contemplate it we are filled with a joy that frees us from our fixation with Antiquity and we experience endless grace and elegance.'[10]

It is surely astonishing that over four centuries ago this architectural marvel should have inspired such a prescient and succinct expression of the presumably timeless aesthetics of modernism.

Philip conceived of the Escorial as the spiritual heart of the Habsburg world within a much broader programme of centralization. He had watched his compulsively peripatetic father destroy his health trying to rule his realms in person and had concluded that henceforth the Empire would have to come to its ruler. In 1561, he permanently moved his court and government to Madrid, which quickly grew into the overcrowded and exciting capital of the Spanish world. The old medieval Royal Palace, the Alcázar, built in the Moorish architectural style known as Mudéjar, became the focus of life for the political and social elites, while Philip and his household frequently escaped to a handful of nearby royal palaces, all set in excellent countryside where he could entertain his passion for hunting.

The Escorial was Philip's favourite in this archipelago of country retreats, the palace where he preferred to spend Easter and often the summer. There, the material world only trespassed on his gloriously otherworldly isolation through the proxy of documents, in the form of words, reports, letters, maps, images, samples and specimens. There was not even a clear view of the surrounding countryside from Philip's desk in the modest apartments where he submerged himself under the paperwork of government. Instead of windows on to the world outside, he looked up from his work to catch the eye of God gazing over him from the middle of Hieronymus Bosch's circular painting, *The Seven Deadly Sins*. Over-burdened by his own Counter-Reformation faith, Philip ruled 'an Empire on which the sun never set' from a monk's cell, relying entirely on written instructions based on other men's reported experience of the reality of his realms. At the Escorial, he could retreat into this virtual sphere of his papers, escaping the hectic, crowded court centred on Madrid.[11]

Paintings were his moral windows on to the world, and he filled the Escorial with important works from his outstanding collection, images he appreciated more for their spiritual and symbolic value than for their aesthetic beauty. The breadth and depth of the collection was breathtaking, yet the works of two very different artists stand out.

Mary of Hungary almost certainly kindled Philip's obsession with Hieronymus Bosch,[12] an obscure painter born at 's-Hertogenbosch in the Netherlands in 1453, who in the words of a leading sixteenth-century Spanish art critic 'painted strange likenesses of things . . . ethical works that show the habits and emotions of men's souls'.[13] His delightfully horrible pictures have done more than those of any other artist to colour our modern popular idea of daily life in the Middle Ages. But his disturbed and disturbingly fantastical moral narratives especially fascinated Philip because they furnished him with a set of ready images against which he compared the world; they were a touchstone for his faith. Father Sigüenza has left us wonderful extended commentaries, setting ajar for us a metaphorical door into Philip's soul, describing Bosch as a revolutionary who 'caught everyone's attention' with his 'range of imagery', but he understood them almost as works of theology, 'artfully made books' filled with 'good sense' in which you can read 'almost all of the sacraments, and the estates and hierarchy of the Church, from the Pope to the most lowly . . . a painted satire on the sins and trespasses of men'.[14]

The best known of Bosch's works is a triptych known as *The Garden of Earthly Delights*, which Philip kept at the Escorial. When closed it shows God the Father presiding over the Creation of the World. When open, the left-hand panel shows Paradise at the moment when Adam and Eve are expelled and the right shows the mouth of hell on the Day of Judgment, which should lead us to interpret the main image in the middle as a 'false paradise'. Yet we suddenly realize how distant we are intellectually and spiritually from Philip's age when we read Sigüenza's explanation that 'the core subject matter is a small flower and one of those little fruits known as strawberries, which are like a *madroño*'.[15] The Prior goes on to refer to the painting as the 'Madroño'. To whom would it occur nowadays, one wonders, to describe this as a painting of strawberries? As one Italian traveller tried to explain, it shows many 'bizarre themes . . . things so pleasing and fantastic that they could not be properly described in any way to those who do not know them'.[16]

Philip's relationship with the work of Titian, his favourite painter, feels only a few degrees nearer to our own experience of art. As a boy, he had grown up knowing his father's likeness from a portrait by Titian better than he had from real life, while Mary of Hungary had taught him a deep appreciation of Titian's skill and had also bequeathed him her excellent collection, which included many of the family portraits Titian painted following the Battle of Mühlberg. Philip came to treat these effigies as though they contained something of the sitter's spirit or were an imprint of the person themselves – so much so that he 'greatly honoured his ancestors by always doffing his hat to their portraits'.[17] That he seems so readily to have blurred the distinction between image and reality is indicative of his ability to live in a virtual world of words and pictures. Titian's realism must have made that easier and, from 1556, he worked almost exclusively for Philip, who paid him a phenomenal annual retainer of 500 ducats. But it was also a personal relationship: Titian had been his father's artist, and legend had it that while 'working on a portrait of Charles V, Titian dropped his paintbrush, which the Emperor picked up. At this, Titian knelt before him, saying, "Sire, a servant of yours does not deserve such an honour," to which Charles replied, "Titian is worthy to be served by Caesar."'[18] At heart, as the leading modern scholar of the artist and his work puts it, 'Charles and Philip were fond of Titian . . . they liked him as a bloke.'[19]

And if the Escorial is solidly emblematic of his and his government's new sense of stasis, then there is no better example of the concomitant dynamism and vision of that new administration than an astoundingly ambitious project known as the *Geographical or Topographical Reports*. Since Philip's return to Spain in 1558, he had been considering compiling a comprehensive atlas of his lands in Castile and the Spanish Indies. Finally, in the 1570s, thousands of copies of a long and detailed questionnaire were distributed to the towns of Castile and settlements in New World with a covering letter:

> Until today no detailed description of the population of these realms has ever been made. And because this would be of great benefit to their government and wealth . . . we charge you with instructing all the councils and officials of the settlements within your jurisdiction to research very well everything contained in the questions and to make their own report.[20]

The results from the New World, containing a kind of Rosetta Stone for indigenous American history – information gleaned from Spanish lords, Indian *caciques* or chiefs, or old and venerable Indians who remembered important details about their traditions – are today scattered across libraries and archives in the Americas and Spain.[21] But the results from Castile were bound together into seven hefty volumes and stored, symbolically enough, in the Escorial library. They contain an overwhelming wealth of potentially fascinating detail. So we know, for example, that in the small village of Esquivias, where Miguel de Cervantes married his wife and on which he modelled the home town of his fantastical, ever dreaming hero Don Quixote, there were 'many vines' and the economy was based on wine, though there was a shortage of firewood and food.[22]

Philip clearly understood that for his centralizing bureaucracy to work he needed clever, perceptive and determined people to be his eyes and ears around the world. That royal promotion of the search for information and its evaluation was part of a much broader culture of inquiry at the time perhaps best exemplified by the great Jesuit historian José de Acosta, whose *Natural and Moral History of the Indies*, published in 1590, contains a brilliant description of the Americas and Americans. However, Crown bureaucracy was jealous of information about the New World, notoriously appropriating Bernadino de Sahagún's meticulous account of Aztec culture in the famous Florentine Codex, a beautiful manuscript filled with vivid illustrations by Indian artists alongside a bilingual commentary in Spanish and native Mexican Nahuatl. Although Philip originally ordered the confiscation of the manuscript because it documented the pagan superstitions of the Indians, once he had the codex in his hands he clearly appreciated it both for its content and for its aesthetic value, ordering a copy of the text to be made, before giving away the sumptuous object itself as a wedding present.[23]

The *Geographical or Topographical Reports* are clearly a consequence of Philip's faith in bureaucracy, but they are also a result of his devotion to knowledge and collecting. Where his father had collected kingdoms by accident of inheritance, Philip amassed objects by design. This was no mere antiquarian desire to own objects, but a way of abstracting his vast empire into an accumulation of seemingly less unmanageable data and ideas. And for Philip, the management of Empire was about divining God's will for his Creation.

Although Philip was neither academic nor intellectual, he was curious about science and inquiry in general. Thus he was readily seduced by Juan de Herrera's obsessive interest in the work of the medieval Majorcan philosopher Ramón Lull, who had developed a holistic theory of the universe based on a kind of cosmic game of Scrabble in which he manipulated letters of the alphabet that symbolized God's moral essence and divine power, associating them with tangible objects, from trees to the planets.[24] One of his results was to affirm that heavenly bodies were bearers of moral qualities, either innate or acquired.[25] His work was closely studied by astrologers and alchemists, researchers whose work reflects the spirit of those times when a rich admixture of science, magic and faith were ready companions in the crucible of reason.

Philip II was very much a man and monarch of that age in which a respected lawyer advised his readers of their moral duty to 'learn about the personality of their children . . . by going to a learned astrologer to have a chart drawn of the position of the heavenly bodies at the moment of the child's birth'.[26] Soon after Philip had his horoscope drawn by Matthias Hacus, in 1550, he had his and Mary Tudor's horoscopes prepared by the English magus John Dee.[27] But Philip could also be highly sceptical, commenting to his secretary, 'I have been meaning to warn the Cardinal of Toledo to get rid of those astrologer-clerics who have done nothing but damage. I am astonished that people believe in them when they clearly do evil, not to mention that it is a mortal sin.'[28] On another occasion, when presented with comments on classical interpretations of comets he pointed out that 'because the Romans were not Christians they believed whatever they liked'.[29]

Alchemy, too, proved alluring, with its twin aspirations of turning base metals into silver or gold and distilling the elixir of life itself through experimentation. Philip was briefly seduced by that mercurial promise of riches when he was forced to suspend interest payments to his bankers in 1557. He attended experiments during which a German alchemist appeared to turn six ounces of mercury into silver and he seriously considered coining whatever alloy had really been produced in order to pay his troops, before realizing his folly and abandoning the idea.[30] But those had been desperate times and he seems to have learnt his lesson to some extent, later describing 'this science' as 'a great hoax'.[31]

But while sceptical about such exaggerated claims, Philip continued to support alchemists interested in medicine and specifically pharmacology, which he hoped would improve his health, even if he could not live for ever. He had eleven rooms at the Escorial fitted out as laboratories with stoves, ovens, a twenty-foot copper distilling tower and a huge pharmacy filled with essences, mineral suspensions and plant extracts. The King made 'frequent orders for the preparation of health-giving quintessences according to the methods of Ramón Lull'.[32]

The consultants who worked at the Escorial epitomized the spirit of adventure, experimentation, empiricism and faith then infusing almost every facet of Spanish and European culture, one aspect, perhaps, of the same spirit of discovery that had launched Spaniards on their conquest of the New World. An English Catholic called Richard Stanyhurst wrote a small tract specially for Philip, *The Touchstone of Alchemy*, explaining how to distinguish between charlatans and the true practitioners of the art. 'Be neither unduly credulous nor wholly disbelieving,' he advised, 'for the Indies would have gone undiscovered if no one had believed Columbus.'[33]

While Philip clearly kept a very open mind about astrology and the wilder claims of alchemy, he was deeply and obsessively superstitious about the power of religious relics. As Protestants across his ancestral domains in northern Europe publicly abandoned their faith in these sacred talismans, he had an army of agents at work acquiring as many desiccated cadavers, heads and other saintly body parts, hairs from the head of the Madonna and pieces of the True Cross as they could find. Luther had joked of the widespread forgery of relics that 300 men would not be enough to carry all the pieces of the Cross then revered across Christendom,[34] and Philip was greatly amused that his enthusiasm had encouraged a flourishing cottage industry forging the full range.[35] This accumulation of sacred bits and pieces was clearly in part a politically charged affirmation of the Council of Trent and the Counter-Reformation. It could also be a demonstration of his centralizing power, as was his compulsory purchase of St Lawrence's head from a convent in Santiago de Compostela in the face of bitter opposition from the nuns and Archbishop.[36] But he also believed. He had amassed 7,449 individual relics by the time of his agonizing death; and, as he lay dying, his body bursting with sores, his blood poisoned, unable to move from his soiled bed, racked by fever and thirst, he sustained himself for an incredible fifty-three days by putting his faith in these objects of devotion. He had St Sebastian's knee, Alban's rib and Vincent Ferrer's arm placed next to his own corresponding and painful body parts as he listened to readings from Teresa of Avila and Fray Luis de Granada.[37]

Amazingly, by the late 1560s, construction work at the Escorial was so far advanced that the King, some of his court and the monks were able to move in. With the quick in residence, it was next the turn of the dead. In 1573 Philip ordered the remains of his deceased family brought to the Escorial: Elizabeth of Valois, tragically killed in a hunting accident, and his insane son Don Carlos were the first to arrive; the following year, Charles V's body was brought from Yuste. The most ghoulish participant in this posthumous pilgrimage was Don John of Austria, who died in the Netherlands in 1578. In order to prevent his cadaver falling into enemy hands, it was dismembered in great secrecy, packed into leather bags, brought overland to Spain, stitched back together again and finally taken to the Escorial to be entombed.[38]

But while monastery and palace were complete, work began on the great basilica only in 1575. The spiritual jewel at the heart of Philip's architectural crown, it is an enormous church, 150 feet square, where the one hundred Hieronymite monks spent eight hours a day singing in the choir, praying for the Habsburg souls. From the outset, Philip wanted this supreme statement about Habsburg and Spanish piety to express the new orthodoxy of the Council of Trent. Spanish churches were (and often still are) cluttered by an excess of haphazardly arranged symbols, an eclectically organic confection of paintings, sculptures, carvings, furniture, silverware and randomly acquired artefacts framed by the anarchy of unplanned architectural history. They could confuse the clergy and bemuse the layman. Philip wanted a majestically simple hymn to God.

So Toledo designed a wondrously solid space that extends into a high dome supported on soaring granite piers from which classical forms loom over you as it reaches for the heavens. But, for Philip, that perfect symmetry must be complemented by the skilful hand and keen eye of artists who could immortalize the saints in perfect harmony with each other and with the building. One has the impression that in the interests of stylistic continuity Philip would have loved a single artist to create every work of art the basilica needed. But he knew that was impossible; instead, he settled on a unifying Italian influence. But while the unrivalled sculptor Leone Leoni and his son Pompeo came eagerly from Milan to create the remarkable bronze statues and major sculptures for the altarpiece, he struggled to persuade the painters whom he wanted to come to Spain.

A handful of Spaniards and a couple of Italians began work on paintings for the minor altars located at the bases of the massive piers supporting the dome and the choir. Each altarpiece was a single painting showing a pair of saints designed to populate the church at ground level with figures from heaven who, barefoot and wearing their robes, would appear dressed like the monks as they attended mass.

But Philip's main concern was the high altar, and he first turned to his beloved Titian, who refused to travel. Instead, Titian painted *The Martyrdom of St Lawrence* as the central image of the altarpiece. It is one of his most beautiful works, a truly virtuoso piece of chiaroscuro, in light and shade, but it would have been impotent amid the massive grandeur of the church; the great Venetian had failed to understand the setting and the painting was hung in a chapel now known as the *iglesia vieja*, the Old Church, where mass could be heard while the basilica was under construction; there it remains to this day.

Once Titian had declined to come to Spain, Philip asked Veronese, Tintoretto and Federico Zuccaro, but none would answer his call. In the meantime, a most unlikely Spanish candidate emerged from the wings, where he had been working on the altarpieces at the base of the great piers. Juan Fernández de Navarrete 'El Mudo', 'the mute', was deaf and dumb from birth and entered a Hieronymite monastery as a child, where he developed into a talented artist. He later travelled and worked in Italy, where legend has it he studied under Titian. That experience enabled him to adapt his own work to suit Philip's attachment to the Venetian style and in 1579 he signed a contract to paint all eight works for the altarpiece. But, days later, on 28 March, he died suddenly while visiting a friend in Toledo.[39] Zuccaro now finally agreed to work on the altarpiece, but Philip rejected his *Martyrdom of St Lawrence* and turned instead to Pellegrino Tibaldi, who had also been working on the minor altars. Tibaldi finally satisfied the King with the action-packed image of figures in movement we see today; done in bold line and colour, set within a pronounced perspective that thrusts the martyrdom in all its painful realism out of the painting towards us, for all its contrived awkwardness when seen in close-up photographs it is strikingly effective *in situ*.

The church was an affirmation of Catholicism in the face of the Reformation. And so, because the Protestants had denied the mystery of transubstantiation, Herrera designed a magnificent tabernacle as the heart of the altarpiece. A light burned permanently beside it, signalling that at all times it contained a consecrated host: at the Escorial, you are always in the real, mysterious presence of God's Supreme Sacrifice. Similarly, while the Protestants denied that good works were a path to salvation, the very act of building the Escorial was obviously a monumental good work. The Protestants had also denied that saints could intervene with God on behalf of mortal souls. But seventy-one saints are represented within the basilica, and, strikingly, relics of those same saints are displayed near by in large reliquary cupboards, forcefully underlining the Council of Trent's decree differentiating clearly between the real saint and the image that is meant simply to inspire the faithful.

Philip II set a fashion by bringing so many artists from Italy to the Escorial, creating a cultural highway that would bring incomparable aesthetic riches to Spain. El Greco was the greatest genius to make that journey, and although 'by any measure' his career 'is one of the strangest in the history of art', he became one of the most famous painters associated with Spain.[40]

Doménikos Theotokópoulos was born on the island of Crete and began painting in a typically Byzantine style, but his obvious talent led him to train in Venice where he studied works by Raphael and Tintoretto; needless to say, the familiar claim has been made that during this period he was also a student of Titian.[41] He moved on to Rome, where he encountered a bewildering range of often conflicting strains of humanist thought and Counter-Reformation theory. The Eternal City teemed with Spaniards: diplomats, cardinals and their entourages and their often more talented hangers-on, men like the great novelist

Miguel de Cervantes, whom he may well have met. Among these self-confident, cosmopolitan Spaniards there was an influential young ecclesiastic called Luis de Castilla, the illegitimate son of the Dean of Toledo Cathedral, Diego de Castilla, who convinced El Greco to abandon his nascent but flourishing career in Italy and move to Spain. According to a contemporary, El Greco arrived in Toledo, in 1577, 'with a considerable reputation and he let it be known he believed his works were the best in the world, and he brought with him such a flamboyant style that its caprice has yet to be equalled'. Moreover, 'he himself was as flamboyant as his pictures'.[42] Such was his arrogance that he poured scorn on Michelangelo.[43]

Diego de Castilla arranged El Greco's first commission, a large canvas of *The Disrobing of Christ* for the Cathedral Chapter of Toledo to hang in the sacristy, where the clergy dressed in their ceremonial robes. The subject is unusual in western art, but was familiar in the Byzantine canon, so it seems likely that El Greco suggested the idea himself. But if the subject matter was unusual, its execution was apparently a shock. The Chapter immediately protested about its lack of decorum: Christ's head was depicted lower down the canvas than other heads; there were other improprieties, and it failed to comply with the strictest interpretation of the decrees of the Council of Trent. But the extent to which the Chapter was truly dismayed is revealed by the fact that the painting still hangs in the sacristy today. In reality, that protest was designed to support a shabby attempt to avoid paying for the painting in full. El Greco sued, with his expert valuer claiming it was worth 900 ducats, while the Chapter priced it at 228. They eventually settled for 317. El Greco had shown himself unwilling to be cowed by a convention that painters and artists should be treated as tradesmen or mediocre artisans by their clients. He was acutely aware of what he called 'the accidents which are the wealth and favours of a prince or king'.[44]

It was not the last time he would do battle with a patron; and, despite these turbulent beginnings, he made his home in Toledo. Nowadays, the old city centre is more museum than reality, a kind of frozen immortality. Deserted at night, by day thousands of tourists amble hither and thither through a warren of narrow streets and lanes that wend to and fro between the high walls of convents, monasteries and seminaries, all intersecting at tiny piazzas over which glowering churches loom. Toledo remains the most important archbishopric in Spain, the religious capital, and ecclesiastics still run the Church from here, while handfuls of monks and clutches of nuns, mostly from India, Africa and South America, are failing to fill the emptiness of the great institutional buildings of their religious orders. One can almost feel faith decompressing here as the sightseers crowd in.

But, when El Greco arrived, hundreds of wealthy churchmen and citizens were eagerly channelling their staggering riches into building, reconstructing and refurbishing the monumental buildings visited by the modern tourists. Now a place of empty cloisters and vacant choir-stalls, it was then 'pullulating with convents', a place of fecund but often reactionary Catholicism.[45] It was so reactionary and politicized that in 1558 the dreaded Inquisition arrested and charged the senior prelate of Spain, the Archbishop himself, former chaplain to both Charles V and Philip II, Bartolomé de Carranza, and imprisoned him for nine years.[46] Castilians may have seen themselves as 'the Lord's chosen nation and champions of His cause',[47] and Toledo may have been the fulcrum for that hubris, but, as we will soon see, it came at the awful price of a society in which the general sense of paranoia about enforcing religious orthodoxy could be ruthlessly exploited by the heavily politicized Church hierarchy.

Toledo may seem an unlikely environment in which so cosmopolitan and experimental an artist as El Greco should have thrived, but the cantankerously supportive society which flourished in the religious capital of conservative Counter-Reformation Spain allowed him to make a success of his career. Hortensio Félix Paravicino, a celebrated ecclesiastic who sat for a captivating portrait by El Greco, wrote in a popular sonnet on the artist's death:

> Crete gave him life,
> But his palette was Toledo born,
> That better homeland where, in death,
> He achieved eternal immortality.[48]

El Greco owed his opportunity to persuade Toledo of his talent to Diego de Castilla, who, as Dean of the Cathedral, reached the height of his power following Carranza's arrest. Although Diego disputed the charges laid against the Archbishop by the inquisitors and gave testimony to the tribunal in which he exalted the piety and probity of his friend, Carranza's absence made him de facto political and spiritual leader of the archdiocese, in addition to his role controlling the finances of one of the richest sees in Christendom. However, it was a curious feature of the early modern Church that religious offices requiring celibacy of their incumbents were sometimes passed down from father to son as though they were some sort of inheritance. Diego was himself the illegitimate son of Ferdinand de Castilla, whom he had succeeded as Dean. Well aware of his sins, he employed El Greco to help atone for the most complicated sin of all: Luis was the offspring of Diego's relationship with María de Silva, the famously beautiful widow of Charles V's Chief Steward, so beautiful, it is said, that the jealous Empress Isabella banished her to a convent. María was a wealthy woman and she named Diego executor of her will. When she died, he immediately set about using her money to establish a magnificent family burial chapel, albeit an unofficial one, by rebuilding the Church of Santo Domingo.

Diego wanted this family chapel to be primarily an appeal for God's forgiveness for his and María's sins: he would build a beautiful church to the greater glory of God with María's money. But it stands to reason that there was another more contentious purpose to this building, for in drawing attention publicly to his relationship with María, it is almost as though he were defying Church orthodoxy and presenting himself and María as somehow legitimately man and wife. Surely Santo Domingo is as much a monument to love as a temple of the Lord?

He appointed the chief architect of Toledo to build Santo Domingo and at one stage involved Juan de Herrera, ensuring a powerful sense of austerity. And he entrusted the all-important decorative iconography, the paintings which would give the altarpiece its symbolic voice, to El Greco. The artist developed such a close relationship with the clandestine Castilla family that when he died, Luis arranged for him to be buried at Santo Domingo as well.

The contract for the paintings specifies the size of the eight canvases to be completed, stipulates that the work could not be subcontracted, that El Greco had to remain in Toledo for the duration of the task and that he was responsible for installation; it includes a schedule of works and a timeframe for payment of the 1,500 ducats agreed as El Greco's fee, as well as some basic penalty clauses. The subject matter of the main paintings was fixed, down to the inclusion of images of Saints Idefonsus and Jerome in the foreground of the two paintings destined for the side altars. Castilla also reserved the right to insist on changes or to reject the work outright.[49] Some art historians have tended to think such 'very careful' supervision and contractual enforcement of both style and content was 'impertinent' micromanagement.[50] But that is nonsense: Castilla, after all, was an expert in Christian iconography, and he also needed the paintings to fit physically into the altarpiece. Beyond these essential requirements, the contract allows El Greco a very free rein in his interpretation of the brief, while ensuring that the client had the final say.

At the centre of the scheme the two men devised are four large narrative paintings depicting the story of Christ as the Redeemer, designed to invoke the idea of Christian salvation, which Diego de Castilla intended for himself, his mistress and their son. *The Adoration of the Shepherds* represented the birth of Christ; there was the miracle of his *Resurrection*; and *The Holy Trinity*, which symbolized God's acceptance of Christ's sacrifice as redeeming humanity; most important of all, *The Assumption of the Virgin Mary* made direct reference to the Madonna as the principal intercessory saint, heaven's leading counsel for sinners who would plead their case with the Lord. The two further intercessory saints-advocate specified in the contract were of particular importance to Diego. Ildefonsus, shown in the *Resurrection*, is the patron saint of Toledo. But Diego, illegitimate himself, had been brought up in a Hieronymite monastery and so had a special personal devotion to St Jerome. El Greco used Diego himself as a model for the Jerome he painted in the foreground of the *Adoration*.[51] This was normal practice and highly desirable for the donor, who thereby ensured that at the deeply mysterious moment in the mass when God's grace transubstantiated the bread and wine of the Eucharist into the real flesh and blood of Christ, the priest would see an image of Diego and be prompted to pray for his soul.

Even as he worked on Santo Domingo, El Greco was drawn to the artistic flame of the Escorial, only to be burned again by the heat of Counter-Reformation orthodoxy. In 1580, he was commissioned to paint an altarpiece for a side chapel in the basilica of the Escorial depicting the *Martyrdom of St Maurice*. Legend had it that in AD 302 Maurice and his men were put to the sword by victorious Romans for refusing to renounce Christianity and pray to the pagan gods of Rome. But El Greco's finished painting was rejected by Philip II for reasons that are unclear and that have been much debated by scholars.

The only contemporary explanation was offered by Prior José de Sigüenza, who reported that:

> the painting did not please His Majesty, which is not surprising, for it pleases few, although there are those who say it is great art . . . for in this there are many opinions and tastes. The difference between works made with reason and art and those that are not, is that the former pleases everyone because art does nothing more than correspond with reason and nature which is imprinted in everyone's soul and therefore gives satisfaction.

In other words it strives to be naturalistic in its representation and logical in composition, 'whereas something badly done with superficial daubs can deceive the uninformed and please the ignorant'.[52] Sigüenza implies that Philip rejected the painting as much for its style as for its form.

Today, scholars dislike the idea that Philip rejected the work for aesthetic reasons. After all, El Greco's very individuality of style is what has attracted modern critics to his paintings. Instead, many have preferred the more prosaic explanation that the Council of Trent had decreed that religious art should be simple to understand and as emotive as possible, which required a dramatic representation of the martyrs actually being brutally put to death in the foreground. El Greco had depicted Maurice and his men discussing whether or not they should pray to the pagan gods and save their lives, while relegating the actual executions to a distant background. So the argument goes that where Philip wanted simplistic melodrama, El Greco gave him 'a Socratic dialogue' in which the 'death' of the martyrs 'has no sting'.[53]

But there is another intriguing and compelling explanation. El Greco included alongside the ancient protagonists of his titular history a handful of contemporary celebrities: the Duke of Savoy who had led the Spanish troops at Saint Quentin, Alessandro Farnese who was even then taking the fight to the Dutch Protestants, the swash-buckling bastard Don John of Austria and, almost indiscernible in the background, a mounted officer with a long beard, unquestionably the Duke of Alba. But there was a terrible problem with this image, for Alba is depicted as one of the executioners, as a pagan Roman beheading a Christian.[54]

During his ruthlessly successful campaign to secure the Portuguese throne for Philip, the ageing Alba reportedly lost control of his Spanish veterans, who ran amok and behaved with their habitual barbarism. Alba had responded by executing hundreds of his own men, so many that he professed to worry that he had 'run out of nooses'. Alba's incessant, monotonous advice to Philip when it came to dealing with traitors was to 'cut off their heads', but to treat his own veterans similarly was especially brutal. Alba was retired in disgrace, but for El Greco to have shown him beheading Christians was a dangerously ill-judged attempt to appeal to Philip in terms of contemporary politics. Alba was one of the greatest generals, and certainly the most loyal, ever to serve the Habsburgs: El Greco was nobody to pass judgment on him, and his arrogance in doing so may well have been what really cost him royal favour.

El Greco returned to Toledo, where he went on to paint an astonishing number of masterpieces, mostly religious subjects and portraits. His work was characterized, especially in his later paintings, by the strange shapes and postures of his flame-like figures who seem to glow and move on the canvas with a wholly otherworldly sense of spirituality, but who have seemed so peculiar to some viewers that it was once seriously suggested they were the result of an astigmatism. Various ingenious rebuttals of this idea have been put forward, mostly flawed or incomplete,[55] although the most obvious objection that he painted a number of portraits without any distortions has been largely over-looked. In reality, El Greco developed that highly distinctive style in Toledo as a very individual response to the artistic tastes of his Spanish patrons.

A century ago, it was obvious to erudite Spaniards that El Greco had been crucially influenced by the greatest Spanish artist of the early sixteenth century, the sculptor Alonso de Berruguete. Indeed, it was felt that Berruguete's own genius had been properly recognized only after his 'follower' El Greco became widely appreciated in the nineteenth century.[56] Two generations ago, one of the greatest Spanish art historians argued that 'there is clearly no more perfect parallel between painting and sculpture than between Greco's glitteringly disturbed fabrics rent asunder by the play of light, and Berruguete's agitated chiaroscuro that animates his fabrics with identically expressive symbolism'.[57]

But such aesthetic judgments are prone to objection and it has become conventional to accept that both men, independently of each other, had clearly been influenced by Michelangelo and that the only traits common to both artists were Italian, traits that El Greco had picked up before reaching Spain.[58] That understanding may have gained currency among specialists, but it is in reality a vague and unsatisfactory thesis that fails to explain why El Greco's work became more like Berruguete's only *after* he came to Spain. Of course he was influenced by Michelangelo's Sistine Chapel and it was self-evidently in Rome that he came to understand Mannerism with its animated figures represented in *contrapposto*, with all the weight thrown on to one foot to give a sense of movement. But El Greco's mature work massively exaggerated the movement of Mannerism, twisting his figures into corkscrew bodies that are contorted way beyond what is usual, desirable or even possible.

In fact, in Italy, El Greco had been concerned with more natural-istic representation, and his *Christ Healing the Blind*, painted in Italy in about 1570, was recognized as being his work only in 1958, having previously been attributed to Tintoretto and later to Veronese. That naturalism reached a climax during his early years in Spain with *The Disrobing of Christ* and *The Adoration of the Name of Jesus*, both painted in 1577 to 1579, in which we see his concern to try and make viewers feel they are beholding a real event.[59]

His distinctive style most obviously began to develop after he had begun working on altarpieces in Castile; and in Castile Berruguete's altarpieces were everywhere, for Berruguete had set the gold-standard in Spanish religious sculpture. Both artists no doubt acquired from Italy a delight in representing colourful figures in contorted and twisted postures with expressive hand movements. But El Greco began to paint those elongated limbs, narrowed faces, vast and upward staring eyes, and began to crowd his figures around one another and view them from unexpected perspectives, the very sort of perspective artfully employed by sculptors of altarpieces, only *after* he had come to Spain and seen Berruguete's work. And, most important of all, only in Spain would he have found patrons ready to appreciate his development because of their own familiarity with Berruguete, patrons enthralled by El Greco's ability to imitate one of the most brilliant sculptors of the sixteenth century in the two dimensions of oil paint.

Berruguete's work sparked in El Greco an understanding of Spanish spiritualism which he then abstracted to new heights of sensuality; and the latter's true genius was perfectly to capture a new sense of mysticism that was invading Spanish religious culture and testing the limits of Counter-Reformation orthodoxy. In that, he complemented in images the words with which the great mystic poets struggled to express their world of intangible visions, hallucinations and ecstasy, the inner life of the Spanish soul.

8

St Teresa, Mystic Poets and the Inquisition

At five in the morning, the thirty-one heretics were brought out by the officials and the friars, there to help die well those who must be burned.

Eyewitness report, 1558

Sixteenth-century Spaniards could choose from a range of scholarly Christian authors who argued that women were the weaker sex and that they should keep their mouths shut. St Paul's Epistle to the Corinthians urged patriarchs: 'Let your women keep silence in the churches: for it is not permitted unto them to speak; but they are commanded to be under obedience, as also saith the law. And if they will learn any thing, let them ask their husbands at home: for it is a shame for women to speak in the church.'[1]

That injunction to keep women silent was extended to writing, so although there were hundreds of women authors writing in Habsburg Spain, almost all are unknown today because so few were published at the time. Over half of these silent writers were nuns who wrote spiritual autobiographies describing their intense mystical experiences for male confessors concerned to assess whether their ecstasies, visions and communion with God were orthodox and Christian, manifestations of madness or the work of the devil.[2]

St Teresa of Avila, 'the greatest woman in Spanish history',[3] was one such nun who first wrote about her spiritual experiences because of worries that her prayers were prey to the devil. She is outstanding among a handful of exceptions to this norm of female silence, a chronically ill mystic who has achieved eternal greatness as a patron saint of Spain thanks to her steadfast pursuit of founding nunneries, her deep spirituality and asceticism and her great accessibility to others, both as a person during her own lifetime and in her writings. She fashioned a wonderful mythology for herself in her autobiography, the *Life*, written in old age as she looked back on a lifetime of service to God and the Carmelite Order. A convent girl with a common touch, she believed that every time she heard a thunderclap God was communicating with her soul.[4]

Teresa Sánchez de Cepeda y Ahumada was born at Avila in 1515, into an affluent merchant family well aware of its Jewish ancestry, not least because her paternal grandfather had been prosecuted by the Inquisition. That persecution encouraged displays of Christian piety which must surely have contributed to Teresa's great childhood faith. As an old woman recalling her childhood, she described reading the lives of the saints and martyrs with her brother and claimed that she thought 'they had paid cheaply to enjoy God's grace and I longed to die the same way, not out of any conscious love of God, but so as to enjoy as soon as possible the pleasures of heaven of which I had read'. But the girl, just like the woman, was a practical creature intent on action: 'I got together with my brother to discuss how to do this and we agreed to go to the land of the Moors and we prayed that for the love of God they would chop off our heads. And I reckon that the Lord would have encouraged us, even at so tender an age, if we had found a way, but our families were the downfall of the plan.' According to another sixteenth-century biographer, when still very young children Teresa and her brother 'left the city by the Adaja gate . . . and crossed over the river by the bridge, but then they ran into an uncle who took them home to their mother, who was very relieved. There had been an anxious search and everyone was afraid the two children must have fallen into a well.' According to another version of this popular anecdote, when their mother 'scolded them, the young boy blamed his sister, saying she had led him on'.[5]

Teresa also remembered deciding to become a hermit and building a hermitage in a nearby orchard out of stones and pebbles, and she wrote of how 'I loved to play at "convents and monasteries" with the other girls, pretending to be nuns.'[6] The old woman deliberately invokes a mundane sense of children's play while hinting at a devoutly fecund imagination deeply imitative of her reading, indeed quixotically so; and she explains that after her mother died, when she was fourteen, she began avidly reading her mother's many books of chivalry. She adds that 'that minor failing of my mother's began to sap my spirit' so that 'I spent hours, day and night, on this vain pursuit, hidden away from my father.' Inspired by the beautiful princesses who populate the genre, 'I began to dress up and I longed to look good. I started to take great care of my hands and hair, I wore perfume, and indulged every vanity you could think of.'[7] Teresa's adolescence would have made a wonderful case study for Jung in his disagreement with Freud over his theory of an Electra Complex: in grief, her mother's books ignited her sexuality and so, even as she dressed the part of a sexually mature woman, she hid her reading from her now sexually available father. But she also remembered that 'as soon as I began to understand my loss, while weeping in my terrible sorrow, I prayed to a devotional image of Our Lady that she should now be my mother'.[8]

At the age of twenty, in 1535, Teresa joined a Carmelite convent and fulfilled her childhood ambition to become a nun, taking the veil two years later. But she suffered from terrible ill-health and soon afterwards became so ill that her father took her to a famous faith healer. She never fully recovered and four years later, she fell into a coma and seemed to be dead; she woke after four days, but for the next three years her legs were paralysed. Later, she began to experience vivid and terrifying hallucinations, she heard voices and saw visions, she went into trances and reached heights of ecstasy through prayer. She embraced asceticism, fasting, scourging herself, spending hours at a time praying. Later, she would write endlessly about pain as central to her experience of communion with God.

Describing God as her 'Spouse', she writes of how 'the Spouse treats her with those delicate and tender ways that come from deep in the soul', of how the soul 'feels deliciously wounded without under-standing how or by whom' and of her realization that she would 'never want to be cured of the wound', for all that it 'is very painful', because it is 'delicious and sweet'. That pain, she insisted, was 'more satisfying than a painless trance brought on by quiet prayer'. And, bearing in mind that she was in part writing to refute any suggestion that her mystical experiences were the work of demons, she notes that 'the devil would never be able to give such delicious pain; he might give a taste of apparent pleasure, but for so much pain to bring such a calm pleasure cannot be his work'.[9]

In the face of bitter opposition, this deeply troubled yet supremely spiritual woman set about establishing a reformed Carmelite order, known as the Discalced (Barefoot) Carmelites, following the examples of Saints Francis and Clare in wearing no shoes as a sign of their strict rule. By her death, in 1582, she had personally founded a further eighteen reformed houses and had influenced the monks of the male order to begin reforming their own. Yet the tensions caused by this reforming zeal eventually brought about a momentous split between the reformed and non-reformed or Mitigated Carmelites that led to vicious rivalry.

In 1567, Teresa met a young Carmelite, John of the Cross, for the first time. He had grown up in genteel poverty, but his mother had managed to send him to school where he became a favourite of the nuns, who thought him 'sharp witted'.[10] He was exactly half Teresa's age – she was almost the same age as his mother. They immediately formed a deep spiritual bond and in 1572 he moved to Avila to become her confessor and had such a profound influence on her that over the following few years Teresa wrote one of her most important spiritual works, *The Interior Castle* or *The Dwelling Places*.

But the vicious political battle between the Mitigated Carmelites and St Teresa's Reformers took a decisive turn in the early hours of 4 December 1577. A group of Mitigated Monks and 'well-armed men' forced their way into the convent and abducted John. They took him to Toledo and imprisoned him in 'a small, dark cell with only an arrow slit high up near the roof' so that in order to read his breviary he had to stand on a stone bench. He was allowed to eat bread and water from the floor of the refectory, but 'when the meal was done, all the brothers encircled him and scourged him; many years later, the scars on the back of the patient father bore testimony' to their cruelty.[11] Teresa wrote immediately to Philip II,[12] but the King, as ever, was slow to act; and in the meantime John managed to escape his captors. But, when Philip finally considered the matter, he concluded that such unholy treatment was irrefutable proof of the need to separate the administration of the two Carmelite factions and, on the King's advice, in 1580 the Pope granted the reformed house independence, a decisive political victory for an exceptional nun.

Just as John in life greatly influenced some of Teresa's most important spiritual writings, so her death inspired him to write the two poems for which he is now best remembered, his *Dark Night of the Soul* and *Flame of Living Love*:[13]

O, flame of living love
Which gently wounds
The deepest centre of my soul!
Now you no longer hide,
If you wish, then be done
And tear the weave of sweet acquaintance.

O sweet prison!
O gift of pain!
O gentle hand, so soft of touch,
O taste of eternity,
You pay all debts
And killing death you turn to life.

O burning lanterns,
Whose brilliance lights
The deepest caverns of a mind
(Once dark and blind),
With strange caresses give
Warmth and brightness to your Love!

My bosom remembers you
As tame and loving.
There you alone dwell secretly
And with your sweet breath
So full of benevolence and grace
How tenderly you make me love.[14]

Today, John's language of love may seem inappropriately sexual for a religious poet still clearly in mourning for the death of an important mother figure with whom he shared such intense spiritual passion. Indeed, Sigmund Freud and Joseph Breur dubbed Teresa 'the patron saint of hysteria', a now outdated psychiatric diagnosis associated almost exclusively with women suffering from a range of symptoms rooted in their sexuality that was treated by a physician or midwife masturbating the patient until she experienced an 'hysterical paroxysm';[15] while Jacques Lacan once flippantly remarked of Teresa's mystical ecstasies that 'you only have to go and look at Bernini's statue of her in Rome to see that she was coming'.[16] But, of course, Bernini was responsible for sculpting Teresa experiencing an eternally Baroque orgasm in bronze and stone. The penultimate word is best given to Teresa, for Bernini had interpreted the following episode from her *Life* in which she described the experience of transverberation, the spiritual piercing of the heart:

It pleased the Lord that I should sometimes see a vision of an angel . . . small and very handsome, with the brilliant face of one of those most exalted angels known as cherubim . . . He held a golden spear in his hands, tipped with a burning iron point. Sometimes, he seemed to thrust it so far into my breast that it penetrated my inner organs. When he withdrew it, it was as though he had disembowelled me and he left me aflame with a great sense of love for God. I moaned a little, for the pain was so fierce, but it was so excessively tender that I did not want it to stop.[17]

But for sixteenth-century religious mystics, the intensity of their faith transcended their sense of sexuality even as they used the language of love to evoke their ineffable experience.

And now, my shepherds, I'll call time
On my sweet song, by heaping praise
On a fearsome genius of whom I'm
Certain he'd better my every word or phrase
And steal a march on my every rhyme
In an ecstasy of lyrical displays.
I speak, of course, of Friar Luis of León
Whom I revere, adore and follow like a son.[18]

Miguel de Cervantes heaped this lyrical praise on the brilliant intellectual and mystic poet Fray Luis de León in *The Galatea* in 1584. A
victim of the political corruption of the Inquistion in his lifetime, León's
work was not published until 1631, when the great satirist Francisco
de Quevedo wrote of the 'moral majesty' and 'illuminating clarity' of
his verse.[19] Another admirer, Francisco Pacheco, the leading Spanish
art theorist of his age and teacher of Diego Velázquez, described 'the
great professor Fray Luis' as 'small of stature, but perfectly formed,
with a large and shapely head covered with plenty of curly hair', and
claimed that 'you could see the nobility of his soul engraved on his
countenance'. 'He was the foremost genius of his age in every science
and art . . . a great poet, he had Latin, Greek, Hebrew, Chaldean and
Syrian . . . and even King Philip II sought his counsel on every important question of conscience.'[20]

Luis de León was born in 1527 at Belmonte, a small town that is still
impressively walled, which sits on the edge of the Spanish plain. The
Inquisition had first cast its shadow over his wealthy family in 1512,
when his maternal grandmother was accused of being a practising
Jew, and they struggled to escape that reputation. At fourteen, Luis
went to study canon law at Salamanca, where he immediately joined
a strict Augustinian community and abandoned the hurly-burly of
secular life among the 7,000 students. The university was then at its
most brilliant thanks to men like Francisco de Vitoria and his influential follower Domingo de Soto, who sponsored the young Luis for his
master's degree.[21]

Luis flourished, winning election to the Chair of St Thomas in 1561.
But, for all his brilliance, he suffered from a sharp-tongued arrogance
and he could not resist baiting his defeated Dominican rival for the

post with taunts about a Dominican heretic who had been burned by the Inquisition for his Lutheran beliefs two years before.[22] Such fate-tempting spitefulness was rash indeed for a theologian whose own Jewish roots were such humiliatingly public knowledge and who excelled above all as a scholar of Hebrew. Luis was vulnerable to calumny and his vicious repartee and intellectual brilliance had made him too many enemies. A Jesuit had reported that Luis 'is held in much higher opinion at the University than the Dominican fathers', which, as Pacheco remarked, 'had excited great envy'.[23]

For Luis, language and creation were intimately linked by their shared divine origin. 'In the beginning was the Word, and the Word was with God, and the Word was God,' according to the Gospel of St John.[24] With an exceptional grasp of the mechanics of vocabulary and grammar, he was fascinated by the most nuanced differences of meaning between one language and the next, and was especially concerned with the almost impossible task of comprehending precisely what ancient cultures had meant by the words that they wrote. He was well equipped to engage in the dangerous business of debating the translation of scripture.

But he was as much a poet as an academician and had imbibed the thrilling new Italianate verse of Garcilaso and Boscán while he was at Salamanca. From them he learnt techniques and skills he would use himself; but most importantly, he was bewitched by the language of earthly desire, which could be so beautifully employed to embrace the love of God.[25] Like all the Spanish mystics, he obsessed over the penultimate book of the Bible, the Song of Songs, the deeply erotic wedding song attributed to King Solomon, filled with very explicit evocations of sexual union. 'Let him kiss me with the kisses of his mouth: for thy love is better than wine,' the verses read; and, as the story of the feast continues, the impatient bride yearns for her lover to 'Comfort me with apples,' in direct reference to the fruit of that forbidden tree, 'for I am sick from love.' In due course, they make love, a number of times:

My beloved is gone down into his garden,
to the beds of spices,
to feed in the gardens,
and to gather lilies.

I am my beloved's,
and my beloved is mine:
he feedeth among the lilies.

. . .

I would lead thee, and bring thee into my mother's house,
who would instruct me:
I would cause thee to drink of spiced wine,
of the juice of my pomegranate.

His left hand should be under my head,
and his right hand should embrace me.

On one level, these can only have seemed like the headiest of lyrics
to a celibate churchman, lyrics that under any other circumstances
would have been censored as the obscene work of the devil. As one
of the most revered Spanish scholars of our own age puts it: given
how much he was influenced by the art and technique of Garcilaso,
the greatest of love poets, Luis can hardly have found 'exploring the
power of an emotion that so motivates men and which is so celebrated
by the arts to be unappetizing. On the contrary, surely it appealed to
a friar in the fullness of masculinity.'[26] But as another exceptional but
very pious modern scholar puts it, 'the Song of Songs contains some
of the most beautiful yet mysterious poetry in the Bible'.[27]

What in heaven's name does it mean? Luis wrote an explanation for
his sister, a nun. He warned that the Song of Songs 'is a difficult book
to read for anyone and especially dangerous for young people and
for those whose sense of virtue is not very developed'. But for those
inured to temptation, 'this lovely song shows God wounded by his
love for us and . . . we see all that passionate lovers usually feel, but
with greater focus and more delicately because divine love is purer
than earthly passion'.[28]

For the mystics, the answer was clear: the Song of Songs is about
the love of God. Its imagery guided the ways in which Saints Teresa
and John of the Cross conceived of their sublime yet ineffable experience of faith. From it, they gleaned the sexually charged language with
which they expressed their spirituality. For Luis, Teresa and John of

the Cross, that intense transmutation of sexuality into mystical spirituality which Lacan poked such fun at in Bernini's statue was the essence of religious ecstasy.

The most influential Spanish cultural historian of the twentieth century, Julio Caro Baroja, remembered that 'as a young child, I happened to see some rolls of parchment inscribed in Hebrew with sacred texts or prayers, which were discovered hidden beneath the leather covering of an eighteenth-century table belonging to a workman employed by my father and which must have once been owned by a pious and very orthodox crypto-Jew who was sufficiently well educated to read Hebrew'.[29] A century earlier, the flamboyant scripture-smuggler George Borrow, who took contraband vernacular Bibles to Spain for the English Bible Society, met a man called Abarbenel who claimed to be a secret Jew and who regularly celebrated Jewish feasts with four high-ranking Catholic churchmen. Borrow also describes a retired official of the Inquisition who remembered 'searching the house of an ecclesiastic' and finding 'a small shrine of silver' under the floorboards containing 'three books in black hog-skin . . . written in Hebrew . . . and of great antiquity'.[30]

Why bind these holy books in filthy, proscribed hog-skin? Could it have been deliberately sacrilegious camouflage? Did Borrow or his informant remember the story inaccurately or simply make the whole thing up? Or could it be that the men or women who originally hid such holy relics had such a disrupted and confused sense of their Jewish past that they were oblivious to the bitter irony of a porcine binding?

Caro Baroja's workman was an accidental and ignorant keeper of the remains of a Jewish past, while Borrow's Jews were simply ghosts in the machine of Spanish culture. But these stories are witness to an enduring obsession among some influential Spaniards with the notion that the spirit of Judaism was quietly but observably alive beneath the Catholic orthodoxy of Spanish society. And that obsession is itself a relic of the particular Spanish mentalities and tempers that led to the foundation of the Inquisition in Spain in 1480.

Those mentalities and tempers are matters of fiery debate and polemic as well as sober scholarship. But the primary motive for the foundation of the Inquisition was simple enough: its purpose was to discover heresy among baptized Christians and reconcile them to the Catholic Church; it was not *designed* to persecute Jews, but in the fifteenth century Judaism *was* its foremost problem.

In the wake of violent rioting across Spain against Jews in the 1390s, many converted to Christianity and during the following century more and more converted out of fear or convenience or for genuine reasons of faith. Abhorred by Jews and treated as inferior believers by Old Christians, these converts developed their own New Christian identity, embracing St Paul's concept of a 'true Israel' that was reborn with Christ while asserting their own direct descent from 'genetic Israel', from the ancient Jews, thereby claiming a blood relationship with Jesus and Mary, the Prophets and the Apostles; they claimed the best of both worlds, setting themselves apart from the neighbouring communities that anyway mistrusted them.[31] That New Christian or *converso* (convert) identity became entrenched, passing from one generation to the next down the centuries.

But many *conversos* embraced Christianity with the same tepid enthusiasm for religion that had allowed them to abandon Judaism in the first place. A leading contemporary chronicler, Hernando de Pulgar, himself a *converso*, complained that in Andalusia 'there are ten thousand young maidens who have never stepped out of their houses since the day they were born and have never heard nor learnt any other doctrine than what they have seen behind the locked doors of their parents' homes'.[32] And he was concerned that behind those doors they saw Jewish cultural practices continued for reasons of tradition and habit, customary behaviours their parents did not think of as Jewish. All no doubt soon learnt the importance of at least appearing to eat pork, but how many knew that they swept rooms away from the walls and towards the centre so as not to foul the blessed threshold? How many continued to cook without milk in a land where there was little milk anyway?

According to Fernández de Oviedo, such lax *conversos* were called *marranos* – not, as is widely thought, because *marrano* meant 'pig', an ironic term of abuse associated with a reluctance to eat pork, but 'because *marrar* in old Castilian meant "to fail", and for a man to fail in what he has promised to do is very shameful'.[33] A *marrano* was a neophyte who failed to embrace Christianity properly. And although evidence suggests that very few *conversos* actually reverted to Judaism or continued to be Jews in secret, there was considerable paranoia among both Old and New Christians alike that many *marranos* had returned to the old religion. And that made them heretics.

The Inquisition was established in 1480 to deal with the persistence of Jewish cultural traits and the perceived problem of wilful Judaizing, or the continued practice of Jewish rites amongst *conversos*. But once the Inquisitors started hunting for crypto-Jews, they seemed to find thousands of them. This was because when they visited a *converso* community, they began by offering a month-long period of grace during which heretics might confess and be reconciled to the Church with all but the mildest punishment. For many, it was much easier to confess than to engage with the impossible task of demonstrating their innocence, not least because there seem to have been many evil characters eager to denounce anyone they wanted out of the way. Queen Isabella personally ordered the arrest of a group of Jews in Toledo who had confessed to perjuring themselves when testifying against a group of *conversos*,[34] while in 1482 Pope Sixtus himself complained that in Spain 'many true and faithful Christians, on the testimony of enemies, rivals, slaves and others ... have without any legitimate proof been thrust into secular prisons, tortured and condemned as relapsed heretics, deprived of their goods and property and handed over to the secular arm to be executed, to the peril of souls, setting a pernicious example, and causing disgust to many'.[35]

Tragically, this self-fulfilling fiction became the official, authorized understanding of the situation. Spaniards began to believe they lived in a land dangerously awash with crypto-Jews and they then logically blamed the Jewish community for encouraging the *conversos* to revert. The Catholic Monarchs felt compelled to act to save their realms and, in 1492, amid the belligerent religious fervour of victory over Islam at Granada, they issued an edict requiring all Jews to leave Spain or convert to Christianity. In reality, relatively few left for ever, but the many who remained or returned were now baptized as Christians, with little or no catechism. Needless to say, these victims of those involuntary and imperfect conversions continued customs and traditions they had grown up with, while many no doubt deliberately kept their ancestral faith in secret. Almost all became potential prey for a newly rapacious Inquisition that in little more than a decade had turned the paranoid fiction of crypto-Judaism into a reality. The Inquisitors had made Jews their enemy, writing another chapter into the history of European anti-Semitism, perpetuating that deep-seated and almost Oedipal need to negate the religion which sired Christianity, that peculiar, seemingly cathartic impetus to see the crucifixion in terms of a phoenix rising from the ashes of Judaism, an impetus that gave the Inquisition its wings as well as its flames.

The Inquisition fostered a distinction between Old and New Christians that gave succour to Spaniards' obsession with their *limpieza de sangre* or 'purity of blood'. Those who could prove that none of their known ancestors had been *conversos* behaved as though their ethnically clean ancestry bestowed an almost noble status upon them, causing a great rift with their neighbours who were known to be descended from Jews. From the mid-fifteenth century, a handful of influential institutions began to exclude New Christians, especially the descendants of people convicted by the Inquisition, fomenting a culture in which notarized documentary proof of *limpieza de sangre* began to gain currency. It especially suited men from humble origins who had risen to positions of power and influence because the poverty of their background often meant that little was known about their ancestry and so their claims to be Old Christians were irrefutable. Purity of blood conferred an almost nationalistic sense of Old Christian identity that gave parvenu peasants an advantage over *converso* competition for university places, government offices and positions within the Church. It even gave them limited leverage over the higher nobility and especially the leading aristocratic families, almost all of which had intermarried with *conversos*.

And so *limpieza de sangre* had numerous powerful and influential opponents who were *conversos*, like Diego de Castilla and Bartolomé de Carranza, but also some who were leading Old Christians such as the Duke of Infantado's sons Pedro González de Mendoza and Álvaro de Mendoza. In 1565, the Pope condemned the concept as being contrary to canon law, while most Spaniards, including Philip II himself, frequently ignored institutional or local statutes of *limpieza* (which prohibited the appointment of *conversos* to specified positions) when it suited them.[36] The Jesuits were famously opposed and Loyola himself reportedly told friends that he would have considered it a divine honour to be Jewish: 'What?' he asked, who would not want 'to be related to Christ Our Lord and to Our Lady the glorious Virgin Mary?'[37]

In 1569, Friar Luis de León was asked to sit on a committee of theologians convened by the Inquisition to examine the orthodoxy of a version of the Bible first published in Paris in 1545.[38] A heated debate ensued between the traditional scholastics and the progressive humanists led by Luis, reflecting the entrenched political positions of Catholics who saw the Council of Trent as an affirmation of long-standing orthodoxy and those who embraced the idea of the Counter-Reformation as a chance to develop the Church.

The most hidebound scholars argued that the Jewish transcribers of the Old Testament had deliberately corrupted the text in order to confound the medieval Christian belief that it prefigured or prophesied the New Testament and so the life of Christ. But humanists could see no reason why Jews would have deliberately perverted one of their own sacred texts, and Luis himself pointed out that the Hebrew text better supported Christian prophecy than St Jerome's seminal Latin translation, the Vulgate.

That was dangerous talk in orthodox Spain, for the Council of Trent had decreed that the 'vulgate edition, by long usage . . . should be held as authentic in public lectures, disputations, sermons and expositions; and no one may dare or presume to reject it under any pretext whatever. Furthermore, in order to restrain petulant spirits, no one shall use his own skill to render the Holy Scripture in his own way that goes against the true sense and interpretation as judged by the Holy Mother Church.'[39]

Needless to say, it was an especially dangerous position for a known *converso*. And, as the debates became more heated, Luis was ever more scathing and sarcastic; he was too good at verbal jousting, too quick, too sharp and too combative for his own good. When the leading traditionalist, León de Castro, accused him of having 'a mind as Jewish as his blood' and threatened to throw him on the Inquisitorial bonfire, Luis smugly retorted that it would be much better to burn Castro's very long and boring book about Isaiah.[40] It had become bitterly personal: in December 1571, one of the Dominican tradition-alists denounced to the Inquisition the three *converso* humanists on the committee. They were accused of asserting that 'Holy Scripture should normally be explained according to the teachings of rabbis, while the writings of the Holy Doctors should be rejected and left out.'[41]

At the outset, the Inquisitors were required by their own rules to appoint a committee of theologians to assess the evidence against the accused. Their decision was critical, for if they advised that there was a case to answer, they effectively shifted the burden of proof on to the accused to demonstrate their innocence. In theory, an official pros-ecutor, or *fiscal*, was then appointed and only then did the constables arrest and imprison the accused, although in one notorious example a group of suspects, including two children of nine and fourteen, were locked up for two years without there being any official case for them to answer.[42]

On 27 March 1572, Luis was taken to the Inquisition jail in Valladolid. At this stage, bailiffs usually impounded all of their victim's chattels, which were valued so that they could be sold off piecemeal to pay for the prisoner's upkeep. In this way, even the few victims who were eventually exonerated were usually ruined. But, as a monk, Luis had surrendered all his worldly wealth to his monastery.

In prison, Luis confronted the first in a trinity of pernicious but ruthlessly effective aspects of Inquisitorial methodology. In exchange for a promise of leniency, he was now invited to confess his crimes, within three days, without being given any indication of the accusations that had been made against him. While Luis could make a reasonable assumption about why he had been arrested, many victims could only guess at what they had been accused of and by whom. This had the effect of baffling the innocent, who could have no idea what they were supposed to have done, and of perplexing the guilty, who had to decide which blasphemies or heresies to confess to.

According to the rules, the prosecution was required formally to charge Luis within ten days, but that process in fact dragged on until 5 May. Defence counsel was appointed, although that role was largely clerical and advisory. The Inquisitors then set about preparing a set of questionnaires that would be used to interrogate as many witnesses as possible, arranging those depositions and collating the documentary records of all those proceedings. Unusually, Luis presented his own questionnaires to the Inquisitors and requested that they also be used. They were not. Finally, on 3 March 1573, the depositions were made public, expurgated of any content by which the witnesses might be identified, and Luis could begin to prepare his defence.

The second incarnation of the pernicious Inquisitorial trinity was the strict anonymity of the witnesses who testified against the accused. But Luis had no doubt who his enemies were and in his defence papers he successfully identified them all. For him, a noble sense of honour and a righteous sense of theology were at stake; indeed, they were more important than expediting a satisfactory resolution. And so, as ever, he was his own worst enemy, for he treated his trial as an intellectual exercise in defending his interpretation of scripture. He belittled the intelligence of his enemies and the Inquisitors, and introduced novel theoretical arguments about the scriptures; he also aroused confusion by recusing some of his own witnesses and caused long hold-ups by calling for testimony from other witnesses who proved difficult to find, including one man who was already dead.

On 28 September 1576, the tribunal finally passed the dreaded sentence of 'indecision', the third incarnation of this evil trinity, for it required that Luis be tortured in order to determine the outcome.

In theory, torture was to be applied 'according to the conscience and will of the appointed judges, following law, reason and good conscience'. Inquisitors were supposed to 'take great care that the sentence of torture is justified'.[43] Morever, no lasting harm should be done, and official overseers and a physician were to be present. In reality, many victims were left with limbs mangled by the rack and other grim machinery; their mental and physical health was often broken, and some died.[44] However, to the consternation of the Inquisitors, it seems a small number of prisoners managed to avoid confessing under torture to either real or imaginary heresies by anaesthetizing themselves with opium, then widely available in apothecaries' shops.[45]

Intriguingly, among the usual tortures employed by the Inquisition was the *toca*. This involved the mouth being held wide open by an iron plug and the *toca*, a strip of linen, being forced down the throat. Water was then poured slowly on to the *toca*, causing a sensation of suffocation in the victim. From time to time the *toca* was removed and the victim urged to tell the truth. Clearly, this is an historic form of waterboarding, and, interestingly, the professional torturers of the Inquisition were not only happy to define it as a form of torture, but by the early 1600s had abandoned it in favour of methods they 'regarded as more merciful'.[46]

Elderly, very frail after years in his cramped cell and suffering from a heart problem, Luis de León would not have survived torture. He claimed that time and again during his incarceration he had sensed death over his shoulder, only to be reprieved by his determination to fight on; and, on 7 December 1576, he finally triumphed: Philip II intervened personally on his behalf and the Inquisitor General himself ruled that Luis be completely absolved. But the twin pillars of his experience, that he was a *converso* and that he had been accused maliciously, perfectly exemplify the evil reality of the Inquisition.

The official abolition of Spanish Jewry and fear of the Inquisition had, within a generation or two, largely suppressed Judaism in Spain, or at least any tangible evidence of Jewish practice. As a result, the

Inquisition became increasingly directionless until, in 1558, to the horror of Charles V and Philip II, Protestant cells were discovered in Valladolid and Seville. The intense persecution of Protestants which followed revitalized the institution and in 1561 a new set of rules for the tribunal was introduced, while the central ceremony during which heretics were reconciled, the notorious auto-da-fé, was redesigned as a public spectacle.[47] As one commentator has put it, for an Inquisitor General who had refused to lend the Crown money for the war against France and so made enemies of Charles and Philip, 'the discovery of Lutheran cells was a gift from heaven'.[48]

In 1558, a vast bonfire of books, known as 'silent heretics', was symbolically burned in Valladolid.[49] But this was merely a prelude to the main auto-da-fé at which thirteen unlucky Protestants were burned at the stake. An eyewitness takes up the story: 'A grand stage was raised high in the main square, with raked seating where the convicts sat in various large divisions according to the seriousness of their crimes,' while the galleries of the City Hall were prepared for the aldermen and other officials. Grandstands were built all around the square, 'for the wives of the Council of Castile, for the Aldermen, and for members of the religious orders', and 'the roofs of all the buildings were removed and replaced' with seating, while the ordinary folk were packed in like groundlings at the theatre. 'So many people came from elsewhere that for two days beforehand it was impossible to walk in the streets.'[50]

The auto-da-fé itself began early. 'At five in the morning, the thirty-one heretics were brought out by the officials and the friars, there to help die well those of them who must be burned.' An armed guard made up of 400 noble cavalry of the King's household and royal halberdiers accompanied the procession as it approached the main square, 'where the Princess Regent, Juana, and our lord the Prince, along with the Heralds at Arms' were waiting.

Among the condemned were many noblemen and aristocratic wives and nuns. There were lawyers, one with his daughter, a silversmith and a couple of peasant girls. But the most important heretic of all was Agustín de Cazalla, a former chaplain to Charles V who had travelled with the Emperor to Holland and Germany in the 1540s. 'They sat him in the highest chair, over to one side, wearing a satin cassock and a *sambenito*,' a penitential tunic, in this case decorated with flames and demons, the sign that he was condemned to burn. Intriguingly, they also brought out an effigy of Agustín's mother, who had once been condemned for Judaizing but never burned.

A Dominican friar preached an hour-long sermon and then Cazalla stepped up to receive sentence from his judges: 'Dr Cazalla, preacher and chaplain of His Majesty, a Jew, descendant of burned Jews and *conversos*', they began before accusing him of being a Lutheran. And then Cazalla confessed: 'I must have read the books of the Lutherans for nine years in order to learn about their errors so as to confound them and refute them . . . But I never found any good in them until 1558. Then, in all my sermons my primary purpose was to promote their false teachings.' He went on to explain in some detail the basic Protestant position. In front of this large crowd, he was invited by the Inquisitorial Prosecutor to expound his belief in the justification of man by faith alone and his denial of good works, purgatory, papal indulgences, days of abstinence (he explained that he always ate meat on Fridays and during Lent), the chastity of the priesthood, the value of confession, transubstantiation of the Eucharist and the graven images of saints. He ended by accusing Charles V of committing a great sin by condemning Luther. It is a peculiar institution indeed that, charged with eliminating heresy, should invite such an able preacher to promulgate so heretical a sermon on so dramatic a platform.

Cazalla was then condemned to the flames, and the effigy of his mother was ordered to be taken away and burned with her bones. So, bizarrely, while Cazalla was sentenced to be burned alive as a Lutheran, his mother was posthumously incinerated as a Jew.

The guard of 400 cavalry and halberdiers accompanied the thirteen men and women who were to be burned and handed them over to the secular officers of justice 'at the usual place outside the Gate of the Campo. A large stage or scaffold had been built to keep back the great crowds, who were so many that since dawn it had not been possible to go through the city gate.'

In fact, Cazalla and eleven others all repented and so were merci-fully garroted before the fires were lit. Only a lawyer from Toro who refused to abjure his heresies was actually burned alive. When Cazalla tried to persuade him to be reconciled to the Church, 'he replied sharply, "you have changed your tune, Cazalla, for death, which is fleeting, has frightened you". And so they tied a rope around his neck and burned him alive. Now he will be wherever he may be, but disabused of his false beliefs,' the eyewitness concludes, 'while the others died as good Catholics, may it please God to pardon their sins.'

The persecution of Lutherans in Spain arose, of course, out of Habsburg dismay at the spread of Protestantism in northern and central Europe and the fear that Spain would be contaminated. Indeed, news of the Spanish cells encouraged foreign Reformers, and over the next decade or so many large consignments of contraband books destined for the heartland of Old Castile were discovered in ports along the Biscay coast and elsewhere; we can only assume that many more went undetected. In Spain, many foreigners were employed operating printing presses. They immediately fell under suspicion and a whole network of heretic printers was identified. At the same time, some Protestants arrived from abroad proselytizing Reform; one Huguenot from Carcassonne claimed to have preached in Saragossa on three separate occasions by 1563. In Barcelona, the Inquisition and civic authorities were unable to cope: 'there are so many very evil foreigners arriving here that some strong remedy is needed', they reported. In 1571 they condemned eighteen French Protestants at a massive auto-da-fé.[51]

But the most intriguing and awful irony in this paranoid perse-cution of Protestants is that so many of them appear to have been *conversos*. The virulently intolerant Archbishop of Toledo in the late 1540s, Juan Martínez Siliceo, had ranted in all seriousness that the 'Lutheran heretics of Germany were nearly all descendants of Jews' and his words were echoed by Philip II himself a decade later. However ludicrous that might seem, that rhetorical abuse takes on a deeply sinister significance when we learn that Siliceo also claimed that 'nearly all the parish priests in his [own] archdiocese [of Toledo] were [also] descendants of Jews'.[52] In articulating this strange fear that heresy must have migrated from Jews to Protestants from one generation to the next, the Archbishop gave voice to an apparently deeply rooted and visceral sense that heresy was inherited by *conversos* and was therefore principally an ethnic problem and not a matter of faith.

9

The Netherlands: 'The Great Bog of Europe'

It is a war such as has never been seen nor heard of even in the remotest lands.

The Duke of Alba, 1572

'The great Bog of *Europe*', a caustic English commentator called the Netherlands in the 1600s, but he went on to describe a place where 'gold is more plentiful than stones'. 'What is it which there may not be found in plenty? They make by their industry all the fruits of the vast Earth their own.' Even 'their knaves are worth a million of ours, for they in a boisterous rudeness can work and live and toil, whereas ours will rather laze themselves to poverty; and like Cabbages left out in winter, rot away in the loathsomenesse of a nauseus sloth.'

Foreigners always marvelled at the wealth of the hard-working, easy-trading Dutch. But the Englishman scoffed at an egalitarian nation of self-satisfied arrivistes where 'escutcheons are as plentifull as Gentry is scarce. Every man is his own Herald; and he that has but wit enough to invent a Coat, may challenge it as his own.' His complaint would have resonated with the stereotypical Spanish *hidalgo* with a preference for poverty over labour, honour over trade, and an obsession with purity of blood. Worse still, the Netherlands seemed a naturally heterodox land, so flat 'it affords the people one commodity beyond all the other Regions: if they die in perdition, they are so low, that they have a shorter cut to Hell . . . And for this cause, perhaps all strange Religions throng thither.' The Dutchmen's permissive attitude to faith would set them at loggerheads with the orthodox Spaniards until 1648.

Introducing the idea of the Netherlands as 'a green Cheese pickled in brine', our Englishman warmed to his new gastronomic theme: 'they are the ingredients of a Black pudding, and want only stirring together'. And, pursuing the inevitable rules of alimentary progress, he described how 'most of their dwellings stand like Privies in moated-houses, hanging still over the water', before allowing the meandering imagery of his metaphor – perhaps inspired by Hieronymus Bosch – to conclude that Dutch 'Soyle is all fat [and] full of veins & bloud, but no bones in't; indeed it is the buttock of the World'.[1]

But the Netherlands were vital to the Spanish economy: over three-quarters of Castilian wool, Spain's only major export, was sold there. And they were of immense sentimental importance to the Habsburgs. Philip's father was born at Ghent, his grandfather at Bruges. Philip was descended from the Burgundian dukes of the great House of Valois, who could trace their lineage back to the Capetian kings of France. From a very early age he was imbued with a deep pride in that direct descent from a legendary dynasty that embodied the virtuous and bellicose spirit of medieval princehood. It proved a poisoned inheritance.

The idea of the Netherlands as a single entity, however, was the artificial construction of imperialist policy. In 1549, Charles V had joined Flanders and Artois to the Dutch- and German-speaking provinces that had formerly been part of the Empire and assumed for himself the title of Lord of the Netherlands. Representatives of the different provinces or States met in a powerful parliament known as the States General, but there was no tradition among them of political unity under a single ruler. Disastrously, Charles isolated the intellectually and spiritually experimental Dutch from the religious tolerance forced upon him in the Empire by the German princes, thus exposing them to decades of autocratic Habsburg intolerance. He negotiated a massive restructuring of the Netherlands Church with the Papacy that was kept secret from the Dutch until it was announced. And he subjected this politically unstable collection of independently minded peoples to nearly crippling levels of taxation.

Philip continued and strengthened his father's policies and permanently stationed garrisons of the dreaded professional Spanish troops known as the *tercios* in the Netherlands. As a result, in an ironic rerun of Charles's experience with the Spanish Comuneros, when Philip returned to Spain in 1559, leaving his illegitimate half-sister Margaret of Parma as Regent in Brussels, the Dutch were incensed: they felt colonized by a haughty Spaniard, a foreigner who imposed his alien will from far away.

So, in 1565, the States General sent one of the most powerful Dutch aristocrats, the Count of Egmont, to Spain, to negotiate directly with Philip. Egmont returned convinced that the King had personally offered a more conciliatory policy towards Protestants and freedom of worship in general. He even had a signed agreement that hinted at further compromise. But within months, in an infamous document now known as the 'Letter from the Segovia Woods', Philip wrote instructing Margaret that no leniency was to be shown to any 'heretic'. Far from introducing a new policy of religious tolerance, he was determined to strengthen the Inquisition in the Netherlands. To make his point, he ordered that six radical Protestant Anabaptists, whom Margaret had hoped to pardon, instead 'be brought to justice' by way of example.[2]

Whatever Philip had really promised Egmont, he now appeared to have broken his word and that made him appear weak and dishonest as well as foreign. Moreover there was a wild card as well, a joker in Philip's deck: his own son and heir, the deranged and deformed Don Carlos.

Charles V had claimed to be delighted when his grandson Don Carlos furiously rebuked him for retreating from battle against the Elector Maurice.[3] But the Emperor privately told his sister that he did not like the boy's 'manners and character' and did 'not know what might become of him'.[4] Don Carlos's dangerously wilful personality was becoming the talk of European courts; a Venetian diplomat described his 'head as out of proportion with his body' and referred to his 'pallid complexion' and his 'cruel character'. 'When he is brought hares or other animals trapped in the hunt,' the Venetian continued, 'he likes to watch them being roasted alive. Once, he was given a giant turtle, which bit his finger, at which he bit off its head with his teeth.'

It was of enormous concern to Philip that this psychotic adolescent was heir to the throne. But in 1561 Don Carlos fell down a flight of stairs while chasing after a gardener's daughter whom he was in the habit of flagellating. He smashed headlong into a door, cracking his cranium so badly that his skull was visible through the wound.[5] Within days, he was running a high temperature and his doctors were very worried. They aggressively cleaned a build-up of pus from the wound and sent urgent word to the King, then at Madrid, who set out at once to be at his son's bedside. The infection spread and the Prince's face puffed up so that he could not open his eyes; it spread to his neck and chest. The great Dr Andreas Vesalius forcefully argued in favour of drilling a hole in the boy's skull to relieve the pressure on his brain. But first they began to administer mild purges. The Prince had already been experiencing frequent bowel movements; now he began defecating up to twenty times a day, 'to the evident satisfaction of everyone except possibly the patient himself'.[6] Across Spain there were religious processions and special masses were said; in Seville, members of the religious confraternities paraded through the streets whipping themselves.[7]

Carlos lapsed into delirium and a famous Morisco doctor was called, but his various caustic ointments only brought the patient closer to death's door. Philip could not bear the suffering and retreated to a nearby monastery to pray. He must have wondered privately to God whether the boy's death might not be for the best. But then the Duke of Alba suggested they bring out the mummified body of a priest, Diego de Alcalá, locally revered as a great healer of the sick both in life and now in death. The desiccated remains were laid down beside the sickbed and the semi-conscious Prince asked that his eyes be forced open that he should see. He reached over and touched the cadaver, 'after which he drew his hands across his diseased face'.[8] Within hours, a miraculous recovery had begun so that a week later the doctors could begin draining pus from the abscesses that had formed around Don Carlos's eyes; five weeks later his recuperation was complete.

But the prolonged trauma made his physical and mental condition worse. Philip II appointed his lifelong friend and political confidant Ruy Gómez, the Prince of Eboli, as senior majordomo in Don Carlos's household. He wrote that he wanted Eboli 'near his son', to care for him, at least until the boy married, 'after which his wife should look after him'.[9]

There was clearly a father's concern behind this arrangement, but it was a politically complicated move. Eboli was the leader of the powerful peace faction at Philip's court, a wily operator fanatically opposed to the Duke of Alba's belligerent approach to foreign policy. Following his father's advice to divide and rule the members of his government, Philip had fostered both parties, but as their positions became ever more entrenched and personal, the King upset the balance by favouring Alba's robust intransigence. If he hoped to remove Eboli from the fray by appointing him to Carlos's household, he had badly miscalculated, for the doves of peace saw an opportunity to woo the Prince as a fount of influence. A Venetian observed that while at first the Prince 'particularly hated Ruy Gómez, such was Gómez's skill that he has managed to win his affection'.[10] Beguiled by Eboli's charisma, Carlos began to believe in his ability to rule and his right to power, a self-belief that stoked his lunacy and delusions. The genie was out of the bottle, and in 1565 Eboli had to disentangle his charge's bizarre plan to go to Aragon and exercise his right to be governor there. The boy was dreaming of insurrection.

When, as a child, Don Carlos had heard that Charles V had arranged matters so that his father's descendants by Mary Tudor would inherit the Netherlands, he declared that 'he would go to war before allowing such a thing'.[11] In his psychotic adolescence, he tried to be as good as his word. When the Duke of Egmont arrived in Madrid to sue for religious concessions in the Netherlands, the Prince began to enter-tain his own fantastical notions about the possibilities offered by this new suitor; and, because Carlos was Eboli's strange prince of peace,

Egmont necessarily wanted to meet him.[12] Don Carlos had gone from being a headache of the future to a very current political liability.

On 5 April 1566, some 300 armed 'confederates', many of them minor nobles or gentry, forced their way into the royal palace in Brussels. In the name of over 400 aristocrats and other leading subjects, they insisted that the Inquisition be suspended in the Netherlands. Margaret of Parma had little choice but to comply, for all that one of her councillors audibly advised her that she had nothing to fear from these 'Beggars' (*Gueux*, or *Geuzen*), who deserved a good thrashing.

Three days later, the confederates enthusiastically co-opted the insult by holding their famous 'Beggars' Banquet'. Once they were 'well and truly drunk', their leader, Hendrik of Brederode, announced that 'as we have been called Beggars, it is reasonable that we carry begging staffs and drink from wooden bowls'. On cue, a page appeared with a vagrant's satchel, which Brederode put over his head. He picked up a roughly hewn wooden bowl full of wine and drank it down, his voice booming: 'I toast the good grace of the Beggars: *Vive les Gueux!*' Then the whole raucous company swore 'by the salt, by the bread, by the satchel, the Beggars will never turn coat!'[13]

This congenially tipsy coalition created a carnival atmosphere in which all sense of hierarchy was undermined. There was a dangerous vacuum of authority, and on 7 July Margaret wrote to Philip about 'the pitiable and miserable state of these Netherlands' and 'the peril we run of total ruin'. The Protestant 'infection has grown to be a general epidemic across the country'. It seems as if everywhere Calvinist preachers were delivering resounding open-air sermons to crowds of thousands, the common people were arming themselves and, to the sound of gunfire, there were shouts of 'Long live the Beggars!'

But the permissive egalitarianism of these clown-like rebels quickly lost ground to the ordered gravitas of Calvinist intolerance, riding high on the shoulders of newly empowered peasants and proletarians. On 3 September, Philip received an explosive letter. 'I have told you about this evil,' Margaret reported to her brother, 'not only the heresy, but the sacrileges and destruction done daily to the churches, monasteries

Titian, *Equestrian Portrait of Charles V at Mühlberg*, 1548. Charles of Ghent, proclaimed King of Kings, the first monarch in history to reign over a truly global Empire.

Alonso Sánchez Coello, *View of Seville*, c. 1580. Seville, the great inland port of southern Spain where the riches of the Americas were landed and which became the cosmopolitan centre of world trade for almost a century and a half.

Cristoph Weiditz, *Indian Travelers to Spain*, 1528. Many indigenous Americans travelled to Spain; and they must have found Europeans as exotic as the Europeans found them.

Mask of the Aztec god Xipe Totec, Our Lord the Flayed One, god of sunset, sacrificial pain and the spring.

Aztec Frog Ornaments, Gold (each piece is almost an inch long), 15th to 16th century.

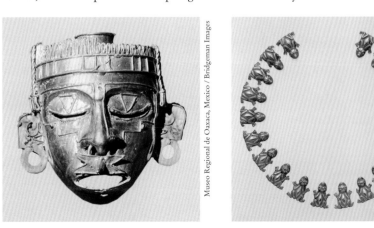

Titian, *Empress Isabella of Portugal*, 1548. Charles V's politically able
Empress, who ruled as regent in Castile during his long absences and
was much loved by her Spanish subjects.

Titian, *Philip II in Armour*, 1550. Pious and ascetic in old age, Philip II brought the art of administration to the government of Spain and her Empire, was briefly King of England and launched the Great Armada.

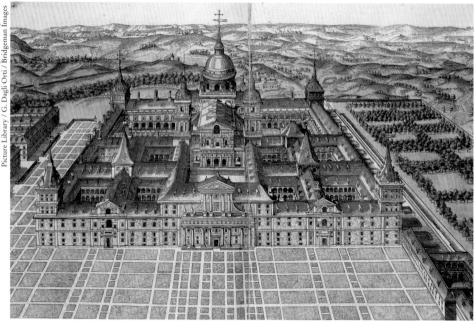

Pedro Perret after Juan de Herrera, *El Escorial*, 1587. Philip II built his massive and austere monastery-palace at El Escorial at the geographical heart of Spain as a centre of government and a pious monument to Habsburg dynasty and monarchy.

Detail from Andrea Vicentino, *Battle of Lepanto*, 1603. Lepanto, in the eastern Mediterranean, was the decisive Christian naval victory over the Ottoman fleet during which Miguel de Cervantes was badly wounded while fighting with exceptional courage.

Francisco Ricci, *Auto-da-fé*, 1683. Prolonged imprisonment, professional torture, the brutal theatre of public penance and the pyre and stake were the tenets of fear used by the Inquisition to terrify the faithful and save the souls of heretics.

Hendrik Cornelisz Vroom, *Day Seven of the Battle with the Armada*, c. 1600. On the stroke of midnight, eight fireships were released into the heart of the Spanish Armada as it sat off Calais and by dawn only five vessels faced the English fleet.

El Greco, *The Burial of the Count of Orgaz*, 1586. The past and the present, this world and the next, Counter-Reformation orthodoxy and humanist inquiry, all rub shoulders in this painting with which El Greco opened the gates of the Golden Age of Spanish art.

and temples, so that all divine mass has stopped.' She added: 'In Antwerp, they have begun to whitewash the church so as to exercise their Calvinist religion. And the Prince of Orange [and others] tell me that these sectarians want to come and murder in my presence all the priests and officers of Your Majesty's Catholic Church.'[14]

The Spanish court was electrified by news of desecrated churches and murdered priests; Flemings were insulted in the streets of Madrid. Philip determined to send a formidable army of mainly Spanish veterans from Italy to restore Catholic order in the Netherlands, but he struggled to find a general willing to accept such a potentially toxic command. Finally, after weeks of negotiations, Garcilaso's great friend, the ever loyal Duke of Alba, acquiesced and agreed to serve as Governor of the Netherlands, which would result in Margaret's resignation the following year.

In the spring of 1566, Alba sailed for Italy with a fleet commanded by the eighty-two-year-old Andrea Doria. The Archbishop of Toledo, Bartolomé de Carranza, was among the passengers, on his way to Rome to clear his name following his release by the Inquisition. Alba told a Spanish cardinal, as they waited to set sail, that 'every hour we delay seems like a year to the archbishop . . . He has been going out of his mind since yesterday thinking that we intended not to take him because we embarked last night' without him.[15]

In the meantime, Philip's heir Don Carlos had descended into hopeless lunacy: according to a reliable diplomatic report, 'he walks hunched over and seems weak on his legs', but is 'much given to violence to the point of cruelty'. On one occasion, he rode his father's prize horse so brutally that the animal died of its wounds. 'He has abandoned himself to such chaos that . . . the joy among the Spaniards at having a native prince is as great as the doubts they have about his ability to govern.' Yet he could be generous, buying the affection and favour even of the servants in his father's household. He borrowed heavily from moneylenders to gamble and especially to lavish gifts on women, notably Philip's attractive young Queen, Elizabeth of Valois.[16]

Philip lived in hope, encouraging Carlos to attend the Council of State, where he seems to have behaved responsibly. But the boy was furious when he heard that his father had appointed Alba to the governorship of the Netherlands, which he had come obsessively to believe was his birthright. He began to plot maniacally, pleading with Don John of Austria to support his claim to rule in the Netherlands. Philip asked Don John to talk some sense into the boy, but his half-brother's report was deeply troubling: the Prince was determined to rebel.

The King was torn between treating the matter as treason and accepting that his heir did not have the capacity for government. Finally, he felt compelled to act: shortly before midnight on 18 January 1568, Philip personally donned his armour and silently led four of his most senior ministers into the Prince's apartment, avoiding a contraption designed by the Prince to drop a heavy weight on intruders. They collected up all his papers and secured the weapons he kept to hand.[17] The King then personally oversaw his son's incarceration; the windows were boarded up, an armed guard was placed on the door.

Marooned in an ocean of his own discontent, the Prince turned his violence upon himself, starving himself almost to the point of death and then swallowing his ring because he thought that diamonds were poisonous. In the relentless heat of the Castilian summer, he ate snow and took to sleeping on a mattress of ice, presumably brought from a nearby ice-house. One evening, he gorged himself on a supper of four partridges and was overtaken by fever; he at last died on 24 July, propelling the court into a year of mourning.[18]

Philip's feelings of relief at the loss of such a troubled heir and distress at the crisis of succession must have been intense, but there were also dark rumours that the King himself had ordered his son's murder.

Alba already had a reputation for brutality gained during years of campaigning in Italy: as we have seen, his favourite advice to Philip, when faced with insurrection, was to go into battle, defeat the rebels and 'cut off their heads'. Now he was marching north to Brussels with his army of 10,000 men-at-arms and an impressive entourage of camp followers, 'four hundred mounted courtesans, as fair and beautiful as princesses, and eight hundred more who went on foot'.[19] As the army approached, two Spanish Protestants published their horrifying

Art of the Holy Spanish Inquisition, offering all Europe an apparently authoritative account of the terrible institutionalization of Spanish religious intolerance that Philip had ordered Alba to impose on the Netherlands.[20] The Flemings were so terrified by this propaganda that the local nobility rallied to the Habsburg cause and began to restore order so effectively that Margaret exhorted Philip to stay Alba's hand. But the die was cast.

There was a toxic atmosphere as Alba entered Brussels, and Margaret's own confessor gave a sermon in the palace chapel denouncing the Spanish presence. But Alba took no notice: his orders were immediately to mete out severe and exemplary punishment. He began with the simultaneous arrest of Egmont and other leading noblemen and instituted a new and draconian tribunal that became known as the 'Council of Blood'.

A terrified peace settled across the Low Countries, but thousands of Netherlanders were fleeing abroad. William of Orange retreated to his ancestral lands in Germany, and others went to France. Eleven thousand weavers from Ghent came to England, and Norwich alone gave succour to 4,000 Flemings; the oldest Dutch Protestant church in continuous use is in Austin Friars, in the City of London.[21] By the spring of 1568, William of Orange, the natural leader of the Dutch patriots in exile, was able to co-ordinate a series of armed incursions, but he was no match for Alba, who kept the patriot army in the field until Orange ran out of money to pay his mercenaries. But Alba also resorted to the only psychological weapon he really believed in: terror. He had Egmont and the Count of Hornes publicly executed for high treason in the main square of Brussels, with 3,000 Spanish troops on duty to keep order. For the next three years, he prosecuted a relentless campaign of persecution against anyone suspected of rebellion or heresy. The figures are staggering: 9,000 were imprisoned, fined or had their property confiscated; as many as 1,700 were executed, ten times as many victims as the Inquisition in Spain would execute during the whole of Philip's reign. Many more fled, perhaps as many as 60,000 in total in 1567 and 1568.[22]

Then, in 1568, with breathtaking arrogance, Alba erected at Antwerp a bronze statue of himself trampling the rebellious Dutch under his horse's hooves, cast from the melted-down cannon he had captured from the patriot army. It was modelled on medieval images of the Spanish patron saint James 'the Moorslayer' riding down Muslims and caused such outrage that Philip had it removed and destroyed. Alba was a brilliant soldier and strategist when it came to battle, but he had no truck with the subtleties of government. At sixty, he was an old man who quickly tired of trying to win the peace.

He is best known from the stunning Titian portrait of 1548, painted after his role in Charles's victory at Mühlberg, in which he already seems almost careworn, with his greying beard and the tiredness evident around his eyes. Twenty years later, his gout was agonizing, while the northern climate left him susceptible to rheumatic fevers; he suffered occasional bouts of intestinal trouble and was often laid up in bed. He repeatedly wrote to Philip asking permission to return to Spain.

Finally, in 1572, the King began the process of bringing his ageing general home. But before he could retire, the Dutch erupted in rebellion. Alba was too sick to direct the Spanish troops in the field and that task fell to his equally psychopathic but extremely inexperienced son Fadrique. Father and son approached the campaign of repression with appalling brutality, only made worse by the riotous mood of the troops, who had not been paid for many months. The soldiers went on the rampage at Mechelen and then put the entire population of Naarden to the sword. There could have been no more powerful encouragement for the Dutch, and when Fadrique advanced on Haarlem he found the citizens steeled for a fight to the death. Even children now helped to break the siege, skimming across the ice on their skates under cover of fog to bring supplies, and 300 armed women played their part in the fighting. Instead of the easy victory they had anticipated, Fadrique's army had to dig in during the harsh winter. In early skirmishing, a contingent of crack troops was devastated when it tried to engage a handful of armed Dutch vessels trapped in the ice. Suddenly, a group of musketeers emerged from the boats wearing skates and slipped fast and sure across the frozen sea, firing volley after volley at their veteran Spanish assailants, who slithered and skidded helplessly. Alba commented that 'it is the most novel business that has ever been heard of' and ordered 7,000 pairs of skates to be made.[23]

The Spanish besiegers became so desperate that even Fadrique suggested raising the siege. 'If you strike camp without the town's surrender,' his father ranted, 'I shall disown you as a son, but if you die in the siege, I shall take your place in person . . . and if we both fail, your mother will come from Spain to do in battle what her son has neither the valour nor patience to achieve.'[24] But assault after assault failed.

During one retreat, John Haring of Horn, in the spirit of brave Horatius, had stood alone with sword and shield on a narrow dyke, where two men could not stand abreast, and faced off the great array. Haring held back thousands, as his men sought safety in the town, for (to borrow Macaulay's classic verse), 'how can man die better than facing fearful odds for the ashes of his fathers and the temples of his gods? And for the tender mother who dandled him to rest and for the wife who nurses his baby at her breast?'

Haring then jumped into the sea, just as Horatius had leapt into the Tiber. Later, a great mock grave was constructed high upon the walls, and the citizens spelled out their motto for the besieging eyes: 'Haarlem is the graveyard of the Spaniard.'

'It is a war such as has never been seen nor heard of even in the remotest lands,' Alba reported to Philip.[25] But it was a war that Alba understood must be won on the water. In late May, the decisive naval battle took place, and before the end of July sorry Haarlem surrendered. The victorious army, still unpaid, unleashed the most heinous carnage. More than 2,000 members of the garrison had their throats cut, and the townsfolk were raped and pillaged. 'In the forty years', Alba lamented, 'that I have led men, I have never seen such dangerous and repellent behaviour. I do not know what to say or do . . .'[26] But Fadrique found a solution: he had the ringleaders of the mutiny arrested and shot his own men by the score. Alba's own commanders now openly talked of 'the abhorrence in which the name of Alba is held'.[27] Fadrique and his father had lost the trust of their most trusted men. Worse still, their riotous behaviour and the senseless slaughter of the garrison confirmed for every Dutch man, woman and child that Spaniards were without mercy. Throughout August and September, the tiny town of Alkmaar held out against Fadrique's army of 10,000 and at the beginning of October he admitted defeat and raised the siege.

On 18 December 1573, Alba finally rose from his sickbed and left Brussels, never to return. On his way home, he brilliantly summarized the reality of the Dutch problem for his King: 'the greater part of the States have always aspired to liberty of conscience and the [principle] that whatever is done in the privacy of one's own home should not be subject to inquiry . . . If Your Majesty grants them freedom of worship, they will pay whatever taxes you demand . . . Neither side . . . wants another ruler . . . but you should understand that they want you to be their ward' under their tutelage.[28] To Alba, any such tolerance of religion was heresy in itself and any dilution of absolute monarchy was anathema. As he said himself, had he been given the resources to stamp out heresy in the Netherlands, he would almost certainly have done so, even if he had to destroy the dykes in order to visit a flood of Catholic seawater upon the heretics, their farms and their cities. He had repeatedly complained to Philip about the impossibility of winning the war because he did not have enough money to pay his troops, but the King retorted that 'I shall never have enough money to satisfy your greed.'[29] Philip had understood that he could not afford to borrow enough money to defeat the Dutch; in fact, Alba's war had bankrupted him.

Banking was in its infancy in the early 1500s. A theologian from Salamanca called Sarabia de la Calle described how bankers:

> travelled from fair to fair, or followed the court from place to place, and set up in the squares or streets with their tables and their coffers and their account books. They openly lend their money and collect interest charges at each fair, or from time to time. They make loans and take deposits, even paying interest, and the first thing that the merchants do when they come to trade at the fairs is hand over their money to these bankers.[30]

Here we see banking in its simplest form, a man with a table, a safe of some sort and a written record of his transactions. Since the Middle Ages, the leading operators of this simple system of lending money and taking deposits had developed a lucrative business offering travellers, merchants and governments a safe way of sending large quantities of money over long distances. Because these bankers were considered so creditworthy and so trustworthy, a banker in, say, Seville could write a kind of cheque or banker's draft known as a bill of exchange which could be drawn on a specific bank in Antwerp by a designated individual; and, because bankers were so effective at accumulating capital, the real money rarely had to be physically moved. They made money by charging a handsome spread on the exchange rate and by lending out the client's deposit while the bill of exchange was in transit. A thriving secondary market in bills of exchange began to emerge, and the great banking families and syndicates sent representatives to a handful of major fairs at which these debts and obligations were bought and sold as well as being settled.

The gold and most importantly the silver that flooded into Spain from the Americas was a massive stimulus to trade across Europe and also brought about the first period in history of sustained price inflation across a large area; the previously independent economies of Europe quickly became inexorably connected. The bankers, who had until then been little more than glorified moneylenders, now found themselves at the centre of a world awash with money, and international merchant banking was born.

The famous Fugger family of Augsburg were the banking heavyweights of the early sixteenth century, borrowing across Europe at relatively low rates of interest in order to lend in the lucrative market at the Flemish city of Antwerp. Their ability to accumulate real money, gold, silver and coin in the strategic centres of Charles V's military operations enabled them to dominate the market in Habsburg sovereign debt. Their bills of exchange, their 'banknotes', were considered so secure that people began to treat them as though they were gold or silver; they became currency. But the Fuggers and the other German bankers were charting, in their account books, a voyage of monetary discovery across an unexplored ocean of financial uncertainty. They overexposed themselves to Charles's borrowing and were hurt badly by his occasional forced reorganizations of his debt, and the risk-averse Germans reduced their involvement. The 'old nobility' of Genoa stepped in to fill the gap, encouraged by the bond that the naval commander Andrea Doria and his family had forged with the Habsburgs: savvy, wily, imaginatively creative, hungry for reward, with a sailor's instinctive relationship with risk, these Genoese developed a variety of financial instruments and services that made them recognizable today as investment bankers in the modern sense.[31]

The Spanish Crown borrowed in two basic ways. The foundation stone of sovereign debt was *juros*, a range of government bonds securitized in one way or another with a guaranteed rate of interest over the life of the loan. The interest was increasingly linked to some specific source of income, perhaps a lien against the *alcabala*, a sales tax raised in Castile on salt, wine and other commodities, or against the rents payable on certain Crown estates, and recovery of the payment was often the responsibility of the bankers themselves. Then there were the *asientos*, a bewildering kaleidoscope of floating debt usually agreed on an ad hoc basis in order to fund some particular project or campaign on which the Crown paid a very high rate of interest for a relatively short period, after which the creditors usually agreed to consolidate *asientos* into *juros*.[32]

Until the 1560s, the bankers who lent money to the Crown largely did so out of their own pockets. But in a world awash with money the Genoese were determined to borrow as much as possible from the tradesmen, merchants, noblemen, farmers and even peasants from across Europe who wanted to lend it to them. They then found all sorts of ways of putting that money to work, but the Spanish Crown was always the major client which drove the whole debt market. In fact, Philip's government was so hungry to fund his huge expenditure that it regularly outbid more useful creditors such as farmers and industrialists, driving up interest rates and contributing to the rampant inflation that devalued the principal of Crown debt but was very damaging to the economy.

The crucial innovation of the Genoese bankers was to create a secondary market in Spanish sovereign debt by selling shares in the *juros* they held to a range of investors, but especially to Spanish ecclesiastical foundations, to the growing middle class, such as lawyers and doctors, and to some noble families. They spread the risk associated with a range of *juros* across a large number of investors, establishing a sort of primitive collateralized debt obligation. The Genoese achieved especially lucrative premiums because the size of their operation allowed them to negotiate on favourable terms with the Crown. As Sarabia de la Calle explained, 'because they are considered so creditworthy, they pay much less interest than the princes who pay at an expensive rate'. But, almost more importantly, they were exceptionally talented at extracting income from the often unreliable sources of revenue put up as security.

The ingenuity of the Genoese in expanding the market for Spanish sovereign debt allowed Philip II to keep his armies in the field and prosecute his wars against the French, the Dutch and the Turks. But the cost of his military operations far exceeded what he could afford: between 1571 and 1575, expenditure in Europe was over eighteen million ducats, while total Crown income in Castile, including bullion and tax receipts from the Americas, amounted to between five and six million.[33] It may be obvious with hindsight that such a deficit must end sooner rather than later in some sort of default. But the bankers and the government were pioneers experimenting on a grand scale with the first ever recognizably modern economy. Even the extent of Crown revenue was so poorly understood that in 1572 Juan de Ovando, the new President of the Council of Finance and an experienced member of the Council of the Indies, described 'the government and administration of the treasury as divided into too many tribunals' and complained that 'in all of them there is much confusion and little, or no, implementation of the work of each office'.[34] Ovando was a very able bureaucrat, but when he tried to assess the Crown's gross income and debt he was unable to come up with consistent, let alone reliable, figures, offering one set of figures in April 1574 and a significantly different set in August.

While Ovando and his officials were failing to understand the detail, matters were coming to a head. Crucially, in the late 1550s almost all Spanish sovereign debt had been converted into *juros* that were to be funded directly by royal receipts from the Americas. The attraction to the creditors is clear: every year they could actually watch their interest being unloaded in glittering piles of gold and silver ingots on to ox-carts at the port in Seville. Year on year, with almost no exceptions, the Crown had banked more and more money from the New World. There seemed no safer bet. But then in the early 1570s American revenues fell significantly and the supposedly safe *juros* lost half their value on the secondary market. Public opinion turned ugly, and there were demands that the Crown should default. The bankers became nervous.

With almost his entire income now tied to the payment of interest, Philip was forced to suspend those payments in order to maintain the Crown's liquidity. At the same time, he had no choice but to default on thirty-six million ducats' worth of loans that had become due for settlement. On 1 September 1575, he effectively declared himself bankrupt, the first sovereign default in history.

The Genoese retaliated by withdrawing his banking facilities in the Netherlands, and Philip's new military commander there complained that he could 'not find a single penny, nor can I see how the king could send money here, even if he had it in abundance. Short of a miracle, the whole military machine will fall in ruins.'[35] It proved to be a perspicacious prophecy. The light cavalry, for example, were owed six years' pay,[36] and in 1576 the soldiers mutinied. After committing a series of terrible atrocities, including the especially brutal sack of friendly Antwerp remembered as 'the Spanish Fury', the Army of the Netherlands mutinied and abandoned the coastal Counties of Holland and Zeeland. The States General worked quickly to unite all Seventeen Provinces of the Netherlands in an act known as the Pacification of Ghent, which established a humiliating general peace that required the removal of all Spanish troops and officials from both the Spanish and Dutch Low Countries. Dutch obstinacy had bankrupted mighty Philip by forcing him to keep such a large army in the field for so long. Now the Dutch had taken charge of themselves;

everything Alba had fought for and every penny he had spent seemed to have gone to waste.

Philip had paid a very high price for insolvency. The negotiations now began for the restructuring of his debts. There can be no doubt that the bankers would have agreed to some solution in due course. Philip may have threatened to go elsewhere for his credit,[37] while his activities underpinned so great a proportion of the European economy that without his borrowing the whole system would have eventually collapsed. But the process would have proved considerably more painful had it not been for the intervention in 1577 of Providence and perhaps of the Madonna herself. That year, silver receipts from the Americas broke every record because one of the great technological developments in the history of silver production, the 'patio method', was now in use in both Peru and Mexico. With the promise of new American riches Philip and his bankers finally reached an agreement known as the *medio general*, which imposed a haircut of almost 40 per cent on nearly fifteen million ducats of short-term debt that was securitized, converted into perpetuities and had its interest rates slashed. Built into the *medio* was the provision of a new loan of five million ducats, and so the cycle of sovereign solvency and default began again.[38]

As ever, American money financed Habsburg aspirations in Europe.

By the 1550s, the primitive mining methods being used in the Americas had all but exhausted the rich and accessible surface deposits at Zacatecas in Mexico and at the legendary, and to the indigenous Andeans sacred, 'Silver Mountain' at Potosí in Peru. But in 1557, in Mexico, a fifty-three-year-old Sevillian merchant called Bartolomé de Medina introduced the technological breakthrough that revolutionized silver production. He claimed that he had 'learned in Spain, through discussion with a German, that silver can be extracted from ore without the necessity for smelting or refining or incurring any other major expense'. He had resolved to go to Mexico in order to test it 'and, having spent much time and money and suffered mental anguish, and seeing that I was not going to be able to make it work, I commended myself to Our Lady . . . and it pleased her to enlighten me and put me on the right path'.[39]

A curious feature – and perhaps the only endearing one – of the usually brutal and greedy Spanish mine owners is that they adopted the language of bread-making to describe Medina's revolutionary process. First, the ore was taken to a 'mill', where it was ground into 'flour' (*harina*). This flour was then well mixed with water, salt and – only slightly less appetizing than yeast – mercury, before being spread out in a thin 'pancake' (*torta*) across a paved yard, or *patio*, surrounded by a wooden or stone kerb, for which reason Medina's method is usually known by the homely name 'the patio process'. The *torta* was then left to rest, sometimes for many months, while the mercury amalgamated with the silver in the ore. The whole mass was then cleaned in a *tina*, a kind of washing machine, a tin vat in which the mixture was stirred around in more water by wooden paddles driven by mules. The heavy amalgam fell to the bottom of this liquid, making it easy to separate out. When the amalgam was heated, the mercury evaporated, leaving almost perfectly pure silver.[40]

It took time to adopt the new technique, but the statistics speak for themselves: silver production in Peru between 1575 and 1580 was four times what it had been between 1570 and 1575.[41] 'A silver boom was born that never died.' Medina's process engendered such economic prosperity that 'it became the financial mainstay of sixty-one viceroys, two emperors and thirty Mexican presidents'. The town of Pachuca has claimed him for a son since the nineteenth century and has named both a street and a theatre after him.[42]

'The Dutch Revolt lasted longer than any other uprising in modern European history,' and rebellion became endemic to daily life for generations.[43] A whole range of factors help to explain why the Dutch so successfully resisted the wealthier, more numerous and much better resourced Spanish Habsburgs. The Army of Flanders was very expensive to keep in the field, while the Dutch were fighting on home soil, and very watery soil at that: the Dutch rebel Sea Beggars were more effective at naval warfare than the Brussels navy. Also, and most importantly, Spain had major commitments elsewhere; she had over-reached herself. In fact, more surprising than the success of ongoing Dutch resistance was Spanish willingness to pursue so obviously unattainable a goal. But that was a matter of inheritance, religious responsibility and Habsburg pride. Any attempt by Spain to cut her losses would have been humiliating. Most curious of all is the failure of one monarch after another to realize that so much might have been achieved by an extended royal visit by the sovereign in person. The Dutch revolt came to an end only after it had become a global conflict being fought in theatres as far afield as Brazil and Indonesia, a global conflict that, in the words of the most accomplished historian of the subject, Geoffrey Parker, 'brought about the collapse of the greatest world empire ever seen'.[44]

The Habsburgs could never have attempted to subdue the Netherlands nor could they have tried to do so for eighty years without the revolutionary effects of American wealth on Spanish finances. But nor would the Dutch have become such an affluent merchant nation had it not been for the revolutionary effects of American wealth on the European economy.

10

Portugal and the Duke of Alba

While he was dying, he showed such spirit that he ridiculed everyone, even death herself.

Hans de Khevenhüller, Imperial Ambassador

On 18 July 1566, at the age of eighty-two, Bartolomé de las Casas died at the Monastery of Our Lady of Atocha, just outside Madrid, and two days later at a well-attended funeral he was buried wearing a simple white robe and with a plain wooden staff.[1] That same summer, the eighteen- or nineteen-year-old Miguel de Cervantes, future stepfather of the modern novel, arrived in the hurly-burly of Philip II's new capital, yet another stop on a lifelong peregrination that had begun in childhood. His father Rodrigo's chaotic propensity for misfortune and misguided projects sired by fantasy had led the family to move again and again about Castile and Andalusia, pursued by their creditors.[2]

Miguel was born in 1547, at the great university town of Alcalá de Henares, where his grandfather, Juan de Cervantes, had briefly enjoyed considerable prosperity following his victory at law over the Duke of Infantado. Yet something went wrong and Rodrigo was forced to abandon the swaggering life of a young gentleman and began to study medicine. But he was deaf and failed to qualify. Instead he became a 'barber-surgeon', a jobbing medic condemned to a life of letting blood, extracting teeth and amputating limbs for the poorest and meanest of clients, and of course offering haircuts and shaves. It was a profession defined by its sharp tools rather than the proficiency of the practitioner.

But when Rodrigo successfully sued his mother's executors, the family was suddenly comfortably off, albeit temporarily. He opened a barber's shop and fell in with a group of wealthy Italians, while his wife set up a boarding house – or maybe it was a genteel bawdy-house, as many a commentator has implied. Soon afterwards, one of the Italians, Giovanni Francesco Locadelo, declared before a Madrid notary that he was 'deeply indebted to Miss Andrea de Cervantes', Miguel's sister, 'for while I have been absent from my native land she has treated me very well and cured me of certain illnesses which I have suffered. I am obliged to remunerate her.' The payment was rich indeed, including seven lengths of yellow and red taffeta, a doublet of silver cloth, two desks, six Dutch cushions and 300 gold *escudos*.[3] Andrea already had an illegitimate daughter by a young nobleman with whom she had dallied in Seville and, given her Aunt María's history with Martín de Mendoza, it is hardly surprising that many have jumped to the conclusion that she had become Locadelo's mistress and had been 'curing' the oldest disease known to man.

Miguel, meanwhile, was absorbed by the lively literary world which thrived in the midst of court life; he also studied at the Madrid municipal academy. In 1567, he had a terrible sonnet publicly displayed on one of many triumphal arches set up to celebrate the birth of Philip II's second daughter, Catherine. A year later, he featured prominently in the school tribute book of verses on the death of Elizabeth of Valois, where the headmaster referred to him as 'our beloved disciple'. Yet by 1570 he was in Rome, where he found short-lived employment in the household of a youthful cardinal.

But why travel to Italy at all, just when life seemed to be settling down for the family in Madrid? Many biographers have evoked his nascent literary genius; surely he was drawn like a bee to the sweet-scented nectars of Italian letters? The land of Petrarch, Bembo, Boccaccio, Ariosto and Tasso had merely to beckon for Miguel to answer their call. What other reason than a passion for culture could have inspired such a great literary figure to undertake such a journey?

In September 1569, a Madrid court ordered the arrest of a student called Miguel de Cervantes who had been sentenced to have his right hand cut off for injuring a man in a duel. Needless to say, the idea that the very hand which wrote down *Don Quixote* might have been cut off in its prime has excited biographers, but the prosaic reality is that there is no proof this was our Miguel de Cervantes. However, such sentences were usually commuted to banishment, which would offer a compelling explanation for his trip to Rome.

While Cervantes was in Italy, in 1570, the Ottoman navy captured Cyprus, terrifying Spaniards, the Italian princes, the Venetians and the Papacy into forming a Holy League to defend the Christian Mediterranean against Islam. Philip's illegitimate half-brother, the dashing Don John of Austria, was appointed Admiral of the enormous fleet which gathered at Messina towards the end of August 1571. Cervantes and his brother Rodrigo enlisted in the company of a captain called Diego de Urbina and took ship aboard the *Marquesa*.

The contemporary historian Ambrosio de Morales described how Don John reviewed his force, 'dressed in the full paraphernalia of war'. Receiving his commanders in his cabin, he 'commended himself to God and touched a crucifix that was hanging from the bedstead'. 'By Christ Our Saviour', he swore 'to engage the enemy fleet'.[4] But he was exasperated by the Venetian ships, which 'are not in the order necessary for the service of God ... You would not believe how badly prepared the soldiers and the sailors are!'[5] 'I do not think that the art of war is any business of merchants,' he fumed.[6]

On 16 September the fleet set sail towards the Greek coast. According to the *Account of the Battle of Lepanto* by Fernando de Herrera, the inspired editor of Garcilaso's poetry, at dusk on Saturday, 6 October, Don John put the fleet under oars and they rowed all night against a light breeze, hoping to engage the enemy. The following morning the fleets were barely ten miles apart when they spotted one another. 'It was a wondrously beautiful sight to see, the whole sea covered in galleys resplendent with so many colourful flags and pennants.'[7] The numbers are staggering: the Ottoman fleet was made up of 230 ships manned by 50,000 men; the Christian fleet of 200 ships had 40,000 men.

Don John's admirals advocated caution; he replied 'that it was no time for councils but to fight'. He 'visited almost every galley in the fleet, preparing the battle order and encouraging the captains and the soldiers, and when a loud and joyous cry went up from the galley slaves, it was taken by all as a sure sign of victory'. At that moment 'Miguel de Cervantes was sick with a fever and his captain and his many friends . . . told him that because he was so ill he should stay down below in the cabin of the galley,' an eyewitness remembered years later. But Cervantes:

> replied angrily: 'On every occasion before now that I have had the chance to fight for His Majesty I have served well, like a good soldier, and so I will do no less today, for all that I am ill; it is better to die in the service of God and King than to go down below.' And he asked the captain to give him the most dangerous station so that he could die fighting there. So the captain ordered him to hold the poop-deck with twelve men, where I saw him fighting very bravely against the Turk until the battle was over.[8]

At eleven in the morning, with the sea as calm as 'a bowl of milk', the Christian galleys opened fire, sending volley after furious volley skimming low across the water, wreaking terrible damage on the Turkish boats. Don John ordered his galley forward to engage the Turkish Pasha's flagship and the two vessels rammed each other with such force that the prow of the Turkish ship crashed up over the bow of the Spanish galley, smashing the buttressing apart. There was a hellish tumult of creaking cables and cracking wood and the screams of the dying and the wounded; the sea boiled with foam and the sky went dark with all the smoke from the flames, and then all you could hear was the endless firing of the guns.

One eyewitness remembered that:

> the main thrust of battle lasted about three hours and it was so bloody and horrendous that the sea and the fire seemed one . . . Many thousands of human bodies, Christian and Turkish, covered the water as far as the eye could see, some smashed to pieces, others floating in the

throes of death; their souls pouring out of them along with the blood from their wounds and the whole sea was dyed red.[9]

On 29 October, at Madrid, news reached Philip of the victory. He ordered a *Te Deum* sung and the city 'exploded in an orgy of celebration'.[10] Cervantes survived, but he was badly wounded in the chest and had his left hand badly mangled by harquebus fire. He had become a hero with a reputation for great bravery.

The Spanish troops wintered on Sicily, where Cervantes recovered from his wounds. In July, he and Rodrigo joined Don John's major expedition to finish off the Turkish fleet, which failed when the pilots got lost; they were also involved in fruitless scrapping for control of Tunis. But in 1575 they were discharged and set sail for Barcelona. Cervantes was carrying glowing letters of recommendation from Don John and a report of his great bravery in battle. He must have had high hopes that Philip II would reward him with a lucrative sinecure in the Americas, upon which he had set his heart. Instead, their galley was attacked by Barbary corsairs from the Ottoman client city of Algiers, home to renegade pirates and the prisoners they hoped to ransom. Both Miguel and Rodrigo were taken prisoner by a Greek renegade called Artrionamy.

With its formidable walls, its turrets, towers and ramparts bristling with artillery, Algiers was an authentic pirate castle, 'home to corsairs and a refuge for robbers' that across the Ottoman world 'they speak of as we talk about the Indies here in Castile', a place to get rich.[11] Miguel and Rodrigo and the other captives were led into the city by way of the harbour gate through the bustle of fishermen bringing their own catches home to market along a street of dirt-poor inns, ruined houses and lime kilns.[12] They had heard many an exaggerated story of the terrible cruelty of the corsairs, the grotesquely embellished reports of mendicant friars who begged funds to ransom Christian hostages and the tall tales told by former captives returning home. Captives were reputedly imprisoned in the infamous *baños*, 'damp and stinking caves, dungeons that were deep below the ground', where they were 'so heavily chained they could not move'. According to a cleric called

Antonio de Sosa who shared imprisonment with Cervantes and became his close friend, 'the streets are always filled with infinite Christians so sick, so thin, so wasted away, so starved and disfigured that they can hardly stand up, nor do they know themselves'. A popular pastime of the Turks, it was said, was to liven up an exhausted Christian slave by making him stand on a burning pyre with his hands tied and then watch him jump around trying to get away.[13]

Sosa also had an eye for ethnographic detail and described the different customs and clothing of the various ethnic groups, Turks, Moors and the Wild Men from the hinterland, mostly Berber shepherds. He even noted that Algerian women dyed their hair dark and bleached their faces white, put rouge on their cheeks and 'used a very black substance made from certain minerals to draw designs on their cheeks, chin and forehead'. Moreover, thus hennaed they were 'forever attending weddings and the feasts organized by hostesses around the year; and not content to dance all day, they dance long into the night as well. A husband', he explained censoriously, 'must be vigilant that his wife returns home.'[14] But Sosa, a Christian cleric, enthusiastically detailed the multiple ways in which the heretics of Algiers embraced all of the Seven Deadly Sins. He seems to have been especially appalled but clearly also intrigued by anal sex, reporting that 'after the Imams sin the sin of sodomy, in great penitence they wash themselves in the sea and not at the bathhouse' and noting that 'when a man sodomizes his wife, which is often, and his wife demands justice of the *Cadi*, or judge, without a word she comes before him and taking her shoe, she puts it down in front of him, with the sole facing upwards, to signify that her husband knows her backwards'.[15]

Cervantes and the other captives were taken through impossibly narrow streets 'along which a man on horseback can barely ride, while two men on foot cannot pass abreast' – a world where the 'houses are so close together, you can pretty much walk around the whole city on the roofs'.[16] That night, the captives slept fitfully in the dungeons.

The Greek renegade Artrionamy soon discovered Miguel de Cervantes's letters of recommendation addressed to Philip II by Don John of Austria and mistook him for an important and wealthy nobleman. He immediately put a price on his head of 5,000 gold *escudos*, a ransom wildly beyond anything that Cervantes or his family would ever be able to afford. We do not know when the Cervantes family first found out that the two brothers had been captured, but by November 1576 their mother Leonor had secured the promise of 120 ducats from the Crown to help buy their release. To elicit sympathy, she claimed to be a 'widow' and said that both brothers had been crippled at Lepanto. By December, thanks to white lies, she had raised a little more money. The following year, she entrusted what she had raised to the Order of Mercedarian Friars who dedicated themselves to the plight of captives in North Africa, raising money to pay ransoms, negotiating their release and bringing them safely home. The Mercedarians went to work, but there was nothing like enough to release Miguel, so they spent all of it on Rodrigo's freedom. Thus, in 1577, one brother was free, but the other remained alone in captivity.

Finally, by 1580, the family had raised a further 300 ducats, which they handed over to a Mercedarian mission led by Fray Juan Gil. During his protracted stay in Algiers, negotiating the release of hundreds of captives, Juan Gil became very friendly with Cervantes. But the ruler of Algiers, Hasan Pasha, was preparing to return to Constantinople and Cervantes was among the captives he chose to take with him. Cervantes was escorted to the port and chained to his oar aboard a galley. But just as the crew were raising the sails, the wily Juan Gil decided that this was the moment when he would get the lowest price he could ever hope to get for a man who had a way with words but whose injured arm would make him next to useless as a galley slave. He agreed to pay 500 *escudos*, making up the difference out of the Mercedarians' own funds. Hasan Pasha agreed.

We can only imagine the relief that Cervantes must have felt, free at last, as he stood on the seashore watching the fleet of a dozen galleys sail away without him, and the sadness too for his unnamed companions in captivity who had not been so lucky.

Miguel de Cervantes now engaged with one of the most revealing bureaucratic processes of the Habsburg administration: he created an official record of his personal merits and service to the Crown known as an *información de méritos y servicios*, by which he hoped to gain a *merced*, or reward, from the King, a sinecure, job or royal contract of some kind. He wanted to capitalize on his injuries and travails.

In the medieval world, valiant subjects and brave soldiers had direct access to their ruler; often they performed their deeds of valour in his very presence, or if not, there were others, close to the King, who could testify on their behalf. But in the 1500s, with the expansion of the Empire, especially into the Americas, it was obvious that the system of royal reward needed reform. Every year, hundreds of men returned to Spain from the Indies and sought an audience with the King or his ministers. They told stirring tales of adventure, of their bravery, their courage, their moral probity, their poverty, and they petitioned and pleaded that they deserved great rewards for all these things. But beyond the hearsay of other colonists who might be to hand, the Crown had no way of gauging the truth or otherwise of these personal autobiographies, these self-serving soldiers' tales filled with bravado and self-importance.

In 1528, as Charles V prepared to travel to Italy, the Council of the Indies concluded that the problem could best be solved by requiring that anyone returning from the Americas in order to seek a reward from the Crown should have had their story authenticated locally by one of the Audiencias. The hopeful petitioner would present a written overview of himself, his circumstances and his services, accompanied by a series of statements that added up to a very full account of his claim and which effectively formed a questionnaire that was then put to a group of witnesses who were asked to confirm the truth of the story the claimant told. A written record of the whole process was then sent to the Council of the Indies so that they could use it to evaluate the claimant's petition when and if he eventually appeared in person in Spain. Spaniards produced thousands of these Reports of Merit and Service and, alongside letters of recommendation and other documents, they became part of the complex bureaucracy of written words by which the King and his government tried to rule over faraway lands.

At some point, Miguel de Cervantes realized that such an account of his service and deeds while captive in Algiers might serve his material interests, and so, on 10 October 1580, he asked Juan Gil to preside over just such a process in the presence of an official notary. The resulting document, known to posterity as the *Información de Argel*, or Algiers Report, tells the story of Cervantes's five years of captivity, and an extraordinary story it is. Told largely in his own words and those of the witnesses he had drilled for the task, and only thinly veiled beneath the often tediously repetitive and formulaic language of the bureaucratic process that gave rise to it, Cervantes offered a thrilling tale of derring-do, of facing danger with Christian stoicism, of pluck and courage and initiative.

The questionnaire asked Cervantes's witnesses to confirm that they knew that Cervantes, 'filled with the desire to escape' and to free many other Christians, had 'found a Moor who would guide them over-land to Oran', a Spanish possession some 120 miles along the coast. 'But, after a few days' travel, the Moor abandoned them and they were forced to go back to Algiers, where Miguel de Cervantes was very badly treated by his owner and from then on was more strictly guarded, more closely confined and better chained.'

Then, as Rodrigo de Cervantes was being ransomed, in 1577, Miguel arranged with his brother for 'an armed frigate to be sent from Spain', so as 'to help many important captive Christian gentlemen to escape'.

Cervantes encouraged 'fourteen leading Christians to hide in a cave outside the city' and during the six months they waited for the boat to arrive, 'he took great care to send them provisions every day, running the risk of being impaled and burned alive' if he was caught. A week before the frigate was due to arrive, he 'joined the others in the cave'. But then, when it finally came, 'the sailors lacked the courage to go ashore in order to get word to the men who were hidden in the cave'. Instead, with salvation so close at hand, 'an evil Christian who knew about the business went to the ruler of Algiers, Hasan Pasha, and told him about the men in the cave, saying that Miguel de Cervantes was the author of the whole escape plan and had woven the whole plot. Because of which,' the Algiers Report explained, 'on the last day of September, the said ruler sent many armed Turkish and Moorish cavalry and infantry to take prisoner Miguel de Cervantes and his companions.'

When the soldiers forced their way into the cave, Cervantes exhorted his companions to let him take the blame, 'promising them that he alone would be condemned', and as the Moors were tying them up, Cervantes shouted out: 'None of these Christians here is at fault in this business, because I alone have been its author, I persuaded them to escape.'

Hasan Pasha sent the guards for Cervantes. As he shuffled through the streets, 'bound hand and foot', the Moors heaped 'insults and offence upon him along the way', almost, one feels, in imitation of Christ on the way to Golgotha. 'Alone and without companions', he was brought before Hasan Pasha, who 'interrogated him about the whole business, threatening him with death and torture. But Cervantes consistently told him that he alone was the author of the whole business and begged His Highness that, if he must punish someone, it should be only him,' taking upon himself the redemption of his fellows. 'He would neither name nor blame a single Christian,' saving the lives 'of the many who had helped him', not least Jorge de Olivar, a friar in the Mercedarian Order whom Hasan Pasha was especially keen to punish. Cervantes was 'chained up in a dungeon' and threatened with terrible punishment.

Strangely, however, the report moves swiftly on to explain that 'after five months, the said Miguel de Cervantes, with the same zeal to serve God and His Majesty and to help Christians, while still imprisoned', was able secretly to send 'a Moor to Oran with a letter for General Martín de Cordoba, Governor of Oran, asking him to send trustworthy men back to Algiers with the Moor' to help him escape along with 'three other important gentlemen whom the ruler had in his dungeon'.

But the Moor was arrested at the very gates of Oran by men loyal to Hasan Pasha and brought back to Algiers where he was impaled alive, but 'died bravely, without revealing anything'. Hasan Pasha 'ordered Miguel de Cervantes to be given 2,000 lashes', a beating that would surely have killed him.

But, wonderfully enough, he lived and 'in 1579, in the month of September', Cervantes began to encourage a renegade Christian from Granada 'to return to the faith of Our Lord Jesus Christ. And he persuaded him that he could do nothing more honourable in the service of God and more acceptable to His Majesty' than return to Spain and there acquire an armed frigate with which to mount yet another a great escape attempt.

The witnesses were now asked to confirm that Cervantes had persuaded a merchant from Valencia, then on business in Algiers, to give the renegade enough money to buy the frigate, which he did. Only then did 'Cervantes, wishing to serve God and His Majesty and help Christians, as he is wont to do, very secretly tell seventy of the most important gentlemen, scholars, priests and Christians who were captive here in Algiers about the plan'.

The whole thing was 'so well advanced there can be no doubt it would have succeeded as planned', but they were betrayed by Juan Blanco de Paz, who claimed to be a Dominican friar, 'as a result of which', the report assures us, 'the said Miguel de Cervantes's life was in great danger'. The terrified Valencian merchant was certain that Cervantes would reveal his part in the whole affair under torture and so, fearing for 'his goods, his freedom and perhaps his life, he tried to persuade the said Miguel de Cervantes to go to Spain on some ships that were ready to leave, saying that he would pay the ransom'.

It was a remarkable opportunity for Cervantes to escape, but instead he 'replied that he was sure that there was no torture, not even death itself, that would be enough to have Hasan Pasha condemn anyone except himself'. Then, 'fearing that if he did not give himself up the ruler would look for someone else to torture', Cervantes surrendered 'of his own free will'.

Hasan Pasha 'threatened him with many tortures in order to find out which people he was planning to take with him. Then, to terrorize him further, he ordered them to put a noose around his neck and to tie his hands behind his back, as though he was going to have him hanged. The said Miguel de Cervantes never once named nor condemned anyone, consistently telling the king that he was the author along with four other gentlemen,' gentlemen who had already been ransomed and were now safely in Spain. For five months, Hasan Pasha 'kept Cervantes chained' in the Moors' jail within his own palace, 'with the intention of sending him to Constantinople, from where he would never be able to gain his liberty'. But Friar Juan Gil, 'moved to compassion by the danger faced by the said Miguel de Cervantes', intervened 'at the moment when the ruler Hasan was hoisting sail in order to go back to Constantinople' and 'he was given his liberty the same day'.

This is Cervantes's story as told in the Algiers Report, first of all by himself and then confirmed and repeated by his witnesses. But it is a curiously quixotic account of escape and the threat of punishment, neatly episodic, rich in literary texture; and at its heart is a glaring contradiction between the narrative tension of repeatedly asserting that Cervantes ran the risk of terrible punishments for his escape attempts, on the one hand, and the bathos in the slow realization that he is never in fact punished, on the other. Sosa reported that 'Hasan Pasha said that as long as he had his "Spanish cripple" well guarded, all his Christians, his ships and even the whole city would be secure,' which goes to show 'how much he feared Cervantes's intrigues'. But 'the strange leniency' shown by Hasan Pasha, 'given the disorder sown by Cervantes among the captives', is puzzling.[17] Why did Hasan Pasha neither execute such a troublesome character nor really lock him up securely, nor ransom him for whatever he could get and be done with it?

Some have suggested that Cervantes was really involved in some diplomatic mission on behalf of Philip II; others that he and Hasan Pasha were gay lovers; or, perhaps most appealingly, as one critic has suggested, it was his ability to tell a good tale that saved Cervantes from the grisly punishments that the story promises, like Scheherazade in the *Arabian Nights*.[18] Another idea is that Cervantes was considered so valuable by his captors that they did not want to risk injuring him. But the fact remains that, in 1578, Hasan Pasha himself paid 500 *escudos* for Cervantes, though it is manifestly not a price that justifies running the risk of tens if not hundreds of valuable prisoners escaping thanks to Cervantes's genius.

The real solution to this conundrum is poetic indeed. At the heart of the Algiers Report was the questionnaire which Cervantes had largely written himself and which, when read question by question, feels like a continuous narrative. But when read along with the responses of the

witnesses, responses given question by question, the theatricality of
the hearing in front of Fray Juan Gil comes alive and we start to get a
sense of drama, a drama orchestrated by Cervantes with the manifest
purpose of presenting an image of himself to the Crown that would
help some future petition for favour.

Given that Cervantes is the subject of scholarly study because he
is considered to be one of the greatest ever writers of prose fiction,
and given that he was also a successful dramatist, it is curious that all
his biographers and critics have unquestioningly accepted as true this
extraordinary story of heroism, exceptional personal bravery in the
face of cruel captors and repeated failed attempts to escape.

The Algiers Report is Cervantes's first known work of fiction, a
dramatic novel, almost a work of theatre, carved from the Spanish
Crown's devotion to bureaucracy by a brilliant imagination, a deliberately marvellous tale filled with moments of wonder and delight,
unreliably narrated and with a plot that does not stand up to logical
scrutiny – a story, in fact, very much like those that Cervantes told
in his many novels and short stories, including, of course, *Don
Quixote*.

Armed with this thrilling piece of paperwork, he finally went home
to Spain.

In 1578, Sebastian I of Portugal had died childless campaigning
in North Africa, leading to the succession of his geriatric uncle,
the Cardinal-King Enrique, the last member of the great house of
Avis to rule the Portuguese people. Fearing a succession crisis, the
pragmatic old Cardinal encouraged candidates to argue their legal
title to the throne. Philip commissioned a scholar called Lorenzo
de San Pedro to plead his cause in a copious document, 310 folios
long. In order to reassure the vehement Portuguese sense of independence, he bizarrely included an engraving illustrating a case of
twin suckling piglets conjoined by a single head that had recently
excited the public imagination in Seville. Then, from his own mental
cabinet of metaphorical curiosities, he extrapolated the notion
that this creature 'split into two perfect bodies and joined at the
nape of the neck into a single head' might serve as a useful symbol

of his determination to maintain a separation of the Spanish and Portuguese crowns and kingdoms despite their having a single ruler. The image was prescient, for the union proved as politically unviable as the presumably short-lived swine were biologically doomed. The alliance fractured sixty years later as the body politic of each kingdom declined and degenerated largely because the single head could not take the strain.[19]

Cardinal Enrique, the nobility and the Church all supported Philip, but the Portuguese Cortes and the common people clamoured for his Portuguese rival, Dom Antonio, the Prior of Crato. It was a clear signal that the people preferred a Portuguese. So Philip brought Alba out of retirement and began to amass a formidable army of 50,000 Spaniards, Italians and Germans at the Portuguese frontier. Alba was old and repeatedly fussed about his duchess's health in his correspondence with Philip, but he was still thirsty for war. 'Your Majesty should bring the Spanish veterans from Flanders, for I would hazard an invasion with them alone,' he wrote to the King.[20]

On 27 June 1580, as a terrifying epidemic of influenza, 'as harmful as the plague', raged across Spain,[21] Alba's army paraded before the King himself and then began crossing the border. Philip exhorted Alba to ensure 'no action be taken about which the Portuguese might complain', but it was an 'impossible' order, as Alba himself pointed out.[22] Sovereign and general were both well aware that the terrifying reputation of the tercios, especially the troops who had served in the Netherlands, was a powerful weapon when negotiating with their enemies: Philip had also ordered Alba to 'behead anyone caught bearing arms against His Majesty', to which his old general replied that 'it pains me to shed the blood of gentlemen and so gain a reputation for cruelty'.[23]

The army advanced towards the Portuguese capital, Lisbon, along terrible roads, harried by a hostile Portuguese peasantry. The soldiers committed the inevitable excesses, but Alba was alive to the problems of negative propaganda, so when his men stole clothing from a monastery that had been left there for safe keeping by private individuals, he made the steward of the monastery officially confirm that nothing had been taken from the monks themselves. 'I tell Your Majesty this', he explained, 'because it may be reported that the monasteries were looted.'[24] But, in truth, the troops were behaving much as an Alba army always had done. Alba reminded Philip that 'it is usual for men on this kind of campaign to have free rein', but as in his final campaign in the Netherlands, he began to punish his own men: 'I am very angry and we have hanged and are hanging so many that I think we shall run out of nooses.'[25] Alba's veterans had once called their beloved general 'the good father of the soldiers', but now it seemed he had abandoned them.[26]

As they laid siege to Belém, an historic suburb of Lisbon, the troops were barely under control. Alba had 'the whole camp shut up, day and night, because for all the men I have hanged and decapitated, or sent to the galleys, whatever I do, nothing seems enough. Yesterday heaps of them were hanged, like every other day, but they take as much notice as if I were giving them their rations.'[27] Again and again, Alba's letters come close to apologizing for the terrible ill-discipline of his troops, and the problem was not just the immorality of the atrocities and the fear of enemy propaganda: now his own officers were openly accusing him of losing authority over his troops because he was so old. Many blamed his failure to expedite the capture of Dom Antonio on that loss of control; his troops, they said, had been so busy pillaging they had ignored his orders.[28]

But as they approached Lisbon itself, Alba's experience began to tell. He allowed the troops to sack the merchants' houses and warehouses in the suburbs, giving rein to their greed, letting them work off their aggression, regaining some of their confidence. Two days later, he 'met with the colonels, aides-de-camp and officers' and gave them a piece of Philip's mind. 'I have sworn to them', he wrote to Philip, 'that if they do not restore order they will wake up one day to find every officer has been discharged and replaced.' He reported that he had sent out his cavalry captains to deal with the riotous soldiers, ordering them 'to fill their luggage with nooses' and sending senior men to bear witness to 'what is done'. He well understood the power of propaganda and reputation: 'if, in future, news of this rioting is to be broadcast throughout the world, then I also want it known that I meted out the most exemplary castigation'.[29] Philip wrote back immediately, sanctioning the harshest punishments.[30]

Alba became the scapegoat, or 'Turk's head', as the Spanish say, for the inevitable excesses of an invading army, a victim of diplomatic hypocrisy. Some of the worst offences were committed by soldiers serving in the Marquis of Santa Cruz's navy. The marquis's cavalrymen stole and broke up 'a beautiful and perfectly worked diamond-studded riding-harness of incalculable value with its many sizeable precious stones collected in India over many years, which was part of the Portuguese crown jewels'.[31] This was truly grave ill-discipline, for this equine jewellery was part of Philip's own Portuguese inheritance. Alba's last campaign has been damned by historians for the breakdown in command and the barbarity of his troops, but in reality it was a very successful invasion concluded with a minimum of fighting.

Ferdinand Álvarez de Toledo, third Duke of Alba, had been 'one of the most renowned and respected generals of his age'. Even his enemies had to admit that 'he was involved in many more important campaigns than anyone else', although he himself regretted 'never having confronted a Turkish army face to face'. He was widely held to be 'a man unrivalled among his peers in competence and experience'. Haughty, rude, arrogant, outspoken, he was the epitome of a chauvinistic Spaniard, a central caricature of the Black Legend. He died on the verge of disgrace, an old man prey to the carrion-eating courtiers and military rivals whom he had never feared to offend. Service to his sovereign had been his only motto. 'While he was dying, he showed such spirit that he ridiculed everyone, even death herself,' which many an evil tongue 'deemed behaviour more appropriate to a pagan Roman than a good Christian'. When, on 11 December 1582, the Imperial Ambassador visited the seventy-seven-year-old scourge of the Dutch, lying on his deathbed, he found the once potent warrior 'so decrepit and weak that like a newborn babe he had to suckle milk from a wet nurse's breast'. Alba turned towards the Ambassador and said: 'now in my broken dotage, I do as I did in my infancy'.[32] His life had come full circle. This child of a disappearing chivalric age had eluded death so often since she first tried to take him as he and Garcilaso rode across

France to serve the Emperor. But by sunset on the following day, she had finally claimed him for her own.

In 1581, Philip was crowned King of Portugal and took up residence at Lisbon, with its huge population of 100,000. Cervantes would eulogize the city in his last novel, *The Adventures of Persiles and Sigismunda*, posthumously published in 1617. There, he wrote,

> you will see the sumptuous churches where God is adored, you will see
> the Catholic masses at which he is praised, and Christian charity in her
> prime . . . you will see the many hospitals, executioners and destroyers
> of disease. Here, love and honesty saunter hand in hand, courtesy
> trumps arrogance, and valour keeps cowardice at bay. The inhabitants
> are friendly, polite and generous, and great lovers of discretion. It is the
> greatest city in Europe, where all the wealth of the Orient is unloaded
> to be distributed across the universe . . . You will wonder at the beauty
> of the women, will fall in love; you will be bowled over by the gallantry
> of the men.[33]

And Cervantes was in Portugal for the coronation, petitioning his King for the post in the New World upon which this pragmatic dreamer appears to have set his sights and perhaps his heart. Instead, Fate's love of irony meant he was sent to Oran, the North African city to which he had so often hoped to escape during his long captivity in Algiers, as one of the team of messengers dispatched to warn Philip's various African possessions not to offer succour to the refugee Dom Antonio, Prior of Crato, the Portuguese people's preferred ruler.[34] By the end of the summer, Cervantes was back in Lisbon, still hoping for a posting in the Indies, but now, it seems, equally ambitious to be recognized as a poet and a playwright. His most influential literary friend, Antonio de Eraso, then a Councillor of the Indies, sent him to Madrid with letters of recommendation, but by the middle of the sixteenth century most positions in the Americas were sold by the Crown and then traded on the open market, so it is difficult to see how Cervantes could have obtained one. In 1582, he wrote to Eraso thanking him, but bewailing the 'little good luck he had had in the business'. 'I must wait for the mail boat to see if there is some other vacancy.' Then he added that 'in the meantime I have kept myself busy raising *La Galatea*, the book I told you I was writing. When it is a bit older, it will come to kiss your honour's hands so you may complete its upbringing and help it come of age in ways that I cannot.'[35] This was the first time we know of that Cervantes used the charming image of a book as a child in need of nurturing and education. Years later, he would introduce *Don Quixote* by announcing that 'it turns out that for all that a father may have an ugly child, without any saving grace, his love makes him blind to those faults . . . But, my dearest reader, although I may seem to be his father, I am in fact Don Quixote's stepfather; and I do not want to follow the usual practice of begging you, as others do . . . to excuse or cover up the mistakes you may see in my son.'[36]

Despite Cervantes's lavish praise and the wealth arriving from its colonies, Lisbon lacked great, monumental buildings. The amateur architect in Philip saw a perfectly primed canvas; the politician in him saw an opportunity to stamp his mark on the very fabric of the Portuguese capital; and so Juan de Herrera led an ambitious programme of construction, including the complete rebuilding of the Royal Palace, the iconic Monastery of São Vicente and the economic powerhouse, the Casa da India. The Portuguese nobility followed suit, putting up a series of new and imposing buildings. Philip's most loyal supporter, the Marquis of Castel Rodrigo, built his residence next to Philip's new palace in Herrera's fashionable style.[37] As part of the Habsburg dominions, Lisbon came of age.

At Lisbon, Philip was in melancholic mood: following the death of Elizabeth of Valois, he had married his niece, Anne of Austria, and fallen deeply in love; but she died suddenly, in 1580, and soon afterwards he lost his son Prince Diego to smallpox. Stoical in his sadness, he could gaze out from the windows of the Royal Palace and meditate on the massive sweep of the great harbour, watching the drama of the Indies fleets arriving battered by the Atlantic storms and the massive galleons coming home from the Far East; he saw them leave, filled with old hands, the merchants' factotums and thousands of would-be colonists. In April 1582, 'following the custom of the Kings of

Portugal', he himself accompained the 'five great ships of the West Indies fleet . . . out of harbour' and 'breakfasted on board his royal galley'.[38] For the first time, with the smell of the sea in his nostrils and the sound of the waves in his ears, Philip seems to have begun finally to realize that his wealth depended on an Atlantic world.

Philip now began to focus his foreign policy on the colonial struggles in America, Asia and Africa, where privateers from northern Europe were waging a kind of guerrilla warfare against his possessions. It seemed that the bellicose English, with their heretical Queen Elizabeth, were the greatest threat of all, a nation of natural pirates who gave help to the Dutch and who had dared to try and settle in the Americas, founding the Virginia Colony, named after their 'Virgin Queen'. Philip had once written to the ailing Alba that the Pope 'has insisted many times that he would like us to undertake the conquest of England . . . for which purpose it would be good to get a foothold in Ireland'.[39] For the first time, he began to think seriously about the great Enterprise of England.

More pressingly, Dom Antonio had taken refuge in the Azores and remained a dangerous threat. In the summer of 1582, the Marquis of Santa Cruz led Philip's navy against the rebels, defeating their French allies at sea. Having wintered on the island of São Miguel, the following year he made a daring assault on Antonio's stronghold at Terceira, disembarking his men in the dangerous waters of a small and rocky cove in the dead of night.

Santa Cruz's quartermaster, Cristóbal Mosquera de Figueroa, a poet and childhood friend of Cervantes, described how 'the Marquis ordered all lights on the galleys extinguished, even the harquebusiers' fuses. Not a shot was to be fired, not a tinderbox touched, not a sound be made.' Soon 'a deep silence reigned over the sea,' broken only by the muffled noises of armed men resting their weapons on the decks. At two o'clock in the morning, with great stealth, the fleet approached the coast under oar and at first light they launched their attack. 'The boats soon reached land and the Spaniards rushed ashore,' under fire from cannon on the high ground. 'The ensign Francisco de la Rúa's boat ran up on the beach and he threw himself into the water with his pennant,' Mosquera reported, 'followed by Captain Luis de Guevara, and Rodrigo de Cervantes, who was later promoted by the Marquis.'[40]

Miguel de Cervantes also claimed to have taken part in this campaign alongside his brother, in which case both of them may have served with another gargantuan figure of Spanish letters, the flamboyant, anarchic, impossibly prolific playwright Félix Lope de Vega y Carpio, whose virulent talents would soon infect Castilian theatre with an epidemic of brilliant storytelling and shameless populism, a rash of dramatic novelty that would spread across the kingdom's stages, laying waste to tradition, raping and pillaging the classics like an Alba army on the march to war. Lope and Cervantes were inexorably linked in life by a friendship and admiration which degenerated into the bitterest and most hateful of rivalries; in death, they are considered paragons of the Spanish literary imagination during the period of astonishing artistic creativity which later generations have called the Golden Age. They may or may not have served Santa Cruz in the Azores, but then how appropriate to be free of certainty when telling the story of these giants of fiction and make-believe.

Lope de Vega lived as colourful a life as lover, poet and playwright as Cervantes did as a soldier and novelist. He wrote thousands of plays and became the most celebrated figure of his age, while his sexual appetite put Don Juan to shame. Yet he later took orders as a priest, after which he fell deeply and faithfully in love, albeit with a woman and not with God; perhaps he felt that to cuckold the Lord was the most daring dalliance of all. Drama and fiction are the stuff of legend, and Lope's world was filled with both as he voraciously ate up life, swallowed it down and then vomited it back out half digested in his plays and poems. Cervantes called him 'a monster of nature'.

And for Cervantes, these were life-changing times. The theatres reopened after a period of mourning for the queen, revivifying the bohemian life of Madrid and Seville. Literary culture was thriving, literacy rates were rising rapidly, reaching 50 per cent or more in some major urban centres, and so book sales were on the increase, attracting foreign printers to Spain, following in the footsteps of the famous Cromberger of Seville (who published Cortés's official accounts of

Mexico), and encouraging the import of works printed in Spanish abroad. The highways and cities of Spain were in thrall to the written word, whether read silently at home or aloud in the taverns, wayside inns and literary salons.[41] In 1580, Herrera published his critical edition of Garcilaso's poetry, with a series of commentaries by a sparkling generation of Sevillian literati, which was the touchstone for a wholly Castilianized style of Italianate verse. Also in 1580, a youthful Luis de Góngora y Argote wrote his first verses, heralding a new age of archly experimental poetry that would captivate some and be excoriated by others.[42]

Cervantes later claimed to have written twenty or thirty plays at this time, which he proudly reported 'were all performed without jeers or whistles, nor were cucumbers and other missiles thrown', implying some degree of success.[43] On 22 February 1584, Antonio de Eraso personally granted a licence for the publication of *La Galatea*, so completing 'its upbringing' as Cervantes had joked. One of Lope de Vega's characters opined from the stage: 'if you want a good book, look no further than *La Galatea*, by Miguel de Cervantes'.[44]

Late in 1584, Cervantes travelled to the small town of Esquivias, in La Mancha, as literary executor to an illustrious friend whose hot-headed young widow had run off with her good-for-nothing lover. There, he met the nineteen-year-old Catalina de Palacios Salazar Vozmediano and three months later they were married in the parish church by her uncle, Juan de Palacios. The following year, Cervantes's only known child was born, a daughter called Isabel. Catalina, however, was not the mother: in the elation of his first, tentative literary success, he had taken up with Ana Villafranca de Rojas, wife of an innkeeper who ran a tavern popular with the writers and dramatists of Madrid. The affair is so shrouded in mystery it has all the appearance of an unfinished work of fiction. Cervantes seems to have kept well clear of a complicated situation until, in 1599, with both Ana and the innkeeper dead, he arranged for Isabel to be taken into service by his sister Magdalena. Only in 1608, at the time of her marriage, do we find him referring to her as his daughter Isabel de Cervantes Saavedra.[45]

In the summer of 1586, Cervantes spent a few weeks in Toledo, where the energetic and charismatic churchman Andrés Núñez de

Madrid, a long-standing friend of his uncle-in-law Juan de Palacios, was the priest of the parish church of Santo Tomé, St Thomas Apostle. Núñez was fresh from successfully prosecuting a claim in the Audiencia of Valladolid against the nearby town of Orgaz, which had owed his parish a bequest worth well over 1,000 *maravedís* a year in perpetuity since the early fourteenth century, but which the municipality had ceased paying in 1564. According to a contemporary compendium of the 'lives of the great saints and illustrious and virtuous men', the Lord of Orgaz who, alongside his wife, had been a great 'servant of God and had lived his life doing Good Works', including rebuilding the Church of Santo Tomé and rehousing some local Augustinian monks, had died in 1312, leaving the annual payment to the parish in his will. History recorded that his 'body was taken to Santo Tomé and placed in the middle of the church', where all the nobility of Toledo gathered around. Then, 'after the clergy had celebrated the office of the dead and were ready to transfer the body to its sepulchre, they witnessed very clearly the glorious Saints Stephen and Augustine descend from on high'. The saints 'approached the body, their faces and clothing recognizable' to the whole assembled company, and 'took him to his grave, saying: "This is the reward for him who serves God and his Saints."' They laid the Lord of Orgaz in his tomb 'and then they disappeared, leaving the church filled with a heavenly fragrance'.[46]

Inspired and empowered by his recent legal victory, Núñez had begun an extensive renovation of the humble chapel at Santo Tomé in which Orgaz had been buried; and, in March 1586, El Greco, now forty-five years old and at the peak of his talents, signed a contract to paint the centrepiece of the new decorative scheme. El Greco's contract clearly instructed him to represent the earthly plain, with the priest and other clergy saying the office of the dead, Saints Stephen and Augustine at the moment of burial and the nobles watching on, while 'above all this' he was to paint 'the heavens opening in glory'.[47] He interpreted this brief faithfully and yet brilliantly, and his *Burial of the Count of Orgaz*, still displayed in Santo Tomé, is considered by many to be the first great painting of the Spanish Golden Age. Moreover, contemporary sources reported that the bold line of noble faces stretching across the middle of the canvas were all real people.

Only five can be identified for certain: some writing on the handker-
chief in the pocket of the kneeling boy labels him as El Greco's son, the
priest officiating is clearly Núñez, while an inscription below the work
states that his assistant is Pedro Ruiz Durón. The two men with grey
beards, one just visible between the two monks on the right, the other
above Ruiz Durón's left shoulder, are recognizable as the two great
humanist brothers Diego and Antonio de Covarrubias.[48] El Greco had
a wondrous intellect and was at the core of a vibrant humanist culture
in Toledo then engaging urgently and creatively with the conservative strictures of the decrees of the Council of Trent. Cervantes must
have been drawn to that circle of lively minds and they must have
opened their arms to a war hero who was becoming one of the most
important literary and theatrical figures of the age. And so, for all that
there is no way to prove the notion that one of the faces in the crowd
of nobles must have been Cervantes, it has been deeply attractive to
many that the greatest writer of the Golden Age should be present in
a painting that heralded such a glittering epoch.[49]

The painting is a tour de force of movement; the glances and
gestures of the figures, the lines of their clothing, the powerful use of
light and colour, all make the viewer's eye dance. But the real skill is in
the structure: the arc of the central image of Stephen, the first martyr,
and Augustine, a doctor of the Church in his mitre, both bending
over to lift Orgaz, perfectly replicates the arc at the top of the canvas
where it fits the vault of the chapel; yet they are not aligned, creating
a strange sense of perspective that thrusts the celestial sphere out
of the painting towards the viewer. But any sense of secure plastic
form which that framework might produce is immediately disturbed
by the three distinct planes of representational style. In the heavens
we see El Greco's extreme Mannerism at its most familiar, an image
composed of simple patches of colour and floating forms; at its heart,
Orgaz's soul is borne by an angel towards the Madonna who will
plead his cause before God so that St Peter may open the Gates of
Heaven with his dangling keys. That celestial world is linked by the
flames of the torches, symbols of the Christian soul, to the central
band of slightly too pointed noble faces and their almost disembodied
heads, in which we see the playful abstraction of reality so typical of

El Greco's portraiture. The miracle itself is shown with a startling hyper-realism of a kind we associate with northern Gothic art or possibly Italian works of the fourteenth or fifteenth centuries. In this way, it points us back in time to the medieval moment when Orgaz was really buried. But at the same time that juxtaposition between the abstract nobles and heavens and the priest officiating at the mass, the saints and the cadaver, all clad in their sumptuous liturgical robes and armour, astonishes us with an almost photographic sense of the reality of the miracle itself. Past and present, this world and the next, Counter-Reformation orthodoxy and humanist inquiry, all rub shoulders in this painting in which El Greco opened the gates of the Golden Age.

Meanwhile, on the grandest of all stages, the Marquis of Santa Cruz, fresh from victory in the Azores, was preparing to play his part in a new script written by Philip II himself and founded on an overconfident belief in the idea of a miraculously Invincible Armada.[50]

11

Pirates, Criminals and Tax Collecting

Non sufficit orbis – the world is not enough.
Imperial coat of arms at Santo Domingo

When Cervantes finally left Algiers for Spain and Portugal in 1580, he returned to the heart of an Empire that with hindsight we now know had reached its zenith, ruled by a sovereign who very obviously seemed at the height of his power.[1] In 1569, Miguel López de Legazpi had begun the settlement of the Philippines, which he named after his sovereign; the Kingdom of Goa came with the Portuguese crown, as did Brazil; Mexico and Peru had long been colonized, as had parts of modern Argentina and Chile; Spaniards even had a tenuous hold on Florida and would soon begin the settlement of New Mexico. But at this moment of almost maximum reach, the Empire was also dangerously overstretched, while back in Spain the population and the economy were on the verge of a slow decline. But none of this would become evident to anyone for a generation, and in 1580 Castilians were in ebullient mood, with many loudly hymning their hopes for that longed-for Christian world ruled over by 'a single shepherd and his monarchy'.[2]

In 1586, the Audiencia of Santo Domingo, on Hispaniola, sent a disturbing report to Philip II: 'Your Catholic Royal Majesty: on 10 January this year, at 10 o'clock in the morning, news reached this city that ships had been sighted heading for the harbour.' There were seventeen English vessels in total, which sowed such fear among the rank-and-file Spaniards that the officials reported that 'the spirits of many began to falter and they started to flee despite the proclamations and other measures taken to prevent them'. The following Saturday, they reported, 'at 12 o'clock, we heard that nine companies of first-rate infantrymen were attacking by land and were half a league away from the city'. Four hundred Spaniards abandoned their posts, leaving the valiant few: 'we mustered about forty horse, and, with an harquebusier seated on each horse's haunches, we set out to do whatever we could'. But when they 'came upon the enemy . . . ten or twelve of us rode to within a musket shot of them, trying to get everyone . . . to attack', but they were 'showered with musket fire' and 'the men's courage failed them . . . and they fled into the bush'.[3]

A handful of officers fired their big guns from the gates of the town and then retreated into the hinterland, abandoning Santo Domingo to the heretics. 'Thus the Spaniards gave us the town for a New Year gift,' one Englishman recalled.[4]

As Philip read on, far away at the Escorial, horror piled up upon horror: the English 'began to commit a thousand abominable deeds, causing great insult and injury to the churches and religious images, all of which they smashed and broke apart, desecrating everything without a second thought'. 'We burned all their images of wood and broke and destroyed all their fairest work within their churches,' the English reported.[5]

And so the disgrace of having to cut a deal with the Protestant pirates began. But when the Spaniards refused the ransom demand of 100,000 ducats, the English 'began to set fire to the city and its churches' with such efficiency that 'in a short time they had burned most of it'. The Spaniards finally agreed a price of 25,000 ducats, and, as the English reported, 'the town during our residence therein, being sacked to the full, with such consideration drawn from them as it was thought good by our General, we all embarked'.[6] They took 'everything with them, including the church bells, the cannon from the fortress, and . . . many black slaves went with them of their own free will', the Audiencia reported to Philip; 'they are now headed for Cartagena'.

'The Captain of these men was Francisco Draque,' baptized 'the Dragon' by Lope de Vega in his epic poem *The Dragontea*, the great navigator and notorious privateer, son of a humble farmer and preacher from Devon in south-west England, who was knighted by Elizabeth I of England as Sir Francis Drake and became a vice-admiral in the Royal Navy.[7]

Philip's Empire was overstretched on almost every front, but it was particularly vulnerable in the Americas. At Santo Domingo, the English had been especially struck by an imperial coat of arms showing the 'whole circuit of the sea and earth, whereupon is a horse standing . . . with a scroll painted in his mouth, wherein was written these words in Latin: *non sufficit orbis* – the World is not Enough'.[8] The official English report exhorted 'the Queen of England' to 'resolutely prosecute the wars against the king of Spain' and force him 'to lay aside that proud and unreasonable reaching vanity'.[9]

But this was more than a fight over colonial wealth and free trade or piracy. Drake's chaplain railed against 'the poisonous infection of Popery . . . wherein (amongst other the like Spanish virtues) not only whoredom, but the filthiness of Sodom' is encouraged among the Indians.[10] With Las Casas's words, which had been published across Europe, metaphorically ringing in his ears, another English pirate accused the Catholics of preaching 'nought else but avarice, rapine, blood, death, and destruction to those naked and sheeplike' Indians.[11] The conflict was increasingly polarized by mutual religious intolerance and, where Philip II might have written off the destruction of Santo Domingo as an inevitable cost of Empire, his piety could not countenance the desecration of churches and holy images by an heretical nation of which he had once been king.

Needless to say, it is an exaggeration to suggest that the Great Armada was assembled because of the exploits of Sir Francis Drake. But with overpowering symbolism he embodied in a single character so many of the geopolitical forces that weighed so heavily on Philip II. In 1585, Queen Elizabeth of England extended her formal protection to the Dutch rebels and sent troops and experienced commanders to help them. That escalation of international tension coincided with Drake's provocatively aggressive voyage to Spain and the Spanish Indies. The same year, Elizabeth approved Sir Francis Walsingham's plan for 'The Annoying of the King of Spain', which involved the destruction of the Spanish fisheries in Newfoundland. The execution of Mary Queen of Scots, on 18 February 1587, was the catalyst to action, for her death left it open to Philip to claim the throne of England for himself.[12] On 2 April 1587, Drake sailed to Cadiz 'to Singe the King of Spain's Beard'. Flying Dutch and French colours, he entered the harbour and destroyed thirty or more vessels before the Duke of Medina Sidonia could muster Spanish defences. 'Their audacity is intolerable,' Philip wrote to the Marquis of Santa Cruz.[13]

At the beginning of *Don Quixote*, the middle-aged hero suffers a mid-life crisis and abandons the fictional Esquivias for a life of adventure as a knight in shining armour, drawing on his extensive library of novels of chivalry for inspiration. In 1587, Cervantes gave his wife power of attorney over their affairs, abandoned the real Esquivias and headed for Seville, still dreaming about America.

Remarkably, at the western edge of a war-torn Europe, Charles V and Philip II had established a lasting peace in Castile following the defeat of the Comuneros. Only major Morisco uprisings in Granada, raids by Barbary and English pirates, occasional French incursions, the invasion of Portugal and the Catalan rebellions disturbed what was, in effect, a *pax hispanica* at home that lasted until the Spanish War of Succession at the beginning of the eighteenth century. A new sense of shared Spanishness emerged among the towns and aristocracy, reinforced by the camaraderie of returning Spaniards who had served abroad. The Crown became synonymous with a range of important institutions – the Cortes, the royal councils, Audiencias, the Treasury, the House of Trade, the Inquisition and the universities. The Crown shared responsibility for maintaining a relatively well-ordered society and for enforcing the law with various other powerful municipal and religious institutions.

Most impressive of all was the ability of such institutions to maintain civic order in a large port city like Seville. By the final decades of the sixteenth century, the official population of Seville had grown to

85,000, while the best estimate suggests a true figure nearer 160,000, swelled by transient merchants, adventurers and ragamuffins, a cosmopolitan influx of Flemings, Germans, French, Italians, Irish, Englishmen, Scotsmen, Moors, Africans, Greeks and even Turks. Perhaps most unexpected were the two contingents of Japanese Samurais, some of whom settled in the nearby town of Coria del Río, where Japón remains a common surname to this day.[14]

This multinational population inhabited a chaotic world of bustling commerce and theatrical street life, a city of packed rental accommodation and myriad taverns and public eating houses, awash with money, teeming with thuggish dandies who called themselves *valientes* and thousands of paupers and hopeful migrants. The noblemen, churchmen and burgers who styled themselves consuls of Ancient Rome clubbed together into bitterly rival political factions, social organizations and official institutions. These city fathers vied with one another and with the Crown for power and prestige, and competed in public displays of wealth and opulence; their squabbling and fighting was constant.

The struggle between the Crown and the municipal authorities was the central rift in the politics of Seville, but it inevitably drew in the Church and a whole range of other institutions and organizations. For example, social welfare had always been administered by a bewildering range of charitable foundations run by religious confraternities of lay brothers, ordinary citizens dedicated to helping the poor, the sick or the spiritually needy. They ran hospitals for lepers, for the syphilitic, for strangers and for Sevillians, their widows, their orphans and their foundlings; there was even a hospital especially for Flemings. Interestingly, the patients and inmates of such institutions appear to have been the first Europeans regularly to eat that quintessentially American tuber, the potato, as part of their normal diet.[15] But in the late 1580s the Crown attempted to wrest control of most of these institutions from the independently minded brotherhoods through a programme of radical rationalization in which seventy-five out of a total of 112 hospitals in the city were forced to merge into two new royal mega-hospitals.[16] That policy was founded on a puritanical moral principle that hospitals should serve the sick alone, and so the city fathers watched on in horror as the many poor, often widowed, elderly, retarded or slightly mad, who had been looked after in one or other of the ramshackle old establishments, were poured out into the streets of the city, where they turned to begging.

In 1597, the Crown appointed the Count of Puñonrostro – literally 'Fist-in-Face' – as *asistente* or Governor of Seville, with instructions to assert royal authority publicly. In response to news of plague spreading across Castile from the north, he ordered the poor of Seville to gather in a field outside the Hospital of the Sangre de Cristo.[17] The following day, over 2,000 arrived, 'the greatest piece of theatre ever seen', according to an eyewitness. 'Some were healthy, others old, there were the lame, the injured and an infinite number of women, all spread out across the field and the courtyards of the hospital.' Then, 'at two o'clock in the afternoon the Governor arrived accompanied by many officers of the law and many doctors'. Over the next three days, they classified this motley collection of broken humanity, dealing first with the women and then with the men. The sick were taken away to be cared for. The 'deserving poor', the lame, the crippled, the otherwise bodily damaged, and the old and infirm had begging licences tied around their necks with white ribbons. We do not have the figures for Seville, but in Madrid, of the nearly 4,000 paupers who were rounded up, only 650 were granted a licence.[18] The 'undeserving poor' were given three days to find employment or leave the city, but if they were found begging without a licence they would be 'given a charitable thrashing'.[19]

Puñonrostro most obviously asserted royal authority through the draconian imposition of law and order in the face of the vested interests of the urban oligarchs. He regularly admonished bullying city bureaucrats; when a poor old woman came to him and complained that she had been cajoled into selling four chickens to a public notary for 64 *maravedís*, though the official list price was 60 a bird, and had then been forced to pay 24 *maravedís* in sales tax, the Governor meted out highly effective summary justice, forcing the notary to pay the woman 2,400 *maravedís* and the tax collector to pay her 800. He also readily took on the powerful Cathedral officials. He questioned a beautiful young girl who was working in an inn and was pregnant;

she had run away from her employers after a canon of the Cathedral had promised to give her a dowry of 100 ducats in exchange for her virginity, but then reneged on the deal. The Governor went home and sent for the canon, and the two men 'greeted one another with a great show of affection and reverence'. The Governor then spoke with astonishing candour: 'Sir, you must know that a certain woman has asked for my help and she has told me how you took advantage of her, promising to pay her a dowry and that you have not been as good as your word.' The canon denied the charge, but the Governor would have none of it: 'Sir, you must fulfil your obligation to this girl, and if not the Cardinal will find out and I will write to the Papal Nuncio in Madrid.' The canon agreed to go and get the 100 ducats immediately, but when he went out into the street he could not find his mule because Puñonrostro had ordered his lackeys to hide it. He rushed back up to complain, but the Governor merely told him that he was holding the animal as collateral, forcing the canon to suffer the humiliation of walking the streets.[20]

The Governor's aggressive campaign was vividly recorded by a diarist called Francisco de Ariño, whose journal reads like the front page of a local newspaper, even containing notices of minor traffic accidents. For example, on Friday, 7 September 1597, Ariño led with a story about 'a black woman and her son who were riding a white pony down the incline of the first section of the bridge as you come from Triana, when the animal caught its hoof in a hole and fell. The mother and child fell into the river, but both were pulled out alive, which was a great miracle.' The bridge seems to have been a dangerous place; in 1604, a man's horse slipped while crossing the bridge 'and fell on top of him and he rolled into the river and although he managed to grab hold of a pole, he drowned. Alonso de Antequera rescued the mare.'

With the authority to mete out a mandatory sentence of 200 lashes for retail misdemeanours, Puñonrostro set about tackling the almost universally flouted byelaws governing the sale of food, arresting well-known personalities from the vibrant street life of hawkers and traders. These characters, known as *regatones* or hagglers, bought up food from stalls and shops at the officially listed price, or imported it from outside the city jurisdiction, and then resold at a premium, which was against the law. On 5 May 1597, days after dealing with the mendicant masses, the Governor had a *regatona* who had concealed butchered goat meat under her skirts sentenced to 200 lashes. As she was paraded through the streets, the hawkers of the city shouted out their protests and there were ugly scenes. The following day it was the turn of a fruit-seller who was overcharging.

Then, on Wednesday 7 May, Ariño reported, 'a gentleman walked to the main meat market or *rastro* . . . and saw a man selling such beautifully fat hindquarters of lamb that he bought two of them along with their testicles. He ordered the testicles roasted for his lunch,' but when his servant 'began removing them, he discovered they had been sewn on . . .' The master sent for his steward, 'who took one look and said, "Sir, this is mutton!" The gentleman immediately had his servant take the meat to the Governor's house, where he explained what had happened.' The following morning the two men went to the market and found the hawker again selling mutton cross-dressed as lamb. But the man turned out to be a servant of one of the city sheriffs. Puñonrostro's job was to tread on such men's toes, and he ordered the crook arrested and jailed. At ten in the morning, he was paraded through the crowded city streets with the offending meat hanging from his neck, while he was given 200 lashes before being banished from Seville. Again, there were raucous protests from the illegal street vendors, while more serious opposition was brewing among the infuriated city fathers.

The unlikely catalyst for the inevitable confrontation was an incident in which a soap seller renowned for her foul mouth refused to serve the slave of a city official, shouting: 'Go on, piss off, I don't want to sell anything to that cuckold master of yours. Does the idiot think I'm going to sell it at the official price?' The slave naturally reported back to her master, who complained to the Governor. The soap seller, called María de la O, took refuge in a church, but she was arrested and jailed.

When the Governor's men came to collect her in order to punish her, they found that María had appealed to the Audiencia, which had

ordered the jail to be locked up and the keys brought to their meeting.
There were angry exchanges outside the prison between the Governor
and representatives of the Audiencia, following which Puñonrostro
ordered a session of the Cabildo, the municipal authority. After much
debate, a special committee was appointed which eventually authorized him to break into the jail in order to carry out the sentence
against María. He sprang into action and his lackeys removed some
bars with pick-axes and then broke the locks on the door. The
constables who had acted for the Audiencia were clapped in irons,
and María was subjected to the usual punishment of 200 lashes while
being paraded through the streets mounted on a donkey and stripped
to the waist.

She may have been the sacrificial victim of an institutional power
struggle, but she was also incorrigible and was soon rearrested. This
time, the atmosphere became so riotous that the Governor ordered a
ban on gathering in the main square. 'And it was quite a sight to see
the terrified people fleeing the square in all directions . . . The hawkers
were amazed,' Ariño reports, but 'no one had a good word to say
about María, and instead many said her punishment was much less
than she deserved.' In true Sevillian fashion, everyone was eager to
proclaim their opinion about what had happened and we can readily
imagine the arguments continuing late into the hot summer night in
the taverns and eating houses. But the Governor clearly had much of
the popular support and soon jaunty *coplas*, or popular ditties, were
being sung all over town:

> Blessed be our holy God,
> For our new Governor,
> Who makes everybody
> Abide by price controls
>
> Making us all equals
> For all we are not judges,
> We now eat as cheap
> As our magistrates.[21]

But anyone familiar with the razor-sharp wit and eye for irony of ordinary Sevillians will hardly be surprised to learn that the popular lyricists also enjoyed poking fun at their squabbling superiors:

> The richly coloured cedars
> Are flamboyant with flowers,
> It's Saintly Peter's Eve and
> The proud pony's trotting,
> Yet the city's up in arms
>
> Whispered rumours are abroad
> About the riotous actions
> Of the Audiencia and *asistente*
> Who're at each other's throats
> For the most trivial of reasons.[22]

The Governor and Audiencia immediately sent representatives to Madrid. In the meantime, the Audiencia took the initiative, fining members of the Cabildo who had been present during the extraordinary session, ordering them to pay for the damage done to the jail and imprisoning them all in the fortress of the Torre del Oro, the iconic dodecagonal Golden Tower built by the Moors to control the river. They also ordered the Governor to pay 500 ducats.

After further shenanigans, during which the Governor kept his head down by claiming to have a fever, a final decision came from Madrid that ruled decisively in his favour. Both sides agreed on a compromise in which the *regatones* would be fined for a first offence, publicly shamed for the second and given 200 lashes for the third. 'And', Ariño reports, 'the *regatones* were well pleased, saying that it was the work of the Audiencia and they ran wildly through the streets claiming "It's nothing, they just want to make money, for if they catch us today and ask us our names we'll just say Pedro and then the next day Juan and so we need not worry about being given lashes by the Governor."' But given that so many of them were very familiar characters this initial optimism may well have proved illusory.

Serious crime was also a major feature of life in Seville during the 1600s and 1700s. A Jesuit called Father Pedro de León kept a record of confessions made to him by remand prisoners and convicts awaiting punishment that, filled with homicide and violence, offers us a chilling account of life in the city and its hinterland.

The constant casual violence is shocking even at the remove of four centuries. When two labourers argued over money, one of them threw a stone at the other, who immediately drew his sword and killed his companion. A fight over a woman between two tradesmen, described as friends, ended in murder. Two gangs of cobblers fought a duel in the main square over a woman, leaving one dead and three seriously wounded. Men fought and killed one another over petty insults: 'the accidental soiling of a cape, the questioning of the quality of olives being sold by a street vendor, an argument over a seat at a public performance could end in sudden death'.[23] Then there is the case of Gonzalo Genis, a racist ruffian from an honourable family, who had asked the white girlfriend of a highly respected and much liked black man: 'How can you shack up with a black man when there are so many white men in the world?' It ended with a knife fight during which the black man was killed. Gonzalo was hanged.[24]

But the hotheads could take a long time to cool down, and the rancour was lasting. León tells the story of an eighteen-year-old Sardinian boy condemned to be drawn and quartered for a grisly murder. While serving as a page in a noble household, the boy had quarrelled with a lackey. And while the two lads were at first supposedly reconciled, resentment burned in the Sardinian. Some time later, he invited the unsuspecting lackey to his lodgings (in what would become the refectory of the English College) to eat a hen for dinner and the two men stayed up chatting. 'It is late for you to go home,' said the pageboy, 'you can sleep here. I have to meet some men further down the lane.' He apologized and went into the street. Oblivious to the coming treachery, the lackey lay down 'and when the page returned he found his enemy asleep, just as he wanted. He took up a paving slab and smashed it on to the lackey's head and then buried him under his bed,' which he then slept in 'as restfully as possible given that he had his enemy interred beneath him'. Needless to say, after a few days the badly buried body began to stink and the shallow grave was soon discovered. The pageboy eventually confessed after he had been tortured by having his hands and feet burned.[25]

Sevillians were nothing if not inventive when it came to improvising murderous objects if violent confrontation took them by surprise. Tradesmen often used their work tools, but 'a large and heavy sea shell, a pumpkin' and a melon are all to be found in the records of murder weapons.[26] And all social classes were involved in violent crime, although skilled tradesmen and journeymen 'seem to have had a predilection for bloodshed'.[27] This may have been because they owned merchandise and materials that needed defending as much as their honour; it may also be that they were relatively well off and could afford to spend more time out and about, getting drunk in the taverns and eating houses.

Such a violent world was difficult and dangerous to police. León records the case of an infamous ruffian called Juan García, who was pursued by a Sheriff with a large posse of armed men. García killed one of them and wounded most of them, shouting 'I am Juan García, and I swear to God that if you don't hold back you'll soon get the message. Show yourselves now if you don't want to die.' The Sheriff and his men took refuge in the Church of Santa Ana, but finally the hooligan was apprehended and executed.[28]

With so little sense of security, criminals and even ordinary citizens looked to armed ruffians and criminal gangs for protection. In one of his best-known short stories, Cervantes describes how two young ragamuffins from northern Spain, Rinconete and Cortadillo, arrived in Seville and soon joined one such well-organized gang, run by the impressive figure of Monipodio, 'who looked forty-five or forty-six, was tall, with a dark complexion, a single bushy eyebrow, a full black beard, sunken eyes, and wearing a shirt, open at the neck, revealing a glimpse of his forest of chest hair . . . with short, hirsute hands, fat fingers . . . and unusually wide and knobbly feet. In short, the most rough and ugly savage imaginable.'[29] But while Cervantes offers up this wonderfully atmospheric but essentially stereotypical image of a pirate chief as his criminal mastermind, he presents the man's organization as though it were a religious brotherhood with strictly enforced rules, carefully kept accounts and its headquarters in a run-down house arranged around a small courtyard. A procession of thieves, prostitutes, corrupt officials and ruffians walk this stage while Monipodio issues orders and passes judgment on members of his criminal confraternity and citizens who have failed to pay their dues or owe money and favours.

There is a tendency among historians to read this story as essentially true and so develop intriguing theories about organized crime in Spanish cities of the time, despite the fact that it is advertised by Cervantes as an 'exemplary novel'. This is in any case to misunderstand what Cervantes was doing: while he may have taken the opportunity to poke fun at whatever embryonic sense of honour there may have been among seventeenth-century Sevillian thieves, in reality this was a grandly theatrical experiment in *agudeza*, literally 'sharpness', which we would translate as 'wit'. For Golden Age Spaniards, the idea behind such a conceit, as explained by another great literary figure, Baltasar Gracián, is the 'intellectual process' stimulated by 'a conceptual artifice that creates concord and harmonious correlation between two or three extremes'. It is, in other words, an unexpected and even inappropriate parallel drawn between two very different concepts or things – such as a gang of criminals and a charitable religious confraternity – and the more extreme the terms of reference 'the more satisfying the result'.[30] And it is as such that we must read this story. The detail may be convincingly realistic, the tricks and artifices of the thieves, their clothes, but the notion that a single boss controlled all crime in the city can be safely enjoyed for the fiction Cervantes intended it to be – albeit exemplary fiction, for this absurd, theatrical novella was intended to satirize the real religious brotherhoods and to highlight corruption and moral hypocrisy in general.

When Cervantes reached Seville in 1587, having left his young wife in Esquivias, he went to stay with an old theatre friend, an actor-turned-entrepreneur called Tomás Gutiérrez de Castro who ran the most magnificent hotel in the city, a luxurious haven where aristocrats and rich merchants were made to feel at home by a legion of slaves and servants, along with the 'damask bedding', the tapestries and meals served on 'silver plate'. It was notoriously expensive: a contemporary street ballad warned guests to 'take account on arrival of what you have to pay per week or month for your room'[31] – a suitably contrary location for Cervantes to have used as headquarters during his explorations of the underbelly of Andalusia. He met Diego de Valdivia, a Sheriff of the Royal Audiencia in charge of securing provisions for the Invincible Armada, who sent him as a Royal Commissioner to Écija and the Cordova hinterland, 'the frying-pan' of Andalusia, at the heart of the rich agricultural land of the Guadalquivir river-system. So Cervantes became an especially unglamorous cog in the malfunctioning imperial machine.

In his play *The Divorce Court Judge*, he described how 'I managed to see myself as other sharp-witted men are seen, holding a staff, riding a small, dry and bad tempered rented mule . . . with saddlebags on its haunches, with a collar and shirt in one, half a cheese, some bread and a wineskin in the other . . . with a commissioner's warrant in his breast pocket'.[32] His mission was to impound wheat, grind it and have it baked into ship's biscuit to supply the Armada. He had the legal power to break into locked property in search of grain, imprison obstructive subjects and sign notes of credit on behalf of the Crown. He was required to keep meticulous accounts for everything, every copper coin spent, every bushel of wheat, every pound of biscuit. He recorded oil bought for lamps, paper, pens and ink, farm implements, fees paid to locksmiths and muleteers, and rent for barns and storage lofts; even the brooms bought to sweep up the chaff went down in his account book.

Écija was 'a spectacularly splendid sight, the beauty of which is unequalled in all Spain', according to one Morrocan ambassador.[33] For Cervantes there was the added attraction that his old friend and Santa Cruz's chronicler, Cristóbal Mosquera de Figueroa, who had described Rodrigo de Cervantes's heroism during the campaign in the Azores, was then coming to the end of his term as *corregidor*, Chief Magistrate of the city; he would be congenial company and might also make harvesting the taxes a less uncongenial task. The city fathers had already surrendered 8,000 *fanegas* of grain (about 14,000 modern bushels of fifty-six pounds) and were in no mood to hand over more. When Cervantes presented his credentials to the Cabildo, the Town Council, he was immediately told he would have to wait because the annual fiesta was about to begin. But Mosquera seems to have acted quickly to broker a deal: on his last day in office, the Council agreed to make representation directly to the Crown and requested that Cervantes impound as little as possible 'because of the great lack of wheat to be found in the city'.[34] Cervantes began to do his job, collecting 4,000 *fanegas*, but was almost immediately excommunicated for sequestering grain from the Church – a familiar tactic in the continual wrangling between Church and Crown that meant he would be refused communion throughout the diocese of Seville.[35] Two months later, Valdivia arrived and the Council agreed to pay a total of 5,400 *fanegas*. Cervantes appointed his cousin Rodrigo as his assistant and he and Valdivia moved on to collect supplies from a handful of small towns in the vicinity.

Cervantes was soon back in Écija, trying to requisition 4,000 *arrobas* of olive oil (thirteen million gallons). But this time he went easy on the city and agreed with the councillors and leading citizens to use his position to present their case to the Crown officials.[36] Most commentators have sentimentally suggested that this reflected Cervantes's humanity, but the most likely explanation is that he had been bribed.

The long months on the byways of Andalusia drew Cervantes into the picaresque world of rural Spain, involving him in the intricacies and intimacies of ordinary Spanish lives, and this was the vividly realistic stage on which he would develop his literary characters. But from time to time he returned to Seville, presumably thirsting for intellectual stimulus. Mosquera de Figueroa was a member of the most important of the many *academias* that thrived in the city, informal gatherings of intellectuals, writers, poets and scholarly noblemen, which took place in the palaces of wealthy patrons.[37] This one had been established in 1566 by Juan de Mal Lara (known as the 'Greek Commander' for his brilliance in classical langauges), because 'in other countries it is a laudable custom for all learned men to assist someone who is writing, and even to have the authors read their work in academies formed for this purpose . . . without publishing the fact that they did him favours'.[38] On Mal Lara's death, Fernando de Herrera, editor of Garcilaso's poetry, took over the leadership of the *academia*, and the mantel passed in turn to the great art theorist Francisco Pacheco, teacher of Diego Velázquez.

Gutiérrez's hotel must have buzzed with the prurient gossip from Madrid. Lope de Vega was in trouble. He had been madly in love with Elena Osorio, the daughter of a businessman, actor and theatre promoter, for whom he had written a number of plays, but Elena had now taken up with a powerful aristocrat, Francisco Perrenot de Granvela. Lope's love turned to passionate hatred and this 'monster of nature' sought revenge in scandalously libellous verse:

> 'A lady's for sale, do I have any takers?
> The highest bidder'll have 'er, any offers?'
> Her father's the hawker, her mother the crier.
> Thirty ducats, silks, satins, a taffeta suit . . . 'any bids, fellas?'
> Then along came a gallant with a handful of songs
> An' plenty o' sonnets . . . which seemed a fair deal!
> Till a friar coughed up thirty doubloons
> The blessed Almighty and his bloody wounds![39]

Suddenly, reams of similarly scurrilous poetry were going the rounds of the Madrid literati, and Elena's father sued for libel. Lope was imprisoned while expert witnesses were instructed to assess the authorship of the lampoons. The literary world was so small and individual verse styles considered so unique that the courts took seriously the aesthetic analysis of the poems as a way of identifying the person who had written them. One witness reported that when Luis de Vargas heard one of the poems, he exclaimed, 'the style of this romance is such that it could only be by one of four or five people', among them 'Cervantes, but he is not here . . . it could be by Vivar, or by Lope de Vega, although Lope would never slander himself to such an extent'. On 7 February 1588, the magistrates sentenced Lope to 'eight years banishment from this kingdom of Castile'.

He fled to Valencia, subject to the Crown of Aragon, but within weeks the Madrid authorities had charged him with abducting a girl called Isabel de Alderete. He resolved this new problem by agreeing to marry her by proxy. According to Juan Pérez de Montalbán's biography, *The Posthumous Homage*, of 1637, 'at the time of the Enterprise of England . . . Lope enlisted, filled with the desire to die' because of this ill-conceived marriage. 'He went to Lisbon, where he embarked with his brother, an ensign, whom he had not seen in a long time' and who was possibly called Francisco.[40]

Years later, Lope remembered, 'in the days when the Armada visited England and I was trying to forget Elena Osorio' (whom he disguised as Phyllis in the verse),

> I walked among the Spaniards
> On a Portuguese beach,
> Shouldering an harquebus,
> Phyllis's letters caught on the wind
> In pieces from the angry barrel.
> And the people hurried
> About the rigging and the decks.[41]

Modern scholars question whether Lope really took part in the Armada.[42] But he himself mentions his service on at least thirteen separate occasions in his work and he even claimed to have written *Angelica's Beauty*, published in 1602, 'amid the rigging, afloat on the galleon San Juan', the vice-flagship.[43] Why, one wonders, was a man who made so many bitter enemies able to get away without having such an ostentatious claim to heroism questioned in his lifetime if it was all a lie? It certainly makes for a better story that he did serve in the Armada.[44]

Cervantes was in Écija when he learnt that the Marquis of Santa Cruz had died on 9 February 1587. The Great Armada was bereft of its architect and admiral, 'a marvellously prudent and experienced general, in whom the soldiers had placed their hopes for a good outcome'.[45] With great reluctance, Alonso Pérez de Guzmán, seventh

Duke of Medina Sidonia, leading grandee of Spain, agreed to take over the command.

Medina Sidonia's notorious complaint that he could not accept the commission because he suffered from sea-sickness is, needless to say, nonsense. Almost everyone had to endure sea-sickness; more importantly, he was worried that he had no experience of naval warfare. He was chosen because he was the only candidate who outranked every one of the other noble officers who had command of the different squadrons and ships. In a world in thrall to the hierarchy of blood, supreme authority was his birthright.

His reluctance to become involved and his prudent approach stand out in contrast to Philip II's increasingly zealous determination to conquer England. In Paris, Henry III's ministers were publicly declaring that Philip had actually gone mad.[46]

Medina Sidonia's orders were to sail up the English Channel and rendezvous near Calais with the Army of Flanders under the command of the Duke of Parma. The Armada would first transport the troops across the strait for a landing on the Kent beaches and then, while Parma marched on London, the fleet would sail up the Thames in a daring double strike by land and sea. The core of the Armada was almost a hundred transport vessels, hulks carrying men, animals and supplies. These were protected by nine massive, 1,000-ton Portuguese warships, eight great galleons of 700 tons drawn from the Atlantic fleets and four towering galleasses from the Naples fleet bristling with awesome firepower, their square-rigged sails painted with great blood-red swords, their fifty-six benches of oarsmen all dressed in crimson.[47]

On 30 May, the vast fleet set sail.

Meanwhile, Cervantes was in Écija in order to have the requisitioned grain milled.[48] The councillors appealed directly to Philip, complaining that 'Your Majesty's Commissary is impounding all the bread we have left and he intends to take everything . . . We beseech you, have mercy upon us.'[49] Cervantes began trawling the surrounding estates with his train of carters, muleteers, day labourers and other hangers-on, with their cargo of sacks and scales.

But, time and again over the coming months, Cervantes seems to have thrown his lot in with the citizens. He repeatedly called on witnesses to declare formally that because the grain had been kept in storage for so long, much of it had been eaten by weevils and other vermin.[50] No doubt there was some such spoilage, but everyone who testified was either a citizen of Écija or a muleteer on his payroll; he did not call a single Crown official. Once again, he was using a bureacratic process in order to construct a plausible fiction, this time so as to explain a marked shortfall between the amount of grain supposedly delivered by the citizens and the amount he recorded as having been milled.

By August, he had moved on to Cordova,[51] where he must have enjoyed the erudite company of Luis de Góngora y Argote, a prebendary canon of the Cathedral and a graduate of Salamanca with a growing reputation for elaborately sophisticated poetry whom Cervantes later described as his favourite poet.[52] Góngora's love of life at the expense of a due reverence for the Church had recently earned him a reprimand from the religious authorities for 'living too youthfully and spending all day and night in lighthearted things'. Among the charges levelled against him were that he 'rarely goes to church and that when he does, he wanders about . . . and talks too much during mass'. To which he replied with appropriately youthful flippancy that 'I have always been as silent during mass as anyone because I have a deaf man on one side of me and someone who never stops singing on the other, so I have to be quiet as I have no one to talk to.' But he was also accused of 'keeping the company of actors and writing secular verses', a charge he not only acknowledged but enthusiastically embraced, claiming that actors particularly enjoyed his hospitality 'because I am a great music lover'.[53]

12

The Great Armada, 1588

For many months there were only tears and laments throughout Spain.

An Escorial monk

On 29 July 1588, the Armada sighted the Lizard, the most southerly part of England. The richly dressed senior officers, mostly old men, and their most trusted advisers boarded the pinnaces and ships' boats and began to gather on the poop deck of the flagship. Their assembly was as much naval court as council of war, beset with rivalries and the all-important trivia of the aristocratic pecking order which sat so uneasily within the rigid hierarchy of military command. Medina Sidonia addressed them confidently, reminding them that their objective was to embark the Army of Flanders. But privately he was worried: 'we have had no message from the Duke of Parma, nor have we had news of him,' he wrote to Philip; 'we are navigating in the dark.'[1]

As the Armada sailed on, warning beacons burst into flame along the clifftops, conveying the news to the English fleet, massed at Plymouth, that the Spaniard had been sighted. Ironically enough, as noted above, while king-consort to Mary, Philip II had advised the Privy Council to strengthen the navy as England's best line of defence, so there were 197 ships at anchor in Plymouth harbour. Medina Sidonia's commanders guessed that within hours their enemy would be ready to sail to meet them, but the tides allowed for more than enough time for Sir Francis Drake to complete his famous game of bowls, if anyone really wants to believe that that is what he did.

At daybreak on 31 July, the Spanish sighted the main body of English ships bearing down on them under the direct command of Lord Admiral Howard. The Armada sailed on in similar rigid formation to that used at Lepanto, with a central bastion flanked by two manoeuvrable horns or *cuernos*. The men prepared for action, Lope de Vega perhaps among them, with his brother Francisco at his side, aboard the galleon *San Juan*.

The first to see action were always the artillery men who manned the big guns, which could fire no more than a broadside or two as the galleys and galleons bore down cumbersomely on an enemy ship. As at Lepanto, the aim was to secure the English ships with grappling irons and board them. After this, battle would be engaged more or less as though on land. There were musketeers with their heavy-calibre hand-held weapons and fancily decorated hats with broad leather brims that could be pulled down to shield their faces from the flash of the charge. There were many more harquebusiers who could work quickly at close quarters during the hand-to-hand fighting after the ships engaged. Grenadiers hurled pottery grenades, filled with explosive, resin and highly flammable spirits, and terrifying pipe-bombs filled with nails. With almost 20,000 fighting men spread across the fleet of 125 ships, armed with 2,431 guns, the Spaniards felt the English had every reason to be fearful.

Howard ordered a small barque, the *Disdain*, to approach the heart of the Armada; the Spaniards watched, wondering. The tiny boat fired a single shot and then dashed for safety. This was no act of bravado, but a deliberately issued challenge, a last vestige of chivalry, a moment of aristocratic calm before the mayhem. And then the English attacked: with the ships snaking along in a line, they cut swiftly across the Spanish rearguard, firing broadside after broadside; but only the *San Juan* was hit, with a score of casualties and damage to a mast. It was a tentative first jab, but Lope de Vega had witnessed the first blood drawn.

The Spaniards proved accident prone: there was a huge explosion aboard the *San Salvador* and, when the Armada stopped to rescue the survivors, the *Rosario* collided with another ship, damaging her steering sails, so that, flailing, she then smashed into yet another vessel, which brought the mainmast crashing down. Medina Sidonia abandoned the *Rosario* to the Fates, who soon arrived in the person of Sir Francis Drake, Vice-Admiral of the Fleet, aboard the *Revenge*. The Spaniards aboard immediately surrendered and Drake and his men 'merrily shared the treasure' and that other great English privateer Martin Frobisher later accused him of forsaking the defence of England 'because he would have the spoil'.[2] His covetous ill-discipline had left the English in disarray, and the Armada sailed on through the long sea-lane of the Channel.

Medina Sidonia was determined to rendezvous with Parma, so, even as the skirmishing continued, the Armada sailed resolutely westwards until, at 4 p.m. on 6 August, it dropped anchor off Calais. That evening, the Admiral received news from Parma for the first time and it was disastrous: the Army of Flanders would not embark for another four days. The Spanish ships were bobbing at anchor like ducks, trapped between the treacherous mudflats of the 'Great Bog of Europe' and the guns of the English fleet.

The following day, Howard ordered eight fireships prepared and, on the stroke of midnight, with the wind behind them, they were released into the heart of the Spanish fleet. Brave Spaniards stationed on tugboats set in a defensive line managed to divert two of the burning, exploding vessels, with their guns firing hither and thither as the heat set off their ready-primed charges. But the other six came unwaveringly onward. There was panic in the ranks, anchor cables were cut, the winds and current dragged boats out of position, and the fleet scattered. By dawn, only five vessels, all ranged around the flagship, faced the entire English fleet.

The *San Juan* was in the thick of the fighting and, according to Montalbán, Lope de Vega's brother Francisco was hit by a bullet and died in his arms.[3] The essence of the battle is distilled in the personal account of the purser aboard the *San Salvador*. 'The enemy bombarded our flagship . . . for nine hours,' hitting 'the starboard flank' and:

the sails . . . more than two hundred times, killing and wounding many. Three pieces of artillery were smashed from their carriages and left useless. The rigging was ripped asunder and the galleon was so holed below the waterline that the two divers could hardly make the repairs with lead and caulking and the pumps were going day and night. The men were exhausted from setting the guns; they had been given nothing to eat.

The enemy did such damage to the galleons *San Mateo* and *San Felipe* that five of the starboard guns aboard the *San Felipe* were knocked off their carriages . . . [When] Don Francisco de Toledo saw his upper deck destroyed and that both his pumps had failed, he ordered grappling hooks to be thrown so as to board any vessel, calling the enemy to fight hand to hand. But they answered by inviting him to surrender under the rules of war. Then an Englishman with his sword and buckler called from the crow's nest: 'Hey, good soldiers, give yourselves up according to the rules of war we are offering.' Instead of responding, a musketeer shot him down in full view of everyone. Then the Maese de Campo ordered the musket and harquebus to fire. When the enemy saw this they retreated and our men called them cowards and chicken and heathens who should return to the battle.[4]

The defeat of the Armada has been convincingly explained as a consequence of the much greater manoeuvrability of the English ships, and their much superior firepower, largely due to better gun carriages which allowed for far more rapid reloading. The purser's story gives us a good sense of how during the battle the English simply pounded the Armada from a distance pretty much until they ran out of shot, while the Spaniards remained immobile, patching up the holes. But in reality the battle at Calais was a stalemate between a handful of ships, while the remainder of the Armada had escaped. In the final reckoning, the Spaniards were defeated not by the English but by the weather. As Montalbán wrote, 'the Fates awoke those tyrannical princes of Neptune's world, disastrous winds and a constant storm, with lamentable results, but which brought our Lope back to Madrid'.[5]

On 9 August, the wind changed direction, carrying the Spanish ships out of the shallows and into the stormy waters of the North Sea. The English were in pursuit, but whenever Howard gathered his ships for an assault, Medina Sidonia slowed to face them and the English wavered. The Spanish continued north into Scottish waters;

they threw their donkeys and oxen overboard to reduce the load, but the Armada was still more or less intact. As the fleet sailed into the North Atlantic, however, the damaged ships began to scatter; some foundered and many sought shelter on the Irish coast where English troops massacred the common soldiers and seamen and, like Barbary pirates, held the officers hostage so as to ransom them later.

On 21 September, in a brilliantly executed manoeuvre through a narrow gap in treacherous reefs, the *San Juan* and another ship took refuge in a sheltered sound at the south-west tip of Ireland. A reconnaissance party went ashore, but was immediately captured by a posse of English. Among the prisoners was a Portuguese seaman who described the conditions experienced by Lope as he was supposedly penning *Angelica's Beauty*. He might well have dreamed of angels!

The Portuguese 'says that out of the ship there died four or five every day of hunger and thirst', and 'eighty soldiers and twenty of the mariners are sick and do lie down to die daily'. 'The rest are very weak, and the Captain very sad and weak. There is left in this flagship but twenty-five pipes of wine, and very little bread, and no water but what they brought out of Spain, which stinketh marvellously, and the flesh they cannot eat, their drought is so great.'⁶ Soon afterwards, another vice-flagship arrived, but hopelessly crippled: 'All her sails were in shreds except the foresail. She cast her single anchor,' but when 'the tide waned . . . we could see that she was going down in an instant . . . She sank with all on board, not a person being saved, a most extraordinary and terrifying thing.'⁷

That same day, 21 September, the first ships began to struggle into Spanish harbours; slowly, the survivors trickled home over the following weeks. One hundred and eighty had died on the flagship alone. A monk at the Escorial described the 'strange emotion felt in all Spain for such a sad and notable disaster . . . and everyone dressed in mourning and there was nothing but tears and laments throughout the land'.⁸ But, although Philip II wept bitterly, he was phlegmatically defiant: 'I give thanks to God, whose generous hand has helped me with strength and troops, and will make it possible for me to raise another armada.'⁹ Even as he raised almost 50,000 ducats to help the sick and wounded, he banned the battered men from demobbing, raised taxes, seized bullion shipments, borrowed eleven million ducats and began rebuilding his navy.[10]

By June 1589, Cervantes had completed his commission and was in Seville, apparently rolling in money. He settled his substantial account with Tomás Gutiérrez and stood guarantor for a woman called Jerónima de Alarcón, who may or may not have been a lover.[11] His meagre backpay did not come close to covering those costs, and the most reasonable explanation is that, like every other tax collector at that time, he had worked the system, although one devoted biographer was convinced that he must have won it at cards.[12] He then disappears from history until the following year, when he submitted the Algiers Information to the Council of the Indies. But his petition failed again: a brief note made by the official who considered his application simply reads: 'Find something over here with which to reward him.' He went back to work as a taxman.

In December 1591, Cervantes was in the splendid seigneurial town of Montilla, close to Cordova, famous for its robust dry fino wine. There he must surely have called upon one of the most fascinating and exotic figures of sixteenth-century Spanish letters: 'El Inca' Garcilaso de la Vega.

'El Inca' Garcilaso was born Gómez Súarez de Figueroa, in 1539, at Cuzco, the Inca capital high up in the remote heart of the Andes, five years after Francisco Pizarro completed his conquest of Peru.[13] His mother was Chimpu Ocllo, a high-ranking *palla* or concubine of royal blood, niece of the last three ruling Inca emperors, whose palatial household was a meeting place for members of the deposed dynasty. 'They mostly talked of the history of their lineage,' he remembered, 'the greatness of their Empire, their conquests and deeds . . . But then they turned from the power and prosperity of the past to the present and wept for their dead sovereigns, their annexed empire and their lost republic. As a young lad I came and went while they conversed and I listened to them, entranced.'[14]

His father, Sebastián Garcilaso de la Vega y Vargas, was related to the dukes of Feria and Infantado, and was a second cousin of Garcilaso, the Prince of Poets. A brave soldier and politically astute, he rose to be a leading figure of the conquistador community at Cuzco. Although he baptized Chimpu Ocllo as Isabel Súarez, he kept her as a *palla* in the Inca fashion and they never married; instead, years later, he took a lowly Spanish wife. Long afterwards, Gómez, writing as 'El Inca', made his feelings felt in an anecdote he recorded about a large group of women who had come from Mexico to marry the wealthy conquistadors of Peru. Soon after they had arrived, one of the women, shocked at the men's war-ravaged aspect, asked: 'Are we meant to marry these rotten old men? They look like they have escaped from hell, all battered as they are, some lame, others crippled, others without ears, others with one eye or half their face missing, the luckiest of them is only slashed up two or three times.' Her friend put her straight: 'we are not marrying them for their beauty, but to inherit their Indians, for being old and worn out they are bound to die soon'. But that venial, ignoble advice from one plebeian Spanish girl to another was overheard by a venerable conquistador, who, 'El Inca' remembered, 'reprimanded the women, warned the other men and then went straight home, sent for a priest and married an Indian noblewoman by whom he already had two natural children'.[15] 'El Inca' Garcilaso the man clearly remembered with bitterness Gómez the boy's rancour at his father's betrayal.

When Gómez's father died, in 1559, he left his son 4,000 *pesos* to go to Spain and acquire an education. As the young man made preparations for this life-changing journey, he went to pay his respects to the incumbent *corregidor*, then writing a history of the Incas. The kindly official said: 'Well, if you are off to Spain, go into that room and you will see some of your ancestors whom I have recently brought to light.' There he found five mummified bodies, his own grandparents among them. 'The corpses were so complete that there was not a hair missing, nor an eyebrow, nor an eyelash. They were wearing the clothes they had worn in life, with nothing but the royal insignia on their royal headdresses, sitting as the Indians usually sit, with their hands crossed upon their breasts and their eyes looking down at the ground.'[16] With that potent image of his American royalty imprinted on his young mind, he set out for his father's continent, never to return.

The young Gómez arrived in Spain, in 1560, as a ward of his father's family and he was sent to live in the household of Alonso de Vargas, a decorated veteran of Charles V's campaigns in Flanders and Italy who had retired to Montilla and married an aristocratic heiress. In 1563, Gómez came of age and now adopted his father's name, calling himself Garcilaso de la Vega, to which he appended the sobriquet 'el Inca', as proud of his Andean royal blood as he was of his Castilian nobility. He served briefly under Don John of Austria during the Morisco uprisings in the Alpuarras of 1570, but then settled into a life of letters.[17] In 1588, he published a translation of the late medieval Jewish poet and philosopher Leo the Hebrew's *Dialogues of Love* out of Italian. At the same time, he was preparing his best-known work, *The Royal Commentaries of the Incas*, published in 1609, which quickly became the standard reference work for all students of the Inca Empire. It has perhaps done more than any other book to create the popular picture of what life was like in the Andes before Europeans came. Today, scholars have begun to question its reliability as a source and instead see it more as a work of propaganda, written by a man who, half Indian and half Spanish, was trying to reconcile these two cultures for his readers. He brought great European erudition to the task of translating his own very personal and particular vision of Inca culture and society for a western audience who had only the vaguest understanding of the New World. And so he turned to the literary models he found around him; he likened the Incas to the Romans, he drew on the Bible, on Renaissance histories and on chivalric romances to communicate his story of the Peruvian past.[18]

He was determined to romanticize a perfect, almost chivalric marriage between the Old World and the New, a union on equal terms, a matrimony of morals and shared ideals, to create a conjunction of two peoples who were caught in a sometimes clumsy, mostly violent courtship. Instead of rape and exploitation he sang a deliberately delusional hymn of destiny to Concordia, the classical goddess of harmony, and a powerful Christian ideal that all men are made in the image of the one and only God who had created the world for the purpose of harmony.[19] Garcilaso expressed this ideal of harmony between the American and European races most poetically in *The Florida of the Inca*, which he was in the midst of writing when

Cervantes was in Montilla and which was published in 1604, a few weeks before the first part of *Don Quixote* came off the presses.

The Florida is ostensibly a history of Hernando de Soto's disastrous attempt to settle the American south-east between 1538 and 1540. Soto was an enormously symbolic figure for Garcilaso because he had been Pizarro's right-hand man during the conquest of Peru. He had returned to Spain fabulously wealthy and was made Governor General of 'La Florida', a then boundless world that theoretically encompassed the whole of the modern United States. But when he went to claim that prize, his vast army was defeated by a lack of food, a woeful sense of geography and ferociously hostile Indians.

Unlike the many personal chronicles of camaraderie, bravery and hardship, *The Florida* is masterful Renaissance storytelling, eclectically embracing elements of chivalric romance, the picaresque, the epic and the nascent novella or short story. It is filled with the kind of literary flourishes that Cervantes played with so successfully, asking us to marvel, almost in disbelief, before grounding us with the pathos of some nitty-gritty detail from the realities of life.[20]

The narrative has a clear symmetry: almost like the phases of the moon herself, that mother of the Inca tradition, the chapters slowly wax in size and importance, reaching a bright, shining climax before waning into the darkness of the expedition's failure. As Soto and his men move north through Georgia, they hear of a mighty, wealthy Indian queen called Cofachiqui and go in search of her marvellous land. Finally they arrive, separated from their goal only by a river; they meet her ambassadors; they wait, as Cortés had done as he bore down on Mexico. And, as Cortés had done, Soto awaits a response from the ruler. She arrives accompanied by eight Indian noblewomen and crosses the river by boat, 'like Cleopatra when she greeted Mark Antony'.

'As soon as the young princess approached General Soto, she paid him her compliments and sat down on a throne they had brought for her.' She offered abundant food and assistance to the Spaniards. And then Garcilaso tells us that 'Soto replied that he was under the greatest obligations to her and that her offers were more than he merited.' The great Hernando de Soto, conquistador of Peru, then one of the richest men in Christendom, is seen here making obeisance to an Indian woman; he does not assert the rights of the Spanish Crown, nor does he proclaim Christianity, but behaves as a vassal doing homage. And Garcilaso 'the Inca' titillates his readers with a vivid rendering of the scene:

> As the Lady of Cofachiqui was discussing these matters with the Governor, she slowly unwound a great string of pearls the size of cobnuts which went thrice about her neck and hung down to her thighs. She took them off slowly and deliberately, all the time that they were speaking, and then, with the pearls in her hand, she stood up so as to personally give them to the Governor from her own hands, and he stretched out his own hand to accept them; then he gave the Lady of Cofachiqui a gold ring set with a beautiful ruby straight from his own finger as a symbol of their peace and friendship; and the great queen took it with great grace and placed it on her own finger.[21]

As much succumbing to the temptation of inventing his own parents' marriage as being seduced by Renaissance narrative norms, Garcilaso, in this sexually charged centrepiece of *The Florida*, conjures up those classic European representations of America in the visual arts as a sultry indigenous beauty luxuriating on the shores of plenty.

It was the kind of rich admixture of fact and fiction upon which Cervantes thrived, produced by one of the most intriguing writers of his age. Garcilaso's *Florida* has long been treated as a work of history, albeit over-embellished and unreliable, but in reality it might be better described as the first thoroughly politicized historical novel. Such a psychologically complex character and fellow conquistador in the world of literary fiction cannot have failed to attract Cervantes. What is more, we know that when Cervantes arrived in Montilla in 1590, Garcilaso was preparing to escape from the tiny town and move to nearby Cordova, drawn to the coterie of literary figures gathering around his aunt's nephew, Luis de Góngora, with whom we know he had business dealings.[22] It is surely inconceivable that these lovers of literature would not have met. And it is pretty to think of Cervantes, Garcilaso and Góngora breaking bread together, eating the little spicy, steamed snails so typical of the region, and drinking the rich and heady Montilla fino wine still made there today.

In 1592, in Seville, Cervantes accepted a commission to write six plays. But then disaster struck: the new *corregidor* of Écija ordered him to 'return and restitute . . . three hundred *fanegas* of wheat he had requisitioned for the galleys on His Majesty's account but which he sold without authority' and to 'sign Crown warrants in payment for the ten *fanegas* of wheat and six of barley he had received', while 'the hundred *reales* he paid himself as salary . . . must be returned unless they already appear in his accounts'.[23] Philip II had ordered a crackdown on the endemic corruption among his tax gatherers; at least five of them would be condemned to the gallows.

Although Cervantes was arrested and briefly imprisoned at Castro del Río, he was free within days and back at work in Écija and Marchena, requisitioning olive oil. But it was a foretaste of a far more serious dispute that brought an end to his career as a taxman, during which he was held in the notorious Royal Prison in Seville.

Now an experienced tax collector, Cervantes agreed a new contract with the Crown to collect unpaid back taxes from a series of provincial towns around the Kingdom of Granada. It had long been a troubled region, a borderland between Christendom and the remains of Spanish Islam. Don John of Austria's brutal suppression of the Moorish rebellions in the Alpujarras mountains, in 1568 and 1570, had brought a kind of peace. But most of the Moriscos were expelled to other parts of Spain and their land given to poor peasants from remote valleys in the north. When Pedro de León visited this area at the same time Cervantes was collecting taxes, he found a dysfunctional world of abject poverty and social deprivation. In his account of his preaching mission to the Valley of Lecrín and the Granada coast in 1592, he describes 'the most needy settlements in the world' inhabited by Christian migrants who were mostly 'absconded criminals with evil ways . . . murderers and thieves, brutal low-lifes, wastrels of evil mien, who would not even let their neighbours' fruit ripen on the vine before stealing it'. He described an infamous curate 'who murdered a married man so as to live with his widow' and lamented that by contrast the Moriscos had been 'trustworthy to a man and would not even steal a chestnut'.[24]

Cervantes travelled through this Godforsaken landscape with the improbable task of raising over 2.5 million *maravedís*; but, slowly, almost miraculously, he managed to collect the tax due. He deposited most of the money with a Seville banker and set out for Madrid to present his accounts. But he seems to have had an unlucky star, and disaster struck yet again: first, the banker went bankrupt and the money could not be recovered until 1597; then, worse still, the royal accountants made an elementary mistake in their book-keeping and so accused Cervantes of owing the Crown 92,307 *maravedís* in addition to what he had actually collected. They ordered a Seville magistrate to arrest him and secure surety for the sum before remanding him to Madrid, but the clerk who filled out the order compounded their mistake by recording a figure of 2.5 million *maravedís* as the sum to be assured. Clearly no one could guarantee such a huge amount and so the magistrate threw Cervantes into the notorious Royal Prison.

Seville had five principal jails. Although life in these institutions must have seemed like an unearthly incarceration in some circle of hell for many prisoners, punishment was not the primary purpose of these prisons. In Cervantes's day, only the criminal clergy and other religious were locked up as a form of penance and as a means to reform. Instead, jails existed to prevent the escape of a whole mix of inmates such as debtors, defendants remanded for trial and convicts awaiting the execution of their sentences.

By far the most important of these jails was the Royal Prison, which received 18,000 prisoners every year, an astonishing 21 per cent of the officially registered residents of the city and 11 per cent or more of the likely total population, and which always had more than 1,800 inmates at any one time.[25] It stood imposingly at the end of the Plaza San Francisco, the main square of Seville, with the sparkling new City Hall standing to the right and the Palace of the Audiencia with its own lock-up to the left. Today, a narrow alley still called Entrecárceles, 'Between-jails', is evidence of where these buildings stood.

The newly arrived prisoners entered by the main door, known to the inmates as the Golden Gate, which gave on to a kind of reception area blocked off at the other end by the Iron Gate, which allowed access to the main part of the jail. It was called the Golden Gate because at this stage those who could afford the fees could pay 'no mean quantity of Gold' to 'stay in the sheriff's accommodation, which is up the stairs on the right', according to Father León.[26] The accommodation was relatively comfortable, with its own roof terrace, and such inmates were largely free to come and go and many were given leave to sleep at home. But most prisoners, Cervantes among them, were led through the Iron Gate by the doorman, who shouted out their crimes so they could be held in the relevant sections, each named with grim irony: 'Blasphemers' was reserved for blasphemers and gamblers, 'Business' for thieves, 'Pleasure' was 'where the ruffians boast of their deeds', 'Yard-Arm' held the galley-slaves, 'Market' was for the fences, 'Greed' for embezzlers and 'Labyrinth' was the name for the area where they kept the career felons with a hand in any and every crime.[27]

Beyond the Iron Gate was the final door, the Silver Gate, where for a ducat or two a prisoner could have his shackles removed. But during the day all the gates seem to have been kept open because of the steady stream of 'men and women who, like ants, come and go with food and bedding and to speak to the prisoners'.[28] And 'anyone who dares to escape is unlikely to be stopped unless his face is well known' to the guards. Many a new prisoner would keep his head down for a fortnight or so and then simply walk out as though he were a visitor, while some more familiar characters who feared being recognized dressed up as women and escaped that way.[29]

In fact the most striking thing about the Royal Prison is how similar it was to the world outside. The Silver Gate gave on to the passage-ways running around the prison yard, a space about 100 feet square, with a large water fountain in the middle with six spouts. Rather like the central square of a small market town, this space was overlooked by galleries, allowing access to the cells, while at ground level there were two taverns, two food stalls and shops selling vegetables, fruit, vinegar, olive oil and, all important in so bureaucratic an environment, paper and ink. These businesses were rented out to entrepreneurs for as much as fourteen or fifteen *reales* per day.

Men passed the day gambling, drinking, arguing and discussing their futures; from time to time they organized their fiestas, when the fiddles, drums and tambourines sounded while the revellers clapped out the rhythm, sang and danced. Fights were continually breaking out, mostly involving the *valientes* or professional thugs and toughs and their gangs who ran prison life. 'There is a species of human in Seville', wrote one contemporary, 'who seem neither Christian, nor Moor, nor Gentile, but whose religion is the adoration of the goddess Bravado.'[30] They took pride in the severity of their sentences, but it was customary among these ruffians to force other prisoners to paint rudimentary donor portraits on their cell walls showing them kneeling piously before an image of Christ. But when one notorious *valiente* saw that the artist had depicted him wearing long trousers, he threatened to kill him and would only calm down after the picture had been adjusted to show him wearing breeches: the uniform of the professional crook consisted of yellow breeches, a fashionably slashed doublet open at the neck, a chunky rosary for a belt, a bracelet and necklace of amber, a dagger, yellow ties in their boots, and sporting a tattoo of a heart in carnation red.

While brawls could happen at any time and for almost any reason, major confrontations were almost an organized sport. The *valientes* and their gangs made their way to the yard concealing beneath their cloaks a vicious arsenal of hardened pointed sticks (which they called shepherds), knives and swords. Others armed themselves with jugs and cooking pots, whatever came to hand. These brawls were usually quickly broken up by the Sheriff and his men and the injured and dying were rushed to the prison infirmary, where they were attended by a permanent barber-surgeon who lived with his wife and family within the prison precinct. As the victims of organized violence were brought in, the constables tried to make them identify their assailants; but there was great honour among these *valientes*. One lawyer remembered witnessing a man so deeply wounded near the kidneys 'that the surgeon's hand fit into it', but when they sent a notary to take a statement, the victim asked: 'What business is this of yours? Did I send for you? I've no idea if I'm wounded or not, for I can't see any wound. If you can see a wound, then write down that you saw a wounded man with whom the law has no business at all for he is one of His Majesty's galley-slaves.'

In one corner of the yard were the latrines, which consisted of a huge cesspool surrounded by stone steps and covered with vaults supported on marble columns. The human waste of all 1,800 prisoners accumulated here and had to be dug out every couple of months. The poorest prisoners charged a small fee for use of the stepping stones they set up at the entrance to this unimaginably foul place. But, for all its filth, many inmates would 'escape a whipping' from the guards 'by immersing themselves in the sewage up to their necks and then riotously throwing handfuls of that evil muck at the jailer and his lackeys'. This tactic was temporarily very effective, resulting in a stand-off that lasted until the fugitives could bear the filth no longer. The newly arrived visitor might have seen one of these men 'stripped naked and washing himself off beneath one of the water spouts of the fountain in the yard'.[31]

The lavatory attendants were the lowest creatures in the prison hierarchy, and there were many other less repellent ways that prisoners could earn money in this brutal market place. There was a thriving trade in old clothes, many of them stolen and then smuggled out to the cheap 'Baratillo' market outside the walls. A number of prisoners made a paltry living as guides, helping lawyers and other visitors find the men they were looking for by shouting out their names at the top of their voices, so loudly, León complained, that the fathers often found it difficult to hear a man's confession.[32]

Literate prisoners were in great demand as letter writers, receiving fees for composing love letters and even poetry.[33] Cervantes must have done a roaring trade; and, intriguingly, in the Prologue to *Don Quixote*, he asked his readers to consider: 'What else could my barren and uncultivated imagination have dreamed up other than this dry and walnut-shrivelled progeny, impetuous and filled with such a variety of unheard of ideas, much like someone sired in a jail, where every discomfort has its place and every sad sound makes its home?'[34]

The final decade of Philip II's reign was a desperately grim period in Castilian history. Modern historians, in their arguments over whether there really was a 'Decline of Spain' at all, have tended to see the rot set in during these years. Contemporaries were similarly gloomy, as well they might have been. God had forsaken Castile's quintes-sentially Catholic crusade, the Invincible Armada, in 1588; in 1596, Protestant English 'pirates' again raided Cadiz; and as the turn of a new century drew near, Spaniards developed the habit of greeting one another with words pregnant with dread: 'May God save you from the plague spreading down from Castile, and the hunger coming up from Andalusia.' The phrase is recorded in the first major picaresque novel, *Guzmán de Alfarache*, written by Mateo Alemán, who delivered his manuscript to the printers in 1597. He was well placed to write about the low life of Spain. The son of the official physician at the Seville jail and a former official at the Treasury, he had written a report about the mercury mines at Almadén which were worked by convicts and which he described as being run with inhuman brutality by the great German bankers, the Fuggers.

The long, two-part *Guzmán de Alfarache* is the fictional autobi-ography of a reformed *pícaro* or picaroon, a word used to describe the thousands of petty criminals and ragamuffins who seemed to be overrunning Spain at the end of the sixteenth century, and from which we get the word 'picaresque'. Writing from aboard a galley where he has been enslaved as punishment for his crimes, Guzmán recalls the story of his life, from his illicit conception in a market garden by the banks of the Guadalquivir at Seville to his eventual imprisonment. The congenial account of a young lad's attempt to make his way in a relentlessly tough but often enjoyable and colourful world is inter-woven with long sermon-like passages heavily overburdened with Christian moralizing. The book, which was hugely successful, is very much of its time. At the moment when the modern novel was begin-ning to emerge as a literary form in Spain, reaching maturity with the publication of *Don Quixote* over the coming decade or so, there is much about *Guzmán* that feels like a novel, most of all the focus on the psychology of a fictional central character set within a vividly real-istic contemporary world. But it also engages with a rising sense of uncertainty that was then beginning to trouble a new generation of Spaniards whose parents and grandparents had grown up supremely confident that their kingdom was a political, financial and military powerhouse at the centre of the world.

When Philip II died on 13 September 1598, Castile still felt itself
to be powerful, but voices of dissent and doubt were beginning to be
raised in the taverns and the salons. Those concerns were inscribed
into a new kind of political literature written by commentators
known as *arbitristas* who, almost like modern bloggers, offered
social and political advice and criticism to the Crown in long tracts
printed for public consumption. Faced with the uncertainty of a new
century and a new ruler, the kingdoms of Spain went into a trance-
like state of celebratory mourning. Within the cavernous Cathedral
in Seville, a vast but temporary monument was put together by
carpenters and plasterers, which reached the roof in layer upon
layer of Baroque flamboyance. Great poets and painters contributed
images and verses. Cervantes, who had finally cleared his name and
was out of jail, attached his own tribute to this ephemeral structure
which seemed to symbolize Spain's terrible descent from greatness
into an underworld of grandiose pretensions and an obsession with
appearance.

By God the terrifying enormity of it!
I'd give a doubloon for words to describe it,
Who can but marvel at such amazing artifice, such wealth and beauty?
Christ alive! Every bit is worth a million,
What a waste if it does not last a century!
Oh Seville, noble spirit of triumphant Rome!
I'll wager that our dead man's soul
Has abandoned eternal heavenly grace
To gaze with pleasure on this place.
A gallant heard me say so:
'The truth, Sir!
'You speak the truth, my man!
'To deny it would be to lie.'
And with that,
He donned his hat,
Gripped his sword,
Glanced this way and that,
And was off, leaving naught.[35]

II

GLITTER

Prologue

In 1610, Gaspar Pérez de Villagrá published his epic poem *The History of New Mexico*, which tells the story of his participation in the settlement of the Upper Rio Grande.[1] The expedition had left northern Mexico under the command of Juan de Oñate in 1598 and established the first city of the Province of Nueva México at San Juan de los Caballeros on 8 September, five days before Philip II died in agony at the Escorial. Today, among the oldest European settlements in the modern USA, San Juan is at the heart of Pueblo Indian country, not far from Taos, where the longest continuously inhabited towns and villages in North America are still lived in by Indians who have been there since time immemorial. There are still corners of this part of the world that feel more like Spain than the United States, and many here pride themselves on their Spanish heritage. The establishment of the remote and impoverished colony of New Mexico was the geographical zenith of imperial expansion, after which Habsburg Spain made no more great conquests or discoveries. It marks the very limits of Spanish imperialism, a final distant conquest of a land and its people at the very edge of the world.

Villagrá set out to tell the story of Oñate's expedition in the spirit of Homer or Virgil, but he was more interested in historical facts than he was an able practitioner of poetic technique and sometimes even interrupted his verse to transcribe passages from some document he felt important. Modern scholars consider his poem to be a largely reliable historical source, but the veracity of his story is less important than the surprising sentiment of national identity he creates for himself and his companions as the poem takes some extremely unexpected twists which reveal the way people living at the very frontiers of the Empire were beginning to feel about themselves.

The poem begins, predictably enough, with a generic picture of conquest and Empire, filled with a strong sense of Christianity and the figures of brave Spaniards, underpinned by references to the monarchy and Philip III's sovereignty:[2]

> I sing of heroes, courage, arms and valour,
> Of brave men who won the West for Spain
> And found there a hidden world, *Plus Ultra*,
> To be claimed for thee, most Christian King,
> Philip o' Spain, holy Phoenix of New Mexico.

But then, as he recounted the momentous departure of Oñate's army from Spanish lands in northern Mexico, instead of lengthy passages alluding to classical mythology and ancient European legends, Villagrá revealed himself to be much more concerned with Aztec history and the mythology of the Mexica ruling class who had founded Tenochtitlán, Mexico City, and who believed that long ago, many generations before the arrival of the first Spaniards, they had come south from the territories that Oñate's army was about to enter:

> From that region, 'tis well known, came forth
> Ancient Mexicans, founders of their eternal city,
> Like Romulus, who traced out the walls of Rome.

> As we struck camp on the frontier of the North,
> Our Aztec allies spoke of ancient images they keep,
> Hieroglyphic histories which recall lineage and descent
> From two valiant, vigorous brothers, filled with brio,
> Whose blood ran royal and noble, the sons of kings,
> Who escaped the harsh depths of their ancestral cave,
> To seek glory and reputation abroad in foreign lands.
> By both the force of arms and the talk of peace,
> They brought lofty lords and kings into obeisance,
> Subjecting them as vassals of a vast and mighty Empire.

Villagrá's perspective was almost more Aztec than Catholic, certainly more American than Spanish or European; indeed, he appropriated pre-Columbian cultural tradition in much the same way that Mexican nationalism would do in the nineteenth century. But, far more surprising than this geographic chauvinism, he then turned his attention to the ancestry of the expedition's leaders. He begins with Hernán Cortés, Marquis of the Valley of Oaxaca:

> The great Marquis of the Valley begat a daughter
> By a princess, one of three girls to Montezuma born,
> Last of those ancient Kings of Mexico to rule his lands.
> The Marquis married this rich prize to Juan de Tolosa,
> Who with two others had found such abundant silver.

Tolosa had discovered the rich silver deposits at Zacatecas in the Sierra Madre of northern Mexico and subjugated the Indian population to Spanish rule alongside the Governor Cristóbal de Oñate, who was, we soon learn:

> Father of Don Juan de Oñate, he who wed
> The great-granddaughter of the Aztec King,
> By whom his own son Cristóbal was born,
> Descendant of the Marquis and all these kings,
> And who, not yet ten years old, sallied with us
> To serve in our conquests like young Hannibal.

Villagrá's determination to explain the Oñate family genealogy in verse makes for confusion as well as poetic inelegance. But clearly what was important to him was that Juan de Oñate had married Cortés's half-Aztec granddaughter and that therefore his own son, named Cristóbal after his grandfather, was descended not just from the great conquistador Cortés, but also from the Aztec Emperor Montezuma himself. He was both Spanish and Indian, noble and royal; and so, among the founders of New Mexico, there was a boy with imperial Aztec blood, returning to the legendary homeland of his ancestors.

This monumentally aggrandizing account of the expedition personnel forcefully expresses a sense of imperial expansion into the American south-west as the work of men born in the New World and who had made their fortunes there. Cortés, Cristóbal de Oñate and Villagrá's own father had all been born in Spain, but Villagrá, like Juan de Oñate, was a child of Mexico. Such men were proud that Aztec blood coursed through the veins of Juan's young son Cristóbal; they were no longer true Spaniards but *criollos* or creoles and so they named their discoveries after their homeland: every land or province conquered in the sixteenth century had been given an old Spanish place name – New Spain, New Granada, New León, Castilla de Oro (Golden Castile) – but these conquistadors called their promised land New *Mexico*.

Just as Garcilaso de la Vega, El Inca, was doing at more or less the same time in his histories of Peru and Florida, Villagrá, in his *History of New Mexico*, was writing from a heart that was as much American as European, a heart that beat in the New World not the Old. This is compelling testimony that people who were born and raised amid the cultural and genetic variety of the American colonies were becoming more and more psychologically detached and temperamentally remote from Spain. The strength of their *criollo* identity is all the more remarkable when we consider that Villagrá had been sent to university at Salamanca, while Garcilaso, of course, lived most of his life in Cordova. In their hearts and minds they were clearly Americans, their sense of pride, honour and glory was rooted in the land of their birth and the people who inhabited it. Villagrá's use of the epic poetry of the Old World to explain the New World to a European audience for whom the realities of the Americas often seemed like something out of chivalric fiction or classical mythology is a fascinating early essay at bridging a widening cultural divide.

The brilliant, irreverent, ever polemical Vine Deloria Jr once recalled that when he was Executive Director of the National Congress of American Indians, 'it was a rare day when some white didn't visit my office and proudly proclaim that he or she was of Indian descent. Eventually I came to understand their need to identify as partially Indian.' But, he observed, 'all but one person I met who claimed

Indian blood claimed it on their grandmother's side.' After all, 'a male ancestor has too much of the aura of the savage', about him; while, on the other hand, 'a young Indian princess? Ah, there was royalty for the taking. Somehow the white was linked with a noble house of gentility and culture if his grandmother was an Indian princess. And royalty has always been an unconscious but all-consuming goal of the European immigrant.'[3]

The first half of the seventeenth century was a time of unusually great upheaval around the world, a period of major climate change known as the Little Ice Age that caused crop failures, famine and demographic collapse.[4] In Europe, the Thirty Years' War lasted from 1618 to 1648, the first major conflict to draw in the whole continent as well as the Ottoman Empire. Historians have fiercely debated the idea of a 'Decline of Spain' during this period and there is no question that the Spanish Crown all but disappeared as a European power, giving way to French ascendancy under Louis XIV. But this is also a period that literary critics and art historians think of as the culmination and zenith of the Spanish Golden Age, when a concentration of exceptionally talented cultural figures produced a dazzling array of brilliant and beautiful things; an Age of Gold had given way to an Age of Glitter.[5] For centuries, this decline of the Spanish Crown was explained in terms of the human failings of first Philip III and then Philip IV, weak rulers who left the business of government to their corrupt and ambitious favourites or *validos*, the Duke of Lerma and the Count-Duke of Olivares,[6] while more recently economic historians have looked at the question of the Decline of Spain in terms of the changing economy of the Empire and a collapse in trade with the Indies.[7]

In 1600, the colonial economy of the Indies was almost wholly based on the export of precious metals to Spain in exchange for wine, olive oil, grain, tools, clothing, African slaves, paper, ink, paintings and the ships to transport them, all of which were imported from the mother kingdom. But the colonial economy depended on Indian labour and agriculture, which it had co-opted through the system of *encomiendas* by which indigenous American social and political groups were reorganized to pay tribute to Spanish masters. As the mining sector grew, that hybrid American colonial and Indian economy expanded. So, by 1650, some 160,000 people were living at Potosí, the vast mining centre in the Viceroyalty of Peru, where the ore was so concentrated that pure silver could almost be scooped out of the ground. Local supply chains spread for hundreds, even thousands of miles; the cultivation of grapes, sugar, wheat and olives developed along the Peruvian coast. Peruvian merchants began importing grain from Mexico, which was also producing sugar, ceramics and furniture for its own markets. Mexico also produced cochineal for export to Spain and became the centre of commerce for the China trade, importing spices, silks, fine porcelains and ivories.[8]

The character of this new economy was defined by the fast-growing colonial population, who began to identify themselves as *criollos* and as distinct from Spaniards. The figures are far from reliable, but with as many as 4,000 Spaniards a year emigrating legally to the Americas and many undocumented arrivals from Spain and elsewhere, the European population of the New World increased five-fold, from about 120,000 in 1570 to 650,000 in 1650, making it about the same size as Catalonia, Aragon and Valencia combined. Over the same period, the combined population of Africans and mixed-race *castas* or 'castes' grew similarly from 230,000 to 1.3 million, roughly the same as the population of Portugal at that time.[9]

But by far the single most important story in the history of colonial Spanish America is the near destruction of the indigenous populations and their cultures. Many were massacred by conquistadors, many were worked to death in the silver mines and sugar mills. With their traditions and culture terribly crippled, many lost the will to procreate; many died of despair, of alcoholism and suicide. Some must have fled to areas not controlled by Spaniards, others had children by Europeans or Africans and so their descendants became part of the *casta* society. But the vast majority were slaughtered by European diseases such as smallpox, measles, typhus, plague and influenza, to which they had no natural immunity, while mumps may have made as much as a third of the adult male population sterile.[10]

Year after year, decade after decade, the indigenous population of one part of America or another was ravaged by innumerable epidemics.

An indigenous Mexican source described the symptoms of sickness when 'plague and death' came to his homeland in the 1540s: 'blood spouted from the victims' mouths and eyes, their noses and anuses. It killed very many people and many noble men and women.' And then, finally, 'wild dogs and hungry coyotes came into the town of Chalco to eat the dead'.[11] The following decade, in Bogotá, the sick 'swelled up until their skin looked like damask silk', and 'worms and maggots went in through their noses, mouths and other orifices and crowded into their bodies'.[12] 'So it was that we became orphans,' the *Annals of Cakchiquels* lament, for 'we were born to die!'[13]

Accurate figures for the population of the Americas before the arrival of Europeans do not exist and so it is impossible to know the extent of the demographic destruction. But a current widely accepted estimate is that numbers of indigenous Americans collapsed by 95 per cent in the first century or two after the arrival of Columbus.[14] Such devastation requires no exact quantification to understand that it had enormous economic as well as social significance. With the new society of *criollos*, newcomers and *castas* growing fast, there were, to put it bluntly and simply, too many colonial *caciques* and not enough Indians.

These massive changes taking place in the Americas affected trans-Atlantic commerce, so that recorded trade between Spain and the Indies seems to have peaked in 1610 and then gone into sharp decline. Although figures for bullion raised through taxation and remitted directly to the Crown held up shakily into the 1640s, these too collapsed dramatically from then on.[15]

The Habsburgs' American geese, it seemed, were beginning to lay many fewer golden eggs. Moreover, those eggs were ever less valuable. Groundbreaking research carried out almost a century ago by an American scholar called Earl J. Hamilton demonstrated that the vast quantities of precious metals pouring into Spain caused massive inflation. In Castile, commodity prices rose by roughly three times during the sixteenth century and then began to fluctuate wildly during the first half of the seventeenth century, although on average they remained more or less the same.[16] As a result, the relative purchasing power of the silver that the Crown received from the Americas during the reigns of Philip III and Philip IV was much less than it had been a generation or two earlier.

With the true value of the all-important source of liquidity falling, the Spanish Crown resorted to raising levels of ordinary taxation that hurt Castile and to adopting a series of extraordinary measures that did even more damage. The most obvious was the repeated devaluation of the copper-based coinage known as *vellón* that was used as everyday currency throughout Castile. The result of such devaluation, needless to say, was the hoarding of silver and the forging of *vellón*, and terrible disruption to the economy because the day-to-day pricing and purchase of life's essentials became uncertain and risky.[17]

There was a silver lining of sorts to these ominous clouds of *vellón* inflation, literally, for the unreliability of *vellón* greatly increased the demand for pure bullion, which must have helped to prevent the average value of the silver during the period from collapsing altogether. But if this benefited the Crown on the one hand because it supported the purchasing power of Crown silver, on the other hand it was one further reason among many for merchants and other private individuals to hang on to their silver by hook or by crook.

To make matters much worse still, in years when the amount of Crown treasure unloaded at Seville fell short of expectations or requirements, the governments of Philip III and IV repeatedly confiscated the privately owned imports of treasure and compensated the merchants to whom it belonged with *vellón* or *juros*. This was disastrous. The merchants responded by investing more of their silver in the growing economy of the Americas and by resorting to massive levels of trans-Atlantic fraud.

Undeclared goods and bullion had always been smuggled across the Atlantic, mostly to Spain, but also abroad; in the first half of the seventeenth century that once small-time illicit traffic now became a massive problem. Of course, the level of fraud is, by its clandestine nature, impossible to assess, but there is every reason to think that the Spanish Crown now lost control of the Indies trade almost completely, and largely because of fraud. One reasonably credible assessment is that, from the 1630s on, in some years well over three-quarters of the treasure shipped across the Atlantic by private individuals went unrecorded and that in most years the proportion was over half.[18]

It has usually been thought that much of this illegal commerce went directly abroad, bypassing Spain altogether. As the ships approached the Spanish coast, treasure was unloaded on to lighter vessels that sailed straight to France and beyond. But Gibraltar also seems to have been an important centre for smuggling, and that suggests that while plenty of silver must unquestionably have been spirited abroad, much of it must surely have been imported into Spain illegally. This makes sense. Major commercial systems do not change easily; the web of relationships, the familiarity of routes and practices that make up their structure are organically conservative. In other words, such is the force of habit that merchants preferred to continue to trade as they had always done; it was just that now this trade was conducted illegally and went unrecorded so as to evade exorbitant and unpredictable levels of taxation and confiscation. In fact, that relatively healthy black economy helps to explain how Philip IV's administration remained militarily potent for almost half a century despite recorded figures that suggest it should have been utterly bankrupt. This clandestine wealth also explains why bankers continued to lend money against the right to raise taxes locally in Spain, why the economy could sustain those taxes and why it survived the pernicious effects of *vellón* manipulation.

And so, where the first part of this book told a history very much underpinned by the power of the Spanish Crown and the central importance of the monarchs Charles V and Philip II themselves, the second part will tell a story during which the power of the Spanish Crown declined both at home and abroad, even as many Spaniards prospered.

As death approached, it had become increasingly obvious to Philip II that the Habsburg Empire had become unmanageably large and that the Netherlands were a problem that needed a local solution as much as Spanish intervention. He settled on a double marriage alliance that would unite Philip III to Margaret of Austria, granddaughter of his uncle Ferdinand, and his beloved daughter the Infanta Isabel Clara Eugenia to the Archduke Albert, son of the Emperor Maximilian II. Philip would rule in Spain, while Isabel would inherit the sovereignty of the Spanish Netherlands, which was to be administered by Albert on her behalf.

In 1599, Philip III and the Infanta travelled to Valencia with an entourage of 600 aristocrats adorned in 'gold, diamonds, pearls and gems' and accompanied by 'innumerable pages, lackeys and servants' to meet Albert and his stern and pious sister, Margaret of Austria, who was to be Philip's queen.[19] The fiestas began in nearby Denia, seat of the marquisate of Francisco Sandoval y Rojas, Philip's *valido*, soon to be elevated to the title of Duke of Lerma. That great rascal playwright Lope de Vega was there in the service of his patron, the future Count of Lemos, himself in Lerma's entourage. Later that year, Lope's *Fiestas of Denia* was published in Madrid, a long narrative poem in praise of the party.

On 19 February the King and Infanta entered Valencia. The city was resplendent, overflowing with royalty and courtiers, all in gregarious and celebratory mood, eagerly looking forward to the double royal wedding. Two days later, the King and his Gentlemen of the Chamber wore masks and fancy dress and went out into the streets to join the carnival crowds. Then, on Shrove Tuesday, Lope himself took centre stage for a comic pageant.

The King's drummers and trumpeters led out two masked riders, the first of whom was soon recognized as Lope, personifying the character of Carnival. 'He was dressed all in red like an Italian clown, with a long black cloak and a velvet cap. He was seated upon a mule, with a host of succulent animals hanging from the saddle: hares, partridges and chickens,' all foods prohibited during the coming weeks of Lent. And his companion, one of the King's jesters, came dressed as a fish to play the part of Lent, 'wearing a headpiece of wooden rings from which eels, bass and salted sardines hung down'. And, as the actors passed the royal palace, Lope addressed Philip and the Infanta Isabel, first in Italian, celebrating the double marriage and then reciting a beautiful ballad in Castilian, which lasted half an hour. And, as the great Lope rode off side by side with the court buffoon, 'the spectators died laughing'.[20]

Amid the exuberant atmosphere, Lope fell in love. Instead of accompanying the royal party to Denia for the reception of Margaret of Austria, he remained in Valencia, where he sired a child called Fernando, who later became a Franciscan preacher.²¹ Ironically enough, he also devoted his time with equal fruitfulness to composing an allegorical religious drama, *The Marriage of the Soul to Divine Love*, to be played in the main square of Valencia during the festivities celebrating Philip and Margaret's wedding, which took place on 18 April, after the end of Lent.

Philip II had tried to prepare his son, Philip III, for government: he made him sit almost daily, from the age of fifteen, on the Council of State, which dealt with foreign affairs; he had him attend meetings of other councils, including Philip's own private and very influential para-governmental executive the Junta de Noche, the Night Cabinet. Philip had thought that while the boy might not understand the complexities of the system, he would at least come to know the ministers and secretaries by seeing them in action.²² So when he succeeded to the throne, at the age of twenty, Philip III had considerable experience of his father's government in action, and what he had actually seen and heard were reports of a kingdom in trouble and an old King who was constantly overwhelmed by paperwork. The defining feature of his father's rule had been an obsession with the disembodied information contained in the reams of documents by which the King interacted with the world from his desk. The boy had looked on as the father tried to assimilate the immense weight and scope of his responsibilities by abstracting them into the virtual world of paper, pen and ink. Yet the old man's experience of reality was staggeringly parochial; away from his desk, he retreated into the easy domesticity of family life, hunting, jousting, his architectural projects and his piety.

So Philip III *may* largely have abandoned this virtual, verbal vision of Empire because he was simply 'the laziest king in Spanish history', but it seems more likely that he sensed that the administration now largely ran itself and so with youthful impatience he felt like a futile element in the process.²³ For a young man born to absolute kingship to discover his relative impotence must have been a bewildering disillusionment, all the more so because his father had seemed to live that lie. What is more, an isolated office in the Escorial was no place for a young man, and the night was no time to be locked away with his government ministers. Philip III wanted to feel his kingship with each of his five senses.

Although, on his succession, Philip III most obviously abdicated responsibility for the dreary day-to-day stewardship of the government to his *valido*, the Duke of Lerma, he also dispensed with the intimate Junta de Noche and devolved power to a much expanded Council of State, which he packed with aristocrats, and to a series of further councils or *juntas* that ran different aspects of the government. A Polish diplomat, in Madrid in 1611, was amazed that 'although the kings of Spain have absolute power, they do nothing and will sign nothing without consulting their Councils, they will not make up their own minds about even the most trivial matters of public interest'. Both Philip and Lerma rarely attended council meetings themselves and only occasionally rejected their councils' advice; mostly, the state was allowed to run itself while Lerma, a deeply Machiavellian mandarin, acquired wealth for himself and exerted influence through tacit understandings and veiled threats made in palace corridors. Instead of ruling, Philip focused on forging a theatrical role for himself as a flamboyantly public monarch by which his subjects could see him reigning: the Pole observed that 'from Corpus Christi [19 May] until the Feast of the Assumption [15 August], the King appeared in public and at church every day and in the afternoons attended the processions at which the Holy Sacrament was shown'.[24]

Philip II's decision to undo the crucial union of the Netherlands and Spain that had existed in the persons of the monarchs themselves was both hugely symbolic and of enormous practical significance, for it formally weakened the Habsburg bond between Spain and the north. As a young man, Philip II had travelled in the Netherlands, he had drunk their ales and loved their women; the Dutch had paid him homage in person; he had received his father's abdication in Brussels and had invested too much energy and money in fighting Lutheran heresy there; he never wavered in his determination to rule over his Dutch subjects. But Philip III was Castilian born and wholly Spanish bred; the Netherlands were a part of the distant virtual Empire he found so intangible and tiresome to comprehend; and if that was true of the heir to the throne, how much more true it was of his favourite and the ministers who governed Spain.

At first, Philip III took his responsibilities towards Catholicism as seriously as he took any matters of state, and he also had his pride as a prince and a Habsburg. In his maiden speech to the Council of State he advocated a policy of defending the faith and waging swift war against his enemies.[25] His government continued to pour money into the Netherlands in support of Albert and Isabel's rule, and the amounts sent and the subsequent success or failure of military campaigns against the rebel United Provinces continued to correlate with the size of the treasure receipts from the Indies.[26] Americans were still paying for the Habsburg wars in Europe.

But many factors combined to confound these early intentions. Albert proved a singularly incompetent regent. He failed both as a politician, despite the close attendance of the brilliant diplomat Baltasar de Zúñiga, and as a military leader, despite being repeatedly rescued by Spanish troops under the command of Ambrogio Spinola, yet another outstanding general who loyally served the Habsburgs in northern Europe. Meanwhile, many Castilians were opposed to spending their revenue to support a now obviously foreign government in a far-off land, and that already waning political enthusiasm for foreign intervention was further undermined by the abject failure of campaigns elsewhere in Ireland and Algiers.[27] But the fundamental problems were Philip's own apathy and Lerma's determination to pursue a policy of peace largely because he had found no satisfactory way of benefiting personally from war.

By the middle of the decade, Spain had again run out of money to support military involvement in the Netherlands. In 1604, peace was secured with England by the Treaty of London, and in 1607 an armistice was concluded with the United Provinces that would be ratified in 1609 as the Treaty of Antwerp, bringing about the Twelve Years' Truce. That long peace would, in due course, prove more favourable to the Habsburgs than to the northern Dutch, whose coalition ruptured now it was no longer cemented together by opposition to Spain. But, in 1609, the Treaty of Antwerp looked to all Europe like a humiliating defeat for Philip III and Spain. One contemporary commentator complained that 'the very name of peace diminishes royal authority' and 'puts the rest of Your Majesty's kingdoms in peril, igniting the hearts of other vassals', giving 'opportunity to other princes to try to weaken your forces'.[28]

In 1603, a young and combative Peter Paul Rubens, then on a diplomatic mission in Valladolid, described Spanish painters as 'wedded to their unbelievable incompetence and carelessness'. Spain was then still a land of decrepit old soldiers and youthful artists, but Rubens also espied the future, conceding that 'the Duke of Lerma is not entirely ignorant of good art, which is why he takes pleasure in his habit of each day admiring works in the Palace or the Escorial by Titian, Raphael and others. I am amazed by the quality and quantity of these, but there are no modern works of value.'[29] The Duke of Mantua, aware of Lerma's reputation as a lover of art, had sent Rubens to Spain charged with transporting forty or more modern copies of classic works made by a number of contemporary Italian artists. The great painter had packed this cargo so carelessly that the pictures arrived badly damaged by torrential rain during his journey across the Spanish plain. He set about repairing and touching them up himself and then hung them in the Royal Palace in preparation for their presentation to Lerma. 'The Duke arrived alone and in house dress, and after the usual compliments, he began to look at them one by one'; after well over an hour he described the works as 'a precious treasure, very much to his taste'. Returning to a portrait of the Duke of Mantua, 'he contemplated every detail very minutely, praised the lively gaze, and the serene majesty of the countenance, the beautiful proportions of the whole, noting that it was easy to tell from the portrait that the duke must have a great soul'.[30]

Lerma recognized Rubens's talent at once and commissioned him to paint the dramatic *Equestrian Portrait of the Duke of Lerma*, which he began in September 1603. In Spain, the young artist could feast his eyes and his mind almost daily on the dazzling royal collection, and he there became 'besotted with Titian's use of colour and light'. This painting marks a crucial development in his style.[31] But while this

may have been one small step for a great artist, it represented an enormously symbolic leap for the Spanish Crown. Titian's great *Equestrian
Portrait of Charles V*, of 1548, was then prominently displayed in the
royal collection, a constant reminder of the great warrior Emperor,
the first Habsburg to rule in Spain.[32] At one level, for Lerma to have
himself depicted in a way that so obviously staked a claim to Habsburg
history was mind-bogglingly arrogant. But it also demonstrates that
he well understood the potential for images as sources of power at
court and beyond.

The advent of rule by favourite not only entailed a restructuring
of government, but also changed the relationship between the Crown
and its subjects. Under Philip III a clear division immediately opened
up within the institution of the Crown between the government and
the monarch. This was a potentially dangerous split because, for all
that Philip the man might abdicate responsibility, the people who now
governed, most obviously the favourite, derived their authority to do
so from the King's sovereignty. So the administration indulged in an
orgy of imagery that showed off the office of the King and icons of
sovereignty across the full gamut of artistic media, in literature, poetry,
drama and, especially, painting and sculpture, as well as in court ritual.
Philip the man and Philip the sovereign were no longer one and the
same. Art had become more potent than life.

Royalty had always exchanged portraits like extravagant postcards,
but now the production of likenesses as part of the administration's
programme of propaganda became almost industrial. In the nine years
between 1608 and 1617, Bartolomé González, one of the Painters
Royal, produced ninety-seven portraits of Philip III and his family. In
1603, Margaret of Austria was depicted very heavily pregnant and the
painting was sent to Austria as evidence of a fecund Spanish branch
of the family. The divine nature of monarchy was emphasized in
Juan Pantoja de la Cruz's *Annunciation* of 1605, in which the Queen
and her daughter were used as models for the Virgin and the Angel
Gabriel. Following the Queen's death, González used her as a model
for a devotional painting of *St Margaret*.[33] Such paintings were copied
as engravings and published in emblem books and collections of prints
that were far more widely owned and viewed than the originals.

The royal family thus set a fashion for portraiture that was quickly embraced by the aristocracy and subsequently became more and more popular; indeed horribly vulgar according to Vicente Carducho, a Painter Royal and influential art critic. Carducho complained that 'I have seen portraits of common men and women who work in trade, standing by a desk or chair below the swathe of a curtain, with such gravitas of bearing that they look like kings or great lords, and others wearing armour, with a staff, as though the Duke of Alba, although they can never have carried such insignia except during some pantomime or other shenanigans.'[34]

The inherent internationalism of the Habsburgs made way for a parochial symbolism easily appropriated by peasants and other plebeians. The personal became public; the human, symbolic; the reality, imaginary or figurative; authority, showmanship; power gave way to imagery.

This was no case of the Emperor wearing no clothes, but of the wardrobe dispensing with the Emperor. Yet this virtual reality was strangely democratic: so much spectacle, so many images, so many words, all invited a response in kind from the sovereign's subjects. It invited a dialogue about the nature of monarchy, and the cultural forces of Castile now combined to answer back.

From around 1600, Spaniards became quickly and acutely aware that image was trumping reality, and that fiction could eclipse truth. Understandably, they were perplexed and troubled by the morality of such a perversion. As today, there were many in the Spanish Golden Age who urged people to be on the lookout for the disturbing charades of life and they gave the name *desengaño*, literally 'disillusionment', to that process by which we come to see the not always palatable substance behind the image. Spaniards became obsessed with trying to perceive the moral truth that underlay superficial reality; they were anxiously searching for real gold among so much glitter.

This preoccupation with *desengaño* was all pervasive. At its most basic, the idea could encompass the revelation in a pair of stitched-on testicles that mutton had been dressed as lamb, but this notion of *desengaño* was curiously like the famous stew of assorted leftovers known as *olla podrida* or 'putrid casserole' that also obsessed Spaniards at the time. Both involved a heady, indeed 'high' mixture of more and less succulent ingredients that had seemingly been cooking for a century or more on the backburners of homes, hostelries and palaces. *Desengaño* was a savoury titillation of the intellectual and emotional taste buds produced by the slow maceration of a plethora of words and writing, of images from the Americas, of the Inquisition's fires, the falsification of ancestry and *limpieza de sangre*, the mysteries of the Catholic mass, of fiction, and Mannerist and Baroque art, the experience of a flourishing theatre and seeing the world as a stage, the travellers' tales of adventure and anthropophagi, and the daily business of worrying about whether there would be enough *olla podrida* and bread to go round in an uncertain world.

At one level, the intellectualization of *desengaño* could take playful delight in blurring the distinction between reality and representation, like the Sevillian aristocrat who had commissioned a portrait from the most fashionable artist which his friends had then criticized in all manner of attention to the detail. Piqued by their slights, the patron called upon a great painter called Luis de Vargas to offer an opinion; he took one look at the portrait and said, 'if it pleases Your Excellency to do as I suggest, you will at least be satisfied that it is a good likeness'.

> Vargas moved the portrait a pace or so into the room and had the windows closed. He drew the curtain a little across the doorway and said: 'Sir, now send for a servant, in all haste and we will wait behind the painting; then you will witness the *desengaño*.' And so it was done. The servant hurried into the large room and after taking six steps, seeing as the portrait said nothing, he simply said to it: 'What does Your Excellency order?'[35]

The process of self-illusion and its denouement in *desengaño* was examined obsessively by political philosophers and moral commentators. They were interested in who they were, how they related to the past and to the distant lands of the Empire. They were interested in what was going on in their immediate vicinity as well as in the intellectual and aesthetic debates of the university men. They complained about problems that they perceived and offered sometimes ludicrous solutions. They read books and each other's writings, they talked, argued, went to the theatre and worked in government offices or as doctors, lawyers, judges; some were bored noblemen, others churchmen and learned scholars. They were truly modern, in other words.

With the succession of Philip III, the arrival of Lerma and the recourse to conciliar rule, the Spanish Empire would for the first time be subject to policies not born of Habsburg sentiment but formulated entirely by Castilians. With their Empire stretched to breaking point, so spread out and diverse it was beyond consolidation or defence, Spaniards still felt themselves to be at the centre of the world, as indeed they were, but they now turned their gaze inward. There was a young King with a love of pageantry, a favourite distributing his own favour, there was peace, there were fortunes to be made and fun to be had at home. The Duke of Lerma and Philip III led what might best be described as a cultural assault on the traditional institutions of monarchy, aristocracy and government, replacing rule and leadership with a strange new authority based on art and display. The dry, virtual world of bureaucracy by which Philip II had clung to control gave way to the intangible influence of image and the power of impression. The aristocracy, almost to a man, completed their degeneration from conspicuous military valour to opulent courtly consumption; they employed poets and painters, they crowded into theatres and collected books, they fought bulls not wars, and left their arms and armour to rust. That noble volte face brought about the seismic shift from a sixteenth-century Spanish Empire built by gold and armies to the politics and glitter of seventeenth-century Spain.

Decadent it may have been, but what fabulous decadence. This was the world of Cervantes's literary success; of the great court painter Diego Velázquez; the 'painter of monks' Francisco de Zurbarán and Bartolomé Esteban de Murillo, two great masters of religious painting and the Baroque; Lope de Vega, Tirso de Molina and Calderón de la Barca, three of the greatest playwrights in the age of Shakespeare, the period that saw Don Juan Tenorio first walk the stage; when Góngora and Quevedo were at their poetic peaks; when Holy Week matured into the great public spectacle it remains today. Part Two of the present work offers a perspective from the arts, from literature, poetry, theatre, painting and public display, which long ago led literary critics and art historians to celebrate this age of supposed decline as the richest decades in 'El Siglo de Oro', the cultural apogee of the Spanish Golden Age.

THE AGE OF PEACE:
PHILIP III AND THE DUKE OF LERMA

13

The First Modern Novel, *Don Quixote*

I assure you it must be the work of some wise magician.

Don Quixote

'It seems our Kingdoms have been reduced to a republic of bewitched men living outside the natural order of things . . . The contradictory truth is that our wealth is all paper blowing in the wind: contracts, bonds, letters of exchange, coins, silver and gold, but nothing fruitful nor productive.' Thus 'the Kingdom is finished, royal revenues have collapsed, there are no more vassals, and the republic is evaporating', complained an obviously perplexed Martín González de Cellorigo in 1600, one of the seemingly endless procession of *arbitristas* or political commentators who had their opinions printed by the burgeoning publishing industry. 'Spain has reached total collapse,' he went on, 'for there were never as many rich vassals as there are today, but never so much poverty among them; nor was there ever such a powerful king, with so much revenue and kingdoms, yet never has there been a king whose estates were so mortgaged.'

This contrary and rather confused spirit in which Spaniards were beginning to doubt themselves even as the Empire reached its greatest extension produced many theories of decline. Some blamed a natural socio-economic cycle of empire, sometimes expressed as the inevitable ageing of a body politic slowly degenerating in geriatric decadence. González de Cellorigo, in his final reckoning, concluded that the underlying problem was that 'Spain has become a nation of

idle rentiers.' This, he complained, was made possible by the interest
paid by the Crown on its bonds and *juros*, but was rooted in the way
work and trade were seen as dishonourable for a nobleman by a nation
obsessed with honour and nobility. The Crown, he suggested, should
instead 'persuade its subjects', rich and poor, noble and plebeian, 'to
work and eliminate the idlers and vagabonds' of every class.[1]

The arrogant ethics of the Age of Chivalry had served Castile well
on the battlefields of Europe and America, but González de Cellorigo
saw with remarkable clarity at the time what we now know to be more
or less true with hindsight: that the realities of Empire had shifted
from the medieval business of conflict to the modern activity of trade.
Castile needed farmers, artisans and merchants, not more aristocrats
and noblemen. In short, it needed a flourishing economy.

It was in this prescient spirit of disillusionment with the ideals of
the past, this aristocratic sense of *desengaño*, that Cervantes let loose
on the world one of the most endearing fictional creations ever to
confront the realities of an uncertain age.

In 2002, at the Nobel Institute in Oslo, the Nigerian-born writer Ben
Okri announced to an audience packed with the literary great and the
good the results of a comprehensive interrogation of one hundred of
the most revered authors from around the globe designed to establish a list of the one hundred most important works in the history
of fiction. Norman Mailer, Nadine Gordimer, Milan Kundera, Doris
Lessing, V. S. Naipaul and Susan Sontag along with their ninety-four
illustrious colleagues singled out only one book for special mention,
determining that *Don Quixote* is 'the best literary work ever written'.[2]
The statistics bear out their opinion: after the Bible, *Don Quixote*
is the most widely translated and most published work in literary
history. Part One was first published in 1604, in Madrid; there was
a second edition before the end of 1605 and another in 1608; there
were nine editions by 1612, printed in Valencia, Lisbon, Brussels and
Antwerp. Thomas Shelton's classic translation into English came out
in 1612, the first French translation in 1614. And the editions kept
on coming. In seventeenth-century England the story cropped up
everywhere: on the stage, in engravings, in songs, in printed, painted

and woven images; there was even a popular dance called the 'Sancho Panza', after Don Quixote's peasant-savant companion.[3] The great revolution that took place in English literary fiction in the eighteenth century is unimaginable without it. Henry Fielding wrote his play *Don Quixote in England* in 1729, when he was only twenty-two years old and he was still so besotted with the book in 1742 that he announced on the title page of *Joseph Andrews* that it was 'written in imitation of the manner of Cervantes'.[4] John Dryden suggested that Milton's Satan of *Paradise Lost* had something of Quixote about him. It was one of Samuel Johnson's three favourite fictions alongside *Pilgrim's Progress* and *Robinson Crusoe*,[5] neither of which would have been written had John Bunyan and Daniel Defoe not been fanatical readers of Cervantes. Likewise, Herman Melville brought something elementally Cervantine to *Moby-Dick*, while we know from Mark Twain's diaries that he was reading *Don Quixote* while writing *Tom Sawyer* and *Huckleberry Finn*.[6] And still it goes on: Paul Auster in the *New York Trilogy* and Salman Rushdie in *Midnight's Children* pay overt homage to their literary heroes. And this is not to mention its influence in other languages, most of all Spanish: Luis Borgés, García Márquez, Vargas Llosa, Isabel Allende, were all suckled on Cervantes's fiction.

Scholars have been aware of Quixote's massive influence on English literature at least since Gerard Langbaine published his *Momus Triumphans, or the Plagiaries of the English Stage* in 1688.[7] Interestingly, the first serious critical edition in Spanish was edited by an eccentric English country clergyman, John 'Don' Bowle, published in six volumes in 1781.[8] In modern times, the greatest of Shakespeare scholars, Harold Bloom, has written movingly and with exemplary integrity that 'perhaps Cervantes's masterwork is the central book of the last half-millennium', for, if:

> Shakespeare pragmatically teaches us how to talk to ourselves, Cervantes instructs us how to talk to one another. Hamlet scarcely listens to what anyone else says . . . But Don Quixote and Sancho Panza change and mature by listening to one another, and their friendship is the most persuasive in all of literature . . . Don Quixote dies in Sancho's loving company, with the wise squire proposing fresh quests to the heroic

knight . . . Cervantes, whose life was arduous and darkly solitary, was able to achieve a miracle that Shakespeare evaded. Where in Shakespeare can we find two great natures in full communion with each other? The reader needs no better company than Sancho and the don: to make a third with them is to be blessed with happiness.[9]

But Lope de Vega was very unhappy about the forthcoming publication of *Don Quixote*, in 1604, which he already knew from a manuscript copy. 'What an age this is for poets, we await a forest of them to bear fruit in the coming year! But at least none of them are as bad as Cervantes nor so stupid as to praise *Don Quixote*,' he wrote to a friend.[10] Lope, it has always been assumed, was furious about a passage in which the curate and the Canon of Toledo discuss the theatre, a passage which has excited scholars into extremes of exegetic ecstasy ever since.

Lope is always credited with having invented the new style of comedy usually known as the *comedia nueva* or 'New Drama', and in 1609 published a short handbook on *The New Art of Writing Plays*. In reality, he was simply the most charismatic and influential of a handful of playwrights who were developing this radically populist approach for the newly burgeoning audiences. In essence, they rejected the long-standing convention that plays should follow a classical model, originating with Aristotle, which rigidly divided performances into five acts set over a twenty-four-hour time frame, and which prohibited characters from different social classes from being represented together. Instead of accepting these incredibly restrictive dictates, the New Dramatists wrote plays that were more representative of the daily realities which their audiences experienced, stories about ordinary folk spiced with variety, humour and unexpected twists and turns of plot. They were, in short, unashamedly populist and this drew harsh criticism from more conservative critics.

Drama had once been the preserve of the Church, a conduit for morality and social conformism, and contemporary Spanish theatre had developed from religious drama that formed part of the liturgy or was performed on holy feast days. Even the great autos-da-fé of the Inquisition itself were conceived in terms of theatre. So, in *Don Quixote*, we find the important character of the curate complaining to the Canon of Toledo that 'foreigners who punctiliously preserve the laws of theatre think us ignorant barbarians', for in an ordered society plays should 'deflect the community from the evils of leisure', leaving the audience 'amused by the jokes, improved by the truths, impressed by what happens, enriched by the wisdom and fables, alert to trickery', and generally 'wary of vice and uplifted by virtue'. But, he laments, 'most plays put on today lack all these things'.

At first, he suggests that the playwrights 'are not at fault, because some of them well know what they are doing wrong and what they ought to do, but because plays have become a commodity to be bought and sold, the promoters will only pay' for something written in the modern style. 'The evidence for this is to be seen in the infinite plays written by a felicitous genius with such verve, such confidence, such elegance of verse, such good sense, and so filled with eloquence that the whole world buzzes with his fame; but not all are as perfect as they should be, for he has bowed to the taste of the promoters.'

As ever with the pronouncements of Cervantes's characters, it would be foolish to assume that this is what he himself really thought. In fact, in the Prologue to a collection of his plays published in 1615, he boasted of his own revolutionary innovations as a playwright when it came to characterization and in cutting down plays from the traditional five acts to a much punchier three. But he went on to explain that he had then found that 'I had other things to do, so I abandoned my pen and the theatre; and then that monster of nature, the great Lope de Vega, arrived and made off with the title Monarch of the Stage. Every actor became his vassal and he filled the world with his own plays, so many that he has written more than ten thousand folios, all of them performed or at least read,' to the exclusion of those who tried to 'share in his glory'.[11] It was both a humble, albeit slightly rancorous admission of Lope's dramatic suzerainty and a statement of his own pride in the part he had played in the New Drama. The curate, it turns out, was as much a critic of Cervantes's drama as he was of Lope; but then Lope had nothing else, while Cervantes had his war wounds and *Don Quixote*.

Lope took extreme umbrage at the curate's critical comments, which he perceived, like most critics since, to be a terrible slight. But Cervantes was simply representing a truly literary churchman's lament that Lope's brilliant potential had been sacrificed by society on the altar of Mammon and celebrity instead of being put to a higher moral purpose. Of course, it takes a very phlegmatic and very self-confident character to accept such criticism as the praise of innate genius, as it was clearly meant to be; but it takes a deeply unpleasant and hotheaded egomaniac to wilfully misunderstand Cervantes's subtlety and respond with pure vitriol: Lope de Vega could be barbaric, nasty, brutish and personal:

> You've never read the Bible, I should say,
> Cervantes, I know not if thou art a cuckold arse,
> But that Lope is Apollo, I confirm; oh dray-
> Horse thou, who draggeth the carriage of his art.
>
> So such a swine could never write again,
> At Lepanto, God crippled thee a hand.
> Oh lummox, thou speaketh, yet sayeth nothing.
> Be off with thee and thy Quixote's evil band.
>
> Honour Lope, thou agèd, self-important hack!
> For he is the Sun, he is the angry rain,
> And thy *Don Quixote* is such worthless crap,
> From arse to arse, shall be the world's refrain,
>
> Purveyor of saffron, spice and Moorish tat,
> Till shat forth, in the cesspit it can lie at rest again.[12]

It is an unfortunate commentary to have made about a book now widely believed to have been the first modern novel and voted the best work of fiction in European literary history. But then Lope is all but forgotten outside Spain today, while Cervantes's laughter continues to peal.

In 1604, Miguel de Cervantes was staying in the bosom of his sisters' coven of courtesan-seamstresses in the heart of Valladolid, a city then overflowing with courtiers and chancers following the Duke of Lerma's decision to make it the capital of Philip III's government. The overcrowded city soon gained a reputation for streets filled with rotting rubbish and an Esgueva River that was effectively an open sewer. The wits dubbed it 'Valleoloroso' or 'Stinking Valley', but the filth seemed to symbolize the very canker at the heart of government. The ever acerbic poet Luis de Gónogra wrote a sonnet in which he asked: 'What do you carry, Mister Esgueva?' Among the answers he proffered were 'the stuff which comes out of the privies ... according to the laws of Digestion', 'the crystalline pee of one lady or t'other' and 'the tears of three eyes', a none too subtle reference to the 'dorsal eye' to which Góngora's great rival, Francisco de Quevedo, wrote his famous *Ode to the Arse's View*.[13]

By 1606, Lerma's experiment had run its course and court and capital returned to Madrid. But in 1604, at stinking Valladolid, Francisco de Robles, entrepreneur and Bookseller Royal, fresh from success with the first ever major work of picaresque fiction, Alemán's *Guzmán de Alfarache*, and with its sequel still wet from the presses, bought the manuscript of Cervantes's daringly experimental piece of storytelling, *The Ingenious Gentleman Don Quixote of La Mancha*.

A clean copy of the manuscript made by a professional scribe was submitted to the Royal Council for approval by the censor and to have an official price established for the sale of each copy. Robles's connections eased that process, and he was already driving a hard bargain with one of the oldest printing houses in Madrid, newly taken over by Juan de la Cuesta. The recent departure of the court to Valladolid had the printer worried, and he agreed to a fee of about 2,000 *reales* for what must have been a significant print run, given that Robles spent 3,500 or 4,000 *reales* on paper alone. Cervantes, it is thought, must have been paid about 1,500 *reales* for his master-piece.[14] By September, the printers had the master manuscript, which was again professionally copied in a legible and uniform hand evenly spaced across the pages so that one of the experienced overseers could assess the task.[15]

Towards the end of Part Two of *Don Quixote*, the novel's unlikely hero, Don Quixote, an avid reader sent mad by his books who is now approaching the twilight of his career, decides like many seasoned adventurers in old age to engage in some unchallenging tourism by taking a walking tour of Barcelona. In one street,

> he saw written in very large letters over a door, 'Books printed here', at which he was hugely pleased, for he had never seen a printers. He went in and saw printing here, correcting proofs there, casting type here, revising there; in short, all the machinery of a great print works. He went up to a type case and asked what it was; the workmen told him and he watched them with wonder.[16]

As well he might. Jan van der Straet's classic engraving of 1600 shows a workshop much like Juan de la Cuesta's in full swing, an image best understood with reference to a detailed contemporary description of a printers' written by Cristóbal Suárez de Figueroa.[17] 'It is fair to say', Suárez writes, 'that the spirit of man slept the deep sleep of ignorance before it was awoken by the invention of printing, because back then the intolerable cost of books meant very few could read, only the rich, while the poor were damned to ignorance. Today, everyone can learn and give themselves up to virtue for books are now moderately priced.'

Published in the same year as Part Two of *Don Quixote*, 1615, Suárez's account succinctly expresses the relatively democratic realities of reading and books a century and a half after the invention of printing. But it remained a labour-intensive trade. There was the *fundidor* who moulded uniform type from solder and lead, fabricating letters, numbers, punctuation, blanks for spaces, decorative capitals, diphthongs and musical notes in different founts. The typesetters can be seen to the left and in the foreground of Straet's engraving, selecting type from the slightly curved type-cases, as they read from pages of the manuscript pinned above them, and then arranging it, symbol by symbol, line by line, fitting each line, one by one, into frames called *galeras*, 'galleys' in English, from which we get the term galley-proofs or galleys. Once the page was set, it was tightened up and then handed to the printer and his assistant who ran off a copy that was read for mistakes by a *corrector*, much as is still done today.

The galleys holding the corrected type were then arranged on the press and kept in place by clips while they were inked up by the printer's assistant using woollen sponges mounted on long handles. The paper was held in place on the tympanum, a frame holding a layer of felt or other cloth. Finally, the printer turned the screw using a handle. Working quickly, he and his team could print 6,000 pages a day. We can tell by comparing different copies of the same edition that it was also quite usual to make corrections during a print run. Moreover, it would have been normal for Cervantes to be present during typesetting. Suárez, with half an eye on his own printers, explained that the whole process 'is incredibly tiring for all the tradesmen and the authors too. Usually, there are more than a few differences of opinion and raised voices among them thanks to the meticulousness of the former and remissness of the latter, although in the end these discussions always end in agreement and gratefulness.' The statement sheds light on a much discussed mistake in Part One of *Don Quixote* when Sancho Panza's ass, which has been stolen and lost for ever, inexplicably reappears in a later chapter, which was almost certainly a result of Cervantes's own lack of vigilance when reordering part of the story. Yet despite this, he disingenuously suggested in Part Two that the whole fiasco must have been the fault of the publishers.[18]

A crucial decision for the publisher then, as today, was to choose the size of edition. Most books were sold unbound, as printed pages. But dimensions mattered. All printing was done on to folios, large sheets of paper, which for luxury editions were printed up with only four pages of text, two on each side, that could then be folded like a modern newspaper into two leaves. But quartos, or quarters, involved printing eight pages on to four leaves, and octavos, sixteen pages on to eight leaves. This required some skill and experience when setting the type so that once folded the text ended up the right way up and continued from page to page in the right order. The advantage of quartos and octavos was, of course, that they allowed for a smaller book that could be easily carried.[19]

The first edition of *Don Quixote*, dated 1605, although the print run was completed by mid-December the previous year, was printed in quarto, with a blazon surrounded by the Latin inscription *post tenebras spero lucem*, 'After dark, I hope for light,' taken from a rather morbid passage in Job 17 that many readers would have been familiar with and which reflects a theme Cervantes picks up on in the Prologue. The seventeenth-century reader would have bought the book unbound; he or she would no doubt have checked the *tasa* recording the regulated price of a copy, would have glanced at the *errata*, would probably have skipped the official licence and may have skimmed over the brief dedication to the powerful Duke of Béjar before settling down to read the Prologue.

'Idle reader,' Cervantes began, 'I need not swear under oath for you to believe that I wish this book, born as it is of my understanding, were unimaginably handsome, dashing and intelligent.' But, he explains, it is not. Moreover, he complains that the Prologue itself has been hard work to write because he fears the 'vulgar public, that ancient lawmaker'. How will they react, he asks, when they see that 'after so many years asleep in the silence of oblivion I have reappeared under the burden of my advanced age with a story as dry as esparto grass'? Cervantes felt this was his chance to return from literary purgatory: *post tenebras spero lucem* was an apt motto for the frontispiece if ever there was one.

The seventeenth-century reader, somewhat taken aback by this intimately confessional opening gambit, would then have been bemused by the preliminary verses. It was usual to have other leading and upcoming authors write laudatory poems at the front of a book, in the same way that puffs pepper modern jackets in the hope they will attract readers. But, claiming to have been unable to find 'anyone foolish enough' to do the usual backscratching, Cervantes wrote his own as an obviously deliberate burlesque of the genre. What, his readers would have been beginning to wonder, was he up to?

The story proper then begins with an unpromising description of the hero of the book's title, who lived recently and near by: 'Not long ago, in a town in La Mancha the name of which I do not remember, there lived one of those old gentlemen whose lance is on its rack, has an old leather shield, a skinny old hack and a fleet greyhound. He ate more beef than mutton, mincemeat of an evening, bubble and squeak on Saturday, lentils on Friday, rewarded himself with pigeon on a Sunday, all of which consumed three quarters of his income.' Poorly dressed, 'he was about fifty years old, gaunt, lean, drawn in the face, an early-riser much given to hunting. It is said that his surname was Quixada or Quexada, although the authors who have written about him differ, and more reliable conjecture suggests he was called Quexana. But it is not important to this tale.'

It was most unusual and disorientating to introduce a character in terms of his very familiar diet and then to suggest that his name was unimportant; and he was anyway a most unusual character to be introducing as the central figure in a work of literature, not least because Cervantes's readers would instantly have recognized a stereotype who was far more familiar from their experience of real life than from their reading (although many will have been aware of a similarly delusional member of the gentry who appears in the unfinished but seminal picaresque tale *Lazarillo de Tormes*, published in 1554). And that sense of realism would immediately have shifted the readers' mindset from books to the world around them, from that ready store of mental images collected from reading fantasy and fiction to their own quotidian existence; some may even have recognized something of themselves in this rather forlorn figure.

When nutritionists at King's College London analysed Don Quixote's diet as described by Cervantes they came up with some worrying results. It is possible to chart how infrequently he seems to eat over the course of the novel and their results implied that his calorie intake must be about a quarter of the bare minimum for a fifty-year-old male with a sedentary lifestyle, let alone a man who spends most of the book travelling across Spain on horseback. They suggested that he would probably have suffered long-term wastage of his flesh and muscles, and Cervantes does indeed describe him as gaunt and lean. But the researchers were equally concerned about the minute levels of calcium and vitamins A, C and E that he was consuming and thought he would have been suffering from osteoporosis and might well have had incipient scurvy. He would certainly have had terrible gum disease; and, although over the course of the novel he apparently avoids breaking any bones despite repeated slapstick batterings, by the end he is described as having lost almost all of his teeth. Most important of all, however, is that the acute lack of vitamins A and E would have led to neurological dysfunction and problems with his vision on top of the lightheadedness he would have anyway been feeling from eating so little.[20]

Needless to say, the nutritional study of meals described in *Don Quixote* was never intended to produce a serious medical assessment of the mental and physical health of a fictional character, but it does very usefully focus our critical attention on the sense of realism that underpins Cervantes's portrait of the apparently absurd figure of Quixote: it is reasonable to assume that contemporary readers would have known intuitively that such a man with such a diet was likely to suffer symptoms of this sort. Indeed, Cervantes must have experienced them himself, for this was an age when most lived on a poor diet from time to time and sometimes suffered extreme hunger.

Cervantes tells us that his presumably almost permanently light-headed and daydreaming character, 'when at leisure, which was almost always, was so fanatically given to reading romances of chivalry that he almost completely forgot about hunting and the business of his estate, becoming so captivated that he sold off many arable fields to buy books'. In other words, he displays the mental symptoms of drug use as well as the social irresponsibility of the addict.

This otherwise genteel but poor and single man, with only a niece to care for and a housekeeper to care for him, with his brain starved of food and his mind wandering in the world of his books, suffers the most delightful nervous breakdown. He collects up his ancient lance and an old sword and cleans up some armour that has been rusting in his barn and prepares to live life according to the tenets of knight errantry, a rulebook he has devised from his obsessive reading.

But the helmet of the suit of armour lacks a visor, so he very slowly and carefully makes one from cardboard. Delighted by its appearance, he takes up his sword and deals two firm blows to the visor:

> with the first he instantly undid the work of a week; he was far from impressed by how easily it had fallen to bits. So, to head off such

dangers, he made a new visor, reinforcing it with iron until he himself was convinced it was sturdy; and then, without testing it again, he put it into service believing it to be a very finely manufactured visor.

This inspired dreamer has learnt his first lesson about treating fiction with care. Cervantes's main character has made his first, wobbling steps into creating a fictional world; it is an appropriately bathos-filled moment to greet the infant modern novel as it toddled into existence. Realizing that names are important for fictional characters, he first decides to call his horse Rocinante, punning the Spanish *rocín*, 'old hack', and *antes*, 'before'. Now, of course, this broken-down old nag has become a trusty steed just as his master has become a bold knight of the kind who won his spurs in the stories of old. This equine baptism sets our strange hero to thinking of a name for himself. For eight days his imagination struggles with the task until he concludes that he will call himself Don Quixote of La Mancha. And, as all knights errant must be faithful to a lady love to whom they can send supplicant giants and magicians they have defeated in single combat, he settles upon the unrivalled beauty Dulcinea del Toboso to fill this role, although Cervantes leads us to believe that she is based on a comely peasant girl his hero once had a crush on called Aldonza Lorenzo.

Saddling up Rocinante at dawn, and without telling a soul, Don Quixote sets out dressed in his ancient armour across the bleached plain of La Mancha under an unforgiving July sun in search of the kind of adventures he has read about in his books of chivalry. 'The sun was so strong and hot that it was enough to melt his brains, had he any.' And as Rocinante plods along, 'a terrible thought' came to Don Quixote: 'he had not yet been dubbed a knight errant'. He immediately decides to find a castle where the sheriff can perform the necessary rites to admit him to the orders of chivalry. Castile is not so called for nothing. La Mancha was the frontier with the Moors for four centuries and is dotted with fortifications large and small. Quixote rides all day dreaming about 'whichever wise magician the task may fall to of being the historian' of the true story of 'the famous gentle-knight Don Quixote of La Mancha'.

Quixote is 'dog tired and faint with hunger' when at dusk he sees the castle he is looking for and hears the bugle call of a dwarf announcing the knight's arrival from the battlements. Two damsels await him at the drawbridge. He speaks: 'Flee ye not nor fear ye injury, for my vows of chivalry permit not such evils, least of all against such noble maidens as yourselves.' The problem is that, as Cervantes explains, the castle is an inn, the bugler a swineherd and the damsels are prostitutes. Don Quixote, we are told, 'has plenty of trouble dismounting, like someone who has been all day without eating'. Nevertheless, he is kindly received by the 'fat and gentle innkeeper' and enjoys his supper of salt cod, which he believes to be exquisite river trout. In due course, Don Quixote asks this amenable sheriff to dub him a knight errant and we learn that the innkeeper 'decided to humour him for the sake of a good laugh'. But he also gives him some important advice, telling him he needs to carry money and ought to have a squire to assist him, like other knights errant. He also apologizes that 'his castle had no chapel where Don Quixote could keep vigil over his arms and armour'. Instead, he could prop them against the well in the castle patio.

During the night, a couple of muleteers try to move his arms and armour out of the way to get water for their animals. An outraged Quixote assaults them, bashing them over the head with his lance and knocking them senseless. This is our introduction to what Vladimir Nabokov called 'the cheerful physical cruelty' in the novel, which, curiously, seems to have mystified the mournful Russian novelist but should have been familiar to him from Punch and Judy, Tom and Jerry or, perhaps more appropriately in a story about the friendship between a jolly fat man and an anxious thin man, Laurel and Hardy.[21] As in these later variations on the same theme, the aggressor is soon the victim, as the muleteers' colleagues rain down a hail of stones and other missiles on a beleaguered Quixote who shelters as best he can beneath his shield. The innkeeper hurriedly goes into action, putting a stop to the violence and performing the rituals required of him by his strange guest in order to get rid of him.

Quixote leaves the inn, well satisfied with his first make-believe sally into the real world. But it is time to go home to collect money and find a squire. On the way, almost Chaplin-like, he picks fights with various people, finally being given a proper beating by a mule-boy. Rescued by a passing neighbour who brings him home, he is put to bed by his distraught housekeeper, who sends for his close friends, the barber and the curate.

They instantly blame his insanity and misfortune on his novels of chivalry. In a daring parody of the Inquisition, Cervantes now shows us these two literate characters working their way through Quixote's almost implausibly extensive library of over one hundred books, offering a literary review of each and every work and handing those they dislike over to their 'secular arm' which takes the form of the housekeeper who adds them to a blazing bonfire she has built for them in the yard outside. One of those saved is *The White Knight* by Joan Martorell, published in Valencia in 1490. 'To tell the truth, *compadre*,' says the curate, 'this is the best book in the world: here the gentle-knights eat and sleep and die in their beds and they make wills and do all sorts of other things this genre usually leaves out.' The curate is a devotee of realism in fiction, that illusive property essential to most definitions of the modern novel: verisimilitude.

And, although he is a professed enemy of fantasy, when he comes to *La Galatea*, he explains that 'this Cervantes, who is better versed in misfortune than in poetry, has been a great friend of mine for many years. His book has some good parts, although he promises much, but offers no conclusions. We will have to wait for the second part he has promised us.' There is nothing Cervantes enjoys more than some unexpected self-referential irony.

The barber and curate now arrange to have the doorway to Don Quixote's library bricked up and plastered over so that the many magicians who have haunted him during the long nights he has spent reading can never escape. When he recovers, he searches in vain for his precious collection but is far from confounded by its disappearance, which he blames on his mortal enemy, the magician Frestón. While his friends hope he will now settle back into genteel poverty, Don Quixote has other ideas and approaches 'a neighbour, a labourer, a man of plenty – if one can say that of a poor man – but lacking in marbles up top', a man called Sancho Panza. 'Among other things,

Quixote told him that if he was happy to travel with him, he might be rewarded for some adventure, maybe with an island of which he would make him governor. And because of such promises, Sancho left his wife and children and signed up to be his neighbour's squire.'

Their adventures begin with a secret dawn tryst, and the two companions set out on to the La Mancha plain, Sancho astride his ass 'like a patriarch', Quixote on Rocinante. As they travel, we readers, already aware of the basic nature of Quixote's condition, get our first taste of Sancho, who, it turns out, has a mind abundantly furnished with a seemingly endless array of aphorisms, folk-sayings and old saws. The idea that such a humble repository of peasant knowledge could be a source of higher wisdom was already well established, and a great compendium of one thousand such sayings had been compiled by the 'Greek Commander', Juan de Mal Lara, the scholar who established the first great academy in Seville, which he published as the *Vulgar Philosophy* in 1568, in emulation of Erasmus' *Collected Adages*.[22] We can therefore now settle down to enjoy this sublime partnership between a scholar of fantastical literature and a credulous rustic with an encyclopaedic knowledge of common-sense dicta.

Quixote immediately begins his illiterate squire's literary education, instructing him in the basics of chivalric romance, beginning with further explanation of the ancient tradition of knights errant rewarding their squires with the governorship of those islands and kingdoms won in battle. And as Sancho contemplates the pleasant prospect of his 'missus' becoming a queen and his daughters *infantas*, the world-famous, eternally notorious windmills appear on a ridge on the horizon, the windmills at which we modern readers know that our hero must inevitably tilt. 'Fortune guides us better than we could have hoped,' says Quixote; 'see there, my friend Sancho Panza, thirty or more riotous giants have shown themselves. I intend to do battle with them.'

'What giants?' asks Sancho.

'Those ones you can see over there, with their long arms.'

'Look, Sir. Those things that have appeared are not giants, but windmills, and those things that look like their arms are the sails which, when blown by the wind, make the grindstone go round.'

'It would seem that you have not yet graduated from the school of adventure.'

And so saying, Quixote spurs on Rocinante and, paying no heed to Sancho's shouts, charges headlong into the fray, dedicating the battle to his beloved Dulcinea del Toboso. Just then, a breeze catches the sails and the arms begin slowly to rotate, and as he attacks the first windmill a great gust sends the sail sweeping round, smashing Quixote's lance to pieces and dragging horse and rider behind it and dashing them to the ground. Temporarily brought to his senses, Quixote informs Sancho that he has been robbed of a great victory by the magician Frestón, who at the last moment must have turned the giants into windmills.

Sancho has witnessed his first practical lesson in early modern knight errantry and begins to digest the experience with the help of a hearty meal and the contents of his wineskin. Quixote, by contrast, fasts, while dreaming up 'flavourful memories' of his beloved Dulcinea, so that the following morning his mind is lean and ready for further adventures. When two Benedictine friars wearing travelling goggles and sunshades appear, coming towards them along the road riding camels alongside a carriage carrying the wife of a rich Basque merchant to Seville, Quixote needs no second thought: 'If I am not mistaken, this will be the most famous adventure ever seen, for those two black forms must be magicians who without doubt have abducted the princess riding in that carriage.'

'This will be worse than the adventure with the windmills,' Sancho mutters, as much to himself and the reader as to his master. It is one thing to serve a madman who engages in random acts of vandalism against property, albeit valuable property; it is quite another should he assault members of the religious orders. Sancho fears trouble from either the Inquisition or the Holy Brotherhood (or Santa Hermandad), the rural police.

Quixote attacks, and the friars flee; he approaches the carriage and asks the princess to return to El Toboso and to present herself before Dulcinea. A rudely rustic Basque servant responds thuggishly and a great battle ensues.

But Cervantes leaves us with a classic cliffhanger, for as Quixote raises his sword to strike dead his opponent, Book One comes to an end with Cervantes explaining that the first author of the story has apologized that he could find no more material to work with.

Cervantes's Book Two (of Part One and not to be confused with Part Two, published in 1615) begins with a spurious literary discussion about sources in which the 'second' author, presumably Cervantes, describes how, while he was shopping in Toledo, 'a young lad turned up trying to sell some old papers to a silk merchant. I instinctively picked up a folder,' the second author explains, 'and saw Arabic script, so I looked about for a Morisco who knew Aljamía.' Toledo had a large Morisco community, so he soon finds an interpreter who notes that 'here in the margin it says that Dulcinea del Toboso was the most skilled woman at salting pork in all La Mancha'.

Because of this passage, it is usually thought that Cervantes was claiming that the original manuscript of Don Quixote was written in Arabic, the alien language of an ancient enemy. But Aljamía was simply Spanish or Portuguese written phonetically in Arabic rather than Latin letters; so it seems likely a contemporary reader would have assumed that the 'original historian' must have been a Morisco, a Spaniard of Muslim descent probably from Toledo and a familiar, homely, neighbourly author. But the narrator then explains that 'the veracity of this story' is doubtful because 'its author was an Arab, a nation much given to mendaciousness'.[23] Such uncertainty is typical of how Cervantes gets his readers to debate the 'truth' or 'reality' of his fiction. But, whether he wrote in Aljamía or Arabic, the 'real truth' is peeking out from behind this curtain, for this mendacious historian has a name, Cide Hamete Benengeli, which interestingly enough is an almost perfect anagram of 'in truth: Miguel de Cervantes'.[24]

Cervantes was toying with his reader's awareness that novels of chivalry were usually presented by their author as the translation of a text from a faraway land written in a remote language. But Don Quixote was simply written either in Castilian, though in a familiar yet foreign script that needed transcribing, or in infidel Arabic; either way, it is an inherently unreliable record of fact. His capacity for intricate satire is breathtaking. To whom, we fail to ask amid so much complexity, did it occur that this might be a true story? But by now he has us thoroughly worried about the factual reliability of a fictional text.

Cervantes must have been influenced by contemporary events and literature. While he was trawling the Granada hinterland as a tax gatherer in the 1590s, the sensational news spread fast that two men supposedly digging for buried Moorish treasure on the long, high hill opposite the Alhambra had found a lead plaque, inscribed with Arabic script that described the martyrdom of a Christian called Meniston during the time of Nero. Over the following months, a score or more of similar 'lead books' were unearthed, along with the cremated remains of most of the martyrs they mentioned. While many, not least the Archbishop of Granada, enthusiastically embraced these self-evident forgeries, many more, including the Pope, recognized them for what they were.[25] We shall return to the lead books shortly, but Cervantes was also influenced by a spurious account of the *True History of King Roderick*, recounting the original Moorish conquest of AD 711, published in two parts in 1592 and 1600 by Miguel de Luna, a Granada physician and translator of Arabic to Philip II, while another Morisco historian of the period had romanticized Muslim Granada as a world of courtly love and chivalric deeds in the *Civil Wars of Granada* of 1595.[26] The mythology of Muslim Spain had form.

Cervantes loved to play around with different levels of fiction, presenting each as apparently true, at least to someone, if only to the madman who has reinvented himself as Don Quixote. But as you strip these different fictions away like the layers of an onion, eventually you are left with nothing but the uncertainty of Cervantes winking at you across the ages.

And so the battle with the Basque servant recommences, with a description of an illustration showing the two combatants frozen in time, as Cervantes has left them. And then the film starts again, with Don Quixote, against all expectation, scoring a knockout blow. In the end, the princess pleads for clemency, the victorious knight errant cannot do otherwise than cede to her will, and a most unlikely murder is avoided.

Part One of *Don Quixote* continues in much the same vein. Sancho and Quixote travel through La Mancha, staying at inns, which Quixote thinks are castles, but most of all engaging with the mundane business of early modern travel and rural realities in the Golden Age. Quixote's approach to each new situation and each new group of characters drives the action, and he does not always come off best as he picks fights with the people he meets. And mindless violence is almost as important in the early stages of this story as it is in novels of chivalry. But Quixote does much more than pick fights. There is a series of 'after-dinner' speeches, when, having eaten well, rather than enact his madness he talks eloquently about the Golden Age of Man or the Dispute Between Arms and Letters, or engages in literary criticism with a canon of Toledo Cathedral.

Superficially, Sancho is a fool, much given to interpreting the world through his repertoire of folk sayings; other characters in the book are amazed that he follows his lunatic master, but we readers have privileged knowledge of Sancho's experience, and we too are voluntarily following Quixote instead of putting the book down. We sympathize because there is excitement and comedy to be had in the company of this highly creative madman. Where else, we ask, will we find the excruciating bathos inherent in a man who, as though the subject of some natural Rorschach test, sees two majestic armies charging into battle in the dust clouds raised by the pitter-pattering hooves of two great transhumant herds of sheep? And then charges into the fray to the dismay of the shepherds?

We also meet interesting or at least intriguing people, all of whom are prefigured by the Inquisition of the Books, for they all seem to have walked out of the pages of one literary genre or another, but who are tinged with realism and live their lives among a profusion of highly realistic low-life characters.

Soon after a convivial meal eaten in the company of a group of goatherds of a most realistic mien, with which Sancho is comfortably familiar, these apparently authentic peasant characters guide the two companions into the midst of a fantastical pastoral drama. The juxtaposition of life and literature is filled with bathos as, suddenly, we all gate-crash the funeral of a classically aristocratic shepherd who has committed suicide over his unrequited love for the ice-hearted Marcela. But we are brought down from the heights of this tragic Olympian idyll when Quixote assaults a humble barber-surgeon who is wearing his shaving-basin as a rain hat. The knight errant, needless to say, believes this to be the golden helmet of Mabrino, and he steals it from the surgeon and begins wearing it instead of his original helmet which has been fictionally suspect from the outset.

When Don Quixote retires to the Brown Mountains to do penance in honour of Dulcinea, he meets a real nobleman apparently crazed by love. Inspired by this deeply romantic hero of Baroque simplicity, he sends Sancho with a missive to Dulcinea. Later, we meet the Captive, who tells his tale of how he has recently been released from prison in Algiers, but, unlike Cervantes in 1580, has returned with a beautiful and wealthy Moorish bride determined to convert to Christianity. Then there is Ginés de Pasamonte, a famous picaroon who, like Guzmán de Alfarache, the anti-hero of Mateo Alemán's groundbreaking picaresque novel, is writing his own autobiography while being escorted to the galleys as part of a chain gang of royal prisoners. Quixote makes a rousing speech about liberty and freedom and then sets the convicts free.

But all good things must come to an end and, as we begin to wonder where the story may be going next, the curate and the barber set out to bring Don Quixote home. Yet they achieve this only by dressing up as chivalric characters, with the curate disguising himself as the Princess Micomicona, and by enlisting the help of some youthful aristocratic lovers recently reconciled after an almost disastrous tiff. In among the vignettes and turns of plot which come thick and fast as the book hurtles towards its anti-climax, Sancho is rescued by the curate and the barber from his impossible task as loyal postman determined to deliver his master's letter to a non-existent Dulcinea: they persuade him to make up a story, to lie. It is a seminal moment in his education in the art of fiction.

Soon afterwards, the whole party arrives at an inn that all of them have visited before and where Don Quixote soon falls asleep. Over a hearty meal, his companions discuss his strange madness with the innkeeper and his family; when the curate explains that he has been sent mad by reading too many novels of chivalry, the innkeeper announces that he has 'two or three' himself, along with 'some other manuscripts which have given me and many others much enjoyment'. He explains that 'at the time of the harvest festival, many reapers stay here and there are always a few who know how to read. So they take up one of these books and more than thirty or so gather around to listen with such pleasure it turns our grey hairs dark again.' So he produces an old valise and the assembled company peruse his diminutive library, which contains a short story with the title 'Impertinent Curiosity' that catches the curate's eye. Everyone pays careful attention as he begins to read the unsettling tale of a jealous husband who so encourages his best friend to test the constancy of his wife that wife and friend end up falling for each other.

These images of Spaniards of all social classes gathered around a man reading aloud from a book, at an inn or in a private house, reflect the reality of early modern Spain. From 1605 onwards, all across Castile, eager listeners would come together in just such a way to listen to *Don Quixote* itself and marvel at the familiarity of the world Cervantes had portrayed for them. For every copy sold, hundreds must have heard the tale.

For almost ten years, Cervantes kept Don Quixote back in his box. But by the end of the decade, he must have been working on Part Two, the sequel that turned a great piece of story telling into the seminal novel of western culture. It is a miracle of ironic imagination.

We remeet Quixote alongside the barber and the curate, 'sitting up in bed, wearing a green baize jerkin, with a red Toledo nightcap, looking as dried up as a mummy'. But his almost religious faith in the precepts of knight errantry is unshaken. After a lengthy discussion of madness and chivalry, the barber and curate leave, and Sancho returns to the stage with some truly titillating gossip: 'Last night, when I greeted Sansón Carrasco, just back from Salamanca where he graduated as a Bachelor, he told me that I have appeared in a history book about you, Sir, called *The Ingenious Gentleman Don Quixote of La Mancha*.'

'I assure you, Sancho, that it must be the work of some wise magician,' says Quixote, excitedly adding, 'I will eat nothing until I know all about it.'

With the arrival of Sansón Carrasco, we real readers are introduced to a type of character who comes to dominate Part Two, a procession of people who have read Part One. Quixote and Sancho are agog, not so much astonished that their meagre exploits should have been published, as anxious to know what has been said about them.

'Tell me, Sir Bachelor, does it include our good Rocinante's story, when he went in search of sweet love?' Sancho says he has asked Carrasco, referring to the wholly unexpected amorous attempt by Quixote's old hack to mount some grazing mares that had resulted in a battering for horse and master from the cowhands in charge. It is an episode embedded within a whole host of tales of unrequited love that end in violence.

'The magician left nothing in the inkwell,' Sansón had replied. 'But there were many', he went on, who, like Nabokov, 'would have preferred it had the authors left out some of the many beatings suffered by Don Quixote.'

'But therein lies the truth of the matter,' an exasperated Sancho had replied.

'It is one thing', said Sansón, plagiarizing Aristotle, 'to write like a poet and quite another as a historian: the poet can sing of deeds not as they were but as they should have been, while the historian must write them not as they ought to have come to pass, but as they were, telling the whole truth and nothing but.'

Then, in the way that interviewers will do with celebrities, Sansón asks Sancho about the unexplained reappearance of his stolen ass.[27]

'I don't know what to say,' Sancho replies, 'except that the historian made a mistake or the printers were careless.'

'And what happened to the 100 *escudos*?' asks Sansón, referring to some gold coins that Sancho and Quixote found by the wayside packed up with some manuscripts in a small travelling case.

'I spent them on myself and my wife and my children, which is why my wife has been so patient about all my travels along the highways and byways in the service of my lord, Don Quixote.'

Inspired by their new celebrity, Quixote and Sancho set out again, determined to visit the jousts to be held at Saragossa. But first Quixote proposes a desperately daring mission to visit Dulcinea in her palace at El Toboso, desperately daring because it is designed to test the very limits of what an author of fiction may be allowed to get away with by his readers. As they approach El Toboso, Quixote is merciless with the pressure he puts on Sancho to find the real Dulcinea. But after a whole book in the company of his master, the servant rises to the task and, as they rest on the outskirts of town, he spies three rude peasant girls riding their mules out into the fields. 'Sir, all you need to do is gee up Rocinante and ride out into the open and you will see your lady Dulcinea.'

Quixote is disbelieving. Cide Hamete tells us that he 'cast his eyes all along the Toboso road but all he could see were three peasant women'. And so Cervantes shifts the burden of his central paradigm of envisioning reality as fiction from Quixote to Sancho: the credulous follower has become the generator of tales. Sancho kneels down in the road before the women and says: 'Queen, Princess and Duchess of beauty, may your highest hugeness be graced to receive the supplications of your captive gentle-knight.' Quixote's eyes are standing out on stalks, the peasant girls are astonished. Sancho has taken control of the script.

From now on they travel as celebrities, for the world has read *Don Quixote* and the world knows who they are and how it expects them to behave. Suddenly, there is nothing strange in Don Quixote mistaking an inn for a castle, for a new literary genre has been born, the modern novel, in which the realism on every page is the stage walked by players cannibalized from a rich admixture of real life and literary precedents. But Quixote and Sancho are developing as well.

After a succession of encounters with make-believe knights errant all imitating Don Quixote and eager for a piece of the action, we readers are confronted with the disturbing episode at the Cave of Montesinos. Led by a scholarly guide into the La Mancha wilderness, Don Quixote ties himself to a rope and is let down into a deep cave. After half an hour, Sancho and the scholar haul in the rope and eventually Quixote appears 'with his eyes shut and showing signs of being asleep'. It takes them a while to wake him and when he does he asks for food. And then, at four in the afternoon, that time of half-sleep and siestas, with the sun poking out from behind the clouds, Quixote tells his tale. He has, he says, descended into an underworld inhabited by the ghosts of all the major characters from the greatest chivalric novels. Like a shaman, he has visited his ancestors, and like a shaman, he has returned with a message from the spirits of the dead.

The message does not make easy listening for Sancho. The great Montesinos, guardian of the desiccated heart of Durandarte, a precious chivalric relic, tells him that Dulcinea has been bewitched and given the appearance of a lowly peasant girl. Sancho must suffer 3,000 lashes in order to break the spell. Sancho takes issue on a point of realism: 'I don't understand how in the short time that you were down there you could have seen so much and conversed so copiously.'

'How long was I down there?'

'An hour or so.'

'That's not possible: night fell and day broke three times.'

Don Quixote's descent into this Hades of chivalric fantasy is his weapon of choice in a developing war over who exactly is in charge of the story. Sancho has very obviously grown in stature as a storyteller since, in Part One, he made a lamentably repetitive attempt to recount a tale involving a shepherd that, with all the characteristics of the incremental chorus of Ten Green Bottles, had quickly descended into a soporific exercise in counting sheep. But, in addition to his developing rivalry with Sancho, more troublingly Quixote has to contend with storytellers in the wider world; and he is soon distracted from his determination to win back dominance over Dulcinea: Cide Hamete tells us that 'coming out of the woods at sunset, Don Quixote gazed across to the far side of a green meadow where he could see a hunting party of falconers. Among them was a beautiful lady mounted on a pure white palfrey adorned in green and with a silver saddle.'

Needless to say, we readers have no idea whether this is what Quixote alone imagines he is seeing. In fact, inasmuch as we can speak of fact in this context, it is an aristocratic hunting party. The lady is a duchess, and she and her duke have read Part One: 'they were very eager to meet Don Quixote and were determined to indulge his lunacy and go along with whatever he desired'.

Here begins the very long central section of Part Two, which takes place at the ducal pleasure palace, soon renamed by Hamete as a castle, which the duke's theatrically minded majordomo converts into a chivalric theme park, quickly filled with the accoutrements and characters usual to the genre. As they arrive at the castle to a flamboyant reception, 'Don Quixote marvelled at it all; and for the first time he believed himself to be a real knight errant, rather than a fantasy.' What, we wonder, are we meant to think of that?

The opportunities for chivalric adventure are legion. At one stage, Quixote and Sancho are blindfolded and invited to mount a wooden horse so that they can literally fly across the heavens to give succour to a distressed damsel. Various props are employed, fires, bellows and the like, to make them feel their take-off, the rushing hot air of the flight through the torrid zone and their bumpy return to earth. When the adventure is over, Sancho claims to have peeked out and seen the earth from on high; the delighted duchess tries to derail this make-believe and Quixote steps in to rescue his squire, ruling that 'as such things come to pass completely outside the natural order, it is no big thing that Sancho should say what he has'. But then he turns to Sancho and says very privately: 'Well, if you want people to believe you about what what you have seen from the sky, so I want you to believe what I have told you I saw in the Cave of Montesinos.' This is a narrative pact if ever I saw one.

But the centrepiece of the visit to this toy-shop castle is the duke's decision to make Sancho governor of an island called Barataria, in reality one of the seigneurial towns on the estate. The spirit of carnival dances throughout the episode as the usual hierarchy is turned upside down and Sancho turns out to be highly competent. But his desire for office has always been essentially visceral and he revels in the prospect of his first meal in power.

Sancho sat at the head of the table, while some personage who must have been a physician stood by. They lifted off a white cloth covering the fruit and a great variety of dishes. A plate of fruit was placed before Sancho, but he had hardly had a bite before the physician touched it with his baton and they took it away. The steward brought another dish, but as Sancho went to taste it, the physician touched it with his baton and as though he had waved a magic wand it was rushed away by a page.

The physician explains that it is his duty to ensure that Sancho has a healthy diet.

'What about those partridges?'

'Over my dead body!'

'If that is the case,' says Sancho, 'Sir Physician, see which of the many dishes on this table will do me good and let me eat it without so much baton waving.'

But the doctor denies him dish after dish until the whole business is brought to a halt by the sound of a cornet announcing the arrival of a letter from the duke about the menace of an imminent attack on Barataria. A terrified Sancho eventually dines on 'dressed beef and some rather high cow heel, which he wolfed down as though they had been the finest game birds of Milan'.

A certain amount of anxiety and dissatisfaction overcomes the reader during the long, long visit to the ducal estate. Sancho and Quixote are separated; moreover they have unquestionably lost control of the story. The characters and their narrative have become the playthings of other, rather vulgar readers. It is like watching a movie of a favourite book, *Don Quixote* itself perhaps, and finding that our beloved friends have been turned into Rex Harrison or Bob Hoskins, that Dulcinea has miraculously materialized as Sophia Loren, and that Cide Hamete has been strangely reincarnated as Orson Welles. The free will of our imagination has been violated.

Quixote and Sancho clearly also feel this painful sense of *desengaño* or disillusionment, because now, each of them, independently and simultaneously, decides to abandon the pantomime created for them by the duke and duchess.

Back on the road, Quixote exclaims: 'Liberty, Sancho, is one of the most precious gifts that God has given man.'

They come to an inn, which Quixote recognizes as an inn, where Sancho asks what there is to eat. The innkeeper replies that he has 'all the birds of the air, every creature of the land, every fish in the sea'.

'We don't need all that,' Sancho replies, 'a couple of roast chickens will do.'

But chicken, he is told, 'is off'.

After further interrogation which exposes the whole extensive menu as fictional, the innkeeper confesses that 'what I really, truly have are two cow heels which look like veal hoofs, stewed up with their garbanzos, onion and bacon, which are crying out to be eaten'.

'Mark them as mine,' says Sancho. 'I'll pay better than anyone!'

The two friends sit down to dinner, reunited as much with us readers as with each other by the familiarity of their surroundings, and with all of us relieved to be free of the painful vanities of the duke and duchess. But suddenly, from the next booth, they hear a voice say: 'Well then, Sir Geronimo, while we are waiting for our dinner, let's read aloud another chapter from Part Two of *Don Quixote*.'

Today, we immediately wonder whether Cervantes may not be playing some ever more complex game and that Part Two has already been fictionally published within the story before being published in the real world. But contemporaries were well aware that a year before the real Part Two came out, someone, possibly Lope de Vega, had published a pirate continuation of *Don Quixote* under the pseudonym of Alonso Fernández de Avellaneda.

'Sir Juan, why on earth would you want to read that rubbish? It is not possible that someone who has read Part One could enjoy this second part,' says Geronimo, voicing Cervantes's own brief appraisal of his rival's efforts.

And then Quixote, Cide Hamete and Cervantes seize control of the story.

Since the outset of Part Two, Quixote and Sancho have been slowly travelling to Saragossa to take part in a tournament there. But when Quixote is told that this is what he and Sancho do in the apocryphal version, he declares, 'I will not set foot in Saragossa so as to make public the lies told by this modern historian.' Instead, they go to Barcelona.

Don Quixote is a book about books and the experience of reading which explores the relationship between reality and fiction. Cervantes seems exuberantly happy in the uncertain, shifting world of life as stage, the world as illusion, society as replete with deception and disillusionment and *desengaño*. He is most at home exploring that familiar and often disturbingly intangible universe of psychological and emotional and moral truths.

Don Quixote is so loved by the literati because it obsessively scratches that familiar scab forever forming and reforming over humanity's common wound of existential angst, but it does so by playing joyfully with the mind's awareness of the limitations of its own perception. The psychoanalyst's morbid fear and mournful search for childhood is here eclipsed by glee, by the sheer delight in human variation. Crippled, luckless, hapless Cervantes laughs and smiles, a man who sees only foibles and frailties, never faults and failings.

Within the ordered chaos of his own creation, he is the arch manipulator and we readers are the subjects of his crazed experiments, his guinea pigs, our melancholic minds recast, re-rendered as successful portraits of Dorian Gray, ever loving, ever youthful, ever unsure, until we close the book and, with a considerable sense of relief, as one character says to another at the end of Cervantes's collection of extended short stories, the *Exemplary Novels*, we may conclude that 'now we have exercised our mind's eye, let us go out into the main square and look at the world with the eyes in our heads'.

Of course, Cervantes soon gives us a half-glance at cruel reality, escorting us into the main square, as he propels us towards Quixote's tragic denouement.

14

Moriscos and Catalans

You well know, Sancho, that His Majesty's Edict of Expulsion issued
against my people was terrifying.

                                        Ricote the Morisco, *Don Quixote*

While Don Quixote is extricating himself from a final, tedious
adventure at the ducal castle, Sancho is given a curious, unusual
episode that is all his own. This may be a book so packed with social
observation that it has inspired cataracts of political interpretation,
but it is rarely overtly political. There is the burning of the books
and its satire on the Inquisition, but otherwise it mostly refrains from
representing politicized realities. Yet as we approach the final chapters a very topical and politically charged character appears among a
group of beggars dressed in French clothing. He approaches the lone
Sancho and exclaims in perfect Castilian: 'Goodness me! Can it be
true that I can stretch out my arms to my dear friend and good neighbour, Sancho Panza?'

Sancho is amazed.

'Brother Sancho, is it possible that you don't recognize your
own neighbour, Ricote the Morisco, the storekeeper of your home
town?'

Without dismounting, Sancho throws his arms around the man's
neck and says: 'Who the hell would recognize you dressed up as a
Frog? And how come you have dared to come back to Spain; if they
catch you it'll be a bad lookout.'

'If you don't give me away, I am safe in this disguise. Let's go and sit down by those elms where my companions are going to eat and rest a while.'

They eat a convivial meal together, which, symbolically enough, includes cured ham and is washed down with plenty of wine; and then Ricote the Morisco begins his tale:

> You well know, Sancho, that His Majesty's Edict of Expulsion issued against my people was terrifying. I decided to leave our village long before it came into effect so as to find a safe place to live with my family, for like all our wise old men I could see this was no mere threat as many claimed, but a real law that would come into force. Oh, how we have cried for Spain wherever we have roamed, for it is the land of our birth!
>
> I left our village and went to France, then Italy, and finally I reached Germany, where it seemed to me a man can live at liberty, for there one can do as one wants, and most of the people live with freedom of conscience.

This may sound like a miraculous American idyll, but for Cervantes it was clearly a reference to the Habsburgs' failure to defeat Protestantism in their German and Dutch lands. It was an age when liberty and freedom, in the wrong hands – and there could be no worse hands than a laxly Christian Morisco – were simply a licence to libertine dissolution and immorality. It was the great poet and writer Francisco de Quevedo who suggested that 'servitude is much better than freedom, at least in as much as they describe licentiousness as liberty'.[1]

'It is now my intention to recover my buried treasure,' Ricote continues, 'and then to go to Algiers where my wife and daughter have gone, for some reason I do not understand, for both of them were good Christians, unlike me, although I am still more of a Christian than a Moor.'

'Look, Ricote, that was out of their hands,' Sancho explains, 'because your wife's brother, Juan Tiopieyo, took them there, fine Muslim that he is!'

Ricote then offers Sancho 200 ducats to help him dig up his treasure, but Sancho refuses because he is terrified of how his wife will react to the news that he has abandoned the governorship of Barataria. Ricote departs along the road, astonished by the literary developments in his old friend's life, but he will reappear along with his daughter, a few chapters later, in Barcelona.

This peculiar and brief encounter refers to the notorious Expulsion of the Moriscos, of 1609 to 1614. But then the Moriscos were a theme to which Cervantes returned from time to time with resolute ambivalence, unable to accept them or condemn them.[2] The great novelist's writings on the subject very much reflected the ambiguity of the times.

The Expulsion of the Moriscos has long been seen as emblematic of the evil stupidity of Philip III's government under the leadership of the Duke of Lerma, but also as evidence of its potential for efficiency. Ever since the fall of Granada, the last Islamic principality in Spain, to the Catholic Monarchs in 1492, the subjects of the newly conquered territories and a residual Muslim population in the rest of Spain left over from earlier phases of Reconquest had all been viewed with great suspicion by a minority of Spaniards. In 1502, there had been some attempt to force Muslims either to convert to Christianity or to leave Spain, but this had been ineffectually enforced and in many areas they were allowed to continuing practising Islam on payment of a tax. The Inquisition was distracted by its obsessive pursuit of crypto-Jews and Protestants, the Crown was apathetic, aristocrats protected valuable vassals irrespective of religion. In Aragon and Valencia even such paltry attempts at religious homogenization as practised in Castile were officially delayed until the 1520s. Many had converted, however, with varying degrees of sincerity, often thanks to the kind of very imperfect catechism described by Padre León in 1592 as he travelled the Granada hinterland.

The Morisco community developed a kaleidoscopic identity, different from place to place, from person to person, and ever changing according to one's perspective on their culture and society. For Sancho and Ricote, religion is clearly of little importance compared to their shared sense of identity in coming from the same place and knowing one another's business and family. The Moriscos were historically Spaniards, tied to the land of their forefathers, as Ricote wails. In fact, many of them were descended from ancestors who had lived in Visigoth Spain before the Moors first came in 711. These Old Moriscos are often called Mudéjars and were as rooted in the soil of Iberia as their Christian neighbours.

But the Turkish Ottoman threat sparked great paranoia; it was feared the Moriscos would help the infidel and loud and powerful voices were raised against them.

Philip II had been persuaded to legislate against the use of traditional 'Arab' dress, which helped to provoke the Alpujarra uprisings of 1568 and 1570 that, in turn, led to the forced dispersal of the still mostly Muslim Moriscos of Granada among the better integrated Mudéjar communities of Castile. The voices of intolerance grew louder still in the overconfident aftermath of the successful annexation of Portugal in 1580. The fundamentalist firebrand Bishop of Valencia, Juan de Ribera, saw the presence of such a heterodox influence in the bosom of Counter-Reformation Spain as an heretical canker that gave succour to the devil: the Moriscos were 'wizened trees, full of knots of heresy' which needed 'tearing up at the roots'.[3] Another bishop advocated transporting them to the Americas, to 'the broad stretch of uninhabited Newfoundland, where they will die out, especially if the men are castrated'.[4]

The Moriscos fought back politically, most obviously and notoriously by forging the peculiar lead books of Granada, with their accounts of ancient Christian martyrdoms recorded in Arabic script.[5] These manifestly fraudulent finds were quickly authenticated by the Archbishop and, in 1608, a collegiate church was founded on the hillside that was officially recognized as the Sacromonte, or 'sacred hill'. The religious confraternities and the guilds of Granada organized a festive procession; over 800 crosses were staked along a route to be lit by bonfires and fireworks, and hundreds of girls and women dressed as angels climbed up to Sacromonte, alongside priests and friars, soldiers and musicians.[6]

Granada may have celebrated, but elsewhere there were many sceptics and the Vatican later described the whole business as 'a mere human fiction'.[7] Why, the sceptics wondered, was so much of the material in Arabic when it was supposed to date from the early Christian period, long before the Moors ruled in Spain? But the lead books were no mere fraud; they were part of a policy to rewrite the history of Islamic Spain that was carefully orchestrated by a powerful network of influential Morisco merchants.[8] Alonso del Castillo, Philip II's own interpreter, seems to have been responsible for the actual falsification and his purpose is clear on reading the texts, which argue for a close affinity between Islam and Christianity and are obviously sympathetic to the Moriscos. In one passage purporting to be from the Gospel of Zebedee, the Madonna declares to St Peter, 'I tell you, the Arabs are an excellent folk, and their language is one of the best. Recently, God has chosen them to help him with his law, after the time they were his enemies. God gave them power, wisdom, and justice for that purpose, because God chooses his servants with compassion.'[9]

The Moriscos had many allies in this cultural rearguard action and it is clear that many, probably most, ordinary Spaniards, as Sancho's behaviour suggests, were sympathetic to their neighbours. A whole genre of heavily romanticized maurophile or 'Moor-loving' literature emerged, which borrowed from books of knight errantry to portray Muslims as noble and chivalrous heroes.[10] That cultural empathy went hand in glove with far more pragmatic reasons to support the Moriscos: modern estimates of the Morisco population suggest it was 300,000, but at the time some thought there might be as many as 600,000, with the majority being New Moriscos in Valencia and Aragon, but with a minority of important historically rooted Mudéjar communities across Castile. At that time, the total population of Spain is thought to have been around ten million at most. To expel around 5 per cent would be madness, devastating local economies, upsetting regional economic balances and ultimately further destabilizing an already precarious Castilian economy. Although Philip II had in principle acquiesced to those arguing in favour of expulsion, he had repeatedly declined to put into practice such an insane policy.

But the Old Mudéjars of Castile were relatively few, and the Council of State was packed with Castilians with an ever more arrogantly Castilian perspective. In 1590, the Council advised rusticating the Moriscos of the main cities to 'hamlets and villages of no importance'. Others urged expulsion to 'Granada from whence they came', displaying a breathtaking ignorance of the complexities of Morisco history. The succession of Philip III encouraged the maurophobes and the Council voted in favour of 'mustering the necessary force to establish in secret an estimate of the number of Moriscos in the kingdom, beginning with Castile'. But as the investigations went ahead, it became increasingly clear that the Castilian Moriscos were well integrated and also had powerful local support. In 1607, for example, the Count of Miranda explained that their labour was essential for agriculture as he sought some kind of compromise that would allow them to stay.[11] Two years later, the Seville City Hall complained bitterly that among the Moriscos 'there are many Catholics of good faith' and 'it is common knowledge how necessary they are to this city, providing services and other work. They do not deserve' to be expelled.[12]

Faced with such resistance, but relentlessly driven by the bigotry of the Archbishop of Valencia, during the first decade of the new century there was a clear shift in policy towards first dealing with Aragon and Valencia, before turning to Catalonia and finally Castile. Lerma was the key to this change, for he had been Philip II's Viceroy in Valencia, had many estates there and was sympathetic to the local nobility. Aware that rents from Morisco tenants had been falling in real terms, he proposed a scheme for expulsion by which the Crown would compensate landowners in Valencia for the loss of their Morisco vassals, offering an easy solution to the financial problems of a fecklessly over-mortgaged aristocracy while expediting the policy of expulsion.

It was one thing, however, to suggest relocating a handful of Castilians to other parts of the Iberian Peninsula where there were already large and not especially integrated Morisco populations; it was something else entirely to propose expelling all of the Moriscos almost without exception. The logistics of such an enterprise are mind-boggling.

Yet by 1609 Philip III's government knew that Spain could no longer afford the War of the Netherlands and agreed to the Twelve Years' Peace. With Catholic Spain being publicly humiliated by Dutch Protestant heretics on the European stage, on 9 April, the very same day that he signed the Treaty of Antwerp, the King also put his name to the Edict of Expulsion of the Moriscos of Valencia, which the Council of Castile had agreed would serve as a precursor to the total expulsion. Religious duty and Christian honour would be restored by cleansing Spain herself of her own impurity.

From the outset, this apparently impossible task was handled amid great confusion. In 1609 the Edict relating to Valencia was published, but nothing was said officially about Castile in the improbable hope that the Moriscos there would not be alarmed. In some places there was calm, but elsewhere there was consternation and panic. Men like Ricote began marrying their daughters to Old Christians (and we know from the parish registers that marriage rates went up), burying treasure and selling their property, seemingly at heavily discounted prices. Many no doubt lost out significantly because of a glut on the market, but there is good evidence that plenty of these sales were made to trusted relatives and friends who qualified as Old Christians; and, because the Crown levied a sales tax on such transactions, it is hardly surprising that the sums reported were very low.[13] Having put their houses in order as best they could, the Ricotes of Castile began to leave, but few took ship for Muslim North Africa. Instead the Crown guaranteed them safe passage by the northern route through Burgos so that they might seek refuge in France, Italy or, as in Ricote's case, in Germany. Thousands of frightened fugitives began making their way to the French border. Then, in 1610, the Edicts of Expulsion from Murcia and Andalusia were issued, followed by those for Aragon and then Castile. The policy, however, remained chaotic, because aristocrats, the Church and many town councils, as well as the Moriscos themselves, fought the expulsion hard in some cases, or at least passively resisted it in others.[14]

History has largely recorded this programme of ethnic cleansing as a disastrous success, in some cases claiming that over 90 per cent of the Spanish Moriscos were removed between 1610 and 1614, when the policy was finally abandoned. But the reality is considerably more nuanced.

In 1627, Philip IV announced a competition to paint a major work depicting the Expulsion of the Moriscos in order to commemorate the only subject that might conceivably be held to glorify his father's notoriously inglorious reign. It was won by the up-and-coming Diego Velázquez, who was rewarded for his artistic victory with the office of Usher of the Royal Chamber, and his painting was hung in the great Hall of Mirrors, alongside some of the most important pictures in the Royal Collection: Titian's equestrian portrait of Charles V and Rubens's portraits of Philip II and III.[15]

Velázquez most probably won because he represented Philip III at the centre of the painting, armed and in white, with the majestic figure of Hispania to his right, dressed as a Roman matron, with a shield and lance in her right hand and a handful of wheat in her left.[16] It is the only occasion we know of when Velázquez included such an allegorical image in one of his paintings,[17] an indication that even for this naturalistic painter, whose lifeblood was intimate realism, the Expulsion of the Moriscos was a subject that needed abstracting into the emblematic fiction of legend.

The painting was lost in a fire that destroyed the Alcázar in Madrid in the eighteenth century, but a preparatory cartoon by Vicente Carducho for his own entry in the competition has survived. It evokes the drama and pathos as soldiers oversee the refugees embarking on to ships that will take them 'home' to North Africa. In the background, a forest of lances symbolizes the military might of the Spanish Crown. It encapsulates the quickly developing iconography of an event imperfectly remembered by many as having finally brought to an end the long history of heathen, Moorish Spain, the glorious conclusion of nine centuries of Reconquest, the spirit of which Lope de Vega perfectly encapsulated in verse:

Those residual relics of the barbarous Moors
Were justly sent to Africa across the seas
Thanks to our third holy Philip's great decrees,
Showing due disdain for proffered heathen treasure.[18]

The latest research is only now beginning to reshape that legend into history by revealing how, along with other Crown propaganda produced at the time, the legend itself has misguided historians ever since. Strangely enough, Cervantes's fiction, written at the time, seems to offer a reliable record; and he trumpeted the fact that he knew what he wrote was potentially seditious by calling Sancho Panza's friend Ricote, a name that would have evoked a history of heroic resistance for contemporary readers.

The Ricote Valley is, even today, a remote and unpromisingly harsh environment in the uplands of the Region of Murcia that was once a separate kingdom lying on the Spanish Levant between Granada and Valencia, at the heart of Morisco country. In the early seventeenth century, it was a poor land of 2,500 peasant farmers and primitive churches, an isolated world whose inhabitants had been hassled from time to time by the Inquisition for their superstitious heterodoxy and the persistence of Islam, and who were thought to be beyond assimilation into the Christian fold.[19] For the most part, these were Mudéjars, among whom there were very few recent migrants from Granada and the Alpujarras. Following the initial Edict of Expulsion for Valencia of 1609, a few inhabitants of the Ricote Valley made preparations to leave, and more began to trickle away following the publication of the Edict for Murcia the following year. But while religious processions celebrated the purification of the kingdom in the streets of the cities, little attempt was actually made to remove Moriscos forcibly from Ricote; at the same time, government officials wrote reports arguing that the Mudéjars should be allowed to remain. The reality of the expulsion, when examined at the level of local detail, begins to look terribly confused, and from 1610 onwards more and more accounts began reaching the Crown that many of the Moriscos who had left of their own accord or actually been expelled had subsequently returned home like Cervantes's Ricote. In many places, the authorities resigned themselves to trying to expel them again.

In 1613, the Count of Salazar, a minor nobleman and enthusiastic administrative stooge, who had been placed in overall charge of the expulsion in Castile, set out himself for Ricote with an armed troop. The removal began as earnestly as it ever would, yet even with Salazar present the local priest was able to establish himself as a kind of savings bank; he allowed his Morisco parishioners to deposit funds with him and agreed to be entrusted with property. The Crown even allowed them to continue to own property themselves and to issue powers of attorney to make possible its administration. Some fled to the hills; all sorts were given dispensation to remain: the old, the infirm, the married and young children. So although the exiles escorted to the coast by Salazar's men may have wept for their homeland as their galleys departed for Italy, they must have had high hopes they would return. And there is plenty of evidence that many of them did indeed soon come home; some of that evidence comes from official records which show that they continued to be troubled by the Inquisition and by the authorities from time to time for years afterwards, although even that harassment mostly abated during the 1620s.[20] By the time Velázquez's painting won Philip IV's competition, no one cared about the Moriscos still living in Spain.

Ricote was clearly a name that for Cervantes symbolized the inefficiency of the expulsion. But Sancho Panza's friend lived in La Mancha, not Murcia nor neighbouring Valencia; and when we turn to La Mancha, we find an even more compelling story showing the almost complete failure of the policy in respect of the Mudéjars.

A bundle of papers was recently discovered at the Provincial Archive of Saragossa, which contains an almost blow-by-blow account of how the powerful Count of Salinas, Lord of Villarrubia de los Ojos and President of the Council of Portugal, strained every legal and administrative sinew and employed a range of obstructive, de facto manoeuvres on the ground in order to thwart Salazar and his officials.[21]

Salinas's opening gambit was deliberately to misinterpret the Edict of Expulsion as applying only to his Moriscos from Granada who, he claimed, 'are very few', before going on to ask that these sacrificial lambs anyway be deported under their own auspices, 'because they were my vassals and have always been good Christians'. Proper patrician that he was, he had thumbed his nose at Crown authority. He then put the royal officials at nearby Almagro on notice that they had no jurisdiction over his seigneurial lands in respect of the expulsion. The town of Villarrubia then wrote to the King, asserting the rights of their Moriscos which they proved had been granted them by the Catholic Monarchs, while Salinas himself pointed out that they did not even live in a separate quarter but were integrated into the rest of the town, though this was in fact stretching a point. He then began lobbying members of the Council of Castile. At the same time, he encouraged his Old Christians to marry the available Morisca girls, evidently mostly marriages of convenience as parish records show that they produced few offspring. There is some suggestion that, at the same time and with mixed success, he encouraged the fabrication of Old Christian ancestry for many Moriscos through the forging of documents and through false testimony in the courts. The Count of Salinas comes across as politically ruthless, but with a twinkle in his eye.

By the summer of 1611, his shenanigans had limited the number forced to leave Villarrubia by Salazar's men to six or seven hundred; but as these refugees were escorted through Madrid on their way to the French border, 250 of them managed to escape their guards and took refuge in Salinas's palace. We know little more about what happened next, but at least some of these fugitives were allowed to go home to Villarrubia.

The whole business of their expulsion was descending into a tragic farce, with officials in the towns along the route to the French border reluctant to accept jurisdiction over Moriscos from elsewhere. There is no record of how many were finally ejected from Spain into France, but by September Salazar lamented that at least 400 had returned to Villarrubia, bringing with them large contingents from neighbouring towns and estates. To cap it all, quite bizarrely it was a Morisco, a man called Alonso Sánchez Terrinces, who, at the end of September, turned up at the city hall of Villarrubia with an order issued by the Chancery Court of Granada relating to a dispute over the appointment and election of various municipal officials traditionally held on St Michael's Day.

In a moment of considerably more chilling irony, the following year the royal commissioners arrived in Villarrubia to remove the Moriscos again, whom they found gathered in church witnessing 150 of their offspring receiving First Communion from the Bishop.[22] But the game of cat-and-mouse went on, with a third round of expulsions in 1613. Yet, by 1617 if not before, Villarrubia was apparently back to normal.[23]

'I lived in my parents' house until I was sixteen or seventeen, perhaps twenty,' a Morisco called Diego Díaz remembered years later, 'working as a labourer, which is what my father did, until the king decreed the Expulsion of the Moriscos. We loaded our belongings on to carts and were escorted to Saint Jean de Luz, in France, where I saw the sea for the first time, but it was a cold and damp place and we longed to come back to Spain.' And so he did, but was apprehended and sent back to France. He tried again, the following year, 'and this time I had more luck, getting home to Damiel, where I began working as a servant to an official of the Inquisition' no less. But he was 'captured again with many others who had returned and we were taken to Cartagena on the Levant coast of Spain. Some were punished in the galleys, but the Lord saved me, for my sins. We were in Cartagena for a few days until the sheriff brought another group of Moriscos and they loaded us on to a ship,' which was supposed to take them to Italy, but which illegally disembarked them in North Africa. They began walking to nearby Algiers and were well received by a troop of Moors, who took them to the city, then teeming with 6,000 refugees from Granada.

Diego claimed that at Algiers he had been circumcised against his will, which nonetheless he considered a terrible sin and which he immediately confessed in secret to a captive Christian priest; although he may, of course, have been circumcised already. He soon escaped aboard a Morisco fishing boat, managing to make his way first to Saragossa and then to France in search of his family. In France he heard that some relatives had died and others had gone home to Spain. But Diego was determined to go to Rome, 'to confess my sins because they had told me that the circumcision ceremony was against the law of Jesus and was a mortal sin that could be pardoned only by the Pope'. En route, two kindly French friars explained to him that Avignon was a papal domain and that the bishop there would be able to absolve him. In Avignon, he found a priest who spoke Spanish and gave him absolution and provided him with written proof of the fact.

Back in Spain, he drifted from Valencia to Alicante before becoming an apprentice butcher. Armed with the tools of his trade, he travelled through Andalusia and La Mancha and then settled in Luis de León's birthplace, the beautifully walled town of Belmonte, where in 1633 he was arrested by the Inquisition. He told his tale to that institution, which is why we have a transcript of it today. Arguing that if he were not a good Christian he would have remained in North Africa, 'where the law of Mohammed rules and which is a land rich in everything', he secured his acquittal in January of the following year.[24]

We can but speculate about how much of Diego's story was true and how much a fabrication convenient to his defence. But it usefully reminds us that while he did indeed come home to Spain, his life had been disrupted by dislocation and uncertainty, he may or may not have had his genitals mutilated, he had certainly had his conscience violated, and his peripatetic picaresque life may well have been a flight from fear of himself as much as a constant evasion of the Inquisition that finally caught up with him. But Diego's expulsion was unquestionably a failure.

Ultimately, the expulsion can be seen as an experiment at the very limits of sovereign authority and of the power of the Crown, the results of which are evidence of the reach and the strength or weakness of the administration. In the past, it was thought that the success of the expulsion was evidence of the robust efficiency of Lerma's administration and the overwhelming power of the monarchy.[25] But it is now clear that in Castile at least, for powerful aristocrats like Salinas and their vassals, the central government was a 'distant irritant to be appeased, if possible'. The reality was that 'the further away from Madrid, the more difficult it was to enforce the dictats and so the easier it was to ignore them. Never was there better evidence of the truth of that well-known Spanish saying: *se obedece pero no se cumple*.'[26] This literally means 'one obeys, but one does not comply', but is best understood as meaning 'I am subject to the rule of law, but I do not abide by the law.'

The evidence from Valencia, however, is more difficult to assess. It was widely said that there were about 135,000 Moriscos living in the

Kingdom of Valencia in the early years of the seventeenth century, and in 1602 the Count of Benavente ordered a census of New Moriscos that recorded 24,695 households in total, which would equate to 100,000 or more. In the course of the expulsion itself, the commanders of the fleet of ships which transported the exiles officially reported carrying a total of 117,521 passengers.[27] At first glance, then, the expulsion from Valencia seems to have been almost total.

But the programme of expelling the Moriscos was officially abandoned in 1614, with the Count of Salazar still haranguing Lerma, Philip and the Council of State about the vast numbers who had returned home or never been thrown out in the first place. That is testimony to the attachment of a people to their landscape and underscores their indigenous identity as Spaniards. Their descendants, the research has shown, are still living in Villarrubia today; and the distinctive influence of their culture is familar across Spain, most obvious and delicious in such classic foods as gazpacho and *ajo blanco* (an almond soup), *albondigas* (saffron-flavoured meatballs), *remojón* (a salad of salt cod and oranges) and the pickled aubergines of Almagro; even paella is rooted in Valencia's Morisco past.

Yet the figure of 117,00 exiles does not take account of those who were expelled but then returned home successfully; and it includes only fifty-seven individuals who had already been expelled and had secretly returned, only to be expelled again, when there must have been many more such cases. However, the most reliable data available show that, in 1650, the rural population of Morisco villages in Valencia was as much as half of what it had been before the expulsion, perhaps 40,000 or so. This was after forty years of sharp decline in population across Spain; and, in fact, the decline in the population of the harsh Valencia uplands, where most of the Morisco villages were located, was similar to that recorded for the harshest lands elsewhere in Spain.[28] This poses the awkward question of who was living there. This has been imaginatively put down to immigration from France, but, when France declared war on Spain in 1634, it was estimated that there were only 10,000 Frenchmen in all Valencia, town and country.[29] So where on earth had the vast majority of the 'new' inhabitants of the old Morisco villages come from? The usual answer is that they were Old Christians from other parts of Spain. But with Europe's population in sharp decline, who, one wonders, would work such land instead of migrating to more forgiving soil that became free as the population fell? As with the rest of Spain, the answer is the people who had always lived there; in this case, the Moriscos.

The successful transportation by boat of 100,000 or more Moriscos from the Valencia ports is certainly evidence of the efficiency of the Spanish military and navy, and it was incalculably disruptive to the Moriscos and their seigneurial lords who were never compensated by the Crown as they had been promised. But it also seems that most of them returned soon afterwards, which is evidence that just as the Crown could send army after army to the Netherlands or armada after armada against England but never managed any permanent victory, so it was similarly unable to impose permanently the expulsion in Valencia or Castile.

Swallows like Ricote and Villarrubia do not a summer make out of the many long winters of discontent of people like Diego Díaz. The discovery that the expulsion largely failed and that much of the damage done was repaired does not detract from the great distress caused to the individuals and the disruption to their traditions and culture. Impotence and incompetence cannot redeem the fundamentalist sentiments that were allowed to bring about the policy of expulsion.

A few chapters further on in *Don Quixote*, soon after their visit to the print shop described earlier, Quixote and Sancho are taken to visit a galley guarding the harbour at Barcelona that, with them still aboard, almost immediately becomes involved in the pursuit of a Barbary corsair. It is as close as Quixote comes to military service. When this ship is captured, it turns out that the captain is in fact a beautiful Morisca girl called Ana Félix, who has disguised herself as a pirate in order to escape Algiers because she is a devout Christian. Needless to say, Ricote soon turns up and recognizes her as his daughter, and she turns out to be betrothed to an aristocratic Old Christian gallant from their home in La Mancha who is currently a captive in North Africa.

It is the Viceroy of Catalonia whose humanitarian voice we now hear: he immediately orders Ricote and his daughter to be treated with the utmost courtesy, 'such was the benevolence and charity with which he was inspired by Ana Félix's great beauty'. In due course, her beloved aristocrat Don Gregorio is rescued, and the Viceroy and Quixote's powerful host, Don Antonio, both agree to initiate the necessary machinations to allow Ricote to remain in Spain and Ana Félix to marry her betrothed. By 1615, when the book was published, such reconciliation was the tacit policy of a Crown that had proved unequal to the task of imposing totalitarian authority on its subjects.

Cervantes wrote his fanfare to the failure of Philip's policy of expelling the Moriscos even as it was happening, but a few chapters earlier he highlighted a completely different context in which the authority of the Crown was severely challenged. Quixote and Sancho travelled to Barcelona, soon after leaving the inn with the disappearing menu; as they entered Catalonia for the first time, they met the only character in the whole book who was very much a real person: the notorious bandit Roca Guinarda, whom Cervantes calls Roque Guinart.

At nightfall, Sancho and Quixote leave the road and dismount in some woods; and, while Sancho sleeps, his master dreams of Montesinos and Dulcinea. In the dead of night, Quixote becomes angry at his squire's lack of enthusiasm for flagellating himself in order to relieve the spell cast over Dulcinea and decides to inflict the necessary lashes himself. But when he starts to unbuckle Sancho's trousers, Sancho wakes and takes refuge behind a tree, where 'he felt someone touching his head and, raising up his hands, he discovered two human feet wearing shoes and socks. Trembling with fear, he went over to another tree, where the same thing happened.' The two friends soon find that 'all of the trees were full of human feet and legs'.

Quixote is quick to reassure Sancho: 'There is no reason to be fearful, for these feet and legs you are touching must belong to robbers or bandits who have been hanged in these trees; around here the justices usually hang them by the score when they catch them, by which I assume that we must be near Barcelona.'

The contemporary reader would have been well aware that this was no Quixotic hallucination, but that policing Catalan banditry was one of the hot political topics of the day. In 1613, the Viceroy of Catalonia boasted that he had 'achieved more than any other viceroy' by establishing an 'indomitable' troop of 'twelve cavalry and thirty infantry' which had pursued Roca Guinarda, 'the worst of robbers'. He went on, 'I have hanged twenty-two of his band alone and I am confident I will hang Roca himself.'[30]

In the morning, Quixote and Sancho see the cadavers hanging from the trees. 'But,' Cervantes tells us, 'if the dead scared them, they were no less perturbed to be surrounded by over forty live bandits' who suddenly appear. As the thieves begin to loot the saddlebags, their leader arrives 'who appeared to be about thirty-four, dark, tough, bigger than average, with a serious expression. He rode a powerful horse and carried four pistols of the kind they call flintlocks. When he saw that his own squires, as they called themselves, were about to rob Sancho, he ordered them not to.' Turning his attention to Quixote, he exclaims: 'Do not be sad, good friend, for you have not fallen into the cruel hands of some Osiris, but into those of Roque Guinart.'

'I am not sad because I have fallen into your hands, valiant Roque, whose fame has no limits, but because your soldiers have captured me with my horse unbridled; for I am obliged by the order of chivalry to be ever vigilant. Oh Roque, would that they had found me in the saddle, with my lance and shield, then they would not have so easily defeated me.'

Roque, of course, has heard of Quixote and is amazed to meet him. The real Roca Guinarda was, at this time, in exile in Italy, where, his biographer has suggested, he will have been tickled pink to discover his own appearance in Part Two of such a famous best-seller.[31]

'Brave knight,' Roque says to Quixote, 'do not blame yourself, nor think you suffer ill luck, for it may be that with our meeting your luck has changed; for the strange machinations of the Heavens often raise up the fallen and enrich the poor.'

At that moment a damsel in distress rides in like the wind and appeals to Roque for help. She has succumbed to the advances of a nobleman whose father belongs to a different bandit gang. The young lad promised marriage, but then took another girl as his wife. The spirited distressed damsel has just shot her jilting lover with a rifle and two pistols. She wants Roque to smuggle her across the French border.

With a twist of the plot, familiar to us from *Romeo and Juliet*, Roque leads the girl to the scene of her crime, where they find the expiring nobleman who explains he has not married the other woman at all. The damsel faints, her lover dies. 'Her lament was so tragic that tears welled up in Roque's eyes, which were unaccustomed to shedding them under any circumstance.'

Back with his gang, Roque orders them to give back everything they have stolen from Quixote and Sancho and then lines his men up so he can distribute the booty of their recent raids and robberies evenly among them. The real Roca Guinarda of contemporary folklore had a reputation for this Robin Hood-like sense of equity towards his men as well as being piously scrupulous about not robbing the Church.[32]

In a remarkable and not entirely plausible tale, a monk called Martín de Perpignan, a lay brother who worked as a jeweller at the Escorial, was returning to Castile along the main trunk road from Barcelona carrying some exquisite pearls for Margaret of Austria, when he was held up by Roca Guinarda and his men.

At first, although they treated him roughly and insulted him, he was not concerned, for while they might take those earthly pearls, 'they could never rob him of the pearls of Christ's wisdom'. Moreover, he hoped 'they might not steal them anyway, because he had taken the precaution of bringing them hidden inside some walnut-shells'. But when 'one of the gang wanted to taste one, the hiding place was discovered'. Guinarda asked him about the pearls and the monk explained that they had been especially chosen by the Queen, adding that now his clever hiding place had failed he humbly hoped that Roca would respect them as royal property. 'It was most strange,' but the bandit and his men not only restored the pearls to the monk but 'escorted him a long way to protect him from further trouble'. As they travelled together, Guinarda confessed 'that he and his men hoped to abandon banditry'. And so the story concluded, 'in the end, the bandits were given a royal passport to go and serve in Flanders'.[33]

As Quixote watches Roque equitably distributing the booty and Sancho marvels at the need for justice even among thieves, a scout appears, announcing that a group of travellers is proceeding along the road towards Barcelona and Roque orders his men to capture them. In the meantime, Don Quixote is so impressed by Roque's admission that he is basically a passive man, but that he has been driven to this life of organized crime by the desire to avenge a wrong once done him, that he suggests that Roque abandon banditry and take up knight errantry.

Quixote and Sancho spend three days with Roque, travelling the back roads to Barcelona. Quixote is astonished by the bandit life: 'here they got up, there they ate; sometimes they fled without knowing from what, other times they waited, without knowing for whom; they slept on the hoof, often waking to move on. It was all about sending out lookouts, listening to sentinels, blowing on the fuses of the harquebus.'

In the dead of night, Roque leaves them on the strand at Barcelona and, at dawn, 'as white Aurora showed her face above the eastern horizon, Quixote and Sancho gazed out upon the sea for the first time'. A group of knights appear and greet them warmly: 'we are all at your service, come with us, we are great friends of Roque Guinart'. The leader of these men, who is to be Quixote's host in Barcelona, is Don Antonio Moreno, 'a rich and intelligent nobleman much given to honest and affable enjoyment'.

In bringing this intriguingly mythologized character from contemporary Catalan reality into the story, Cervantes manages to sketch the crippled state of Catalonia at the beginning of the seventeenth century.

In 1615, the Chastelain of Amposta reported that:

it is well known to His Majesty and ministers that the whole of the Principality of Catalonia is divided into two bands, the Nyerros and

Cadells, and that these two groups pursue their ancient enmity with such a fury inherited from their forefathers that for that reason alone they take up arms against each other, committing murder, theft, robbery so that to this day no remedy can be found with which to uproot this barbaric tradition.[34]

The Chastelain's picture of Catalonia as dominated by two brigand bands is not much of a simplification, and it well conveys the terrifying reality of a lawless land left behind by Castilian modernization in which a whole host of ruffians – commoners, gentry and nobles alike – did indeed loosely associate themselves with the two great 'Mafia' families, the Nyerros and the Cadells. Catalonia was poor, its nobles and the oligarchs in Barcelona were fiercely protective of their vested interests, epitomized by a paranoid determination to uphold their traditional laws and rights that brought them into almost constant conflict with Habsburg kings who were regarded as Castilian interlopers. As one nationalistic adviser reminded the Catalan Generalitat or Governing Council, 'the affairs of Catalonia must not be judged by those of other kingdoms and provinces, where the kings and lords are sovereign lords, with such power that they make and unmake laws . . . In Catalonia, the supreme power and jurisdiction over the province belongs . . . to His Majesty and the three estates of the province.'[35] One equally fervent political commentator explained to Philip IV that the medieval *fueros*, or laws, were a contract 'between Your Majesty and your vassals' by which 'Your Majesty must observe their laws and privileges'.[36]

The Habsburgs, hobbled by their limited power in an uninvitingly impoverished province, mostly kept away; the titled aristocrats migrated to the political centre in Castile, leaving the lesser nobility to putrefy on decaying estates where they fell in with and fomented local banditry. In the 1580s, a Dutch traveller passed through a small town ruled over by a lord who 'seemed more villain than nobleman' and lived in 'a ruined castle to the west of town' but was often away in Barcelona, where he was 'suing his vassals over the rights to the town butcher's shop; which', the amazed Dutchman explained, 'is quite usual among the gentry of this land, who are frequently the reason that their impoverished vassals turn up as highwaymen along the main roads'.[37]

This desperate class of petit-gentry, the *cavallers*, clearly had much in common with Don Quixote; but where he is a humorous character from fiction, whose sometimes riotous actions on the roads of Castile were the foolish forays of a lunatic into the world of the picaresque literary genre, the Catalan gentry took to the highways for real as robbers in search of a fast ducat as much as adventure. Quixote may have recognized some underlying kindred spirit in Roque Guinart, but there was never any danger that Cervantes's hero would end up hanged from a tree.

One morning, as Don Quixote rides along the beach at Barcelona wearing his armour and carrying his lance, he sees another knight errant riding towards him. 'Honoured knight,' the rider shouts out, 'I am the Knight of the White Moon. I have come to challenge thee, for my own lady, whoever she may be, is more beautiful than Dulcinea. If I am victorious, I shall seek no other satisfaction than that thou abandoneth knight-errantry and returneth peacefully to thy village for a year.'

Don Quixote is taken aback. 'Knight of the White Moon, I am sure you have never laid eyes on Dulcinea.'

With the Viceroy officiating alongside Don Antonio, the two knights take the field, wheel round on their steeds and charge. As they come together, the Knight of the White Moon does not bother to lower his lance but instead crashes into Rocinante with such force that Don Quixote is knocked to the ground.

'Thou art defeated, gentle knight,' says the Knight of the White Moon, holding his lance to Quixote's throat.

'Oh gentle knight, presseth home thy lance and taketh my life as thou hast taken my honour,' Quixote replies.

The Knight of the White Moon turns out to be the university graduate Sansón Carrasco, and the whole escapade is a ruse to force Don Quixote and Sancho to go home. Defeated, Quixote slowly makes his way back to La Mancha and although, along the way, he plays with the idea that he and Sancho might become shepherds and live the life of a pastoral novel, the reality is that Sansón's dubious victory proves a death sentence to Don Quixote. 'Whether because of melancholy brought on by his defeat or because it was thus ordained in heaven,' Cervantes explains, 'he fell sick with a fever that kept him in bed for six days.'

'My mind is now clear and free,' Quixote finally explains to his niece, and he sends for his friends. 'Congratulate me, gentlemen,' he tells them, 'for I am no longer Don Quixote of La Mancha, but Alonso Quijano,' and he goes on to repudiate novels of chivalry. 'Sancho, my friend,' he says, 'forgive me for allowing you to seem as much of a madman as I.'

'Ay!' replied a weeping Sancho. 'Don't die, Sir. Take my advice and live many years more. Get up from your bed and let's go out into the countryside dressed as shepherds and maybe behind some bush we'll find Dulcinea unbewitched. If you are dying because you were defeated, then blame me for not tightening the straps on your saddle.'

But Sancho's pleas are in vain. Quixote makes his will and receives the last rites and dies.

In the Prologue to his final great novel, *The Adventures of Persiles and Sigismunda*, published posthumously in 1617, Cervantes wrote:

> It came to pass, beloved reader, that as two friends and I were coming from the well known town of Esquivias, famed for a thousand reasons...
> I heard someone clip-clopping up behind me in a great hurry, as though he were hoping to catch us up. We waited for him and he turned out to be a student riding a donkey

They fall into conversation. Then:

> scarcely had the student heard the name Cervantes than he dismounted ... and came towards me; and gripping me by the left hand he said: 'Yes, yes, this is the healthy cripple, famed throughout the world, that happy bard, the final joy of all the muses.'
>
> 'Many other avid readers have made the same mistake in their ignorance. Sir, I am Cervantes, but neither the joy of the muses, nor any of the other things your grace describes.'

Cervantes explains that he is very ill: 'My life is coming to an end at the rhythm of my pulse's whimsy, which will have run its course by this coming Sunday at the latest.'

Hours later, he wrote a brief foreword to the book addressed to his powerful patron, the Count of Lemos, President of the Council of Italy: 'Yesterday they gave me Extreme Unction and today I write these words. Time is short, my worries grow, hope fades, and so I live longer than my will to live . . .'

The following Saturday, 23 April 1616, he died.

Two years earlier, on 31 March 1614, the seventy-three-year-old El Greco, 'lying sick in bed', declared to a notary that 'because of the gravity of my illness I am unable to make a will' and he signed a power of attorney in favour of his son. A week later, he died. He was honoured with a splendid funeral mass that was attended by the confraternities of Holy Charity and Our Lady of Sorrows and by leading figures from his parish of Santo Tomé; he was entombed at Santo Domingo, alongside his most benevolent patrons.[38]

Two of the most unlikely celebrities of the Spanish Golden Age were dead.

15

Holy Week: Art and Illusion

The God of Wood.

Sobriquet of Juan Martínez Montañés

The same year that Part Two of *Don Quixote* was first published, 1615, in Seville the religious Brotherhood of Christ's Passion, the Hermandad de Pasión, commissioned an image of Christ carrying the Cross from the greatest sculptor then working in the city, Juan Martínez Montañés, who was also an *hermano* or brother of the confraternity. It is one of the greatest examples of an almost all-consuming trend towards startlingly lifelike religious images of Christ, the Madonna and the saints which achieved a sublime brilliance in Spain during the first half of the seventeenth century. Carved in wood and carefully painted to look real, these works mark an emotional and psychological apogee in western sculpture after which all else seems tastefully bland or excessively vulgar.

Antonio Palomino, the 'Spanish Vasari', wrote in the early 1700s that Montañés had created the breathtaking image of the *Christ of the Passion* 'with such an anguished expression that it excited the devotion of even the most lukewarm heart and it is said that when they carried this sacred image in procession during Holy Week, the artist himself went from street to street to watch it, exclaiming that it was impossible that he should have made something so wondrous. There is also a *Calvary* by him,' Palomino went on, 'in which Christ Our Lord is speaking to the Good Thief, so lifelike that it is as though one can hear His voice.'[1]

Known to his contemporaries as the 'God of Wood', Montañés worked at that vibrant and thrilling yet perilous artistic juncture where the emotionally charged extreme realism of high Spanish Baroque seems to peer into the gargantuan abyss of kitsch perdition. Palomino's anecdote obviously fits into the fashionable delight that was taken in artifice and *desengaño* alongside the story of a Sevillian aristocrat who tricked his servant into believing a portrait to be real. In a similar scene set in Barcelona, Don Quixote and Sancho Panza are invited by Don Antonio to meet a miraculous 'talking head'. It is a bronze bust of a man connected by a speaking tube to a room below, where the operator can hide. Quixote and Sancho are apparently deceived by this device and engage it in simple conversation, much to the amusement of their host and his friends. This was not the product of Cervantes's imagination, however, for such things were real: according to one eyewitness, in the Royal Palace in Madrid, there was 'the head of a Satyr which could move its eyes and ears around aggressively', shaking its hair, 'and opening its mouth with such powerful groans that it shocked and frightened anyone who had not been forewarned, as I once saw happen to a man who, terrified out of his wits, jumped more than four paces'.[2]

At one level, such objects are vulgar fairground humour, humble slapstick jocularity for the not always sophisticated aristocracy; but with Don Antonio's 'talking head' Cervantes highlights the far more complex and profound series of questions that the makers and owners of such objects wanted to inquire into first hand, questions about the meaning of perception, reality and truth, about the essence of life itself, about the anxious intangibility of *desengaño*. The comic yet terrifying theatricality of these artful, almost artistic machines reflects the fact that this was an age when men and women were obsessed with representation and the drama of illusion. These heads, like Montañés's religious sculptures, were almost actors on a stage. And such heads also highlight Spaniards' relish for sudden revelation that something apparently real and concrete was, in fact, merely a man-made imitation of nature, of God's Creation. But, they asked, was it a fiction?

What they desperately desired were marvellously vivid dreams filled with moral truths, but they wanted their reality as well.

It may be true that Montañés did indeed marvel at the naturalism of his *Christ of the Passion* as it was carried in procession, but Palomino's example fits a tradition in art history of stories about illusion established since classical times and constantly referred to by Golden Age artists and patrons. Pliny the Elder, in his *Natural History*, tells the story of a competition between the great artistic showman Zeuxis of Heraclea and Parrhasius that had taken place in the third century BC. Zeuxis had created a painting of such succulent-looking grapes that the birds came down to eat them, 'whereupon Parrhasius produced such a realistic picture of a curtain that Zeuxis, proud of the verdict of the birds, requested that the curtain be drawn and the picture displayed'. Amazed that Parrhasius' curtain was so realistic that it had even tricked a great artist like himself, Zeuxis conceded first prize to his rival.[3]

At its mythological limits, this idea of art as illusion crosses a Rubicon into a divine sphere where creation and life itself are considered to be forms of art. We need only think of Pygmalion, the sculptor in Greek mythology whose marble statue of a beautiful woman was brought to life by Aphrodite in answer to his prayers.[4] In the Christian tradition, God himself is the sculptor of life, as we are well aware: 'God created man to his own image and formed man of the slime of the earth, and breathed into his face the breath of life, and man became a living soul.'[5] But Montañés was not simply threatening to trespass in the Garden of Eden when he sculpted such lifelike images. If we stop to think about the subject matter of the *Christ of the Passion*, we quickly realize that there was something dangerously ironic in dubbing Montañés the 'God of Wood'.

The Sevillians are still excitably gregarious, seemingly compelled to gather at any opportunity for conviviality and conversation. Devoted to the drama of real life, *la calle*, the street, is their stage and they are both players and audience. Nowadays, from Palm Sunday to Easter Sunday, the city teems with a heterodox crowd of pious spectators, curious observers, more or less respectful tourists and casual merrymakers drawn to the sixty-one confraternities which process from their chapels to the Cathedral and back in the course of the week. Some are humble and poor, some venerably old, some are rich charitable institutions with great political influence. All are proud inheritors of a tradition which reached maturity in the Golden Age.

Each day during Holy Week double files of figures dressed in long robes or *tunicas* and distinctive pointed hoods called *capirotes* shuffle through the streets. They are known as *nazarenos*, and their priestly clothes evoke the ascetic Nazarene sect to which Jesus belonged. During the day they often stand in the hot spring sunshine or the cold rain; at night they light the long and heavy candles they carry all day. These were historically *hermanos de luz*, 'brothers of light', who lit the way for the penitents. Today, the barefoot penitents wear hoods that flop down behind their heads, *capirotes* without the conical support structure, and they carry wooden crosses, bringing up the rear of the procession. At the heart of the display are the *pasos*, massive Baroque floats; the first of these bears an effigy of Christ, the last houses the weeping Madonna below the *palio*, a canopy strewn with roses and supported by files of silver columns, slender like banisters, and lit by a forest of candles. In between, there may be other *pasos*, called *misterios*, 'mysteries', on which scenes from the Passion are displayed, and there are marching bands with brass and drums, while dozens of men dressed as Roman legionaries accompany a *paso* showing Pontius Pilate washing his hands.

If Holy Week in Seville, for all its sober veneer, seems to express the joy of human salvation as much as mourning for Christ's sacrifice, then the equally impressive processions in Valladolid are an overwhelmingly sombre lament for the sins of man which required such a violent redemption. These two cities are the best-known examples in Spain of this unbroken tradition of penitentiary religious processions, especially associated with Easter, which today are found across the Hispanic world. The powerful attraction of the cult is perhaps best illustrated by the endurance of the Penitentes in New Mexico. It is difficult to think of any other continuous, living tradition in western culture that remains as strong and as central to a society as Holy Week does to the life of Seville. There is no better place to feel the long reach of the Spanish Golden Age than among these crowds.

Penitential self-mortification in public was, of course, nothing new. For Christians it is rooted in the cult of martyrdom in the face of the pagan persecution of the early faithful in the Ancient Roman Empire, but it is common to many cultures. Likewise, religious processions and other forms of pageant have no doubt been celebrated since time immemorial. In the Middle Ages, a confraternity devoted to the True Cross had been established within the Monastery of St Francis in Seville. The guilds organized processions during which they displayed images of their patron saints, usually on their feast day. Flagellant processions had been celebrated across Europe, and many *fraternite dei battuti* emerged in Italy under the auspices and jurisdiction of the civic authorities.[6] Over the course of the fifteenth and sixteenth centuries, the sacramental confraternities became especially important and their members paraded consecrated communion bread through the streets, most splendidly at Corpus Christi but on other occasions as well. These often formed part of welfare programmes, such as the Ronda de Pan y Huevo, the Egg and Bread Patrol, which distributed food to the Madrid poor, beautifully depicted by El Greco's protégé Luis Tristán. Others concerned themselves with taking the sacrament to the sick and the dying, such as the Hospital of Charity in Seville. The dramatic example of the Inquisition must have helped to foster a cult for putting penance on parade, while the devastating crop failures and plague which terrified Spain in the final years of the sixteenth century gave extra impetus to this cult of piety. In 1599, processions were organized and the flagellants 'scourged themselves and prayed, asking God to bring the city health in the face of the evil contagion'.[7] Cosmopolitan Seville was a hugely important religious centre filled with wealth and poverty and vice. In an age when people believed that military defeat and natural disasters were God's punishment for national sinfulness, the penitential confraternities were asserting themselves as public custodians of civic moral worth.

The Marquis of Tarifa is usually credited with being the catalyst for this outpouring of popular piety, most enthusiastically expressed at

Easter. During that long unholy summer of 1519, as Cortés prepared his golden gift for Charles V, and the German Electors were bribed by bankers to vote him Holy Roman Emperor, as Oviedo and Pedrarias squabbled in Darien, and as the Comuneros' anger turned to fury, when Garcilaso seized his love child from a hospital in Toledo, the first Marquis of Tarifa was on an altogether more spiritual mission as a pilgrim-tourist in the Holy Land. In the heat of August, at Jerusalem, he carefully followed the Via Crucis, the route of the Passion, the path trodden by Christ wearing the Crown of Thorns and carrying the Holy Cross to Calvary, the Hill of Golgotha, 'the Place of the Skull', where he was crucified.

The marquis meticulously measured the route to be 1,321 paces (about 1,100 yards) long and on his return to Seville he set about laying out a re-creation of the Via Crucis from his house, which has become known as the Casa de Pilatos, after Pontius Pilate, to a place outside the walls known as the Cruz del Campo, the Cross in the Field, after a shrine originally erected in the fourteenth century by the Cofradía de los Negros, a charitable brotherhood open only to black Africans and today the oldest of the confraternities in the city.[8] Nowadays, the shrine is dwarfed by the Cruzcampo brewery to which it gave its name and which makes the excellent, refreshing beer available in almost every bar in Seville.

The association of piety and inebriation is appropriate enough. The marquis organized a series of processions to set out from the Chapel of the Scourge within his palace, on the Friday of Lent, Holy Friday, and a handful of other holy days associated with the Cross throughout the year. These soon attracted crowds of penitent participants atoning for their sins and enthusiastic spectators. Franciscan friars lined the route to encourage piety and decorum. The penitents wore white or black hooded tunics and carried hefty wooden crosses. Others whipped their bare backs as they processed, others still went manacled and in chains, with hair shirts, vice-like cilices and other instruments of pain and self-mortification. Some came as individuals or in groups of friends, but others attended with members of their confraternities, carrying devotional images from their chapels and hospitals. But as night fell and the crowds of men and women, many still wearing masks, made their way back to the city by the light of blazing torches and candles, sin slowly stirred awake in the darkness. By their very presence, these penitents had proven the weakness of their flesh, and, as one resigned ecclesiastic complained, 'the enemy of all mankind', the devil, often intervened, causing 'a worthy edification of the population' to degenerate into evil, licentious debauchery.[9]

Interestingly, the popularity of Holy Week grew just as the creole colonial culture in the Americas was developing its sense of identity. Indeed, the earliest-known depiction in art of a penitent Holy Week procession is a fresco in a Franciscan monastery in Huejotzingo in Mexico. Painted in the late 1500s it shows barefoot penitents scourging themselves and some hooded *nazarenos* holding up the towel given to Christ by Veronica on to which his sweat imprinted an image of his *Santa Faz* or 'Holy Face'; at the back images of Christ, two martyrs and the Madonna are carried on *pasos*.[10] The Spaniards were greatly impressed by the Aztecs' love of public spectacle and by their skill and artifice in reproducing realistic scenes of forests and lakes on which to stage such theatre. The early missionaries discovered that this enthusiasm for dramatic enactment was a wonderful way of communicating the gospels, but also of including their neophytes in church activities. The relationship was unsettlingly complicated because self-mortification and human sacrifice were central to Aztec religion, as was a whole Olympus of graven images. But this shared cultural ground became the mainstay of many programmes of evangelization. It is usual to think that the cultural traffic was all from Spain to the colonies, but it is intriguing to speculate that the American enthusiasm for Holy Week may have travelled in the other direction and contributed impetus to the rise of processional confraternities in the capital of the Atlantic trade.

The crucial characteristic of Holy Week in Seville is the large number of confraternities or *cofradías* which take part, so that throughout the week every detail of Christ's Passion as recorded in the gospels is on display. The exponential emergence of this multiplicity of religious brotherhoods is absolutely central to the whole culture because it engendered a deeply ingrained spirit of rivalry and competition that continues to energizes the brothers today. They vie for superiority in the number of *nazarenos*, the order of seniority in which they process, the beauty of their images, the richness with which they decorate their *pasos* and, for the true aficionados, the dexterity with which the *pasos* are carried through low church doorways or around the telegraph stanchions, balconies and street lamps of the narrow lanes. Blogs, chatrooms and the bars and cafés of the city are filled with an excited hangover of critical memories in the days following Holy Week as adherents and private commentators offer their interpretation of recent events. YouTube is filled with video clips of moments of high drama and great skill, with images of ornately adorned Madonnas to whom the beautiful, haunting laments of praise called *saetas* are sung in doleful *cante jondo*. In 1604, in Plaza Salvador, one confraternity attacked another, 'armed with stones, swords, daggers, knives and other offensive weapons . . . stabbing and slashing everyone they could', sending their rivals 'fleeing into the houses and the church' so that they 'abandoned their sculpture and *pasos*'.[11]

This defining fragmentation of secular piety seems to have come about as a result of the consolidation of 'charitable' hospitals that began in the 1570s on the orders of Philip II, discussed in Chapter 11 above. In Seville, seventy-five out of the hotchpotch of 112 privately run charitable hospitals that had offered varying degrees of assistance to the poor and sick were rationalized into two major extra-mural institutions run by the state. In addition to providing for the needy, most of these home-spun hospitals also functioned as gathering places for their sponsors. Sometimes attached to guilds or other institutions, or run by well-off burghers for the good of their souls, not quite trade associations, they were like social clubs in which to meet with friends and make new acquaintances, but they were also places of personal sanctuary and community spirit. It is surely no coincidence that between 1579 and 1602, when these institutions were being closed by the dozen, the number of penitential confraternities dedicated to Holy Week in Seville tripled.

By 1600, the iconography and pageantry of Holy Week was established with the basic form and content that it has today. Each confraternity associated itself with a particular station of the Cross so that over the course of Holy Week the complete narrative of the Passion is acted out in a marathon of community street theatre. And during the Golden Age the principal roles in that drama came to be played not by human actors, but by divine images created by sculptors and painters collaborating with one another.

A seventeenth-century Sevillian clergyman described another exquisite work by Montañés, his *Expiring Christ*:

> it is a thing of wonder to see the public devotion to this sacred image . . . it is carried from the Convent of Mercy, followed by many devotees all staring at that holy image, which is life size and moves wondrously, inspiring faith; and simply looking at it moves the people; for, although it is always on display in a chapel in the convent, when it is carried in public it causes great spiritual emotion to all those who see it; and they say it seems to them as though they are watching the real moment when Christ expired.[12]

While Palomino's story about Montañés's amazement at his *Christ of the Passion* clearly fits into a long tradition in the history of art about the limits of realism, both secular and sacred, his amazement can be more prosaically explained, making the story itself entirely plausible as fact rather than legend. For while Montañés had sculpted the image, another artist, Francisco Pacheco, had then painted and decorated it. In fact, Montañés's amazement, far from being a spontaneous display of self-congratulatory hyperbole, would have been understood by contemporaries as theatrical homage to Pacheco's brilliant completion of the work.

Montañés and Pacheco forged the greatest and one of the most enduring collaborations between sculptor and painter perhaps of all time, but curiously Pacheco has rarely been given due credit for his role in that partnership by modern art historians in the way that Montañés had done so publicly in 1615. In fact, Pacheco is usually remembered today as the teacher of Diego Velázquez, a painting master who wrote an important work of art theory, *The Art of Painting*, published posthumously in 1646, but whose own rather wooden pictures are of little interest and who was also a rather pedantic and tedious bureaucrat, the inspector of paintings for the Inquisition and the City Hall. But as Pacheco not disinterestedly tells us himself in the *Art*: 'sculpture is entirely dependent on painting for every aspect of its realism and imitation of nature, because it derives its form from the art of drawing and its colours are of paint'.[13]

St Teresa of Avila's confessor, the mystic poet St John of the Cross, had been apprenticed to a sculptor in childhood and, aware that God had been the divine sculptor of human form, he understood terrestrial workshops as potential models of virtuous organization where the work was arranged in orderly fashion according to the abilities of the craftsmen involved:

> Not everyone who can hew a block of wood is able to carve an image; nor is everyone who can carve it able to outline and polish it; nor is he that can polish it able to paint it; nor can he that is able to paint it complete it with the final touches. Each of these working upon an image, can do no more than that with which he himself is familiar, and, if he tries to do more, he will only ruin his work.[14]

St John's portrait of the workshop as systematic and mechanical reflected the reality that sculptures were the result of a collaborative process between a range of artisans.

In Seville, as elsewhere in Spain, a strict guild system distinguished between painters, who had their own guild dedicated to St Luke, and sculptors, whose professional home was among carpenters under the patronage of St Joseph. As a result, the production of all polychrome sculpture was divided between two workshops. The master sculptor began by discussing the work with the client, which led to a contract being drawn up that specified the size and posture of the final image, the types of material to be used and whether any of the limbs were to be articulated; the sculptor, as the main contractor, then took charge of the construction and carving. But such contracts were vague about the paint finish, which was dealt with by a separate contract between the client and the master painter. So the sculptor, when finished, entrusted the carved masterpiece to a painter whose team primed it and then applied the lifelike skin tones and dazzling colours to sculpted clothing.[15]

Despite the strict rules imposed by the guilds, in 1621 Montañés contracted to create the main altarpiece or *retablo* for the Convent of St Clare, including the gilding and the painting. In that relentlessly litigious age, no great professional relationship would be complete without at least the threat of a lawsuit and Pacheco, wearing his cap of bureaucratic authority, immediately brought an action against his friend and collaborator on behalf of the painters' guild.[16] He then wrote a kind of epistle 'To Professors of the Art of Painting' in support of the painters' case, which concludes with a succinct explication of the city by-laws advising sculptors who wanted to complete their own works to sit the various painting examinations.[17] (Another of his talented pupils, Alonso Cano, later did just that.) Whether Montañés was trying to get away with it unnoticed or was deliberately trying to buck the status quo, Pacheco's regulatory line drawn in the protectionist sand of the guild system held sway. Montañés quickly backed down and subcontracted the painting to an artist called Baltasar Quintero. For Pacheco, this contretemps was an opportunity to advocate the official recognition of the nobility of painting, a long-standing ambition of artists; but it was primarily a business dispute that seems to have caused little animosity between the two colleagues in the long run, for Montañés continued to engage Pacheco to do his paintwork for years to come.

The real skill of the great sculptors like Montañés, of course, lay in their ability to visualize the subject in three dimensions and to carve that mental hologram into the wood. And, within the constraints of tradition and training, master sculptors no doubt developed their own idiosyncratic approaches to their work. In general, however, he or she (and Luisa Roldán became one of the greatest in the late 1600s) began with a drawing and often a model. It was usual for the body to be carved from a single block of wood that was then hollowed out to reduce its weight. The head, the arms and the hands and feet were all carved separately, so drawings were needed to show how these pieces were to be assembled together. Where the contract specified that limbs were to be articulated, they needed to plan and design the joints carefully. The pieces were finally put together under the supervision of professional *ensembladores* who preferred to connect the parts using glue and wooden pegs rather than metal nails, which caused the wood to crack with changes in humidity and temperature.

Montañés's *Christ of the Passion* is relatively simply articulated so that the arms can be either arranged to carry the Cross, which is how it is carried in procession, or crossed in front of him to depict Christ Captive. These changes in posture from one context to the next obviously add to the sense of animation, but such artifice reached an apogee in the late sixteenth-century fashion for eerie images of Christ crucified that could be taken down from the Cross, in full view of the spectators, with the legs and arms moving at shoulder, elbow and knee, sometimes with the joints covered with leather painted to look like skin. However, this fad was short lived because the ecclesiastical authorities were, it seems, as unnerved by the idea as we are today.[18]

Pacheco announced in his *Art* that 'there is plenty to be said about the fleshing out of sculpture, which belongs to the category of oil painting, and is not to be undervalued'. He goes on to explain the process in great detail, which conforms closely to the reality discovered by modern researchers during the painstaking restoration of such works. The whole sculpture was first painted with liquid plaster known as gesso, after which the exposed flesh was treated differently to areas of sculpted clothing that was intended to appear sumptuously rich. The clothing was first covered with linen and then further layers of different types of plaster were added, then bole, a red mineral used as a primer for gilding, giving the finished surface a rich red tint; it was then covered in gold leaf over which a layer of dark pigment known as *estofado* was painted; finally this *estofado* was incised in brocade-like patterns, carefully revealing the gold beneath. The parts to be fleshed out or *encarnado*, literally 'incarnated', had only one or two further layers of plaster, each carefully sanded and smoothed, before the master painter set to work with his oil paints.

Pacheco himself had been one of the first, in 1600, to introduce a new type of matte finish that he believed to be more realistic than the traditional gloss, which he dismissed as 'glazed crockery', although others clearly disagreed for gloss continued to be used. He goes into great detail explaining how to mix the different consistencies of plaster and paint (some involving unexpected ingredients like garlic and bread), the type of bole needed, and even noting that in the high heat of the Seville summer 'very good' paint can be made 'by mixing powdered red lead and white lead into the oil and leaving it in a glass jar in the sunshine for fifteen days, shaking it daily, and then straining it'. He describes the careful use of colour and contrast to create realistic hair-lines, explaining how to give the impression of shadow. 'Always begin with the forehead and the eyes . . . colouring the eyebrows first of all,' he advises, before telling us that he prefers to paint them on 'with loving brush strokes', adding that he would never 'use real eyelashes', which he finds 'crudely' detract from the sculpture.[19]

As we read Pacheco, we get a vivid idea of just how important a contribution the artist made to polychrome sculpture. 'Given that sculpted faces always seem flat if they are simply painted a flesh colour because they have little sense of relief, I have made use of more or less gentle shading . . . and I believe that I am the first to have done this.'[20]

Many orthodox observers were worried by the whole spectacle of Holy Week. An official of the Seville Inquisition complained about its frivolity: the populace 'entertain themselves watching the confraternities and then get in the way of people going to church to pray . . . and there are so many processing on Maundy Thursday from midday all night and then all of Good Friday and so many people look for places to watch them that as a result there is more rumpus than devotion'.[21] Even John of the Cross, despite his childhood apprenticeship as a sculptor, developed an ambivalent, almost negative attitude to the processional images themselves: he invoked the Council of Trent's approval of images as 'important to holy worship and very necessary for inspiring devotion', but immediately warned against devotion to the 'graven image' itself, suggesting that 'many enjoy the painting and ornamentation and not what is represented'. It may be 'good to like having images which inspire devotion in the soul', but the way to 'perfection is not to be so attached to them that you are saddened if they are taken away'. He particularly disliked the newly fashionable but 'abominable tendency . . . to adorn images with the clothing [and jewellery] that vain people have invented to entertain their vanities', which he dismisses as a victory for the devil.[22] A Sevillian commentary sheds further light on this problem by complaining that 'they dress the Madonna in layers of coloured brocade, with an imperial crown and other finery, which may be permissible in joyful seasons . . . but cannot be said to be appropriate to a mystery from the Passion of Christ'.[23]

St John was particularly concerned here with *imagenes de vestir* or 'clothed images', which, like the *Christ of the Passion*, were designed to be shown wearing real clothes. However, where Christ was dressed with obvious decorum in notionally biblical costume, with the appearance of liturgical vestments, the Madonna wore something akin to contemporary fashion, the long bell-shaped skirts of Habsburg women. While these were usually relatively unadorned and in the white or black of mourning, it is clear that the modern custom of bedecking the image as richly as possible is rooted in the Golden Age. But while *imagenes de vestir* were all the rage in Seville, they did not become popular further north: a typically austere Castilian commentator called Juan de Avila was appalled by the use of modern clothing in the south: 'they dress the Madonnas as profanely as secular women, which leads to evils best left unspoken, and such injury you would not believe'.[24]

There were two clear strands to this cult of realism. On the one hand, the clothing and bejewelling of Christ and especially the Madonna were developing into a ritual of offering and ostentatious display that challenged the Church and which many observers clearly felt had descended into vulgarity. On the other hand, but in a parallel trend, sculptors began to introduce more and more hyper-realistic elements to processional images, adding wigs of actual hair and real or carved ivory teeth, and creating startling glass eyeballs and teardrops to be affixed to weeping faces.

Fascinatingly, these later images that incorporate real human elements are far less effective in creating the illusion of reality than were the masterly works of Montañés and his contemporaries. To understand why, we need to appreciate something of how the human mind processes images.

Our eyes are not camera lenses and our brains are neither film nor pixels. The images we see are created by our minds, which, according to our expectations, make a coherent whole out of the innumerable glimpses and glances gathered by our vision from the world immediately about us. Our eyes are constantly scanning, but only our brains can attempt to build up a whole picture. As a result, our previous experience is crucial to this process because it determines what we are expecting to see. Cervantes, of course, played with this idea: Don Quixote is not simply a case of 'life imitating art', but a sublimely transcendental (and astonishingly postmodern) example of art invading or perhaps colonizing reality: of course he sees inns as castles, for there are no inns in his books; of course he sees giants not windmills, for there are no windmills in *Amadis of Gaul*. And of course he sees armies not flocks, for there are no sheep in pastoral novels, only shepherds and shepherdesses. Cervantes was exploiting his instinctive understanding of the way our brains try to make sense of the pictures our eyes relay to us. We tend to rely more on our sensory experience of the real world than on our experience of literature in order to formulate the world we think we are seeing, but we can easily be deceived: we have surely all had the experience of fleetingly mistaking one thing for another, even in broad daylight.

When we deeply contemplate a lifelike image in which all the elements are artistic creations, we somehow subliminally enter into a kind of artistic pact with the image and its creator. We agree to believe it, we embrace the idea of the deception, however temporarily. This is what the brilliant Viennese art historian Ernst Gombrich called the 'beholder's share' in the artifice of art. But if you give a wooden statue real hair and eyelashes and hyper-realistic eyes and teeth, and if you then clothe it in real textiles, however brilliantly it has been covered in plaster and then artfully decorated with perfect skin tones, the statue can never look as real as the hair, the eyelashes or the teeth. The real human elements suddenly look disembodied, the sculpture looks statuesque. Think of our own experience of wax museums such as Madame Tussauds in London: despite the clever lighting effects used on some models, these never seem lifelike and real when we are actually in the museum. It is only afterwards when we look at the photographs that we almost see ourselves standing next to the celebrities and notorious figures from history. Only the bland naturalism of the photograph tricks our mind into failing to distinguish between the plastic clone and our own reality.

To make the sacred real, the artist must engage the viewer's imagination, for it is in the mind of the viewer that this remarkable metamorphosis takes place, just as it is the faith of the Catholic that allows the bread and wine of communion to transubstantiate into the real flesh and blood of Christ. And just as the bells and incense of the mass are conducive to this miracle, so too do the crowds and candles and music of Holy Week allow the artist's image to carry the mind into the spiritual eternity of the heavenly canopy. Images look real only in context and the backdrop to Holy Week is not everyday reality, it is surreal, supremely theatrical. The sculpted figures are life-size in order to appear naturalistic, but they are elevated on the *pasos*; they are kept at an all-important psychological distance like actors on a stage. Indeed, during the sixteenth century, a new kind of morality play or *auto sacramental*, literally 'sacramental scene', was developing out of the medieval tradition of liturgical drama and becoming an integral part of the Corpus Christi celebrations. Real actors played out religious vignettes as they were carried on carts or floats drawn through the streets by beasts of burden; it is the same tradition to which the primary school nativity play belongs.

And so, just as the theatre was becoming more elaborate over the course of the seventeenth century, we find the drama of Holy Week developing theatrically. The sense of observing reality, of absolute naturalism experienced by spectators watching the images as they are moved through the streets, is an illusion. These sculptures are abstracted from reality by the experience of Holy Week; we need the crowds, to be weary, to feel aching limbs, the flickering light, the music and the constant smell of frankincense in order to be deluded. Most of all, viewers and spectators need practice and experience to perfect the illusion for themselves.

This was the very Spanish, specifically Sevillian cultural background in which three of the greatest Baroque painters developed their sense of vivid realism. I will come to the story and art of Bartolomé Esteban Murillo in due course, but first I will touch on Francisco de Zurbarán and look at Diego Velázquez in some depth.

16

Velázquez and Zurbarán

> Pacheco's home was a gilded prison of art, the academy and school
> of the greatest minds in Seville.
>
> Antonio Palomino, *Vidas*

Diego Rodríguez de Silva Velázquez was born in Seville in 1599, and was apprenticed to Francisco Pacheco in 1611; he would become the greatest painter of his generation, one of the greatest artists of all time, the equal of Titian and Rubens, Rembrandt and Vermeer. His art brought him close to Philip IV and he developed into a model courtier and an able diplomat. He was the first Spanish artist to be ennobled by the King and admitted into the Order of Santiago. His work would be a seminal influence on generations of great painters, including Chardin, Manet, Picasso and Bacon.

The young Diego grew up surrounded by the rich daily street life of Seville and the flourishing world of public spectacle. There was the secular theatre and religious mystery plays and *autos sacramentales*. Bullfights were beginning to develop formal characteristics, bringing something of the rural and the wild to the heart of urban life. Diego grew up in the centre of global trade, at the commercial heart of the Spanish Empire, at the fulcrum of the modern world.

Holy Week must have left an indelible impression on his young imagination and on his developing artistic vision. And he grew up with an even more acute understanding of the abstracted aesthetic of Holy Week than the average Sevillian, for learning how to prime and paint these polychrome images was, of course, a core subject in the formal curriculum of a painter and one of the key exams that had to be passed, and with Pacheco as his master he would have had to pay special attention to that work, for, as we have seen, he was learning from the best. Pacheco's exceptional vision of the relationship between two- and three-dimensional imagery in oil paint coloured Velázquez's experience from the outset and it profoundly affected his approach to portraying the human form within the wider world.

Polychrome saints in varying states of nakedness, undress and dismemberment surrounded him as he began learning about the human form: first by copying engravings and paintings, but soon graduating to unpainted sculpture, before working from religious sculpture itself; it is thought he sketched from Pietro Torrigiano's *St Jerome Penitent* which was revered by Sevillian artists as a model of naturalism and which helped to set the trend towards realism in religious imagery.[1]

But it is also important to remember Gombrich's idea of the 'beholder's share', because the success of an artist depends on the extent to which his or her representation of the world resonates with the vision of his viewers. So, just as El Greco's patrons in Toledo had been prepared for his distorted naturalism by Berruguete's sculpture, the same vibrant imagery of life and art that so stimulated painters in Seville in the early 1600s was also the visual playground and artistic classroom of the aristocratic patrons and bookish critics who could make or break a reputation. Gombrich put a subtle psychological spin on the principle of life imitating art by appealing 'to an experience most of us have had. We go to a picture gallery, and when we leave it after some time, the familiar scene outside, the road and the bustle, often look transformed and transfigured.' We are here dealing with the same experience, but under normal conditions, that Cervantes exaggerated in Don Quixote's vision of the world through the lens of his novels of chivalry. 'Having seen so many pictures in terms of the world, we can now switch over and see the world in terms of pictures.'[2] But we need not stop here, for in the never-ending cycle of art and life feeding off one another pictures are part of the world that we see in terms of pictures. Or, to put it another way, artists and patrons not only sometimes see the real world in terms of art, but they therefore inevitably see works of art in a way that is influenced by seeing the real world in terms of art.

Velázquez and his contemporaries, then, began to develop an eye for people based on polychrome sculpture, which in turn affected how they looked at portraits. And Velázquez's brilliant reputation largely depends on his genius as a portrait painter, a genre which requires of the artist an elusive, almost mercurial, deeply contradictory admixture of ingredients. On the one hand, the creation of a true likeness of the sitter, faithfulness to that personal reality, is the necessary starting point; even Picasso began with reality. On the other hand, success depends on an ineffable expressive truthfulness that breaths life into that likeness as God did to Adam and Pacheco to Montañés. Velázquez's artistic alchemy fused the essential ingredients of the Spanish Baroque: the recreation of physical reality that was somehow glossed by a psychological essay on moral truth. And he did it by exploiting the tendency in all of us to look at paintings of people in terms of other representations of the human form.

In order to help understand how polychrome sculpture was the keystone of Velázquez's portraiture, it is instructive to look briefly at the work of his almost exact contemporary, Francisco de Zurbarán, often known as the 'painter of monks' because of his many works done for religious orders.

A daring exhibition held at the National Gallery in London and National Gallery of Art in Washington, in 2010, brought polychrome sculpture to the untutored eye of an English and American audience. The show was a dazzling visual essay on the relationship between these unfamiliar and often disturbingly vivid and violent sculpted images and the more familiar medium of painting from the period, all supported by a groundbreaking article in the catalogue which showed conclusively the relationship between the two by focusing on Zurbarán's work.[3]

Zurbarán was the son of a shopkeeper, born in 1598, in a tiny farming village in the harsh province of Extremadura where so many famous conquistadors had come from, including Cortés. Although he studied painting in Seville at the same time as Velázquez, he returned to his native province and set up as a jobbing artist in the market town of Llerena. Almost nothing is known of his early works, but his contract with a local monastery to carve and paint a life-size cruci-fixion in 1624 has been discovered.[4] That commission allowed him to break into a lucrative and growing market for paintings made for monasteries in Seville; two years later, he contracted to paint a series of twenty-one pictures for the Dominican monastery of San Pablo in the city at the knockdown price of 4,000 *reales*, little more than a quarter of the going rate and clearly an attempt to establish a foothold in the secure market working for religious institutions. The following year, 1627, the Dominicans commissioned him to paint a life-size *Christ on the Cross*, to be displayed in a small chapel within the sacristy.[5]

Christ on the Cross immediately brought Zurbarán fame and celeb-rity. Palomino describes 'a crucifix by him which they display with the chapel gate kept closed, and there is little light, and everyone who sees it and is not forewarned thinks it must be a sculpture'.[6] Zurbarán had made the most of these unpromising conditions in which to show off his skills as an artist. He produced a vast painting, about nine feet by five, that would dominate the tiny sacristy chapel, which was just seventeen feet by twelve. The narrow, dark space was lit only by two windows on the right-hand side, and so Zurbarán painted the pale, blood-drained body of the dead Christ and the dark wood tones of the Cross as though intensely lit from high up on the right. He was meticulous in his attention to detail in the highlighting and shading of every strained sinew and stretched muscle, every fold in the loincloth. This incandescent image is thrust forward towards the viewer by the contrast of a deeply intense black background. Zurbarán leaves us in no doubt that this *trompe l'oeil* trickery was intended, for at the very bottom of the painting he has depicted a piece of bright white paper pinned to the foot of cross where he has signed his name, a detail so convincingly painted that for a moment we question whether it may not really be a label stuck on to the painting.[7]

Zurbarán had captured the artistic vision of the time, bringing an intense feeling of spirituality to this realism partly through his lighting effects, but also through a deep sense of calm achieved by the remarkable use of triangular forms in his modelling which became characteristic of his style. This effect is especially easy to see in *Christ on the Cross* because it is here formulated around the geometry of the Cross itself. We see the two right-angle triangles formed by the Cross, with Christ's arms as the hypotenuses. Together, they form a not quite equilateral triangle with a right angle below the chin. There is the strong, almost equilateral form of the loincloth, open on the hypotenuse to reveal the half-lit legs. Through this simple device he gently guides the viewer's gaze about the painting, inviting contemplation, creating an atmosphere of almost monastic tranquillity.

Further significant commissions led a local oligarch to suggest that 'as painting is one of the greater ornaments of a republic' the 'City Council should invite the painter Zurbarán to move permanently to Seville'. The councillors agreed. But, needless to say, because he had not passed the requisite exams in Seville, this resulted in Pacheco's pupil Alonso Cano making a claim against him on behalf of the painters' guild, which was only resolved by the City Council pulling rank on the painters and insisting that Zurbarán be allowed to work in peace.[8]

Contemporaries evidently perceived the superficial brilliance of Zurbarán's *Christ on the Cross* in terms of his ability to make the painting look like a sculpture and not the real thing. But there was more to it than straightforward *trompe l'oeil*. They clearly felt, as we do today, that Zurbarán had transcended artifice to create an illusion that was deeply spiritual – an illusion, nonetheless, that he achieved only by making reference to sculpture, and that could happen only because his viewers already had a powerful relationship with sculpted images of Christ crucified.

Velázquez took this relationship between sculpture and realism one step further in the most astonishing way. This is most easily seen in a number of his earliest works, an important group of tavern and kitchen scenes known as genre works, or *bodegones* in Spanish, apparently showing ordinary people going about their daily existence surrounded by the kind of objects we would associate with still life, all painted while he was still a young artist in Seville. Although the representation of plebeian life had been popular in Dutch art throughout the sixteenth century, it was a subject new to Seville. Velázquez would have seen a few examples of those Dutch paintings and from the bound collections of engravings that every artist coveted at the time

he would have gained a good idea of the range of subject matter represented in such works, which often included some kind of religious
scene.[9] In 1526, Erasmus had complained about the way Dutch artists
'portray Mary and Martha receiving Our Lord to supper, the Lord
speaking with Mary and John as a youth talking secretly in a corner
with Martha, while Peter drains a tankard . . . Or again, Peter already
rubicund with wine, yet holding the goblet to his lips'.[10] It seems
likely that the leading Sevillian art patron and collector, the third
Duke of Alcalá, may have encouraged Velázquez to develop these
bodegones, and there is good if inconclusive evidence that he owned
the *Kitchen Scene with Christ in the House of Martha and Mary*.[11] But
as we shall soon see, instead of Dutch bawdiness Velázquez's painting
was an exemplum of probity of which Erasmus would have greatly
approved.

Whatever the catalyst, Velázquez almost certainly began painting
these *bodegones* as an exercise which his master saw as a challenging
task to set a pupil: Pacheco explains that still-life objects such as dead
fish, birds and animals, foods, fruits and crockery are 'easy to imitate
because they hold the same position chosen' by the artist, whereas
live animals 'cause the painter more work because they move around',
movement that is both difficult to capture and more difficult to represent. Humans obviously belong to an intermediate category as they
will sit reasonably still for a portrait, but where they are engaged in
some activity the painter has somehow to show them in motion. When
still very young, Velázquez 'used to pay an apprenticed country boy
to model for him, moving about or adopting various unforgivingly
difficult poses, now crying, now laughing'. The particular challenge
of the genre scene was consequently to represent active humans and
live animals in a way that looked realistic alongside the easily painted
still-life objects. Pacheco recorded the story of his friend Pablo de
Céspedes, who invited a group of critics to look at his newly complete
Last Supper; but the guests all 'greatly praised a [large water] jar painted
in [the foreground] without paying attention to anything else', which
so enraged the artist that he shouted to his servant, 'Andrés, rub out
that jar and take it away. Can it be possible that no one pauses to
examine all those hands and heads I have worked on so carefully, yet
they all admire this impertinent jug?'[12] The ornate jar remains part

of the painting to this day, however. This is, of course, an analogous problem to the use of glass eyes, real hair, eyelashes and ivory teeth in polychrome sculpture; it was a way of showing up even the slightest failing in the representation of the figure. Velázquez solved this problem by arranging his figures almost as though they were polychrome sculptures on a Holy Week *paso*, as we can see in two of the best known of these works, *The Waterseller of Seville* and *An Old Woman Cooking Eggs.*

Velázquez himself valued the *Waterseller* at 400 *reales* in an inventory he made on the death of Philip IV's Head Chaplain, the Sevillian nobleman Juan de Fonseca y Figueroa, in 1627, a good indication that these *bodegones* were quickly appreciated by the cognoscenti.[13]

Watersellers were a common sight in the streets of Seville, collecting water from one of the newly refurbished drinking fountains fed by a Roman aqueduct known as the *Caños de Carmona* and selling it door to door and in the street. Velázquez painted one of his large earthenware jars jutting out of the middle foreground. Water percolated slowly through the unsealed pottery and evaporated, cooling it all down; we can see beads of 'sweat' that have condensed on the jar, evoking the heat of summer. (Such jars are still widely used for drinking water in Andalusian petrol stations.) A young boy appears to be handing the waterseller a glass containing a purple bulb, once thought to be a fig, but actually a decorative addition made by a skilled glassblower.[14]

The strong effect of light coming from the left is obviously related in style, albeit less intense in execution, to Zurbarán's *Christ on the Cross.* The ways it falls on the two faces, the boy's collar, the jars and the waterseller's white shirtsleeve are highlighted by the very dark ground. The painting gains an enormous sense of depth from the way this light focuses our attention on a series of objects and figures each in its own plane. In the very foreground, we see the jug bulging towards us out of the painting and feel we can stretch out and touch it, but as we focus on it we see almost nothing else. Then the shirtsleeve draws our eye upwards, first to the waterseller's chiselled features and then to the boy's realistic face framed by his collar, and then to the glinting glass, before we look down at the table and the other pots painted with such detail and come full circle to the earthenware jar again. We can tell from a copy of the painting that when the very indistinct figure drinking in the background could be seen properly, there was an even greater sense of depth to the image.

But it is a strange experience to discover that it is almost impossible to see this painting as a whole. The eye skips from each of these highly naturalistic elements across planes of uniform colour that are without all but the most basic shape and form. There are faces and hands, fleshed out with all the realism of a polychrome sculpture, but the clothes and the background are abstracted almost out of existence. And then the relationship between the figures is distant: the faded character in the background stares out at us from behind his cup (he has nothing to do with the rest of the picture); and, although the boy and man are joined by the fragile transparency of the glass, the water-seller seems to have almost unseeing eyes while the boy stares intently at nothing.

If the *Waterseller* is majestic, then the most eye-catching of these *bodegones* is *An Old Woman Cooking Eggs*. Dated 1618, it shows the same boy and a striking-looking woman arranged in a similar way to the figures in the *Waterseller*. Again, only the flimsiest of connections is made between these characters at the point where the old woman's hand appears to brush the glass wine jug the boy is holding; otherwise, she too seems almost unseeing, while the boy again stares intently, almost awkwardly, perhaps about to catch our eye. The white and brown of the old woman's clothing, her lined and sculpted face, the way she holds her hands, and the earthenware stove all have much in common with the *Waterseller*. Here, too, the eye travels from each sharply realistic feature to the next across planes of colour and shade; here, too, it is impossible to hold the whole image at once within a single glance.

In this work we can actually see how Velázquez has followed Pacheco's directions for shading the hairline of polychrome sculpture with brushstrokes made away from the dark hair towards the light flesh. The striking effect of the lighting again depends on a very dark background and an intense light source. This type of painting, known in English as chiaroscuro, from the Italian, and called *tenebrismo* in Spanish is closely associated with Caravaggio. Velázquez may or may not have known Caravaggio's work directly; art historians have struggled to document that influence beyond simply arguing that he must have at least seen works influenced by the Italian. By contrast, the connection between Spanish *tenebrismo* and the lighting effects of hundreds of candles flickering, at night, below the sculpted figures carried on the *pasos* of Holy Week is unquestionable.

The groups of figures in the *Waterseller* and the *Old Woman* are almost disconcertingly static for such three-dimensional images. They seem to lure the viewer inside the painting in the hope of being able to walk around them, letting the changes in perspective lend them the sense of movement they seem to lack, just as you would do with a sculpture in order to bring it to life. Although impossible, Velázquez comes close to making this happen by forcefully suggesting that the eye move around the painting in particular ways, anchoring our vision to the highly realistic elements, the faces and objects, but discouraging it from settling for long with the desert areas of near blankness, the clothing and the background. This is how Velázquez achieved the sense of movement and instability that is the essence of Baroque art; he understood intuitively what modern psychology now knows is the way in which the human mind sees what the eye records. In other words, how vision works. The 'optical act' of viewing a painting begins with a brief, almost cursory overview, and then, because we see 'clearest and sharpest on the foveal axis', at the centre of our vision, we begin 'scanning' the image, moving the focus of this centre vision around the picture. At first, 'the gait of the eye' is quicker and wider, leaping about as we get our bearings, but then we start to settle on different aspects of the image, stopping for a quarter or a fifth of a second and moving the focus of our gaze by 'three to five degrees'.[15]

So Velázquez's ability to make paintings that seem to compel our vision to follow a particular route and to pause in particular places is crucial to creating the illusion of reality. But equally crucial is that he asks us to experience this effect from an overwhelmingly intimate perspective; he uses the same wide-angle lens, as it were, that we find in modern smartphone cameras intended primarily for photographing our friends at parties. Even Titian never brings us this close to what is going on. When looking at these paintings, we are drawn into the scene, invited in by the still-life objects that we feel we could reach out and touch and which therefore act as a bridge between the real world and the image.

Velázquez also instinctively realized that we look at the real world using variations on this theme of scanning and flitting. He had understood that to paint all of what was actually there, as a photograph does, fails to create an illusion of realism because that is not how we look at the world. When eating with friends, at a candle-lit dinner party perhaps, we are likely to focus on their faces, the serving dishes sometimes, our own plates and wine glasses, maybe the candlesticks. The tablecloth, the chairs, the rest of the room, the paintings, the furniture, all disappear into a background blur. That is partly chiaroscuro at work in the real world, but it is also because when we eat with friends we are emotionally compelled to focus on the food and the company.

And so Velázquez added to this sense of intimacy by populating these paintings with a recurring set of figures who, almost like a troupe of actors, walk the stage of every canvas in various guises. What is more, for contemporaries these characters would, it seems, have been intimately familiar.

The old woman cooking eggs looks a lot like a somewhat older woman in a painting thought to be a self-portrait by Pacheco of himself with his wife.[16] And there is also some similarity between Pacheco and the waterseller. These identifications admittedly appear tenuous until we turn our attention to Velázquez's *Christ in the House of Martha and Mary*, in which we find the same old woman still in the kitchen but now alongside a girl traditionally referred to as a 'serving maid'. Christ appears in a small scene in the top right-hand corner that has excited much debate over whether it is a mirror, a painting or a window on to another room. Whatever Velázquez's intention, if any, it most resembles a rather poor painting done with terrible perspective illustrating the moment in the Gospel of St Luke when Martha complained that she was doing all the housework while Mary, who in the seventeenth century was thought to be Mary Magdalene, did nothing but sit at Christ's feet and listen. 'And the Lord answering, said to her: Martha, Martha, thou art careful, and art troubled about many things. But one thing is necessary, Mary hath chosen the best part, which shall not be taken away from her.'[17]

Christ was frequently painted in the house of Martha and Mary in celebration of matrimony, for Martha is the patron saint of housewives. A wife was queen of the domestic sphere, of the kitchen and, of course, of the bedroom. It may seem absurdly bawdy today, but the pestle and mortar would have immediately and decorously signified to Pacheco or Velázquez both the sexual and culinary functions of a wife. There is nothing debauched about this painting, unlike the contemporary Dutch genre scenes that inspired these works; fish was a well-known sign of the early Christians, the eggs evoke a meal of abstinence. It is homely and pious, an image of proper domesticity.

And here Velázquez has painted the girl in the foreground wearing almost identical seventeenth-century clothes to Martha, in the background, while Christ and Mary are dressed in biblical robes. This connection between foreground and background is reinforced by the way the naturalistic, symbolically homely crockery shares the two spaces; it seems to evoke Teresa of Avila's famous observation that 'God walks among the cooking pots.'[18] Velázquez painted this picture, dated 1618, in the same year he married Pacheco's daughter Juana. Suddenly, the notion that the old woman is indeed Pacheco's wife and that the 'serving maid' might actually be her daughter whom she is offering up, as it were, to her son-in-law starts to seem an entirely plausible interpretation. And the girl does look a bit like the Madonna presenting the Christ child to the Three Kings in his *Adoration of the Magi* painted the following year, soon after their first child was born; not surprisingly, it has been suggested that Velázquez used wife and daughter, Francisca, as models in this painting as well.[19]

Remarkably, we have a contemporary description of Velázquez's wedding breakfast in the form of a terrible poem by the otherwise unknown Baltasar de Cepeda, which does, however, conjure up the atmosphere of the party and illustrates the stimulating and privileged intellectual and artistic environment in which Velázquez grew up as

Pacheco's apprentice. Towards the end of the poem, Cepeda describes the entrance of the radiant couple:

> We ate admirably well,
> And drank not a little,
> For we fancied our fill,
> Of the plenteous fare.
> Then grace was recited
> And the tables vacated.
> Came the bride and her groom,
> From their nuptial bedroom,
> The festivities started and
> The wit, Bezón, sang sweetly
> In that excellent voice of his,
> A musical toast, much finer
> Than Bacchus's wine, for he
> Toasted this Siren (and I make
> No mistake in calling her so)
> For her singing bewitches.
> So honest and beautiful,
> Such a wonderful look,
> Now the Queen of her world,
> Lady o'er her spouse's house.

He then goes into a long description of Juana Pacheco's dancing, which the ever witty Bezón seems to have compared to Salomé, although Cepeda notes that it was a very 'proper' version, before deciding to cut short his detailed account of Bezón's long nuptial song, for, as he says:

> I seem to have forgotten
> The newlywed couple,
> Who are very deserving
> Of my plentiful praise:
> For the sun was eclipsed,
> By the eyes of the bride, which
> Like two planets obscured it.[20]

One gets the sense that this doggerel may have been written in the heat of the moment, very much in an end-of-party spirit. Fortunately, ever the diligent scholar, Pacheco preserved it for posterity, and, for all its failings, it paints us an intimately vivid picture of an early modern Sevillian fiesta. We see the couple reappearing to the tipsy and excitable company having consummated the marriage, and all attention turns to the glowing bride, whose astral eyes eclipse the sun. She glows with such sexuality that 'the wit' Bezón, presumably 'rubicund with wine', likened her to Salomé: according to the Gospel of St Mark, Salomé danced so sensuously for Herod's assembled guests that he agreed to grant her any wish within his power; Salomé, of course, asked him for the head of John the Baptist, who had criticized her mother's marriage to Herod as illegal because she had divorced Herod's brother.[21] It was, needless to say, a provocatively inappropriate image to conjure up given that Salomé was clearly a symbol of upset to the sacrament of marriage, not to mention baptism. But, in recording Bezón's 'musical toast', Cepeda offered Juana to his readers as a paragon of sexual vitality, dancing gaily at a great feast, surrounded by an abundance of wine and food: she epitomizes Martha's two essential roles in the bedroom and the kitchen as patron saint of housewives.

Cepeda included a limited but fascinating guest list from which we learn that this was something of a minor society wedding. Francisco de Rioja was there, who would become the closest confidant of Philip IV's almost all-powerful favourite, the Count-Duke of Olivares. Pacheco's great friend Sebastián de Acosta came, and the Carmelite Pedro de Frómesta, not to mention Bezón. Cepeda goes on to describe at length a 'competition among the wits, a cacophony of scholars' whom he likened to the Council of Trent, all 'quoting from books worth their weight in gold'.[22] The guests at this wonderful party seem mostly to have been members of a group of intellectual and scholarly friends that is today known as 'Pacheco's Academy'.

'Pacheco's home was a gilded prison of art, the academy and school of the greatest minds in Seville, where Diego Velázquez lived happily, painting with great expressive genius,' according to Palomino,[23] referring to the quasi-formal gatherings first encouraged in 1568 by Juan de Mal Lara, the 'Greek Commander', and then hosted by Hernando de Herrera until Pacheco took on the leadership of this group in about 1600, sharpening its interest in and understanding of both classical and contemporary art. It became the cultural centre of the Sevillian world at a moment when the city was at the zenith of her wealth and power. The Cathedral was now complete, with its grand new Baroque campanile built on top of the former minaret and called the Giralda after the 'gyrating' weathervane placed on its ultimate pinnacle. Across the way, the imposing bulk of Juan de Herrera's Merchants' Exchange stood as a monument to trade. Nearby, the solid Royal Mint received gold and silver from the Americas, while the House of Trade was not far away, meeting in newly built rooms within the Alcázar, the royal palace and fortress in which Charles V had married Isabella of Portugal. The magnificent Italianate City Hall, which had been under construction throughout most of the sixteenth century, had finally been completed in the 1590s, although repairs were already under way to secure the galleries.[24]

The Sevillians who walked this grand, monumental stage were repeatedly described by contemporaries as 'proud, arrogant', 'witty, intelligent', 'loquacious' and 'of good bearing, very polite and serious, servile in nothing, but lordly, high-spirited and generous'. 'Full of verve and a combative spirit, they loved all kinds of weapons and wielded them well.' Diego Hurtado de Mendoza, a brilliant poet-soldier and contemporary of Garcilaso de la Vega, Prince of Poets, had noted perceptively that because they were so 'well off, carefully managing their wealth or working at some trade, and so comfortable in themselves, few of them go off in search of a better life elsewhere'.[25] This was a supremely self-assured city with a powerful oligarchy of aristocrats and gentry who did not shun involvement in trade and who must have truly felt that they were at the very centre of the world. They were brash and landed, Europe's nouveau-super-riche of established noble families who competed with each other relentlessly at every level.

These showy oligarchs turned Seville into a city of sumptuous palaces, filled with all kinds of riches; but these magnificent houses are strangely homely, cobbled together from medieval buildings that were extended and adapted to fit whatever irregularly shaped neighbouring lots might come up for sale. For centuries, Sevillian architecture had been rooted in Islam's love of very private, inward-looking living spaces, homes arranged around secret courtyards filled with plants and fountains. From the fifteenth century onwards, windows were cut into the bare outside walls and grand doorways were opened to create tantalizing vistas for passers-by in the narrow streets, glimpses of the calm, cool oases within. These buildings are still one of the great pleasures of an early-evening stroll through the old city.

Despite their haphazard individuality, these grand houses share basic common characteristics. They are usually two storeys of grand rectangular rooms arranged around one or more central courtyards, or *patios*, with their columns and arcades supporting a gallery running around the upper level on two or three of the sides. In general, the cooler ground floor was used during the heat of summer, while the family would retire to the upper level in winter. Most of them squeezed ornamental gardens, orchards and vegetable patches within their walls.[26] These were palaces to be lived in and enjoyed, not grandiose personal monuments to be admired, but homes.

Pacheco's Academy quickly became closely associated with one of the most important and iconic of these palaces, the Marquis of Tarifa's Casa de Pilatos, which had passed by inheritance to his great-nephew, the third Duke of Alcalá, the most important of the many enthusiastic patrons of the arts in the city. He had assembled one of the most impressive private libraries in Spain, and, an enthusiastic amateur painter himself, he commissioned Pacheco to paint a series of mythological scenes for his newly constructed library-study. He had also put together an extraordinary collection of Roman art and antiquities, including many important sculptures and statues, some of which are still on display in the Casa de Pilatos today. Pacheco brought his pupils to draw and paint these sculptures as an important part of their training, getting them to observe and then record how light and shadow fell on the still, stone features. It is likely that the duke often played host to Pacheco's Academy at the Casa de Pilatos, and that the young Velázquez was a frequent onlooker and later a participant.

Cepeda mentions that Velázquez's illustrious wedding guests discussed the two major cultural issues that were dominating the political debates of the day, both, interestingly enough, about the representation of women in religion. First, they debated the pros and cons of the highly contentious but powerful lobby agitating to have Teresa of Avila made joint patron saint of Spain alongside the long-standing Apostle James, 'Santiago'. They then turned their attention to the disputed Doctrine of the Immaculate Conception which was then *the* burning civic and political issue that had captured the imagination of everyone in Seville.

It can be very difficult to grasp just how alien and different to our own were the ideas, concerns and vision of the past. So often, we recognize our shared humanity, the food, wine and song of a wedding, the slightly pompous intellectual banter of scholars whom we might still find in a university common room, the military concerns of an overstretched superpower or the private struggle of a would-be playwright. Occasionally we glimpse the differences, the obsession with dynasties rather than individuals, and most of all the role of religion and faith in a world unencumbered by secular scepticism. Teresa of Avila did not speak to a tiny minority of extreme believers when she made her remark about 'God' walking 'among the cooking pots'.[27] And in no other context, perhaps, can we better see just how different was that world of all-pervasive faith than in the so-called Marian Wars that broke out in Seville in 1613.

At the outset, it is essential to distinguish the Immaculate Conception from the moment when the Angel Gabriel announced to Mary that she was now with child by the Holy Ghost, which is known as the Annunciation. The Immaculate Conception refers not to the conception of Jesus, but to the conception of Mary herself; it is about the sex life of her parents, Saints Anne and Joachim. The conception of Mary is hugely important because Catholics believe that since Eve persuaded Adam to eat the apple and God cast them out of the Garden of Eden, every human being has subsequently been born in a state of Original Sin, the Original Sin intrinsic to the sexual intercourse that engenders each and every one of us. Thankfully, people are cleansed of Original

Sin through baptism, which is why in an age of high infant mortality this sacrament was traditionally performed within days of birth. And the cleansing power of the holy water and oils works only because God sacrificed his son Jesus on the Cross in order for our souls to be saved through the purification that comes with the sacrament of baptism. Otherwise, we should all go straight to hell.

But if Original Sin could be washed away only after Christ's crucifixion, then, theologians had pointed out since at least the third century, Mary must have been born in a state of Original Sin, which was no state for the Mother of God to be in. And so the notion that Mary had been conceived 'immaculately', whatever that might mean in practice, became a matter of relatively obscure theological debate.

But during the Middle Ages the subject became contentiously politicized when the great medieval Dominican theologian Thomas Aquinas argued that Mary was cleansed of Original Sin only after conception but before birth, while in the womb; and that settled the matter as far as his holy order was concerned. By contrast, the Franciscans, who had officially recognized the Feast of the Conception in the thirteenth century, asserted forcefully that the Mother of God must have been conceived without Original Sin. The question became an important political symbol of rivalry between these two powerful religious orders. But in Spain the Immaculate Conception became especially popular and was enthusiastically supported by the Catholic Monarchs, Ferdinand and Isabella. Juana the Mad established a convent in Mallorca under the patronage of La Immaculada, while Charles V had an image of the subject displayed on his armour and was closely associated with confraternities devoted to the doctrine. And when Protestants derided the idea, this only fuelled fervent support among the Counter-Reformation Spaniards.[28]

Then, in 1606, the Madonna appeared twice in one week to Francisco de Santiago, Confessor to Margaret of Austria, prophesying the popular veneration of her own immaculacy, but warning him that an evil campaign would soon be waged against the doctrine and that he should enlist the support of the King and Queen; she also identified 'the son of Father Mata' in Seville as an important ally.[29] Soon afterwards, Diego de Castro, the Archbishop of Granada who had so enthusiastically asserted the authenticity of the notorious forged lead books, was promoted to the see of Seville and began adamantly to promote the Immaculate Conception using material gleaned from these very obviously spurious texts. That inevitably invited derision from scholarly opponents and was deeply embarrassing to serious proponents of the doctrine who recognized the lead books as the fraud they were. As an advocate, Castro became a liability.

Matters came to a head in Seville in 1613, on the Feast of the Birth of the Madonna, when a Dominican preacher publicly denied the doctrine in a deliberately inflammatory sermon. This 'was such a firm tenet of faith among the souls of the whole city', the historian Ortiz de Zúñiga reported less than a century later, that 'public outrage was most notable, with everyone taking it personally, as though they had been poked in the eye, and great care had to be taken to prevent the outraged public attacking the family' of the preacher, who 'was chased and vilified through the streets'.[30] Archbishop Castro led the Dean and Chapter in organizing a great procession through the city in support of the doctrine and 'later, fiestas were organized by all the confraternities and guilds, and every nation, of every colour', and 'the *mulattos* and the *negros* amazed the whole city with such sumptuous processions as had never before been seen'.[31]

The following year, 1614, Francisco de Santiago arrived in Seville and went to pray at Father Mata's tomb at the Church of the Incarnation. God gave him to understand that the ally whom he sought was Bernardo de Toro, who happened to be in a confessional in the church at this moment. Although the two men had never before met they recognized their common purpose and they were soon joined by Mateo Vázquez de Leca, Archdeacon of Carmona and a nephew of one of Philip II's most powerful secretaries. These three natural publicists commissioned a popular song, more a jingle, which they set to music and had sung in the streets and taught tirelessly in the schoolhouses until it rang out from the lips of every child:

> Everybody's singing out
> Shouting about their Queen,
> To tell of your conception
> That's without Original Sin![32]

With Archbishop Castro's support, they left the city in procession, singing this ludicrous but effective ditty, and headed for Madrid, where Philip III gave them letters of introduction to the Pope. In October of 1616, they set out for Rome to lobby for a papal ruling on the doctrine.[33] Meanwhile, the city threw itself into a frenzy of devotion that erupted into exultant celebrations a year later when the news arrived that the Vatican had issued an edict 'favourable to the holy mystery and ordering that nobody dare to affirm the contrary position'. This was only an interim victory and the doctrine was, in fact, recognized as dogma only in 1854. But in 1616 the Feast of the Immaculate Conception, 8 December, was celebrated with an outpouring of piety and a very long solemn mass was said in thanksgiving at the Cathedral, while all the church bells were rung, and the ships on the river fired their guns in salute.[34]

If the religious rejoicing organized by the ecclesiastical authorities was exuberantly pious, then the secular celebrations of the nobility were riotously extravagant, with fireworks, masques and jousting. But the centrepiece was a bullfight arranged by Don Melchor del Alcázar on 19 December. The Church authorities took an ambivalent attitude to this increasingly popular public spectacle, with some condemning the needless loss of human life, while others recognized the massive appeal of such exciting entertainment. Moreover, bullfighting was beginning to take on some of the formal characteristics recognizable today, and many clergymen enjoyed the pageantry, the danger and the skill.

Soon after midday, the city fathers had taken their places in the Plaza San Francisco, and the ladies and gentlemen were watching from the windows of the surrounding buildings or from their seats in the makeshift stands. The public thronged into the great square, which was grandly adorned with drapes and tapestries. The Royal and City Sheriffs made their entry, and then the *asistente* took his seat and gave the order for the first bull to be released into the square. In total, seven were fought by commoners, *valientes* and others, who tested their wits against this ferocious breed of Iberian bovine, *Bos taurus*, descended from the terrifying aurochs that roamed the savannahs of prehistoric Europe. Chaotic scenes ensued as many of the plebeian protagonists were tossed high over the heads of the bystanders; but once this free-for-all was over and the animals dispatched by a thousand murderous cuts, the square was cleared by the Sheriff's men and the mounted noblemen arrived full of pomp and swagger.

They were all dressed alike, with long cloaks, all embroidered with a wave design of plaited silver threads, worn over toughened silver lamé. Their crimson coats were edged with silver tassels and worked in thick cabling. They wore black velvet *monteras*, still the name given to a bullfighter's distinctive hat, with silver decoration and rosettes of white and red feathers; and their capes were embroidered with arabesques and a bundle of darts. 'It was generally held that this was the finest display of livery seen in Seville within living memory, as much for the joyful colours as for the rich novelty of the array.'

They entered in procession, alongside their assistant lackeys, with tawny rosettes and silver ribbons on their lances. The square was full of toreadors when the first bull came out, and the Marquis of Ayamonte's twelve brave lackeys managed to lance it six times. Then Fernando Ponce daringly provoked it from close up against a wooden barrier. The bull charged, Ponce's lance broke and the animal drove its horns deep into his horse which staggered and died. Sebastián de Olivares rescued his friend by bravely driving home his sword to kill the beast.

This bloodthirsty action was followed by some 'light relief enjoyed by everyone: Juan de Cazalla, Melchor del Alcázar's dwarf, who was so short they had to hang the stirrups from a harness in front of his saddle, appeared on a white horse with a specially made bridle'. He was dressed in black and white, with some decorative silver touches here and there, while 'his lackeys were four blacks who were so tall that they were head and shoulders above everyone else, all wearing similar robes'. Cazalla entered the square 'very self-confidently, laughing gracefully and doffing his cap to the city fathers, and the ladies and gentlemen'. He went to the middle of the ring and waited. Then, they let out the next bull, which tossed and gored a lad; when Fernando Ponce went to save him, another of his horses was badly injured and he had to be rescued again himself, this time by a whole posse of noblemen. The bull rushed hither and thither across the square, from corner to corner, with the noblemen chasing after it and, as it passed Cazalla, he managed to get his lance a hand's width into the hide. The bull was finally finished off by the lackeys. Then another was released, and a number of the mounted noblemen managed to make some impressive passes close to the horns, stopping the animal suddenly in its tracks by using long sticks called *garrochas* – a skill still practised in open fields today. Finally, with the bull waiting to one side of the square, Cazalla provoked it to charge from close up, 'as though the greatest toreador, touching its horns with the steel tip of his lance. He did this twice, but then retreated, realizing that this was a very aggressive bull.' 'The public was better entertained and had a better time than ever before', Ortiz de Zúñiga reported, 'from the moment the mounted noblemen appeared until the bullfight was over.'[35]

And so, the city fathers of Seville celebrated a papal ruling about the immaculacy of Mary's conception with a grand fiesta involving plenty of gaily dressed noblemen, the sacrifice of a handful of bulls, a few dead horses, the odd gored human, a bullfighting dwarf and some very tall Africans. That is the world in which the protagonists of this story learnt to think and live.

Clearly, the Immaculate Conception was an enormously emotive tenet of faith, but it was not a concept that readily lends itself to its representation in art. In the Middle Ages, it had often been implied by showing Saints Joachim and Anne as too old to have children, depicting their first meeting at the Golden Gate in Jerusalem, or by the representation of their 'miraculous kiss' in which Joachim pecks his wife on the cheek. But none of these solutions was satisfactory, because all implied that in some way Mary was not conceived by sexual intercourse. The Church was quite clear that she had been and that the theological problem lay in explaining how that sex had been immaculate.

And so a new orthodoxy emerged for the representation of the Immaculate Conception based on the Revelation of St John the Divine and his vision, at Patmos, of the Lady of the Apocalypse:

And a great sign appeared in heaven: A woman clothed with the sun, and the moon under her feet, and on her head a crown of twelve stars:

And being with child, she cried, travailing in birth, and was in pain to be delivered. And there was seen another sign in heaven: and behold a great red dragon, having seven heads, and ten horns: and on his head seven diadems: And his tail drew the third part of the stars of heaven, and cast them to the earth: and the dragon stood before the woman who was ready to be delivered; that, when she should be delivered, he might devour her son. And she brought forth a man child, who was to rule all nations with an iron rod: and her son was taken up to God, and to his throne.[36]

The Lady of the Apocalypse is clearly an allegory of the Virgin Mary, but she must also be understood as a figure of opposition to the Whore of Babylon, described a few verses earlier, to whom Martin Luther had likened the Catholic Church, infuriating the Pope and Charles V. Theologians understood the mystery of St John's vision in terms of the key medieval concept of *figura*, by which characters and events in the Old Testament were understood as allegorically prefiguring the New Testament. The most obvious example is Eve, who, as it were, gave birth to Original Sin, and was therefore associated with the Whore. The Madonna, however, gave birth to the Lord, who is Our Saviour from Original Sin. But medieval scholars took this symbolic play a stage further; they especially enjoyed this example of *figura* because in Latin Eva is a palindrome of Ave, as in Hail Mary, the salutation with which the Angel Gabriel greeted the Madonna at the Annunciation. Thus the Lady of the Apocalypse metaphorically embodies Eve and Mary and their relationship with Original Sin.

For this reason, Pacheco advised that representations of the Immaculate Conception should 'follow the mysterious woman seen by St John the Divine, with all the associated symbols'. But he goes on to point out that because 'God honoured her with his infinite power and his ardent love and deep wisdom . . . this Lady must be painted in the flower of youth, at twelve or thirteen, a beautiful girl, with kind and serious eyes, perfect nose and mouth, and rosy cheeked, with golden hair'. Diverging slightly from St John's vision, he explains that the Madonna had appeared to a pious Portuguese woman, who later founded a religious house in Toledo, wearing a 'white tunic' which should be visible beneath her crimson robe and blue mantle, 'all set against an oval, white and ochre-coloured sun, crowned by twelve stars in a circle'. 'She should be wearing an imperial crown and under her feet a fully circular moon, transparent to reveal the background landscape below, but with a clearly visible crescent moon at the top with its points facing down.' He particularly insists on this, noting that mathematicians had determined that this would have been the phase of the moon visible at Patmos when St John had his vision. But, he concludes, although some do so, 'I never like to paint the beast, our common enemy, whose dominion the Madonna crushed when she defeated Original Sin.'[37]

Without much variation, this is how Spanish painters represented the Immaculate Conception, with perhaps the most moving results achieved not by Velázquez but by Bartolomé Esteban Murillo, who came to dominate Sevillian art while Velázquez was to become Court Painter and an important confidant of Philip IV. This solution to representing the intangible and ineffable through subtle symbolism and vividly painted imagery is the essence of the Spanish Baroque in the visual arts, creating a sense of colour in motion behind which lies a fundamental moral truth. But as we have seen in *Don Quixote*, this interplay of image and *desengaño* was as important to literature as to art; and it reached its apotheosis in poetry, most obviously the work of Luis de Góngora.

17

Politics and Poetry: Góngora and Quevedo

Nowadays, Greed is helmsman.
> Luis de Góngora y Argote, The First *Soledad*

L uis de Góngora y Argote, perhaps the most brilliant poet of the Spanish Baroque, certainly the most controversial, was lauded by some as inheritor of Garcilaso's title 'Prince of Poets' and excoriated by others as a pretentious practitioner of impenetrable verse. His work epitomizes the contradictory and deeply contrary spirit that came to dominate Spain in the first half of the seventeenth century. We see a broken and self-delusional political society reflected and refracted in the many facets of his poetical diamonds, but a society that was at times excruciatingly self-questioning and racked with doubts, insecurities and a supreme sense of pride in its past. We see a strange world in which reality and fiction were blurred in the minds of many, in which a desperate attachment to tradition made the past and the future indistinguishable.

Born into the scorching heat of a southern summer in 1561, Góngora was the eldest son of illustrious and aristocratic parents. He was raised and lived most of his life in personal pomp amid the genteel provincial poverty of Cordova. He was wealthy thanks to a very lucrative prebendary position as *racionero* at the Cathedral, a kind of endowed canonical office that did not require him to be ordained. It was clear from a very early age that he was precocious intellectually and creatively, so he was sent to Salamanca, where he took a cursory interest in his legal studies but developed a passion for verse and a love of public spectacle: there he lived an epicurean life of *afición* for the theatre, bullfighting, good food, wine and the convivial company of likeminded aesthetes. As he avoided the law, so he attended lectures by a brilliant classical humanist known as El Brocense, who had published an important commentary on Garcilaso de la Vega's poetry in 1574. University was a deeply formative experience that provided him with a fluent knowledge of the classics and of literary theory, an understanding that ran as deep as it was broad.

But he returned from Salamanca to continue his leisured life of local luxury in dusty Cordova, where the records show he continued to enjoy the company of actors, gambled, watched bullfights, wrote his poetry and listened to music, especially appreciating the ringing of the church bells; and, as we have seen in Chapter 12, he must have met Cervantes and befriended 'El Inca' Garcilaso. But, from time to time, his prebendary office forced him to travel. From what we know of these early forays across Spain, from poems and letters, he comes across as very much the Andalusian abroad, a tourist who compared everything to home and mostly found it wanting.[1] But as a result of these official trips he made three important extended visits to court. The first, in 1585, we know little about, but during the second, in 1603, after which he lampooned Valladolid as 'Stinking Valley', we know that he fell in with an animated group of poets and literary figures, including Lope de Vega and the brilliant but equally troubled and troublesome literary satirist and poet Francisco Quevedo. But while that experience must have slowly rekindled some of the excitement and sense of intellectual adventure he had felt at Salamanca, he came filled with his own aristocratic conceit and Andalusian arrogance. He never assimilated, but remained a proudly provincial southern wit, asking in verse:

> Beautiful ladies . . .
> Who doesn't look 'pon an Andalusian kindly,
> For who can reject the favours of an Andalusian?
> Who hurls his spear in the arena,
> Kills all the bulls, wins the *juego de cañas*?
> And at the balls, who most often,

> gets to dance gazing into the sweetest eyes,
> other than the gallants of Andalusia?[2]

At the same time, he thought the court a Babylon, with filthy rivers into which grandiose arses emptied themselves, a 'Valley of Tears', a town where he had walked from 'wall to wall and found courtly deceit living in every street' and 'grubby Mandarins who were once fine yeomen'.[3]

The young Francisco Gómez de Quevedo Villegas, who had grown up an orphan at court, now riding a wave of recent success and with a profound sense of his own Castilian nobility, responded with a series of poems attacking Góngora's poetry; but, fatally, also attacking him personally, even suggesting that a 'poet who sings so much of arses must be queer'.[4] Góngora retorted with some verses hinting at Quevedo's small-time delinquency, his brawling in taverns, his flights from the constables and his sordid support for the Duke of Osuna in a scandalous intrigue with a playwright's daughter.[5] And so a childishly inelegant poetic rivalry spilled over into unbridled lyrical rancour. Quevedo now accused Góngora of having Jewish ancestry and there-fore having an unclean bloodline:

> In all the dirt you sing,
> While by your massive nose,
> And the nonsense you spout,
> All can see you are not clean . . .
> Inventors of the Passion . . .
> Your ancestors all bear the stain
> Of the blood of the Heavenly King.[6]

In 1609, Góngora again returned to court, this time full of ambition. But despite harbouring the highest of hopes for preferment by first the Count of Lemos and then the Duke of Feria, both men went abroad to serve the Crown without him:

> My Lord the Count, he's gone to Naples,
> My Lord the Duke, he's gone to France:
> Princes, bon voyage! for today's the day

I'll give some trouble to the snails.
As there are so many learned Spaniards,
I did not offer up my Muse to either,
But to a humble home, in Andalusia,
Which has defeated the greatest . . . Suns that is.[7]

The world of liars and cheats had chewed him up and spat him out.

Drying off the metaphorical spittle in the southern sunshine while enjoying the classic Cordovan snack of snails in piquant sauce, he then began writing the two major poetical works for which he is lauded today, works described by one leading Spanish critic as 'the loftiest peaks of artistic creation in all Spanish poetry', but which proved highly controversial at the time.[8] The first, *The Fable of Polyphemus and Galatea*, drew directly on the stock-in-trade myth of the Cyclops's murder of a water spirit out of jealousy for the nymph, taken from Ovid's *Metamorphoses*.

The second, the *Soledades* or 'Solitudes', flabbergasted his rivals with its daring poetical experimentation. José Ortega y Gassett, perhaps the most brilliant European intellectual of the twentieth century, once wrote that 'Góngora is the *Soledades*,' a work of pure invention and imagination that defined him as a poet and a person.[9]

As Góngora's creative life progressed, he had adopted a fledgling poetic trend known as *culteranismo* or 'erudition' and began adapting it according to his own love of sophistication. At its most basic, this obviously involved the use of vocabulary derived directly from Latin. In fact, he borrowed much of this vocabulary from medieval and Renaissance Castilian poetry. It was certainly nothing new, and Garcilaso and Herrera had both done the same, which had clearly been an important influence on Góngora. Intriguingly, the great Spanish scholar Dámaso Alonso demonstrated over half a century ago that most of the vocabulary that was roundly criticized by Góngora's contemporaries for being excessively *culterano* and obscure is now in current usage; in fact, he only found two dozen examples of Latinate words in all Góngora's works that would have been unfamiliar to a normally educated Spaniard of the 1940s.[10]

Góngora also took from Garcilaso and his followers a Latinization of word order known as hyperbaton, which will be familiar to students of the English metaphysical poets, but which most of us would immediately associate with Shakespeare: 'Uneasy lies the head that wears a crown' (*Henry IV Part 2*), as opposed to 'The head that wears a crown lies uneasy.' Or Aristotle's adage: 'One swallow does not a summer make' rather than 'One swallow does not make a summer.'

Classical and Renaissance literary Latin was richly fluid and versatile, and Góngora clearly wanted that freedom in Spanish, embracing it with exaggerated panache. Where his contemporaries and predecessors had been content with a few inversions of words, he took this affectation to its logical, perhaps illogical, Baroque extreme: nouns, adjectives, subordinate clauses and the verbs and even articles to which they would normally be attached migrate great distances across the page, playfully forcing the reader or listener to recover the relationship between them in order to make sense of the poem. This deeply promiscuous and libertine sense of syntax allows for an overwhelming musicality about his language, which, in its dislocated state and with its meaning often obscure, begins to sound like the notes of a score rather than words on a page. It moves towards celestial choral perfection. This his versifying beyond translation must assuredly make.

But if Góngora's poetry is viscerally musical, it is also a visually intoxicating dance, filled with vibrant imagery drawn from the whole canon of western verse: from the Ancients, especially Homer, Ovid and Virgil, to the Renaissance greats like Petrarch and Tasso, and deeply influenced by the Spaniards Garcilaso, Boscán and Herrera. As a result, his readers need an even more encyclopaedic knowledge of the classics and the models he drew on than did the previous generation of literati.

But his most glorious indulgence and the Baroque essence of *gongorismo*, Góngorine *culteranismo*, was the way he used that imagery as a poetic vocabulary, for he always sings his song in layer upon layer of metaphor drawn from his models. He did not choose his words and images for the meanings Spaniards usually ascribed to them, but required his readers and listeners to work out what he wanted them to signify on the basis of the context. And so a bird stands for a person, either a coquette or a rapacious man, a castle for the courtly world, and excrement for human endeavour. He wrote in a kind of code, setting up beautiful, sonorous, richly coloured puzzles to be solved by recourse to a love of erudition and a devotion to form. He was the supreme master of metaphor.

The First *Soledad* begins with a potently scene-setting image:

> It was the floweréd season of the year
> When Europa's deceitful, disguiséd thief
> – His half-moon horns upon his forehead,
> The celestial orb in every sunbeam of his hair –
> Shining honour of the sky
> Where stars in sapphire fields are grazing . . .

Góngora leaves the reader to decipher the metaphors thus: we must know from classical mythology that Jupiter abducted and raped Europa having taken the form of a bull; acutely aware of the bovine form from watching bullfights, seventeenth-century Spaniards would have been familiar with the crescent or half-moon shape of a bull's horns, which are presented in the sky alongside the sun; from this, a society still tacitly in thrall to astrologers would quickly have deduced that we are under the sign of Taurus and therefore in late April or early May. Moreover, it is early evening or late afternoon, for the stars which form the constellation of Taurus (and can therefore be described as 'grazing') are visible at the same time as the sun itself, set against the deep, sapphire-coloured sky.

At this stage, so much classical ornamentation to explain that the poem opens late on a warm afternoon in spring may seem absurdly self-indulgent and hopelessly unnecessary, but as we shall soon see, the underlying sentiments or themes of this imagery soon resurface in the poem: we have been most subtly prepared for rape and violence in an idyllic bucolic setting; and, incredibly, those themes arise in the context of an extraordinary head-on assault on Spanish imperialism in the New World. In this, he must surely have been influenced by

'El Inca' Garcilaso and also his father's lively correspondence with
Juan Ginés de Sepúlveda about various legal issues including the rights
of indigenous Americans.[11] Such an unpatriotic attitude earned him
opprobrium well into the twentieth century and must surely have
poured paraffin onto Quevedo's already blazing furnace of outrage
and anger.

The First *Soledad* describes how the survivor of a shipwreck,
conventionally referred to by the scholarly critics as 'the Pilgrim',
reaches those springtime strands in the late-afternoon sun and,
having dried himself, climbs the cliffs to behold a beautiful landscape. He is drawn to the light of a campfire, where he is given a
rustic meal by some goatherds and is befriended by an Old Man
'whose eyes, gentle tears did fill . . . and with grave white hairs
spoke thus . . .'

The Old Man embarks on his long soliloquy with an attack on the
whole classical history of navigation itself, which he associates with
conflict, specifically Paris's abduction of Helen and the resulting Siege
of Troy; the magnetic compass, he explains, is made of the very same
iron as the armour worn by Mars, the god of war. Making reference to
Jason and the Argonauts and Aeneas, he brings us up to the present:

> Nowadays, Greed is helmsman, guiding,
> Not a handful of masts, but floating forests,
> Which did first leave the Ocean, father of all waters,
> – In whose monarchy
> The Sun, each day
> Is born and dies among his waves –
> Grey-haired with foaming surf . . .

He is here at first playing on the word *arbol*, which means tree as well
as mast; the image of a great fleet as a floating forest was a familiar
one, used for example by Lope de Vega in his description of the
Great Armada. This floating forest, as it sails, wears down the Ocean,
leaving it looking grey and aged by throwing up foam and surf. Then,
having evoked the vastness of these waters with the idea that the sun

rises and sets in them, he soon turns his attention to Columbus' three little craft which made the first fateful crossing of the Atlantic:

> [Greed's] three fir-trees raped Neptune's
> Trident-sceptred realm,
> To force himself upon the world,
> And stomp o'er the other side,
> Then as yet inviolate by any other . . .

The image of raping the Sea God's kingdom clearly picks up on the image of Jupiter raping Europa with which he opened the poem, and also on the story of Helen of Troy. In the process, we travel from Greek mythology, through distant Greek history, to the harsh reality of 'stomping' on newly discovered lands. Not that these lands are welcoming: it was 'despite the flying asps', a terrifying metaphor for the notorious poisoned arrows of the native Caribs, that 'Greed's ever glorious banners, ever fluttering, defeated the Laestrygones', a cannibal people of Ancient mythology thought to live on Sicily and a clear reference to the man-eating reputation of the New World Indians.

He then moves on to the discovery of the Pacific, which 'rendered unto Greed, not only the white children of her beauteous shells', a reference to the pearl trade, 'but also those homicidal metals that Midas knew not how to get'. Midas was, of course, the ruler who asked the gods that anything he touch be turned to gold, only stupidly to touch his daughter with the inevitable consequences, and then discover that the same thing happened to his food and drink. The vehemence of the expression 'homicidal metals' needs no explanation, and the language continues in the same vein: 'that this element', water, 'sent sharks and killer whales, raised foamy fortifications, or has had her beaches dishonoured' by the evils of the 'first daring' expeditions – expeditions 'which made even the vultures weep' – yet those watery defences were not enough to put a stop to further exploration in search of 'pearls' and 'secret mines'. Even the Magellan Strait becomes 'the hinge of fugitive silver', suggesting that the homicidal metals themselves tried to flee the rapacious onslaught of the Spanish conquistadors.

In an eclogue on the death of the Duke of Medina Sidonia, written soon afterwards, Góngora evoked an eye-catching image of America that nuances this sense of anti-colonialism with some insightful commentary on the role of Genoese bankers:

> Great America, with her veins of gold,
> And bones of silver, which happily
> A Genoese sailor gave
> To Spain,
> Genoese interest drains,
> Today, her ruby blood,
> And sucks out her marrow . . .[12]

At times, Góngora's handling of his imagery, his ability to turn it into a kind of pictorial story as he makes one theme lead on from another, is as breathtaking as the imagery itself. In the First *Soledad*, as the Old Man's invective draws to a close, he evokes the Caribbean Virgin Islands, which had been named by Columbus after the medieval tradition of St Ursula who had been martyred along with 11,000 virgins at Cologne in the fifth century (the anti-imperialist metaphor remaining rhetorically relentless). At first, Góngora writes of 'an immobile fleet' of 'solid islands' in 'the dawn sea', 'which because of their number, because of their pleasing beauty, and because of the sweet confusion of their variety, even if they are not lascivious, might well . . .' and then he leaves us to wonder what they might well do while he follows this new thread of metaphor made up of water and innumerable virgins.

He goes on: 'in the white ponds of the Eurotas River, the nude and virginal hunters' – a reference which would at once have alerted his readers to Ovid's tragic account of the huntsman Actaeon who surprised Diana and her nymphs while bathing, for which she turned him into a deer, leading him to be killed by his own hounds. (Woe betide a man or nation that, like Columbus and Spain, spies virgin territory.) But for Góngora so simple a reference is just a beginning. With his metaphors and images of these island-virgin-nymphs, he has brought together elements of nature, Christianity and classical mythology: three of the four key philosophical axes of the Baroque world. Now he describes these beautiful, virginal characters as 'forming reefs of marble or stiff ivory with their beautiful bodies'. Marble and ivory immediately introduce the idea of sculpture, and so art, artifice and the imitation of nature, the core characteristics of *desengaño*, of course. And only at this point does he allow us to know what it was that they might well do – the kind of exaggerated cliff-hanger of a hyperbaton that so infuriated his critics – and this, it turns out, is to 'cause Actaeon to lose himself among them'. Even here there is a rather crude double-entendre, for in Spanish 'to lose oneself' can also mean to become sexually overexcited. At one level, he is repeating the idea of America being raped by colonialism. But this deliberately lewd wink also serves as a prelude to a return to the main action of the poem: within a few verses, the Old Man concludes his soliloquy and invites the Pilgrim to 'follow a feminine troop', 'a beautiful army of mountain women' on their way to a peasant wedding.[13]

As Federico García Lorca put it with his own peculiarly Baroque sense of precision, Góngora 'was the first to devise a new way of hunting down Castilian metaphors and crystallizing their meaning, for he believed that there was eternity in the quality and structure of poetic imagery'.[14]

In the Second *Soledad*, the Pilgrim arrives in a sinister, courtly world instantly evoked by the image of 'an ancient castle made of gleaming white Parian marble', which stands 'majestically' on a hill rising above a rocky shoreline stained 'purple with the blood of seals'. To the sound of a trumpet, a group of 'green-dressed hunters' suddenly emerges from this ethereal edifice in great confusion across a draw-bridge, 'an agitated troop, armed against the air' with a huge squadron of trained birds of prey. These are then enumerated, bird by bird, and their characteristics explained, including the goshawk, a typically British hunting bird that Góngora describes as 'generous with its time in the terrorism of Daedalus's nephew'. His poetry always needs detailed explication: Daedalus was the father of Icarus and uncle to Perdix, who invented the serrated saw and measuring compasses, which made Daedalus so envious that he pushed his nephew off a cliff. The goddess Athene came to the rescue by turning Perdix into a partridge (ironically allowing him to fly while his cousin Icarus, of course, fell to his death trying to do so): the etymology is even more obvious in Spanish in which the word for partridge is *perdiz*. And so we can deduce that goshhawks, *azor britano* in Spanish, were good at hunting partridges because they had plenty of the necessary stamina and so could afford to be 'generous with their time' as they 'terrorized' their prey.[15]

Suddenly, Góngora fills the air with every conceivable variety of hawk and falcon, even an owl, hunting down a range of prey, including a flycatcher and a whole rookery of crows: such a multitude of greedy raptors that the sky was almost too limited an arena for the chase. Suddenly, a gerfalcon is unblinkered and it soars high above the crowd, a veritable 'Harpy of the North'.

The Pilgrim finally stops staring at the action when his boat lands at a pathetically poor shoreside hamlet where clucking, frightened hens protect their featherless chicks and peck around in the dirt. Suddenly, this new and equally filmic scene of apocalyptic bathos is interrupted by the whinnying of the hunting party's 'hot sweating' horses, and with this desperately disconcerting image Góngora brought the *Soledades* to a close, apparently left unsatisfyingly and confusingly unfinished.

Hand-copied manuscripts of the *Soledades* were devoured by the rapacious Madrid literati and the critical fervour reached a terrible climax with many leading poets competing to spill as much corrosively vitriolic ink as possible by way of reply, with Francisco de Quevedo's the most sulphuric quill of all.

Góngora retreated into his Cordovan carapace, writing in response to all the criticism of the *Soledades*, in an epistle to be broadcast in the courtyard of the Madrid Alcázar, that 'at my age I'm as much given to truth as to wit: I'll befriend anyone who befriends me; and if that's no one, then Cordova, 3,000 ducats a year, my dinner-table, my breviary, my barber, and my mule will be solace enough against every rival I have'.[16] Many a Madrid wit must have likened him to Don Quixote putrefying in the supposed cultural desert of a hot provincial nowhere.

Quevedo's irrational hostility towards Góngora was clearly in large part one of those inexplicable personal antipathies; but it was also rooted in a deep sense of insecurity in the face of a terrifyingly talented poetic rival. Quevedo might pursue him with the same stamina as an *azor britano* does a partridge, but Góngora always slipped away to triumph. Other leading detractors of Góngora's poetry tended to focus their attention on the pretentious Latinate language, the complexity and obscurity of his metaphors and his inappropriate use of verse form. He himself had preached extreme poetic elitism by advocating verse that was so obscure it could be understood only by the most highly educated audience. But he insisted on roughing up that over-erudite constituency: in the *Soledades* he broke a deeply ingrained norm by using an epic verse form, long reserved for great acts of aristocratic heroism, to describe pastoral scenes populated by peasants. He had upset the decorum of social hierarchy.

And so, although his verse is rooted in the Renaissance and classical traditions, Góngora was determinedly anti-establishment, a poetic revolutionary who very obviously did violence to tradition; he was the thinking man's Lope de Vega. His more vociferous enemies were outraged and even many of his literary friends took issue with these aspects of his work, but he also had eloquent and influential supporters; the greatest literary theorist of the age, Baltasar Gracián, who memorably thought 'a sharp wit, the food of the soul', was a deeply reflective admirer of Góngora's work. In his persistently searching exploration of Baroque sensibilities, *The Sharpness of Wit and Artifice of Genius*, published in 1642, he turns to Góngora's poetry time and again for examples that can clarify and crystallize his ideas. 'Genius is not merely content with the truth, like a judge's ruling, but aspires to beauty,' Gracián wrote, as he struggled to explain the essence of 'wit' or *agudeza*. He cites Ovid, who addressed onyx as *nix, flamma mea* or 'Oh snow, my flame!' evoking the cool of the marble and its flamboyant colour, before attempting a much quoted definition: 'So the conceptual artifice [of wit] consists, then, in an act of comprehension that, thanks to some exquisite association, manages to make real a harmonious correlation between two or three recognizable opposites.' His point here is that the beauty is in the eye of the beholder, that it requires an 'act of comprehension' on the part of the viewer or listener. And, he goes on, that 'act of understanding expresses the correspondence between things'.[17]

Quevedo was himself a brilliant poet with a rebellious streak and a sharp quill that led him, on occasion, to be rusticated to his estates and eventually bullied to destruction by the Count-Duke of Olivares. Like Gracián, he recognized the lyrical beauty, intellectual inquiry and spiritual grandeur of Góngora's playful approach to tradition. Acutely sensible to the Baroque love of inversion as a way of thought, he intuitively understood the irony that while he might be the rising star at the court which had rejected Góngora, that court was so parochial and introspective that his own talents had not flourished. Strangely, his metropolitan poetic reputation was threatened by the work of a provincial nobody that was fresh with emotive beauty and enthralling complications, the work of a poet who had so obviously discarded the shackles of conservatism. Quevedo appreciated the innately Andalusian character of that revolution, as Federico García Lorca would do, three centuries later, when he explained Góngora in terms of the 'popular imagery of Andalusia that reaches extremes of finesse and marvels of sensibility with its utterly gongorine metaphors', the work of 'people who make their poetry as they walk along country tracks not sitting at some desk'.[18] Quevedo could not ignore Góngora's native Andalusian sense of freedom and that enchanting enthusiasm for describing the world and events using surprising and entertaining simile and metaphor.

Modern critics have confidently acclaimed Góngora as having captured 'the essence of the Baroque' in 'the most expressive and accomplished way',[19] but the idea of the Baroque itself remains refreshingly free of precise categorization. It has evaded its academic and intellectual huntsmen, goading them to ever more elaborate speculation as the majestic Baroque itself reigns at liberty, an elusive, slippery queen of the psychological and sensual jungle, the very qualities that make it so attractive in the first place – the ghost in the creative machine.

To manifest the ineffable is a self-evidently quixotic task, but it is possible to sketch the basic characteristics of the Spanish Baroque and link them to a sense of some overarching character of Castilian intellectualism in the early seventeenth century. The Baroque is

most immediately familiar as the kind of wedding-cake architecture featuring an excess of decoratively scrolling curlicues and
assorted carved images set within a more or less classical framework of corkscrew columns and hefty pediments that produces
an overwhelming sense of busyness and movement. Without
stretching the point with one's own excess of Baroque effusion, it
should be relatively easy to see that this is almost exactly the same
thing as Góngora was doing in his poems: he has a classical framework on to which he paints one layer after another of imagery,
some of it primarily decorative like the scrolls and curlicues, but
much of it filled with symbolic meaning like the carved images of
an altarpiece or a church façade. The violence that his extreme use
of hyperbaton did to his word order forces his reader to shift his
or her mind's eye hither and thither about the verse, exploring and
analysing the confusing array of possibilities just as the viewer's
gaze roams about the ornamental orgy of a grand Baroque salon or
hall, seemingly in random agitation, while in reality guided by the
movement of the forms. In essence, it is the same mental movement
so effectively exploited by Velázquez and so essential to a Holy
Week procession.

And it is that sleight of hand that makes the Baroque the Baroque,
the ability to evoke an immediate sense of confusion and anarchy –
and so uncertainty – while, in reality, the artist, architect or poet
gently lures us to follow almost unwittingly. As we follow, we are
drawn in directions that have a strong sense of form that is at first
concealed from us and of which we become aware slowly as we join
in the aesthetics of the dance, like a Spanish fighting-bull that charges
the cape again and again with only the dimmest awareness of the matador's part in the drama.

But just as in bullfighting there is a 'moment of truth' when the
matador folds up the cape, reveals himself to the bull and, face to face
with his adversary, thrusts himself between and over the horns to kill
with a sword thrust to the heart, so there is a 'moment of truth' in
the Baroque. In Góngora, this is the moment of acute understanding
when the superficial meaning of the metaphors, the complexities of the
hyperbaton and the classical erudition all fall into place and somehow

the soul of the verse reveals itself. It is the moment of definitive *desengaño* in an age defined by artifice and illusion.

In 1617, Góngora's life changed completely when he was appointed Chaplain of Honour to Philip III. At the beginning of the summer, he arrived in Madrid eager to compete in the courtly obstacle race of ostentatious display. The most plausible theory for this otherwise incredible and unexplained reversal in his fortunes is that his great patron in Cordova, Francisco del Corral, had canvassed the support of Rodrigo Calderón, the Duke of Lerma's right-hand man, the favourite's favourite.[20] Moreover, it was said that the extrovert cultural courtier and leading poet the Count of Villamediana, who had publicly praised Góngora's poetry, had sent his own carriage to collect him from Cordova.[21] It may be that even at this early date Olivares also had a hand in furthering the career of so erudite an Andalusian with the sharp intellect and gilded wit so lacking among the stern Castilians. Whatever the reasons for this new turn of the Fates, by July Góngora was writing home to Corral to say that 'thanks to good guidance and the favour of my patrons, I have begun to seek some modest applause at court'.[22]

Góngora is remembered today for his poetry, but he saw himself as first and foremost the scion of an illustrious aristocratic family with a long tradition of service to the Crown. His ambitions at court reflected a sense of entitlement that he should be near his sovereign and at the heart of power: a life of ostentatious display was his birthright and he arrived determined to shine; such pretensions nearly bankrupted him. They sent Quevedo into paroxysms of poetic rage and he scribbled out a sonnet filled with apoplectic vitriol that would have been better burned as soon as it had been penned:

> I'll spread my works with lard,
> So you don't chew them, little Góngora,
> Bitch among the illustrious Castilians,
> Ragamuffin Professor of Obscenities.
> Barely a man, you're the meanest of priests,
> Who learned your profession without Christ.

> Coarse mule-hand from Cordova and Seville,
> And buffoon-at-court of strange divinity,
> Why do you criticize Ancient Greek,
> When you are a rabbi of Jew's Hebrew,
> To which your nose bears witness?
> Write no more verse, 'pon my life . . .[23]

In the summer of 1617, Quevedo's hateful rage against Góngora must have been exacerbated by the political situation and his own recent personal experience. Quevedo arrived in Madrid, at the end of July, as the political envoy of the Duke of Osuna, Viceroy of Naples, charged with the important mission of pitching plans for a comprehensive naval and military campaign against a hostile Venice that was now in league with the Dutch, while also dealing with the delicate matter of Osuna's growing unpopularity with the Neapolitan elite. In effect, Quevedo was now serving as advocate for a new bellicose approach in the Mediterranean that would inevitably unsettle a Council of State accustomed to the peaceful policies of the Duke of Lerma. That August, with the connivance of Lerma's own son, the Duke of Uceda, Quevedo was granted a long audience with Philip III, which allowed him to circumvent the Council of State and Lerma as he pressed his master's suit. Soon afterwards, he became openly embroiled in prickly poetic duel with Lerma himself.[24]

Deeply involved with the machinations of the 'war party', his personal and public situation was an uncomfortable one at a time of great political uncertainty: he must have been horrified to arrive in the capital to find that the 'peace party' was now favouring Góngora, whose *Soledades* seemed to sing to a profoundly anti-imperialist spirit.

Interestingly, Góngora was Cervantes's favourite poet and, strikingly, the action of the *Soledades* takes place on a series of stages that it shares with *Don Quixote*. There are goatherds and huntsmen in the mountains, a peasant village at the heart of an agricultural region, there is a wedding, an island and an aristocratic castle populated by noblemen falconers. And, for all that Góngora too complained about effete aristocrats, laughing that dukes were no longer *dux*, or leaders, he himself, like Don Quixote, came from illustrious and ancient lineage that had won its nobility and its spurs in the stories of old on the battlefields of the Middle Ages. Yet, like Don Quixote, and unlike Cervantes, Góngora never wielded a weapon in anger, he never fought a military campaign, but instead enjoyed the controlled and civilizing violence of the *juego de cañas* or the bullfight or the modern flights of fancy falconry. And, just as Quixote was obsessed with ensuring that a historian should write down the story of his adventures and so was, in a sense, the author of his own book, so Góngora was a creature of pen, ink and paper.

The *Soledades* require the reader to indulge in a process of inquiry and reasoning that leads to this epic moment of truth, a moment of revelation about the depressing reality of contemporary Castile. This is most obvious in their condemnation of colonialism in the New World and the romanticizing of a peasant idyll reminiscent of so much discourse about the Noble Savage that was associated with the Americas. But our clue to understanding the sinister maelstrom of hawks and falcons with which the *Soledades* concludes is in *Don Quixote*, whose protagonist also came across just such an aristocratic hunting party; as a result, he was invited by a duke to a castle that turned out to be a mere pleasure palace, a place of entertainment, a glittering marble monument of inconsequential reality. And curiously, like Góngora himself when he finally found a place at court, Quixote at first embraced the illusion, before he and Sancho Panza abandoned such an overwhelming sense of fiction as they reached that all-important Baroque climax of *desengaño*. In the end, Góngora too would return home to Cordova to die, disillusioned.

By far the most historically influential frequenter of Pacheco's golden circle was Don Gaspar de Guzmán, third Count of Olivares, future favourite of Philip IV. Immediately elevated by the young sovereign, on his accession in 1621, to the rank of grandee, this physically vast, psychologically troubled, larger-than-life character at once became the most powerful man in Christendom.

Olivares was born on Epiphany 1587 in Rome, where his hard-working father was Philip II's Ambassador to the Vatican, and was brought up to become the ferociously ambitious scion of an embittered minor branch of the great house of Medina Sidonia. His grandfather had unsuccessfully contested at law the inheritance of the mighty seventh duke, the man appointed Admiral of the Armada in 1588.

Fired with that historic spirit of righteous resentment and a determination to outshine his more illustrious cousins, young Gaspar went up to study at Salamanca with a personal household of twenty-one servants. He was a bright, intelligent and lazy student, but already clearly a consummate politician so that in his second year he was elected Rector of the university by the student body. It is said that he died deliriously murmuring, 'When I was Rector, when I was Rector!' The magisterial twentieth-century Spanish physician and historian of unrivalled reputation Gregorio Marañón wrote that, for Olivares, 'dreaming of greatness was as natural a bodily function as breathing'.[25]

In 1607, he succeeded to his father's title and went to court, where he is said to have spent 300,000 ducats on a mind-boggling display of ambition which won him the hand in marriage of his cousin Doña Inés de Zúñiga y Velasco, lady-in-waiting to the Queen, granddaughter of the Constable of Castile and daughter of his uncle the Count of Monterrey, Viceroy of Peru.

Having won Doña Inés at such expense, he failed to find favour with the King and retired from the outlandishly costly court to Seville, where 'there is every indication that he lived the typical life of a young Andalusian nobleman of the period, with its cheerful blending of hospitality, whoring and horsemanship'.[26] He also found time to become a regular presence in Pacheco's enchanted world of erudition; and there he met and clearly came to trust Francisco de Rioja, Pacheco's friend, guest at Velázquez's wedding, who would become one of Olivares's closest confidants. And so, when the Duke of Alcalá took issue with Rioja's advice to Pacheco on the labelling of the Holy Cross in an image of the crucifixion, Olivares eagerly encouraged the prevailing spirit of jovially cantankerous intellectual bickering by funding the printing of Rioja's definitive public reply.[27] He also wrote poetry himself, in both Latin and Castilian, which he later burned as juvenilia but which Rioja would describe as 'miraculous'. What survives, however, was assessed by Marañón as 'frankly awful'. According to the usually acerbic court wit Francisco de Quevedo, he 'always wrote our language with great facility' and was an especially brilliant author of politically didactic prose that should be 'treasured for generations to come'.[28] He must have also watched Velázquez emerging on to that nurturing, private, very Sevillian stage, for the artist's meteoric rise and subsequently astral career owed as much to Olivares's and Rioja's inculcation of artistic taste in Philip IV as it did to Velázquez's remarkable talents.

These years in Seville were formative and enjoyable for a frustrated and by turns deeply depressive and effervescently enthusiastic young nobleman; they offered Olivares an intellectual environment that stimulated his interest in theories of statecraft and moral principle in comfortable isolation from Lerma's mandarin world of intrigue and backstabbing. He would thereafter always identify himself as a 'child of Seville', and claim that the city always felt like home.[29]

But, in 1615, Lerma finally called Olivares to court to take up a long-coveted position in the newly established household of the Crown Prince, the future Philip IV. He approached the post with exuberant panache. Quevedo, so often an irascible and incorrigibly caustic court commentator, reported that as the royal entourage returned from the double marriage of Prince Philip to Isabel of France and Louis XIII to the Infanta Ana, which had taken place at the frontier, 'the grandeur of the royal wedding continues, not to mention the grandeur of the Duke of Lerma who is as enthusiastic as ever . . . The Duke of Sessa made a stirring entry into the town, accompanied by a whole house-hold of cavalry and gentlemen, and bringing Lope de Vega with him, while the Count of Olivares threatened to outdo him by bringing two poets in his entourage,' one of them Rioja, the other perhaps Quevedo himself.[30] Yet for all this swagger, ingratiating himself with his future monarch could be a profoundly humiliating experience: on one occasion, the Prince announced that he was bored with Olivares who, as Groom of the Stool, had the presence of mind to kiss the royal chamber pot he was carrying at the time and withdraw.

The position of Groom, however, gave him great influence and he was instrumental in having his uncle Baltasar de Zúñiga appointed to the Council of State and then as tutor to Prince Philip during a state visit to Portugal in 1619. Zúñiga was a very experienced career diplomat who had desperately tried to represent Spanish interests in the Netherlands during the disastrous regency of Archduke Albert, and his voice soon became the most powerful among his peers on the Council at a crucial juncture in Spanish foreign policy. For although Lerma had long advocated the maintenance of peace in the face of the bellicose rhetoric of many a proud Castilian nobleman, as his star began to wane the winds of conflict were waxing all across a troubled Europe on the cusp of the Thirty Years' War.

In the early summer of 1618, news reached Madrid of a terrible outrage committed by some of the leading Protestants of the Kingdom of Bohemia, a powerful principality of the Holy Roman Empire. On 23 May, the four Catholic lords regent of Bohemia had attended morning mass at St Vitus's Cathedral, in Prague, and then climbed the steep stair to their chancery chamber in a high tower in the famous castle at the heart of the city, where they were due to hear the grievances of the Protestant Estates. Soon afterwards, the Protestant lords arrived in belligerent mood and accompanied by a rowdy mob of lackeys and hangers-on. When the regents tried to postpone responding to some of the key questions put to them, the Protestants turned on two of the Catholic lords, accusing them of being 'enemies of us and our religion', enemies who had 'horribly plagued your Protestant subjects . . . and tried to force them to adopt your religion'. Suddenly, the riotous nobles grabbed hold of the two men; at first the victims thought they were being arrested, but they realized the awful truth as they were dragged towards an open window, sixty feet above the moat below. They knew only too well that almost exactly two centuries earlier a Czech rebellion in Bohemia ended with seven councillors being thrown to their deaths from a tower. Mercilessly ignoring their pleas to be confessed, the Protestant lords threw the first man out of the window and then turned their attention to the second; he was hanging on to the fixtures and fittings for dear life, so they smashed his fingers and hurled him into the moat below as well. Finally, seemingly as an afterthought, they tossed out the men's protesting secretary. But, miraculously, all three men survived, thanks to the 'intercession of our dear and most distinguished Lady, the Virgin Mary, who slowed' at least one man's 'fall with her outstretched cape', or so one of the victims claimed later. Protestant sources reported that they had survived because they landed in a soft and heady sludge of rotting rubbish and excrement.[31] For all the farce of the happy ending, this attempted murder of noblemen by noblemen because of religious intolerance – which became known as the Defenestration of Prague – was discussed and debated across Europe.

These were the opening acts of a great war fought over religion, power and national identity that dragged all the European powers into its vortex and which has become known as the Thirty Years' War. The Prague Protestants quickly issued a long complaint that was published across Europe about religious suppression in which they prominently blamed 'the Jesuit sect, whose impetuses, writings and endeavours have always been aimed primarily toward fraudulently subjugating not only His Majesty, but also all Protestant residents and estates of this entire kingdom under the lordship of the Roman See'.[32] But in Rome the General of the Society of Jesus described the three victims' salvation in providential terms as a 'wonderful' sign of God's favour towards the Catholic cause, and the Jesuits understood the Thirty Years' War as a Holy War.[33]

Lerma tried to avoid embroiling Spain in the Bohemian problem, a sense of parochialism that only contributed to his coming downfall, while Zúñiga argued forcefully for intervention and managed to persuade Philip III to send 300,000 ducats to the Empire that summer. The arguments for war and peace abroad were matched by the most Machiavellian of machinations at the heart of government, and Olivares and Zúñiga positioned themselves perfectly during Lerma's fall from grace in the summer of 1618. Lerma's son, the Duke of Uceda, and his own right-hand man, the hated Rodrigo Calderón, immediately filled the vacuum of domestic power, but it was Zúñiga who, under these most fraught conditions, took control of foreign policy. In May 1619, Spain sent 17,000 troops from the Netherlands and Italy to support the Emperor Ferdinand. In July, the Duke of Feria marched from Milan to support a Catholic uprising in northern

Italy and seized control of one of the key passes into Germany. But in August the rebels deposed Ferdinand as King of Bohemia and in November, Frederick, the Elector of the Palatinate, reluctantly agreed to be crowned in his stead. And so, in August the following year, the brilliant Habsburg general Ambrogio Spinola led a further 22,000 troops into the Rhine Palatinate, and in November Spanish and imperial troops easily defeated the main Protestant army and occupied Prague. The Bohemian rebellion was over, but the Empire was now plunged into war.[34]

With the German lands descending into a vicious sectarian conflict, the Habsburgs were also facing French aggression in Flanders and an impious league between Venice and the Ottoman Turks; but looming ever more darkly, the Twelve Years' Truce with the Dutch was due to expire in 1621. Zúñiga spoke with deeply pessimistic clarity of the near impossibility of financing any kind of resumption of the war in the Netherlands, but there were ever louder voices raised against him. The Treaty of Antwerp had been humiliating for Spain and there was a lingering sense of shame at the damage done to national pride, honour and *reputación*. The treaty had also been disastrous for the Portuguese imperial possessions, allowing the Dutch such freedom of expansion that they quickly became the dominant European force in the East Indies. Spain, already struggling to assert her power in the Americas against the Dutch and the English, had sacrificed Portuguese Asia on the altar of pragmatism. But the Dutch also made such inroads into the Brazil trade that they claimed that two-thirds of it was theirs by 1620. The Dutch had treated peace as an invitation to inveigle their way into the Iberian Empire. As a result, the true theatre of war and mercantile competition was shifting from Europe to the colonial world.[35] Not surprisingly, then, in Madrid the Councils of Portugal and the Indies advocated strongly a resumption of the war against the Dutch as the primary line of defence in Spain's battle for the world.

THE AGE OF DECLINE: PHILIP IV AND
THE COUNT-DUKE OF OLIVARES

18

Drama: Olivares and Don Juan

Now everything is mine!

The Count-Duke of Olivares

'But, to deal with the beginning of our pain and the end of this history,' wrote Matías de Novoa, the Toledan historian and avowed enemy of Lerma,

> just when [King Philip III] had gloriously restored the Empire of Germany through the force of diplomacy and arms and with all his enemies defeated and put to flight . . . with [Lombardy] rid of its Protestant tyranny . . . and just when, weary of truce, he energetically set his sights on war with Holland . . . on 1 March [1621], he was afflicted by a burning and evil ague . . . and the sickness worsened until he was weak, exhausted by a humour which filled his heart.

The doctors dithered in despair, the King confessed his sins and prepared for death; he commended himself time and again to God and the saints, he prayed that the Pope should rule definitively on the Immaculate Conception; the Patriarch of the Indies gave him the last sacrament;[1] and, as he awaited extreme unction, Olivares addressed the dying monarch, or so, at least, Quevedo reported: 'Sir, I ask that in the midst of your distress, Your Majesty might honour my family and house, not out of ambition, but to alleviate your conscience, for that is how you can best settle the debt you owe to my father and grandfather.'

'His Majesty is in no state to deal with anything that might afflict him,' the Duke of Uceda is said to have replied, but then himself immediately urged the King to sign a pardon for a long list of prisoners and convicts, among whom was, needless to say, the Duke of Lerma.[2]

'On 31 March, at nine in the morning,' Quevedo wrote, 'His Majesty the King "passed on to a better life", as the just and the pious so elegantly and consolingly like to refer to Death . . . Everyone lamented his life almost as much as his death' and 'the whole kingdom rejoiced at the change of lord, without knowing anything about the successor other than that he was new.' With his usual biting sarcasm, he left his readers to ponder whether he was writing of Olivares or Philip IV.[3]

Twelve years later, Philip IV himself wrote movingly:

at that time, God saw fit to take my lord and father the King unto himself, and his death affected me as you would expect; I lost a father whom I loved dearly and a lord whom I served with all my fealty and obedience. I assumed the responsibilities of my rank – of which there are so many no pen could record them – and with little or no idea of how to accomplish such important duties . . . and so found myself afloat on this sea of confusion and this ocean of problems.

As he explained, 'I had been too young for the King to have introduced me to the business of monarchy.'[4]

And as Philip III died, Olivares, already the Prince's firm favourite, supposedly said: 'Now everything is mine!'

'Everything?' Uceda asked.

'Yes, everything without exception.'[5]

But Olivares was patient and cunning as well as bold and he persuaded the young King Philip III to appoint Zúñiga as his First Minister; Olivares himself, for the time being, would remain closer to the throne than the government. He became Philip's constant companion, his friend, his confidant, but also his tutor in the business of monarchy and rule. Years later, Philip himself described how, because he was too young to attend Council meetings, Olivares devised a simple system to educate the sovereign: 'little windows were opened up giving on to the Council chambers with such thick screens that my coming or going could not be sensed, nor my presence, so that I could listen to the most important business . . . and perhaps hear something that they otherwise would not dare to say to me'. Philip may have thought his officials would be more forthright, but for Olivares the constant threat of secretive royal surveillance was a powerful way to silence the more recalcitrant and rebellious councillors. Philip also described the reading list Olivares and Rioja had set for him, from which he learnt that 'History . . . is the real school of Princes and Kings, in which we find examples to follow, matters of note, and ways of getting good results in the business of monarchy.'[6]

Influenced by his own family's rancorous history, Olivares was devoted to an ideal of dynasty that defined every aspect of his approach to his *de facto* role as favourite – a term he disliked and avoided using, for he claimed to be simply a minister – and in particular his under-standing of the concept of sovereignty. History, preferably heavily mythologized, is, of course, the handmaiden of dynasty; and so, when Olivares looked at the King as the vessel of sovereignty and therefore the fount of authority and power, he saw in Philip a bloodline that led directly from Ferdinand and Isabella to Charles V and Philip II. He looked to these ancestors as the role models for the conception of a monarchy that must be conserved in its own image.[7]

Olivares was determined to orchestrate the formation of the King as part of a whole programme for the formulation of the royal image that encompassed history, art and spectacle. Philip would be moulded to fit Olivares's conception of monarchy. But this vision was greatly complicated by a striking contradiction arising out of his own deep personal relationship with Philip, for Olivares was both a subject of and father figure to the King, his teacher, his guide and also his friend, a man that Philip looked up to. And Olivares was a great teacher, so that in 1630 he could claim, almost as a proud father, that:

in all Spain there is not a single private person who can ride in both styles of the saddle like our master, the king, while performing all the eques-trian exercises I have described with almost equal skill. And although

they did not teach him much Latin, he has some; and his knowledge of
geography is outstanding. He understands and speaks French, he understands Italian and Portuguese as well as he understands Castilian.[8]

He had made Philip fit for government.

But Olivares's instinct to control led him to influence obsessively
every single aspect of Philip's development. In time, the King might
assert his independence, but as much as possible he would owe his
whole conception of the world to Olivares. And so the favourite
was as aware of the importance of his Prince's private pastimes and
personal diversions as he was of his regal responsibilities.

Under this watchful paternalism, Philip learnt a love of parties,
dancing and the theatre, sang songs, learnt to play musical instruments, fought bulls and laughed at his jesters and his dwarves. But
almost everything he did had some higher purpose, so that even a
game of bowls or billiards was glossed with a veneer of education and
symbolic meaning. A contemporary account described how:

> the Prince has one bowl or ball, and a servant or confidant the other.
> On the Prince's are written the words *majesty* and *affability* . . . while
> his confidant's ball has *clemency* and *justice* . . . The two players then
> bowl their balls and when they stop, if, for example, the Prince's ball
> reads *majesty* and the servant's *clemency*, then the Prince wins because
> *majesty* with *clemency* is a good thing in a Prince . . . But if the monarch's
> reads *affability* and the servant's ball *clemency*, then the servant wins . . .
> because to be clement and affable will lead a Prince to lose respect.

And so it went on, covering each possible combination.[9]

Like all the Habsburgs, the adolescent Philip was most devoted to
hunting: he was an excellent shot with an harquebus and he shared a
love of horses and riding with Olivares, who secured for himself the
role of Master of the Horse. That allowed him to share in the King's
youthful joys of the chase, but by 1633 Olivares had become so obese
and 'so racked by illness' that he complained 'that when I tried to
mount a horse the other day I simply could not manage it. This is the
worst thing that could happen, because I always used to recover my

spirits and vitality once I was on horseback.'[10] Worse still, of course, this disability denied him access to the King at play, enjoying his favourite sport.

In Madrid, rumour was rife that Olivares and the King shared a passion for another kind of chase, and the Archbishop of Granada wrote to Olivares urging him 'to prevent the King going out at night and to consider that the people largely blame you for this, for they say openly that you go with him and encourage him'. The vast figure of Olivares must have been conspicuous enough in the seedy taverns and bordellos for which the King was supposedly developing a politically unhealthy enthusiasm. But there was a particularly salacious rumour abroad in Madrid that one of the Gentlemen of the Chamber had introduced Philip to an especially beautiful Benedictine nun at the Convent of the Incarnation, popularly known as San Plácido. Night after night, the young King went out in disguise and made love to the girl – in the old-fashioned sense – through the grille in the entranceway of the convent. After protracted negotiations between Olivares, the Abbess and the girl, Philip, 'aflame with a fiery appetite', was finally allowed inside, accompanied by Olivares and the Gentleman of the Chamber, gaining access through the coal cellar. When the ardent suitor pushed open the door of the monastic cell, the nun, in protest at her coming sacrifice, 'appeared richly dressed in blue and white, the attire of the Immaculate Conception', as the gossips pointed out, 'turning the whole sacrilegious business into pure heresy'.[11] 'Not surprisingly', the Granadan prelate had scolded Olivares that rumours of his night-time adventures with the King 'upset the people, for it seems to them that Your Excellency thus destroys the great hope that there was at the beginning of the reign . . . In truth, this predilection is not good because of the many opportunities for damage that arise and the liberties which his vassals take in talking about various things that undermine the decorum of the Monarch.'

Olivares retorted that he could 'see no problem in a young king going out and about to see properly with his own eyes the many things that if he did not see them, might get twisted in the reports he hears; his grandfather began to learn about the world when young and so he turned out to be a great king.' By contrast, he wrote, Philip III had been brought up in a protective isolation that had left him prey to the Duke of Lerma.[12] The Spanish Ambassador in Paris observed that 'there is nothing in this life for which men will not find some excuse'.[13]

While our knowledge of Philip IV's nocturnal adventures among the low-life of Madrid can never be more than educated conjecture, we do have an excellent documentary record of his breathtaking collection of erotica which Velázquez and quite probably Rubens helped him to hang on his walls over the course of the next decade.

In 1626, the Papal Legate's secretary and arch-aesthete, Cassiano dal Pozzo, wrote a description of his visit to the newly completed Summer Apartments in the Madrid Alcázar, the most private part of the palace where the King lived surrounded by his household, which the Count of Gondomar, the former Ambassador to London, thought 'the most comfortable house in the world'.[14] As he went from room to room, Pozzo saw a range of paintings, but he was most impressed by the Rubens and especially the Titians, rapturously applauding the latter's *Adam and Eve* and the *Battle of Lepanto with Philip II Offering Prince Fernando to Victory*.[15] Pozzo's description is particularly useful in light of an official inventory made in 1636, because, although the paintings mostly seem to have been the same, their arrangement was revealingly different.

In between those two dates, in 1628–9, Rubens made an extended visit to Spain, during which he was fêted by Philip and was allowed to spend long hours copying and sketching from the collection in the Summer Apartments. He immediately developed an intimate friendship with Velázquez, born of respect for one another as the greatest painters, old and young, of their age. Given Philip's reliance on Velázquez's advice during this period and his admiration for Rubens, it is difficult to believe, albeit impossible to prove, that this new arrangement was not largely due to these two great artists.[16]

By 1636, the pictures were displayed according to what today seems a rather contrived scheme themed on the function of the rooms. The most public areas, the stairway and royal conference room and study, were hung with a handful of mostly military landscapes or battle scenes and a large number of portraits of princes and rulers. The King's reading room was adorned with a range of erudite and religious works that might be said to allude to the kind of texts he read. While in his bedroom Philip could contemplate a sobering series of royal relatives including Titian's portraits of Charles V, Isabel of Portugal and Philip II, as well as paintings of his grandmother Anne of Austria and his father Philip III, while Titian's *Venus of the Mirror* 'with her bare breasts and a crimson dressing gown' drew attention to the dependence of dynasty on sexuality. His two dining rooms contained a dynamic hunting scene of hounds chasing a hart by Frans Snyders, presumably to whet his appetite, but also a *Noah's Ark* and *Creation* by the Venetian master Jacopo Bassano, each filled with an abundance of farm animals ripe for the slaughter and the table, but very obviously the gift of God. There were also copies of the main panels of Bosch's *Garden of Earthy Delights* and, bizarrely, as if intended to put the King off his food, Jan van Hemessen's gruesome *Stone Operation* in which a charlatan barber-surgeon pretends to remove a stone from his victim's bloody forehead with a cut-throat razor.

And then we come to the 'last of the vaulted rooms . . . where His Majesty retires after luncheon'.[17] This room was hung with nine works by Titian: an *Adam and Eve*, in which Cupid helps the Serpent tempt Eve into plucking the apple while Adam tries to discourage her, and a cycle of eight highly sensual works conjuring up scenes of sexual exploitation and violence from classical mythology, including the six *poesies* or 'poetries in paint' depicting scenes from Ovid's *Metamorphoses* which the artist painted for Philip II between 1551 and 1562. In 1640, Philip bought the spectacularly high Baroque *Garden of Love* from Rubens's executors, and he and Velázquez hung it in this most private of rooms alongside the Titians which had inspired it.[18]

Taken individually, the subject matter of these works was both very familiar and potentially morally instructive. The range of meanings suggested by modern interpreters of the *poesies* is astonishing in quantity and ingenuity[19] but is also bewildering when it comes to understanding what Philip himself may have thought as he relaxed after lunch. For example, *Danaë and Jupiter* depicts the moment at which the king of the gods took the form of Golden Rain in order to impregnate the daughter of the King of the Phoenicians. But might Philip have really concluded that Titian had shown the Golden Rain as a shower of coins in order to suggest prostitution?[20]

We cannot know. But it does seem likely that the young 'Planet King' would have been tempted to identify himself with Jupiter in this work and also in the *Rape of Europa* and *Diana and Callisto*, in each of which we see the moment when the king of the gods conquers a different victim by subterfuge and force. In the former, he transformed himself into a bull so as to win Europa's trust; in the latter, he has taken on the guise of the goddess of the hunt in order to abduct the nymph Callisto. At first glance, these works might suggest Philip's *droit du seigneur*, albeit a pagan right to fornicate with his vassals' womenfolk, while another of Philip's Titians that was hung near by, *Venus and Cupid with an Organist*, seems to underline that sexuality is simply a rather messy fact of life, even among princes and gods. However, although none of those offers anything much in the way of moral commentary, some sense of more exemplary behaviour was perhaps suggested by another work, *Perseus and Andromeda*, in which we see Perseus, the son of Jupiter and Danäe, saving the daughter of the King of Ethiopia who has chained her to a rock as a sacrifice to Poseidon. And there certainly was an obviously emphatic moral message in *Tarquin and Lucretia*, which depicts the moment at which the Crown Prince of Rome raped the wife of an important courtier, an act of betrayal that led to bloody rebellion and the overthrow of the House of Tarquin. Even more telling, given the voyeurism intrinsic to pornography, is *Diana and Actaeon*, in which the unfortunate hunter surprises the goddess of the hunt while she is bathing. And so Philip may have read some sort of exhortation to turn away from so many invitations to sensual pleasure in *Venus and Adonis*, which showed him the moment at which Adonis struggles free from the sensual clutches of the goddess of love. Last but not least, the moral meaning of *Adam and Eve* of course speaks for itself.

However Philip may or may not have tried to intellectualize these works, it seems reasonable to conclude that as he relaxed after lunch his mind must have wandered about the images before his eyes rather than among the ideas they may or may not have symbolized.

When viewed as a group, these paintings effervesce with an almost overwhelming abundance of naked female flesh, a bounteous array of beautiful Baroque nudes, posing from front and back, bathing, reclining, embracing, all set off by a background of vibrant land-scapes filled with blue skies, fluffy white clouds and crimson textiles. The overall effect is more harem than bordello, more Olympian than perdition, but it oozes with sexuality nonetheless. Someone had even considerately thought to hang a medium-sized mirror in the room as well, to complete our picture of Philip's postprandial enthusiasm for licentious abandon. Thus Philip IV retired for his private siestas to a room in which he was surrounded by some of the most erotic muses of classical mythology, a room which had discreet access to and from the palace gardens and the outside world.

Felipe de Guevara, the most authoritative Spanish art commentator of the mid-sixteenth century, had treated the business of nude paintings with utmost brevity, merely recording the curiously matter-of-fact cultural observation that 'Venetian painters depict the female nude as excessively fleshy,' which 'stems from their popular belief that no woman can be perfectly beautiful unless she is very fat; so all their notions and fantasies in this respect are of grossly corpu-lent figures'.[21] However, before we nod too eagerly in agreement, it is worth remembering that he was, of course, primarily writing about Titian's mythological paintings, done for Philip II, that were the foundations of a fashion for both the naked female and to a lesser extent the male form that burgeoned across Europe during the seven-teenth and eighteenth centuries. In 1601, one especially scandalized critic complained that the fashion for paintings of nudes 'has caught on so fast that the sitting rooms and galleries of Princes' palaces are full of such filth, as are the parlours and bedrooms of every class of person, for they all think such indecent decoration is more jolly and pleasant than any other kind of image'.[22]

Velázquez's *Rokeby Venus*, painted in about 1650 and acquired by the Duke of Eliche, marks the apogee of that fashion: it is surely the most stunning image of a naked woman ever executed in paint. Today it is viewed as a beautiful painting rather than an exceptionally titillating example of early modern erotica. Yet as recently as 1914 it was symbolically slashed by the leading suffragette Mary Richardson protesting against such a public display of pornography. And a similar if differently motivated outrage was felt by many early modern Spanish churchmen who railed against the fashion; indeed, one of Philip's Confessors Royal frequently visited aristocratic houses offering to remove their collections of nudes and replace them, free of charge, with religious paintings of a similar size.[23] Women particularly, the moralists felt, were best protected from such sights; so, as Cassiano dal Pozzo remarked sardonically, 'whenever the Queen approaches the [summer] apartments, all the paintings of nudes have to be covered up before she arrives'.[24]

Just as it was felt that Queen Isabel would be offended by her husband's glittering display of pornographic old masters, so too – or so it was said – was she deeply hurt and troubled by his nocturnal egress from the palace in search of socially enlightening illicit pleasures. As the Archbishop of Granada's letters became public, the anti-Olivares faction flocked around the Queen in a display of moral outrage and sentimental sympathy for a slighted wife. But in a world awash with decadent hypocrisy, even as they rallied to Isabel, the palace gossips were all agog at the antics of the flamboyant Postmaster General, the Count of Villamediana, who was, according to some, himself openly courting the aggrieved Queen and doing so with her encouragement.[25] Years later, one admittedly extremely unreliable source reported that Villamediana had appeared at court dressed in a suit sewn all over with *reales*, or 'royal' silver pieces, and he wore a sash bearing the legend 'My love is *real*' – real or royal depending on how you interpret it – a very dangerous pun to have coined.[26] As the Archbishop of Granada had been at pains to emphasize, the problem was not what royalty might really be doing, but the damage that gossip could do to the monarchy's *reputación*.

On 21 August 1622, Villamediana arrived late in the evening at the Alcázar, surrounded by an unusually large entourage of servants and lackeys, just as Philip and Luis de Haro were returning from mass at a nearby convent. According to Quevedo, Zúñiga was also present and,

Detail from Juan Pantoja de la Cruz, *Philip III*, 1606. Philip III wanted to feel his kingship with each of his five senses and he loved the theatre of sovereignty, but he abdicated responsibility for the dreary day-to-day stewardship of the government to his *valido*, the Duke of Lerma.

Peter Paul Rubens, *Duke of Lerma*, 1603. The Duke of Lerma was a deeply Machiavellian mandarin largely interested in increasing his own fortune.

Francisco de Zurbarán, *Christ on the Cross*, 1627. Palomino describes 'a crucifix by Zurbarán which they display at Santo Domingo with the chapel gate kept closed and everyone who sees it thinks it must be a sculpture.'

Bartolomé Esteban Murillo, *Immaculate Conception of Los Venerables*, 1678. The nature of the Madonna's own conception was a fiercely debated question of great political, as well as religious, importance and her purity or immaculacy was especially celebrated in Spain and Seville.

Theodoor Galle after Jan Van der Street, *The Development of Printing*, c. 1550. Don Quixote 'went in and saw printing here, correcting proofs there, casting type here, revising there; in short, all the machinery of a great print works... and he watched with wonder.'

Diego Velázquez, *Kitchen Scene with Christ in the House of Martha and Mary*, 1618. Velázquez seems to have used his fiancée and future mother-in-law as models for this striking genre scene in which the hyperrealism of the mundane foreground contrasts with the abstracted vision of the spiritual world in the background.

Diego Velázquez, *Philip IV of Spain*, 1644. In time, the King might assert his independence, but he owed almost his whole conception of the world to Olivares.

Diego Velázquez, *Equestrian Portrait of the Count-Duke of Olivares*. If the relationship between Olivares and Philip IV is most obviously like that of an aging father and a growing son, there is also a flavour of marriage about it, or at least a peculiar partnership that verged on obsession.

Diego Velázquez, *The Surrender of Breda*, 1634. The defeat of the Dutch and capture of Breda in 1625 by the great Genoese general Ambrogio Spinola was one of a handful of seemingly miraculous Habsburg victories during the reign of Philip IV.

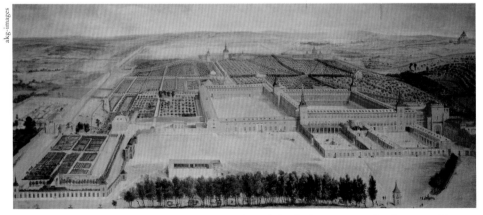

Jusepe Leonardo, *The Buen Retiro*, 1637. Olivares built the Buen Retiro just outside Madrid as a pleasure palace for Philip IV, but the project was driven by his own very personal notions of the past, of Habsburg identity and even his own family history.

Diego Velázquez, *Las Meninas (the Maids of Honour)*, 1656. Velázquez's greatest painting shows the artist himself at work, surrounded by the Infanta Margarita of Austria and her maids, servants, dwarf and dog, with the King and Queen reflected in a mirror in the background. But what was Velázquez in the process of painting on the canvas before him?

Juan Valdés Leal, *In Octu Oculi*, c. 1672, one of the striking pair of paintings which greet visitors to the Hospital of Charity in Seville. *In ictu oculi, finis gloriae mundi*: in the twinkling of an eye, the end of all worldly things.

'as though playing the part of Villamediana's guardian angel, warned him: "Be on the lookout, for your life is in danger." "That sounds more like a threat than a warning," the Count replied obstinately.' He then insisted that Haro join him for a ride in his carriage. But Haro refused. Villamediana insisted so vehemently that, according to one contemporary commentator, 'it was as though he were trying to force him to come along as witness to his murder'.[27]

Haro climbed into the carriage and the two men went for a drive, 'talking of this and that, of horses, music and poetry'. Góngora reported that as the carriage was nearing the count's home, 'on Main Street, a man came out from under the arcaded pavement at San Ginés and approached the coach from the left, where the Count was travelling'. Suddenly, 'wielding a terrible knife – to judge by the wound – he slashed him down the left side and arm, dealing him such a blow as would be horrifying even in a fighting-bull. The Count flew at him . . . gripping his sword, but as he realized he was too weak to hold it, he cried: out "'Tis done, gentlemen; I commend myself to God," and he collapsed.'[28]

At this point, the accounts differ as to the extent of Villamediana's contrition and whether the last rites were duly administered, a matter of great importance for his soul and so fuel for malicious gossip. As Quevedo explained, 'his death was more applauded than lamented' thanks to his 'licentious pen and sharp tongue'. In fact, his death certificate shows he died two days later, which supports the more plausible claim that he indeed received the final sacrament and was anointed with the holy oils of extreme unction, as Góngora reported. But Quevedo also hinted at the true darkness of the intrigue: 'some got so carried away they blamed the King . . . while others suggested he should have died at the hands of Justice . . . for neither in life nor in death could he do anything that was not a sin and he sought his own punishment with his whole body'.[29]

This remark would not have seemed cryptic to contemporaries who were well aware of an ongoing investigation into a group of homosexuals associated with Villamediana, the Duke of Alba's household in Naples and another senior figure in the post office, a royal messenger called Silvestre Nata Adorno. In an age when sodomy was 'a crime against nature' and known as the Nefarious Sin, this was a serious business and in December five young men, including a royal buffoon and personal servants of both Villamediana and the Duke of Alba, were convicted and burned at the stake in Madrid.[30] But Adorno was to be lucky, for the case against him depended on evidence that proved Villamediana's guilt, evidence that the King himself had ordered his prosecutor to suppress 'so as not to bring infamy upon the dead'.[31] Quevedo does not clarify whether the gossips thought the King had had Villamediana murdered out of jealousy over the Queen or to prevent the evidence against him coming out at the trial of the homosexuals. What other powerful figures, one wonders, might have feared that their own 'sinning against nature' might be revealed unless Villamediana's silence was ensured?

Olivares and Zúñiga had predicated the public image of Philip's new government on a moralizing break with the political corruption and licentious reputation of his father's court and administration. In 1621, they had established a powerful Council of Reform charged with rooting out the perceived widespread immorality of the kingdom under a hawkish career administrator, Francisco de Contreras, who had been born during the reign of Charles V. This puritanical agency was a key part of a propaganda campaign designed to demonstrate the sea-change supposedly taking place at the heart of government. The same year, they also hoped to show that clear difference of image between the old and the new regimes through the trial and execution of Lerma's right-hand man, Rodrigo Calderón, on 14 July. But a well-known account published at the time reported how, instead of dying like a traitor, as the new regime intended, Calderón had behaved with exemplary piety, commending himself to God and spending the three months between his conviction and execution at prayer. At the gallows, to the horror of the crowd, he was denied the last rites.[32] But by far the most moving account of his death was written by Góngora, who probably owed his elevation to a life at court to Rodrigo Calderón.

It was typical of Góngora's innate sense of quixotic nobility that, despite the risk of angering the new regime, he spoke up for his former protector in verse. But in a moving letter to Francisco de Corral in

Cordova, he was more explicit still, describing how Calderón 'listened to his sentence with such bravery that the secretary and witnesses were moved to compassion; he showed no emotion, but simply said: "God be praised, blessed be Our Lady."' He was spending four to six hours a day with a Carmelite friar, who 'broadcast how reconciled he was to his fate' with the result that 'everyone was distraught and his enemies were disconcerted'. Góngora describes how Calderón's father and wife had pleaded with Zúñiga, Olivares and the King, each of whom was unable to respond to them without bursting into tears. 'I myself have been so affected I have been unable to write until now,' he went on.[33] On the scaffold, on 14 July, Calderón was courteous to the executioner, spoke movingly and faced death with supremely understated bravery.[34]

Calderón and Villamediana had been Góngora's most important supporters at court and his hopes might have died with these last remnants of the old regime. But he had watched the changing political situation at the accession of Philip IV and the rise to prominence of Olivares with the zeal of a neophyte to the faith of courtly intrigue. He felt he might find a place to shine in Olivares's brave new Andalusian firmament and hope once again blossomed in his bosom: as one biographer put it, he began to 'think life was a bed of roses', or, as the Spanish saying goes, 'that the hillside was covered in oregano'.[35] For all that he 'could barely write for the cold', in January of 1622 he had reported home that 'until today I have merely wandered this court . . . but things are better now, for I have been given an audience by my King and his senior ministers, and at least one of them' – he was referring to Olivares – 'has looked upon me kindly'. Both Zúñiga and Olivares had by now promised to make Góngora's nephew a Knight of Santiago and he was convinced that he was about to be granted permission to appoint another knight to the order, a concession which he could use as a dowry for his niece. But, for all that optimism, in his letters home he constantly pleaded with his friend and steward to send him money because, he claimed, his credit had run out and he could not even afford food. Such a state of affairs, he suggested acerbically enough, clearly with his mind on the recent demise of Rodrigo Calderón, 'would be to behead my own reputation'.[36]

The business of politics was so strange and uncertain that this revolutionary poet whose verse sang of a courtly world that was putrid to the marrow was now invited to the whole rotten banquet, a banquet that, like Sancho Panza's disappearing dinner when he was governor of the island of Barataria, is nothing but disillusionment and *desengaño*: for Góngora, art and reality had collided in witnessing the terrible violence of Calderón's and Villamediana's deaths. The hawks and falcons of the Olivares regime had their prey; Góngora was thankful they had not come for him.

This unpalatable atmosphere of moral decadence and abuse of power was the backdrop to the first ever appearance, on the Madrid stage, of the most enduring and strangely endearing character in the history of western literature: Don Juan Tenorio, 'the Trickster of Seville', another corrupt aristocratic Andalusian and an assassin to boot.

Don Juan is surely the most iconic secular figure in western culture. He is a byword for a disturbingly alluring and utterly unbridled sexuality, a frighteningly compelling and unscrupulous master of seduction. Since he first walked the Madrid stage against the backdrop of Olivares's regime, his character has been reinvented and rewritten more than 1,700 times. These multiple reincarnations are the work of the most creative minds of every generation. Molière, Mozart, Byron, Shaw, Bergman, Bardot, Depp and even Bill Murray and their directors have all remade Don Juan for their own times, casting him in their own images, moulding him to their own ideas and desires. Over the centuries, during this strange story of a constantly mutating myth, he has been a libertine philosopher, a slave to his own desire, a helpless victim, an anti-establishment hero and a wanderer in search of the seemingly impossible, the perfect woman. On occasion, he has inspired horror, pity, envy, admiration and desire. He is today the troubled protagonist of an awful 'groundhog day' of sin and rebellion; ultimately, he is a victim of his own endless resurrections across the centuries. He has become, it seems, a celebrity who can never die.

This monumental figure was in origin the confection of Gabriel Téllez, 'dark and high of forehead', who had become a monk at the age of nineteen in 1600 and went on to study law at Salamanca and then theology in Toledo. By 1610, he had begun to write successful plays with more than a twist of ribaldry about them under the pseudonym of Tirso de Molina, one of the greatest playwrights of the Golden Age. In 1616, he went to Hispaniola as a missionary, but by 1618 he was back in Spain, living in the Mercedarian monastery in Madrid, a city then experiencing the political upheaval of Lerma's fall from power. He was largely known for his comedies, and his keen wit was suddenly quick with the injustice of the colonies and the immoral vicissitudes at the heart of the body politic. Against that fascinatingly sordid backdrop, he wrote *The Trickster of Seville, or the Stone Guest*. We must imagine one of the *corrales de comedia* or courtyard playhouses overflowing with excited spectators on a Madrid afternoon.

From the early seventeenth century, the theatre had been bursting into life across Europe as populations exploded and people poured into the towns and cities, a tide of immigrants hungry for entertainment and a sense of community. Almost everyone had enough money to buy a ticket and audiences were drawn from all walks of life and almost every social echelon, reflecting the diversity of the urban population. Like their English counterparts in Shakespearian London, Spaniards in places like Seville and Madrid quickly developed a keen taste for drama, going to plays regularly and keeping up a vociferous demand for new productions. Plays had short runs, a handful of performances at most; actors were worked hard and the playwrights like Lope de Vega worked harder still; Lope owed his success as much to the quantity of plays he wrote as to their quality, the only dramatist of his age who could keep up with demand, satisfying his fans with something new on an almost weekly basis.

The close-knit if not always convivial community of actors, directors and impresarios was a rare opportunity for Spaniards to escape their highly conservative world, in which the three main careers were traditionally the Church, the law and the army. There was a feeling of freedom in the travelling and the liberal lifestyle, but there was also a sense of security in the camaraderie of the profession. The world of theatre, as it has always done, attracted innovative and imaginative minds, individuals well suited to the task of bringing excitement and adventure, but also commentary and reflection, to a self-confident but uncertain world.

As it became evident that staging plays could be a lucrative business, a number of permanent theatres were established. The first of these playhouses opened its doors in Seville in 1574 and was run by one of the religious brotherhoods in order to raise funds for a charitable hospital they ran for the poor and needy of the city. Madrid followed, building two theatres in 1579 and 1582. Soon, charitable institutions, town councils and all sorts of entrepreneurs were setting up theatres across Spain. Companies of actors became a familiar sight on the main roads as they travelled the the kingdom performing stock favourites from their repertoire in the smaller towns and bringing fashionable new productions to the cities.[37]

The new theatres that grew up quickly were known as *corrales de comedia* because they were 'enclosed' within the internal courtyards formed where the buildings of a city block backed on to each other, a space similar to a London court. In recent decades, historians have thoroughly researched the history of these *corrales*, piecing together archaeological and documentary evidence which gives us a very good idea of what it must have been like to go to a performance in one of these open-air theatres embedded within the bowels of the city fabric. In 1950, an original *corral*, dating from 1628, was discovered at the small town of Almagro, in the heartland of central Spain, during minor building work at an inn. Following major restoration and reconstruction, it was reopened as a functioning theatre in 1952.

The seats in the Almagro *corral* are far from comfortable, but they are seats nonetheless; there is no standing room today, there are no steeply raked tiers with narrow wooden benches. There is no official *apretador*, or 'squasher', a man whose job it was to squeeze each patron into the tiny space allotted. Showers and deodorant have changed for ever the heady smell of a once strongly perfumed but unwashed throng who considered it ungodly to bathe. In Lope's day, performances were in the afternoon, but people gathered early, arriving from midday onwards, milling around, socializing and showing off. They came fancily dressed and even the cobblers and the shopkeepers wore their capes and their swords as though they were fine gentlemen, one foreign traveller observed.[38] Then, as more and more patrons appeared and the crowd swelled, the old hands began jostling and shoving, and soon everyone was jockeying for position, intent on getting into the theatre and finding a good spot from which to see the play. When the doors were thrown open, the men entered from the street along passageways, or even through the ground-floor rooms of one of the houses. These opened out on to a narrow *patio*, or yard, the 'pit', open to the skies, but partially covered with canvas awnings, a modicum of shade against the bright sunlight.

At the opposite end of this yard, the stage rose six to ten feet above the ground. The more sophisticated theatres had a remarkable range of special effects to draw on. The front of the stage was open, but an area at the back could be curtained off, while a gallery ran around the top of the stage, which could represent a tall building, a mountain or some other high point. The windows and balconies of houses backing on to the stage could be used as well and were especially effective for representing heaven. Meanwhile, a series of trapdoors in the stage allowed characters and objects to appear and disappear; fires, flares and fireworks could be lit in the space underneath, creating a powerful image of the entrance to hell itself, an image with which Tirso's *Trickster of Seville* would end on that first night.

A Florentine nobleman who visited Spain in the 1680s described how the crowd packed into the standing room in the yard and on the steep wooden *gradas*, or 'steps', to each side. 'When it rains,' he noted, 'it is highly disagreeable to be anywhere near the middle of that area, because it has no roof so as to allow the light in, and the water turns it into a real farmer's yard.'[39]

Entry to this muddy *patio* was very cheap – scholars estimate that it cost about a fifth of the average workman's daily wages, or enough to buy half a dozen eggs – and it filled with a noisy mixture of poorer patrons, the groundlings, known as *mosqueteros*, literally 'musketeers', labourers, artisans, students and youthful aristocrats enthusiastically slumming it with the masses. These *mosqueteros* could make or break a play with their heckling and rowdiness. Near the entrances, at the back, were the bar and the fruit stalls, handy sources of fuel and ammunition for rowdy and disgruntled patrons.

At first-floor level, opposite the stage, there was an area popularly known as the *cazuela*, or 'stewpot', set aside for 'women of doubtful virtue', according to one French noblewoman, 'and to which all the great lords flock in order to talk to the girls'. 'Sometimes,' she goes on, 'they make such a noise that you couldn't hear a thunderclap; and they come out with such funny comments that you would die laughing, for they have no sense of decency at all.'[40]

Directly above these garrulous comediennes in their stewpot, there was a tier of seating reserved for clergymen, while above them and along the sides the rich hired private boxes, some purpose built, but many of them really just rooms in houses overlooking the *corral*.

Rich and poor, men and women, aristocrats and soldiers, lawyers and thieves, prostitutes and clergymen, all crammed into this claustrophobic melting pot – each with their social pretensions, their personal hopes and, of course, their enthusiasm for the New Drama. The social hierarchy of the Spanish Golden Age was laid out before the actors on the stage, from the high born to the most lowly, as they played their parts, each character drawn from the motley public for whom they were performing.

The actors had to compete with their audiences to be the centre of attention in a colourfully competitive world obsessed by grandiose public display, honour, reputation and self-importance.

Suddenly, it is the dead of night. Somewhere near the back of the stage, two figures are barely visible, standing near a bed. One speaks; she sounds like a young woman, she seems to be wearing a nightdress: 'Duke Octavio, you can leave safely this way.'

Now we hear the voice of a young man: 'Duchess, we'll be married soon,' it says.

'Do you promise? Can it really be true?'

'I promise.'

'Wait,' says the girl's voice. 'I am going to get a light.'

'Why, what for?' says the other voice; it sounds concerned.

'I want to see you. I want to look into your eyes and see your soul. I want my soul to know the good faith I hear in your words.'

By the dim light of a lantern, we catch a glimpse of a very beautiful but dishevelled girl. Then a spotlight falls briefly on the bearded features of a youth in his early twenties. He is obviously alarmed and withdraws into the shadows, whispering violently: 'Kill that light at once or I'll kill it for you!'

'Good God! Who the devil are you?' she asks, her voice distorted with horror.

'Who am I?' he asks defiantly. 'A man without name.'

'You're not the duke!'

'No, I am not the duke.'

'Help! Guards! Guards!' the girl shouts.

'Wait, duchess, give me your hand,' says the youth.

'Don't tell me to wait, you bastard! Guards, guards! Call the King!'

The King of Naples rushes on, carrying a flaming torch. He peers across the stage, as though straining to see through the darkness.

'Oh my God! It is the King,' the girl wails. 'I am lost.'

The King shouts: 'What's going on? What the hell is this?'

Showing unbelievable insolence to the monarch, the youth replies:

> What on earth did you think it was going to be,
> but a man and a woman, Your Majesty?

The King of Naples orders the Spanish Ambassador, Don Pedro Tenorio, and the guards to arrest the intruder, but the young man swears that he will fight to the death rather than be taken alive. 'I am a Spanish gentleman,' he states. 'I want to speak to the Ambassador alone.'

Don Pedro and the intruder are left on the stage. Don Pedro threatens his quarry: 'Now we are alone, show me that you can fight with courage.'

'I am courageous enough, Uncle Pedro,' the youth says, 'but I will not fight with you.'

'Tell me who you are!'

'Your nephew . . . Oh, uncle, I am young, just as you once were. So, seeing as you too tasted love, forgive me my own love. I'll tell you the truth, for I tricked Duchess Isabella into having sex with me.'

'How did you trick her?'

'I pretended to be her fiancé, Duke Octavio.'

Pedro is furious, but as he says: 'If the King finds out I'll be finished.' He tells his nephew to jump from a balcony and make good his getaway; Pedro then arrests Octavio and charges him with the crime, but allows him to escape before he can be so unjustly punished. The audience still had no idea what the audacious protagonist might be called. He was Don Juan.

The story continues apace. Don Juan and his creepy servant Catalinón – Sevillian slang for 'Big Turd' – are washed up on a Spanish shore just as a beautiful fisher-girl is expounding her 'joy at being free from all the bitterness of love'. But she falls victim to Don Juan, for Catalinón has told her that 'Don Juan Tenorio . . . is the son of the Chamberlain to the King of Spain,' and Don Juan soon promises to marry her. She tells him:

> If you break that promise, as you know well,
> God will punish you in death, and you'll burn in hell.

'Death's a long way off!' Don Juan replies. It becomes his refrain in this most moralizing of licentious plays.

But Catalinón has a buffoon's words of wisdom for his master:

> With your tricks and lies you bring women strife,
> But you will pay for it all in the afterlife.

'That's a long way off!' Don Juan replies.

Meanwhile, in Seville, the King of Spain, Alfonso XI, enters, which would have alerted the audience to the fact that the play was set in the fourteenth century, during one of the most troubled periods in Spanish dynastic history. King Alfonso has agreed with the Constable of Castile, Gonzalo de Ulloa, to marry the Constable's daughter, the beautiful Doña Ana, to Don Juan. But when Uncle Pedro arrives with the scandalous news from Naples, they decide to betroth her to Duke Octavio instead.

Later, somewhere in the streets of Seville, Don Juan meets an old friend, the Marquis of Mota, an intentionally humorous interloper from the real seventeenth-century court. As they discuss the pox-ridden whores they have tricked in the past, Mota boasts that he is hopeful Doña Ana 'has shown some interest'. But while Mota is off whoring, Don Juan tricks his way into Doña Ana's house disguised in his friend's cloak. 'Impostor! You are not the marquis,' she cries out. 'You have tricked me, you liar!' We have no idea how far the tryst has gone.

Don Gonzalo appears: 'That's Ana's voice.'

'Won't anybody kill this traitor who has murdered my honour?' Doña Ana shouts.

'Has someone dared to dishonour my daughter. Oh God, and she keeps shouting about her "dead honour" – she might as well ring a bell to announce the fact.'

'Kill him!' Doña Ana now shouts.

'Let me through,' Don Juan orders.

'Let you through? I'll run you through with this sword, you traitor,' shouts Don Gonzalo.

Don Juan mortally wounds Don Gonzalo and escapes.

In due course, the King orders the arrest of the Marquis of Mota, who is taken to a dungeon to await execution in the morning. The King of Spain then orders a statue to be made to honour the murdered Don Gonzalo de Ulloa: 'Bury him with pomp and ceremony and due gravitas; then have a bust made of bronze and stone in his honour. This monument shall be inscribed: "May the Lord take revenge on the traitor who murdered this loyal knight."'

In the next scene, Don Juan seduces a peasant girl at her own wedding, thanks to her father's gullibility in believing that he intends to marry her. As he says:

Before I do the real damage, I'm going to set things straight. For a peasant always thinks he holds his honour in his own hands, so I'm going to get permission for my crime from Gaseno himself, the bride's father.

> May the stars bring me luck in this deed,
> And I'll pay for my crime when I'm dead,
> For Death's a long way off!

But Catalinón is worried: 'I hope we get out of this alive!'

'What are you afraid of?' Don Juan asks. 'My father is the King's favourite; he dispenses justice in this land!'

'God takes his revenge on men who favour wrongdoing. Be careful! Life seems very short at the moment when Death overcomes us; and a different emperor rules in the afterlife!'

'Death is a long way off! Long live deceit and trickery!'

Don Juan and Catalinón now return to Seville, where they find Don Gonzalo's tomb. 'This is whom I killed,' says Don Juan, laughing. 'They've given him an impressive tomb. Look, here it asks God to revenge his death! Is that meant to be a warning, you silly old man?' Don Juan asks the statue, pulling at the stone beard in imitation of the most insulting gesture one Spanish aristocrat could make to another. 'Tonight you will dine with me at my inn.'

The scene changes. Two servants are laying the table in the empty dining room of an inn. There is a loud knock at the door. Don Juan shouts: 'Who goes there?'

'I do,' replies a deep, resonant voice.

'Who are you?'

'I am the honourable gentleman you invited to supper.'

'There will be dinner for two tonight,' says Don Juan, turning to his servants. He orders Catalinón to sit at table, but the man is speechless with fear. 'How absurd,' Don Juan continues, 'what have you to fear from a dead man, you pathetic, imbecilic peasant?'

The two aristocrats dine, the mortal Don Juan, a man of flesh and bone, eats and drinks for the two of them, while Don Gonzalo, immortal and made of stone, remains silent. When the meal is over, the stone statue tasks Don Juan: 'Give me your hand. Remember I am an Ulloa. Do not be afraid!'

'Afraid! I'd go with you to hell itself!'

'Will you give me your word as a gentleman that you will dine with me tomorrow night at ten o'clock?'

'I will be your guest tomorrow. Where?'

'In the chapel.'

'I give you my word as a Tenorio.'

As the play nears its finale, Juan and Catalinón go into the darkened church. A figure comes towards them out of the blackness. 'Who goes there?' Don Juan asks.

'I do,' Don Gonzalo replies. 'I want to invite you to dinner,' the statue explains, but 'you'll have to open up this tomb.'

The statue, Don Juan and Catalinón sit down to eat. A choir begins to chant:

> Every debt owed will always be paid,
> Even those who God punishes late in the day,
> For Death is never a long way off!

'Give me your hand, Don Juan,' the statue says. 'The wonders of God, Don Juan, are ever present. And God wants you to pay for your crimes at the hands of a dead man; that is how you will pay for all the girls you have tricked and cheated. This is God's justice!'

Catalinón looks on as Don Gonzalo and Don Juan disappear along with the tomb as it sinks into the stage aflame with hellfire.

Don Juan was, in reality, Tirso de Molina's artful collage. His character was pieced together from a range of sources, but with life breathed into him by the moral reality of his times, rather as Dr Frankenstein would do with his monster. At its core, there are two parts to his character: the sexual predator who tricks and lies his way to conquest and a criminally violent yet brave young man who defies death. There has been plenty of scholarly conjecture about the roots of Tirso's story in medieval Spanish traditions, and plentiful folktales have been identified about mythical murderers and ne'er-do-wells who suffered divine punishment, often in a graveyard, for disrespecting the dead.[41] Intriguingly, the great medieval English poet Geoffrey Chaucer included in *The Canterbury Tales* the story of a priest called Daun John who seduces the wife of a miserly merchant. Clearly, by the fourteenth century the name was already associated with assaulting the divine sacrament of matrimony and this, for Tirso, was his character's greatest sin. But there had been a real Juan Tenorio, and Tirso's choice of the name immediately located the action in medieval Seville.

At one stage in the play, Don Juan describes himself as 'a noble gentleman of the House of Tenorio, ancient conquerors of Seville', clearly identifying himself as a member of a real family, with an illegitimate royal bloodline, which had its power base in Seville from 1248 when Pedro Tenorio played a key role in the Christian conquest of the city from the Moors. The family developed into one of the most prominent and powerful aristocratic clans in Andalusia, but in 1295 Ruy Pérez Tenorio (the great-uncle of the real Don Juan) fled Seville, having murdered a geriatric military commander and poet, a hero of the conquest of Seville, a war veteran who had fought alongside Pedro Tenorio. It is an especially ignominious episode in the Tenorio family history that clearly inspired Tirso's account of Don Juan's murder of the venerable old soldier Don Gonzalo. The endgame in the real medieval story is more prosaic than Tirso's dinner between the animated statue and Don Juan on the threshold of hell. The retribution was royal rather than divine: in 1295, one of the royal princes personally hunted down and murdered the fugitive Tenorio as he headed for the Portuguese border.

These are compelling clues, of course, to Tirso's use of medieval Castilian royal chronicles as his sources. But *The Trickster* is set in the reign of Alfonso XI, who married his cousin María of Portugal, despite being denied papal dispensation for the match. But by the time the Pope, faced with this fait accompli, had regularized the situation the following year, Alfonso had embarked on a disastrous relationship with 'a widow living in Seville called Doña Leonor . . . rich in her own right and very much a noblewoman, and the most beautiful woman in the whole realm', the chronicler reported.[42] The Pope wrote to María of Portugal describing her King's 'actions as an offence against our divine majesty himself'. The chronicler squarely blames Alfonso for the long time it took for the Queen to fall pregnant because he was always with Leonor instead. And, disastrously, while María bore him one son, the future Pedro the Cruel, Leonor gave birth to a dynasty of twelve siblings upon whom Alfonso lavished titles, lands and honours. In 1369, the fourth son of this brood, Henry of Trastamara, great great-grandfather of both Ferdinand of Aragon and Isabella of Castille, usurped Pedro's crown and became King of Castile.

But with Alfonso and Pedro it was like father, like son, and the real Juan Tenorio came to the fore as the Falconer Royal and one of Pedro's most trusted courtiers thanks to his role in introducing the young King to a minor noblewoman, possibly a relative, called María de Padilla, petite, dark and famous for her beauty. By Tirso's day, myth and reality were becoming blurred and Pablo de Espinosa's *History of Seville*, of 1627, reported that 'it is commonly held and traditional in Seville that Doña María lived in this city with her uncle Don Juan de Henestrosa, in a house that can still be seen in the parish of San Gil'.[43] It was said 'that the King saw her on his return from the hunt', presumably in the company of his Falconer, Don Juan, 'and he fell in love with her. He explained how he felt to her uncle, but she would not agree to please the King unless she was properly married. And so they say that he married her and that he took her to the Alcázar as his wife.' It was then thought, Espinosa explained, that Juan Tenorio was related to the Padilla family.[44]

In *The Trickster of Seville*, Tirso poured into the character of Don Juan all the immorality of the medieval reigns of Alfonso XI and Pedro I as described by the Castilian chroniclers in which the violation of marriage lay at the heart of a brutally cynical and ambitious political class and ultimately led to dynastic disaster. His choice of the Tenorio family as his archetype firmly associated this atmosphere of malaise with over-influential courtiers from Seville. At Philip IV's court, febrile with salacious gossip about an arrogant and aristocratic Andalusian favourite, the implications of the themes running through Tirso's great play would not have been lost on its audience. In 1625, Tirso fell foul of Olivares's Junta de Reformación or Council of Reform. Plays, the Council advised, were 'a great danger because so many are performed and so often, and because of their evil plots which make them such a bad example to the general public'. And then the minutes of their meeting turn to the 'notorious . . . scandal caused by a Mercedarian friar called Gabriel Téllez, also known as Tirso de Molina, who writes profane plays which set an evil example'. They agreed to put the matter before the King, advising that the relevant religious authorities be required to banish Tirso to 'one of the order's remotest monasteries and that he be threatened with excommunication so that he writes no more plays nor any other kind of profane verse'. Although Philip never countersigned the order, the following year Gabriel Téllez was moved to the Mercedarians' monastery in distant and isolated Trujillo.[45]

And then in 1623 a most unexpected English lover arrived in Madrid under cover of darkness, a theatrically chivalrous Lothario rather than a Don Juan. His suit was ultimately unsuccessful, but it caught the romantic imagination of seemingly every Spaniard in the realm, except for Olivares.

19

The Prince of Wales in Madrid

As soon as the Infanta saw the Prince, her colour rose very high,
which we hold to be an impression of Love and Affection.

James Howell, English Cosmographer Royal

At ten o'clock in the evening of Friday, 7 March 1623, under cover
of darkness, two Englishmen rode their mules discreetly into
the heart of Madrid, looking for the very appropriately named Street
of the Infanta. They dismounted outside the famous House of the
Seven Chimneys, the residence of the English Ambassador, the Earl of
Bristol. One of them knocked at the door and presented himself to the
servant as Mr Thomas Smith. He went inside carrying his own luggage
and quickly explained that he had hurt his leg and could not climb the
stair, requesting that Bristol come down to meet him. Meanwhile, the
other man, who went by the name of John Smith, 'stay'd on t'other
side of the Street, in the dark'.[1]

When Bristol appeared, he was amazed to find that Thomas Smith
was in fact King James's favourite, the Marquis (later Duke) of
Buckingham, who quickly explained that the story about his injured leg
was simply a way of ensuring correct etiquette: as John Smith began to
hurry across the street, Buckingham told the astounded Ambassador
that his companion was in reality none other than Charles, Prince
of Wales, heir to the thrones of England and Scotland. 'Bristol, in a
kind of Astonishment, brought him up to his Bed-chamber, where he
presently called for Pen and Ink and dispatch'd a Post that night to

England to acquaint His Majesty how in less than sixteen days he was come safely to the Court of Spain.'[2]

The utterly unexpected arrival of the heir to the British thrones at the fastidiously formal Spanish court was an extraordinary breach of protocol described by one leading journalist of the day as 'almost beyond belief' and 'quite beyond all reason'.[3] But Charles had come to woo the Infanta María, sister of Philip IV, and his daring incognito journey caught the Spanish imagination as a bizarre yet endearingly chivalric gesture. Góngora hymned the Prince as a 'bird from King Arthur's realms' who was drawn to the sunshine of 'María's august splendour'.[4] A marriage alliance between Spain and England had been mooted since the beginning of the century and Philip III's able anglophile Ambassador to London, the Count of Gondomar, had long worked hard for it.[5] The Venetian Ambassador reported the widespread belief that 'the prince was burning with a love ... kindled by the reports of Gondomar and in his desire to bring about the marriage he thought he could compel it by his presence'.[6] Gondomar had perhaps worked too hard and had given the Stuarts too much hope: most problematically, the Spaniards immediately interpreted the secrecy surrounding the journey as a sure indication of Charles's intention to convert to Catholicism, and that vain hope proved fatal to the match. And beyond the quixotic charm of his daredevil demonstration of a flaming passion for an Infanta he knew only from a painting and from hearsay, there was clearly an element of desperation about such unseemly haste. James was trying to force Philip IV's hand in an attempt to secure a reconciliation between Spain and his errant and now defeated son-in-law, the Elector Frederick of the Palatinate. As the journalist put it, James 'well knew the power of the Catholic King, his diligence towards his alliances, and the jealousy and fear he inspired across Europe'.[7]

Charles had set out for Spain from Buckingham's house, Newhall, in Essex, on 18 February, with a tiny entourage; both men were disguised in false beards and the Prince also wore an eye-patch. Unused to the ordinary business of daily life, they had set out without any small change and had to pay a whole guinea to a delighted ferryman in order to cross the Thames at Gravesend. Then, on the trunk road to Dover, they had to make their horses jump the hedges and cross some fields in order to avoid the French Ambassador who was coming in the other direction; and at Canterbury they were arrested by the suspicious Mayor, forcing Buckingham to take off his beard and pull rank. The following day, after a stormy crossing, they landed in France and made straight for Paris, for Charles was determined to see the famously flamboyant French court. And so, 'for the better veiling of their visages, his Highness and the Marquis bought each of them a perriwig, somewhat to overshadow their foreheads', and thus disguised they bribed their way into the banqueting hall and from the public galleries watched the royal family eating. Charles wrote to his father that he was so taken with the great beauty of Ana, Louis XIII's Spanish Queen, 'that it hath wrought in me a greater desire to see her sister', the Infanta María.[8]

There is no record of their journey across Spain, but their experience must have been very similar to that of Richard Wynn, a member of their official entourage which would arrive in their wake at the beginning of April. Wynn was surprised by the way the proud Spaniards loafed around while the women did all the hard work, was unimpressed by the lack of glass in the windows and was amazed at the rudimentary food and cooking arrangements on the Spanish roads. On one occasion, riding on ahead of the main party and having passed up the opportunity to visit El Toboso, 'a poor Village where the famous Dulcinea lived', he and his companion asked where they might get wine and food and were 'directed to a House in a Wood'. There a woman 'made us a Pancake of Eggs and Bacon, all fryed together'. But, 'she having covered a little Stool, and layd on the Table two Loaves of Bread, of a suddain there comes out of the Wood two black Swine, overthrow the Stool, and each carries away a Loaf'. The following night, however, in a village where the womenfolk 'lamented that we were not Christians', he 'had as good a Hen and Bacon as ever I eat'. As Sancho Panza put it to Don Quixote: 'hunger is the best sauce for food'.[9]

Whether Charles and Buckingham enjoyed the liberty of the road as much as Philip and Olivares enjoyed their libertine Madrid nightlife has gone unrecorded, but Charles's letters home to his father suggest an excited young man revelling in the adventure. There can be little doubt that most of the Englishmen who ended up in Madrid in Charles's meagre entourage, while unimpressed by 'accommodation' that was 'very scurvy', must have been taken with the beautiful women, 'who, whether from the constitution or the customs of the city', or out of sheer exoticism, the Englishmen 'noted to be much more lascivious and meretricious than in other places', and 'if some pretended to be driven to it by necessity . . . others certainly were drawn to it by their inclinations'. However, while they were 'very crafty' and 'their discourse very ingenious . . . their bodies were generally infectious', which rather suggests that this particular commentator may have been unlucky or overindulgent in his visits to the brothels.[10]

For Bristol, the excitement of the Prince's arrival must, at first, have been a matter of high anxiety, for it breached almost every conceivable norm of diplomatic etiquette. But he quickly recovered his composure and, realizing there was only one thing to be done, drove immediately to Gondomar's lodgings, telling him only that Buckingham had arrived. Gondomar returned with him to the House of the Seven Chimneys; he too was now subjected in person to the astonishing presence of the Prince; he too realized that there was only one course of action to be followed and drove immediately to Olivares's apartments.

Olivares was eating his supper as Gondomar arrived 'in so obviously a joyous mood' that he asked, 'What news does Your Grace bring me here at this hour and in such a good mood that you might as well have brought the King of England to Madrid?'

'Perhaps not the King,' Gondomar admitted, 'but the Prince of Wales in person.'

'Olivares did not know what to think, but was dumbfounded by a mixture of joy and uncertainty at such extraordinary news.' Deeply perturbed, Olivares went to give Philip his bizarre report. 'The King, like all prudent men', assumed that Charles's secrecy foretold a desire to 'resolve the conflicts of religion' and was 'overjoyed'. In fact, if we believe Olivares's own account of the scene, Philip appears to have immediately grasped the precarious political reality of the situation.

Understanding that the marriage depended on some sort of religious compromise, he instantly turned to a 'crucifix hanging at the head of his bed' and swore an oath: 'Lord, I vow . . . that I be resolved not to waver in any way over matters relating to religion as determined by Thy Vicar, the Roman Pontiff, even were I thereby to lose my Kingdoms.'[11]

The oath cast some important political dice by ensuring that the Pope and his cardinals would dictate the religious terms on which Philip might consent to his sister's marriage to a Protestant prince and thereby removed control of the matter from Spain. This had two crucial advantages for Olivares, for it rendered his political rivals in Madrid impotent, while deflecting the blame for any failure in the business on to the Papacy and away from Philip and Spain. In fact, the Vatican was already close to dictating terms that might have proved workable; but Olivares, through a lively and secret correspondence with Rome, now set about ensuring that the Pope dictated new terms that would be so onerous as to make the match all but impossible for Charles to accept. From now on, the whole escapade was doomed.

There were many reasons why Olivares may have opposed the match, but perhaps the most obvious is that the immediate reaction of a man so controlling and jealous of power to such a breathtaking display of chivalric bravado was an implacable determination that it should fail. He was simply not prepared to let Charles, James, Buckingham and Gondomar steal a march on him. He was henceforth rude to the Prince, refusing to cover his head at their first meeting despite repeated requests to do so; and he cultivated an ugly and dysfunctional relationship with Buckingham so that both men came to despise one another by the end of the summer.

King Philip had at once ordered Olivares to ensure 'all the Prince's wishes are gratified in consideration of the obligation under which he has placed us by coming'. And so the count stayed up all night, planning the festivities with which the Prince of Wales would be fêted and how his household was to be arranged within the Alcázar.[12] No expense would be spared, recently introduced austerity measures prohibiting the wearing of expensive clothes and jewellery were suspended,

Madrid would throw her royal guest a summer of banquets, tourneys and spectacles, which were scheduled to begin with the Prince's official entry into the city the following weekend.

On the Sunday following his arrival, Charles was allowed his first sight of the Infanta. He waited in a covered carriage just outside the city on the fashionable promenade of the Prado until Philip, the Queen and the Infantes, all curious to see the Prince, came by in the royal carriage, with 'the Infanta herself sat in the Boot with a blue ribbon about her Arm of purpose that the Prince might distinguish her'. According to the English accounts, Charles was so taken with her beauty that Gondomar had to stop him from leaping out of the coach to greet the royal party, while 'as soon as the Infanta saw the Prince, her colour rose very high, which we hold to be an impression of Love and Affection'.[13]

The grandeur of the official royal reception is powerfully evoked by the journalist's account of the outlandish pyrotechnics that greeted the Prince: the 'many rockets, foot-burners, thunder-flashes, barrel-bombs, Catherine-Wheels, lanterns' and other exotic fireworks the precise explosive nature of which is no longer known; there was even a 'flaming mountain from which bulls, goats, rams, serpents, horses and wild boar rushed forth', all of which lasted over half an hour. That night, a re-creation of Troy was attacked and burned by invading Greeks, a deliberately less than tactful reference to Paris's foolhardy kidnapping of Helen from Agamemnon which delighted the cynically poetic wits at court who later documented the irony in verse.[14]

This cynical symbolism was surely the work of Olivares. Henceforth, he did everything he could to keep Charles away from the Infanta, to the point that when the news was released that she 'had fallen sick with a slow fever', foreign diplomats reported that while some observers optimistically said 'it was real and due to her great perturbation, others claimed it was feigned to provide an excuse for delay'. The gossips were quick to notice that the Prince, who 'professed himself deeply in love', was 'growing tired and resentful' of the situation.[15]

Olivares settled on Palm Sunday as the perfectly unromantic opportunity to allow Charles another brush with his prey. The Prince of Wales dressed in gala finery and bedecked himself with jewellery. But his Spanish household insisted that his blue trousers were excessively jaunty for such a solemn holy day; the Prince resisted until one senior courtier had the presence of mind to ask for them as a present, a request that could not properly be refused; Inés de Zúñiga then lent him some appropriately sombre clothing and a few fashionable Spanish collars.[16] After vespers, Philip collected the now suitably attired Charles and accompanied him to the Queen's apartments, where, with a crowd of grandees and courtiers looking on, the smitten Englishman was allowed to approach the Infanta and pay his respects. By all accounts, María remained stony-faced during her brief conversation with the Prince, a display of self-control that was interpreted differently by the spectators. The English were optimistic that this was a sign of concealed affection, with one senior diplomat suggesting, with characteristically English crudeness, that 'without a doubt she will be with child before she gets into England'.[17] The Venetian Ambassador, however, thought that Charles had been forced to finish his suit 'sooner than he wanted' and described how the onlookers 'spoke with universal astonishment' at 'how composed she remained throughout . . . for it is notorious that she regards this marriage with extreme aversion and dread'.[18]

Although many observers were beginning to detect a breakdown in trust between the two sides, the King and the Prince seem to have developed a strong friendship based on their mutual love of art and culture. Charles clearly had a naturally aesthetic eye, but it was while looking at the royal collections alongside Philip that he became an educated connoisseur, soon to be one of the great collectors of his day. Indeed, following his execution, in 1649, Philip's agents discreetly acquired many of his best pieces. Charles and Buckingham both relished their sojourn at the Spanish court as a unique opportunity to acquire many paintings, sculptures, books and other curios; they sent James a gift of two asses, five camels, a horse and a dipsomaniac elephant that went on to live in St James's Park consuming a gallon of wine a day at considerable expense to the Exchequer.[19] But even as they indulged in this orgy of material acquisition, it was becoming ever clearer that the marriage would never happen.

Charles, still impetuous, was not easily discouraged, and, to the horror of his hosts, he determined to make one last dramatic gesture for the Infanta's hand, a gesture inspired by a work of literature. This time, he did not, however, emulate a chivalric novel, but instead chose the late-medieval Spanish classic *La Celestina*, translated into English as *The Spanish Bawd*. This early best-seller, first published in 1499, recounts the story of a young man who turns to a witch-like procuress to arrange a tryst with the recalcitrant object of his lust, Melibea, but falls to his death from a ladder while trying to climb out of her father's walled garden, causing the grief-stricken girl to commit suicide.

As the heat of summer came on, in late June, Charles learnt that the Infanta habitually drove out to the King's summer house, the Casa de Campo, where she gathered flowers among the trees. So one morning, 'he rose betimes and went thither' and was 'let into the House and . . . Garden. But the Infanta was in the Orchard; and there being a high partition-wall between, and the door doubly bolted, the Prince got on the top of the wall and sprung down a great height, and made towards her; but she spying him first of all the rest gave a shriek and ran back.'[20]

As the summer dragged on in an endless round of irksomely decorous festivities while everyone was all too aware that the marriage had foundered on the difference of religion, it slowly dawned on the English that Charles was now practically a hostage. The Spaniards in general clearly still hoped he might be persuaded to convert and swear to protect British Catholics, while Olivares hoped to persuade him to marry an Austrian Habsburg bride, the Emperor's eldest daughter.[21] It would not be easy to leave without the dangerous provocation of riding roughshod over protocol.

But Charles had had enough and was determined to retreat home at any cost; the price he paid was an act of desperate duplicity. In early July, he again astonished everyone by agreeing to each of the impossible terms and conditions that Olivares had convinced the Papacy to require of him. It may have been a last throw of the dice in hope that he might be allowed to go home with his Spanish bride. Needless to say, he was not. But there was now no reason for Philip to refuse him permission to leave Madrid and so, through gritted teeth, Olivares was forced to watch his prisoners depart, along with the hated Buckingham, even as the rest of the court celebrated the implausible Damascene conversion. Charles left Madrid at the end of August, still promising to marry the Infanta by proxy, but by the time he set sail from the Santander on 18 September, he had already instructed Bristol not to go through with the ceremony. His peculiarly chivalric adventure had ended in abject failure and most unromantic subterfuge.

A presumably satisfied if weary Olivares now turned his attention to taking the King on an important journey of his own to visit Andalusia and to see Seville, that jewel in his economic crown, and to try and do something to reverse the drastic decline in revenue from the Americas.

Many historians have followed the contemporary commentators who pictured Lerma and Olivares as Machiavellian political monsters who orchestrated the courtly world with a patriarchal, godlike omnipotence. They controlled their kings by overwhelming them with layer upon layer of Baroque grandeur, keeping their minds constantly occupied by splendid spectacles and courtly rituals, while their emotions were regularly thrilled by the hunt or the pursuit of pleasure. And so the King became a symbol of monarchy, his purpose simply to underpin the authority of the Crown, his authority actually exercised by the favourite: the favourite ruled while the King reigned.

Olivares's relationship with Philip IV was more emotionally complicated than that. Olivares was a megalomaniac, but he was far from omnipotent and his control over the kingdom and many of its institutions was at best tenuous and often non-existent. He was a deeply delusional personality, lacking in psychological stability, who came to believe his own propaganda about Habsburg history. He had more than a touch of Don Quixote about him as, with flabbergasting political naivety, he tried to force on to Castile his own hopelessly unrealistic agenda for reform.

Abroad, he pursued an insanely bellicose foreign policy, blundering into as many foreign conflicts as might arise in the belief that Habsburg history would prevail over the present-day European reality. He seems genuinely to have believed that the past could somehow win the wars of the present; the fact that, despite the Crown's almost permanent bankruptcy, Castile was able to carry on fighting until the 1640s is

testimony to the resilience of the whole Spanish system; an infrastruc-
ture of postal services, banking facilities, food supplies, established
routes for the movement of troops, ports, shipping and the mental
habits of so many Italians, Flemings and Germans for whom Spain
had for so long been the centre of the world. The Spanish monarchy
was undergoing an extended period of precipitous decadence, but
Castile remained the keystone of a worldwide economic system.

At home, in Spain, Olivares aspired to a Union of Arms that would
open up roles in the Madrid government for Valencian, Catalan and
Aragonese aristocrats in return for contributions to the defence of
all Philip's realms; he envisaged a modern sense of Spain. 'The most
important business of your monarchy', he explained to Philip, 'is
to make yourself King of Spain . . . and work and secretly scheme
to reduce the kingdoms of which Spain is composed to the laws of
Castile, with no . . . borders nor customs posts, and the power to
convoke the Cortes . . . wherever is desirable.'[22] Ultimately, this
fantastical ambition would destroy him, but even Olivares was not
mad enough to try to force through such a policy in the face of
regional hostility at the outset of the reign.

Instead, he focused on a programme of reform at home founded on
three basic and sensible objectives: to stimulate trade and economic
growth, to rationalize taxation and to push through a massive
austerity drive to direct investment away from luxury. These were
all areas of pressing failing and Olivares's aims were in themselves
entirely rational. But the policies he hoped would achieve these aims
were radical, bold and brash: to bolster the economy, he advocated
a state-organized banking system to be subsidized by the towns, a
series of tax incentives to encourage immigration from abroad and to
encourage couples to marry and have children, and the establishment
of trading companies similar to the Dutch East India Company and
its English equivalents. He railed against the iniquities and inefficien-
cies of the *milliones*, a tax on various basic foodstuffs, still voted by
the Cortes on behalf of the municipalities, and tried to introduce a
fairer and better system that would place the burden on the wealthier
cities rather than the hard-pressed peasantry. He tried to set about
butchering the vast and corrupt municipal administration, proposing

a reduction of two-thirds in the number of bureaucratic posts in every town.

In the idyllic, utopian Castile of his deranged imagination anything appeared to be possible. But he seems to have had as little grasp, perhaps even less than his monarch, of the political realities. The entire programme of reform led him into a head-on collision with the towns and so the Cortes: he asked the towns to capitalize the new banks, without any guarantee the money would not immediately be sequestered by the Crown; he wanted the commercial monopolies long enjoyed by the urban oligarchs to be undermined by the new trading companies that would operate in the interests of the Crown; and the burden of the new taxation system was to lie most heavily with these same urban oligarchs. It was a programme designed to allow the Crown to usurp the power of the kingdom. More insane still, the need for the towns' *procuradores* to vote the *milliones* represented a stranglehold over Crown finances and it was inconceivable they would surrender that power. But Olivares blithely pursued these reforms with a surreal dogmatism that was doomed to failure and his most eloquent publicist, Quevedo, gave the programme enthusiastic support, celebrating the count as the saviour of Castile, in his *Satirical Epistle against the Present Customs of the Castilians*; it was an ominous title that rode roughshod over tradition in a way that seemed to evoke the causes of the Comunero Revolt.

In 1623, Olivares's ability to gloss over his delusional fictions resulted in the spectacular vote he wrested from the Cortes of sixty million ducats over five years in addition to twelve million outstanding. The sum was unprecedented, but the towns had limited the powers of their *procuradores* to ensure that the grant still had to be ratified at municipal level, and so the negotiation continued. They insisted that the tax be raised in the customary manner and then, on 2 February 1624, it was made a condition of the grant of the *milliones* that the Crown itself capitalize the new banking sector.

At the outset, the towns had forced Olivares to abandon both his tax and banking reforms; even the promise of seventy-two million ducats began to seem like a fiscal windmill waving tantalizingly on a hazy horizon. The last hope for reform was borne by the lone and

forlorn figure of a lawyer called Baltasar Gilimón de la Mota, who
rode out across Castile, charged with abolishing two-thirds of the
municipal offices of every town, compensating those affected directly
and distributing the remaining third by lot. Sancho Panza might have
had more chance of success.

Olivares was a man of movement as much as action. On 8 February
1624, he set out with Philip IV for Andalusia. The royal progress 'was
organized so fast that no sooner was it announced than they had set
off'.[23] Out of respect for the notion of austerity, the entourage was
impressively small by Habsburg standards; even so, it consisted of
a whole host of aristocrats and courtiers, ambassadors and senior
officials of the royal household. There were in addition 200 servants
and soldiers, including biscuit makers, candlemakers, tailors, a soup
chef, a pastry chef, a watercarrier, some falconers and hunters, thirteen archers, two altar boys, a farrier and three washerwomen. It was
decided that Philip would make his royal entries into the cities in a
coach, also to save money, but perhaps also to avoid the risk of dissent.
Despite terrible gales and pouring rain, the party made good speed to
Andújar, where the Guadalquivir was in flood and they had to wait
before they could cross.

For Olivares, Philip's progress through Andalusia was a personal
mission to introduce the King to the part of Spain he felt was his
homeland; it was also designed to force the King, his court and his
government to witness with their own eyes the tangible wealth and
power of the region and so understand just how important it was
to the whole monarchy. But, most urgently, he hoped that the presence of Philip and the royal entourage would help to bring round the
great Andalusian cities that had been the most recalcitrant opponents
of his programme of reform in the Cortes. The arrival at Cordova
in such tempestuous weather was a discouraging omen. Góngora's
home seemed so miserably poor that Olivares quickly abandoned any
attempt to browbeat the city fathers into embracing policies that they
could clearly not afford. Philip saw the great Cathedral and former
mosque, the Mezquita, visited some monasteries and attended a

bullfight and some *juegos de cañas*. After four days, the royal party moved on to Écija, where there was a masked ball.

On 1 March, Philip entered Seville, described by the expedition chronicler as 'the universal powerhouse of Spain'.[24] During the eleven-day visit, he stayed in the Alcázar and there were the usual spectacles and fireworks. He must surely have visited the great collection of the Duke of Alcalá at the Casa de Pilatos; it is equally hard to believe that he did not wonder at some of Montañés's great sculptures, or the paintings of Zurbarán, or discuss art theory with Pacheco. Seville was filled with beautiful works of art that must have thrilled this aesthete monarch, but there is, sadly, no record of what he saw nor of his reactions. We do know that he spent time at a country estate, downriver, known as the Palace of Pedro the Cruel, at the invitation of the Count of Niebla, heir to the Duke of Medina Sidonia.[25] We can only assume that he inspected the Tierra Firme Fleet, soon to sail for Portobello in Panama, from whence merchandise would be laboriously transported by barge and mule to the Pacific for shipping to Lima; and where it would pick up as much as two-thirds of the Peruvian silver sent to Spain.[26]

Meanwhile Olivares was working hard to convince the oligarchs of his home town to at least ratify the promised *milliones* even if they rejected his reforms. As Sheriff of the Alcázar, he himself had a seat on the City Council and, allying himself with the Royal Governor, the *asistente*, he finally persuaded the city to approve the monies voted at the Cortes. But it was yet another empty victory: the populace was furious and rioting broke out as soon as the royal party had moved on;[27] no other Andalusian city would confirm the *milliones*. The city had treated Olivares, a proud Sevillian in his own mind, almost as an outsider.

But while Olivares's government policy was in tatters, at least his own dynastic ambitions were well served by his Sevillian sojourn. The visit allowed him to conclude the purchase of a rich estate in the Seville hinterland centred on the town of Sanlúcar la Mayor, which the King allowed him to entail and so leave in perpetuity to his heirs. The following January, of 1625, Philip made him Duke of Sanlúcar and, already Count of Olivares, he immediately began styling himself the Count-Duke.

The royal party now travelled down the olive-green waters of the Guadalquivir to that other and more illustrious Sanlúcar, Sanlúcar de Barrameda, fiefdom of the dukes of Medina Sidonia, which the chronicler called 'such a wealthy possession its lord seems like a second king thanks to the wonders of the sea and its port which so enrich it'. Here Niebla welcomed 'His Majesty with ten companies of militia who were drawn up in formation at the harbour, and another was drawn up in the main square through which His Majesty had to pass on his way to the palace'. It was a potent display of local power and authority perhaps intended as a threat and a warning to Olivares and his King. But, in contrast to so much military vigour, the grand old duke himself was ill and ageing and could barely rise from his sickbed to greet his monarch. It was a bitter moment for the broken grandee; for Olivares, with his new estates and titles, was clearly in the ascendant and had even recently defeated Medina Sidonia in a long-running court battle worth 300,000 ducats that dated back to 1576.[28]

From Sanlúcar, Philip moved on to inspect the New Spain Fleet and then sailed to Cadiz where he was able to spend time with his naval commanders before he went on to review the coastal defences as far as Gibraltar and Malaga.[29] He then returned to Madrid by way of Granada, where he was enchanted by the Alhambra and could contemplate his great-grandparents' victory over Islam.[30]

Olivares was well aware that the century-old cycle by which Castile paid for Habsburg ambitions across a divided Europe had come up against the bleak new reality in which revenue from the Americas appeared to have gone into steep decline. He sensed that corruption was the cause and intended the royal visit to strengthen his position in reforming the powerful Andalusian institutions he believed were at the heart of the problem.

In 1617, a report had been presented to the Council of State detailing the way vast quantities of contraband bullion and goods were smuggled off the Americas fleets just before they made landfall in Spain and were loaded on to French, English, Flemish and Dutch craft for immediate export.[31] Similarly, enormous quantities of goods were smuggled aboard the fleets before they set sail for the Indies. Olivares, very much in character, wanted to tackle the problem head-on; he decided to make an example of the Tierra Firme Fleet which the King had seen being prepared and loaded at Seville.

This fleet sailed for Panama in March 1624, reaching the largely temporary trading town of Portobello in June. There a local official called Cristóbal de Balbas, whose grandfather had served Cortés during the conquest of Mexico, and who was presumably acting with the secret encouragement of Olivares, turned whistleblower. He claimed that 85 per cent of the merchandise carried by the fleet was contraband and in the immediate furore the Audiencia of Panama arrested Balbas for fraud and embezzlement himself and sent him to Spain in chains.[32]

But once in Seville he was quickly transferred to Madrid and, now under royal protection, he was allowed to make his case. The evidence he produced was overwhelming; yet the Council of the Indies was reluctant to pursue the matter, advising the Crown that 'we must weigh up against these problems a whole host of others so great that it would be better to cover up these excesses as has always been done'.[33] And no wonder they were concerned: the merchants' organization in Seville, the powerful Consulado, had warned that this business might cause that year's Tierra Firme Fleet not to be unloaded, and, 'worse still', might prompt 'instructions not to send silver from Peru for fear that it might be sequestered'.[34] The Consulado also wrote a long letter to the Crown explaining that, because so much trade went undeclared, it had long been customary to charge tax on imports of between 100 and 350 per cent of the silver that the merchants had officially recorded in the registers. The corruption was self-evidently formalized. 'What possible good can come of these ruinous accusations?' they asked.[35] Olivares now dispatched Balbas to Seville in the company of a magistrate and with an armed guard; and so the haggling began, and both sides soon agreed that the Consulado would pay a fine of 206,000 ducats in settlement of the dispute.[36]

Olivares had taken Philip south with high hopes that he could revive Crown revenues from the Indies trade. Instead, he had learnt that the government in Madrid was powerless to enforce the law and that all he could hope to do was haggle over money with the powerful institutions of the kingdom like the towns and the Consulado. This significant and very costly loss of control over the Indies trade was only made worse when, from time to time, the Crown, desperate for funds, confiscated privately owned bullion that had been transported on the treasure ships in exchange for government debt or the debased copper *vellón*, as it had done as recently as 1620. Such arbitrary and draconian taxation was a guarantee that avoidance and evasion would increase. Typically, Olivares had recognized the problem, but had addressed it with a grand gesture that failed, at which point he gave up and turned his attention elsewhere.

20

Triumph and Disaster

My soul surrendered to a pain which racked me with such strength
that all my feelings were numbed . . .

                              The Count-Duke of Olivares

Olivares's unhealthy passion for power was rooted in a single-
minded pursuit of dynasty and reputation. With his elevation to
the dukedom of Sanlúcar la Mayor and the right to entail his estates,
the House of Olivares had eclipsed the dukes of Medina Sidonia. But
just as his own stellar orbit was subject to the gravitational flux of the
Planet King, so too the House of Olivares itself was palpably fragile:
malicious tongues in Madrid suggested that the Count-Duke's union
with Inés de Zúñiga was political and not physical, that they had
surrendered their hearts to power and not to the heights of passion.
Olivares had sired a single daughter, María, and with only the slightest
chance of a male heir, he necessarily made her the centrepiece of his
plans for the future of his dynasty.

On 9 January 1625, he married María to an impoverished and rustic
thirteen-year-old aristocrat, the Marquis of Toral, to the astonishment
of the court and the chagrin of the many pretenders to her hand. Toral
may have seemed an obscure choice to the court, but he was an obvious
choice for Olivares, for Toral claimed the senior line of the House of
Guzmán, the family name of the Medina Sidonia: Olivares's grandsons,
men of his bloodline, would become the titular heads of the dynasty.
Over the coming years, Olivares trained his son-in-law well and he

became a brilliant courtier and diplomat; he was raised to the dukedom of Medina de las Torres, a title pregnant with Baroque symbolism: Sanlúcar de Barrameda was the ancestral home of the Medina Sidonia, and now a 'Medina' would inherit Sanlúcar la Mayor. There would be poetry in Olivares's dynastic victory over his cousins.

By early 1626 it was clear that the sixteen-year-old María was with child by the still adolescent Toral and Olivares was filled with 'hope for the preservation of my line'. At the beginning of July, she went into labour; but the birth was difficult and the infant, named Isabel María, died almost immediately. María's own life now hung in the balance. At first, she seemed to recover and Olivares described how he could 'wipe away his tears' at the loss of the babe, 'taking comfort in seeing María get better after such grave danger'. But then, he lamented, 'God chose to reward her before her time and carried her off just as we thought her saved.' His only child was dead.

> My soul surrendered to a pain which racked me with such strength that all my feelings were numbed and gave way to the rational thought that such things happen either as punishment or as a test . . . And so, although I felt utterly alone, I rendered unto God what He had given me by His Hand despite the Countess's grief, and the loss and anguish of the Marquis, and the pain of everyone, for even total strangers suffered much.[1]

Olivares's family emblem was a stout olive tree, and a rather clumsy letter of condolence sums up the dynastic disaster as 'the tragic sight of such an illustrious tree being cut down, nay ripped up at the root'.[2]

Most serious contemporary commentators felt that the Count-Duke never fully recovered his anyway fragile sanity after this terrible blow, while court gossips engendered dark rumours on the streets of Madrid. It was said that Olivares was so desperate to sire an heir that on the suggestion of a witch he took Inés at night to the infamous 'San Plácido and in a chapel there he had sex with her while the nuns fumigated them with incense, after which her belly swelled up, and after eleven months a great deal of water and blood burst forth'. There were stories of child sacrifice and of a workman who disappeared after discovering the cadaver of an infant in a blocked culvert.[3]

This personal tragedy would prove to be a harbinger of trouble across the whole monarchy and usher in a politically precarious period in Olivares's career.

Sixteen-twenty-five seemed a year of miraculous victories for the Spanish Habsburgs, the most famous being the capture of Breda by the great Genoese general Ambrogio Spinola, celebrated years later by Velázquez in his breathtaking painting *The Surrender of Breda*. But the Duke of Feria forced the French to retreat across the Alps; the Marquis of Santa Cruz managed to raise the siege of Genoa; and an English attack on Cadiz was successfully repulsed. Philip IV crowed to the Council of Castile that, with all the powers of Europe lined up against Spain, the monarchy had maintained 800,000 troops in the field. But the joy was short lived. In 1627, the French had stolen a march on Spain and the Empire when the Duke of Nevers married the young heiress of Mantua and so was able to lay claim to that strategically important duchy on the death of her uncle. Between 1628 and 1631 Olivares's world seemed to collapse. He had made no preparations for the death of the old duke and because Mantua was a client of the Empire he reacted angrily to what he saw as French trespassing; he sent in Spanish troops from Milan. Meanwhile, Spinola arrived in Madrid arguing determinedly for a peace with the United Dutch Provinces. Again, Olivares saw this as an affront to honour and reputation, but found himself isolated as the rest of the Council of State and even the King himself listened to Spinola and agreed with him. Spain was beginning to recognize the futility of the Dutch stalemate. But Olivares's sense of history could not abide defeat and he was wily enough to delay the implementation of any change in policy. For now, the conflict would continue. But by the end of 1628 soldiers in the field in both Flanders and Mantua were becoming restless at the lack of pay; the bankers would not release funds until there was certain news of the New Spain treasure fleet.

Then, on 22 December, after weeks of rumour, definite reports finally arrived in Madrid that a Dutch privateer, Piet Heyn, had launched a daring raid on the fleet, when still in port in Cuba, and had captured the entire treasure. By now Olivares had become so unpopular that Rubens could write home that although 'the loss of the fleet has caused great discussion here', and although 'according to the general opinion the loss is enormous, it is imputed to folly and negligence rather than misfortune, since no precautions were taken, in spite of many timely warnings against the threatened disaster. You would be surprised to see', he explained, 'that almost all the people here are very glad about it, feeling that this public calamity can be set down as a disgrace to their rulers.'[4]

While Madrid was aflame with indignation, Louis XIII burned with ambition and anger at the Spanish intervention in Mantua: as soon as he heard that Spain would struggle to pay the troops in Italy, he began raising an army which he led in person, that winter, over the Alps and which then inflicted a humiliating defeat on the Spanish army. But Olivares refused to accept reality and began raising money to renew the military effort. The Tierra Firme Fleet arrived promisingly early, in May 1629, but with a depressingly meagre four million ducats of which only one million was due to the Crown; Olivares ordered the forced conversion of one and a half million ducats' worth of the private funds into a government loan and seized the bullion. It was a desperate and disastrous measure that convinced the Atlantic merchants to entrust almost no revenue to the official fleets for the next three years.

That summer, a piece of chillingly incisive invective against the regime was circulated in Madrid and was read by Philip himself. For all Olivares's good intentions, it said, 'he has an insatiable appetite for rule', yet his policies are all 'fantasies and illusions', his actions corrupt and dangerous. He 'tyrannizes the King's will . . . keeping His Majesty locked away as a person to be manipulated so that he can exercise the office of kingship himself. His Majesty is simply a ceremonial king, loved by his vassals for himself, but loathed for his government.'[5]

Philip was stung into action and began to exercise his own will in matters of state. In June, Olivares presented him with a questionnaire about various matters of state which was designed to lead Philip to the conclusions he desired. But when it came to Flanders, Philip ignored the advice and wrote instead that he believed the war to be a waste of time and resources, before astonishing everyone by stating that he would send an army to Italy and that 'I would like to be a part of it, as I say, and once I am in Italy with the army and this campaign is over I will be able to do what I want with the world, God willing. Think it through and make it happen by whatever means necessary, for to my mind I cannot win honour without leaving Spain.' Louis XIII had set a tempting precedent. Olivares had clearly discussed this beforehand with Philip and in an effort to dissuade him had raised the spectre of the Comunero Revolt. But he had taught his pupil too well and Philip knew his history: 'for all you tell me that the Spaniards may be worried by the departure of their King, I want to tell you that when the greatest trouble broke out here [with the Comuneros] there was neither King nor royal successor, but with God's favour I will have an heir and the Queen will govern well'.[6] As far as Philip was concerned, his Queen Isabel would be just as effective a regent as Charles V's Empress had been. He too could argue from his own dynastic past: a policy of peace with the Dutch and to lead an army in person in outright war against the French in Italy was very much in the mould of his great-grandfather; and he clearly saw that his favourite knew it too.

But Olivares feared he would be unable to hang on to power without Philip's immediate presence. Although this was a reasonable concern were the King to go abroad, it developed into a monstrous paranoia. The Infanta María Ana, now married to the King of Hungary, the eldest son of the Holy Roman Emperor, Ferdinand III, by proxy, was due to set out on her journey to her new home. Philip naturally wanted to accompany his sister on the early stages of her travels across Spain, but Olivares was implacably opposed. In a long, ranting complaint about his waning influence, sent to the Count of Castro, he lamented that 'for three years since, I have scarcely been in [the King's] company for more than a quarter of an hour each day'. And 'in this business of the Queen of Hungary's journey, everyone', he wrote, 'points out how the travelling would put his life in danger'. It was the utterly absurd claim of an almost deranged mind and Philip had already put his foot down on the matter, writing to Olivares 'to say that I have made my point two or three times, or more, and that now it was my job to obey him and do what he orders'. 'Never before', Olivares fumed, 'have I met a man whose mind is as immune to influence.'[7]

Then Philip went down with one of his periodic bouts of malaria and agreed to postpone the journey until later in the year. Olivares's obstinate determination to control the King's own body, or at least be seen to do so, is yet another sign of how irrational he was becoming. The Emperor, unable to comprehend the delay in the Queen's departure, was so infuriated and suspicious that he now threatened war at the very moment when Spain needed the support of the Empire most.[8]

All Madrid followed the story as Philip, in public defiance of Olivares, left his capital on 26 December and accompanied his sister first to Guadalajara, where he had agreed to take his leave and return to Olivares's side. But instead he decided that he would continue; the royal party carried on and crossed the border into Aragon. The King only finally turned around after a brief sojourn at Saragossa. 'It was', according to one malicious observer, 'the first time Philip had deceived Olivares during his whole period as favourite and it deeply wounded him to the heart, which the court and all the world enjoyed . . . and set all Europe a-talking.'[9]

Philip was destined never to leave Spain, his own chivalric pretensions as fantastical as his favourite's policies. But late in 1629 Spinola was sent to Mantua, setting sail with Velázquez who was embarking on his first trip to Italy thanks to the encouragement of Rubens. The experience would help Velázquez to define the looser, mature style which makes him one of the finest painters in history. His first truly great work in this new hand was the *Surrender of Breda*, painted in 1634, depicting Spinola's finest triumph. But Spinola himself was destined to die in Italy a deeply embittered man. Just when he was on the verge of victory, despite being poorly supplied with money and men, Olivares had suddenly stripped him of his powers to negotiate for peace. Broken and sick, he was visited by a papal diplomat to whom the veteran soldier delivered a venomous tirade against Olivares and the King, 'who have robbed me of my honour'. Then, interrupting his own diatribe, he asked feebly for some nearby chapel or hermitage where he could hide his shame from the world and die far away from other men. He died three weeks later, and Quevedo commented acerbically that 'they buried all Spain's military experience and valour with his corpse'.[10]

By the following year, the dreadful folly of the Mantuan war was evident to all. Olivares had isolated Spain: he had alienated Urban VIII, the longest serving and most cultured of popes, the Emperor had agreed a peace with France without consulting Madrid, while the war in the Netherlands had dragged on disastrously and losses in Flanders had led to 'fury and rage against every Spaniard' across the loyal provinces in the words of the experienced diplomat and soldier Don Carlos Coloma. Presumably having got wind of Philip's hopes for personal glory, Coloma had pleaded for the 'royal leadership that is needed here', leadership that should be 'as royal as possible'.[11] Olivares's foreign policy of bellicose intervention had been a failure, the economy at home was in deep depression, Castile was almost bankrupt, none of his reforms had been enacted and Philip had shown a disturbing willingness to experiment with independence, perhaps even to the extent of dispensing with his favourite altogether.

But Rubens had written home very perceptively indeed, in 1629, that Philip had aroused his sympathy, for he 'is endowed by nature with all the gifts of body and spirit . . . and would surely be capable of governing under any conditions, were it not that he mistrusts himself and defers too much to others'.[12] The King would continue to rely on Olivares for another dozen years. The obvious question is why?

If we discount salacious rumours that were then doing the rounds in Madrid that Olivares had cast a spell over Philip,[13] we are left with the logical interpretation that the root of the King's dependency is to be found in the interplay between their particular personalities. For even the most amateur psychoanalyst, Philip's struggle with Olivares for control over an increasingly barren matrix of Spanish sovereignty, authority and power must of course appear almost classically Oedipal. It certainly created an atmosphere of great tension and suspense which thrilled the court and which was worthy of a Greek tragedy. But if their relationship is most obviously like that of an ageing father and a growing son, there is also a flavour of marriage about it, or at least a peculiar partnership that verges on a kind of possession. When contemporaries suggested that Olivares had bewitched Philip they were reacting to what they saw.

Courtiers were used to a strong sense of separation between the image of the King and its human incumbent; and this was not simply a separation of the office from the man, but extended into the public and private world of the royal person, most obviously in the uncomfortably close proximity of the Groom of the Stool. The King's body was not entirely his own, but instead he shared it with the monarchy and his subjects. That is why Philip's struggle with Olivares was brought most sharply into focus over the question of the King's geographical whereabouts. For a psychoanalyst, the favourite's intimate involvement with the King's defecation would obviously lead to an emerging sexual tension, while historians will be well aware of a long tradition of the favourite as royal lover so familiar from the stories of Piers Gaveston and Edward II, Elizabeth I and Essex, Buckingham and James I, or Juan II of Castile and his notorious fifteenth-century favourite Álvaro de Luna.

There is no suggestion that Olivares was Philip's lover, but his reputation as the royal *alcahuete* or 'pimp' shows the breadth of his control over the King's body. We will never know the extent to which his control over Philip's sexuality may have helped Olivares to gain a psychological hold over him, but we do know that while he had begun his reign with Zúñiga and Olivares in many ways acting as though they were regents, caretakers of the monarchy for a young ruler, they had also been educating him, teaching him, inculcating him with a sense of kingship based on the simple ideology of Habsburg dynasty. The master had trained the student to think in likeminded fashion; it was a kind of brainwashing.

But here we must shift our attention away from Philip's psychological weaknesses and on to those of Olivares. It is clear that Olivares had long reciprocated Philip's filial attachment, finding in him the son and heir he longed for. Tellingly, on the death of María in 1626, he resigned the crucial position of Groom of the Stool to his son-in-law, placing the heir to the Olivares dynasty in the most intimate official relationship imaginable with his surrogate son and the Habsburg incumbent. Quite how Olivares's troubled mind conceived of these powerful bonds is beyond reach, but it is clear that he was at least beginning to see the two dynasties in parallel and was probably beginning to blur the boundaries between them at some deep psychological level.

Olivares now inhabited Philip's mind, and his son-in-law and heir was unavoidably close to the King's human body. No wonder, then, that contemporaries gossiped about the black arts. Philip was evidently aware that such profound and all-pervading psychological and physical proximity between the Habsburgs and the Olivares was problematic, for all that he proved unequal to the task of extricating himself. The favourite, by contrast, clearly became pathologically deluded by the emotional intensity of these close personal bonds. His jealousy over control of the King's whereabouts and his determination to keep Philip close at hand go beyond political expediency. It is almost as though Olivares felt that the royal body was in some way an extension of himself.

Gregorio Marañón, the great twentieth-century Spanish physician, historian and biographer of Olivares, remarked on his subject's strange tendency to go beyond exercising sovereign power and authority in the name of the King and actually emulate royalty himself. Marañón saw this in the equestrian portrait Velázquez painted of him, in his dress and in his construction of the Convent of Loeches near Madrid which has a façade that is an exact imitation of the royal Convent of the Incarnation.[14] But, as just explained, it seems not only that Olivares had pretensions to styling himself royally in his accoutrements and behaviour, but that at some level he had deluded himself into believing that he was in some way a part of the Habsburg dynasty. He seems really to have felt that Philip was his *alter ego*, that he was the disembodied political mind of the physically present King.

And so Olivares began to behave as though he were a Habsburg monarch, himself attempting to complement the ceremonial role he had created for Philip. In doing this, he adhered to his own ideological conception of the dynasty, an ideology that was relentlessly communicated through display, images and words: public spectacle, hunting, poetry, drama and painting. Where the sixteenth-century Habsburg past had been a reality, Olivares's seventeenth-century Habsburg present became a pastiche of that past. It was a glittering illusion, a sparkling fiction, backward-looking, hopeful, full of wonder and marvels, but ephemeral, without substance.

Olivares's most spectacular and whimsical demonstration of his disturbing brilliance was the slow and haphazard evolution of an idea to build a great royal palace and bucolic haven on the outskirts of Madrid, a pleasure complex which became known as the Buen Retiro, or 'Good Retreat'. Its construction had all the characteristics of a highly imaginative child playing with his toys: the work went ahead at unbelievable speed, it grew almost intuitively as whole structures were put up only to be knocked down and replaced with something bigger, developing with an *ad hoc* immediacy that baffled contemporaries.

All that remains of the capricious Buen Retiro are a couple of unspectacular annexes of the Prado Museum, the Casón and the Salón de los Reinos. Most of it was destroyed at the beginning of the nineteenth century during the Peninsular War, and even today the park bears almost no resemblance to the gardens that Olivares had laid out with such enthusiasm and energy. The almost total absence from the modern Madrid landscape of any trace of this massive construction project is symbolic enough of the favourite's own transience. Interestingly, there is a magnificent painting by Velázquez of the young heir to the throne, the Prince of Asturias Baltasar Carlos, riding a black horse outside the Retiro Palace with Olivares, who had been in charge of teaching him to ride, prominent in the mid-ground; but there is another, almost identical painting, a copy, in the Wallace Collection, in London, from which the figure of Olivares has been removed, presumably after his fall from grace.[15]

The Buen Retiro project was directly associated with Baltasar Carlos from the outset. Since the birth of Philip II, the nobles and Cortes of Castile had sworn an oath of allegiance to the Crown Prince at the Monastery of St Jerome, just outside the walls, where Charles Prince of Wales had stayed before his official entry into Madrid. So, when Baltasar Carlos was born in 1629, Olivares had himself appointed Sheriff of the Royal Apartments of St Jerome and immediately set about enlarging the very modest accommodation in time for the ceremony, which took place on 7 March 1632.

That early building work was limited, little more than an extensive remodelling project that appropriated some of the monks' cells as an apartment for the Queen. But something about it fired Olivares's imaginative ambition. Because the monastery was dedicated to St Jerome, his mind would have immediately turned to the Escorial, Philip II's monumental Hieronymite retreat; and, perhaps, as he looked out across the olive groves to the east and north, he was reminded of his own name and dynasty. Already so crippled by gout and corpulence that he could not ride easily, he must have rued the King's frequent retreats to his hunting lodges and thought about creating an alternative, a park suitable for old men.

Over the summer of 1632, Olivares began a slightly more ambitious development involving a new wing and a new set of rooms arranged around a courtyard, while the gardens were laid out, including a great lake, a large cage for a menagerie of wild animals and a gigantic aviary. The work continued apace and was finished by the spring of the following year, but at the expense of quality. The English Ambassador 'wished it had been built with less haste . . . for the security thereof'; a Tuscan diplomat complained that 'they have only paid attention to comfort and finishing quickly, not to the majesty and durability of the work'; while the wags of Madrid had been attracted by the sight of the vast aviary and began calling the whole building the 'Hen Coop'.[16] Olivares's many enemies seized on this banter, publishing a torrent of broadsides ridiculing the whole jerry-built project.

That clearly stung the favourite and his King and somehow money was found to embark, at breakneck speed, on a massively ambitious new expansion. The bemused Tuscan, Bernardo Monanni, who followed the development with great critical interest, observed with amazement that over a thousand workmen had begun digging up the newly completed formal gardens and levelling the hillside in preparation for the construction of an immense courtyard to the north of the recently finished building, part of which also had to be demolished. 'As they build, they expand the project, which is not the one they started with . . . changing their plans and making it bigger,' he reported; yet 'they have only laid the foundations for what has already been built, so they will find it difficult to enlarge in the future'.[17]

But they did keep enlarging and, with up to 1,500 men working round the clock and on holidays and Sundays, on 1 December 1633 Olivares was able to present the King and Queen with the keys to the complex, which he now officially proclaimed was to be called the Palace of the Buen Retiro. The centrepiece was the huge courtyard where, five days later, a bullfight was held in the pouring rain, followed by jousting, and then a great banquet. But, unbelievably, this courtyard was not large enough for all the spectacles Olivares wanted to put on, and by August the following year work was well ahead on a new, larger plaza to the north. Over the coming years a ballroom and a theatre were also added to the east of the main palace, although Olivares's dream of cladding the frontage in a marble façade never became a reality.

Monanni complained that 'the architecture, in general, is not pleasing because they have not followed the advice of the architects, although they were Italian and eminent', so that, on the inside, he felt the rooms 'too long', while on the outside it was 'too low, too small, simple and ordinary'. He concluded that it 'looks more like a monastery than a royal dwelling'.[18] Clearly, he had failed to understand that the external austerity of the Buen Retiro was inspired by the Escorial, so it was meant to look like a monastery; nor does he seem to have understood that the rooms were built long, tall and narrow because they were conceived as art galleries and for courtiers and diplomats to view the spectacles which took place in the courtyards below. He evidently judged the project in terms of his experience of the princely suburban villas then fashionable in Italy. In reality, the Buen Retiro is best understood as essentially Andalusian in character, sitting on a hill just outside Madrid just as the Alhambra overlooks Granada from its heights, while Olivares's piecemeal approach to construction reflected the kind of architectural space typical of the palaces of Seville. The form and function of the palace were rooted in the easy intimacy of a building adapted and remodelled to suit some immediate whim or necessity that would have been reassuringly familiar to a homesick Andalusian aristocrat.

In 1635, the Chief Steward of the Retiro, Diego de Covarrubias, published a collection of verse filled with anodyne praise for the palace as a kind of poetic programme or handbook to whet the appetites of courtiers and see off as much caustic criticism as possible. It is dedicated to Olivares and, while formulaically recognizing the building as 'His Majesty's work', it makes it quite clear that the Count-Duke was 'in charge' and had 'worked so hard to make His Majesty's idea shine' and bring the project to fruition. Interestingly, he suggests it surpassed Diocletian's amphitheatre, indicating its purpose as a sporting arena and place of spectacle and entertainment. In general, the poems are a mixed bag, describing the palace in the most general terms as 'a house of the Sun' 'without rival', but also as a 'theatre of the Graces and the joyful Muses in which the gods delight', while one poet addressed it with the lines: 'Oh Theatre, you represent the glories of Spanish monarchs; and Painting, you show off an Empire of illustrious artifice and beauty.'[19]

Olivares's outlandishly capricious approach to the construction of the Buen Retiro was matched and underpinned by an almost implausibly contradictory sense of single-mindedness in his conceptualization of the purposes to which he intended to put the eccentric collection of spaces he had created. In an age when the popularity of the theatre forced playwrights to be propagandists and publicists as much as they were entertainers, in a world in which the strength of images and illusions allowed fiction to trespass on to an increasingly fickle sense of reality, in a world acutely literate in the language of symbols and metaphor, Philip IV's favourite had an overriding vision of a palace complex in which everywhere was a stage and every feature an element in the drama. It was that single-mindedness of function that conquered the confusion of architectural form. And at a time when stage sets and scenery were increasingly complicated and spectacular, Olivares paid closest attention to the backdrop against which his protagonists would act their parts.

Just as the verdant grounds with their waterways and fecund flowerbeds, orchards and kitchen gardens were a paradise that sharply contrasted with the barren surroundings of scrubland and olive groves, in the same vein visitor after seventeenth-century visitor recorded his or her initial amazement at the outward austerity and lack of grandeur of the poor-quality buildings, only to describe being dazzled by their contents. One of the best accounts we have is by a Frenchman who was so wonder-struck that abandoning his Gallic chauvinism he declared that 'there was more there than in all of Paris'.

He visited the gardens and was then taken into the palace proper by way of some annexes containing 'all the most precious treasures produced in the Indies, by which I mean rugs made from tree bark, suits of clothes worn by the Aztecs and Incas, strange cabinets, polished stone mirrors, curtains made of feathers, and a thousand other furnishings I have no idea about nor know the names of'. But these marvels of Empire were a mere *amuse-bouche* to the visual banquet of European opulence he found inside the palace, where he was 'immediately surprised by the number of pictures' and soon recognized their quality as well. He says he had been lost in admiration for three hours and describes the bewitching effects of the great realism and beauty of the works so that he began talking to himself and imagining himself transported within the scenes. He claims he could easily have stood in the same place gawking in ecstasy all day had he not been ushered around with the words 'Can't you keep moving?' ringing in his ears.[20]

Olivares put together a massive collection of art for the Buen Retiro at tremendous speed. At first he forced a host of Spanish aristocrats to sell works from their own private collections, reportedly reducing to tears the great aesthete and his own relative and ally the Count of Leganés as he requisitioned painting after painting. He also sent word to his ambassadors and agents in the Netherlands, Rome and Naples to buy and commission new works of sculpture, tapestries, furniture and silverware, much of it of first-rate quality.[21] Few expenses were spared: the ageing master Pietro Tacca was contracted to sculpt and cast an equestrian statue of Philip IV, now in the Plaza del Oriente in Madrid, to complement his statue of Philip III on horseback that is now in the Plaza Mayor. The new work was so ambitious, in requiring him to create a statue with the horse rearing on its hind legs, that he called in Galileo Galilei to help devise a method of casting it. Montañés was brought from Seville to carve a bust of the King to be sent to Tacca to ensure an adequate likeness; Velázquez's famous portrait of Montañés shows him at work on this commission.[22]

It seems that from early on Olivares had decided he wanted the Buen Retiro to work as an art gallery and it is surely significant that he commissioned thirty-four works depicting the history of Rome as the largest series of pictures with a single unifying theme that would be made specifically for the palace. This most obviously appealed to the usual readiness of western empires to liken themselves to the Romans and specifically the long-standing association of Spain and the Habsburgs with the Roman Empire. But the subject must have had very personal appeal for Olivares because he had himself been born in Rome; and all of this group of paintings, in one way or another, can be linked to the contemporary neo-Stoic philosopher Justus Lipsius, whose work had been a huge influence on Olivares and Francisco de Rioja since their days at Pacheco's Academy in Seville.[23]

Rioja was now closely involved in the project and, while both he and Olivares may have conceived of paintings as the soul of the Buen Retiro, it must have become apparent early on that a palace so ephemeral in character needed some solid central focus. They instructed their architects and builders to create a Salón Grande, or 'Great Hall', as the ceremonial and political heart of the complex. It was designed to complement the great exterior courtyards and was located between them so that it could overlook them both. Although it hosted the opening session of the Cortes in 1638, Carducho called it 'that magnificent hall for soirées and festivities',[24] and it was mostly used as a theatre and ballroom.

Modelled on the Great Hall of the Alcázar, this now much remodelled grand entertainment space was over a hundred feet long, thirty wide and twenty-five high, with five large windows along each long wall, above which a wide gallery ran round most of the room at about sixteen feet, with a stretch of smaller windows above this. At each end, doors led into smaller adjoining halls. The squinches of the vaulted ceiling were adorned with twenty-four brightly painted heraldic blazons representing the twenty-four kingdoms of the Spanish Habsburgs and it quickly became known as the Salón de Reinos, or the 'Hall of Realms'. The focal point of the room was the suitably sumptuous throne, inlaid with mother of pearl and topped with a canopy, which was located at one end. The room was furnished with a dozen or so heavy jasper tables and twelve rampant silver lions, commissioned at 2,000 ducats a piece, that would be melted down in 1643 in order to help pay for the war effort in a hugely symbolic act of contrition made by Philip in the same year that he finally dismissed Olivares from his court and government.

The Hall of the Realms was decorated in great haste between 1634 and 1635 according to a decorative scheme devised by Rioja and Velázquez to which Olivares appended a daringly arrogant footnote. The two ends walls were filled with five canvases by Velázquez depicting the most dynastically iconic members of the immediate Habsburg family. Two large, almost square equestrian portraits of Philip III and Margaret of Austria, apparently riding out of the pictures and into the room, filled the west wall. They were matched in the east by similarly sized images of the reigning monarchs, Philip IV and Isabel, also on horseback, but riding towards one another, across the canvas, as Titian had portrayed Charles V in the equestrian portrait with which the fashion originated. Between the King and Queen, over the central door, was a smaller painting of Prince Baltasar Carlos, also on horseback.

Three generations of Habsburgs thus dominated the length of the room but in allegorical orbit about Philip IV, the Planet King, for the royal throne was also at the east end. And so, when Philip and Isabel were in attendance, the real, physical presence of royalty was displayed in direct juxtaposition to Velázquez's brilliant paintings. There was also a screen at this end of the room which was ostensibly so that Baltasar Carlos could watch the goings-on but leave discreetly if childish fidgeting got the better of him. However, Olivares is recorded as accompanying the boy and also remaining behind the screen even when the Prince had left;[25] it was as close as the favourite could come, in the real world, to actually joining the royal family.

The rigidity of court etiquette was recorded by a Frenchman who attended a play in the Hall of the Realms. The royal family were led in by a lady-in-waiting carrying a candlestick, he explained; and then as the King came in, he took off his hat in deference to the ladies present and then sat with the Queen to his left and the Infanta to her left. 'Throughout the whole play, the King moved neither his legs nor his hands nor his head, except to look sideways from time to time, and he sat alone with the exception of a dwarf.' Afterwards, the ladies present 'stood up and left, walking one by one from each side and meeting in the middle like the canons of some cathedral . . . They held hands and bowed, all of which took a quarter of an hour,' until, 'finally, the King rose and made his bows to the Queen and the Queen curtsied to the Infanta, and taking one another by the hand', *exeunt*.[26]

Velázquez must have understood that in the juxtaposition of these statuesque royals and his lively portraits, especially at night when the room was lit by torches and candles, he could approach the same kind of effect of transcending reality that he had seen during his childhood on the theatrical streets of Seville. It was certainly the sort of sensual illusion that hovered between playful delight and disconcerting *desengaño* that Olivares would have appreciated. Perhaps for this reason, Zurbarán, by now the leading painter working in Seville, was brought to Madrid to create a curious series of canvases depicting the Labours of Hercules, which were hung high up on the long, lateral walls, above the windows and just below the gallery. They have a strikingly incongruous impressionist quality about them, almost as though they were left unfinished; so strange and unpolished, indeed, that they were attributed to another artist until conclusive documentary evidence was discovered in the 1950s which showed that Zurbarán had been paid for them.[27] In fact, he was in Madrid for only a year, during which he also painted the masterfully executed *Defence of Cadiz* and two other fine paintings of contemporary legal scholars; and, although the original commission was for all twelve labours in the cycle, he delivered only ten; so it is not inconceivable that much of the work was left to an apprentice or another painter. But a more compelling explanation is that they were deliberately ethereal and otherworldly in order to make the royal portraits seem palpably real by contrast with the quasi-abstract demi-god. Hercules was associated with the mythology of a distant Spanish past, so the paintings were meant to be symbolic and not representative. Instead, the imitation of nature, which had so bewitched the French art lover, was reserved for the immediate Habsburgs and, of equal importance, the main cycle of twelve canvases, which celebrated the great Spanish military victories of Philip IV's reign. This is, of course, effectively the same idea for creating a kind of hierarchical relationship between a spiritual plane, a representation of the present and the reality inhabited by the viewer – in which, in this case, the real King and Queen were on display – that Velázquez had used in his *Christ in the House of Martha and Mary* with its secondary image of Christ preaching in the distant background.

So while there was a Renaissance tradition of 'halls of princely virtue' that glorified a ruler's dynasty and right to rule, the Hall of the Realms was firmly dedicated to Olivares's deluded vision of the jingoistic present, a present in which Olivares clearly saw himself as being as much the centre of the world as Philip.

The Andalusian artistic triumvirate of Olivares, Rioja and Velázquez may well have been influenced by Pannemaker's great tapestries of Charles V's Tunis campaigns in their theme for the twelve key paintings for the Hall of the Realms that would flank the tall windows of the north and south walls.[28] The Habsburg Spanish monarchy and the Spanish Empire may have been under desperate pressure across Europe and under threat in the Indies, but Olivares was determined to create a place to which he, the King and the court could retreat into an alternative reality of his own creation; and so the cycle was, pragmatically enough, a pictorial vindication of foreign policy.

Today, the most famous of these twelve victory paintings is unquestionably Velázquez's *Surrender of Breda*, in which the artist depicted Spinola magnanimously, almost tenderly, receiving the keys of the city from the Dutch Governor on 3 June 1625. The painting is also often known as *The Lances* because of the way Velázquez evoked the sense of a massive army by painting twenty-nine long lances behind the throng of figures in the middle ground. This is one of his greatest works, showing the influence of his recent trip to Italy, but it also retains the intimacy of his earliest works in the figure of a Dutch musketeer whose puzzled gaze is directed out of the canvas towards us. It is a portrait of somebody, possibly Velázquez himself.

The device of multiple lances was also used by Jusepe Leonardo in *The Relief of Breisach* and *The Surrender of Jülich*, which are both formally very similar to *The Surrender of Breda*. In fact, although these works are often referred to as 'battle paintings', almost all conform to a basic design in which the peaceful moment at which the enemy surrendered to an identifiable Spanish commander dominates the foreground with, in some cases, only the most cursory reference to the actual fighting itself which is shown in the distance set in a bucolic landscape. They are more accurately described, then, as victory paintings. There were only two exceptions to this rule: Carducho's *Battle of Fleurus*, which is completely out of tune in showing the Spanish generals charging into battle and skirmishing in the foreground; and Fray Juan Bautista Maino's *Recapture of Bahía*, unquestionably the most important painting in the group as far as Olivares was concerned.

Maino had studied in Italy and then practised in Toledo before becoming Philip IV's drawing tutor and subsequently joining the Dominicans, an order to which Olivares was especially attached. He clearly got on with both Philip and his favourite, who greatly respected his artistic judgment and asked him to oversee the competition to paint *The Expulsion of the Moriscos* held in 1627, which was won by Velázquez largely thanks to Maino. The Andalusians clearly liked him and it is fascinating that he was chosen over Velázquez to paint the only work for the Hall of the Realms in which Olivares appears, and we have absolutely no idea why.

The Recapture of Bahía celebrates Don Fadrique de Toledo's successful expedition of 1625 to wrest the rich Portuguese colony of Bahía, in Brazil, back from the Dutch following its capture by Piet Heyn the year before. Within weeks of the news reaching Spain, this important assertion of imperial power had been trumpeted by Lope de Vega in his play *Brazil Regained*, performed only days after the great court playwright Pedro Calderón de la Barca's *Siege of Breda*. In Lope's dramatized account, the victorious Fadrique explained to his Dutch captives that 'I am not inclined to treat for clemency, for my King has sent me to punish them. But I know that in his breast that divine Monarch is as much a merciful father as a harsh judge and so I will speak with him, from here, for I have his portrait in my tent. So, while I speak with him, kneel down.'

At that moment a portrait of Philip IV was revealed on stage. Fadrique turned to it reverently: 'Great Philip, these people ask for pardon, does Your Majesty want us to pardon them this time? Aha, it seems he says yes.'[29] The implication, of course, is that contemporary audiences would have accepted the notion of a painting that was animated by sovereignty to the point of effectively being a nearly live proxy for the King. It was exactly the kind of dramatization of imagery which lay behind the whole conception of the Hall of the Realms, and Maino recreated an almost identical scene in his painting, either adapting the material directly from Lope's play or else drawing on a common source.

The foreground of *The Recapture of Bahía* is dominated by Portuguese refugees, including a number of children, looking on as a nurse attends to a Spanish soldier who has been shot in the chest, another scene apparently borrowed from Lope. The emphasis is clearly on the horrors of war, while in the background the naval battle rages. But the second plane of the foreground, which evokes the dominant theme of the whole series, clemency and peace, is the most fascinating. The defeated Dutch are shown kneeling before a dais on which Fadrique stands, gesturing towards a life-size portrait of Philip IV that is set under a canopy as though it were the King himself. In this picture within a picture, Philip holds a palm of peace in one hand and his staff of justice in the other, a self-evident testimony to his clemency. To his right and a little behind him, the Roman goddess of victory, Minerva, holds a laurel wreath above his head; to his left, the unmistakable figure of the Count-Duke of Olivares extends his right arm to help the goddess with the wreath, while in his left hand he holds the sword of the Catholic Monarchs, a further symbol of royal justice, from which an olive branch appears to be sprouting, at once a sign of peace and, of course, the heraldic blazon of his own dynasty.

This is the only painting directly evoked in Covarrubias's anthology of poetic praise for the Buen Retiro, which otherwise contains nineteen poems that mention the grandeur of the Hall of Realms and is full of general but unspecific praise for the pictures. Indeed, Maino's *Recapture of Bahía* is mentioned in four different sonnets;[30] self-evidently, the intention was to draw attention to the one image in which Olivares himself appeared and to portray him, in the words of another poem, as 'the splendour of the Guzmans who protects such fortunate Majesty'.

Olivares could not take centre stage, but he had very discreetly eclipsed his Planet King.

Pedro Calderón de la Barca, born in Madrid in 1600, was a consummate courtier and the most polished playwright of his generation. We must imagine his most accomplished work, *La vida es sueño*, or *Life is a Dream*, being played for the first time in the Hall of the Realms to an eager courtly audience. This important play, still the most performed and studied of his works, explored the great existential questions about the meaning of reality and perception that so preoccupied Spaniards during the Golden Age. But, daringly, it did so within a plot that hinges on burning moral questions about power, government, tyranny, rebellion and social order, the very questions then being raised by ever louder and ever more numerous dissenting voices in Madrid.

Life is a Dream tells the story of Prince Sigismondo, rightful heir to the Crown of Poland, who has been imprisoned from birth by his father King Basilio in a fairy-tale tower in a mysterious forest because his horoscope predicted that he would become an evil tyrant. Under the watchful eye of a faithful retainer who has sole control over his education, he has been raised in bestial discomfort, chained up and dressed in animal skins, until he is discovered by the beautiful Rosaura. But at this moment Basilio is racked by doubt and he decides to test the astrologers' predictions by having Sigismondo drugged with opium and then brought to the royal palace, where he comes round in the King's bed and is appointed ruler for the day. He immediately throws an aristocratic servant out of the window, attacks his former jailer with a dagger and tries to rape Rosaura. The horoscope is thus vindicated and, drugged again, Sigismondo is returned to his tower. As he struggles back to consciousness, he dreams of defeating his father and murdering his jailer:

> Oh, unrivalled valour, let's
> Walk the great broad stage together,
> That theatre of the world, and frame
> The symmetry of my revenge.[31]

But no sooner is he awake than he begins to speculate on his strange experience. Is he still asleep and dreaming, he wonders, or has he woken up? But rather than drawing a concrete conclusion, he offers a supremely slippery Baroque answer:

> There can't be much deception,
> For, if what I saw as palpable
> Has been nothing but a dream,
> Then all I see is mutable;
> And there's no capitulation,
> For I can see in my sleep
> What I dream when awake.
>
> What is life? Mere caprice.
> What is life? Mere illusion,
> A shade, shadow, or fiction . . .
> For the whole of one's life's a dream,
> And dreams are nothing but dreams.[32]

But his wise jailer advises him 'to lose no opportunity to be good, even when dreaming'.

In the final act, Sigismondo is co-opted by a popular uprising of 'plebs and peasants', whom he leads in the conquest of Poland. But now that he can exercise free will, he is magnanimous towards his humbled father and forgiving of his jailer, marries Rosaura to her philandering fiancé, thus preserving her honour, himself marries his Princess cousin and incarcerates the leader of the popular rebellion in the tower. And so, in a trice, Sigismondo presides over the complete restoration of order and hierarchy, perfecting a transition from bestial wild man to paragon of royal virtue.

Life is a Dream has a tiny cast of mostly aristocratic or royal characters and takes place almost entirely in a courtly world obsessed with parochial matters of honour and hierarchy. Played in the Hall of the Realms or the ballroom of the Alcázar, it was very much an allegorical tale performed against the backdrop of a theatrical court. It was a play within a play for an audience so attuned to reading signs that it would have been lost on almost no one that Basilio was an allegory of incompetent government and deluded political advice and that Sigismondo symbolized inherent princely virtue. It certainly cannot have been lost on Olivares that a popular uprising had restored order; after all, he had himself evoked the spectre of the Comuneros in his efforts to keep Philip under control.

There is no record that anyone drew any parallel between Philip IV and this captive Prince whose sovereignty has been emasculated nor between Olivares and Sigismondo's all-powerful jailer, nor between Basilio in hock to his astrologers and magicians and either Philip III or Olivares. That these parallels are there to be drawn is not evidence that anyone drew them, but they were unquestionably the building blocks of Calderón's plot precisely because they were the burning issues in contemporary politics; he had captured and harnessed the Zeitgeist.

But he also set that political Zeitgeist within a matrix of philosophical angst about reality and illusion. In a courtly world that was so obviously a broad stage on which every actor played a part, Sigismondo's decision to abandon all hope of distinguishing between life and dream would have made disturbing sense, all the more disturbing in that he abdicates his sovereignty over empirical reality and fiction precisely because he recognizes the overriding importance of moral truth. It is of no consequence to distinguish between dream and reality so long as you do the right thing.

For Olivares, the Buen Retiro was always meant to be a 'picture palace', in the sense that it was laid out and decorated as an art gallery in which to display a stunning collection, but we can also invoke the sense that it was a place of moving images created by the royals and courtiers who walked his stage. The paintings and tapestries were both a backdrop to the drama and a commentary on the meaning of that drama, as well, ultimately, as an attempt to fix in paint and thread the ephemeral spectacle of sovereignty in a desperate bid to make so much theory and ideology seem real. The formality of the court made human movement wooden, giving it a sense of stasis, an almost sculptural quality. At the same time, the fluidity and realism of the paintings that so enchanted visitors like the French traveller, its energetic Baroque vibrancy, gave the two-dimensional backdrop a feeling of mobility. Olivares's palace was a temple in which to celebrate the high mass of sovereignty, it was an act of faith in monarchy, a good work done in the name of the King by a donor who aspired to the heavenly ranks of royalty. One of Covarrubias's poets sang of 'Guzmán's Religion' that was even 'learned in the art of painting', while another arrived 'like a pilgrim' at the Retiro's 'religious threshold'. And so, orchestrated by the fancy of the favourite's imagination, art and life communed in mutual imitation, transcending reality and representation in an orgy of gorgeous imagery.

In the final reckoning, there is something about the story of Olivares's Buen Retiro that is both deeply allegorical and tangibly representative of the times. That the palace no longer exists and the garden has changed beyond recognition, that his monument has all but vanished, is testimony to the wholly ephemeral atmosphere surrounding a project that, in retrospect, clearly owed much more to the kind of temporary architecture so typical of the age than it did to any sense of permanent intent. It is properly remembered among the triumphal arches made of wood and plaster through which royals made their entries into cities, as Charles V and the Empress Isabella had done in Seville, or categorized alongside the pompous catafalque that soared towards the heavens in Seville Cathedral in memory of Philip II, about which Cervantes had written his acerbic verse. A modern analogy would be an Olympic Park or a World Trade Expo, a hurriedly cobbled-together place of entertainment and networking that leaves behind a few featureless traces, making a mark that is more conundrum than identity. The Buen Retiro was the conceit of a man driven by very personal notions of the past, of Habsburg identity and his own family history; a man obsessed by dynasty who, in the cruel-lest and most untimely twist of Fate, had reached for the skies and then, at the very zenith of that celestial trajectory, had all sense of a meaningful future ripped from his hopes and memories with the death of his daughter and the end of his bloodline. All had come to naught, and it is the madcap nature of his grief at the death of a dynasty that explains the Buen Retiro. The project was in part an attempt to rewrite the reality of history, a strange experiment in bringing an imaginary Habsburg past into the present, both for his own personal benefit and for the public image of the Crown. In Richard Kagan's words, 'the royal favorite rarely hesitated to treat Clio', the classical muse of history, 'as if her only task was to promote the reputation of Spain's Habsburg monarchy, both at home and abroad' or to justify his own policies.[33] But this was no wily subterfuge, for he believed, or at least desperately wanted to believe, in his own propaganda. And so the Retiro was, as its name indicated, a place of retreat and escape. Like the Alhambra, it was inward-looking, a place where dreams would never be challenged by a contrary reality: it was as quintessentially quixotic an enterprise as Olivares's own life itself had proved to be. It was the most splendid windmill on the Spanish plain.

21

Death and Defeat

For many days, the Count-Duke has continually requested me to allow him to retire because of very poor health.

Philip IV

Towards the end of 1625, Olivares had begun seriously to contemplate pitching his policy of a Union of Arms to the kingdoms of Aragon, Catalonia and Valencia. He decided that the King should preside in person over the Cortes of each of these independently minded nations and hoped that the logic of his own arguments would sway their leaders. But both Aragon and Valencia were painfully under-populated lands and immediately rejected any form of military service that would take invaluable human resources overseas; instead, under extreme pressure, they agreed to vote financial subsidies. Philip and Olivares moved on to Catalonia.

Although the Castilian Viceroy in Barcelona, the Duke of Albuquerque, had restored some semblance of order to Catalonia during the final years of Philip III's reign, it remained at heart an ungovernable land of noblemen-bandits, churchmen who readily resorted to violence and the self-interested merchant oligarchs of Barcelona. The Catalan Corts reflected that innate spirit of anarchic individualism in the characters of the deputies, in its fierce protection of the traditional Catalan liberties and in the political machinery of its working practices. The Corts was quite different to the Castilian Cortes. Its primary purpose was to make laws and act as a tribunal to which Catalans could bring any grievance, and it paid particular attention to any claims made against royal officials. It could act as a very powerful curb on royal power. Only as an afterword would the deputies consider granting subsidies to the King.

Such an instinctive autocrat as Olivares was unlikely to find a way of working with such an independent institution, let alone sympathize with its byzantine systems. But he did at least comprehend that he would have to wait a long time before he could even begin to broach the subject of a Union of Arms. First, the deputies had to address a long procession of local issues, including the seemingly endless grievances brought before them by the subjects of a barely functional kingdom. These were studiously assessed and considered, but as a decision-making body the Corts was hamstrung by a labyrinth of hierarchies and procedures designed to undermine any executive authority. The most startlingly impractical of these was a political instrument known as the act of *dissentiment*, a mechanism by which a lone deputy could bring all other business then being dealt with to an immediate halt while a single supposedly burning issue was discussed and resolved. It was a recipe for blackmail that rewarded individual intransigence and brinkmanship and, when it collided with Olivares's insistent impatience, it rendered the whole system utterly dysfunctional.

Needless to say, when the idea of the Union of Arms was first raised in such a bloody-minded environment there was general uproar. The Corts was an institution designed for and accustomed to making demands not concessions. But Olivares was wily and he must have realized that by raising the subject he would invite the inevitable act of *dissentiment*. That, at least, gave discussion of the only policy that interested him priority over everything else. He had also been sensible enough to realize that he needed to commute his demands to payments made in lieu of military service rather than try and secure a commitment to raise men-at-arms, thereby turning the whole discussion into an argument about money.

At the same time, the Catalans were separately demanding that Philip IV forgo the royal fifth, the 20 per cent tax raised on all imports into the kingdom, which they had anyway not paid for fifteen years. So Olivares requested that the Corts vote an utterly unrealistic subsidy of three million ducats, which resulted in an intractable stalemate in which neither side showed any signs of being prepared to consider the other's demands. But then Olivares acted with his usual bullish decisiveness. For weeks, the King had repeatedly warned the Corts that the hot and humid Barcelona summer would be very dangerous for his health. This concern may have been exaggerated for political effect, but he suffered from malaria and an acute attack was a real possibility. Olivares, concerned about Philip's health, having lost all patience with the Corts and no doubt worried about the huge expense of prolonging the royal visit, decided that the King must leave. And so, on 4 May, at six in the morning, Philip's entourage slowly made its way out of Barcelona and began heading back to Madrid.

The Corts could not continue without him; so now the deputies could do no business at all. The Council of Barcelona, the Consell de Cent, panicked. Olivares had cunningly given them hope that he might be prepared to make concessions on the question of the royal fifth, which was naturally of great interest to the merchants of Barcelona. They sent a representative rushing after the King with about 40,000 ducats in cash as an immediate loan to cover the expenses of his journey and made overtures for his return. Pressure was brought to bear on the great estates, the aristocracy and the Church, and their deputies soon began to vote a range of subsidies despite still being under the act of *dissentiment* that prohibited them from doing so. A total of seventy other *dissentiments* were immediately withdrawn, an indication of the ludicrous level of abuse. Olivares, by removing their ruler, had cowed the Catalans. But, instead of negotiating a deal, Philip and his favourite simply took the money proffered by the Barcelona merchants and continued their journey back to Madrid. Each side had proved itself as ineptly uncompromising as the other. No productive Union of Arms could ever be forged out of this unhappy marriage.

The Catalans had now seen at first hand how Olivares lived by a strange chivalric code of Habsburg hubris. In the following years, they were further troubled by reports of the almost universally bellicose approach of the regime; one influential Catalan commentator in Madrid wrote home that 'no one understands this method of governing Spain'.[1] But by 1632 Olivares was keen to revive the failed Corts in the hope of raising desperately needed funds. A placatory approach from a new viceroy brought promising signs of detente; the Catalans seem to have been willing to negotiate, and various towns voted small sums of money to support the war in Italy. Then, in May, Philip and Olivares visited Barcelona briefly so that the Cardinal Infante Don Fernando, the King's brother, could be invested as President of the Corts and Viceroy of Catalonia. And this time the Corts failed because of a farcical dispute about hats.

The councillors of Barcelona insisted that they were tradition-ally allowed to keep their heads covered in the presence of the King; Olivares was disinclined to concede them the honour, which was a hugely important symbol of status otherwise only granted to the grandees of Castile. An ingenious solution was devised by which the Catalan Duke of Cardona, who was also a Castilian grandee, would remove his hat during the Cardinal Infante's investiture as Viceroy, thereby obliging the councillors to do the same. The ceremony proceeded with protocol duly observed and honour maintained by all sides. But when the populace heard that their representatives had behaved so pusillanimously there was uproar. By early June, Barcelona had decided to pull out of all official functions until the matter had been resolved in person by Philip, who was now again in Madrid. By October, Philip and Olivares, in despair, suspended the Corts.

In 1635, the United Dutch finally convinced France to declare war on Spain. This pitted Olivares against his able French counterpart, Cardinal Richelieu, favourite of Louis XIII. With Habsburg posses-sions surrounding France on almost every land border, war began to open up on multiple fronts. Spanish troops had the better of the initial skirmishing, but failed to press home their advantage; and in the summer of 1638, a French army invaded north-west Spain and laid siege to the border fortress at Fuenterrabía. The fighting raged until early September, when the French were finally forced to retreat by a Spanish army that included Portuguese, Italians, Valencians and Aragonese, and 1,500 Irishmen. It was a very tangible step towards Olivares's dream of a Union of Arms. But the Catalans were conspic-uous by their absence, once more invoking their traditional laws that exempted them from military service outside their own land. What is more, although the Portuguese had sent troops to Fuenterrabía, the Portuguese aristocracy had objected to demands for military service and raising troops to be sent abroad; and in 1637 the proposed Union of Arms had been the touchstone to tax riots in the important Portuguese city of Evora. But such dissatisfaction was rooted in a perceived failure by Castile to offer any protection for Portugal's possessions in the East and West Indies. Dutch incursions into Brazil, with her rich sugar trade, were at the heart of the problem, but resentment also built up at the continued exclusion of Philip's Portuguese subjects from his Spanish possessions in America.[2]

By now, all Europe was at war: the Swedes had invaded Germany, tying up the Empire; the Spanish army in Flanders was under pressure from the Dutch and the French. The crucial transport routes from Italy to Flanders were under threat and the Spanish navy had twice suffered horrible defeat in the English Channel. Even the Papacy had once again started to show a pro-French bias; Naples was restless. Most gravely of all, in the summer of 1639, a strong French force invaded Catalonia and captured the strategically vital fortress of Salces that controlled the Roussillon border.

Francisco de Quevedo, who had so often served as Olivares's hired pen, now patriotically turned his satire on a regime he clearly believed was destroying Spain with its unbridled policy of war. In 1639, he wrote a scathing series of verses about the state of the kingdom, known as the *Memorial*, which was smuggled onto the King's dining table folded up in his napkin. When Olivares learnt that the King had seen this document, he acted immediately; two sheriffs were dispatched to the residence of the Duke of Medinaceli where Quevedo was staying. He was arrested, thrown into a coach and, under heavily armed guard, driven away under cover of darkness. He was taken to the Monastery of San Marcos in distant León, where he was imprisoned for the next four years. Medinaceli's house was ransacked and Quevedo's papers were seized, among them the manuscript of a vicious satire with the title *The Island of Monopantos*. It described a colony ruled by a governor called Pragas Chincollos, an anagram of Gaspar Conchillos, who is clearly intended to be recognized as Olivares himself and which was an obvious reference to his descent from the *converso* Lope Conchillos; the Governor was supported by a council of Jews, which was an only slightly more oblique reference to his increasing reliance on Portuguese bankers of Jewish origin. Quevedo's former patron responded ruthlessly; he was thrown into solitary confinement in a foetid cellar at San Marcos and left to rot, as good as dead.

The rebellion of a once loyal figure of such prominence was evidence of how isolated the regime had become; but the forever over-confident Olivares seems to have been incapable of heeding a warning. Instead, he now saw a chance to kill two birds with one stone; by engaging the French in Catalonia itself he believed he could force the Catalans to contribute to the war effort and that, he also seems to have believed, would be enough to secure a decisive victory. He now decided to launch a massive assault on France from Catalonia itself and ordered the Royal Army, including some of the most experienced *tercios* outside Flanders, to march into Catalonia, where the notori-ously violent and lawless troops would be billeted over the winter.

The greatest concentration of soldiers settled into the area around Gerona ready for a spring offensive against Salces. At the end of April 1640, after months of abuse by the troops, the resentment of the local population spilled over into violence. At the mountain town of Santa Coloma, the villagers rioted and a royal official was burned to death. A detachment of troops sent to punish the rioters itself went on the rampage and more or less razed the place to the ground. Fury raged across Catalonia and the peasants rose up in revolt, organizing themselves into a well-armed and determined army that confronted a detachment of crack Spanish troops and put them to flight.

Then, at Corpus Christi, the usual unruly crowd of seasonal day labourers turned up in Barcelona, their numbers bolstered by rebel militiamen who had been fighting the royal troops. The tense atmo-sphere almost immediately deteriorated into brutally vindictive rioting during which the Viceroy tried to flee. At first, he prepared to board a Genoese galley that was standing off in the harbour, but he hesi-tated too long. The rioters burst into the dockyards, and the crowd of nobles and servants accompanying the Viceroy panicked and scattered. The mob seized control of the artillery and began firing at the galley, forcing it to retreat. The now terrified Viceroy escaped towards the famous hill of Montjuïc with a small group of loyal retainers; but with no hope that the galley could reach them, they set off in the blazing sunshine along the rocky shoreline. Old and fat, the Viceroy struggled to keep going. He stumbled repeatedly, he stopped to rest, he forced himself to carry on, but then he slipped and fell; he fainted. The rebel mob caught up with him. The first man on the scene was uncertain what to do, but as he dithered, an impetuous young sailor soon caught up; he immediately and gleefully disembowelled his prey.

All semblance of royal authority in Catalonia was at an end; and such was the hatred felt for Olivares that there were many in Madrid who rejoiced at the news. But Catalonia was now a failed principality. In the towns, the anarchic rioters turned their anger on the rich and powerful, sacking their houses, burning their books and furniture, raping and pillaging at will. The Catalans fell under the auspices of the rural militias, which soon aligned themselves according to their traditional allegiances to the Nyerros and Cadells. Anyone accused of treachery and of being in league with the Crown feared for their lives. The impoverished gentry and even well-off peasants became targets of this feral coalition of brigands, petty criminals and the poorest of the poor. And finally, of course, this bestial throng began to turn upon itself.

The Catalan ruling classes went into hiding. The obdurate conservatism and short-sighted self-interest of their merchants, the parochial independence of an ineffectual aristocracy and, above all, their lack of any sense of collective will had left them living in a backward remnant of the Middle Ages. Now, with their tenuous hold on power usurped by popular banditry, the crippled Catalan nobility finally acknowledged the need for outside help. But Castile could no longer provide the military might necessary to restore order. Instead, Cardinal Richelieu had been watching patiently, his network of spies carefully and quietly persuading the Catalans' rulers that only France could bring some semblance of order to their mayhem. They were deeply troubled by an alliance with France, but as they hesitated, arguing and negotiating with the French, Olivares began to raise a rag-tag Castilian army of *hidalgos* and peasants, an army of Quixotes and Sanchos, a medieval army to reconquer a medieval land. Spain was travelling back in time. And so the Catalans capitulated to the inevitable and accepted the tutelage of the King of France; they allowed French ships use of their ports and agreed to pay for an army of 3,000 French troops to defend a principality they could not hope to defend themselves. Catalonia had become a French colony. Much of it remains a part of France today.

Then, at Lisbon, on 1 December 1640, the Duke of Braganza was proclaimed King Joao IV of Portugal. The Portuguese nobility had finally decided to break with Castile.

Olivares had to accept that he did not have the resources to prosecute any but the most cursory campaign against Portugal, and he retreated into his anxious paranoia while his enemies in Madrid pared their quill pens into razor-sharp barbs. Meanwhile, in the south, the ninth Duke of Medina Sidonia, grandson of the Admiral of the Armada, was plotting a rebellion that would lead to him being proclaimed King of Andalusia. This was probably only ever intended as a way of forcing Philip IV's hand into removing Olivares, but it was treason within Olivares's own noble lineage nonetheless. He sent for his errant distant cousin and, explaining that 'it is impossible for your reputation to suffer without the ruin of my own', he forced him to join the campaign against the Portuguese.[3] Quevedo's criticism had been as nothing beside the threat of such aristocratic sedition.

Philip IV must have known his favourite was mortally wounded and he himself now attempted to rise to the impossible challenges facing his monarchy. In April 1642, he set out for Catalonia determined to lead his armies to victory over the French, but he was hobbled from the outset by a chronic lack of funds. Olivares was deeply despondent as he struggled to squeeze the money out of an economy rapidly descending into hyper-inflation. But by the end of July both King and favourite were installed at Saragossa, a long way from the main theatre of action that was still centred around Roussillon, but well placed for a massive attack on the nearby city of Lérida, which had fallen to the French earlier in the year. When the strategically crucial city of Perpignan fell in September, Philip was furious and immediately ordered that the assault on Lérida begin. It was led by Olivares's cousin and close confidant, the art-loving Marquis of Leganés. On 7 October, the two armies met outside the town and after a day of very fierce fighting the French force of 13,000, which included 1,000 Catalans, defeated over 20,000 Castilian troops, a quarter of whom lost their lives.

At the beginning of December, Philip and favourite turned tail and went back towards Madrid. At Alcalá de Henares, the students openly insulted Olivares in the streets and, on the night of 6 December, the two men scuttled back into the capital city under cover of darkness and by a little-used gate. The monarchy had been utterly humiliated.

Throughout Christmas and the New Year Madrid effervesced with excited rumour until, finally, on 23 January, Olivares ate his last meal in the Alcázar, alone and in complete silence. He then left in secret for his country estate to the north-east of Madrid at Loeches, passing the Buen Retiro for the last time as he went.[4] The following day, the King formally addressed his expectant privy councillors.

> For many days, the Count-Duke has continually requested me to allow him to retire because of very poor health . . . but I have been so satisfied by his zeal, care, attention and incessant hard work . . . that I have made him wait. But, recently, he has pressed me so hard that I have given him permission to retire whenever might suit him; he has already left . . . and I hope that with some peace and quiet he will recover his health and return to my service.[5]

Olivares died two years later, threatened with investigation by the Inquisition. His final fever sent him into the incoherent ramblings of a fatal delirium brought on, Marañón explains, by the total collapse of his cardio-renal system. 'When I was Rector,' he remembered, thinking of his first ever political success at the University of Salamanca, 'when I was Rector!'[6]

In the immediate aftermath of removing such a maniacal tyrant from the heart of his government, Philip IV clearly longed to come of age as statesman himself: 'it seems to me', he announced to his privy councillors, 'that this is the moment to advise my Council that in the absence of such a good minister I am the only person who can replace him, for the straits in which we find ourselves require all my attention.'[7] But Philip's ardent desire to fill the shoes of his strange mentor and nemesis soon buckled under the pressures of his collapsing Empire and the complexities of the administration. The grandees and bureaucrats began to assert themselves, while a broad range of other characters now came into view as vital elements in the government. Luis de Haro now became his de facto favourite, but with a far more discreet presence and a much lighter touch. Also, slowly but surely, Olivares's son-in-law Medina de las Torres emerged as the most influential political figure in Madrid; he returned to the Council of State and, at Haro's death in 1661, assumed the role of First Minister, energetically prosecuting a foreign policy based on peace and alliances with England and the Empire that he had advocated since at least 1639.[8]

Philip himself now turned for advice to a most unusual counsellor. While travelling to Saragossa on his way to campaign in Catolonia, the King had spent the night at the remote town of Ágreda. There he visited Sister María, the Abbess of the Convent of the Immaculate Conception, who was famous for miraculously materializing in New Mexico and Texas in order to help with the evangelization of the Jumano Indians while her body was still asleep in her convent in Spain. Philip was clearly drawn to this sensational story and he seems to have found in Sister María a feeling of personal contact with God. For the next twenty-four years, until both correspondents died in 1665, the King exchanged over 600 letters with this mystic nun. She became Philip's closest confidante, frankly advising him on spiritual and moral matters, as one might expect, but also offering advice on international politics and the business of government and even volunteering detailed opinion on military strategy.[9]

From 1641 onwards, it had been ever more apparent in Madrid that Spain needed peace in the Netherlands. But it was difficult to negotiate with the now ascendant Dutch, who, once united in their hatred of Spain, had begun to argue among themselves with the result that the preparations for formal peace talks disappeared into an 'intricate maze of . . . disparate interests'.[10] And, as the Dutch squabbled, the more bellicose among them produced a mass of warmongering rhetoric and victorious anti-Spanish propaganda. In Zeeland particularly, there seemed no appetite for peace. So, in 1646, Madrid began to capitulate, agreeing to the absolute independent sovereignty of the United Provinces. Finally, the negotiators gathered at Münster, where they proceeded to define the borders to be drawn in the Netherlands and discuss the detail of trade agreements relating to the American colonies. Spain abandoned all pretence of defending Portuguese claims to lands in Brazil and Africa previously captured by the Dutch, but resolutely resisted opening up Spanish America to Dutch merchants. The Portuguese had paid a heavy price for their rebellion. In the end, the Peace of Münster was formally signed on 30 January 1648.[11]

The peace treaty publicly recognized the failure of four generations of Spanish Habsburgs to root out Protestant heresy in the United Provinces. The following year, 1649, a wrathful Catholic God, it seemed, began to wreak the grimmest of vengeance upon the Spanish people and he struck most cruelly at the economic heart of Castile, at Seville. For two or three years, there had been worrying reports of sporadic outbreaks of bubonic plague in the poverty-stricken east of Andalusia; then, over the winter of 1648–9, there had been cases in the Cadiz ports. The astrologers read signs of malevolence in the movement of the planets, and in February the Archbishop of Seville died. It was a fearful omen.[12]

'The year 1649', wrote Ortiz de Zúñiga, the great Andalusian historian, was 'the most tragic in the history of Seville', a year when the city faced 'utter destruction'. Over the winter, isolated cases of plague in the city itself had the authorities on alert. But torrential spring rains brought flooding, 'the air became infected' and 'everyone fell sick with . . . diarrhoea, vomiting and other gastric accidents'. Ortiz de Zúñiga at first rather formally cited his source as a contemporary account by the Senior Pilot of the House of Trade, but then, in a moving passage, continued: 'and I can confirm it from what I myself witnessed with my own eyes and what my closest relatives and I experienced ourselves'.

As April went on, 'Death's executives – violent fevers, swellings, tumours, buboes and other vehement and deadly complications – struck furiously.' A Council of Health was convened that requisitioned the Hospital of the Five Wounds, with its 1,200 beds. For a month and a half detailed records were kept, but by the end of May it was thought that as many as 80,000 had died; 'the whole city was now a Hospital', filled with the dead and the dying. One morning, over ninety cadavers were found piled up between the Cathedral and the Merchant's Exchange. As most of the citizens fled for the countryside, the priests, monks and 'ministers braved the worst of the danger and incessantly carried the sick to the Hospital', but every 'morning dawned with the streets and the doors of the churches piled high with those who had died in their houses'. Across this 'horrendous' and 'ghastly' landscape of 'wailing' and 'misery', 'you could see carts overloaded with bodies leaving the city and dumping them, in great crowds, into the ghastly, badly covered mass graves that gave off an intolerable stench'.

Twenty-four prebendary canons of the Cathedral were slaughtered by this divine retribution, among them Mateo Vázquez de Leca who had done so much to promote the Immaculate Conception. So many churchmen died that mass could not be said in many of the churches, the offices were sung at strange times if they were sung at all, and many victims did not receive the last rites and extreme unction. But the authorities gathered their strength; there were constant prayers and a handful of major religious processions were organized, desperate but 'marvellous displays of the republic's Christianity'. And in July, the mortality rate began to relent and by October the end of the Great Plague was officially proclaimed. Whole families had been wiped out, thousands of houses were left vacant, whole parishes were left without parishioners. According to Ortiz de Zúñiga, there had been 200,000 victims.

Modern historian have disputed this figure because the total population of Seville in 1648 cannot be reasonably estimated at more than 150,000. The best-informed guess, and that is all it was, made by the great twentieth-century Sevillian historian Antonio Domínguez Ortiz, was that 60,000 died, nearly half the population of the city. Moreover, by comparing figures for receipts from taxation, he was able to show that in the years following the plague the economy of the city roughly halved in size, while the population stabilized at 80,000 and did not recover its 1648 level until the nineteenth century.[13] But if Ortiz de Zúñiga's figure of 200,000 were intended to include the extended Seville hinterland and not just the city, it in fact seems a reasonable estimate for the total loss of life in the province.

This ghastly massacre was inexorably followed by famine, for there had been no one to sow the crops or till the fields. Harvests had failed abroad and the price of wheat rose fourfold by 1652. The Archbishop and the Dean of the Cathedral began a massive programme of charitable handouts, but as thousands of hungry peasants flocked into the city in search of assistance, there were outbreaks of sporadic unrest and rioting, much of it directed at the profiteering bakers. The discontent gained momentum and the mob forced the Archbishop and various city officials to join a rowdy house-to-house search for food. They sacked the armoury and for a week in May the situation hung in the balance. But then the nobility rallied under the leadership of Martín de Ulloa and managed to defuse the situation by feeding wine and cheese to the rioters, before finally restoring an uneasy order by organizing a series of armed militias.[14]

Seville never recovered from these political and God-sent disasters. Spain was no longer the centre of the world, and the Crown's already declining control over the Indies trade became weaker still. Mercantile activity was increasingly concentrated on the Atlantic ports, where smuggling was endemic and goods could easily be re-exported. Under pressure from foreign merchants the Crown capitulated to capitalism and the House of Trade effectively shifted its administrative centre to Cadiz in 1680. Seville, symbol of the royal monopoly over the Indies trade, that great European Babylon of the long sixteenth century, once as cosmopolitan as modern London or New York and richer still, transcended that past to become a deeply religious and very beautiful provincial backwater, a place of quiet lanes and courtyards, jasmine flowers, orange blossom, grand monuments, ghosts, memories and vivid traditions.

Francisco de Zurbarán, the talented artist from Extremadura whose uncannily sculptural *Christ on the Cross* had won the approval of the

Seville Artists' Guild, was one of the most prominent members of the newly well-off urban class of artisans and traders whose businesses were victim to the vicissitudes of artistic tastes, the Indies trade and the effects of plague.

Following his brief stay in Madrid working on *The Labours of Hercules* and *The Defence of Cadiz* for the Buen Retiro, Zurbarán was inundated with commissions from religious institutions and private patrons in Seville. He also enthusiastically embraced the commercial possibilities of New World markets with an authentically entrepreneurial spirit. He established a large workshop staffed by a team of skilled craftsmen. While he created the templates for different subject matters, he relied on these employees actually to produce the pictures. Each man specialized in a particular subject, representing clothing or jewellery or painting hands and feet; the most talented did the faces. This production line made fifty to a hundred works a year for export to America, mostly for sale in Peru. In contrast to Zurbarán's commissions done for rich and powerful patrons, this Indies venture was at first entirely speculative, as we know from a court action he brought against a ship's captain called Diego de Mirafuentes in 1640. Four years earlier, he had entrusted one of his first consignments of paintings for sale in the Portobello trade fair to Mirafuentes and they had agreed in advance a list of prices to be achieved for the paintings. But the drunken sailor had unpacked them during the voyage to decorate his ship during a fiesta he held in mid-Atlantic, causing them to be lost or irrevocably damaged; so Zurbarán had sued him.[15] Zurbarán was not deterred by this unhappy beginning and went on to sell vast numbers of often very indifferent works into the American market. But he had learnt his lesson and henceforth he contracted directly with Portobello merchants who agreed to buy the works wholesale on delivery, and few sea-captains would cross those all-powerful market-makers of the Peru trade.[16]

But the plague and famine severely affected his workshop, presumably killing many of the artists and disrupting the productivity of the survivors. For similar reasons, the Indies trade generally fell off very sharply in the decade after 1648 and the export of paintings appears to have virtually ceased altogether.[17] The recessionary effects of God's ire were then disastrously compounded by Protestant piracy when

English privateers captured the Treasure Fleets of 1656 and 1657, ships that would have been carrying payment for consignments of paintings Zurbarán had sent in 1650 or even before.[18]

At the same time, by the 1650s, Zurbarán's sober simplicity of line and palette was gradually becoming outmoded as a young artist called Bartolomé Esteban Murillo was revolutionizing the aesthetic tastes of Sevillian patrons with a new style of painting that has come to be called *vaporismo*, or 'misty-eyed'. The pain of 1648 took people in different ways. Murillo began to portray saints with a richly sentimental soft focus and Madonnas who float on billowy clouds, glowing with golden hues and gleaming cobalt blues and shining whites. And everywhere, it seems, he conjured up angelic children with blond curls and enchanting smiles and blue eyes that look longingly out of his paintings with the vibrant stare of a happy, much loved Labrador puppy. The brushwork is as loose as Rubens's, the images as controlled as Velázquez's, the artistic vocabulary simple and accessible. Filled with movement and life and feeling, this extraordinary explosion of aesthetic emotion was the very sort of romantic and otherworldly reality that the battered people of Seville hankered for in a troubled age.

During the early 1650s, Zurbarán struggled by. He had built up a small portfolio of prime residential and commercial real estate comprising four or more properties, some of which he owned and some of which he leased and then sub-let; he continued to paint a few portraits for the nobility and a number of important works for religious institutions, but he struggled to find major commissions. He did, however, paint three truly great paintings for the Seville Charterhouse, including his *St Hugo in the Refectory*, completed in 1655, in which he perfectly captures the serene calm of the famously austere Carthusians, the only monastic order to remain so faithful to their severe vows of poverty, chastity and silence that it was never reformed.

The Carthusians were devout vegetarians, believing that they would live longer by eating very little and by refusing all forms of meat, including fowl, and so could spend their longevity in prayer. The painting illustrates one of the foundation myths of this refusal to eat meat. Soon after St Bruno had established the first Charterhouse high in the Chartreuse Mountains in 1084, Hugo, Bishop of Grenoble,

sent the friars a meal of some meat, but it arrived on the Sunday before
Ash Wednesday, the beginning of Lent, when all Christians should
abstain from flesh. They then began such an intense theological discussion about whether they should eat it that they fell into a deep sleep.
They woke up six weeks later, on Palm Sunday, unaware they had
been asleep for so long and prepared to tuck into the same meal. At
this moment, Hugo arrived in person and was horrified to discover
the friars sitting down before a meal of what, in Zurbarán's painting,
looks like roast lamb. He immediately remonstrated with the Prior,
who was astonished to discover that Easter was upon them, and Hugo
was only convinced by their story when he touched the cooked flesh
and it instantly turned to ashes.[19]

In the summer of 1656, Zurbarán defaulted on the rent of a large
property where he seems to have been living with his family but which
was attached to a bakery that he was renting out.[20] Scholars have long
interpreted these signs of financial trouble as evidence that he was
losing work to Murillo and to another rising star of the new Baroque
style, Juan Valdés Leal. But, for all that the master's star was waning,
Zurbarán's workshop seems to have survived plague and piracy and
contributed to a marked revival in the export of paintings to the New
World that began in 1658.[21] Indeed, in 1659, he was able to put up a
typical bundle of about twenty mass-produced works as surety against
his rent arrears, presumably while he waited for the treasure fleet to
arrive the following year; and five years later, he noted in his will that
his daughter had taken payment of 8,000 *reales* for paintings presumably sold to the Indies trade.[22]

Now an old man, Zurbarán travelled to Madrid, where he found
work with the help of Velázquez, and the following year he again
defaulted on his rent in Seville and moved permanently to the capital.
There he produced a very significant number of paintings and found
other jobs, such as valuing the Polish Ambassador's art collection, a
strenuous workload for a veteran of faltering strength and health.[23]
He died in Madrid in 1664 at the age of sixty-six. It has become
commonplace to report that he died in great poverty because he grum-
bled in his will that he could not afford to bequeath his widow her
own dowry and that she had been forced to pawn the family silver

in order to pay for his medical bills and the funeral. But these facts alone do not evince penury. First of all, the probate inventory is filled with luxury goods such as a Cairo carpet, tablecloths, napkins, a full wardrobe, plenty of good-quality furniture and much art paraphernalia including a number of paintings and tapestries.[24] The total value of his estate, including outstanding debts, was about 20,000 *reales* or fifteen years' rent on a prime house in Seville. And that was what his widow declared to the authorities; none of the silver she had pawned, including 'two goblets, a serving dish, salt-cellar, pepper pot, sugar bowl, a plate, two candlesticks, half-a-dozen spoons and a fork', was valued in the probate inventory because it was conveniently with the pawnbroker where it could presumably be redeemed for well below its true value.

Zurbarán died neither rich nor poor, still at work and away from home. It is a mundane, melancholy end, but it was not the death of a pauper: his cadaver had not been piled high with others in the street and tipped into a mass grave.

By contrast with Zurbarán's relative obscurity, Velázquez's career was in the ascendant thanks to Philip's constantly developing passion for painting. In 1645, Velázquez had taken charge of turning the state rooms of the Madrid Alcázar into a great picture gallery. Then, in 1648, the King gave him the chance to travel again to Italy; in his capacity as a Gentleman of the Chamber, he joined the embassy sent to bring Mariana of Austria back to Spain as Philip's new bride following the death of Isabel the year before. But while Velázquez went as a diplomat, his real mission was to acquire art and antiquities for the royal collection. He travelled across Italy, to Venice, Parma, Modena and Rome, where he made his famous portrait of Pope Innocent X, for which, according to Palomino, he practised by painting a bust of his black slave, Juan de Pareja, a well-respected painter in his own right.[25] During this visit to Italy, Velázquez also painted his only surviving female nude, the stunning *Rokeby Venus*, and it is thought that he achieved its quiet eroticism by using his mysterious Italian mistress as his model. The name of this beautiful muse has gone unrecorded, but we know that she bore him a son called Antonio.[26]

Following his return to Madrid, Velázquez continued to paint a variety of subjects, and it was during this final period of his working life that he conceived and completed *Las Meninas*, 'The Maids of Honour', a portrait of the Infanta Margarita Teresa, Philip and Mariana's eldest child, surrounded by her most intimate household, her maids, her dwarfs and her dog, which is generally considered his greatest work and which inspired Goya and Picasso to copy and experiment with it. The subject matter of the painting is dominated by the presence of the artist himself: Velázquez stares out at the viewer, a vast canvas in front of him, his palette and brushes in hand, a playful conceit that has provoked endless questions about the meaning of images and representation. The mystery of what he might be painting has elicited all sorts of elaborate speculation. In the background, a portrait of Philip IV and Mariana hangs on the wall, as though surveying the scene, and the most commonly held view is that we see the scene through the eyes of Philip and Mariana, who are the subjects of his painting, and that their portrait on the back wall is in fact meant to be a reflection in a mirror.[27] Indeed, Palomino suggested that the mirror reflected the image of the King and Queen which Velázquez was in the process of painting, while another suggestion is that the portrait on the back wall is a deliberately anachronistic representation of the unseen work in progress.[28]

We will never know what Velázquez really wanted us to think he had depicted himself as painting in *Las Meninas*, if he had anything in mind at all, other than the playfulness so typical of the age. But the painting does unquestionably show Velázquez in splendid grandeur and wearing the red cross on his breast signifying that he had become a knight of the great military Order of Santiago. The painting affirms the rise of a poor boy from Seville to the heights of the nobility and to an intimate familiarity with the royal family; it even hints at his friendship with the King himself. Palomino recorded the rumour that Philip IV had personally painted this cross onto the picture after the artist's death 'as encouragement to practitioners of this noble art'.[29] That remark gave rise to a long-standing belief that Velázquez finally succeeded in ennobling the art of painting in Spain, thereby concluding a long struggle conducted by artists such as El Greco, Carducho and

Pacheco to gain recognition of painting as a liberal art. But the reality is more prosaic: the powerful Knights of Santiago had, in fact, objected strongly to his membership, believing him disqualified on the grounds that he had earned money from manual labour, as an artist, and that, being Portuguese, he was suspected of having Jewish ancestry. Only Philip's personal intervention on his behalf and special dispensation from the Pope forced the Order of Santiago to accept the painter as a knight, in 1659.[30] It was very clearly a personal victory for Velázquez thanks to his friendship with the King and his service in the royal household, but it was far from being a great triumph for the art of painting.

In 1659, peace was finally agreed between France and Spain, to be secured by the marriage of the Infanta Margarita to Louis XIV, which took place in the summer of 1660, at the Isle of Pheasants, on the border with France. Velázquez was now an old man, but as Royal Steward or *aposentador* he was responsible for organizing accommodation for the royal entourage and devising the temporary structure where the wedding ceremony would take place. The task exhausted him and within weeks of returning to Madrid he fell gravely ill with the fever that killed him within days; a week later, his wife Juana de Pacheco died as well. With their deaths, the spirit of Seville faded from the heart of courtly life.[31] But so rich and grand a city as Seville faded slowly and, in the 1660s, Murillo was at the height of his artistic powers.

Bartolomé Esteban Murillo was baptized in Seville on 1 January 1618, the youngest of fourteen children. His father, a barber-surgeon, died in 1627, and he was quickly apprenticed to one of the many artists' workshops then flourishing in the city. Talented and versatile, in the 1640s he travelled to Madrid where he was greatly influenced by Velázquez's increasingly Italian style with its looser brushwork and bright palette. Back in Seville, in 1645, he married and gained his first major commission for the Franciscans, which allowed him to show off his virtuoso sentimentality. He also painted secular vignettes of happy, healthy children on the cusp of adolescence. Generally but inaccurately referred to as paintings of 'Beggar Boys', these in fact offer a deceptively appealing vision of the working youth of Seville at play or negotiating the price of a meal. After 1648, such images were a welcome escape from reality.

Following the death of his wife in 1663, he began a prolific period of production during which he created his most mature and important work, including the series done for the Hospital of Charity and a large number of pieces commissioned as a direct or indirect result of his friendship with Justino de Neve, a great collector of Murillo's work who lived near him in Seville and whom the artist would name as an executor of his will.[32]

Neve, the son of a wealthy Flemish merchant who had settled in Seville, was an exemplary canon of Seville Cathedral, with a special devotion to the Immaculate Conception, who immersed himself in the charitable life of the Chapter, and who reportedly died beating his chest and kissing a crucifix in search of forgiveness for his sins.[33] We know him best from a very fine portrait by Murillo, in which his serious and confident expression belies his youthful countenance with its carefully barbered beard and moustache and dark, close-cropped hair. Dressed in his black canonical robes, he looks up from his books, his finger holding his place, a man of learning; an ornate clock sits on his table, a reminder that life is temporal, but a sign of his wealth; a silver bell to call his slaves and servants is to hand. At his feet, his pet dog gazes at him loyally. He is the perfect patrician.

In 1662, he was charged with supervising the reconstruction of the small church of Santa María la Blanca, especially popular with slaves and free blacks, which was a dependency of the Cathedral. In the past, it had been a mosque and then a synagogue, and some features of that primitive building remain. But Neve set about fitting on to this cramped urban lot a typical temple of the high Baroque, rich in decorative plasterwork, gilding and a series of colourful frescoes devised by the sculptor Pedro Roldán.[34] He must have felt a special bond with a church dedicated to the Madonna of the Snows, both because of his devotion to the Madonna and because his own surname meant snow. This was a project in which he wanted to shine for both worldly and spiritual motives, so he commissioned Murillo, then the leading artist working in Seville, to devise the entire decorative scheme. He

particularly needed Murillo's inventive handling of form and colour
to solve the aesthetic problem of painting four large lunettes or half-
moon-shaped paintings to hang high up below the small, voluptuously
ornate dome and at the ends of the side aisles.

The paintings under the dome had to depict the story of the fourth-
century Roman patrician and his wife who had dreamed that the
Madonna had asked them to build a church dedicated to her on the
Esquiline Hill. The following day, the patrician sought the advice
of the Pope and the whole party went to the divinely proposed site
where they found the plan of the church traced out by a miraculous
summer snowfall. Murillo illustrated this legend in the *Dream of the
Patrician and his Wife* and the *Patrician and his Wife before the Pope*.
The first of these images shows the couple fully clothed, she wearing
the red and blue associated with the Madonna, while he has a fine coat,
with stockings on his feet, and is partly wrapped in a cape or blanket.
A book on the table evokes the gospels, while a shawl, cushions,
sheets, laundry basket, a dog and a richly ornate bed all conjure
up an image of comfortable and intimate domesticity. Curiously, as
a leading Spanish art historian has pointed out, to anyone familiar
with Seville at the height of summer the scene evokes the siesta rather
than night-time.[35] What is more, the half-sleep of a long siesta is especially conducive to this kind of vivid dreaming. The marked curvature
of form Murillo has given to this group and strong chiaroscuro
lighting project the image out of the painting; above them, the
Madonna herself hovers, pointing to the snow-covered building lot,
brightly lit and animated among the Baroque cushioning of heavenly
clouds, almost like a hologram watching over the scene. This exagger-
atedly three-dimensional formulation of the key images deals with the
problems of perspective for viewers far below, looking up at an angle
from the floor of the church at this awkwardly shaped and very large
canvas, seventeen feet wide.

Neve's other major project to which Murillo made an important contribution was the Hospital de los Venerables Sacerdotes, or
Hospital for Geriatric Priests, a charitable institution that he founded
for poor and destitute clergymen on the site of a former theatre. Among
the 'superb paintings by Murillo', one excited traveller reported, 'the

Immaculate Conception on a throne of angels and clouds is thought to be one of his most excellent works', and by the nineteenth century it was widely considered his best work, largely because it had been acquired by the Louvre, where it was admired by Balzac and Zola.[36] The painting had belonged to Justino de Neve, who displayed it in public during the festivities to celebrate the founding of Santa María la Blanca in 1665.[37]

Epilogue

In ictu oculi, finis gloriae mundi.
In the twinkling of an eye, the end of all worldly things.

In 1665, Philip IV received two psychologically fatal blows. In April, Sister María de Ágreda died, and then, over the summer, the Portuguese won the decisive victory which ensured independence from Spain. The King himself was in faltering health, surviving on a diet of ass's milk; on 17 September, he died, the Spanish Habsburg who had finally surrendered the dynastic inheritance in northern and central Europe for ever.

Philip IV also bequeathed Castile a four-year-old heir, his only surviving son Carlos II, a weak and sickly child in both body and mind, who matured into an imbecile, a tragic creature who would become for ever known as 'Carlos the Bewitched'. The Queen Mother, Mariana of Austria, was installed as Regent, but the business of her dysfunctional government was conducted by her pious Jesuit favourite in the face of almost total opposition among the Castilians until he was removed by Philip IV's illegitimate son, known as Don John of Austria like his great-uncle, in 1669, at the head of a detachment of 400 cavalry. In the aftermath of this palace contretemps, Don John retired to Aragon, but a new and equally unpopular favourite emerged and, in 1677, Don John led the great aristocratic houses of all Spain in a violent military *coup d'état*; Mariana was exiled and her political faction suppressed. But Don John too proved to be an autocratic and incompetent ruler, a capable soldier but not a statesman. Finally, on his death in 1679, Spain found a competent ruler and administrator in the Duke of Medinaceli.

Meanwhile, Carlos II lived out his strange life, playing spillikins for hours on end with his beautiful queen, the French Princess María Luisa. Thankfully, he proved unable to procreate; in 1688, a French diplomat reported that 'a Dominican monk had a revelation that the King and Queen were bewitched', which he claimed explained Carlos's impotency or infertility. 'The question of breaking the spell then arose, but the procedure was horrifying: the King and Queen must be stark naked while the monk in vestments performed the exorcism in an infamous manner, after which, in the monk's presence, they must test whether the spell had been broken.' María Luisa refused. Carlos would produce no heir and the Spanish branch of the House of Habsburg would soon be eclipsed for ever; he was a broken ghost of a monarch for a kingdom that seemed to be in the throes of death.[1]

The life of Miguel Mañara Vicentelo de Lecca seems to epitomize the spirit of that age. He lived through the dramatic trauma of plague and Seville's precipitous decline from metropolitan Babylon at the centre of world trade into obsessive piety and provincial poverty. He developed an apocalyptic vision of the world, and an obsession with the dying and the dead led him to evoke in words, pictures and deeds the terrible scenes he had witnessed in 1648 and to invest his whole soul in alleviating such horrid suffering.

Mañara's father was a Corsican nobleman who had made a fortune in the Americas and returned to Seville, where he was one of the handful of very powerful figures who ran the Consulado and who helped to develop a lucrative secondary market extending credit to the Crown and financing the official treasure ships.[2] Miguel, born in 1627, was the youngest of ten siblings and he grew up, by his own account, leading the notoriously dissolute life of the Andalusian aristocracy. 'I served the devil that prince of Babylon,' he claimed, 'by committing countless sins and crimes of abominable arrogance and thousands of adulteries, profanities, scandals and thefts, whose sins and crimes are beyond counting.'[3] This self-denunciation had such a powerful effect on a handful of French nineteenth-century historians that they claimed he had been Tirso de Molina's model for Don Juan in *The Trickster of Seville*, first performed, of course, before Mañara was born. In reality, this poetic self-flagellation was an extreme example of the kind of exaggerated Baroque expression that came to characterize Mañara's morbidly obsessive later life during which he danced with death herself.

He had already lost his two elder brothers and five sisters, when, in 1648, his father also died, probably an early victim of the plague, leaving Miguel as titular head of the family and bequeathing him one of the largest fortunes in Seville. Four months later, he married Jerónima Carillo de Mendoza, a noblewoman from Guadix in the impoverished Granada hinterland. For the next thirteen years he played his part in the civic life of Seville: he was a member of the Order of Calatrava, acted as Sheriff of the rural police force, the Santa Hermandad, and joined the official delegation sent by the city to congratulate Philip IV on the birth of his ill-fated and epileptic son Felipe Próspero. But then, in September 1661, Jerónima died childless while they were summering at their estate near the ancient mountain town of Ronda.

Mañara retreated into mourning at a nearby Carmelite monastery known as the Desert of Snows, where he made a full confession of his sins. The following year, he returned to Seville, where he joined the Holy Brotherhood of Charity, La Caridad, determined to devote his life to good works. Filled with divine zeal and a practical dynamism, he set about revivifying this stale, staid organization that was run by a handful of lay brothers drawn from the highest echelons of the aristocracy.

La Caridad had been founded in the fifteenth century with the specific purpose of giving a Christian burial to executed convicts whose cadavers were otherwise left to rot by the gallows, and they soon began performing the same service for paupers and the homeless. Their chapel, dedicated to St George, was just outside the walls of the city, where it had a magnificent view of the Arenal, the river, the suburb of Triana across the water, and the life of the port. But the brotherhood had all but ceased to exist after the royal consolidation of the

Seville hospitals during the reign of Philip II and, by 1640, the chapel was in ruins. During the 1640s, the brothers began slowly rebuilding, but the works had progressed little by the time of the Great Plague in 1649 and La Caridad was wholly unprepared for the massive demand on its traditional services.

By the time Mañara joined in 1662, that abject attempt at revival had withered. But he arrived determined to turn the brotherhood into a monument to human mortality, frailty and the dignity of poverty and charity. Like Olivares at the Buen Retiro, he had no coherent plan from the outset, but launched into a successful ad hoc campaign to expand the number of brothers and the remit of the organization. His fellow brothers were initially wary, but soon welcomed his energy and force of character, so much so that the following year they elected him Senior Brother, or *hermano mayor*. He got down to work. Between 1663 and 1679, as Spain seemed poised for civil war, 500 new members were admitted, including leading painters like Murillo and Valdés Leal, turning this preserve of aristocrats into a fashionable charitable organization with a very broad reach. But the keystone of Mañara's policy was to expand the remit of the brothers' rule to include caring for the sick and the dying as well as the dead. In 1644, he negotiated a long lease on one of the deep vaults in the massive Royal Arsenal, the Atarazanas, next door to the ruined Church of St George. This vault was immediately converted into a hospice, and over the next fifteen years three infirmaries were added, piecemeal. Nowadays, the Hospital of Charity is still functioning as a hospice and old people's refuge, an eloquent legacy for this driven man.

But most modern visitors to La Caridad come to see the compact church, the heart of the complex, with its disturbing paintings and sculpture that evoke charity and death, a decorative scheme devised by Mañara himself with Murillo as his muse. By 1663, the church was 'in very bad condition. The floor was earth, the roof untiled and open to the sky; a flock of pigeons came and went through these holes, flying among the rafters . . . so that the floor was revoltingly filthy.'[4] Mañara set about completing the existing structure, but most importantly he still had to negotiate the purchase of land for the sanctuary and the high altar with the royal wardens of the Armoury. The brotherhood's councillors at first balked at the 300 *reales* a month rent, but Mañara convinced them to go ahead anyway, supposedly claiming that Providence would provide. No doubt the truth of the matter is that he was ready to pay out of his own pocket, but myth and legend stick to Mañara like Pacheco's paint to a Montañés sculpture: the story goes that a beggar visited Mañara one morning and insisted on donating the pitiful inheritance his wife had left him, despite every attempt to dissuade him. The wily Mañara, who had clearly inherited his father's instincts for money, used this convenient story to raise funds from the legion would-be brothers anxious to join, and work had soon begun on the extension.[5]

The façade of the church rises brilliant white, topped by an imperious campanile in classic colonial style, decorated with blue-and-white ceramic tiles depicting Faith, Hope and Charity, Santiago and St George. On one occasion, Mañara, an amateur artist himself, became so absorbed in overseeing the installation of these images that he missed his footing and fell from a scaffold.[6]

That personal involvement and attention to detail ensured that the decorative scheme inside has an eye-wateringly forceful sense of coherence, but even Mañara could not have achieved such a dramatic effect without the close involvement of Murillo.

In the late 1660s, Mañara commissioned from Murillo a series of six paintings to illustrate for the brothers of La Caridad the daily acts of mercy that were the core of their charitable responsibilities to the living and which had been succinctly outlined by Christ himself: 'I was hungry, and you gave me to eat; I was thirsty, and you gave me to drink; I was a stranger, and you took me in; naked, and you covered me; sick, and you visited me; I was in prison, and you came to me.'[7]

Murillo illustrated these acts of charity with familiar images from the gospels, such as *The Feeding of the Five Thousand* for giving food to the hungry and *Moses Sweetening the Waters at Mara* for satiating the thirsty.[8] Although he was paid piecemeal for these works over the coming years, they were in place by 1670, the first paintings completed for the church. They were close to Mañara's heart because they depicted the tangible aspect of his newly expanded rule, the practical outcomes he wanted to achieve. But as soon as they were hung, he had Murillo paint two further works. The first of these, *The Charity of St John of God*, was personally and emotionally important to him because it was intimately associated with his wife's home of Granada, where an important hospital complex was dedicated to the saint. The second, *St Elizabeth of Hungary Healing the Sick*, depicted a well-known story of the thirteenth-century Princess who, on being widowed, established a hospital at Marburg where she personally attended on the poor and the sick. This illustrated a core value of La Caridad that noblemen should themselves work in the hospital, but it also, of course, reminded everyone of the origin myth that Mañara's own pious work was inspired by widowerhood.

As the focal point of the church, Mañara and Murillo commissioned *The Entombment of Christ* from the leading sculptor then working in Seville, Pedro Roldán, who had worked on Santa María la Blanca. This centrepiece of the scheme, which stands out in its bold three dimensions in contrast to the surrounding paintings, most obviously symbolized the founding purpose of La Caridad to give Christian burial to executed convicts and the poor; Roldán's scene shows Nicodemus and Joseph of Arimathea, dressed in all their finery, tenderly carrying Christ's lifeless body by the shoulders and the legs and laying it carefully in the tomb. It closely follows La Caridad's rule which instructed the brothers to gather the cadaver of the convict from the gallows 'as Joseph and Nicodemus had done with Christ'; it then instructed them to hand the corpse over to the Senior Brother, prefigured in the sculpture by St John the Baptist who is shown lovingly receiving Christ's body from his companions.[9] The effect was to focus the brothers' minds on the relationship between the quick and the dead, and, of course, on death itself. So conscientious were Mañara's brothers that the great English diarist Samuel Pepys, visiting Seville in 1683, commented that in Spain 'a man hanged has the finest burial'.[10]

And in that context this iconic sculptural group at the heart of the altarpiece took on a much darker and more personal symbolism for Mañara. In a starkly and startlingly complementary location at the diametrically opposite end of the church, in the atrium through which the brothers entered, he erected his own tomb, where the visitor was greeted with the inscription: 'Here lie the bones of the worst man ever to have lived in the world. Pray to God for him.'[11]

Beyond this overpoweringly personal monument to mortality, the visitor is brutally confronted to left and right – on both arrival and departure – by two of the most startling and horrifying images in the whole phantasmagoric pantheon of high Baroque art: *Finis Gloriae Mundi*, the End of Worldly Glories, and *In Ictu Oculi*, In the Blink of an Eye. Commissioned by Mañara from Valdés Leal, who painted them in a vividly hyper-realistic, almost photographic style, these 'hieroglyphs of the end times' stare back at the viewer in stark and shocking contrast to Murillo's gently sentimental images of earthly mercy and human charity. They are a ferocious reminder of death; but then Mañara was so obsessed by death and decay as an invitation to piety and good works that he spelled out his ghastly catechism in his *Discourses on the Truth*, published in 1670. This relentless exhortation to a constant awareness of mortality and piety lays out his vision of death as the spiritual driving force behind true humanity and La Caridad. It is also a fascinating insight into Mañara's orchestration of Valdés Leal's art. 'We should see our own death-shrouds every day,' Mañara told his readers and his brethren, 'to remind us we will be covered in dirt and trodden on by everyone, for you will soon forget your honours and status in this world.'[12]

The *Finis Gloriae Mundi* accomplishes that purpose by depicting the grim reality of a catacomb or crypt. In the foreground, the cadaver of a bishop rots in its coffin, dry skin taut across the bones, lips withered and parted by a rictus grin, white hair at his temples and his brow. Mañara's church greets you with the palpable presence of death just as his *Discourses* begin with the same bleak imagery familiar from Ortiz de Zúñiga's account of the plague. 'What can be as horrible as a dead man?' Mañara asks. 'A ghostly illusion to his friends, a horrendous sight for his loved ones.'[13]

Even the wood of the bishop's coffin shows beneath its no longer sumptuous leather lining, while beetles crawl across his mitre and chasuble and other insects feast on his putrid flesh. The corpse of a Knight of Calatrava, always identified as Mañara himself, lies next to the bishop, and in the background there is a pile of skulls and bones and a skeleton lying in a coffin.

'Consider the base maggots that must eat your body,' Mañara urged, 'and how ugly and abominable it will be in the tomb, and how your eyes that are reading these words, must be eaten by the earth, and your hands must be eaten and shrivelled, and the silks and fine clothes you wear today will become a putrid shroud, your perfumes become stench . . . What silence! You can hear nothing but the gnawing of the beetles and the worms.'[14]

Movingly, he wrote of how 'beauty and gentility' are consumed by 'earthworms' and how 'family and lineage' decay 'into the greatest loneliness. Think of your parents or your wife, if you have lost her,' and how 'the lady who wore fine clothes and brocades and diamonds on her head has the skulls of beggars as companions'.[15] Thus he evoked his own endless mourning of his dear departed Jerónima, but his message is loud and clear: death is the great leveller. 'Visit some ossuary full of skeletons and pick out the rich from the poor, the wise from the foolish, and the great from the small; they are all but bones and skulls that look the same.'[16] And, in the painting, an all-seeing owl looks out at the viewer, while in the centre at the top Christ's disembodied but wounded hand dangles a pair of scales in which symbols of sin and piety hang in the balance.

On 25 May 1681, the last great literary celebrity of the Spanish Golden Age, the virtuoso court playwright Pedro Calderón de la Barca, died in Madrid aged eighty-one. Five days earlier, drawing up his will, he wrote the stage directions for his own funeral: he asked to be buried 'wearing the Franciscan habit and rope, an Augustinian belt . . . a Carmelite scapular . . . and laid out on the cloak of Santiago'. His cadaver was to be carried to the Church of San Salvador 'uncovered, so as to compensate for the vanities of a life so publicly ill-spent through this public discovery or *desengaño* of my death'.[17]

How wonderful that the greatest dramatist in a generation should have gone to his grave in costume and on display; for Calderón, in both life and death, the world was always a stage. But for the erstwhile

master of theatrical illusion, the purpose of that final performance
was to allow his public to see the ephemeral trappings of his celebrity
humbled by the tangible permanence of death, and that denouement
was intended to be a moment of moral revelation. In his greatest play,
Life is a Dream, the captive Prince Sigismondo laments:

> In this rustic forest desert,
> Where I live so miserably,
> A living skeleton, am I,
> Animate cadaver of the dead.[18]

To contemporaries this strange 'wild man' would have evoked a soul
in Purgatory or Limbo, a human beyond the boundaries of life, an
actor with neither stage nor part; he seemed to promise that the terrifying uncertainties of life would continue in the eternity of death until
the End Times.

Calderón's splendidly clad cadaver rotting in an open coffin like the
bishop of Valdés Leal's *Finis Gloriae Mundi* was a ghoulish invitation
to similar speculation about the uncertainties of human reality.

But *Life is a Dream* and Calderón's final performance were
primarily provocations designed to help discover eternal moralities
and Christian truths that were obscured by the endless illusion of
reality. This was, in part, because reality had become overwhelmingly
depressing and often terrifying; so Spaniards tried to escape the world
or disguised its ugliness with pretty pictures. But it was also a political and philosophical phenomenon. As Spanish power was eclipsed,
with Castile bankrupt, with Seville simply now the crippled carapace
of commerce long disappeared abroad, all that Spaniards had left to
them was the illusion that is history: they were haunted by the ghosts
of Empire more than the grim reality of a broken homeland. There
was nothing left for Spaniards to do, no deeds to perform, no adventures, no conquests, no trade. Without a globe to make their own, they
retreated into a brave new world of words and pictures, representations, fictions, memories and religious obsession; a world in thrall to a
playwright's posthumous display of piety.

The following year, 1682, in Seville, in the week after the Easter
pageant to sacrifice and resurrection had been celebrated, Bartolomé

Esteban Murillo was at work in his studio on a painting of St Catherine when he fell from his scaffolding; he was sixty-five. Fatally injured, he called for a notary and began to dictate his will, but before he could finish, on 3 April, a priest gave him his last rites and administered extreme unction, and then the last great artist of the Spanish Golden Age was dead.[19]

Returning to La Caridad to gaze once more at Valdés Leal's *In Ictu Oculi*, I have come to realize that it is the perfect symbol for the 'end times' of Spanish imperialism. It is a hieroglyph, a symbol to be interpreted, an image to be read like an epitaph of Empire, in which Valdés Leal captures all the fear and desperation in an age of relentless decline and defeat. He had painted, in essence, a still life in which objects of a very Sevillian kind of material grandeur and clear imperial association are heaped upon a stone sarcophagus. There are books, works of literature and religion and expensive crimson cloth, but there are also a baton of justice, heavy gold and silver chains of office, arms and armour, an ornate sword, a papal robe and mitre and a cardinal's ornate golden crosier; for some reason only a work of art is missing, a painting or a sculpture. Culture, gold, glory and religion, each a facet of terrestrial power and influence and so of human spiritual folly, are on display. But the painting is dominated by the sinister figure of Death herself, a looming skeleton, strangely animated, her eyeless sockets leering from her skull as she grins out a gap-toothed smile; she carries a shroud instead of clothes, a plain wooden coffin rather than a carved sarcophagus, and a simple scythe. She stretches out the bare, brown bones of her right arm and pinches out the candle-flame of life.

Death's left foot rests upon a globe – where Habsburg Spain's once mighty Empire, upon which the sun once never set, had proved as temporal as life itself and now barely gleamed in its own twilight. Death, we are reminded, will for ever rule with universal equity in the realms of gold. Spain had aspired to Death's dominion and under Philip II had shone at the zenith of a troubled global heaven, the first world superpower in human history. But as the sun dipped in the western sky, Spain ceased to shine and instead glittered in the golden beams until it faded into darkness.

The mast and furled topsail of a ship are visible, depicted on the globe, a doomed reflection of the ships that Mañara, Murillo and Valdés Leal would have seen through the doorway of the church, all lined up on the banks of the Guadalquivir. We have come back to the Arenal where that first consignment of Montezuma's treasure was landed by Cortés's men in 1519, a place that for so long had indeed been the Centre of the World.

'Life is like a ship that sails quickly,' Mañara had written, 'leaving no trace nor mark where it has been. What happened to all those earthly Kings and Princes who ruled the world? Where is their majesty now?'[20]

Notes

Abbreviations

ADA   Archivo del Duque de Alba, Madrid
ADF   Archivo de los Duques de Frías, Toledo
ADM   Archivo del Duque de Medinaceli, Toledo/Seville
AGI   Archivo General de Indias, Seville
AGS   Archivo General de Simancas, Valladolid
AHN   Archivo Historico Nacional, Madrid
AMS   Archivo Medina Sidonia, Sanlúcar de Barrameda
AMT   Archivo Municipal, Toledo
ANTT   Archivo Nacional Torre do Tombo, Lisbon
APAS   Archivo del Palacio Arzobispal, Seville
ARCV   Archivo de la Real Chancillería de Valladolid
ASF   Archivio Storico del comune di Firenze, Florence
BCB   Biblioteca Central, Barcelona
BCS   Biblioteca Colombina, Seville
BL   British Library, London
BNE   Biblioteca Nacional de España, Madrid
CDI   *Colección de documentos inéditos relativos al descubrimiento,*
          conquista y organización de las antiguas posesiones españolas
          de América y Oceanía, ed. Joaquín F. Pacheco, Francisco
          de Cárdenas and Luis Torres de Mendoza, 42 vols (Madrid:
          1864–84)
CODOIN   *Colección de documentos inéditos para la historia de España*,
          ed. Martín Fernández Navarrete et al., 112 vols (Madrid:
          1842–95)
IVDJ   Instituto de Valencia de Don Juan, Madrid
RILCE   *Revista Instituto de Lengua y Cultura Españolas*.

Epigraph

1   Miguel de Cervantes Saavedra, *The History and Adventures of the Renowned
    Don Quixote*, trans. Tobias Smollett (London: 1796).

    All other translations are my own unless quoted from an English secondary
    source.

Part I   Prologue

1   *CDI*, 12:155–60, Letter of Juan de Rojas, 11 September 1519.
2   John Tate Lanning, 'Cortes and his First Official Remission of Treasure to Charles V', *Revista de Historia de América*, 2 (1938), 5–9; AGI: Contratación 4675; Pascual de Gayangos, *Cartas y relaciones de Hernán Cortés al Emperador Carlos V* (Paris: 1866), pp. 28–34.
3   The gold disc weighed 39lb and the silver one 24lb.
4   Gonzalo Fernández de Oviedo y Valdés, *Historia general y natural de las Indias*, ed. Juan Pérez de Tudela Bueso, 5 vols (Madrid: 1959 [1535]), 4:10.
5   Viktor Frankle, 'Hernán Cortés y la tradición de las *Siete Partidas*', *Revista de Historia de América*, 53–4 (1962), 9–74.
6   John H. Elliott, *Imperial Spain, 1469–1716* (London: 1963), p. 135; Hugh Thomas, *The Conquest of Mexico* (London: 1993), p. 347.

1   Realms of Gold

1   John M. Headly, 'The Emperor and his Chancellor: Disputes over Empire, Administration and Pope (1519–1529)', in José Martínez Millán and Ignacio J. Ezquerra Revilla (eds), *Carlos V y la quiebra del humanismo político en Europa (1530–1558)*, 4 vols (Madrid: 2001), 1:21–36, p. 23 n. 4 refs C. Bornate (ed.), 'Historia vite et gestorum per dominum magnum cancellarium', in *Miscellanea di storia Italiana*, 48 (1915), 233–568, p. 405.
2   Ramón Carande, *Carlos V y sus banqueros*, ed. Antonio-Miguel Bernal (Barcelona: 2000 [1943]), p. 300; Richard Ehrenberg, *Capital and Finance in the Age of the Renaissance: A Study of the Fuggers and their Connections*, trans. H. M. Lucas (New York: 1928 [1922]), pp. 77–8.
3   Raymond Turner, 'Oviedo's *Claribalte*: The First American Novel', *Romance Notes*, 6 (1964), 65–8.
4   Bartolomé de las Casas, *Historia de las Indias*, ed. Agustín Millares Carlo, 3 vols (Mexico City and Buenos Aires: 1951), 2:441–4.
5   Ibid., 3:340–4.
6   Oviedo, *Historia*, 3:62–3.
7   Las Casas, *Historia*, 3:311–12.
8   Oviedo makes the claim in his *Batallas y Quinquagenas*, quoted by Juan Pérez de Tudela Bueso, 'Estudio preliminar: vida y escritos de Gonzalo Fernández de Oviedo', in Oviedo, *Historia*, 1:v–clxxv, pp. xxiii–xxiv; the claim is disputed by Álvaro Félix Bolaños, 'El primer cronista de Indias frente al "mare magno" de la crítica', *Cuadernos Americanos*, 20:2 (1990), 42–61, pp. 48–50; also see J. G. Cobo Borda, 'El Sumario de Gonzalo Fernández de Oviedo', *Cuadernos Hispanoamericanos*, 427–30 (1986), 63–77, pp. 63–4; and Juan Pérez de Tudela Bueso, 'Rasgos del semblante espiritual de Gonzalo Fernández de Oviedo: la hidaguía caballeresca ante el nuevo mundo', *Revista de Indias*, 17 (1957), 391–443, pp. 413–15.
9   Oviedo, *Historia*, 1:198.
10 Whom John Keats famously confused with 'stout Cortez' in his sonnet 'On First Looking into Chapman's Homer', published in 1816.
11 Oviedo, *Historia*, 3:276–7.

12 Ibid., 3:62; Manuel Ballesteros Gabrois, *Gonzalo Fernández de Oviedo* (Madrid: 1981), p. 106.

13 Ernesto J. Castillero, 'Gonzalo Fernández de Oviedo y Valdés, veedor de Tierra Firme', *Revista de Indias*, 17 (1957), 521–40, p. 536.

14 Juan Boscán, *Obras*, ed. Carlos Clavería (Barcelona: 1991 [1543]), p. 392:

> Garcilaso que al bien siempre aspiraste:
> y siempre con tal fuerça le seguiste,
> que a pocos passos que tras él corriste,
> en todo enteramente l'alcançaste . . .

15 Antonio Gallego Morell, *Garcilaso de la Vega y sus comentaristas* (Granada: 1966), pp. 15–16, 25–7; María de la Cinta Zunino Garrido, 'Boscán and Garcilaso as Rhetorical Models in the English Renaissance: The Case of Abraham Fraunce's *The Arcadian Rhetorike*', *Atlantis*, 27:2 (2005), 119–34.

16 Frank Goodwyn, 'New Light on the Historical Setting of Garcilaso's Poetry', *Hispanic Review*, 46:1 (1978), 1–22.

17 Paul Julian Smith, 'Garcilaso's Homographesis', in *Estudios de literatura española del Siglo de Oro dedicados a Elias L. Rivers* (Madrid: 1992), 243–52, and 'Homographesis in Salicio's Song', in Marina S. Brownlee and Hans Ulrich Gumbrecht (eds), *Cultural Authority in Golden Age Spain* (Baltimore: 1995), 131–42; Aurora Ermida Ruiz, book review, Richard Helgerson, *A Sonnet from Carthage: Garcilaso de la Vega and the New Poetry of the Sixteenth Century* (Philadelphia: 2007), *Modern Philology*, 108:3 (2011), E158–61, p. E160.

18 Francisco de Borja de San Román y Fernández, 'Documentos de Garcilaso en el Archivo de Protocolos de Toledo', *Boletín de la Real Academica de la Historia*, 83 (1918), 515–36; and 'Garcilaso, desterrado de Toledo', *Boletín de la Real Academia de Bellas Artes y Ciencias Históricas de Toledo*, 2:5 (1919), 193–5.

19 Carmen Vaquero Serrano, *Garcilaso: Poeta del amor, caballero de la guerra* (Madrid: 2002), pp. 19–22.

20 *Calendar of State Papers: Spanish, 1509–1525*, p. 307.

21 David Starkey, *The Queens of Henry VIII* (London: 2003), p. 185.

22 Juan Ginés de Sepúlveda, *Obras completas*, vol. 1, *Historia de Carlos V: libros I–V* [c.1556], ed. and trans. E. Rodríguez Peregrina (Pozoblanco: 1995), bk 2, ch. 10, pp. 40–2.

23 Joseph Pérez, *La revolución de las comunidades de Castilla (1520–1521)*, trans. Juan José Faci Lacasta (Madrid: 1979 [1970]), pp. 141–5; AGS: Estado 16, f. 416.

24 Henry R. Wagner, 'Translation of a Letter from the Archbishop of Cosenza to Petrus de Acosta', *Hispanic American Historical Review*, 9:3 (1929), 361–3.

25 Peter Martyr d'Anghiera, *De Orbe Novo*, trans. Francis A. McNutt, 2 vols (New York and London: 1912), 2:38–9, 46.

26 Alonso de Santa Cruz, *Crónica del Emperador Carlos V*, 4 vols (Madrid: 1920 [c.1550]), 1:223.

27 Fray Prudencio de Sandoval, *Historia del Emperador Carlos V, Rey de España*, ed. Gregorio Urbano Dargallo, 9 vols (Madrid: 1846 [1634]), 2:32.

28 Santa Cruz, *Crónica*, 1:224.

29 Sandoval, *Historia*, 2:33–5.

30 AGI: Indiferente, 420, l.8, ff. 173v–175r; *CODOIN*, ed. Martín Fernández Navarrete et al., 112 vols (Madrid: 1842–95), 1:472, see note attributed to Juan Bautista Muñoz.

31 Pérez, *Revolución*, pp. 148–50, 150 n. 135.

32 Frank Goodwyn, 'Garcilaso de la Vega, Representative in the Spanish Cortes', *Modern Language Notes*, 82:2 (1967), 225–9, pp. 227–8 n. 7 refs Gonzalo de Ayora, 'Relación de lo sucedido en las Comunidades . . .', BNE: Ms 1779, ff. 25–25v; in fact, the speech is attributed to Garcilaso, which seems extremely unlikely, albeit not impossible.

33 Pérez, *Revolución*, p. 154 n. 148.

34 John Adamson, 'Introduction: The Making of the Ancien-Régime Court, 1500–1700', in John Adamson (ed.), *The Princely Courts of Europe: 1500–1750* (London: 1999), 7–41.

2 Holy Roman Emperor

1 José María de Azcárate, *Alonso de Berruguete: Cuatro Ensayos* (Valladolid: 1963), appendix 1.

2 *Calendar of State Papers: Venetian, 1520–1526*, p. 35.

3 David Loades, *Mary Tudor: The Tragical History of the First Queen of England* (Kew: 2006), p. 18.

4 Albrecht Dürer, *Albrecht Dürer: Diary of his Journey to the Netherlands, 1520, 1521*, ed. J. A. Goris and G. Marlier (London: 1970), p. 37.

5 Sandoval, *Historia*, 2:277–87; Karl Brandi, *The Emperor Charles V*, trans. C. V. Wedgwood (London: 1965 [1939]), p. 123.

6 Lewis Hanke, *All Mankind is One: A Study of the Disputation between Bartolomé de las Casas and Juan Ginés de Sepúlveda in 1550 on the Intellectual and Religious Capacity of the American Indians* (DeKalb, Ill.: 1974), p. 6.

7 Richard Maurice, *Martin Luther: The Christian between God and Death* (Cambridge, Mass. and London: 1999), pp. 285–7; Gerhard Brendler, *Martin Luther: Theology and Revolution*, trans. Claude R. Foster Jr (New York and Oxford: 1991), pp. 188–9; The Holy Bible, Vulgate, Revelations 17:1–4, Douay–Rheims translation: http://www.drbo.org/chapter/73017.htm.

8 Marcel Bataillon, 'Un problema de influencia de Erasmo en España. El *Elogio de la locura*', in *Erasmo y Erasmismo*, trans. Carlos Pujol (Barcelona: 1977 [1971]), 327–46.

9 Abridged from Henry C. Bettenson, *Documents of the Christian Church*, 4th edn (Oxford and New York: 1986), pp. 212–14.

10 Brandi, *Charles V*, pp. 131–2.

11 Vaquero Serrano, *Garcilaso*, p. 64

12 Stephen Haliczer, *The Comuneros of Castile: The Forging of a Revolution, 1475–1521* (Madison and London: 1981), pp. 3–4, 3.

13 Pedro de Alcocer, *Relación de algunas cosas que pasaron en estos reinos desde que murió la reina católica doña Isabel, hasta que se acabaron las comunidades en la ciudad de Toledo* (Seville: 1872), p. 42.

14 Ibid., p. 44.

15 Bethany Aram, *Juana the Mad: Sovereignty and Dynasty in Renaissance Europe* (Baltimore: 2005 [2001]), p. 126.

16 Pérez, *Revolución*, pp. 185–6.

17 Aram, *Juana*, p. 127.

18 Ibid., p. 83.

19 Ibid., pp. 54–5.
20 Sandoval, *Historia*, 1:84–94.
21 Aram, *Juana*, pp. 100–1, 132.
22 Ibid., p. 101.
23 Santa Cruz, *Crónica*, 1:282–93.
24 Manuel Angel Fernández Álvarez, *La España del emperador Carlos V (1500–1558: 1517–1556)*, vol. 18 of *Historia de España*, ed. Ramón Menéndez Pidal (Madrid: 1979 [1966]), p. 30.
25 Santa Cruz, *Crónica*, 1:293–328, 294, 314.
26 Pérez, *Revolución*, pp. 305–7, 307; Manuel Danvila y Collado, *Historia crítica y documentada de las Comunidades de Castilla*, 5 vols (Madrid: 1897–9), 3:430, 558.
27 Sepúlveda, *Carlos V*, 1:73.
28 Vaquero Serrano, *Garcilaso*, pp. 80–1.
29 Antonio Gallego Morell, *Garcilaso: documentos completos* (Madrid: 1976), doc. 4; AGS: Continos, leg. 5.
30 Daniel Heiple, *Garcilaso de la Vega and the Italian Renaissance* (University Park, PA: 1994), p. 223.
31 I quote and paraphrase from Ignatius Loyola, *The Autobiography of St. Ignatius*, ed. J. F. X. O'Conor (New York: 1900), pp. 19–28.
32 Elliott, *Imperial Spain*, p. 149.
33 Aurelio Espinosa, *The Empire of the Cities: Emperor Charles V, the Comunero Revolt, and the Transformation of the Spanish System* (Leiden and Boston: 2008), pp. 84ff.; Henry Kamen, *Spain, 1469–1714: A Society of Conflict* (London and New York: 1983), p. 79.
34 Vaquero Serrano, *Garcilaso*, p. 94.

3 Isabella of Portugal

1 Contrast, for example, Elliott, *Imperial Spain*, p. 159, and A. W. Lovett, *Early Habsburg Spain, 1517–1598* (Oxford: 1986), p. 39, with: Pérez, *Revolución*; Haliczer, *The Comuneros of Castile*, esp. pp. 209–35; and Kamen, *Spain, 1469–1714*, p. 81.
2 Aurelio Espinosa, *Empire*, esp. pp. 17–33.
3 Santa Cruz, *Crónica*, 2:81.
4 Sandoval, *Historia*, 4:220.
5 Helen Nader, *Liberty in Absolutist Spain: The Habsburg Sale of Towns, 1516–1700* (Baltimore and London: 1990), p. 34.
6 Santa Cruz, *Crónica*, 2:436.
7 Juan José López and Carmen Vaquero Serrano, '¿Garcilaso traicionado? María de Jesús, hija de Guiomar Carrillo', *Lemir*, 14 (2010), 57–68.
8 María del Carmen Mazarío Coleto, *Isabella de Portugal* (Madrid: 1951), p. 3.
9 Jorge Sebastián Lozano, 'Choices and Consequences: The Construction of Isabel de Portugal's Image', in Theresa Earenfight (ed.), *Queenship and Political Power in Medieval and Early Modern Spain* (Aldershot: 2005), 145–162, p. 152.
10 Ibid., p. 150 n. 11 refs Pietro Aretino, *Lettere*, ed. Paolo Procaccioli, *Edizione nazionale delle opere di Pietro Aretino*, 4 vols (Rome: 1997), 3:42; this was probably the work by William Scrots now in the National Museum of Poland at

Poznan, see *Tiziano*, exhibition catalogue, ed. Miguel Falomir (Madrid: 2003), cat. 30.

11   Sebastián Lozano, p. 153 n. 25 refs Joanna Woodall, 'An Exemplary Consort: Antonis Mor's Portrait of Mary Tudor', *Art History*, 14:2 (1991), 81–103.

12   *Tiziano*, ed. Falomir, cat. 30.

13   Mónica Gómez-Salvago Sánchez, *Fastos de una boda real en la Sevilla del quinientos (estudios y documentos)* (Seville: 1998), p. 56 n. 56 refs Gonzalo Fernández de Oviedo, 'Relación de lo sucedido en la prisión del rey de Francia', in *CODOIN*, 38:404–530, p. 447; and p. 56 n. 57 refs Francisco de Andrada, *Cronica do mvyto alto e mvito poderoso rey destes reynos de Portugal dom Ioao III deste nome* (Lisbon: 1613).

14   Gómez-Salvago, *Fastos*, pp. 56–7 nn. 164 and 165 ref. Luis de Sousa, *Anais de D. Joao III*, 3 vols (Lisbon: 1938), 1:270–1.

15   Gómez-Salvago, *Fastos*, p. 60 n. 175 refs Andrada, *Cronica*, ff. 113r–v.

16   Gómez-Salvago, *Fastos*, p. 60 n. 178 refs Oviedo, 'Relación', p. 448.

17   Fernando Checa Cremades (ed.), *Los inventarios de Carlos V y la familia imperial/The Inventories of Charles V and the Imperial Family*, 3 vols (Madrid: 2010), pp. 1214ff.

18   Sebastián Lozano, 'Choices', pp. 145–62.

19   Checa Cremades (ed.), *Los inventarios*, pp. 1222–4.

20   Florence Lewis May, 'Spanish Brocade for Royal Ladies', *Pantheon*, 23 (1965), 8–15, p. 12.

21   Gómez-Salvago, *Fastos*, p. 75 n. 249 refs Sousa, *Anais*, p. 272.

22   Except where an alternative source is indicated in the notes, the following is abridged and paraphrased from Santa Cruz, *Crónica*, 2:224–30.

23   Oviedo, 'Relación', p. 450; 'Recibimientos que fueron hechos al invictíssimo César don Carlos V', in Gómez-Salvago, *Fastos*, doc. 23, pp. 247–60, BCS: Ms 59–1-5, f. 22v.

24   'Recibimientos', ff. 22r–v, in Gómez-Salvago, *Fastos*, doc. 23.

25   Oviedo, 'Relación', p. 452.

26   Mazarío Coleto, *Isabella de Portugal*, p. 48 n. 35 refs ANTT: Corpo Cronológico 1ª-33–114.

27   Alonso Enríquez de Guzmán, *Libro de la vida de Alonso Enríquez de Guzmán*, ed. Howard Keniston (Madrid: 1960), p. 72.

28   Antonio Rodríguez Villa, 'El Emperador Carles V y su Corte', *Boletín de la Academia de la Historia*, 42–4 (1903–5): Letter of 24 September 1530; Mazarío Coleto, *Isabella*, pp. 170, 103.

29   Vaquero Serrano, *Garcilaso*, pp. 153–8.

30   Ibid., p. 152.

31   Santa Cruz, *Crónica*, 2:249.

32   Vaquero Serrano, *Garcilaso*, p. 159.

33   Gallego Morell, *Garcilaso: documentos*, docs 18, 19, 21, 88.

34   Antonio Gallego Morell, 'La corte de Carlos V en la Alhambra en 1526', in *Miscelánea de estudios dedicados al profesor Antonio Marín Ocete*, 2 vols (Granada: 1974), 1:267–94, pp. 272, 275.

35   Ibid., p. 274 refs Adolf Hasenclever, 'Die tagebuchartigen Aufzeichnungen des pfälzischen Hofarztes D. Johannes Lange über seine Reise nach Granada im Jahre 1526', *Archiv für Kulturgeschichte*, 5:4 (1907), 385–439, p. 420.

36 Christoph Weiditz, *Das Trachtenbuch des Christoph Weiditz von seinen Reisen nach Spanien (1529) und den Niederlanden (1531/32)*, ed. Theodore Hampe (Berlin and Leipzig: 1927), plate 37/38.
37 Mazarío Coleto, *Isabella*, pp. 79–86.
38 Joan Boscán, *Las obras de Boscán y algunas de Garcilaso de la Vega repartidas en quatro libros* (Barcelona: 1543), f. 20.
39 Heiple, *Garcilaso*, pp. 77ff.
40 Richard Helgerson, *A Sonnet from Carthage: Garcilaso de la Vega and the New Poetry of Sixteenth-Century Europe* (Philadelphia: 2007), p. 5.
41 Santa Cruz, *Crónica*, 2:267–8.
42 Gallego Morell, 'La corte', pp. 275–6.
43 Fernando Marías, 'El palacio de Carlos V en Granada: formas romanas, usos castellanos', in M. J. Redondo Cantera and M. A. Zalma (eds), *Carlos V y las artes: promoción artística y familia imperial* (Valladolid: 2000), 107–28, p. 112 n. 20 refs Real Academia de Historia: Colección Salazar y Castro, B 75, ff. 50–1v.
44 Earl E. Rosenthal, *The Palace of Charles V in Granada* (Princeton: 1985), p. 18 n. 91, Letter dated 8 June 1526.
45 Marías, 'Palacio de Carlos V', p. 114.
46 M. Gómez-Moreno, 'Juan de Herrera y Francisco Mora en Santa María de la Alhambra', *Archivo español de arte*, 14:40 (1940), 5–18, pp. 10–11.
47 Rosenthal, *Palace*, Documentary Appendix.
48 Ibid., p. 265, Documentary Appendix, doc. 1, BNE: Ms 3315, ff. 294r–v, 30 November 1527, Charles V to Luis Hurtado de Mendoza, and pp. 265–6, doc. 2, AGS: Estado 16, f. 401, February 1528, Luis Hurtado de Mendoza to Charles V.

4   Arms and Letters: Garcilaso and Alba

1 Sandoval, *Historia*, 5:43–4.
2 Alejandro Coreleu, 'La contribución de Juan Ginés de Sepúlveda a la edición de los textos de Aristoteles y de Alejandro de Afrodisias', *Humanistica Lovaniensia: Journal of Neo-Latin Studies*, 43 (1994), 231–45; and 'The *Fortuna* of Juan Ginés de Sepúlveda's Translations of Aristotle and of Alexander of Aphrodisias', *Journal of the Warburg and Courtauld Institutes*, 59 (1996), 325–32.
3 Sepúlveda, *Carlos V*, 2:36, 7.4–5.
4 Ibid., 2:37, 7.7 and 2:34, 7.1–2.
5 Ibid., 2.38–40.
6 Santa Cruz, *Crónica*, 2:434–48.
7 Sandoval, *Historia*, 5:215, 228–30.
8   No las francesas armas odiosas,
         en contra puesta del airado pecho,
         ni en los guardados muros con pertrecho
         los tiros y saetas ponzoñosas;
         no las ascaramuzas peligrosas,
         ni aquel fiero ruido contrahecho
         d'aquel que para Júpiter fue hecho
         por manos de Vulcano artificiosas,
         pudieron, aunque más yo me ofrecía

a los peligros de la dura guerra,
quitar una hora sola de mi hado;
mas infición de aire en solo un día
me quitó al mundo y m'ha en ti sepultado,
Parténope, tan lejos de mi tierra.

9 Santa Cruz, *Crónica*, 2:454–8.

10 Peter Marzahl, 'Communication and Control in the Political System of Emperor Charles V: The First Regency of Empress Isabella', in Wim Blockmans and Nicolette Mont (eds), *The World of the Emperor Charles V* (Amsterdam: 2004), 83–96.

11 Sandoval, *Historia*, 5:343.

12 Gallego Morell, *Garcilaso: Documentos*, doc. 22; Frank Goodwyn, 'New Light on the Historical Setting of Garcilaso's Poetry', *Hispanic Review*, 46:1 (1978), 1–22.

13 Gallego Morell, *Garcilaso: Documentos*, doc. 23.

14 *Calendar of State Papers: Spanish, 1529–1530*, p. 668.

15 Eustaquio Fernández de Navarrete, *Vida del célebre poeta Garcilaso de la Vega* (Madrid: 1850), p. 208; Gallego Morell, *Garcilaso: Documentos*, doc. 24.

16 Brandi, *Charles V*, p. 316.

17 Gallego Morell, *Garcilaso: Documentos*, doc. 46.

18 The journey is recorded in Eclogue II, lines 1433–1511; see Garcilaso de la Vega, *Obras completas con comentario*, ed. Elias L. Rivers (Madrid: 2001 [1981]); the translation is my own, but draws on J. H. Wiffin (ed. and trans.), *The Works of Garcilasso de la Vega Surnamed the Prince of Castilian Poets* (London: 1823), pp. 251–5.

19 Los montes Pyreneos, que se 'stima
de abaxo que la cima está en el cielo
y desde arriba el suelo en el infierno,
en medio del invierno atravesava.
La nieve blanqueava, y las correintes
por debaxo de puentes cristalinas
y por eladas minas van calladas ...

20 Luego pudiera verse de traviesso
venir por un espesso bosque ameno,
de buenas yervas lleno y medicina,
Esculapio, y camina no parando
hasta donde Fernando estava en lecho;
entró conpie derecho, y parecía
que le restituía en tanta fuerça ...

21 Con amorosos ojos, adelante,
Carlo, César triumphate, le abrazava
quando desembarcava en Ratisbona
[...]
estava el magisterio de la tierra
convocado a la guerra [...] y en el punto
que a sí le vieron junto se prometen
de quanto allí acometen la vitoria.

22 Henry Kamen, *Empire: How Spain became a World Power, 1492–1763* (New York: 2003), p. 71.
23 Garcilaso, *Obras completas*, Canción II, lines 27–9.
24 Gallego Morell, *Garcilaso: Documentos*, doc. 67.
25 Henry Kamen, *Philip of Spain* (New Haven and London: 1997), pp. 4–7.
26 Javier Lorenzo, 'After Tunis: Petrarchism and Empire in the Poetry of Garcilaso de la Vega', *Hispanofilia*, 141 (2004), 17–30.
27 Gervasio de Artiñano y Galdácano, *La arquitectura naval* (Madrid: 1920), pp. xxxiv, 190–1.
28 Hendrik J. Horn, *Jan Cornelisz Verymeyen: Painter of Charles V and his Conquest of Tunis: Paintings, Etchings, Drawings, Cartoons & Tapestries* (Doornspijk: 1989), Introduction.
29 Sepúlveda, *Historia*, 1:xxxii–xxxiii.
30 Ibid., 10:27–8, 11:6, 11:7.
31 Garcilaso, *Obras completas*, Sonnet 33.
32 Santa Cruz, *Crónica*, 3:270.
33 Sepúlveda, *Historia*, 10:30, 12, 10.
34 Hugh Thomas, *The Golden Age: The Spanish Empire of Charles V* (London: 2011), p. 366.
35 Kamen, *Empire*, p. 72.
36 Gallego Morell, *Garcilaso: Documentos*, docs 72–82.
37 Vaquero Serrano, *Garcilaso*, p. 296.
38 Ibid., pp. 300–1.

5 Rule of Law

1 Anon., *Cortes de los antiguos reinos de León y de Castilla*, 5 vols (Madrid: 1861–1903), 4:538.
2 Aurelio Espinosa, *Empire*, pp. 207ff.
3 Richard L. Kagan, *Lawsuits and Litigants in Castile: 1500–1700* (Chapel Hill: 1981), p. 14 n. 34 refs ARCV: Libros Civiles, caja 63.
4 Kagan, *Lawsuits*, p. 84 n. 12 refs AMT: Pleitos, Navahermosa (1577).
5 Kagan, *Lawsuits*, pp. 12–13.
6 Ibid., p. 12 nn. 23 and 24 ref. ADF: leg. 190, n. 11; AHN: Osuna, leg. 249, secc. 1, f. 1.
7 Kagan, *Lawsuits*, p. 12 n. 26 refs AMS: secc. II, *carpeta* 201.
8 Kagan, *Lawsuits*, p. 68 n. 167 refs AGS: CC, leg. 2715, *Visita* to the chancillería of Valladolid (1554).
9 Kagan, *Lawsuits*, p. 37 n. 58 refs John B. Owens, 'Despotism, Absolutism, and the Law in Renaissance Spain: Toledo versus the Counts of Belalcázar (1445–1574)', Ph.D., University of Wisconsin, 1972.
10 Kagan, *Lawsuits*, pp. 7 fig. 1, and 16–17, 17.
11 Ibid., pp. 100–1, 100 n. 58 refs AGS: CC, leg. 2715.
12 Francisco Lyana Serrano, *El Palacio del Infantado en Guadalajara* (Guadalajara: 1996), p. 50; Antonio Márquez, *Los alumbrados: Orígenes y filosofía, 1525–1559* (Madrid: 1972).
13 Most of the documents recording the case were published by Narciso Alonso Cortés, *Casos cervantinos que tocan a Valladolid* (Madrid: 1916), pp. 23–53; those

and additional documents are in Krzysztof Sliwa, *El licenciado Juan de Cervantes: Efemérides del licenciado Juan de Cervantes, documentos y datos para una biografía del abuelo paterno del autor del* Quijote (Kassel: 2001), pp. 145–71.

14   Kagan, *Lawsuits*, p. 36.

15   Antonio de Remesal, *Historia general de las Indias occidentales y particular de la gobernación de Chiapas y Guatemala*, ed. Carmelo Sáenz de Santa María, 2 vols (Mexico City: 1988 [1619]), 1:212ff.; Oviedo, *Historia*, 1:38–9.

16   Papal Encyclicals Online: http://www.papalencyclicals.net/Paul03/p3subli. htm.

17   Richard Kagan, 'Universities in Castile, 1500–1700', *Past & Present*, 49 (1970), 44–71.

18   Francisco de Vitoria, *Political Writings*, ed. Anthony Pagden and Jeremy Lawrance (Cambridge: 1991), pp. 259–63.

19   Ibid., pp. 287–90.

20   Ibid., p. 278.

21   James Brown Scott, *The Spanish Origin of International Law: Francisco de Vitoria and his Law of Nations* (Oxford: 1934).

22   Martti Koskenniemi, 'Empire and International Law: The Real Spanish Contribution', *University of Toronto Law Journal*, 61 (2011), 1–36, pp. 11–12.

23   James Boswell, *The Life of Samuel Johnson*, 4 vols (London: 1823), 1:387; quoted on his title page by Scott, *The Spanish Origin of International Law*.

24   *Leyes y ordenanzas nuevamente hechas por S. M. para la gobernación de las indias, y buen tratamiento y conservación de los indios*, at Biblioteca Virtual Miguel de Cervantes: http://bib.cervantesvirtual.com/servlet/SirveObras/06922752100647273089079/p0000026.htm.

25   Juan Cristóbal Calvete de Estrella, *Rebelión de Pizarro en el Perú y Vida de D. Pedro Gasca*, 2 vols (Madrid: 1889), 1:98–9.

26   Hanke, *All Mankind*, p. 60.

27   Anthony Pagden, *The Fall of Natural Man: The American Indian and the Origins of Comparative Ethnology* (Cambridge and New York: 1982), p. 109.

28   Demetrio Ramos, *Ximénez de Quesada en su relación con los cronistas y el Epítome de Conquista del Nuevo Reino de Granada* (Seville: 1972), p. 199.

29   Biblioteca Virtual Miguel de Cervantes: http://www.cervantesvirtual.com/bib/historia/CarlosV/7_4_testamento.shtml.

30   Vitoria, *Political Writings*, pp. 233–8.

31   Quoted in Hanke, *All Mankind*, p. 67.

32   Felipe Pereda, 'The Shelter of the Savage: "From Valladolid to the New World"', *Medieval Encounters*, 16 (2010), 268–359.

33   Juan Ginés de Sepúlveda, *Demócrates Segundo o de las justas causas de la guerra contra los indios*, ed. and trans. Ángel Losada (Madrid: 1984 [c.1548]).

34   Pagden, *Fall*, pp. 113, 112.

35   Ibid., p. 114.

36   Sepúlveda, *Demócrates Segundo*, pp. 35, 33.

37   Ibid., pp. 28–9.

38   Ibid., p. 38.

39   Hanke, *All Mankind*, p. 80.

40   Ibid., p. 84.

41 Ibid., p. 92 n. 43.

42 Ibid., pp. 97–8 n. 53.

43 Lewis Hanke, *Aristotle and the American Indians* (London: 1959), p. 40.

44 William Bradford (ed.), *Correspondence of the Emperor Charles V and his ambassadors at the courts of England and France: from the original letters in the imperial family archives at Vienna; with a connecting narrative and biographical notices of the Emperor and of some of the most distinguished officers of his army and household; together with the Emperor's itinerary from 1519–1551* (London: 1850).

45 David C. Goodman, *Power and Penury: Government, Technology and Science in Philip II's Spain* (Cambridge: 1988), p. 2 n. 3 refs BL: Egerton Ms, 442, ff. 144–6.

46 Leonard Francis Simpson (ed. and trans.), *The Autobiography of the Emperor Charles V. Recently discovered in the Portuguese language by Baron Kervyn de Lettenhove* (London: 1863), pp. 143–50.

47 Brandi, *Charles V*, pp. 569–70; Pierre Bourdeille (Seigneur de Brantôme) and André Vicomte de Bourdeille, *Oeuvres complètes*, ed. J. A. C. Buchon, 2 vols (Paris: 1838), 1:27.

48 Sheila Hale, *Titian: His Life* (London: 2012), p. 493.

6 *Death of the Emperor*

1 Goodman, *Power and Penury*, p. 2 n. 3 refs BL: Egerton Ms, 442, ff. 144–6.

2 J. M. Rodríguez-Salgado, 'The Court of Philip II of Spain', in Ronald G. Asch and Adolf M. Birke (eds), *Princes, Patronage and the Nobility: The Court at the Beginning of the Modern Age, 1450–1650* (New York: 1991), 205–44, p. 206; Adamson, 'Introduction', pp. 7–8.

3 Adamson, 'Introduction', pp. 28–9.

4 David Starkey, 'Representation through Intimacy: A Study in the Symbolism of Monarchy and Court Office in Early-Modern England', in Ioan Lewis (ed.), *Symbols and Sentiments: Cross-cultural Studies in Symbolism* (London: 1977), 187–224, pp. 213, 204, 211.

5 Gonzalo Fernández de Oviedo, *Libro de la cámara real del príncipe don Juan, oficios de su casa y servicio ordinario*, ed. Santiago Fabregat Barrios (Valencia: 2006 [c.1548]), pp. 94, 87, 110.

6 Baltasar Castiglione, *Los quatro libros, del cortesano compuestos en italiano por el conde Balthasar Castellon, y agora nueuamente traduzidos en lengua castellana por Boscan* (Barcelona: 1534), Prologue.

7 Juan Christóval Calvete de Estrella, *El felicísimo viaje del muy alto y muy poderoso Príncipe don Phelippe*, ed. Paloma Cuenca (Madrid: 2001 [1552]), p. 41.

8 Vicente Álvarez, *Relation du Beau Voyage que fit aux Pays-Bas en 1548 le Prince Philippe d'Espagne*, trans. M. T. Dovillée (Brussels: 1964 [c.1551]), p. 42; Calvete de Estrella, *Felicísimo*, p. 72.

9 Álvarez, *Relation*, pp. 42–3.

10 Calvete de Estrella, *Felicísimo*, pp. 71–3; Álvarez, *Relation*, p. 43 records the time as 4 a.m.

11 Hale, *Titian*, pp. 512–13.
12 Álvarez, *Relation*, pp. 56, 57; Calvete, *Felicísimo*, p. 108.
13 Álvarez, *Relation*, pp. 64, 65.
14 Calvete, *Felicísimo*, pp. 126–34.
15 Álvarez, *Relation*, pp. 77–8.
16 Xavier de Salas, *El Bosco en la literatura española: discurso leído el día 30 de mayo de 1943 en la recepción pública de Don Savier de Salas en la Real Academia de Buenas Letras de Barcelona* (Barcelona: 1943), p. 11.
17 Calvete, *Felicísimo*, pp. 325–44, 326.
18 Ibid., pp. 342–4.
19 Charles O'Malley, 'Some Episodes in the Medical History of the Emperor Charles V: An Imperial Problem and the Problem of an Emperor', *Journal of the History of Medicine and Allied Sciences*, 13:4 (1958), 469–82, p. 478 n. 27 refs William van Male, *Lettres sur la vie intérieure de l'empereur Charles-Quint*, ed. J. de Reiffenberg (Brussels: 1843 [1550]), p. 38.
20 Goodman, *Power and Penury*, p. 4.
21 Brandi, *Charles V*, p. 598.
22 Fernand Braudel, *The Mediterranean and the Mediterranean World in the Age of Philip II*, trans. Siân Reynolds, 2 vols (London: 1972 [1949]), p. 916; Brandi, *Charles V*, p. 600.
23 Marino Cavalli, 'Relación de Marino Cavalli' [1551], in José García Mercadal (ed.), *Viajes de extranjeros por España y Portugal*, 3 vols (Madrid: 1952), 1:1054; O'Malley, 'Some Episodes', p. 479 n. 31 refs Eugenio Albèri (ed.), *Relazioni degli ambasciatori veneti al senato*, 15 vols (Florence: 1839–63), series 1, vol. 2, p. 211.
24 Agustín García Simón, 'Los años críticos', in Martínez Millán and Ezquerra Revilla (eds), *Carlos V y la quiebra del humanismo político*, 2:321–34.
25 *The Canons and Decrees of the Council of Trent*, trans. Rev. H. J. Schroeder (London: 1978), 25th Session.
26 Sandoval, *Historia*, 8:439.
27 Braudel, *Mediterranean*, pp. 903–31.
28 Lisa Jardine and Jerry Brotton, *Global Interests: Renaissance Art between East and West* (London: 2000), ch. 2; Jerry Brotton, 'Buying the Renaissance: Prince Charles's Art Purchases in Madrid, 1623', in Alexander Samson (ed.), *The Spanish Match: Prince Charles's Journey to Madrid, 1623* (Aldershot: 2006), 9–26, p. 15.
29 Kamen, *Philip of Spain*, p. 58; Andrés Muñoz, *Viaje de Felipe Segundo a Inglaterra*, ed. Pascual Gayangos (Madrid: 1877 [1554]), pp. 97, 113.
30 E.g. Martin A. S. Hulme, *Philip II* (London: 1906), p. 40.
31 Martin and Parker, *Armada*, p. 51.
32 Loades, *Mary Tudor*, pp. 143–4.
33 Sandoval, *Historia*, 9:104, 111.
34 *CODOIN*, 2:493–6, Philip to Ferdinand, 29 August 1557.
35 Patrick Frazer Tytler, *England under the reigns of Edward VI, and Mary, with a contemporary history of Europe*, 2 vols (London: 1839), 2:493.
36 Vicente de Cadenas y Vicent, *Carlos de Habsburgo en Yuste* (Madrid: 1990), pp. 55–7; William Stirling, *The Cloister Life of the Emperor Charles the Fifth* (London: 1853), p. 208.

37 Fray José de Sigüenza, *Fundación del Monasterio de el Escorial por Felipe II* (Madrid: 1927 [1605]), pp. 171–2.

38 Tellechea Idigoras, J. J., *Fray Bartolomé de Carranza. Mis treinta años de investigaciones Carrancianas*, 6 vols (Salamanca: 1962–81), 5:71–2; M. J. Rodríguez-Salgado, 'Charles V and the Dynasty', in Hugh Soly (ed.), *Charles V and his Time, 1500–1558* (Antwerp: 1999), 26–111, p. 110 n. 139.

39 Goodman, *Power and Penury*, p. 2 n. 3 refs BL: Egerton Ms, 442, ff. 144–6.

40 Juan Pérez de Tudela Bueso, 'Vida y escritos de Gonzalo Fernández de Oviedo', in Oviedo, *Historia*, 1:v–clxxv, p. clxvi.

41 Juan de Vandenesse, 'Diario de los viajes de Felipe II', in García Mercadal, *Viajes*, 1:1080.

7 El Escorial and El Greco

1   Miguel de Unamuno, *Andanzas y visiones españolas* (Madrid: 1922), pp. 48–9.

2   Fray Julián Zarco Cuevas (ed.), *Documentos para la Historia del Monasterio del San Lorenzo el Real de El Escorial*, 7 vols (Madrid: 1917) 2:71–140, pp. 71–2.

3   José Javier Rivera Blanco, *Juan Bautista de Toledo y Felipe II: La implantación del clasicismo en España* (Valladolid: 1984), pp. 85–100.

4   Henry Kamen, *The Escorial: Art and Power in the Renaissance* (New Haven and London: 2010), p. 77 n. 96 refs BL: Add. 28350 f. 100.

5   Rivera Blanco, *Juan Bautista*, pp. 35–6 nn. 83 and 84 ref. AGS: C. y S.R. leg. 247–1, ff. 61–2.

6   Eugenio Llaguno y Amirola and Agustín Ceán Bermúdez, *Noticias de los arquitectos y arquitectura desde su restauración . . .*, 5 vols (Madrid: 1829), 2:333.

7   George Kubler, *Building the Escorial* (Princeton: 1982), p. 26.

8   Catherine Wilkinson, 'The Escorial and the Invention of the Imperial Staircase', *Art Bulletin*, 57:1 (1975), 65–90.

9   Amancio Portabales Pichel, *Los verdaderos artifices de El Escorial* (Madrid: 1945); J. B. Bury, 'Juan de Herrera and the Escorial', *Art History*, 9:4 (1986), 428–49, p. 442; see also Rivera Blanco, *Juan Bautista de Toledo y Felipe II*, p. 22.

10 Sigüenza, *Escorial*, p. 10.

11 Geoffrey Parker, *The Grand Strategy of Philip II* (New Haven and London: 1998), esp. pp. 13–75.

12 Salas, *El Bosco en la literatura española*, p. 12.

13 Felipe Guevara, *Comentarios de la pintura* (Madrid: 1778 [1564]), pp. 41–4.

14 Sigüenza, *Escorial*, pp. 519–26.

15 The *madroño* is a type of arbutus tree; a bear attempting to eat its fruit is the symbol of Madrid.

16 Antonio de Beatis, *The Travel Journal of Antonio de Beatis: Germany, Switzerland, the Low Countries, France and Italy, 1517–1518*, ed. J. R. Hale, trans. Hale and J. M. Lindon, Hakluyt Society, 2nd series, no. 150 (London: 1979), p. 94; and see Ernst Gombrich, 'The Earliest Description of Bosch's Garden of Delight', *Journal of the Warburg and Courtauld Institutes*, 30 (1967), 403–6.

17 Francisco Pacheco, *Libro de descripción de verdaderos retratos de ilustres y memorables varones* (Seville: 1983 [1599]), p. 302.

18   Charles Hope, 'Titian as a Court Painter', *Oxford Art Journal*, 2 (1979), 7–10, p. 7.

19   Charles Hope, in conversation, 10 February 2013.

20   Carmelo Viñas Mey and Ramón Paz (eds), *Relaciones histórico-geográfico-estadisticas de los pueblos de España hechas por iniciativa de Felipe II, Provincia de Toledo* (Madrid: 1951), at http://www.uclm.es/ceclm/b_virtual/libros/Relaciones_Toledo/index.htm.

21   Alfonso Caso, 'El mapa de Teozacoalco', *Cuadernos Americanos*, 8 (1949), 145–81; Howard F. Cline, 'The Relaciones Geograficas of the Spanish Indies', *Hispanic American Historical Review*, 44:3 (1964), 341–74; Manuel Carrera Stampa, 'Relaciones Geográficas de Nueva España, siglos XVI y XVIII', *Estudios de Historia Novohispana*, 2:2 (1968), 1–31, at www.ejournal.una.mx/ehn/ehn02/EHN00212.pdf; Manuel Orozco y Berrera, 'Apuntes para la Geografía de las Lenguas y Carta Etnográfica de México', *Anales del Ministerio de Fomento* (Mexico), 6 (1881), 155–62.

22   *Relaciones histórico-geográfico-estadisticas*, pp. 398–404.

23   Bernardino de Sahagún, *Códice florentino (Historia general de las cosas de Nueva España)*, facsimile edn (Mexico City and Florence: 1979 [c.1545–90]); Francisco Fernández del Castillo (ed.), *Libros y libreros en el siglo XVI* (Mexico City: 1982), p. 513; Walden Browne, *Sahagún and the Transition to Modernity* (Norman, OK: 2000), pp. 26–36.

24   René Taylor, 'Architecture and Magic: Considerations on the Idea of the Escorial', in *Essays in the History of Architecture Presented to Rudolf Wittkower* (London: 1967), 81–107, p. 82.

25   Frances Yates, 'The Art of Ramon Lull: An Approach to It through Lull's Theory of the Elements', *Journal of the Warburg and Courtauld Institutes*, 17:1–2 (1954), 115–73.

26   Francisco Bermúdez de Pedraza, *Arte legal para estudiar la iurisprudencia* (Salamanca: 1612), p. 11.

27   Goodman, *Power and Penury*, pp. 3–4 nn. 10 and 11.

28   Gaspar Muro, *La vida de la princesa de Éboli* (Madrid: 1877), appendix 62.

29   Goodman, *Power and Penury*, p. 6 n. 20 refs IVDJ: 61(ii)/19.

30   Goodman, *Power and Penury*, p. 12 n. 45 refs Eugenio Albèri (ed.), *Relazioni degli ambasciatori veneti al senato*, 15 vols (Florence: 1839–63), series 1, vol. 3, p. 367.

31   Goodman, *Power and Penury*, p. 13 n. 52 refs BL: Add. Ms 28,357 f. 41.

32   Goodman, *Power and Penury*, p. 14 n. 57 refs IVDJ: 99/303.

33   Goodman, *Power and Penury*, p. 15 n. 64 refs BNE: Ms 2058, 'Toque de Alchimia'.

34   Paul Gillingham, 'The Strange Business of Memory: Relic Forgery in Latin America', *Past & Present*, Supplement 5 (2010), 199–226.

35   Miguel Morán and Fernando Checa, *El coleccionismo en España: De la cámara de maravillas a la galería de pinturas* (Madrid: 1985), p. 177.

36   Guy Lazure, 'Possessing the Sacred: Monarchy and Identity in Philip II's Relic Collection at the Escorial', *Renaissance Quarterly*, 60 (2007), 58–92, p. 77.

37   Ibid., p. 59; Kamen, *Philip of Spain*, p. 314.

38   Kamen, *El Escorial*, pp. 66–7.

39 Francisco Fernández Pardo, 'Reseña biográfica de Navarrete "el Mudo"', in *Navarrete 'el Mudo', pintor de Felipe II (Seguidores y Copistas)*, exhibition catalogue (Logroño: 1995), 19–140, pp. 33–5; Bernice Davidson, 'Navarrete in Rome', *Burlington Magazine*, 135:1079 (1993), 93–6, p. 94; Joaquín Yarza Luaces, 'Aspectos incograficos de la pintura de Juan Fernández Navarrete, "el Mudo" y relaciones con la contrareforma', *Boletín del Seminario de Estudios de Arte y Arqueología de la Universidad de Valladolid*, 36 (1970), 43–68.

40 Jonathan Brown, *Painting in Spain, 1500–1700* (New Haven and London: 1998), p. 62.

41 Jusepe Martínez, *Discursos practicables del nobilísmo arte de la pintura*, ed. María Elena Manrique Ara (Madrid: 2006 [1675]), p. 289.

42 Ibid., p. 290.

43 Fernando Marías and Agustín Bustamante García, *Las ideas artísticas de El Greco (Comentarios de un texto inédito)* (Madrid: 1981), pp. 80, 226.

44 Ibid., pp. 103, 229.

45 David Davies, 'El Greco's Religious Art: The Illumination and Quickening of the Spirit', in *El Greco*, exhibition catalogue, ed. David Davies (London: 2003), 45–71, p. 60.

46 Henry Kamen, *The Spanish Inquisition: An Historical Revision* (London: 1997), pp. 160–3.

47 John H. Elliott, 'El Greco's Mediterranean', in *Spain, Europe, and the Wider World 1500–1800* (London: 2009), p. 26.

48 'Creta le dio la vida y los pinceles / Toledo mejor patria donde empieza / a lograr con la muerte eternidades', in Alfonso Pérez Sánchez, 'El Greco y Toledo', in José María Llusiá and Antonio Fernández de Molina (eds), *Marañon in Toledo: sobre elogia y nostalgia de Toledo* (Cuenca: 1999), 107–36, p. 119.

49 Francisco de Borja de San Román y Fernández, 'Documentos del Greco, referentes a los cuadros de Santo Domingo del Antiguo', *Archivo Español de Arte y Arqueología*, 28 (1934), offprint, pages numbered 1–3.

50 San Román, 'Documentos', p. 2; Richard G. Mann, *El Greco and his Patrons: Three Major Projects* (Cambridge: 1986), p. 22.

51 Mann, *El Greco*, p. 24.

52 Rosemarie Mulcahy, *The Decoration of the Royal Basilica of El Escorial* (Cambridge and New York: 1994), p. 57 n. 10.

53 Davies, 'El Greco's Religious Art', p. 51.

54 John Bury, 'A Source for El Greco's "St. Maurice"', *Burlington Magazine*, 126:972 (1984), 144–7, p. 147 n. 4; Brown, *Painting in Spain*, p. 67.

55 This nonsense is adequately dealt with by P. Trevor Roper, *The World through Blunted Sight: An Inquiry into the Influence of Defective Vision on Art and Character* (London: 1970), pp. 49–51.

56 D. Elías Tormo, review of Ricardo de Orueta, *Berruguete y sus obras* (Madrid: 1917), in *Boletín de la Sociedad Española de Excursiones: Arte, Arqueología, Historia*, 26 (1918), 61–4, p. 64 n. 1.

57 José Camón Aznar, *Dominico Greco*, 2 vols (Madrid: 1950), 2:1239.

58 Harold E. Wethy, *El Greco and his School*, 2 vols (Princeton: 1962), 2:61.

59 Davies, 'El Greco's Religious Art', pp. 45–51.

8 St Teresa, Mystic Poets and the Inquisition

1 1 Corinthians, 14:34–5.
2 Ronald E. Surtz, *Writing Women in Late Medieval and Early Modern Spain: The Mothers of Saint Teresa of Avila* (Philadelphia: 1995), p. 1.
3 Allison E. Peers, *Saint Teresa of Jesus and Other Essays and Addresses* (London: 1953), p. 15.
4 Teresa de Jesús, *Castillo interior, o las moradas*, in *Obras completas*, ed. Luis Santullano, 11th edn (Madrid: 1970), morada 6, ch. 2, p. 434.
5 Teresa de Jesús, *Vida de Santa Teresa de Jesús*, in *Obras completas*, pp. 54–5; Allison Peers, *Studies of the Spanish Mystics*, 3 vols (London: 1951–60), 2:111 n. 1 refs Francisco de Ribera, *Vida de Santa Teresa de Jesús*, ed. P. Jaime Pons (Barcelona: 1908 [1590]), pp. vi & 55 n. 1.
6 Teresa, *Vida*, p. 55.
7 Ibid., p. 56.
8 Ibid., p. 53.
9 Teresa, *Castillo*, pp. 434–5.
10 Jean Baruzi, *San Juan de la Cruz y el problema de la experiencia mística*, trans. Carlos Ortega (Valladolid: 1991), p. 103 nn.1, 6–7 ref. BNE: Ms 12738, f. 613r and p. 112 n. 34 refs BNE: Ms 8568, f. 371r.
11 Baruzi, *San Juan*, pp. 203–4 nn. 108–16 ref. BNE: Ms 13460 bk 1, chs 31 and 33; 12738 ff. 1215v, 997v, 229.
12 Teresa, *Obras completas*, Letter 104, pp. 998–1000.
13 Father John the Evangelist was in the Carmelite monastery of Granada while John of the Cross was Prior; see Baruzi, *San Juan*, pp. 223–4 nn. 6–7 ref. BNE: Ms 12738, ff. 1431r, 1435.
14 San Juan de la Cruz, *Poesía*, ed. Domingo Ynduráin (Madrid: 1992), p. 263:

> 1.
> ¡Oh llama de amor viva,
> que tiernamente hieres
> de mi alma en el más profundo centro!;
> pues ya no eres esquiva,
> acaba ya, si quieres;
> rompe la tela de este dulce encuentro.
>
> 2.
> ¡Oh cauterio suave!
> ¡Oh regalada llaga!
> ¡Oh mano blanda! ¡Oh toque delicado!,
> que a vida eterna sabe
> y toda deuda paga;
> matando, muerte en vida la has trocado.
>
> 3.
> !Oh lámparas de fuego,
> en cuyos resplandores
> las profundas cavernas del sentido,
> que estaba oscuro y ciego,
> con estraños primores
> calor y luz dan junto a su querido!

4.

!Cuán manso y amoroso
recuerdas en mi seno
donde secretamente solo moras,
y en tu aspirar sabroso
de bien y gloria lleno
cuán delicadamene me enamoras!

15 The phrase is apparently Breuer's: see Sigmund Freud and Joseph Breuer, *Studies on Hysteria*, trans. James and Alix Strachey (Harmondsworth: 1974), p. 312.

16 Jacques Lacan, *Écrits: A Selection*, trans. Alan Sheridan (New York: 1977), p. 147.

17 Teresa, *Vida*, p. 177.

18 Miguel de Cervantes Saavedra, *La Galatea*, ed. Francisco López Estrada and María Teresa López García-Berdoy (Madrid: 1995 [1585]), bk 6, p. 583:

Quisiera rematar mi dulce canto
en tal sazón, pastores, con loaros
un ingenio que al mundo pone espanto
y que pudiera en éxtasis robaros.
En él cifro y recojo todo cuanto
he mostrado hasta aquí y he de mostraros:
fray Luis de León es el que digo,
a quien yo reverencio, adoro y sigo.

19 Francisco de Quevedo, 'Dedicatoria a Olivares', in *Quevedo y su poética dedicada a Olivares: Estudio y edición*, ed. E. L. Rivers (Pamplona: 1998), p. 37.

20 Pacheco, *Libro de retratos*, pp. 43–6.

21 Colin Thompson, *The Strife of Tongues: Fray Luis de León and the Golden Age of Spain* (Cambridge: 1988), pp. 6–7; Manuel Durán, *Luis de León* (New York: 1971), pp. 24, 28–9.

22 Thompson, *Strife of Tongues*, p. 6.

23 Ángel Alcalá (ed.), *Proceso inquisitorial de fray Luis de León* (Valladolid: 1991), p. xvii n. 3 refs Letter of Montemayor to Aquaviva (Prior General of the Jesuits) in Antonio Astrain, *Historia de la Compañía de Jesús en la Asistencia de España*, 6 vols (Madrid: 1912–29), 4:226; Pacheco, *Libro de retratos*, pp. 43–6.

24 John 1:1.

25 Fernando Lázaro Carreter, 'Fray Luis de León y la clasicidad', in *Fray Luis de León: Historia, humanismo, y letras*, ed. Víctor García de la Concha and Javier San José Lera (Salamanca: 1996), 15–28, pp. 17, 21–2.

26 Ibid., p. 17.

27 Thompson, *Strife of Tongues*, p. 26.

28 Luis de León, *Traducción literal y declaración del Cantar de los Cantares de Salomón* (Madrid: 1798 [c.1561]), Prologue, at http://bib.cervantesvirtual.com/servlet/SirveObras/p268/12147297718948273987213/index.htm.

29 Julio Caro Baroja, *Los judios en la España moderna y contemporanea*, 3 vols (Madrid: 1961), 1:388, and *Razas, pueblos y linajes* (Madrid: 1957), pp. 127–8.

30 George Borrow, *The Bible in Spain* (London: 1923 [1842]), chs 11 and 17, pp. 159–61 and 247–8.

31 Benzion Netanyahu, *The Origins of the Inquisition in Fifteenth Century Spain* (New York: 1995), pp. 934–7.

32   Angus MacKay, 'The Hispanic-Converso Predicament', *Transactions of the Royal Historical Society*, 5th series, 35 (1985), 159–79, p. 175 n. 75 refs F. Cantera Burgos, 'Fernando de Pulgar y los conversos', *Sefarad*, 4 (1944), 295–348, p. 308.

33   Gonzalo Fernández de Oviedo y Valdés, *Las Quinquagenas de la Nobleza de España*, ed. Vicente de la Fuente, 2 vols (Madrid: 1880), 1:279: 'Marrano propiamente quiere decir falto, porque marrar quiere dezir faltar en lengua castellana antigua; e faltar e ser falto el ombre de lo que promete es cosa de mucha vergüença.'

34   Kamen, *Spanish Inquisition*, p. 18.

35   Ibid., p. 49.

36   Ibid., pp. 236–40.

37   Ibid., p. 245 n. 56 refs Eusebio Rey, 'San Ignacio Loyola y el problema de los "Cristianos Nuevos"', *Razón y Fé*, 153 (1956), 117–204.

38   This was published by Robert Estienne and edited by the great Hebrew scholar François Vatable.

39   *Canons and Decrees*, 4th Session.

40   Alcalá, *Proceso*, p. xxv.

41   Ibid., p. 3.

42   Kamen, *Spanish Inquisition*, p. 183.

43   Ibid., p. 188 n. 52 refs AHN: Inquisition 497, f. 45.

44   Ibid., p. 191 n. 63 refs Michèle Escamilla-Colin, *Crimes et châtiments dans l'Espagne inquisitoriale*, 2 vols (Paris, 1992), 1:593–7.

45   Victoria González de Caldas, *El poder y su imagen: la Inquisición Real* (Seville: 2001), pp. 130–7.

46   Henry Charles Lea, *A History of the Inquisition of Spain*, 4 vols (New York and London: 1906–7), 3:19–20, refs AHN: Inquisición 1226, ff. 605–9.

47   Mary Elizabeth Perry, *Crime and Society in Early Modern Seville* (Hanover and London: 1980), p. 4 n. 4 refs Marcelino Menéndez y Pelayo, *Historia de los heterodoxos españoles* (Madrid, 1928), p. 112; Werner Thomas, *Los protestantes y la Inquisición en España en tiempos de Reforma y Contrarreforma* (Leuven: 2001), p. x.

48   Werner Thomas, *La represión del protestantismo en España, 1517–1648* (Leuven: 2001), p. 217.

49   Clive Griffin, *Journeymen-Printers, Heresy, and the Inquisition in Spain* (Oxford: 2005), p. 5.

50   My account here follows the 'Relación de lo que pasó en el auto que la santa inquisición hizo en la villa de Valladolid, en veinte [sic] de mayo de 1559 años, que fué domingo de la Trinidad', AGS: Estado 137, ff. 5 and 6, in José Luis González Novalín, *El inquisidor general Fernado de Valdés (1483–1568)*, 2 vols (Oviedo: 1971), 2:239–48.

51   Thomas, *Represión*, p. 242 n. 133 refs AHN: Inquisición 730, f. 23.

52   Kamen, *Spanish Inquisition*, pp. 236–8.

9   *The Netherlands: 'The Great Bog of Europe'*

1   Owen Feltham, *A Brief Character of the Low Countries under the States* (London: 1660); quotations are, in order, pp. 1, 6, 62, 41, 18, 1, 3, 2, 5. Parker uses the chapter heading 'The Great Bog of Europe' in *Grand Strategy*, p. 115.

2 Philip wrote to his sister from Segovia in French and Spanish on 17 and 20 October 1565; the quotations are from *CODOIN*, 4:328–9; AGS: Estado 525.

3 Federico Badoaro, 'Relación de España', [1557] in García Mercadal, *Viajes*, 2:1104–33.

4 Louis-Prosper Gachard, *Don Carlos et Philippe II*, 2 vols (Brussels: 1863), 1:23.

5 Two of his physicians have left accounts of the illness: Dionisio Daza Chacón, 'Relación Verdadera de la herida del Príncipe D. Carlos', in *CODOIN*, 18: 537–63; and Diego Santiago Olivares, 'Relación de la enfermedad del Príncipe . . .', in *CODOIN*, 15:554–74. For an excellent account in English see L. J. Andrew Villalón, 'Putting Don Carlos Together Again: Treatment of a Head Injury in Sixteenth-Century Spain', *Sixteenth Century Journal*, 26:2 (1995), 347–65.

6 Villalón, 'Don Carlos', p. 354.

7 Susan Verdi Webster, *Art and Ritual in Golden-Age Spain: Sevillian Confraternities and the Processional Sculpture of Holy Week* (Princeton: 1998), p. 29 n. 100 refs 'Memorias de Sevilla [1698]', BCS: Ms 84-7-19, ff. 320v–321v.

8 Villalón, 'Don Carlos', p. 356.

9 Saint-Sulpice to Catherine de Medici, Madrid, 7 October 1564, quoted in James M. Boyden, *The Courtier and the King: Ruy Gómez de Silva, Philip II, and the Court of Spain* (Berkeley: 1995), p. 132 n. 79.

10 Antonio Tiepolo, 'Relación de España', [1567] in García Mercadal, *Viajes*, 2:1147–54, p. 1152.

11 Miguel Suriano [Venetian Ambassador], 'Relación de España', [1559], in García Mercadal, *Viajes*, 2:1135–45, pp. 1144–5.

12 Boyden, *Courtier*, p. 132.

13 Henk van Nierop, 'A Beggars' Banquet: The Compromise of the Nobility and the Politics of Inversion', *European History Quarterly*, 21 (1991), 419–43, pp. 420–1; follows P. Payen, *Mémoires de Pontus Payen*, ed. Alexandre Henne, 2 vols (Brussels and The Hague: 1861), 1:139–43.

14 Enno van Gelder (ed.), *Correspondance française de Marguerite d'Autriche, Duchesse de Parme, avec Philippe II*, 3 vols (Utrecht: 1941). The quotes as follows: 2:245, Margaret to Philip, 7 July 1566; 258–64, 19 July; 326–32, 29 August.

15 Fernando Álvarez de Toledo, *Epistolario del III duque de Alba, Don Fernando Álvarez de Toledo*, 3 vols (Madrid 1952), 1:636; Kamen, *Alba*, p. 174 n. 71.

16 Tiepolo, 'Relación', p. 1152; Kamen, *Philip of Spain*, p. 120.

17 Ann Lyon, 'The Mad Heir Apparent and the Spanish Succession: The Fate of the Infante Don Carlos', *Liverpool Law Review*, 30 (2009), 225–45, pp. 239–40.

18 Kamen, *Philip of Spain*, p. 122; Lyon, 'Mad Heir Apparent', p. 243.

19 Kamen, *Alba*, p. 79.

20 Kamen, *Inquisition and Society*, p. 307.

21 John J. Murray, 'The Cultural Impact of the Flemish Low Countries on Sixteenth- and Seventeenth-Century England', *American Historical Review*, 62:4 (1957), 837–54, pp. 839 and 840 nn. 5 and 8 ref. Norman G. Brett-James, *The Growth of Stuart London* (London: 1935), p. 18, and Thomas Fuller, *The History of the Worthies of England* (London: 1652, 1659 etc.), 2:274.

22 Kamen, *Alba*, pp. 91–3.

23 John Lothrop Motley, *The Rise of the Dutch Republic* (London: 1876 [1856]), pp. 502–3.

24 Kamen, *Alba*, p. 115.

25 Motley, *Rise*, p. 511.

26 Alba to King, Utrecht, 2 August 1573, in Álvarez de Toledo, *Epistolario*, 3:486.

27 Kamen, *Alba*, p. 116.

28 Alba to King, Vireton, 2 January 1574, in Álvarez de Toledo, *Epistolario*, 3: 575–9.

29 Kamen, *Alba*, p. 121 n. 59 refs Duque de Berwick y Alba, *Discurso del Duque de Berwick y de Alba* (Madrid: 1919), p. 65.

30 Carande, *Carlos*, p. 128.

31 Ibid., pp. 128–55; Braudel, *Mediterranean*, pp. 318–22; Elvira Vilches, *New World Gold: Cultural Anxiety and Monetary Disorder in Early Modern Spain* (Chicago and London: 2010), pp. 145–209; Stanley J. Stein and Barbara H. Stein, *Silver, Trade, and War: Spain and America in the Making of Early Modern Europe* (Baltimore and London: 2000), pp. 40–56.

32 The following account of Castilian finance and the bankruptcy of 1575 draws on Lovett, *Early Habsburg Spain*, pp. 219–35, and 'The Castilian Bankruptcy of 1575', *Historical Journal*, 23:4 (1990), 899–911.

33 Lovett, 'Castilian Bankruptcy', p. 900.

34 Stafford Poole, *Juan de Ovando: Governing the Spanish Empire in the Reign of Philip II* (Norman, Okla.: 2004), p. 169 n. 29 refs IVDJ, Madrid: Envío 72, caja 99, tomo 1, f. 33v.

35 Parker, *Grand Strategy*, p. 143 n. 103 refs IVDJ: 37/72, Requeséns to Zúñiga, 12 November 1575.

36 Geoffrey Parker, *Spain and the Netherlands, 1559–1659: Ten Studies* (Glasgow: 1992 [1979]), p. 110.

37 Lovett, 'Castilian Bankruptcy', p. 911, refutes the suggestion that the bankruptcy was a deliberate attempt by Philip to replace his Genoese bankers with Italian competitors.

38 Mauricio Drelichman and Hans-Joachim Voth, 'The Sustainable Debts of Philip II: A Reconstruction of Spain's Fiscal Position, 1560–1598' (December 2007), CEPR Discussion Paper No. DP6611, SSRN, http://ssrn.com/abstract=1140540.

39 Alan Probert, 'Bartolomé de Medina: The Patio Process and the Sixteenth-Century Silver Crisis', in Peter Bakewell (ed.), *Mines of Silver and Gold in the Americas*, vol. 19 of *An Expanding World: The European Impact on World History* (Aldershot: 1997), 96–130, originally published in *Journal of the West*, 8:1 (1969), 90–124, of which p. 90 n. 1 refs Francisco Fernández del Castillo, 'Algunos documentos nuevos sobre Bartolomé de Medina', in *Memorias de la Sociedad Alzate*, vol. 47 (Mexico: 1927), 207–51, p. 231.

40 Peter J. Bakewell, *Silver Mining and Society in Colonial Mexico: Zacatecas 1546–1700* (Cambridge: 1971), pp. 138–41.

41 Ibid., p. 138 n. 4.

42 Probert, *Bartolomé de Medina*, pp. 97–8.

43 Parker, *Spain and the Netherlands*, p. 45.

44 Ibid., p. 62.

10 *Portugal and the Duke of Alba*

1 Isacio Pérez Fernández, *Cronología documentada de los viajes, estancias y actuaciones de fray Bartolomé de las Casas* (Puerto Rico: 1984), pp. 892–5.

2 For the details of Miguel de Cervantes's life, unless otherwise indicated I have followed the monumental accumulation of data in Luis Astrana Marín, *Vida ejemplar y heroica de Miguel de Cervantes Saavedra con mil documentos hasta ahora inéditos y numerosas ilustraciones y grabados de época*, 7 vols (Madrid: 1948).

3 Krzysztof Sliwa, 'Andrea Cervantes, nieta más querida de la abuela paterna, Leonor Fernández de Torreblanca, y Constanza de Ovando y Figueroa, la simpática sobrina de Miguel de Cervantes Saavedra', *RILCE*, 20:1 (2004), 241–54, p. 245.

4 Ambrosio de Morales, *La Batalla de Lepanto (Descriptio Belli Nautici et Expugnatio Lepanti per D. Ioannem de Asutria)*, ed. Jernao Costas Rodríguez (Madrid: 1987), pp. 42–4.

5 Letters of 25 and 30 August to García de Toledo quoted by Astrana Marín, *Vida*, 2:292–3.

6 Morales, *Batalla*, pp. 42–4.

7 I have followed Fernando de Herrera's very literary account for the details of the battle unless otherwise indicated: 'Relación de la guerra de Cipre y suceso de la batalla naval de Lepanto, escrita por Fernando de Herrera' (Seville: 1572), in *CODOIN*, 21:243–383; see also Jack Beeching, *The Galleys at Lepanto* (London: 1982).

8 AGI: Patronato 253, R.1, 'Expediente de méritos y servicios: Miguel de Cervantes'; Pedro Torres Lanzas (ed.), *Información de Miguel de Cervantes* (Madrid: 1905).

9 Quoted by Astrana Marín, *Vida*, 2:334–5 (without citation of his source).

10 Kamen, *Philip of Spain*, p. 139.

11 Diego de Haedo [Antonio de Sosa], *Topographia e historia general de Argel* (Valladolid: 1612), f. 116v.

12 Ibid., ff. 8r, 9v.

13 Ibid., ff. 118r, 119r, 116r–v [sic: mispaginated for 120r–v].

14 Ibid., ff. 27r–v, 28v–29r.

15 Ibid., ff. 36r–39r, 32r, 35r.

16 Ibid., f. 7v.

17 Daniel Eisenberg, '¿Por qué volvió Cervantes de Argel?', in Ellen M. Anderson and Amy R. Williamsen (eds), *Essays on Golden Age Literature for Geoffrey L. Stagg in Honour of his Eighty-Fifth Birthday* (Newark, DE: 1999), 241–53. For a more detailed version of the following analysis see R. T. C. Goodwin, 'Origins of the Novel in Cervantes's *Información de Argel*', *Bulletin of Hispanic Studies*, 83:4 (2006), 317–35.

18 Haedo, *Topographia*, f. 185r; Eisenberg, '¿Por qué volvió?', pp. 241–53, 242; Jean Canavaggio, *Cervantes* (Paris: 1986), pp. 97–8; Emilio Sola and José F. de la Peña, *Cervantes y la Berbería: Cervantes, mundo turco-berberisco y servicios secretos en la epoca de Felipe II* (Madrid and Mexico City: 1995); R. Rossi, *Escuchar a Cervantes: Un ensayo biográfico* (Valladolid: 1988);

Alonso Zamora Vicente, 'El cautiverio en la obra cervantina', in Francisco Sánchez-Castañer (ed.), *Homenaje a Cervantes*, 2 vols (Valencia: 1950), 2:237–56, p. 242.

19 Anon., 'Diálogo llamado Philippino donde se refieren cien congrvencias concernientes al derecho que sv Magestad del Rei D. Phelippe nuestro señor tiene al Reino de Portugal', quoted by Fernando Bouza Álvarez, cat. 87, in *Felipe II: un monarca y su época. Las tierras y los hombres del rey*, exhibition catalogue (Valladolid: 1998), p. 283, and *Imagen y propaganda: capítulos de historia cultural del reinado de Felipe II* (Madrid: 1998), 74–82, p. 81.

20 Alba to Secretary Delgado, 20, 22, 23 February 1580, *CODOIN*, 32:14, 16, 18; AGS: Guerra, Mar y Tierra, leg. 97.

21 Luis Cabrera de Córdoba, *Historia de Felipe II, Rey de España*, ed. José Martínez Millán and Carlos Javier de Carlos Morales, 3 vols (Valladolid: 1998), 2:947.

22 Alba to King, 18 July 1580, *CODOIN*, 32:277; AGS: Estado 413.

23 Alba to King, 1 August 1580, *CODOIN*, 32:349; AGS: Estado 413.

24 Alba to King, 26 August 1580, *CODOIN*, 32:465; AGS: Estado 413.

25 Alba to King, 18 July 1580, *CODOIN*, 32:278; AGS: Estado 413.

26 Pierre Bourdeille and André Vicomte de Bourdeille, *Oeuvres complètes*, 1:31.

27 Alba to King, 17 August 1580, *CODOIN*, 32:420; AGS: Estado 413.

28 Hans de Khevenhüller, *Diario de Hans Khevenhüller: embajador imperial en la corte de Felipe II*, ed. Sara Veronelli and Félix Labrador Arroyo (Madrid: 2001), p. 218.

29 Alba to King, 28 August 1580, *CODOIN*, 32:482; AGS: Estado 413.

30 King to Alba, 31 August 1580, *CODOIN*, 32:482; AGS: Estado 413.

31 Cabrera de Córdoba, *Historia de Felipe II*, p. 9147.

32 Khevenhüller, *Diario*, p. 261.

33 Miguel de Cervantes, *Los trabajos de Persiles y Sigismunda*, ed. Juan Bautista Avalle-Arce (Madrid: 1969 [1617]), bk 3, ch. 1, p. 277.

34 Astrana Marín, *Vida*, 3:142–3.

35 González de Amezúa, 'Una carta desconocida e inédita de Cervantes', *Boletín de la Real Academia Española*, 34 (1954), 217–23; also Astrana Marín, *Vida*, 6:511–12, and Sliwa, *Vida*, p. 390.

36 Cervantes, *Don Quijote*, 1:prólogo al lector.

37 F. A. Baptista Pereira, cat. 83, in *Felipe II: un monarca y su época*, pp. 278–9.

38 *Calendar of State Papers: Venetian, 1581–1591*, p. 33.

39 King to Alba, 31 August 1580; *CODOIN*, 32: 508; AGS: Estado 425.

40 Cristóbal Mosquera de Figueroa, *Comentario en breve compendio de disciplina militar* (Madrid: 1596), ff. 53v–58r.

41 Serafín de Tapia Sánchez, 'La alfabetización de la población urbana castellana en el Siglo de Oro', *Historia de la Educación*, 12–13 (1993–4), 274–307; Richard Kagan, *Students and Society in Early Modern Spain* (Baltimore and London: 1974); Trevor Dadson, 'Literacy and Education in Early Modern Rural Castile: The Case of Villarrubia de los Ojos', *Bulletin of Spanish Studies*, 81:7–8 (2004), 1011–37, p. 1013; Luisa Cuesta Gutiérrez, 'Los tipógrafos extranjeros en la imprenta burgalesa, desde Alemán Fadrique de Basilea al italiano Juan Bautista

Veresi', *Gutenberg Jahrbuch* (1952), 67–74; William Pettas, 'A Sixteenth-Century Spanish Bookstore: The Inventory of Juan de Junta', *American Philosophical Society*, 85:1 (1995), 1–247; Clive Giffin, *Los Cromberger: La historia de una imprenta del siglo XVI en Sevilla y Méjico* (Madrid: 1991).

42 Arthur Terry, *Seventeenth-Century Spanish Poetry: The Power of Artifice* (Cambridge: 1993), p. 65.

43 Miguel de Cervantes, *Ocho comedias y ocho entremeses nuevos nunca representados* [Madrid: 1615], Prologue, at www.cervantesvirtual.com/obra/ocho-comedias-y-ocho-entremeses-nuevos-nunca-representados – o.

44 Félix Lope de Vega y Carpio, *La viuda valenciana*, in *Comedias*, Part 15 (Madrid: 1620 [c.1600]), Act 1.

45 Cristóbal Pérez Pastor (ed.), *Documentos cervantinos hasta ahora inéditos*, 2 vols (Madrid: 1897–1902), 1:131, 135, 146–7; docs 36, 37, 41, 42.

46 Alonso de Villegas, *Flos Sanctorum . . . y historia general en que se escriven las vidas de santos extravagantes y de varones ilustres en virtud . . .* (Madrid: 1675 [1588]), p. 518.

47 Francisco de Borja de San Román y Fernández, *El Greco en Toledo o nuevas investigaciones acerca de la vida y obras de Dominico Theotocópuli* (Madrid: 1910), p. 142.

48 Francisco Calvo Serraller, *El Greco: The Burial of the Count of Orgaz*, trans. Jenifer Wakelyn (London: 1995), pp. 19–20.

49 Astrana Marín, *Vida*, 3:586–96.

50 I borrow the language from the title of Neil Hanson's *The Confident Hope of a Miracle: The True Story of the Spanish Armada* (London: 2003).

11 Pirates, Criminals and Tax Collecting

1 Kamen, *Philip II*, p. 242.

2 As phrased by the poet Juan Rufo, quoted by Henry Kamen, *Spain's Road to Empire: The Making of a World Power, 1492–1763* (London: 2002), p. 304; published in the USA as *Empire: How Spain Became a World Power, 1492–1763* (New York: 2003).

3 AGI: Santo Domingo, 51 R.9 N.87.

4 Mary Fear Keeler, *Sir Francis Drake's West Indian Voyage, 1585–86* (London: 1981[1588–9]), p. 194: Document 10: The *Primrose* Journal, BL: Royal Ms 7 C p. xvi, ff. 166–73.

5 Ibid.

6 Keeler, *Drake's Voyage*, p. 103: Document 6: The Record kept aboard the Ship *Tiger*, BL: Cotton Ms Otho E. VIII, ff. 229–34.

7 Félix Lope de Vega y Carpio, *La Dragontea* (Valencia: 1598).

8 Keeler, *Drake's Voyage*, Document 11: *A Summarie and True Discourse of Sir Frances Drake's West Indian Voyage* (London: 1589).

9 Ibid.

10 William S. Maltby, *The Black Legend in England* (Durham, NC: 1971), pp. 30–1 n. 4 refs Francis Fletcher, *The World Encompassed by Sir Francis Drake*, in Hakluyt Society Publications, series 1, no. 16 (London: 1854 [1682]), p. 109.

11 Maltby, *Black Legend*, p. 69.

12 *Armada, 1588–1988: An International Exhibition to Commemorate the Spanish Armada*, exhibition catalogue, ed. M. J. Rodríguez-Salgado (London: 1988), cat. 6.21, *Arbol de la succession de Inglaterra*.

13 M. J. Rodríguez-Salgado, 'Philip II and the "Great Armada"', in *Armada, 1588–1988*, p. 22 n. 3 refs AGS: GA. 208 f. 366.

14 Antonio León Pinelo, *Anales de Madrid, desde el año 447 al de 1568* (Madrid: 1971), p. 132 and Fundación Lázaro Gaidiano: M 1-3-21, at http://www.bibliotecavirtualmadrid.org/bvmadrid_publicacion/i18n/consulta/registro.cmd?id=3526; Diego Ortiz de Zúñiga, *Anales eclesiásticos y seculares de la muy noble y muy leal ciudad de Sevilla*, 5 vols (Madrid: 1796), 4:240; Antonio Domínguez Ortiz, *Orto y ocaso de Sevilla: estudio sobre la prosperidad y decadencia de la ciudad durante los siglos XVI y XVII* (Seville: 1966).

15 Earl J. Hamilton, *American Treasure and the Price Revolution* (Cambridge, Mass.: 1934), p. 196; Radcliffe Salaman, *The History and Social Influence of the Potato* (Cambridge and New York: 2000 [1940]), pp. 68, 143.

16 Antonio Hermosilla Molina, 'Los hospitales reales', in Fernando Chueca Goitia (ed.), *Los hospitales de Sevilla* (Seville: 1989), 35–52, p. 48.

17 Juan Ignacio Carmona García, *El extenso mundo de la pobreza: la otra cara de la Sevilla imperial* (Seville: 1993), p. 177; Francisco de Ariño, *Sucesos de Sevilla de 1592 á 1604* (Seville: 1873), pp. 45–7.

18 Carmona García, *Extenso mundo*, p. 177.

19 Ariño, *Sucesos*, p. 47

20 Ibid., pp. 1–120; for what follows see esp. pp. 50–93.

21 Ibid., p. 66: 'Decirse cuerpo de Dios / Bien haya el nuevo asistente, / Pues hace guardar la tasa / A toda suerte de gente. / A todos nos hace iguales, / Pues que no siendo jueces / Nos hace comer barato / Como el oidor y el regente.'

22 Ibid., p. 73: 'Cuando su color el cedro / Y la flor hermosa brota / Y el potro gallardo trota / La víspera de San Pedro / Esta ciudad se alborota. / El audencia y asistente / Arman grandes divisiones / Por mínimas ocasiones / De que mormura la gente / Viendo las rebeliones.'

23 Ruth Pike, 'Crime and Criminals in Sixteenth-Century Seville', *Sixteenth Century Journal*, 6:1 (1975), 3–18, p. 8; Pike made a study of an inquiry ordered by Philip II in 1572 into criminality in Seville, AGS: Diversos de Castilla, legs. 28 and 29.

24 Pedro de León, *Grandeza y miseria en Andalucía: testimonio de una encrucijada histórica (1578–1616)*, ed. Pedro Herrera Puga (Granada: 1981), ff. 522–3, 326r–v.

25 Ibid., ff. 395–7, 220v–221v.

26 Pike, 'Crime', p. 9.

27 Ibid., p. 6.

28 León, *Grandeza*, ff. 485–6, 298r.

29 Miguel de Cervantes, *Novela de Rinconete y Cortadillo*, in *Novelas ejemplares*, 1:189–240.

30 R. O. Jones, *A Literary History of Spain: The Golden Age of Prose and Poetry* (London and New York: 1971), p. 143; Lorenzo Gracián [Baltasar], *La agudeza, y el arte de ingenio*, in *Obras completas* (Barcelona: 1757), 2:6.

31 Astrana Marín, *Vida*, 4:131 n. 1 and 133 n. 1 ref Adolfo Rodríguez Jurado, *Discursos leídos en la Real Academia Sevillana de Buenas Letras, Proceso seguido a instancias de Tomás Gutiérrez* . . . (Seville: 1914), 81–197.

32 Miguel de Cervantes Saavedra, *El juez de los divorcios*, at http://cervantes.tamu.edu/english/ctxt/cec/disk7/ENTREMES.html.

33 'Un embajador marroquí' [1690–1], in García Mercadal, *Viajes*, 2:1217–77, p. 1225.

34 Rodríguez Marín, *Nuevos documentos cervantinos*, 2 vols (Madrid: 1897–1902), 1:192.

35 Ibid., 1:315, 320–1.

36 Ibid., 1:214–15.

37 José Sánchez, *Academias literarias del Siglo de Oro español* (Madrid: 1961).

38 Juan de Mal Lara, *Philosophia vulgar* (Seville: 1568), 'A los lectores', quoted from Jonathan Brown, *Images and Ideas in Seventeenth-Century Spanish Painting* (Princeton: 1978), p. 22.

39 Félix Lope de Vega y Carpio, 'Una dama se vende' [c.1587], in *Cancionero de obras de burlas provocantes a risa*, ed. Eduardo de Lustonó (Madrid: 1872), p. 278:

> Una dama se vende, ¿hay quien la quiera?
> En almoneda está, ¿quieren compralla?
> Su padre es quien la vende, que aunque calla,
> Treinta ducados pide y saya entera
> de tafetán, piñuela o añafalla,
> y la mitad del precio no se halla
> por se el tiempo estéril en manera.
> Mas un galán llegó con diez canciones,
> cinco sonetos y un gentila cabrito,
> y aqueste tespondió ser buena paga.
> Mas un fraile le dio treinta doblones,
> y aqueste la llevó. ¡Sea Dios bendito,
> muy buen provecho y buena pro le haga!

40 Juan Pérez de Montalbán, *Fama postúma a la vida y muerte del doctor frey Felix Lope de Vega Carpio* (Madrid: 1636), p. 4.

41 Quoted in Rudolph Schevill, 'Lope de Vega and the Year 1588', *Hispanic Review*, 9:1 (1941), 65–78, p. 75.

42 Antonio Sánchez Jiménez, 'Lope de Vega y la Armada Invencible de 1588. Biografía y poses del autor', http://uva.academia.edu/AntonioSanchezJimenez/Papers/857038/Lope_de_Vega_y_la_Armada_Invencible_de_1588.

43 Félix Lope de Vega y Carpio, *La hermosura de Angélica* (Madrid: 1602): 'sobre las aguas, entre las jarcias del galeón San Juan y las gleras del Rey Católico, escribí'.

44 The same argument has been used to support Lope's claims to have studied at the prestigious University of Alcalá de Henares: Hugo A. Rennert and Américo Castro, *Vida de Lope de Vega (1562–1635)* (Madrid: 1919), p. 16.

45 Antonio de Herrera y Tordesillas, *Tercera parte de la historia general del mundo* (Madrid: 1612), bk 4, p. 93.

46 Rodríguez-Salgado, 'The Court of Philip II of Spain', p. 205.
47 Colin Martin and Geoffrey Parker, *The Spanish Armada* ([London]: 1988), pp. 36–44.
48 Astrana Marín, *Vida*, pp. 223–4.
49 Rodríguez Marín, *Nuevos documentos*, doc. 90, pp. 222–4.
50 Pérez Pastor, *Documentos*, 2:148–56, doc. 43 refs AGS: Contaduría General, leg. 1475.
51 Rodríguez Marín, *Nuevos documentos*, doc. 92, p. 227.
52 John Beverley (ed.), 'Introducción', in Luis de Góngora y Argote, *Soledades* (Madrid: 2007), pp. 17–18.
53 Emilio Orozco, *Introducción a Góngora* (Barcelona: 1984 [1953]), p. 33.

12   *The Great Armada, 1588*

1   Martin and Parker, *Armada*, p. 28 n. 1 refs AGS: Estado 455/492, Medina Sidonia to King, 31 July 1588.
2   Quoted by ibid., pp. 169, 170.
3   Pérez de Montalbán, *Fama postúma*, p. 4.
4   J. Paz, 'Relación de la "Invencible" por el contador Pedro Coco de Calderón', *Revista de archivos, bibliotecas y museos*, 3rd series, 1 (1987), appendix 1; for the name Francisco see José Florencio Martínez, *Biografía de Lope de Vega, 1562–1635: Un friso literario del Siglo de Oro* (Barcelona: 2011), p. 85.
5   Pérez de Montalbán, *Fama postúma*, p. 4.
6   Quoted in Martin and Parker, *Armada*, p. 237.
7   Marcos de Arambaru, *Account of Marcos de Arambaru*, trans. W. Spotswood Green, in *Proceedings of the Royal Irish Acadamy*, 27 (Dublin and London: 1908–9).
8   Zarco Cuevas, *Documentos*, 4:59.
9   Kamen, *Philip II*, p. 275.
10 Rodríguez-Salgado, 'Philip II and the "Great Armada" of 1588', p. 35 n. 6 refs AGS: GA.235 f. 71; Kamen, *Philip II*, p. 275, mentions him raising 50,000 crowns.
11 José María Asensio, *Nuevos documentos para ilustrar la vida de Miguel de Cervantes* (Sevilla: 1864), doc. 3, pp. 8–10; and Pérez Pastor, *Documentos*, doc. 48.
12 Astrana Marín, *Vida*, 4:375–87.
13 I draw here on Aurelio Miró Quesada, *El Inca Garcilaso y otros estudios garcilasistas* (Madrid: 1971), and – a good read – John Grier Varner, *El Inca: The Life and Times of Garcilaso de la Vega* (Austin and London: 1968).
14 El Inca Garcilaso de la Vega, *Comentarios reales de los Incas*, ed. Carlos Araníbar, 2 vols (Mexico City: 1991 [1609–17]): Garcilaso published a history of Peru in two parts which is usually known as the *Comentarios reales* or *Royal Commentary*; in fact, the first part, which is a history of the Incas, was published as the *Comentarios Reales de los Incas* (Lisbon: 1609), while the second part was published as *Historia General del Perú* (Cordova: 1617). That historical distinction is made in the citations here; see Garcilaso, *Comentarios*, bk 1, ch. 15.

15 Garcilaso, *Historia General*, pt 2, bk 2, ch. 1.

16 Garcilaso, *Comentarios*, pt 1, bk 5, ch. 29.

17 Raúl Porra Barrenechea, *El Inca Garcilaso en Montilla (1561–1614)* (Lima: 1955), pp. xxiii–xxiv, xxiv.

18 Frances G. Crowley, *Garcilaso de la Vega, el Inca and his Sources in* Comentarios Reales de los Incas (The Hague and Paris: 1971); also Margarita Zamora, *Language, Authority, and Indigenous History in the* Comentarios reales de los incas (Cambridge: 1988), pp. 7–8.

19 Keith Whitlock, *The Renaissance in Europe* (New Haven and London: 2000), pp. 20–1; Juan Bautista Avalle-Arce, *El Inca Garcilaso en sus* Comentarios (Madrid: 1964), p. 20.

20 David Henige, 'The Context, Content, and Credibility of La Florida del Ynca', *Americas*, 43:1 (1986), 1–23, p. 21.

21 El Inca Garcilaso de la Vega, *La Florida del Inca* (Lisbon: 1605), bk 3, chs 10, 11.

22 Robert Jammes, *La obra poética de Don Luis de Góngora y Argote* (Madrid: 1987), p. 14 n. 52 refs Rafael Ramírez de Arellano, *Ensayo de un catálogo biográfico de escritores de la provincia y diócesis de Córdoba...*, 2 vols (Madrid: 1922–3), 1:256; José de la Torre, 'Documentos gongorinos', *Boletín de la Real Academia Española*, 18 (1927), 65–218, doc. 61.

23 Quoted in Astrana Marín, *Vida*, 5:32.

24 León, *Grandeza*, pp. 102, 104, 119, 121.

25 Cristóbal de Chaves, 'Relación de la cárcel de Sevilla', in Aureliano Fernández-Guerra y Orbe (ed.), *Noticia de un precioso codice de la Biblioteca Colombina* (Madrid: 1864), 51–65; Alonso de Morgado, *Historia de Sevilla* (Seville: 1587), p. 194.

26 León, *Grandeza*, p. 373, 208v.

27 Ibid., p. 374, 210r.

28 Ibid., p. 379, 212r.

29 Chaves, 'Relación', p. 52.

30 Vicente Espinel, *La Vida de Marcos de Obregón* (Barcelona: 1881 [1617]), p. 211.

31 Chaves, 'Relación', p. 56.

32 León, *Grandeza*, p. 375, 210v.

33 Chaves, 'Relación', p. 58.

34 Miguel de Cervantes Saavedra, *Don Quixote*, Part One, Prologue.

35 Antonio Feros and Fernado J. Bouza Alvarez (eds), *España en tiempos del Quijote* (Madrid: 2004), p. 44:

> Voto a Dios que me espanta esta grandeza
> y que diera un doblón por describilla,
> porque ¿a quién no sorprende y maravilla
> esta máquina insigne, esta riqueza?
> Por Jesucristo vivo, cada pieza
> vale más de un millón, y que es mancilla
> que esto no dure un siglo, ¡oh gran Sevilla,
> Roma triunfante en ánimo y nobleza!
> Apostaré que el ánima del muerto

por gozar este sitio hoy ha dejado
la gloria donde vive eternamente.
Esto oyó un valentón y dijo: 'Es cierto
cuanto dice voacé, señor soldado,
Y el que dijere lo contrario, miente.'
Y luego, incontinente,
caló el chapeo, requirió la espada
miró al soslayo, fuese y no hubo nada.

Part II Prologue

1 Gaspar Pérez de Villagrá, *Historia de la Nueva México*, trans. and ed. Miguel Encinias, Alfred Rodríguez and Joseph P. Sánchez (Albuquerque: 1992 [1610]).

2 The handful of 'verses' that follow, from cantos 1 and 6, are very abridged and freely translated, but are intended to convey succinctly the spirit and language of the original.

3 Vine Deloria Jr, *Custer Died for your Sins* (London and New York: 1969), pp. 2–3.

4 Geoffrey Parker, *Europe in Crisis: 1598–1648* (Brighton: 1980).

5 E. J. Hobsbawm, 'The General Crisis of the European Economy in the 17th Century', *Past & Present*, 5 (1954), 33–53, and 'The Crisis of the 17th Century – II', *Past & Present*, 6 (1954), 44–65; John H. Elliott, 'The Decline of Spain', *Past & Present*, 20 (1961), 52–75; Henry Kamen, 'The Economic and Social Consequences of the Thirty Years' War', *Past & Present*, 39 (1968), 44–61; 'The Decline of Spain: A Historical Myth?', *Past & Present*, 81 (1978), 24–50; and 'The Decline of Spain: A Historical Myth?: A Rejoinder', *Past & Present*, 91 (1981), 181–5; J. I. Israel, 'The Decline of Spain: A Historical Myth?', *Past & Present*, 91 (1981), 170–80.

6 E.g. the classic account by Antonio Cánovas del Castillo, *Historia de la decadencia de España desde el advenimiento de Felipe III al Trono hasta la muerte de Carlos II* (Madrid: 1910 [1854]).

7 John Lynch, *The Hispanic World in Crisis and Change* (Oxford and Cambridge, MA: 1992 [1969]), pp. 229–347.

8 Lyle N. McAlister, *Spain and Portugal in the New World, 1492–1700*, vol. 3 of *Europe in the Age of Expansion* (Minneapolis: 1984), pp. 375–81.

9 Ángel Rosenblat, *La población indígena y el mestizaje en América, 1492–1950*, 2 vols (Buenos Aires: 1954), 1:59.

10 The subject is well summarized by Noble David Cook, *Born to Die: Disease and New World Conquest, 1492–1650* (Cambridge and New York: 1998).

11 Francisco de San Antón Muñón Chimalpahin Cuauhtlehuanitzin, *Relaciones de Chalco Amaquemecan*, ed. and trans. S. Rendón (Mexico City and Buenos Aires: 1965 [c.1600–50]), 'Séptima relación', pp. 160–1.

12 Cook, *Born to Die*, p. 112.

13 *Annals of the Cakchiquels*, [1559–1581], quoted by ibid., p. vi.

14 Jared Diamond, *Guns, Germs and Steel: A Short History of Everybody for the Last 13,000 Years* (London: 2005 [1997]), p. 211.

15 The monumental study of the Atlantic trade by Pierre Chaunu and Huguette Chaunu, *Séville et l'Antique (1504–1650)*, 12 vols (Paris: 1962) is more accessible in an abridged form: *Séville et l'Amérique aux XVIe et XVIIe siècles* (Paris: 1977), with the most relevant graphs on pp. 260–2; Earl J. Hamilton's important essay 'Monetary Inflation in Castile, 1598–1660', *Economic History (A Supplement to the Economic Journal)*, 2 (1930–3), 177–211, is reproduced in context along with an expanded set of tables and graphs in his *American Treasure*, pp. 73ff.; also see A. García-Baquero González, 'Andalusia and the Crisis of the Indies Trade, 1610–1720', in I. A. A. Thompson and Bartolomé Yun Casalilla (eds), *The Castilian Crisis of the Seventeenth Century: New Perspectives on the Economic and Social History of Seventeenth-Century Spain* (Cambridge: 1994), 115–35.

16 Hamilton, *American Treasure*, table 1 and chart 1, pp. 34–5, and chart 20, p. 301.

17 Ibid., pp. 73–103 and table 7 and chart 4, pp. 96–7, and 'Monetary Inflation', table 1 and chart 1, pp. 203–5.

18 Michel Morineau, *Incroyables gazettes et fabuleux métaux: Les retours des trésors américains d'après les gazettes hollandaises (XVIe–XVIIIe siècles)* (London and New York: 1985), table 41, p. 242.

19 Francisco Herrera y Maldonado, *Libro de la vida y maravillosas virtudes del Siervo de Dios Bernardino de Obregón* (Madrid: 1634), f. 211r.

20 Henri Mérimée, *Spectacles et comédiens à Valencia (1580–1630)* (Toulouse and Paris: 1913), pp. 95–6; Felipe de Gauna, *Relación de las fiestas celebradas en Valencia con motivo del casamiento de Felipe III*, ed. Salvador Carreras Zacarés, 2 vols (Valencia: 1926).

21 Martínez, *Biografía de Lope de Vega*, p. 178.

22 Paul C. Allen, *Philip III and the Pax Hispanica, 1598–1621: The Failure of Grand Strategy* (New Haven and London: 2000), pp. 3–4.

23 Lynch, *Hispanic World*, p. 8.

24 Javier Liske, *Viajes de extranjeros por España y Portugal en los siglos XV, XVI, XVII* (Madrid: 1878), pp. 261–2, 262.

25 Allen, *Philip III*, pp. 13–19.

26 Lynch, *Hispanic World*, pp. 53–5.

27 Allen, *Philip III*, p. 75.

28 Ibid., pp. 234–41; p. 240 n. 23 refs BNE: Ms 18721, 'Como se deve qualquier Principe poderoso guiar en los consejos de pazes con sus enemigos . . .'

29 Gregorio Cruzada Villaamil, *Rubens, diplomático español* (Madrid: [1874?]), p. 72: Peter Paul Rubens to Annibal Chieppo, Valladolid, 24 May 1603, first published as 'Rubens, diplomático español', *Revista Europea*, 1:6–17 (1874), 7–519 (intermittently).

30 Cruzada, *Rubens*, pp. 81–3: Iberti to Duke of Mantua, Valladolid, 18 July 1603.

31 Alexander Vergara, *Rubens and his Spanish Patrons* (Cambridge: 1999), pp. 11–12; quotation from David Davies, in conversation, 25 September 2012.

32 Matteo Mancini, '*El emperador Carlos V a caballo en Mühlberg* de Tiziano, un icono para la Historia del Arte', in *La restauración de El emperador Carlos V a caballo en Mülhlberg de Tiziano*, exhibition catalogue (Madrid: 2001), 103–16, pp. 109–12.

33 Rosemarie Mulcahy, *Philip II of Spain, Patron of the Arts* (Dublin: 2004), pp. 285–7, 228–9; J. Moreno Villa and F. J. Sánchez Cantón, 'Noventa y siete retratos de la familia de Felipe III por Bartolomé González', *Archivo Español de Arte y Arqueología*, 13:38 (1937), 127–56.

34 Vicente Carducho, *Diálogos de la pintura, su defensa, origen, escencia, definición, modos y diferencias*, ed. Francisco Calvo Serraller (Madrid: 1979 [1633]), 336–7.

35 Francisco Calvo Serraller (ed.), *La teoría de la pintura en el Siglo de Oro* (Madrid: 1981), p. 504.

13   The First Modern Novel, Don Quixote

1   Martín González de Cellorigo, *Memorial de la política necesaria y útil restauración de la república de España* (Valladolid: 1600), ff. 29v, 25r, 2r–v, 4ff, 22r–30v, 23r–v.

2   '100 prominent authors from more than 50 different nations have elected The Library of World Literature: "The 100 Best Books in the History of Literature"', in *Bokklubben din Nettbokhandel*, at http://www.bokklubben.no/SamboWeb/side.do?dokId=65500&klubbid=WB.

3   Dale B. J. Randall and Jackson C. Boswell, *Cervantes in Seventeeth-Century England: The Tapestry Turned* (Oxford: 2009), pp. xxxii, ix–x.

4   Ronald Paulson, *Don Quixote in England: The Aesthetics of Laughter* (Baltimore and London: 1998), pp. ix–x.

5   Ibid., pp. ix, 5.

6   Olin Harris Moore, 'Mark Twain and Don Quixote', *Proceedings of the Modern Language Association of America*, 37:2 (1922), 324–46.

7   Randall and Boswell, *Cervantes in Seventeeth-Century England*, p. xvii.

8   R. W. Trueman, 'The Rev. John Bowle's Quixotic Woes Further Explored', *Cervantes: Bulletin of the Cervantes Society of America*, 23:2 (2003), 9–43.

9   Harold Bloom, 'Introduction', in Harold Bloom (ed.), *Modern Critical Interpretations: Cervante's* Don Quixote (Philadelphia: 2001), pp. 1–2.

10 Lope de Vega y Carpio, *Cartas*, ed. Nicolás Marín and Luis Fernández de Córdoba (Madrid: 1985), p. 68: Letter dated 14 August 1604.

11 Cervantes, *Ocho comedias*, Prologue.

12 Quoted in Daniel Eisenberg, 'Cervantes, Lope, and Avellaneda', in *Josep María Solà-Solè: Homage, Homenaje, Homenatge*, ed. Antonio Torres-Alcalá, 2 vols (Barcelona: 1984), 2:171–83, p. 174; at users.ipfw.edu/jehle/deisenbe/cervantes/lope.pdf.

13 Jammes, *Obra poética*, p. 97; Luis de Góngora y Argote, *Obras completas*, ed. Juan Millé y Giménez and Isabel Millé y Giménez (Madrid: [1900]), no. 121, pp. 331–3.

14 Francisco Rico, 'Prólogo', in *Don Quijote de la Mancha*, ed. Francisco Rico et al., 2 vols (Madrid: 2005 [1604–15]), 1:ccxxi–ccxxii.

15 Sonia Garza Merino, 'La cuenta del original', in Pablo Andrés and Sonia Garza (eds), *Imprenta y crítical textual en el Siglo de Oro* (Valladolid: 2000), 65–95, pp. 65–6.

16 *Don Quixote*, 2.62.

17 Cristóbal Suárez de Figueroa, *Plaza universal de todas ciencias y artes* (Madrid: 1615), Discurso 111, 'De los impressores'.

18 *Don Quixote*, 2.4; R. M. Flores, 'Cervantes at Work: The Writing of *Don Quixote*, Part I', *Journal of Hispanic Philology*, 3 (1979), 135–60, and 'The Loss and Recovery of Sancho's Ass in *Don Quixote*, Part I', *Modern Language Review*, 75:2 (1980), 301–10.

19 Garza Merino, 'La cuenta', p. 67.

20 B. W. Ife, 'Don Quixote's Diet', Occasional Paper Series, no. 34 (Department of Hispanic, Portuguese and Latin American Studies, University of Bristol) (Bristol: 2000).

21 Vladimir Nabokov, *Lectures on Don Quixote*, ed. Fedson Bowers (London: 1983), pp. 51–2.

22 Mal Lara, *Philosophia vulgar*; Desiderius Erasmus Roterodamus, *Collectanea Adagiorum* (Paris: 1500).

23 A leading American Cervantes specialist was working on this at his untimely death: Carroll B. Johnson, *Transliterating a Culture: Cervantes and the Moriscos*, ed. Mark Groundland (Newark, DE: 2009), pp. 203–30.

24 I find it hard to believe that this is coincidence, although it is difficult to explain why he did not make the match perfect. At that time, bee, vee and u were frequently interchangeable, as were eff and aitch. So we get: en fe, Mig[u]el de Ce[r]bante[s], with e and i surplus.

25 Kaite A. Harris, 'Forging History: The Plomos of the Sacromonte of Granada in Francisco Bermúdez de Pedraza's *Historia Eclesiastica*', *Sixteenth Century Journal*, 30:4 (1999), 945–66; Thomas E. Case, 'Cide Hamete and the *Libros Plúmbeos*', *Bulletin of the Cervantes Society of America*, 22:2 (2002), 9–24.

26 Francisco Márquez Villanueva, 'La criptohistória morisca (los otros conversos)', in Agustin Redondo (ed.), *Les Problèmes de l'exclusion en Espagne (XVIe–XVIIe siècles)* (Paris: 1983), 77–94, p. 86 n. 27 – Márquez Villanueva defends Luna, citing Ramón Menéndez Pidal, *Floresta de leyendas heroícas epsañolas*, vol. 2: *Rodrigo, el últimoo godo* (Madrid: 1926), 2:48 – and Ginés Pérez de Hita, *Guerras civiles de Granada* (Cuenca: 1595–1616).

27 See note 18 above.

14 *Moriscos and Catalans*

1 Alejandro Ramírez-Araujo, 'El morisco Ricote y la libertad de conciencia', *Hispanic Review*, 24:4 (1956), 278–89, p. 280 n. 8 refs Francisco de Quevedo Villegas, *Obras completas*, ed. Astrana Marín (Madrid: 1947), 1419a.

2 René Quérillacq, 'Los moriscos de Cervantes', *Anales Cervantinos*, 30 (1992), 77–98.

3 Benjamin Ehlers, *Between Christians and Moriscos: Juan de Ribera and Religious Reform in Valencia, 1568–1614* (Baltimore: 2006), p. 134 n. 35 refs Colegio de Corpus Cristi, Valencia: 1: 7, 8, Moriscos 1, 27(3), ff. 20, 1.

4 Pascual Boronat y Barrachina, *Los moriscos españoles y su expulsión. Estudio histórico-crítico*, 2 vols (Valencia: 1901), 1:633–4.

5 Harris, 'Forging History', 945–66; Case, 'Cide Hamete', 9–24.

6 Harris, 'Forging History', p. 947 n. 3 refs Adan Centurión y Córdoba, Marquis of Estepa, *Información para la historia del Sacromonte . . . Primera parte* (Granada, 1623).

7 Miguel José Hagarty, *Los libros plúmbeos de Sacromonte* (Madrid: 1980), p. 27; also see 'Los libros plúmbeos y la fundación de la Insigne Iglesia Colegial del Sacromonte', in *La Abadía del Sacromonte: Exposición artístico-documental: Estudios sobre su significación y orígenes* (Granada: 1974).

8 William Childers, 'An Extensive Network of Morisco Merchants Active Circa 1590', in Kevin Ingram (ed.), *The Conversos and Moriscos in Late Medieval Spain and Beyond*, 2 vols (Leiden and Boston: 2012), 2:135–60; and Kevin Ingram, 'Introduction to this Volume', in Ingram (ed.), *The Conversos and Moriscos*, 2:6–7.

9 Hagarty, *Libros*, p. 124.

10 Barbara Fuchs, 'Maurophilia and the Morisco Subject', in Ingram (ed.), *The Conversos and Moriscos*, 1:269–85.

11 Quoted by Trevor J. Dadson, *Los moriscos de Villarrubia de los Ojos (siglos XV–XVIII)* (Vervuert: 2007), p. 294 nn. 9 and 10 ref. AGS: Estado 165, papel no. 351, and Manuel Danvila y Collado, *La expulsión de los moriscos españoles: Conferencias pronunciadas en el Ateneo de Madrid* (Madrid: 1998), pp. 240, 295–6, 296 n. 14 refs Boronat y Barrachina, *Los moriscos y su expulsión*, 2:110.

12 Quoted by Manuel F. Fernández Chavez and Raveale M. Pérez García, 'The Morisco Problem and Seville (1480–1610)', in Ingram (ed.), *The Conversos and Moriscos*, 2:75–102, p. 101 n. 83 refs AMS: Actas Capitulares, libro H-1694, ff. 31r–32r.

13 L. Lisón Hernández, 'Mito y realidad de la expulsión de los mudéjares murcianos del Valle de Ricote', *Areas. Revista de Ciencias Sociales*, 14 (1992), 141–70, p. 150.

14 Dadson, *Villarrubia*, pp. 289–342.

15 Martínez, *Discursos practicables*, pp. 239–40.

16 The great court painter to Carlos II and Philip V, Antonio Palomino, describes it: Antonio Palomino, *Vidas [Museo pictórico. Tercera parte: El Parnaso Español Pintoresco Laureado]*, ed. Nina Ayala Mallory, 2 vols (Madrid: 1986 [1724]), 2:162.

17 Carl Justi, *Velázquez y sus siglo*, trans. Pedro Marrades (Madrid: 1953), p. 234.

18 Félix Lope de Vega y Carpio, *Corona trágica, vida y muerte de la serenissima reyna de Escocia María Estuarda a Nuestro Padre Urbano VIII* (Madrid: 1627):

> Por el tercero santo, el mar profundo
> al Africa pasó (sentencia justa)
> despreciando sus bárbaros tesoros,
> las últimas reliquias de los moros.

19 Juan Bautista Vilar, 'La expulsión de los moriscos del Reino de Murcia. Sus efectos demográficos y económicos sobre la región de origen', in *L'expulsió dels moriscos: conseqüències en el món ilsàmic i el món cristià* (Barcelona: 1994), 86–95, p. 88.

20 Lisón Hernández, 'Mito y realidad', pp. 151–3.

21 For the following see Dadson, *Villarrubia*, pp. 343–93.

22 Ibid., pp. 428–9.

23   The title of Dadson's chapter 10, ibid., pp. 593–654.
24   Ibid., pp. 459–63 refs R. Bénitez Sánchez-Blanco, 'La odisea del manchego Diego Díaz', in R. García Cárcel (ed.), *Los olvidados de la historia: Herejes* (Barcelona: 2004), 214–36.
25   Henrí Lapeyre, *Géographie de l'Espagne morisque* (Paris: 1959).
26   See Dadson, *Villarrubia*, pp. 30, 28.
27   Damián Fonseca, *Relación de la expulsión de los moriscos del reino de Valencia* (Valencia: 1878 [1612]), p. 163; Lapeyre, *Géographie*, p. 67 and appendices 1, 2, 3, 4.
28   Ángel García Sanz, *Desarrollo y Crisis del Antiguo Régimen en Castilla la Vieja. Economia y Sociedad en Tierras de Segovia, 1500–1814* (Madrid: 1977); Angel Rodríguez Sánchez, *Población y Comportamiento Demográficos en el Siglo XVI* (Cáceres: 1977); Vicente Pérez Moreda and David Sven Reher (eds), *Demografía histórica en España* (Madrid: 1988).
29   Lapeyre, *Géographie*, pp. 67–73; James Casey, *The Kingdom of Valencia in the Seventeenth Century* (Cambridge: 1979), pp. 6–7.
30   Jaime Villanueva, *Viage literario a las iglesias de España*, 22 vols (Valencia: 1821), 7:131–2.
31   Lluís Soler i Terol, *Perot Roca Guinarda: Història d'aquest bandoler* (Manrèsa: 1909), pp. 356–7.
32   Henry Kamen, *The Phoenix and the Flame: Catalonia and the Counter Reformation* (New Haven and London: 1993), p. 208.
33   Francisco de los Santos, 'La vida del Padre Fr. Andrés de los Reyes y de un Hermano de los Legos llamado Fray Martín de Perpiñan, hijos de S. Lorenzo', in *Quarta parte de la Historia de la Orden de San Gerónimo* (Madrid: 1680), ff. 763–4.
34   Soler i Terol, *Perot Roca Guinarda*, p. 413, pp. 412–13 n. 6 refs Arxiu de la Corona d'Aragó, Lligall 843, Letter, 18 July 1615.
35   John H. Elliott, *Revolt of the Catalans: A Study in the Decline of Spain* (Cambridge: 1963), p. 45 n. 2 refs BCB: Fullet Bonsoms, no. 12, *Per los Diputats del General de Catalunya* (Barcelona: 1622), f. 2.
36   Elliott, *Revolt of the Catalans*, p. 45 n. 1 refs BCB: Fullet Bonsoms, no. 15, *Discurso y memorial . . . por Fr Francisco de Copons* (Barcelona: 1622), ff. 8, 9.
37   Enrique Cock, 'Anales del año ochenta y cinco . . .' [1585], in García Mercadal, *Viajes*, 1:1293–1445, p. 1376.
38   José Álvarez Lopera, *El Greco: estudio y catálogo*, 2 vols (Madrid: 2005), 1:283–7, 309–11; José Camón Aznar, *Dominico Greco*, 2 vols (Madrid: 1950), 1:198ff.

15   Holy Week: Art and Illusion

1   Palomino, *Vidas*, n. 72.
2   Carducho, *Diálogos*, Dialogue 8, f. 153r.
3   Pliny the Elder, *Natural History*, trans. H. Rackham, Loeb edn, 10 vols (London: 1952), bk 35.68, pp. 310–13.
4   Ovid, *Metamorphosis*, bk 10, at http://www.mythology.us/ovid_metamorphoses_book_10.htm.
5   Genesis 1:27, 2:7.
6   Webster, *Art and Ritual*, p. 17.

7   Ibid., p. 29 n. 101 refs APAS: *Hermandades*, leg. 13, 'Libro de Cabildos de Montesión', f. 52r.

8   Isidoro Moreno, *La antigua hermandad de los negros de Sevilla: etnicidad, poder y sociedad en 600 años de historia* (Seville: 1997), p. 25.

9   Manuel Chaves, *Cosas nuevas y viejas: apuntes sevillanos* (Seville: 1904), pp. 104–5; quote: Abad Alonso Sánchez Gordillo, *Religiosas estaciones que frecuenta la religiosidad sevillana*, ed. Jorge Bernales Ballesteros (Seville: 1983 [1635]), p. 54.

10 Elena Estrada de Gerlero, 'El programa pasionario en el convento franciscano de Huejotzingo', *Jahrbuch für Geschichte von Staat, Wirtschaft und Gesellschaft Lateinamerikas*, 20 (1983), 642–62; Susan Verdi Webster, 'Art, Ritual, and Confraternities in Sixteenth-Century New Spain', *Anales del Instituto de Investigaciones Estéticas*, 70 (1997), 5–43.

11 Webster, *Art and Ritual*, p. 45 nn. 165 and 167 ref. APAS: *Hermandades*, leg. 94, 'Auto de la cofradía y hermanos de nuestra señora de la antigua . . .'

12 Sánchez Gordillo, *Religiosas estaciones*, p. 44.

13 Francisco Pacheco, *El arte de la pintura*, ed. Bonaventura Bassegoda i Hugas (Madrid: 1990 [1646]), p. 133.

14 Saint John of the Cross, *Complete Works*, ed. Allison Peers, 3 vols (London: 1935), 3:89.

15 Ronda Kasl, 'Painters, Polychromy, and the Perfection of Images', in *Spanish Polychrome Sculpture 1500–1800 in United States Collections*, exhibition catalogue, ed. Suzanne L. Stratton ([New York]: [1994]), 32–49, p. 34.

16 José Hernández Díaz, *Juan Martínez Montañés (1568–1649)* (Seville: 1987), pp. 194–6, nn. 148–152 ref. Celestino López Martínez, *Retablos y esculturas de traza sevillana* (Seville: 1928), pp. 48, 53, 55; and *Desde Jerónimo Hernández a Martínez Montañés* (Seville: 1929), 262–5; Antonio Muro Orejón, *Documentos para la escultura sevillana. Artífices sevillanos de los siglos XVI y XVII*, Documentos para la historia del Arte en Andalucía, vol. 1 (Seville: 1927), p. 208.

17 Francisco Pacheco, 'A los profesores del arte de la pintura. Opúsculo impreso en Sevilla el 16 de Julio de 1622', in Calvo Serraller (ed.), *La teoría de la pintura*, 179–91.

18 Webster, *Art and Ritual*, pp. 65–7.

19 Pacheco, *Arte de la pintura*, pp. 497, 495–6, 500.

20 Ibid., p. 500.

21 Webster, *Art and Ritual*, pp. 164–5.

22 San Juan de la Cruz, *Subida del monte Carmelo*, ed. Eulogio Pacho, bk 3, ch. 35, at http://es.catholic.net/santoral/147/2519/articulo.php?id=2058.

23 Webster, *Art and Ritual*, p. 117 n. 20 refs Sánchez Gordillo, *Religiosas estaciones*, p. 171.

24 Webster, *Art and Ritual*, p. 118 n. 22 refs Juan de Ávila, *Obras completas*, ed. Francisco Martín Hernández, 6 vols (Madrid: 1971), 6:74.

16   Velázquez and Zurbarán

1   Peter Cherry, 'Artistic Training and the Painters' Guild in Seville', in *Velázquez in Seville*, exhibition catalogue, ed. David Davies (Edinburgh: 1996), 66–75, p. 72.

2   Ernst Gombrich, *Art and Illusion* (London: 1960), p. 258.

3 Xavier Bray, 'The Sacred Made Real', in *The Sacred Made Real: Spanish Painting and Sculpture, 1600–1700*, exhibition catalogue, ed. Xavier Bray (London: 2010), 15–44.

4 Ibid., p. 18 n. 12 refs Odile Delenda and Luis J. Garraín Villa, 'Zurbarán Sculpteur: aspects inédits de sa carrière et de sa biographie', *Gazette des Beaux-Arts*, 131 (1998), 125–38.

5 Brown, *Painting in Spain*, pp. 132–3.

6 Palomino, *Vidas*, p. 198.

7 Xavier Bray, '*Christ on the Cross, 1627*', in *The Sacred Made Real*, cat. 25, p. 160.

8 José Gestoso y Pérez, *Ensayo de un diccionario de los artífices que florecieron en Sevilla desde el siglo XIII al XVIII inclusive*, 3 vols (1899–1909), 2:124–6 refs AMS: Papeles del conde del Águila, sección 11, tomo 38, no. 23.

9 *Velázquez in Seville*, cats 17–20.

10 See P. K. F. Moxey, 'Erasmus and the Iconography of Pieter Aertsen's *Christ in the House of Martha and Mary* in the Boymans-Van Beuningen Museum', *Journal of the Warburg and Courtauld Institutes*, 34 (1971), 335–6, and Erwin Panofsky, 'Erasmus and the Visual Arts', *Journal of the Warburg and Courtauld Institutes*, 32 (1969), 200–7.

11 Jonathan Brown and Richard Kagan, 'The Duke of Alcalá: His Collection and its Evolution', *Art Bulletin*, 69:2 (1987), 231–55.

12 Pacheco, *Arte de la pintura*, pp. 518, 527–8, 521.

13 *Velázquez in Seville*, cat. 31.

14 *Velázquez*, exhibition catalogue, ed. Dawson W. Carr (London: 2006), cat. 8.

15 Michael Baxandall, *Patterns of Intention: On the Historical Explanation of Pictures* (New Haven and London: 1985), pp. 3–4.

16 *Velázquez*, exhibition catalogue, ed. Antonio Domínguez Ortiz, Alfonso E. Pérez Sánchez and Julián Gállego (Madrid: 1990), cat. 4.

17 Luke 10:38–42.

18 Teresa, *Libro de las fundaciones*, in *Obras completas*, ch. 5, p. 545.

19 *Velázquez*, ed. Domínguez Ortiz, Pérez Sánchez and Gállego, cat. 8.

20 William L. Fichter, 'Una poesía contemporánea inédita sobre las bodas de Velázquez', in *Varia velazqueña: homenaje a Velázquez en el III centenario de su muerte 1660–1960*, 2 vols (Madrid: 1960), 1:637–9.

21 Matthew 14:1–12.

22 Fichter, 'Poesía', 1:637–9.

23 Palomino, *Vidas*, p. 155.

24 Alfredo J. Morales, *La obra renacentista del ayuntamiento de Sevilla* (Seville: 1981), pp. 135–6.

25 M. Herrero García, *Ideas de los españoles del siglo XVII* (Madrid: [1928]), pp. 169–89; Diego Hurtado de Mendoza, *Guerra de Granada* (Valencia: 1776 [1627]), pp. 275–6.

26 Teodoro Falcón Márquez, *El Palacio de las Dueñas y las casas-palacio sevillanas del siglo XVI* (Seville: 2003).

27 Teresa, *Libro de las fundaciones*, in *Obras completas*, ch. 5, p. 545.

28 Suzanne L. Stratton, *The Immaculate Conception in Spanish Art* (New York: 1994).

29 Ortiz de Zúñiga, *Anales eclesiásticos*, 4:245.

30 Ibid., 4:234–5.

31 Ibid., 4:236–8.

32 Ibid., 4:235:

> Todo el mundo en general
> A voces, Reina escogida,
> Diga que sois concebida
> Sin pecado original.

33 Ibid., 4:248–56.
34 Ibid., 4:263–8.
35 Ibid., 4:269–75.
36 Revelations 17:1–5.
37 Pacheco, *Arte de la pintura*, pp. 576–7.

17   Politics and Poetry: Góngora and Quevedo

1 Jammes, *Obra poética*, pp. 97–100.
2 The *juego de cañas* was a martial sport in which teams of riders, taking turns, threw light cane javelins at one another and defended themselves with shields. Góngora, *Obras completas*, no. 273, pp. 485–6:

> Hermosas damas . . .
> ¿quién con piedad al andaluz no mira,
> y quien al andaluz su favor niega?
> ¿Quién en la plaza los bohordos tira,
> mata los toros, y las cañas juega?
> ¿En saraos, quién lleva las más veces
> los dulcísimos ojos de la sala,
> sino galanes de el Andalucía?

3 Góngora, *Obras completas*, nos 275–7, 279, pp. 486–9.
4 Quevedo, 'Ya que coplas componeis', at http://www.franciscodequevedo. org/index.php?option=com_content&id=83%3Aya-que-coplas-componeis-826&Itemid=59:

> sois poeta nefando
> pues cantáis culos así.

5 Góngora, *Obras completas*, no. 22, pp. 430–2; and see Pablo Jauralde Pou, *Francisco de Quevedo (1580–1645)* (Madrid: 1999), pp. 906–8.
6 Quevedo, 'en lo sucio que has cantado', at http://www.franciscodequevedo. org/index.php?option=com_content&view=article&id=77%3Aen-lo-sucio-que-has-cantado-827&catid=35%3Adecimas&Itemid=59:

> En lo sucio que has cantado
> y en lo largo de narices,
> demás de que tú lo dices,
> que no eres limpio has mostrado.
>
> Eres hombre apasionado;
> y por saber que es corona
> la Pasión en tu persona,
> es punto más necesario
> que esté en el monte Calvario
> puesta de hoy más tu Helicona.

Traducir un hombre al rey
de francés en castellano,
mandándolo por su mano,
es justo, y por justa ley;
mas no [a] la plebeya grey
ni al rey por dinero ruego,
como tu pariente ciego;
y no hagas desto donaire;
que mi culpa es cosa de aire,
pero la tuya, de fuego.

Por muy pequeña ocasion
sé que en perseguirme has dado:
de aquellos lo has heredado
que inventaron la Pasión.
Satírico no es razón
ser un hombre principal
que tiene sangre real;
yo lo sé: que tus pasados
fueron todos salpicados
con la de un Rey Celestial.

7 Góngora, *Obras completas*, no. 312, p. 507:

El Conde mi señor se fué á Napóles;
el Duque mi señor se fué a Francia:
príncipes, buen viajes, que este día
pesadumbre daré a unos caracoles.
Como sobran tan doctos españoles,
a nunguno ofrecí la Musa mía:
a un pobre albergue sí, de Andalucía,
que ha resistido a grandes, digo Soles.

8 Orozco, *Introducción*, p. 42.
9 José Ortega y Gassett, *Obras completas*, 13 vols (Madrid: 1983), 3:585.
10 Dámaso Alonso, *La lengua poética de Góngora* (Madrid: 1950), pp. 67–87.
11 Jammes, *Obra poética*, p. 66.
12 Góngora, *Obras completas*, no. 404, p. 616.
13 Luis de Góngora y Argote, *Soledades*, ed. Robert Jammes (Madrid: 1994), lines 366–525.
14 Federico García Lorca, 'La imagen poética de don Luis de Góngora', in *Obras completas*, ed. Arturo del Hoyo, 2 vols (Madrid: 1980 [1954]), 1:1036.
15 The long-standing riddle of what Góngora meant by 'generous terror' has only recently been solved; see Humberto Huergo Cardoso, 'Algunos lugares oscuros de las *Soledades* de Góngora', *Bulletin of Hispanic Studies*, 87 (2010), 17–41, esp. pp. 30–1.
16 Góngora, *Obras completas*, Epistolario 2, pp. 955–8, 958.
17 Baltasar Gracián, *La Agudeza y arte de ingenio*, ed. Evaristo Correa Calderón, 2 vols (Madrid: 1969 [1642]), p. 55.
18 García Lorca, 'Imagen poética', p. 1032; and see Jauralde Pou, *Quevedo*, p. 910.
19 Orozco, *Introducción*, p. 13.

20 Jammes, *Obra poética*, p. 277.

21 Orozco, *Introducción*, p. 47 n. 56 refs José de la Torre, 'Documentos gongorinos', *Boletín de la Real Academia de Ciencias, Bellas Letras y Nobles Artes de Córdoba*, 18 (1927), 65–218, doc. 95.

22 Góngora, *Obras completas*, Epistolario 5, pp. 961–2.

23 Quevedo, 'Yo te untaré mis obras con tocino', at http://www.franciscodequevedo. org/index.php?option=com_content&view=article&id=913%3Ayo-te-untare- mis-obras-con-tocino-829&catid=47%3Asonetos-sarcasmos&Itemid=59:

> Yo te untaré mis obras con tocino
> porque no me las muerdas, Gongorilla,
> perro de los ingenios de Castilla,
> docto en pullas, cual mozo de camino;
>
> apenas hombre, sacerdote indino,
> que aprendiste sin cristus la cartilla;
> chocarrero de Córdoba y Sevilla,
> y en la Corte bufón a lo divino.
>
> ¿Por qué censuras tú la lengua griega
> siendo sólo rabí de la judía,
> cosa que tu nariz aun no lo niega?
>
> No escribas versos más, por vida mía;
> aunque aquesto de escribas se te pega,
> por tener de sayón la rebeldía.

24 Jauralde Pou, *Francisco de Quevedo*, pp. 351–62.

25 Gregorio Marañón, *El Conde-Duque de Olivares (La pasión de mandar)* (Madrid: 1936), p. 25: 'el soñar así era para él función tan natural como la respiración'.

26 John H. Elliott, *The Count-Duke of Olivares: The Statesman in an Age of Decline* (New Haven and London: 1986), p. 20.

27 Brown, *Images and Ideas*, pp. 60–1.

28 Marañón, *Conde-Duque*, pp. 31, 143.

29 Elliott, *Count-Duke*, p. 28.

30 Francisco Quevedo y Villegas, *Epistolario completo de don Francisco de Quevedo Villegas*, ed. Luis Astrana Marín (Madrid: 1946), Letter 10, to the Duke of Osuna, 1615, pp. 23–6, 23.

31 Jaroslav Martinitz, 'Beschreibung der Böhmischen Rebellion in anno 1618', Knihovna Nárdního Muzea, Praha, Sign. VI G. 2, in Tryntje Helfferich (ed. and trans.), *The Thirty Years War: A Documentary History* (Indianapolis and Cambridge: 2009), doc. 1, pp. 14–19; Martinitz was the first man to be thrown out of the window.

32 Peter Milner von Milhausen, *Apologia oder Entschuldigungsschrift . . .* (Prague: 1618), in Helfferich (ed. and trans.), *Thirty Years War*, doc. 2, pp. 20–2.

33 Robert Bireley, *The Jesuits and the Thirty Years War* (Cambridge and New York: 2003), p. 35.

34 Parker, *Crisis*, pp. 165–9.

35 Lynch, *Hispanic World*, pp. 77–82.

18   *Drama: Olivares and Don Juan*

1   Matías de Novoa, *Historia de Felipe III, Rey de España*, in *CODOIN*, 60 and 61, 61:328–43.

2   Francisco de Quevedo, 'Grandes anales de quince días. Historia de muchos siglos que pasaron en un mes' [1621], ed. Victoriano Roncero López, in *Obras completas en prosa*, ed. Alfonso Rey, 3 vols (Madrid: 2005), 3:44–115, p. 59.

3   Ibid., pp. 65, 61.

4   'Autosemblanza de Felipe IV', appendix 2 in Carlos Seco Serrano (ed.), *Cartas de Sor María de Jesús de Ágreda y de Felipe IV*, 2 vols (Madrid: 1958), 2:231–6, p. 232.

5   Juan Antonio de Vera y Figueroa, Count of La Roca, *Fragmentos históricos de la vida de D. Gaspar de Guzmán*, in Antono de Valladares de Sotomayor (ed.), *Semanario Erudito*, vol. 2 (1787), 145–296, p. 162.

6   'Autosemblanza', 2:232.

7   Richard Kagan, *Clio and the Crown: The Politics of History in Medieval and Early Modern Spain* (Baltimore: 2009), pp. 201–3.

8   John H. Elliott and José F. de la Peña, *Memoriales y cartas del Conde Duque de Olivares*, 2 vols (Madrid: 1978–80), 2:doc. XIIa, Olivares to Archbishop of Granada.

9   Fernando Bouza Álvarez, 'Semblanza y aficiones del monarca: Música, astros, libros y bufones', in *Felipe IV: El hombre y el reinado*, ed. José Alcalá-Zamora y Queipo de Llano (Madrid: 1996), 27–44, p. 28 n. 5 refs A. Remón, *Entretenimientos y juegos honestos y recreaciones . . .* (Madrid: 1623).

10   Jonathan Brown and John H. Elliott, *A Palace for a King: The Buen Retiro and the Court of Philip IV* (New Haven and London: 1980), p. 22 n. 25 refs ADM: leg. 79, 21 January 1633.

11   Basilio Sebastián Castellanos de Losada (ed.), *El bibliotecario y el trovador español . . .* (Madrid: 1841), p. 59: 'Relación de lo sucedido en el convento de la Encarnación . . .'

12   Antonio Valladares (ed.), 'Carta que el ilustrísimo señor don Garceran Alvarez, arzobispo de Granada, maestro que fue del rey don Felipe IV escribió al Conde-Duque de Olivares', in *Semanario erudito* (Madrid: 1787), 3:64, 66.

13   Elliott, *Count-Duke*, p. 112 n. 109 refs BNE: Ms 18,428, f. 30, Mirabel to Gondomar, 10 March 1622.

14   Mary C. Volk, 'Rubens in Madrid and the Decoration of the King's Summer Apartments', *Burlington Magazine*, 123:942 (1981), 513–29, p. 519.

15   Cassiano dal Pozzo, *Il diario del viaggio in Spagna del Cardinale Francesco Barberini*, ed. Alessandra Anselmi (Madrid: 2004), pp. 99–100.

16   Volk, 'Rubens', pp. 513–29.

17   Gloria Martínez Leiva and Ángel Rodríguez Rebollo (eds), *Qvadros y otras cosas que tienen su Magestad Felipe IV en este Alcázar de Madrid, Año de 1636* (Madrid: 2007).

18   Volk, 'Rubens', p. 513.

19   See the literature survey in Jane Clinton Nash, 'Titian's *Poesie* for Philip II', Ph.D. thesis, Johns Hopkins University, 1981, pp. 33–156.

20   Ibid., pp. 179–83.

21 Javier Portús Pérez, *La Sala Reservada del Museo del Prado y el coleccionismo de pintura de desnudo en la Corte Española, 1554–1838* (Madrid: 1998), pp. 16–17 refs Felipe de Guevara, *Comentarios de la pintura* (Madrid: 1778 [1564]), pp. 16–17.

22 Portús Pérez, *Sala Reservada*, p. 36 n. 35 refs José de Jesús María, *Primera parte de las excelencias de la virtud de la castidad* ([Madrid]: 1601).

23 Portús Pérez, *Sala Reservada*, p. 40.

24 Ibid., p. 91 n. 66 refs Volk, 'Rubens in Madrid', p. 526.

25 Luis Rosales, *Pasión y muerte del conde de Villamediana* (Madrid: 1969).

26 François Bertaut, 'Diario de Viaje a España' [1669], in García Mercadal, *Viajes*, 2:417.

27 Rosales, *Pasión y muerte*, p. 88 n. 19 refs Gonzalo de Céspedes y Meneses, *Prima parte de la historia de D. Felipe el IV, Rey de las Españas* (Lisbon: 1631), p. 239.

28 Gongora, *Obras completas*, Epistolario 100, pp. 1095–6.

29 Quevedo, *Grandes anales*, pp. 107–8.

30 Rosales, *Pasión y muerte*, p. 34 refs BNE: H.97, f. 112.

31 Rosales, *Pasión y muerte*, p. 36.

32 Fernando Manoio, *Relación del muerte de Rodrigo Calderón* (Madrid: [1621]).

33 Góngora, *Obras completas*, Epistolario 68, p. 1052.

34 Manoio, *Relación*.

35 Orozco, *Introducción*, p. 50 n. 59 refs Miguel Artigas, *Don Luis de Góngora y Argote: Biografía y estudio crítico* (Madrid: 1925), p. 178.

36 Góngora, *Obras completas*, Epistolario 80, pp. 1067–9, 1067.

37 A useful overview of Golden Age Spanish theatre in English is Jonathan Thacker, *A Companion to Golden-Age Drama* (London: 2007).

38 François Bertaut, 'Diario' [1669], in García Mercadal, *Viajes*, 2:550–688, pp. 642–3.

39 Cosimo III de Medici, Grand Duke of Tuscany, 'Viaje por España', in José María Diez Borque (ed.), *La vida española en el Siglo de Oro según los extranjeros* (Barcelona: 1990), p. 225.

40 Marie Catherine le Jumel de Barneville, Mme D'Aulnoy, 'Relación del viaje a España', in García Mercadal, *Viajes*, 2:920–1104, pp. 1037–8.

41 Luis Díaz Viana, 'En torno al origen legendario de "El convidado de piedra"', *Cuadernos de trabajo* (Centro Cultural de Estudios Folklóricos: Valladolid), 2 (1980), 77–126.

42 Diego Catalán (ed.), *Gran crónica de Alfonso XI: Fuentes cronísticas de la historia de España IV* (Madrid: 1976), 1:366.

43 Pablo Espinosa de Monteros, *Historia y grandezas de Sevilla*, 2 vols (Seville: 1627–30), 1:50–1.

44 Alfredo Rodríguez López-Vázquez, 'Don Pedro y Don Juan', in Francisco Ruíz Ramón and César Oliva (eds), *El mito en el teatro clásico español: Ponencias y debates de las VII jornadas de teatro clásico español (Almagro, 25 al 27 de septiembre, 1984)* (Madrid: 1988), 192–5.

45 Ángel Gónzalez Palencia, 'Tirso y las comedias ante la Junta de Reformación', *Boletín de la Real Academia Española*, 25 (1946), 43–84; Ruth Lee Kennedy, *Studies in Tirso, I: The Dramatist and his Competitors, 1620–26* (Chapel Hill: 1974), pp. 85ff.

19 The Prince of Wales in Madrid

1 Anon., 'Relación de la llegada del Principe de Gales', in José Simón Díaz (ed.), *Relaciones breves de actos públicos celebrados en Madrid de 1541 a 1650* (Madrid: 1982), 197–9; James Howell, *Epistolae Ho-Elianae: The Familiar Letters of James Howell*, ed. Joseph Jacobs (London: 1890), bk 1, Letter XV, p. 164. The background to and story of Charles's journey to Madrid is brilliantly explained in Glyn Redworth, *The Prince and the Infanta: The Cultural Politics of the Spanish Match* (New Haven and London: 2003).

2 Howell, *Epistolae*, p. 164.

3 Andrés Almansa y Mendoza, *Obra periodística*, ed. Henry Ettinghausen and Manuel Borrego (Madrid: 2001), Relación 1, p. 330.

4 Góngora, *Obras completas*, no. 382, p. 546.

5 Almansa y Mendoza, *Obra*, p. 334.

6 *Calendar of State Papers: Venetian, 1621–1623*, p. 613.

7 Almansa y Mendoza, *Obra*, p. 331.

8 Henry Ellis (ed.), *Original Letters Illustrative of English History*, series 1, 3 vols (London: 1825), 3:123–4 in the footnotes quotes 'Life and Death of the Duke of Buckingham', in *Reliquiae Wottonianae* (London: 1651), pp. 81–9 and Letter CCLXXIV, Charles and Buckingham while incognito at Paris to the King, BL: Ms Harl. 6987, art. 6, pp. 121–2; for the eye-patch see Anon., 'Relación de la llegada . . .', p. 198.

9 Richard Wynn, 'Account of the Journey of Prince Charles's Servants into Spain in the Year 1623', in *Historia Vitae et Regni Ricardi II*, ed. Thomas Hearne (Oxford: 1729), 297–340, pp. 298–308.

10 Robert Bargrave, *The Travel Diary of Robert Bargrave, Levant Merchant (1647–1656)*, ed. Michael G. Brennan (London: 1999), p. 206.

11 Juan Antonio de Vera y Figueroa (Conde de la Roca), 'Extract from "Fragmentos historicos de la vida de Con Gaspar de Guzman . . ."', in Francisco de Jesús, *El hecho de los tratados del matrimonio pretendido por el Príncipe de Gales . . .*, ed. & trans. Samuel Rawson Gardiner (London: 1869), appendix 10, pp. 325–6.

12 Ibid.

13 Howell, *Epistolae*, p. 165.

14 Almansa y Mendoza, *Obra*, p. 342; e.g. the poet Francisco López de Zárate, *Obras varias*, ed. José Simón Díaz, 2 vols (Madrid: 1947), 1:74.

15 *Calendar of State Papers. Venetian, 1621–1623*, pp. 637–9.

16 Ibid., p. 639.

17 Redworth, *Prince*, p. 98.

18 *Calendar of State Papers: Venetian, 1621–1623*, p. 638.

19 Ellis, *Original Letters*, pp. 146–7: Letter CCLXXXVII, Buckingham to the King, Ms Harl. 69867, art. 40; Redworth, *Prince*, p. 112 n. 2 refs John Bowle, *Charles I: A Biography* (London, 1975), p. 75.

20 Howell, *Epistolae*, Letter XVIII, p. 169.

21 Redworth, *Prince*, pp. 99, 123.

22 Elliott and Peña, *Memoriales y cartas*, 2:96.

23 Jacinto Herrera y Sotomayor, *Jornada que Su Magestad hizo a la Andaluzia* (Madrid: 1624), f. 1r.

24 Ibid., f. 3r.
25 Bernardo Mendoza, *Relación del lucimiento y grandeza con que el Duque de Medina Sidonia festejó Su Magestad en el bosque llamado Doña Ana* (Madrid: 1624), f. 1r.
26 Enriqueta Vila Vilar, 'Las ferias de Portobelo: apariencia y realidad del comercio con Indias', *Anuario de Estudios Americanos*, 39 (1982), 275–340, p. 275.
27 Elliott, *Count-Duke*, pp. 153–4.
28 Herrera y Sotomayor, *Jornada*, f. 4v; Elliott, *Count-Duke*, pp. 164–5.
29 Mendoza, *Relación*, f. 2r.
30 Herrera y Sotomayor, *Jornada*, f. 6r.
31 Elliott, *Count-Duke*, p. 156.
32 For what follows on fraud and the decline of the Atlantic trade see Vila Vilar, 'Ferias de Portobelo'.
33 Ibid., pp. 326–7; p. 327 n. 148 refs AGI: Panama 1, Consulta del Consejo, Madrid, 21 March 1626.
34 Ibid., p. 327 n. 149 refs AGI: Panama 1, Madrid, 26 March 1926.
35 Ibid., pp. 327–8; p. 328 n. 148 refs AGI: Consulado, 110, Carta del Consulado, Seville, 18 March 1626.
36 Elliott, *Count-Duke*, pp. 156–7; Vila Vilar, 'Ferias de Portobelo', p. 327 n. 149 refs AGI: Panama 1, Consulta del Consejo, Madrid, 8 January 1627.

20   *Triumph and Disaster*

1   Marañón, *Conde-Duque*, pp. 282–3; p. 283 n. 46 refs BNE: Ms 41–11.263 and ADA, G-96–14; Olivares to unknown recipient, 4 September 1626.
2   Marañón, *Conde-Duque*, pp. 280–1 n. 44 refs BNE: Ms 10.857–44, f. 105bis, Fray Antonio Pérez, Letter of Condolence, 30 July 1626.
3   Castellanos de Losada (ed.), *Bibliotecario*, p. 72bis [68]: 'Vida licenciosa y hechos escandalosos y sacrilegios . . .'
4   Ruth Saunders Magurn (ed. and trans.), *The Letters of Peter Paul Rubens* (Cambridge, MA: 1955), p. 295; Rubens to Gevaerts, Madrid, 29 December 1628.
5   Matías de Novoa, *Historia de Felipe IV*, 4 vols (Madrid: 1878), 1:73–6.
6   Elliott and Peña, *Memoriales y cartas*, 2:19–23.
7   Ibid., 2:47–8.
8   Elliott, *Count-Duke*, p. 384.
9   Novoa, *Historia de Felipe IV*, 1:89–90.
10 Antonio Rodríguez Villa, *Ambrosio Spínola: primer Marqués de los Balbases* (Madrid: 1904), pp. 592–5, 592, 595.
11 Ibid., pp. 564, 567.
12 Magurn, *Letters of Rubens*, p. 295: Rubens to Gevaerts, Madrid, 29 December 1628.
13 Castellanos de Losada (ed.), *Bibliotecario*, p. 71bis [67]: 'Vida licenciosa y hechos escandalosos y sacrilegios . . .'
14 Marañón, *Conde-Duque*, p. 105.
15 *Velázquez*, ed. Dominguez Ortiz et al., cat. 41, p. 253.
16 Brown and Elliott, *Palace*, p. 71 n. 66 refs BL: Egerton Ms 1820, f. 286, Hopton to Coke, 26 October 1632; n. 65 ref. ASF: Mediceo, filza 4959, 15 January 1633 and 3 December 1633; and p. 59.

17 Brown and Elliott, *Palace*, p. 60 n. 28.

18 Ibid., p. 60 n. 28 and p. 71 n. 65 ref. ASF: Mediceo, filza 4959, 15 January 1633 and 3 December 1633.

19 Diego Covarrubias y Leyva (ed.), *Elogios al Palacio Real del Buen Retiro escritos por algunos ingenios de España* (Madrid: 1635).

20 Muret, Letter of 10 January 1667, in García Mercadal, *Viajes*, 2:710–33.

21 Brown and Elliott, *Palace*, pp. 116–18.

22 Ibid., p. 111.

23 Andrés Úbeda de los Cobos, 'The History of Rome Cycle', in Andrés Úbeda de los Cobos (ed.), *Paintings for the Planet King: Philip IV and the Buen Retiro Palace* (Madrid and London: 2005), 169–89.

24 José María de Azcárate, 'Una Variante en la edición de los *Diálogos* de Carducho con noticia sobre el Buen Retiro', *Archivo Español de Arte*, 95 (1951), 261–2.

25 José Álvarez Lopear, 'The Hall of Realms: The Present State of Knowledge and a Reconsideration', in Úbeda de los Cobos, *Paintings for the Planet King*, 91–111, p. 94.

26 Ibid., p. 94 n. 31 refs Françoise Langlois de Mottevill, *Mémoires pour servir à l'histoire d'Anne d'Autriche . . .* (Amsterdam: 1723), 5:58–9.

27 María Luisa Caturla, 'Cartas de pago de los doce cuadros de batallas para el salón de reinos del Buen Retiro', *Archivo Español de Arte*, 33 (1960), 333–55, pp. 341, 343.

28 Brown and Elliott, *Palace*, pp. 149–50.

29 Lope de Vega, *El Brasil Restituido: Obras de Lope de Vega XXVIII*, ed. Marcelino Menéndez Pelayo (Madrid: 1970), p. 294, Act 3; see Brown and Elliott, *Palace*, pp. 186–7.

30 Alvarez Lopear, 'The Hall of Realms', p. 107 n. 94.

31 Pedro Calderón de la Barca, *La vida es sueño*, ed. Ciriaco Morón (Madrid: 1983 [1635]), lines 2072–5:
    Salga a la anchurosa plaza
    del gran teatro del mundo
    este valor sin segundo,
    porque mi venganze cuadre.

32 Ibid., lines 2101–7 and 2182–7:
    Y no estoy muy engañado; porque si ha sido sñado,
    lo que vi palpable y cierto,
    lo que veo será incerito;
    y no es mucho que rendido,
    pues veo estando dormido,
    que sueñe estando despierto.
    . . .
    ¿Qué es la vida? Un frenesí.
    ¿Qué es la vida? Una ilusión,
    una sombra, una ficción,
    . . .
    que toda la vida es sueño,
    y los sueños, sueños son.

33 Kagan, *Clio and the Crown*, p. 202.

21   *Death and Defeat*

1   Elliott, *Revolt of the Catalans*, p. 253 n. 4 refs Jeroni Pujades, *Dietari*, Biblioteca de la Universidad de Barcelona: Ms 975, [vol. 4], f. 94v.

2   Lynch, *Hispanic World*, pp. 150–4.

3   Letters of 29 August and 1 September in Anon., *Memorial Histórico Español: colección de documentos, opúsculos y antigüedades*, 16 (1862), pp. 161–5.

4   Elliott, *Count-Duke*, pp. 637–9, 650–1.

5   Marañón, *Conde-Duque*, appendix 28.

6   Ibid., pp. 398–404.

7   Ibid., appendix 28.

8   R. A. Stradling, *Spain's Struggle for Europe, 1598–1668* (London and Rio Grande: 1994), pp. 147–76, 283–5.

9   Sor María de Ágreda, *Cartas de la venerable madre Sor María de Ágreda y del Señor Rey Don Felipe IV*, ed. Francisco Silvela, 2 vols (Madrid: 1885).

10 Jonathan I. Israel, *The Dutch Republic and the Hispanic World, 1606–1661* (Oxford: 1982), p. 353.

11 Laura Manzano Baena, *Conflicting Words: The Peace Treaty of Münster (1648) and the Political Culture of the Dutch Republic and the Spanish Monarchy* (Leuven: 2011).

12 For this and what follows I have used the account in Ortiz de Zúñiga, *Annales eclesiasticos*, 4:395–416.

13 Dominguez Ortiz, *Orto y ocaso*, pp. 85–7.

14 Ortiz de Zúñiga, *Annales eclesiasticos*, 5:77–99.

15 *Zurbarán y su obrador: pinturas para el Nuevo Mundo*, exhibition catalogue, ed. Benito Navarrete Prieto (Valencia: 1998), 19–31; J. M. Palomero Páramo, 'Notas sobre el taller de Zurbarán: un envío de lienzos a Portobelo y Lima en el años de 1636', in *Actas del congreso: Extremadura en la Evangelización del Nuevo Mundo* (Madrid: 1990), 313–30.

16 Duncan T. Kinkead, 'Juan Lazón and the Sevillian Painting Trade with the New World in the Second Half of the Seventeenth Century', *Art Bulletin*, 66:2 (1984), pp. 303–10.

17 Lutgardo García Fuentes, *El comercio español con América, 1650–1700* (Seville: 1980), table 34, p. 505.

18 Duncan T. Kinkead, 'Last Sevillian Period of Francisco de Zurbarán', *Art Bulletin*, 65:2 (1983), 303–15, p. 308.

19 Fray Juan de Madariaga, *Vida del seráfico padre San Bruno, Patriarca de la Cartuja* (Valencia: 1596), ff. 147r–48r.

20 Luis Manuel Calzada and Luys Santa Marina, *Estampas de Zurbarán* (Barcelona: 1929), 31.

21 García Fuentes, *Comercio*, table 34, p. 505.

22 Kinkead, 'Last Sevillian Period', p. 306; María Luisa Caturla, *Fin y muerte de Francisco de Zurbarán* (Madrid: 1964), p. 13.

23 Kinkead, 'Last Sevillian Period', p. 306; Caturla, *Fin y muerte*, p. 8.

24 Caturla, *Fin y muerte*, pp. 15–23.

25 Palomino, *Vidas*, p. 175.

26 Enriqueta Harris, *Velázquez* (Oxford: 1982), pp. 136–7; Jennifer Montagu, 'Velázquez Marginalia: His Slave Juan de Pareja and his Illegitimate Son Antonio', *Burlington Magazine*, 125:968 (1983), 683–5, pp. 684–5.

27 Harris, *Velázquez*, pp. 172–4.

28 Palomino, *Vidas*, p. 182.

29 Ibid.

30 Ángel Aterido Fernández (ed.), *Corpus velazqueño*, 2 vols (Madrid: 2000), 2:344–451.

31 Alfonso E. Pérez Sánchez, 'Velázquez y su arte', in *Velázquez*, ed. Domínguez Ortiz, Pérez Sánchez and Gállego, 21–56, p. 54.

32 Peter Cherry, 'Documentary Appendix on Justino de Neve', in *Murillo and Justino de Neve*, 143–68, pp. 156–66.

33 Peter Cherry, 'Justino de Neve: Life and Works', in *Murillo and Justino de Neve*, 31–45, p. 31.

34 Teodoro Falcón Márquez, 'The Church of Santa María la Blanca in Seville, Meeting Point between Murillo and Justino de Neve', in *Murillo and Justino de Neve*, 61–72, pp. 66–7.

35 Diego Angulo Íñiguez, *Murillo: su vida, su arte, su obra*, 3 vols (Madrid: 1981), 1:329.

36 Antonio Ponz, *Viage de España, en que se da noticia de las cosas más apreciables . . .* (Madrid: 1947 [1771–94]), p. 794; Peter Rogers, *The Mystery Play in Madame Bovary: Moeurs de Province* (Amsterdam: 2009), p. 42.

37 Elena Cenalmor Bruquetas, 'The Immaculate Conception of the Venerables Sacerdotes', in *Murillo and Justino de Neve*, cat. 7.

Epilogue

1 Arsène Legrelle, *La mission de M. de Rébenac à Madrid et la mort de Marie-Louise, reine d'Espagne (1688–1689)* (Paris: 1894), Rébenac to Louis XIV dated 23 December 1688; John Nada, *Carlos the Bewitched: The Last Spanish Habsburg, 1661–1700* (London: 1962), p. 130.

2 Enriqueta Vila Vilar, 'El poder del Consulado Sevillano y los hombres del comercio en el siglo XVII: una aproximación', in Enriqueta Vila Vilar and Allan J. Kuethe (eds), *Relaciones de poder y comercio colonial: nuevas perspectivas* (Seville: 1999), 3–34, pp. 28–9.

3 Juan de Cárdenas, *Breve relación de la muerte, vida y virtudes del venerable caballero D. Miguel Mañara . . .* (Seville: 1903), p. 377.

4 Ibid., p. 42.

5 Jonathan Brown, 'Hieroglyphs of Death and Salvation: The Decoration of the Church of the Hermandad de la Caridad, Seville', in *Images and Ideas*, 128–46, p. 134.

6 E. Valdivieso and J. M. Serrera, *El Hospital de la Caridad de Sevilla* (Seville: 1980), p. 11.

7 Matthew 25:35–6.

8 Valdivieso and Serrera, *Hospital de la Caridad*, p. 71.

9 Ibid., p. 72.

10   W. Matthews, 'Samuel Pepys and Spain', *Neophilologus*, 20:3 (1935), 120–9, p. 129.

11   Valdivieso and Serrera, *Hospital de la Caridad*, p. 66.

12   Miguel Mañara Vicentelo de Leca, *Discurso de la Verdad* (Madrid: 1878 [1670]), p. 13.

13   Ibid., p. 26.

14   Ibid., pp. 13–14.

15   Ibid., pp. 14, 25.

16   Ibid., p. 25.

17   Cristóbal Pérez Pastor (ed.), *Documentos para la biografía de D. Pedro Calderón de la Barca*, vol. 1 (Madrid: 1905), doc. 188, pp. 375–6.

18   Calderón, *Vida es sueño*, lines 199–203:
      este rústico desierto
      donde miserable vivo,
      siendo un esqueleto vivo,
      siendo un animado muerto.

19   Palomino claims he died in Cadiz, but as his will was made *in extremis* and is dated in Seville on the same day as his death, that is all but impossible; see Nina Ayala Mallory, *Bartolomé Esteban Murillo* (Madrid: 1983), p. 31.

20   Mañara, *Discurso*, p. 12.

A Note about Currency and Monetary Values

In the sixteenth and seventeenth centuries, the basic unit of account in Castile was the *maravedí*. The word may be corruption of *morabotín*, the name given to a gold *dinar* minted in Moorish Spain in the Middle Ages.

1 copper *blanca*	½ *maravedí*
1 copper *cuarto*	4 *maravedís*
1 silver *real*	16 *maravedís*
1 crown	350–612 *maravedís*
1 gold *escudo*	330–612 *maravedís*
1 doubloon	2 *escudos*
1 gold ducat	375–429 *maravedís*
1 *castellano*	
or *peso de oro*	442–576 *maravedís*

The business of money and currency in Spain – not to mention across Europe and the Americas – during the period covered by this book is complex and at times bewildering. So much so that many standard textbooks largely ignore the subject. The same name was often used at different times or in different places to describe different coins of differing or sometimes similar values. Conversely, coins of similar or identical value might be known by different names in different places or at different times. If this were not confusing enough, the values of coins changed in relation to each other, which might be by royal diktat, but primarily because of fluctuations in the relative values of gold, silver and copper, the metals used to mint coins. Matters become further complicated in the seventeenth century when the Spanish Crown began issuing much debased copper *vellón* with little or no silver content or devaluing existing coins in circulation. The table above shows a basic range of values for coins in circulation over the period, with the lower values more or less accurate until the seventeenth century, when values move around very significantly.

Bibliography

Literary Texts

Ávila, Juan de, *Obras completas*, ed. Francisco Martín Hernández, 6 vols (Madrid: 1971).

Boscán, Juan, *Obras*, ed. Carlos Clavería (Barcelona: 1991 [1543]).

Calderón de la Barca, Pedro, *La vida es sueño*, ed. Ciriaco Morón (Madrid: 1983 [1635]).

Castiglione, Baltasar, *Los quatro libros, del cortesano compuestos en italiano por el conde Balthasar Castellon, y agora nueuamente traduzidos en lengua castellana por Boscan* (Barcelona: 1534).

Cervantes Saavedra, Miguel de, *Don Quijote de la Mancha*, ed. Francisco Rico et al., 2 vols (Madrid: 2005 [1604–15]).

—, *La Galatea*, ed. Francisco López Estrada and María Teresa López García-Berdoy (Madrid: 1995 [1585]).

—, *The History and Adventures of the Renowned Don Quixote*, trans. Tobias Smollett (London: 1796).

—, *El juez de los divorcios* ([Madrid: 1610–15]), at http://cervantes.tamu.edu/english/ctxt/cec/disk7/ENTREMES.html.

—, *Novelas ejemplares*, ed. Harry Sieber, 2 vols (Madrid: 1991 [1613]).

—, *Ocho comedias y ocho entremeses nuevos nunca representados* [(Madrid: 1615]), at www.cervantesvirtual.com/obra/ocho-comedias-y-ocho-entremeses-nuevos-nunca-representados-o.

—, *Los trabajos de Persiles y Sigismunda*, ed. Juan Bautista Avalle-Arce (Madrid: 1969 [1617]).

Covarrubias y Leyva, Diego (ed.), *Elogios al Palacio Real del Buen Retiro escritos por algunos ingenios de España* (Madrid: 1635).

Garcilaso de la Vega, El Inca, *La Florida del Inca* (Lisbon: 1605).

Garcilaso de la Vega, *Obras completas con comentario*, ed. Elias L. Rivers (Madrid: 2001 [1981]).

Góngora y Argote, Luis de, *Obras completas*, ed. Juan Millé y Giménez and Isabel Millé y Giménez (Madrid: [1900]).

—, *Soledades*, ed. John Beverley (Madrid: 2007).

—, *Soledades*, ed. Robert Jammes (Madrid: 1994).

Gracián, Baltasar, *La Agudeza y arte de ingenio*, ed. Evaristo Correa Calderón, 2 vols (Madrid: 1969 [1642]).

John of the Cross, Saint, *Complete Works*, ed. Allison Peers, 3 vols (London: 1935).

[John of the Cross, Saint] Juan de la Cruz, San, *Poesía*, ed. Domingo Ynduráin (Madrid: 1992).

—, *Subida del monte Carmelo*, ed. Eulogio Pacho, bk 3, ch. 35, at http://es.catholic. net/santoral/147/2519/articulo.php?id=2058.

León, Luis de, *Traducción literal y declaración del Cantar de los Cantares de Salomón* (Madrid: 1798 [*c.*1561]), at http://bib.cervantesvirtual.com/servlet/SirveObras/ p268/12147297718948273987213/index.htm.

Lope de Vega y Carpio, Félix, *El Brasil Restituido: Obras de Lope de Vega XXVIII*, ed. Marcelino Menendez Pelayo (Madrid: 1970 [1625]).

—, *Cartas*, ed. Nicolás Marín and Luis Fernández de Córdoba (Madrid: 1985).

—, *Corona trágica, vida y muerte de la serenissima reyna de Escocia María Estuarda a Nuestro Padre Urbano VIII* (Madrid: 1627).

—, 'Una dama se vende' [*c.*1587], in *Cancionero de obras de burlas provocantes a risa*, ed. Eduardo de Lustonó (Madrid: 1872), p. 278.

—, *La Dragontea* (Valencia: 1598).

—, *La hermosura de Angélica* (Madrid: 1602).

—, *La viuda valenciana*, in *Comedias*, Part 15 (Madrid: 1620 [*c.*1600]).

López de Zárate, Francisco, *Obras varias*, ed. José Simón Díaz, 2 vols (Madrid: 1947).

Mal Lara, Juan de, *Philosophia vulgar* (Seville: 1568).

Mañara Vicentelo de Leca, Miguel, *Discurso de la Verdad* (Madrid: 1878 [1670]).

Ovid, *Metamorphosis*, Book 10, at http://www.mythology.us/ovid_metamorphoses_ book_10.htm.

Pérez de Hita, Ginés, *Guerras civiles de Granada* (Cuenca: 1595–1616).

Quevedo y Villegas, Francisco de, 'En lo sucio que has cantado', at http: //www.franciscodequevedo.org/index.php?option=com_content&view= article&id=77%3Aen-lo-sucio-que-has-cantado-827&catid=35%3Adecimas& Itemid=59.

—, *Epistolario completo de don Francisco de Quevedo Villegas*, ed. Luis Astrana Marín (Madrid: 1946).

—, 'Grandes anales de quince días. Historia de muchos siglos que pasaron en un mes' [1621], ed. Victoriano Roncero López, in *Obras completas*, ed. Alfonso Rey, 3 vols (Madrid: 2005), 3:44–115.

—, *Obras completas*, ed. Alfonso Rey, 3 vols (Madrid: 2005).

—, *Obras completas*, ed. Astrana Marín (Madrid: 1947).

—, *Quevedo y su poética dedicada a Olivares: Estudio y edición*, ed. E. L. Rivers (Pamplona: 1998).

—, 'Ya que coplas componeis', at http://www.franciscodequevedo.org/index. php?option=com_content&id=83%3Aya-que-coplas-componeis-826&Itemid=59.

—, 'Yo te untaré mis obras con tocino', at http://www.franciscodequevedo.org/index. php?option=com_content &view=article&id=913%3Ayo-te-untare-mis-obras- con-tocino-829&catid= 47%3Asonetos-sarcasmos&Itemid=59.

Teresa de Jesús, *Obras completas*, ed. Luis Santullano, 11th edn (Madrid: 1970).

Tirso de Molina [Gabriel Téllez], *El burlador de Sevilla o el convidado de piedra* (Madrid: 1630).

Primary Sources

The Holy Bible; all references are to the Douay–Rheims translation of the Latin Vulgate of 1605, at http://www.drbo.org/chapter/01001.htm.

AGI: Patronato 253, R.1, 'Información de Argel de Cervantes Expediente sobre méritos y servicios: Miguel de Cervantes'.

AGI: Santo Domingo, 51 R.9 N.87, 'Cartas de Audiencia'.

Ágreda, Sor María de, *Cartas de la venerable madre Sor María de Ágreda y del Señor Rey Don Felipe IV*, ed. Francisco Silvela, 2 vols (Madrid: 1885).

Albèri, Eugenio (ed.), *Relazioni degli ambasciatori veneti al senato*, 15 vols (Florence: 1839–63).

Alcalá, Ángel (ed.), *Proceso inquisitorial de fray Luis de León* (Valladolid: 1991).

Alcocer, Pedro de, *Relación de algunas cosas que pasaron en estos reinos desde que murió la reina católica doña Isabel, hasta que se acabaron las comunidades en la ciudad de Toledo* (Seville: 1872).

Almansa y Mendoza, Andrés, *Obra periodística*, ed. Henry Ettinghausen and Manuel Borrego (Madrid: 2001).

Álvarez, Vicente, *Relation du Beau Voyage que fit aux Pays-Bas en 1548 le Prince Philippe d'Espagne*, trans. M. T. Dovillée (Brussels: 1964 [c.1551]).

Álvarez de Toledo, Fernando, *Epistolario del III duque de Alba, Don Fernando Álvarez de Toledo*, 3 vols (Madrid: 1952).

Andrada, Francisco de, *Cronica do mvyto alto e mvito poderoso rey destes reynos de Portugal dom Ioao III deste nome* (Lisbon: 1613).

Anon., 'Diálogo llamado Philippino donde se refieren cien congrvencias concernientes al derecho que sv Magestad del Rei D. Phelippe nuestro señor tiene al Reino de Portugal', in *Felipe II: un monarca y su época*, exhibition catalogue, cat. 87.

—, *Memorial Histórico Español: colección de documentos, opúsculos y antigüedades*, vol. 16 ([Madrid]: 1862).

—, 'Relación de la llegada del Principe de Gales', in Simón Díaz (ed.), *Relaciones breves de actos públicos celebrados en Madrid de 1541 a 1650* (Madrid: 1982), 197–9.

—, 'Relación de lo que pasó en el auto que la santa inquisición hizo en la villa de Valladolid, en veinte [sic] de mayo de 1559 años, que fué domingo de la Trinidad', [AGS: Estado 137], in Novalín, *El inquisidor*, 2:239–48.

Arambaru, Marcos de, *Account of Marcos de Arambaru*, trans. W. Spotswood Green, *Proceedings of the Royal Irish Academy*, 27 (Dublin and London: 1908–9).

Aretino, Pietro, *Lettere*, ed. Paolo Procaccioli, *Edizione nazionale delle opere di Pietro Aretino*, 4 vols (Rome: 1997).

Ariño, Francisco de, *Sucesos de Sevilla de 1592 á 1604* (Seville: 1873).

Asensio, José María, *Nuevos documentos para ilustrar la vida de Miguel de Cervantes* (Sevilla: 1864).

Bargrave, Robert, *The Travel Diary of Robert Bargrave, Levant Merchant (1647–1656)*, ed. Michael G. Brennan (London: 1999).

Beatis, Antonio de, *The Travel Journal of Antonio de Beatis: Germany, Switzerland, the Low Countries, France and Italy, 1517–1518*, ed. J. R. Hale, trans. Hale and J. M. Lindon, Hakluyt Society, second series, number 150 (London: 1979), 'Diary', in Ludwig Pastor, 'Die Reise des Kardinals Luigi d'Aragona durch Deutschland, die Niederlande, Frankreich und Oberitalien, 1517–1518', *Erläuterungen und Ergänzungen zu Janssens Geschichte des deutschen Volkes*, IV:4 (Freiburg: 1905).

Bermúdez de Pedraza, Francisco, *Arte legal para estudiar la iurisprudencia* (Salamanca: 1612).

Bettenson, Henry C., *Documents of the Christian Church*, 4th edn (Oxford and New York: 1986).

Bornate, C. (ed.), 'Historia vite et gestorum per dominum magnum cancellarium', in *Miscellanea di storia Italiana*, 48 (1915), 233–568.

Borrow, George, *The Bible in Spain* (London: 1923).

Boswell, James, *The Life of Samuel Johnson*, 4 vols (London: 1823).

Bourdeille, Pierre (Seigneur de Brantôme) and André Vicomte de Bourdeille, *Oeuvres complètes*, ed. J. A. C. Bouchon, 2 vols (Paris: 1838).

Bradford, William (ed.), *Correspondence of the Emperor Charles V and his ambassadors at the courts of England and France: from the original letters in the imperial family archives at Vienna; with a connecting narrative and biographical notices of the Emperor and of some of the most distinguished officers of his army and household; together with the Emperor's itinerary from 1519–1551* (London: 1850).

Cabrera de Córdoba, Luis, *Historia de Felipe II, Rey de España*, ed. José Martínez Millán Carlos Javier de Carlos Morales, 3 vols (Valladolid: 1998).

Calendar of State Papers: Spanish, 1509–1525.

Calendar of State Papers: Spanish, 1529–1530.

Calendar of State Papers: Venetian, 1520–1526.

Calendar of State Papers: Venetian, 1581–1591.

Calendar of State Papers: Venetian, 1621–1623.

Calvete de Estrella, Juan Christóval, *El felicísimo viaje del muy alto y muy poderoso Príncipe don Phelippe*, ed. Paloma Cuenca (Madrid: 2001 [1552]).

Calvo Serraller, Francisco (ed.), *La teoría de la pintura en el Siglo de Oro* (Madrid: 1981).

The Canons and Decrees of the Council of Trent, trans. Rev. H. J. Schroeder (Rockford, IL: 1978).

Carducho, Vicente, *Diálogos de la pintura, su defensa, origen, escencia, definición, modos y diferencias*, ed. Francisco Calvo Serraller (Madrid: 1979 [1633]).

Castellanos de Losada, Basilio Sebastián (ed.), *El bibliotecario y el trovador español* (Madrid: 1841).

Catalán, Diego (ed.), *Gran crónica de Alfonso XI: Fuentes cronísticas de la historia de España IV* (Madrid: 1976).

CDI: Colección de documentos inéditos relativos al descubrimiento, conquista y organización de las antiguas posesiones españolas de América y Oceanía, ed. Joaquín F. Pacheco, Francisco de Cárdenas and Luis Torres de Mendoza, 42 vols (Madrid: 1864–84).

Centurión y Córdoba, Adan, Marquis of Estepa, *Información para la historia del Sacromonte . . . Primera parte* (Granada: 1623).

Céspedes y Meneses, Gonzalo de, *Prima parte de la historia de D. Felipe el IV, Rey de las Españas* (Lisbon: 1631).

Chaves, Cristóbal de, 'Relación de la cárcel de Sevilla', in Aureliano Fernández-Guerra y Orbe (ed.), *Noticia de un precioso codice de la Biblioteca Colombina* (Madrid: 1864).

Chaves, Manuel, *Cosas nuevas y viejas: apuntes sevillanos* (Seville: 1904).

Checa Cremades, Fernando (ed.), *Los inventarios de Carlos V y la familia imperial/ The Inventories of Charles V and the Imperial Family*, 3 vols ([n.p.]: 2010).

Cherry, Peter, 'Documentary Appendix on Justino de Neve', in *Murillo and Justino de Neve*, exhibition catalogue, 143–68.

CODOIN: Colección de documentos inéditos para la historia de España, ed. Martín Fernández Navarrete et al., 112 vols (Madrid: 1842–95).

Cortes de los antiguos reinos de León y de Castilla, 5 vols (Madrid: 1861–1903).

Covarrubias y Leyva, Diego (ed.), *Elogios al Palacio Real del Buen Retiro escritos por algunos ingenios de España* (Madrid: 1635).

Daza Chacón, Dionisio, 'Relación Verdadera de la herida del Príncipe D. Carlos', in *CODOIN*, 18:537–63.

Dürer, Albrecht, *Albrecht Dürer: Diary of his Journey to the Netherlands, 1520, 1521*, ed. J. A. Goris and G. Marlier (London: 1970).

Elliott, John H. and José F. de la Peña, *Memoriales y cartas del Conde Duque de Olivares*, 2 vols (Madrid: 1978–80).

Ellis, Henry (ed.), *Original Letters Illustrative of English History*, series 1, 3 vols (London: 1825).

Erasmus Roterodamus, Desiderius, *Collectanea Adagiorum* (Paris: 1500).

Espinosa de Monteros, Pablo, *Historia y grandezas de Sevilla*, 2 vols (Seville: 1627–30).

Feltham, Owen, *A Brief Character of the Low Countries under the States* (London: 1660).

Fernández de Oviedo y Valdés, Gonzalo, see Oviedo.

Fernández del Castillo, Francisco, 'Algunos documentos nuevos sobre Bartolomé de Medina', *Memorias de la Sociedad Alzate*, vol. 47 (Mexico, 1927): 207–51.

Fichter, William L., 'Una poesía contemporánea inédita sobre las bodas de Velázquez', in *Varia velazqueña: homenaje a Velázquez en el III centenario de su muerte 1660–1960*, 2 vols (Madrid: 1960), 1:636–9.

Fletcher, Francis, *The World Encompassed by Sir Francis Drake*, in Hakluyt Society Publications, series 1, no. 16 (London: 1854 [1682]).

Fonseca, Damián, *Relación de la expulsión de los moriscos del reino de Valencia* (Valencia: 1878 [1612]).

Fuller, Thomas, *The History of the Worthies of England* (London: 1652, 1659 etc.).

Gallego Morell, Antonio, *Garcilaso: documentos completos* (Madrid: 1976).

García Mercadal, J., *Viajes de extranjeros por España y Portugal*, 3 vols (Madrid: 1952–62).

Garcilaso de la Vega, El Inca, *Comentarios reales de los Incas*, ed. Carlos Araníbar, 2 vols (Mexico City: 1991 [1609–17]).

Gauna, Felipe de, *Relación de las fiestas celebradas en Valencia con motivo del casamiento de Felipe III*, ed. Salvador Carreras Zacarés, 2 vols (Valencia: 1926).

Gayangos, Pascual de, *Cartas y relaciones de Hernán Cortés al Emperador Carlos V* (Paris: 1866), 28–34.

Gelder, Enno van (ed.), *Correspondance française de Marguerite d'Autriche, Duchesse de Parme, avec Philippe II*, 3 vols (Utrecht: 1941).

Gómez-Salvago Sánchez, Mónica, *Fastos de una boda real en la Sevilla del quinientos (estudios y documentos)* (Seville: 1998).

González de Amezúa, 'Una carta desconocida e inédita de Cervantes', *Boletín de la Real Academia Española*, 34 (1954), 217–23.

González de Cellorigo, Martín, *Memorial de la política necesaria y útil restauración de la república de España* (Valladolid: 1600).

Guevara, Felipe, *Comentarios de la pintura* (Madrid: 1778 [1564]).

Guzmán, Alonso Enríquez de, *Libro de la vida de Alonso Enríquez de Guzmán*, ed. Howard Keniston (Madrid: 1960).

Haedo, Diego de [Antonio de Sosa], *Topographia e historia general de Argel* (Valladolid: 1612).

Hasenclever, Adolf, 'Die tagebuchartigen Aufzeichnungen des pfälzischen Hofarztes D. Johannes Lange über seine Reise nach Granada im Jahre 1526', *Archiv für Kulturgeschichte*, 5:4 (1907), 385–439.

Helfferich, Tryntje (ed. and trans.), *The Thirty Years War: A Documentary History* (Indianapolis and Cambridge: 2009).

Herrera, Fernando de, 'Relación de la guerra de Cipre y suceso de la batalla naval de Lepanto, escrita por Fernando de Herrera' (Seville: 1572), in *CODOIN*, 21: 243–383.

Herrera y Maldonado, Francisco, *Libro de la vida y maravillosas virtudes del Siervo de Dios Bernardino de Obregón* (Madrid: 1634).

Herrera y Sotomayor, Jacinto, *Jornada que Su Magestad hizo a la Andaluzia* (Madrid: 1624).

Herrera y Tordesillas, Antonio de, *Tercera parte de la historia general del mundo* (Madrid: 1612).

Howell, James, *Epistolae Ho-Elianae: The Familiar Letters of James Howell*, ed. Joseph Jacobs (London: 1890).

Hurtado de Mendoza, Diego, *Guerra de Granada* (Valencia: 1776 [1627]).

Jesús María, José de, *Primera parte de las excelencias de la virtud de la castidad* ([Madrid]: 1601).

Keeler, Mary Fear, *Sir Francis Drake's West Indian Voyage, 1585–86* (London: 1981 [1588–99]).

Khevenhüller, Hans de, *Diario de Hans Khevenhüller: embajador imperial en la corte de Felipe II*, ed. Sara Veronelli and Félix Labrador Arroyo (Madrid: 2001).

Langlois de Mottevill, Françoise, *Mémoires pour servir à l'histoire d'Anne d'Autriche* ... (Amsterdam: 1723).

Las Casas, Bartolomé de, *Historia de las Indias*, ed. Agustín Millares Carlo, 3 vols (Mexico City and Buenos Aires: 1951).

Legrelle, Arsène, *La mission de M. de Rébenac à Madrid et la mort de Marie-Louise, reine d'Espagne (1688–1689)* (Paris: 1894).

León, Pedro de, *Grandeza y miseria en Andalucía: testimonio de una encrucijada histórica (1578–1616)*, ed. Pedro Herrera Puga (Granada: 1981).

León Pinelo, Antonio, *Anales de Madrid, desde el año 447 al de 1568* (Madrid: 1971), and see Fundación Lázaro Gaidiano: M 1-3-21, at http://www.bibliotecavirtualmadrid.org/bvmadrid_publicacion/i18n/consulta/registro.cmd?id=3526.

Leyes y ordenanzas nuevamente hechas por S. M. para la gobernación de las indias, y buen tratamiento y conservación de los indios, at Biblioteca Virtual Miguel de Cervantes: http://bib.cervantesvirtual.com/servlet/SirveObras/06922752100647273089079/p0000026.htm.

Liske, Javier, *Viajes de extranjeros por España y Portugal en los siglos XV, XVI, XVII* (Madrid: 1878).

Loyola, Ignatius, *The Autobiography of St. Ignatius*, ed. J. F. X. O'Conor (New York: 1900).

Madariaga, Fray Juan de, *Vida del seráfico padre San Bruno, Patriarca de la Cartuja* (Valencia: 1596).

Magurn, Ruth Saunders (ed. and trans.), *The Letters of Peter Paul Rubens* (Cambridge, MA: 1955).

Male, William van, *Lettres sur la vie intérieure de l'empereur Charles-Quint*, ed. J. de Reiffenberg (Brussels: 1843 [1550]).

Manoio, Fernando, *Relación del muerte de Rodrigo Calderón* (Madrid: [1621]).

Martínez, Jusepe, *Discursos practicables del nobilísmo arte de la pintura*, ed. María Elena Manrique Ara (Madrid: 2006 [1675]).

Martinitz, Jaroslav, 'Beschreibung der Böhmischen Rebellion in anno 1618', Knihovna Nárdního Muzea, Praha, Sign. VI G. 2, in Helfferich (ed.), *The Thirty Years War*, doc. 1, pp. 14–19.

Martyr d'Anghiera, Peter, *De Orbe Novo*, trans. Francis A. McNutt, 2 vols (New York and London: 1912 [1511–25]).

Mendoza, Bernardo, *Relación del lucimiento y grandeza con que el Duque de Medina Sidonia festejó Su Magestad en el bosque llamado Doña Ana* (Madrid: 1624).

Milhausen, Peter Milner von, *Apologia oder Entschuldigungsschrift . . .* (Prague: 1618), in Helfferich, *The Thirty Years War*, doc. 2, pp. 20–2.

Mosquera de Figueroa, Cristóbal, *Comentario en breve compendio de disciplina militar* (Madrid: 1596).

Motolinia, Fray Toribio de Benavente, *Memoriales (Libro de oro, MS JGI 31)*, ed. Nancy Joe Dyer (Mexico City: 1996).

Muñoz, Andrés, *Viaje de Felipe Segundo a Inglaterra*, ed. Pascual Gayangos (Madrid: 1877 [1554]).

Muro Orejón, Antonio, *Documentos para la escultura sevillana. Artífices sevillanos de los siglos XVI y XVII*, Documentos para la historia del Arte en Andalucía, vol. 1 (Seville: 1927).

Novoa, Matías de, *Historia de Felipe III, Rey de España*, in *CODOIN*, 60 and 61.

—, *Historia de Felipe IV*, 4 vols (Madrid: 1878), 1:73–6.

Olivares, Diego Santiago, 'Relación de la enfermedad del Príncipe . . .', in *CODOIN*, 15:554–74.

Ortiz de Zúñiga, Diego, *Anales eclesiásticos y seculares de la muy noble y muy leal ciudad de Sevilla* (Madrid: 1796).

Oviedo, Gonzalo Fernández de, *Historia general y natural de las indias*, ed. Juan Pérez de Tudela Bueso, 5 vols (Madrid: 1959 [1535]), 4:10.

—, *Libro de la cámara real del príncipe don Juan, oficios de su casa y servicio ordinario*, ed. Santiago Fabregat Barrios (Valencia: 2006 [c.1548]).

—, 'Relación de lo sucedido en la prisión del rey de Francia', in *CODOIN*, 38: 404–530.

—, *Las Quinquagenas de la Nobleza de España*, ed. Vicente de la Fuente, 2 vols (Madrid: 1880).

Pacheco, Francisco, 'A los profesores del arte de la pintura. Opúsculo impreso en Sevilla el 16 de Julio de 1622', in Calvo Serraller (ed.), *La teoría de la pintura*, 179–91.

—, *El arte de la pintura*, ed. Bonaventura Bassegoda i Hugas (Madrid: 1990 [1646]).

—, *Libro de descripción de verdaderos retratos de ilustres y memorables varones* (Seville: 1983 [1599]).

Palomino Velasco, Antonio, *Vidas [Museo pictórico. Tercera parte: El Parnaso Español Pintoresco Laureado]*, ed. Nina Ayala Mallory, 2 vols (Madrid: 1986).

Payen, P., *Mémoires de Pontus Payen*, ed. Alexandre Henne, 2 vols (Brussels and The Hague: 1861).

Paz, J., 'Relación de la "Invencible" por el contador Pedro Coco de Calderón', *Revista de archivos, bibliotecas y museos*, 3rd series, 1 (1987), appendix 1, at http://www. armada.mde.es/html/historiaarmada/tomo3/tomo_03_30_apendices.pdf.

Pérez de Montalbán, Juan, *Fama postúma a la vida y muerte del doctor frey Felix Lope de Vega Carpio* (Madrid: 1636).

Pérez de Villagrá, Gaspar, *Historia de la Nueva México, 1610*, trans. and ed. Miguel Encinias, Alfred Rodríguez and Joseph P. Sánchez (Albuquerque: 1992 [1610]).

Pérez Pastor, Cristóbal (ed.), *Documentos cervantinos hasta ahora inéditos*, 2 vols (Madrid: 1897–1902).

—, *Documentos para la biografía de D. Pedro Calderón de la Barca*, vol. 1 (Madrid: 1905).

Pliny the Elder, *Natural History*, trans. H. Rackham, Loeb edn, 10 vols (London: 1952).

Ponz, Antonio, *Viage de España, en que se da noticia de las cosas más apreciables . . .* (Madrid: 1947 [1771–94]).

Pozzo, Cassiano dal, *Il diario del viaggio in Spagna del Cardinale Francesco Barberini*, ed. Alessandra Anselmi (Madrid: 2004).

Rachfahl, F., *Le registre de Franciscus Liscaldius, trésorier général de l'armée espagnole aux Pays-Bas de 1567 à 1576* (Brussels: 1902).

Remesal, Antonio de, *Historia general de las Indias occidentales y particular de la gobernación de Chiapas y Guatemala*, ed. Carmelo Sáenz de Santa María, 2 vols (Mexico City: 1988 [1619]).

Remón, A., *Entretenimientos y juegos honestos y recreaciones . . .* (Madrid: 1623).

Ribera, Francisco de, *Vida de Santa Teresa de Jesús*, ed. P. Jaime Pons (Barcelona: 1908 [1590]).

Sahagún, Bernardino de, *Códice florentino (Historia general de las cosas de Nueva España)*, facsimile edn (Mexico City and Florence: 1979 [c.1545–90]).

—, *Historia general de las cosas de Nueva España* (Mexico City: 1999 [c.1545–90]).

San Antón Muñón Chimalpahin Cuauhtlehuanitzin, Francisco de, *Relaciones de Chalco Amaquemecan*, ed. and trans. S. Rendón (Mexico City and Buenos Aires: 1965 [c.1600–50]).

San Román y Fernández, Francisco de Borja de, 'Documentos de Garcilaso en el Archivo de Protocolos de Toledo', *Boletín de la Real Academica de la Historia*, 83 (1918), 515–36.

—, 'Documentos del Greco, referentes a los cuadros de Santo Domingo del Antiguo', *Archivo Español de Arte y Arqueología*, 28 (1934), unnumbered offprint.

Sánchez Gordillo, Abad Alonso, *Religiosas estaciones que frecuenta la religiosidad sevillana*, ed. Jorge Bernales Ballesteros (Seville: 1983 [1635]).

Sandoval, Fray Prudencio de, *Historia del emperador Carlos V*, ed. Gregorio Urbano Dargallo, 9 vols (Madrid: 1846 [1634]).

Santa Cruz, Alonso de, *Crónica del Emperador Carlos V*, 4 vols (Madrid: 1920 [c.1550]).

Santos, Francisco de los, 'La vida del Padre Fr. Andrés de los Reyes y de un Hermano de los Legos llamado Fray Martín de Perpiñan, hijos de S. Lorenzo', in *Quarta parte de la Historia de la Orden de San Gerónimo* (Madrid: 1680), ff. 763–4.

Seco Serrano, Carlos (ed.), *Cartas de Sor María de Jesús de Ágreda y de Felipe IV,* 2 vols (Madrid: 1958).

Sepúlveda, Juan Ginés de, *Demócrates Segundo o de las justas causas de la guerra contra los indios*, ed. and trans. Ángel Losada (Madrid: 1984 [c.1548]).

—, *Obras completas*, vol. 1: *Historia de Carlos V: libros I–V [c.1556]*, ed. and trans. E. Rodríguez Peregrina (Pozoblanco: 1995).

Sigüenza, Fray José de, *Fundación del Monasterio de el Escorial por Felipe II* (Madrid: 1927 [1605]).

Simón Díaz, José (ed.), *Relaciones breves de actos públicos celebrados en Madrid de 1541 a 1650* (Madrid: 1982).

Sousa, Luis de, *Anais de D. Joao III*, 3 vols (Lisbon: 1938).

Suárez de Figueroa, Cristóbal, *Plaza universal de todas ciencias y artes* (Madrid: 1615).

Sublimus Deus, at Papal Encyclicals Online: http://www.papalencyclicals.net/Paulo3/p3subli.htm.

Testamento político del Emperador: Instrucciones de Carlos V a Felipe II sobre política exterior (Augusta a 18 de enero de 1548), at Biblioteca Virtual Miguel de Cervantes: http://www.cervantesvirtual.com/bib/historia/CarlosV/7_4_testamento.shtml.

Torres Lanzas, Pedro (ed.), *Información de Miguel de Cervantes* (Madrid: 1905).

Valladares, Antonio (ed.), 'Carta que el ilustrísimo señor don Garceran Alvarez, arzobispo de Granada, maestro que fue del rey don Felipe IV escribió al Conde-Duque de Olivares', in *Semanario erudito*, vol. 2 (Madrid: 1787).

Vera y Figueroa, Juan Antonio de (Conde de la Roca), 'Extract from "Fragmentos historicos de la vida de Don Gaspar de Guzman . . ."', in Francisco de Jesús, *El hecho de los tratados del matrimonio pretendido por el Príncipe de Gales . . .*, ed. and trans. Samuel Rawson Gardiner (London: 1869).

—, *Fragmentos históricos de la vida de D. Gaspar de Guzmán*, in Antono de Valladares de Sotomayor (ed.), *Semanario Erudito*, vol. 2 (1787), 145–296.

Villegas, Alonso de, *Flos Sanctorum . . . y historia general en que se escriven las vidas de santos extravagantes y de varones ilustres en virtud . . .* (Madrid: 1675 [1588]).

Viñas Mey, Carmelo, and Ramón Paz (eds), *Relaciones histórico-geográfico-estadisticas de los pueblos de España hechas por iniciativa de Felipe II, Provincia de Toledo* (Madrid: 1951), at http://www.uclm.es/ceclm/b_virtual/libros/Relaciones_Toledo/index.htm.

Weiditz, Christoph, *Das Trachtenbuch des Christoph Weiditz von seinen Reisen nach Spanien (1529) und den Niederlanden (1531/32)*, ed. Theodore Hampe (Berlin and Leipzig: 1927).

Wynn, Richard, 'Account of the Journey of Prince Charles's Servants into Spain in the Year 1623', in *Historia Vitae et Regni Ricardi II*, ed. Thomas Hearne (Oxford: 1729).

Zarco Cuevas, Fray Julián (ed.), *Documentos para la Historia del Monasterio del San Lorenzo el Real de El Escorial*, 7 vols (Madrid: 1917).

Exhibition Catalogues

Armada, 1588–1988: An International Exhibition to Commemorate the Spanish Armada, ed. M. J. Rodríguez-Salgado (London: 1988), 205–44.

El Greco, ed. David Davies (London: 2003).

Felipe II: un monarca y su época. Las tierras y los hombres del rey (Valladolid: 1998).

Murillo and Justino de Neve: The Art of Friendship, ed. Gabriele Finaldi (Madrid, Seville and London: 2012).

Navarrete 'el Mudo', pintor de Felipe II (Seguidores y Copistas), June 14 to July 16, 1995, Saragossa (Logroño: 1995).

La restauración de El emperador Carlos V a caballo en Mülhlberg *de Tiziano* (Madrid: 2001).

The Sacred Made Real: Spanish Painting and Sculpture, 1600–1700, ed. Xavier Bray (London: 2010).

Spanish Polychrome Sculpture 1500–1800 in United States Collections, ed. Suzanne L. Stratton ([New York]: [1994]).

Tiziano, ed. Miguel Falomir (Madrid: 2003).

Velázquez, ed. Dawson W. Carr (London: 2006).

Velázquez, ed. Antonio Domínguez Ortiz, Alfonso E. Pérez Sánchez and Julián Gállego (Madrid: 1990).

Velázquez in Seville, ed. David Davies (Edinburgh: 1996).

Zurbarán y su obrador: pinturas para el Nuevo Mundo, ed. Benito Navarrete Prieto (Valencia: 1998).

Secondary Sources

Adamson, John, 'Introduction: The Making of the Ancien-Régime Court, 1500–1700', in Adamson (ed.), *The Princely Courts of Europe*, 7–41.

Adamson, John (ed.), *The Princely Courts of Europe: 1500–1750* (London: 1999).

Allen, Paul C., *Philip III and the Pax Hispanica, 1598–1621: The Failure of Grand Strategy* (New Haven and London: 2000).

Alonso Cortés, Narciso, *Casos cervantinos que tocan a Valladolid* (Madrid: 1916).

Álvarez Lopera, José, *El Greco: estudio y catálogo*, 2 vols (Madrid: 2005).

—, 'The Hall of Realms: The Present State of Knowledge and a Reconsideration', in Úbeda de los Cobos (ed.), *Paintings for the Planet King*, 91–111.

Andrew Villalón, L. J., 'Putting Don Carlos Together Again: Treatment of a Head Injury in Sixteenth-Century Spain', *Sixteenth Century Journal*, 26:2 (1995), 347–65.

Angulo Íñiguez, Diego, *Murillo: su vida, su arte, su obra*, 3 vols (Madrid: 1981).

Anon., '100 prominent authors from more than 50 different nations have elected The Library of World Literature: "The 100 Best Books in the History of Literature"', in *Bokklubben din Nettbokhandel*, at http://www.bokklubben.no/SamboWeb/side.do?dokId=65500&klubbid=WB.

Aram, Bethany, *Juana the Mad: Sovereignty and Dynasty in Renaissance Europe* (Baltimore: 2005 [2001]).

Artigas, Miguel, *Don Luis de Góngora y Argote: Biografía y estudio crítico* (Madrid: 1925).

Artiñano y Galdácano, Gervasio de, *La arquitectura naval* (Madrid: 1920).

Astrain, Antonio, *Historia de la Compañía de Jesús en la Asistencia de España*, 6 vols (Madrid: 1912–29).

Astrana Marín, Luis, *Vida ejemplar y heroica de Miguel de Cervantes Saavedra con mil documentos hasta ahora inéditos y numerosas ilustraciones y grabados de época*, 7 vols (Madrid: 1948).

Aterido Fernández, Ángel (ed.), *Corpus velazqueño*, 2 vols (Madrid: 2000).

Aurelio Espinosa, *The Empire of the Cities: Emperor Charles V, the Comunero Revolt, and the Transformation of the Spanish System* (Leiden and Boston: 2003).

Avalle-Arce, Juan Bautista, *El Inca Garcilaso en sus* Comentarios (Madrid: 1964).

Ayala Mallory, Nina, *Bartolomé Esteban Murillo* (Madrid: 1983).

Azcárate, José María de, *Alonso de Berruguete: Cuatro Ensayos* (Valladolid: 1963).

—, 'Una Variante en la edición de los *Diálogos* de Carducho con noticia sobre el Buen Retiro', *Archivo Español de Arte*, 95 (1951), 261–2.

Bakewell, Peter J., *Silver Mining and Society in Colonial Mexico: Zacatecas 1546–1700* (Cambridge: 1971).

Ballesteros Gabrois, Manuel, *Gonzalo Fernández de Oviedo* (Madrid: 1981).

Baruzi, Jean, *San Juan de la Cruz y el problema de la experiencia mística*, trans. Carlos Ortega (Valladolid: 1991).

Bataillon, Marcel, 'Un problema de influencia de Erasmo en España. El *Elogio de la locura*', in *Erasmo y Erasmismo*, trans. Carlos Pujol (Barcelona: 1977), 327–46.

Baxandall, Michael, *Patterns of Intention: On the Historical Explanation of Pictures* (New Haven and London: 1985).

Beeching, Jack, *The Galleys at Lepanto* (London: 1982).

Bennassar, Bartolomé, *La España de los Austrias (1516–1700)*, trans. Bernat Hervàs (Barcelona: 2001).

—, *La España del siglo de oro*, trans. Pablo Bordonava (Barcelona: 1983 [1982]).

Benzoni, Gino (ed.), *Il Mediterraneo nella seconda metà de '500 all luce di Lepanto* (Florence: 1974).

Berwick y Alba, Duque de, *Discurso del Duque de Berwick y de Alba* (Madrid: 1919).

Beverley, John (ed.) 'Introducción', in Luis de Góngora y Argote, *Soledades* (Madrid: 2007).

Bireley, Robert, *The Jesuits and the Thirty Years War* (Cambridge and New York: 2003).

Bloom, Harold, 'Introduction', in Harold Bloom (ed.), *Modern Critical Interpretations: Cervante's* Don Quixote (Philadelphia: 2001).

Bolaños, Álvaro Félix, 'El primer cronista de Indias frente al "mare magno" de la crítica', *Cuadernos Americanos*, 20:2 (1990), 42–61.

Boronat y Barrachina, Pascual, *Los moriscos españoles y su expulsión. Estudio histórico-crítico*, 2 vols (Valencia: 1901).

Boscán, Joan, *Las obras de Boscán y algunas de Garcilaso de la Vega repartidas en quatro libros* (Barcelona: 1543).

Bouza Álvarez, Fernando, *Imagen y propaganda: capítulos de historia cultural del reinado de Felipe II* (Madrid: 1998).

—, 'Semblanza y aficiones del monarca: Música, astros, libros y bufones', in *Felipe IV: El hombre y el reinado*, ed. José Alcalá-Zamora y Queipo de Llano (Madrid: 1996).

Bowle, John, *Charles I: A Biography* (London, 1975).

Boyden, James M., *The Courtier and the King: Ruy Gómez de Silva, Philip II, and the Court of Spain* (Berkeley: 1995).

Boyer, Richard, 'Mexico in the Seventeenth Century: Transition of a Colonial Society', *Hispanic American Historical Review*, 57:3 (1977), 455–78.

Brandi, Karl, *The Emperor Charles V*, trans. C. V. Wedgwood (London: 1965).

Braudel, Fernand, *The Mediterranean and the Mediterranean World in the Age of Philip II*, trans. Siân Reynolds, 2 vols (London: 1972 [1949]).

Bray, Xavier, 'Christ on the Cross, 1627', in *The Sacred Made Real*, exhibition catalogue, cat. 25.

—, 'The Sacred Made Real', in *The Sacred Made Real*, exhibition catalogue, 15–44.

Brendler, Gerhard, *Martin Luther: Theology and Revolution*, trans. Claude R. Foster Jr (New York and Oxford: 1991).

Brett-James, Norman G., *The Growth of Stuart London* (London: 1953).

Brotton, Jerry, 'Buying the Renaissance: Prince Charles's Art Purchases in Madrid, 1623', in Alexander Samson (ed.), *The Spanish Match: Prince Charles's Journey to Madrid, 1623* (Aldershot: 2006), 9–26.

Brown, Jonathan, 'Hieroglyphs of Death and Salvation: The Decoration of the Church of the Hermandad de la Caridad, Seville', in *Images and Ideas in Seventeenth-Century Spanish Painting* (Princeton: 1978), 128–46.

—, *Images and Ideas in Seventeenth-Century Spanish Painting* (Princeton: 1978).

—, *Painting in Spain, 1500–1700* (New Haven and London: 1998).

Brown, Jonathan, and John H. Elliott, *A Palace for a King: The Buen Retiro and the Court of Philip IV* (New Haven and London: 1980).

Brown, Jonathan, and Richard Kagan, 'The Duke of Alcalá: His Collection and its Evolution', *Art Bulletin*, 69:2 (1987), 231–55.

Browne, Walden, *Sahagún and the Transition to Modernity* (Norman, OK: 2000).

Bury, J. B., 'Juan de Herrera and the Escorial', *Art History*, 9:4 (1986), 428–49.

Bury, John, 'A Source for El Greco's "St Maurice"', *Burlington Magazine*, 126:972 (1984), 144–7.

Cadenas y Vicent, Vicente de, *Carlos de Habsburgo en Yuste* (Madrid: 1990).

Calvete de Estrella, Juan Cristóbal, *Rebelión de Pizarro en el Perú y Vida de D. Pedro Gasca*, 2 vols (Madrid: 1889).

Calvo Serraller, Francisco, *El Greco: The Burial of the Count of Orgaz*, trans. Jenifer Wakelyn (London: 1995).

Calzada, Luis Manuel, and Luys Santa Marina, *Estampas de Zurbarán* (Barcelona: 1929).

Camón Aznar, José, *Dominico Greco*, 2 vols (Madrid: 1950).

Canavaggio, Jean, *Cervantes* (Paris: 1986).

Cánovas del Castillo, Antonio, *Historia de la decadencia de España desde el advenimiento de Felipe III al Trono hasta la muerte de Carlos II* (Madrid: 1910 [1854]).

Cantera Burgos, F., 'Fernando de Pulgar y los conversos', *Sefarad*, 4 (1944), 295–348.

Cárdenas, Juan de, *Breve relación de la muerte, vida y virtudes del venerable caballero D. Miguel Mañara . . .* (Seville: 1903).

Carmona García, Juan Ignacio, *El extenso mundo de la pobreza: la otra cara de la Sevilla imperial* (Seville: 1993).

Caro Baroja, Julio, *Los judios en la España moderna y contemporanea*, 3 vols (Madrid: 1961).

—, *Razas, pueblos y linajes* (Madrid: 1957).

Carrera Stampa, Manuel, 'Relaciones Geográficas de Nueva España, siglos XVI y XVIII', *Estudios de Historia Novohispana*, 2:2 (1968), 1–31, at www.ejournal. unam.mx/ehn/ehno2/EHNoo212.pdf.

Case, Thomas E., 'Cide Hamete and the *Libros Plúmbeos*', *Bulletin of the Cervantes Society of America*, 22:2 (2002), 9–24.

Casey, James, *The Kingdom of Valencia in the Seventeenth Century* (Cambridge: 1979).

Caso, Alfonso, 'El mapa de Teozacoalco', *Cuadernos Americanos*, 8 (1949), 145–81.

Castillero, Ernesto J., 'Gonzalo Fernández de Oviedo y Valdés, veedor de Tierra Firme', *Revista de Indias*, 17 (1957), 521–40.

Caturla, María Luisa, 'Cartas de pago de los doce cuadros de batallas para el salón de reinos del Buen Retiro', *Archivo Español de Arte*, 33 (1960), 333–55.

—, *Fin y muerte de Francisco de Zurbarán* (Madrid: 1964).

Cenalmor Bruquetas, Elena, 'The Immaculate Conception of the Venerables Sacerdotes', in *Murillo and Justino de Neve*, exhibition catalogue, cat. 7.

Chaunu, Pierre, and Huguette Chaunu, *Séville et l'Amérique aux XVIe et XVIIe siècles* (Paris: 1977).

—, *Séville et l'Antique (1504–1650)*, 12 vols (Paris: 1962).

Checa Cremades, Fernando, *Carlos V: la imagen del poder en el Renacimiento* (Madrid: 1999).

Cherry, Peter, 'Artistic Training and the Painters' Guild in Seville', in *Velázquez in Seville*, exhibition catalogue, 66–75.

—, 'Justino de Neve: Life and Works', in *Murillo and Justino de Neve*, exhibition catalogue, 31–45.

Chevalier, François, *La formation des grands domaines au Mexique: Terre et société aux XVIe–XVIIe siècles* (Paris: 1952).

Childers, William, 'An Extensive Network of Morisco Merchants Active Circa 1590', in Ingram (ed.), *The Conversos and Moriscos*, 2:135–60.

Cline, Howard F., 'The Relaciones Geograficas of the Spanish Indies', *Hispanic American Historical Review*, 44:3 (1964), 341–74.

Cobo Borda, J. G., 'El Sumario de Gonzalo Fernández de Oviedo', *Cuadernos Hispanoamericanos*, 427-30 (1986), 63–77.

Cook, Noble David, *Born to Die: Disease and New World Conquest, 1492–1650* (Cambridge and New York: 1998).

Cooper, J. P. (ed.), *The Decline of Spain and the Thirty Years War, 1609–48/59: The New Cambridge Modern History*, vol. 4 (Cambridge: 1970).

Coreleu, Alejandro, 'La contribución de Juan Ginés de Sepúlveda a la edición de los textos de Aristoteles y de Alejandro de Afrodisias', *Humanistica Lovaniensia: Journal of Neo-Latin Studies*, 43 (1994), 231–45.

—, 'The *Fortuna* of Juan Ginés de Sepúlveda's Translations of Aristotle and of Alexander of Aphrodisias', *Journal of the Warburg and Courtauld Institutes*, 59 (1996), 325–32.

Crowley, Frances G., *Garcilaso de la Vega, el Inca and his Sources in Comentarios Reales de los Incas* (The Hague and Paris: 1971).

Cruzada Villaamil, Gregorio, *Rubens, diplomático español* (Madrid: [1874?]).

—, 'Rubens, diplomático español', *Revista Europea*, 1:6–17 (1874), 7–519 (intermittently).

Cuesta Gutiérrez, Luisa, 'Los tipógrafos extranjeros en la imprenta burgalesa, desde Alemán Fadrique de Basilea al italiano Juan Bautista Veresi', *Gutenberg Jahrbuch* (1952), 67–74.

Dadson, Trevor J., 'Literacy and Education in Early Modern Rural Castile: The Case of Villarrubia de los Ojos', *Bulletin of Spanish Studies*, 81:7–8 (2004), 1011–37.

—, *Los moriscos de Villarrubia de los Ojos (siglos XV–XVIII)* (Vervuert: 2007).

—, *Tolerance and Coexistence in Early Modern Spain: Old Christians and Moriscos in the Campo de Calatrava* (Woodbridge: 2014).

Dámaso, Alonso, *La lengua poética de Góngora* (Madrid: 1950).

Danvila y Collado, Manuel, *La expulsión de los moriscos españoles: Conferencias pronunciadas en el Ateneo de Madrid* (Madrid: 1998).

—, *Historia crítica y documentada de las Comunidades de Castilla*, 5 vols (Madrid: 1897–9).

Davidson, Bernice, 'Navarrete in Rome', *Burlington Magazine*, 135:1079 (1993), 93–6.

Davies, David, 'El Greco's Religious Art: The Illumination and Quickening of the Spirit', in *El Greco*, exhibition catalogue, 45–71.

Delenda, Odile, and Luis J. Garraín Villa, 'Zurbarán Sculpteur: aspects inédits de sa carrière et de sa biographie', *Gazette des Beaux-Arts*, 131 (1998), 125–38.

Deloria, Vine Jr, *Custer Died for your Sins* (London and New York: 1969).

Diamond, Jared, *Guns, Germs and Steel: A Short History of Everybody for the Last 13,000 Years* (London: 2005).

Díaz Viana, Luis, 'En torno al origen legendario de "El convidado de piedra"', *Cuadernos de trabajo* (Centro Cultural de Estudios Folklóricos: Valladolid), 2 (1980), 77–126.

Díaz-Plaja, Guillermo, *El espíritu del Barroco* (Barcelona: 1983 [1940]).

Diez Borque, José María (ed.), *La vida española en el Siglo de Oro según los extranjeros* (Barcelona: 1990).

Domínguez Ortiz, Antonio, *El antiguo régimen: los reyes católicos y los Austrias* (Madrid: 1974).

—, *Crisis y decadencia de la España de los Austrias* (Barcelona: 1969).

—, *The Golden Age of Spain, 1516–1659*, trans. James Casey (London and New York: 1971).

—, *Orto y ocaso de Sevilla: estudio sobre la prosperidad y decadencia de la ciudad durante los siglos XVI y XVII* (Seville: 1966).

Drelichman, Mauricio, and Hans-Joachim Voth, 'The Sustainable Debts of Philip II: A Reconstruction of Spain's Fiscal Position, 1560–1598' (December 2007), CEPR Discussion Paper No. DP6611, SSRN, at http://ssrn.com/abstract=1140540.

Durán, Manuel, *Luis de León* (New York: 1971).

Ehlers, Benjamin, *Between Christians and Moriscos: Juan de Ribera and Religious Reform in Valencia, 1568–1614* (Baltimore: 2006).

Ehrenberg, Richard, *Capital and Finance in the Age of the Renaissance: A Study of the Fuggers and their Connections*, trans. H. M. Lucas (New York: 1928).

Eisenberg, Daniel, 'Cervantes, Lope, and Avellaneda', in *Josep María Solà-Solè: Homage, Homenaje, Homenatge*, ed. Antonio Torres-Alcalá, 2 vols (Barcelona: 1984), 2:171–83.

Eisenberg, Daniel, '¿Por qué volvió Cervantes de Argel?', in Ellen M. Anderson and Amy R. Williamsen (eds), *Essays on Golden Age Literature for Geoffrey L. Stagg in Honour of his Eighty-Fifth Birthday* (Newark, DE: 1999).

Elías Tormo, D., review of Ricardo de Orueta, *Berruguete y sus obras* (Madrid: 1917), in *Boletín de la Sociedad Española de Excursiones: Arte, Arqueolgía, Historia*, 26 (1918), 61–4.

Elliott, John H., *The Count-Duke of Olivares: The Statesman in an Age of Decline* (New Haven and London: 1986).

—, 'The Decline of Spain', *Past & Present*, 20 (1961), 52–75.

—, 'El Greco's Mediterranean', in *Spain, Europe, and the Wider World 1500–1800* (London: 2009).

—, *Imperial Spain, 1469–1716* (London: 1963).

—, *The Revolt of the Catalans: A Study in the Decline of Spain* (Cambridge: 1963).

Ermida Ruiz, Aurora, review of Richard Helgerson, *A Sonnet from Carthage: Garcilaso de la Vega and the New Poetry of the Sixteenth Century* (Philadelphia: 2007), *Modern Philology*, 108:3 (2011), E158–61.

Escamilla-Colin, Michèle, *Crimes et châtiments dans l'Espagne inquisitoriale*, 2 vols (Paris, 1992).

Espinel, Vicente, *La Vida de Marcos de Obregón* (Barcelona: 1881).

Estrada de Gerlero, Elena, 'El programa pasionario en el convento franciscano de Huejotzingo', *Jahrbuch für Geschichte von Staat, Wirtschaft und Gesellschaft Lateinamerikas*, 20 (1983), 642–62.

Falcón Márquez, Teodoro, 'The Church of Santa María la Blanca in Seville, Meeting Point between Murillo and Justino de Neve', in *Murillo and Justino de Neve*, exhibition catalogue, 61–72.

—, *El Palacio de las Dueñas y las casas-palacio sevillanas del siglo XVI* (Seville: 2003).

Fernández Álvarez, Manuel, *Carlos V. Un hombre para Europa* (Madrid: 1974).

—, *La España del emperador Carlos V (1500–1558: 1517–1556)*, vol. 18 of *Historia de España*, ed. Ramón Menéndez Pidal (Madrid: 1979 [1966]).

—, *Felipe II y su tiempo* (Madrid: 1998).

—, *La sociedad española en el siglo de oro*, 2 vols (Madrid: 1989).

Fernández Chavez, Manuel F., and Raveale M. Pérez García, 'The Morisco Problem and Seville (1480–1610)', in Ingram (ed.), *The Conversos and Moriscos*, 2:75–102.

Fernández de Navarrete, Eustaquio, *Vida del célebre poeta Garcilaso de la Vega* (Madrid: 1850).

Fernández del Castillo, Francisco (ed.), *Libros y libreros en el siglo XVI* (Mexico City: 1982).

Fernández Pardo, Francisco, 'Reseña biográfica de Navarrete "el Mudo"', in *Navarrete 'el Mudo'*, exhibition catalogue, 19–140.

Feros, Antonio, *Kingship and Favoritism in the Spain of Philip III, 1598–1621* (Cambridge: 2000).

Feros, Antonio, and Fernando J. Bouza Álvarez (eds), *España en tiempos del Quijote* (Madrid: 2004).

Flores, R. M., 'Cervantes at Work: The Writing of *Don Quixote*, Part I', *Journal of Hispanic Philology*, 3 (1979), 135–60.

—, 'The Loss and Recovery of Sancho's Ass in *Don Quixote*, Part I', *Modern Language Review*, 75:2 (1980), 301–10.

Frankle, Viktor, 'Hernán Cortés y la tradición de las *Siete Partidas*', *Revista de Historia de América*, 53–4 (1962), 9–74.

Freud, Sigmund, and Joseph Breuer, *Studies on Hysteria*, trans. James and Alix Strachey (Harmondsworth: 1974).

Fuchs, Barbara, 'Maurophilia and the Morisco Subject', in Ingram (ed.), *The Conversos and Moriscos*, 1:269–85.

Gachard, Louis-Prosper, *Don Carlos et Philippe II*, 2 vols (Brussels: 1863).

Gallego Morell, Antonio, 'La corte de Carlos V en la Alhambra en 1526', in *Miscelánea de estudios dedicados al profesor Antonio Marín Ocete*, 2 vols (Granada: 1974), 1:267–94.

—, *Garcilaso de la Vega y sus comentaristas* (Granada: 1966).

García Fuentes, Lutgardo, *El comercio español con América, 1650–1700* (Seville: 1980).

García Lorca, Federico, 'La imagen poética de don Luis de Góngora', in *Obras completas*, ed. Arturo del Hoyo, 2 vols (Madrid: 1980 [1954]).

García Sanz, Ángel, *Desarrollo y Crisis del Antiguo Régimen en Castilla la Vieja. Economia y Sociedad en Tierras de Segovia, 1500–1814* (Madrid: 1977).

García Simón, Agustín, 'Los años críticos', in José Martínez Millán and Ignacio J. Ezquerra Revilla (eds), *Carlos V y la quiebra del humanismo político en Europa (1530–1558)*, 4 vols (Madrid: 2001), 2:321–41.

García-Baquero González, A., 'Andalusia and the Crisis of the Indies Trade, 1610–1720', in I. A. A. Thompson and Bartolomé Yun Casailla (eds), *The Castilian Crisis of the Seventeenth Century: New Perspectives on the Economic and Social History of Seventeenth-Century Spain* (Cambridge: 1994), 115–35.

Garza Merino, Sonia, 'La cuenta del orginal', in Pablo Andrés and Sonia Garza (eds), *Imprenta y crítical textual en el Siglo de Oro* (Valladolid: 2000), 65–95.

Gestoso y Pérez, José, *Ensayo de un diccionario de los artífices que florecieron en Sevilla desde el siglo XIII al XVIII inclusive*, 3 vols (Seville: 1899–1909).

Gillingham, Paul, 'The Strange Business of Memory: Relic Forgery in Latin America', *Past & Present*, Supplement 5 (2010), 199–226.

Gombrich, Ernst, *Art and Illusion* (London: 1960).

—, 'The Earliest Description of Bosch's Garden of Delight', *Journal of the Warburg and Courtauld Institutes*, 30 (1967), 403–6.

Gómez-Moreno, M., 'Juan de Herrera y Francisco Mora en Santa María de la Alhambra', *Archivo español de arte*, 14:40 (1940), 5–18.

González de Caldas, Victoria, *El poder y su imagen: la Inquisición Real* (Seville: 2001).

Gónzalez Palencia, Angel, 'Tirso y las comedias ante la Junta de Reformación', *Boletín de la Real Academia Española*, 25 (1946), 43–84.

Goodman, David C., *Power and Penury: Government, Technology and Science in Philip II's Spain* (Cambridge: 1988).

Goodwin, R. T. C., 'Origins of the Novel in Cervantes's *Información de Argel*', *Bulletin of Hispanic Studies*, 83:4 (2006), 317–35.

Goodwyn, Frank, 'Garcilaso de la Vega, Representative in the Spanish Cortes', *Modern Language Notes*, 82:2 (1967), 225–9.

—, 'New Light on the Historical Setting of Garcilaso's Poetry', *Hispanic Review*, 46:1 (1978), 1–22.

Griffin, Clive, *Journeymen-Printers, Heresy, and the Inquisition in Spain* (Oxford: 2005).

—, *Los Cromberger: La historia de una imprenta del siglo XVI en Sevilla y Méjico* (Madrid: 1991).

Hagarty, Miguel José, *Los libros plúmbeos del Sacromonte* (Madrid: 1980).

—, 'Los libros plúmbeos y la fundación de la Insigne Iglesia Colegial del Sacromonte', in *La Abadía del Sacromonte: Exposición artístico-documental: Estudios sobre su significación y orígenes* (Granada: 1974).

Hale, Sheila, *Titian: His Life* (London: 2012).

Haliczer, Stephen, *The Comuneros of Castile: The Forging of a Revolution, 1475–1521* (Madison and London: 1981).

Hamilton, Earl J., *American Treasure and the Price Revolution* (Cambridge, MA: 1934).

—, 'Monetary Inflation in Castile, 1598–1660', *Economic History (A Supplement to the Economic Journal)*, 2 (1930–3), 177–211.

Hanke, Lewis, *All Mankind is One: A Study of the Disputation between Bartolomé de las Casas and Juan Ginés de Sepúlveda in 1550 on the Intellectual and Religious Capacity of the American Indians* (DeKalb, IL: 1974).

—, *Aristotle and the American Indians* (London: 1959).

Hanson, Neil, *The Confident Hope of a Miracle: The True Story of the Spanish Armada* (London: 2003).

Harris, Enriqueta, *Velázquez* (Oxford: 1982).

Harris, Kaite A., 'Forging History: The Plomos of the Sacromonte of Granada in Francisco Bermúdez de Pedraza's *Historia Eclesiastica*', *Sixteenth Century Journal*, 30:4 (1999), 945–66.

Headly, John M., 'The Emperor and his Chancellor: Disputes over Empire, Administration and Pope (1519–1529)', in José Martínez Millán and Ignacio J. Ezquerra Revilla (eds), *Carlos V y la quiebra del humanismo político en Europa (1530–1558)*, 4 vols (Madrid: 2001), 1:21–36.

Heiple, Daniel, *Garcilaso de la Vega and the Italian Renaissance* (University Park, PA: 1994).

Helgerson, Richard, *A Sonnet from Carthage: Garcilaso de la Vega and the New Poetry of Sixteenth-Century Europe* (Philadelphia: 2007).

Henige, David, 'The Context, Content, and Credibility of La Florida del Ynca', *Americas*, 43:1 (1986), 1–23.

Hermosilla Molina, Antonio, 'Los hospitales reales', in Fernando Chueca Goitia (ed.), *Los hospitales de Sevilla* (Seville: 1989), 35–52.

Hernández Díaz, José, *Juan Martínez Montañés (1568–1649)* (Seville: 1987).

Herrero García, M., *Ideas de los españoles del siglo XVII* (Madrid: [1928]).

Hobsbawm, E. J., 'The Crisis of the 17th Century – II', *Past & Present*, 6 (1954), 44–65.

—, 'The General Crisis of the European Economy in the 17th Century', *Past & Present*, 5 (1954), 33–53.

Hope, Charles, 'Titian as a Court Painter', *Oxford Art Journal*, 2 (1979), 7–10.

Horn, Hendrik J., *Jan Cornelisz Vermeyen: Painter of Charles V and his Conquest of Tunis: Paintings, Etchings, Drawings, Cartoons & Tapestries* (Doornspijk: 1989), at http://cervantes.tamu.edu/english/ctxt/cec/disk7/ENTREMES.html.

Huergo Cardoso, Humberto, 'Algunos lugares oscuros de las *Soledades* de Góngora', *Bulletin of Hispanic Studies*, 87 (2010), 17–41.

Hulme, Martin A. S., *Philip II* (London: 1906).

Ife, B. W., 'Don Quixote's Diet', Occasional Paper Series, no. 34 (Department of Hispanic, Portuguese and Latin American Studies, University of Bristol) (Bristol: 2000).

Ingram, Kevin (ed.), *The Conversos and Moriscos in Late Medieval Spain and Beyond*, 2 vols (Leiden and Boston: 2012).

Ingram, Kevin, 'Introduction to This Volume', in Ingram (ed.), *The Conversos and Moriscos*, 2:1–13.

Israel, Jonathan I., 'The Decline of Spain: A Historical Myth?', *Past & Present*, 91 (1981), 170–80.

—, *The Dutch Republic and the Hispanic World, 1606–1661* (Oxford: 1982).

Jammes, Robert, *La obra poética de Don Luis de Góngora y Argote* (Madrid: 1987).

Jardine, Lisa, and Jerry Brotton, *Global Interests: Renaissance Art between East and West* (London: 2000).

Jauralde Pou, Pablo, *Francisco de Quevedo (1580–1645)* (Madrid: 1999).

Johnson, Carroll B., *Transliterating a Culture: Cervantes and the Moriscos*, ed. Mark Groundland (Newark, DE: 2009).

Jones, R. O., *A Literary History of Spain: The Golden Age of Prose and Poetry* (London and New York: 1971).

Justi, Carl, *Velázquez y su siglo*, trans. Pedro Marrades (Madrid: 1953).

Kagan, Richard, *Clio and the Crown: The Politics of History in Medieval and Early Modern Spain* (Baltimore: 2009).

Kagan, Richard, *Students and Society in Early Modern Spain* (Baltimore and London: 1974).

—, 'Universities in Castile, 1500–1700', *Past & Present*, 49 (1970), 44–71.

Kamen, Henry, 'The Decline of Spain: A Historical Myth?', *Past & Present*, 81 (1978), 24–50.

— 'The Decline of Spain: A Historical Myth?: A Rejoinder', *Past & Present*, 91 (1981), 181–5.

—, 'The Economic and Social Consequences of the Thirty Years' War', *Past & Present*, 39 (1968), 44–61.

—, *Empire: How Spain became a World Power, 1492–1763* (New York: 2003).

—, *The Escorial: Art and Power in the Renaissance* (New Haven and London: 2010).

—, *Philip of Spain* (New Haven and London: 1997).

—, *The Phoenix and the Flame: Catalonia and the Counter Reformation* (New Haven and London: 1993).

—, *Spain, 1469–1714: A Society of Conflict* (London and New York: 1983).

—, *The Spanish Inquisition: An Historical Revision* (London: 1997).

Kasl, Ronda, 'Painters, Polychromy, and the Perfection of Images', in *Spanish Polychrome Sculpture*, 32–49.

Kelsey, Harry, *Philip of Spain, King of England* (London and New York: 2012).

Kennedy, Ruth Lee, *Studies in Tirso, I: The Dramatist and his Competitors, 1620–26* (Chapel Hill: 1974).

Kinkead, Duncan T., 'Juan Lazón and the Sevillian Painting Trade with the New World in the Second Half of the Seventeenth Century', *Art Bulletin*, 66:2 (1984), 303–10.

—, 'The Last Sevillian Period of Francisco de Zurbarán', *Art Bulletin*, 65:2 (1983), 303–15.

Koskenniemi, Martti, 'Empire and International Law: The Real Spanish Contribution', *University of Toronto Law Journal*, 61 (2011), 1–36.

Kubler, George, *Building the Escorial* (Princeton: 1982).

Lacan, Jacques, *Écrits: A Selection*, trans. Alan Sheridan (New York: 1977).

Lapeyre, Henri, *Géographie de l'Espagne morisque* (Paris: 1959).

Lázaro Carreter, Fernando, 'Fray Luis de León y la clasicidad', in *Fray Luis de León: Historia, humanismo, y letras*, ed. Víctor García de la Concha and Javier San José Lera (Salamanca: 1996).

Lazure, Guy, 'Possessing the Sacred: Monarchy and Identity in Philip II's Relic Collection at the Escorial', *Renaissance Quarterly*, 60 (2007), 58–92.

Lea, Henry Charles, *A History of the Inquisition of Spain*, 4 vols (New York and London: 1906–7).

Lewis May, Florence, 'Spanish Brocade for Royal Ladies', *Pantheon*, 23 (1965), 8–15.

Lisón Hernández, L., 'Mito y realidad de la expulsión de los mudéjares murcianos del Valle de Ricote', *Areas. Revista de Ciencias Sociales*, 14 (1992), 141–70.

Llaguno y Amirola, Eugenio, and Agustín Ceán Bermúdez, *Noticias de los arquitectos y arquitectura desde su restauración . . .*, 5 vols (Madrid: 1829).

Loades, David, *Mary Tudor: The Tragical History of the First Queen of England* (Kew: 2006).

López, Celestino, *Desde Jerónimo Hernández a Martínez Montañés* (Seville: 1929).

—, *Retablos y esculturas de traza sevillana* (Seville: 1928).

López, Juan José, and Carmen Vaquero Serrano, '¿Garcilaso traicionado? María de Jesús, hija de Guiomar Carrillo', *Lemir*, 14 (2010), 57–68.

López Estrada, Francisco (ed.), *Siglos de Oro: Renacimiento*, vols 2.1 and 2.2 of *Historia y crítica de la literatura española*, ed. Francisco Rico, 8 vols (Barcelona: 1980).

Lorenzo, Javier, 'After Tunis: Petrarchism and Empire in the Poetry of Garcilaso de la Vega', *Hispanofilia*, 141 (2004), 17–30.

Lovett, A. W., 'The Castilian Bankruptcy of 1575', *Historical Journal*, 23:4 (1990), 899–911.

—, *Early Habsburg Spain, 1517–1598* (Oxford: 1986).

Lyana Serrano, Francisco, *El Palacio del Infantado en Guadalajara* (Guadalajara: 1996).

Lynch, John, *The Hispanic World in Crisis and Change* (Oxford and Cambridge, MA: 1992).

—, *Spain 1516–1598: From Nation State to World Empire* (Oxford and Cambridge, MA: 1991).

—, *Spain under the Habsburgs*, 2 vols (Oxford: 1969).

Lyon, Ann, 'The Mad Heir Apparent and the Spanish Succession: The Fate of the Infante Don Carlos', *Liverpool Law Review*, 30 (2009), 225–45.

McAlister, Lyle N., *Spain and Portugal in the New World, 1492–1700*, vol. 3 of *Europe in the Age of Expansion* (Minneapolis: 1984).

MacKay, Angus, 'The Hispanic-Converso Predicament', *Transactions of the Royal Historical Society*, 5th series, 35 (1985), 159–79.

Maltby, William S., *The Black Legend in England* (Durham, NC: 1971).

Mancini, Matteo, '*El emperador Carlos V a caballo en Mühlberg* de Tiziano, un icono para la Historia del Arte', in *La restauración de* El emperador Carlos V a caballo, exhibition catalogue, 103–16.

Mann, Richard G., *El Greco and his Patrons: Three Major Projects* (Cambridge: 1986).

Manzano Baena, Laura, *Conflicting Words: The Peace Treaty of Münster (1648) and the Political Culture of the Dutch Republic and the Spanish Monarchy* (Leuven: 2011).

Marañón, Gregorio, *El Conde-Duque de Olivares (La pasión de mandar)* (Madrid: 1936).

Marcos Martín, Alberto, *España en los siglos XVI, XVII y XVIII. Economia y sociedad* (Barcelona: 2000).

Marías, Fernando, 'El palacio de Carlos V en Granada: formas romanas, usos castellanos', in M. J. Redondo Cantera and M. A. Zalma (eds), *Carlos V y las artes: promoción artísica y familia imperial* (Valladolid: 2000), 107–28.

Marías, Fernando, and Agustín Bustamante García, *Las ideas artísticas de El Greco (Comentarios de un texto inédito)* (Madrid: 1981).

Márquez, Antonio, *Los alumbrados: Orígenes y filosofía, 1525–1559* (Madrid: 1972).

Márquez Villanueva, Francisco, 'La criptohistória morisca (los otros conversos)', in Agustin Redondo (ed.), *Les Problèmes de l'exclusion en Espagne (XVIe–XVIIe siècles)* (Paris: 1983), 77–94.

Martin, Colin, and Geoffrey Parker, *The Spanish Armada* ([London]: 1988).

Martínez, José Florencio, *Biografía de Lope de Vega, 1562–1635: Un friso literario del Siglo de Oro* (Barcelona: 2011).

Martínez Leiva, Gloria, and Ángel Rodríguez Rebollo (eds), *Qvadros y otras cosas que tienen su Magestad Felipe IV en este Alcázar de Madrid, Año de 1636* (Madrid: 2007).

Martyr d'Anghiera, Peter, *De Orbe Novo*, trans. Francis A. McNutt, 2 vols (New York and London: 1912).

Marzahl, Peter, 'Communication and Control in the Political System of Emperor Charles V: The First Regency of Empress Isabella', in Wim Blockmans and Nicolette Mont (eds), *The World of the Emperor Charles V* (Amsterdam: 2004), 83–96.

Matthews, W., 'Samuel Pepys and Spain', *Neophilologus*, 20:3 (1935), 120–9.

Maurice, Richard, *Martin Luther: The Christian between God and Death* (Cambridge, MA and London: 1999), 285–7.

Mazarío Coleto, María del Carmen, *Isabella de Portugal* (Madrid: 1951).

Menéndez Pidal, Ramón, *Floresta de leyendas heroícas españolas*, vol. 2: *Rodrigo, el último godo* (Madrid: 1926).

Menéndez y Pelayo, Marcelino, *Historia de los heterodoxos españoles* (Madrid: 1928).

Mérimée, Henri, *Spectacles et comédiens à Valencia (1580–1630)* (Toulouse and Paris: 1913).

Miró Quesada, Aurelio, *El Inca Garcilaso y otros estudios garcilasistas* (Madrid: 1971).

Montagu, Jennifer, 'Velázquez Marginalia: His Slave Juan de Pareja and his Illegitimate Son Antonio', *Burlington Magazine*, 125:968 (1983), 683–5.

Moore, Olin Harris, 'Mark Twain and Don Quixote', *Proceedings of the Modern Language Association of America*, 37:2 (1922), 324–46.

Morales, Alfredo J., *La obra renacentista del ayuntamiento de Sevilla* (Seville: 1981).

Morales, Ambrosio de, *La Batalla de Lepanto (Descriptio Belli Nautici et Expugnatio Lepanti per D. Ioannem de Asutria)*, ed. Jernao Costas Rodríguez (Madrid: 1987).

Morán, Miguel, and Fernando Checa, *El coleccionismo en España: De la cámara de maravillas a la galería de pinturas* (Madrid: 1985).

Moreno, Isidoro, *La antigua hermandad de los negros de Sevilla: etnicidad, poder y sociedad en 600 años de historia* (Seville: 1997).

Moreno Villa, J., and F. J. Sánchez Cantón, 'Noventa y siete retratos de la familia de Felipe III por Bartolomé González', *Archivo Español de Arte y Arqueología*, 13:38 (1937), 127–56.

Morgado, Alonso de, *Historia de Sevilla* (Seville: 1587).

Morineau, Michel, *Incroyables gazettes et fabuleux métaux: Les retours des trésors américains d'après les gazettes hollandaises (XVIe–XVIIIe siècles)* (London and New York: 1985).

Mosquera de Figueroa, Cristóbal, *Comentario en breve compendio de disciplina militar* (Madrid: 1596).

Motley, John Lothrop, *The Rise of the Dutch Republic* (London: 1876).

Moxey, P. K. F., 'Erasmus and the Iconography of Pieter Aertsen's *Christ in the House of Martha and Mary* in the Boymans-Van Beuningen Museum', *Journal of the Warburg and Courtauld Institutes*, 34 (1971), 335–6.

Mulcahy, Rosemarie, *The Decoration of the Royal Basilica of El Escorial* (Cambridge and New York: 1994).

—, *Philip II of Spain, Patron of the Arts* (Dublin: 2004).

Muro, Gaspar, *La vida de la princesa de Éboli* (Madrid: 1877).

Murray, John J., 'The Cultural Impact of the Flemish Low Countries on Sixteenth- and Seventeenth-Century England', *American Historical Review*, 62:4 (1957), 837–54.

Nabokov, Vladimir, *Lectures on Don Quixote*, ed. Fedson Bowers (London: 1983).

Nada, John, *Carlos the Bewitched: The Last Spanish Habsburg, 1661–1700* (London: 1962).

Nader, Helen, *Liberty in Absolutist Spain: The Habsburg Sale of Towns, 1516–1700* (Baltimore and London: 1990).

Nash, Jane Clinton, 'Titian's *Poesie* for Philip II', Ph.D. thesis, Johns Hopkins University, 1981.

Netanyahu, Benzion, *The Origins of the Inquisition in Fifteenth Century Spain* (New York: 1995).

Nierop, Henk van, 'A Beggars' Banquet: The Compromise of the Nobility and the Politics of Inversion', *European History Quarterly*, 21 (1991), 419–43.

Novalín, José Luis González, *El inquisidor general Fernado de Valdés (1483–1568)*, 2 vols (Oviedo: 1971).

O'Malley, Charles, 'Some Episodes in the Medical History of the Emperor Charles V: An Imperial Problem and the Problem of an Emperor', *Journal of the History of Medicine and Allied Sciences*, 13:4 (1958), 469–82.

Orozco, Emilio, *Introducción a Góngora* (Barcelona: 1984 [1953]).

Orozco y Berrera, Manuel, 'Apuntes para la Geografía de las Lenguas y Carta Etnográfica de México', *Anales del Ministerio de Fomento* (Mexico), 6 (1881), 155–62.

Owens, John B., 'Despotism, Absolutism, and the Law in Renaissance Spain: Toledo versus the Counts of Belalcázar (1445–1574)', Ph.D., University of Wisconsin, 1972.

Ortega y Gassett, José, *Obras completas*, 13 vols (Madrid: 1983).

Pagden, Anthony, *The Fall of Natural Man: The American Indian and the Origins of Comparative Ethnology* (Cambridge and New York: 1982).

Palomero Páramo, J. M., 'Notas sobre el taller de Zurbarán: un envío de lienzos a Portobelo y Lima en el años de 1636', in *Actas del congreso: Extremadura en la Evangelización del Nuevo Mundo* (Madrid: 1990), 313–30.

Panofsky, Erwin, 'Erasmus and the Visual Arts', *Journal of the Warburg and Courtauld Institutes*, 32 (1969).

Parker, Geoffrey, *Europe in Crisis: 1598–1648* (Brighton: 1980).

—, *The Grand Strategy of Philip II* (New Haven and London: 1998).

—, *Spain and the Netherlands, 1559–1659: Ten Studies* (Glasgow: 1992).

Paulson, Ronald, *Don Quixote in England: The Aesthetics of Laughter* (Baltimore and London: 1998).

Peers, Allison E., *Saint Teresa of Jesus and Other Essays and Addresses* (London: 1953).

—, *Studies of the Spanish Mystics*, 3 vols (London: 1951–60).

Pereda, Felipe, 'The Shelter of the Savage: "From Valladolid to the New World"', *Medieval Encounters*, 16 (2010), 268–359.

Pérez, Joseph, *La revolución de las comunidades de Castilla (1520–1521)*, trans. Juan José Faci Lacasta (Madrid: 1979).

Pérez de Tudela Bueso, Juan, 'Estudio preliminar: vida y escritos de Gonzalo Fernández de Oviedo', in Oviedo, *Historia*, 1:v–clxxv.

—, 'Rasgos del semblante espiritual de Gonzalo Fernández de Oviedo: la hidaguía caballeresca ante el nuevo mundo', *Revista de Indias*, 17 (1957), 391–443.

Pérez Fernández, Isacio, *Cronología documentada de los viajes, estancias y actuaciones de fray Bartolomé de las Casas* (Puerto Rico: 1984).

Pérez Moreda, Vicente, and David Sven Reher (eds), *Demografía histórica en España* (Madrid: 1988).

Pérez Sánchez, Alfonso, 'El Greco y Toledo', in José María Llusiá and Antonio Fernández de Molina (eds), *Marañon in Toledo: sobre elogia y nostalgia de Toledo* (Cuenca: 1999), 107–36.

Pérez Sánchez, Alfonso E., 'Velázquez y su arte', in *Velázquez*, ed. Domínguez Ortiz, Pérez Sánchez and Gállego, exhibition catalogue, 21–56.

Perry, Mary Elizabeth, *Crime and Society in Early Modern Seville* (Hanover and London: 1980).

Petrie, Charles, *Philip of Spain* (London: 1963).

Pettas, William, 'A Sixteenth-Century Spanish Bookstore: The Inventory of Juan de Junta', *American Philosophical Society*, 85:1 (1995), 1–247.

Pike, Ruth, 'Crime and Criminals in Sixteenth-Century Seville', *Sixteenth Century Journal*, 6:1 (1975), 3–18.

Poole, Stafford, *Juan de Ovando: Governing the Spanish Empire in the Reign of Philip II* (Norman, OK: 2004).

Porra Barrenechea, Raúl, *El Inca Garcilaso en Montilla (1561–1614)* (Lima: 1955).

Portabales Pichel, Amancio, *Los verdaderos artífices de El Escorial* (Madrid: 1945).

Portús Pérez, Javier, *La Sala Reservada del Museo del Prado y el coleccionismo de pintura de desnudo en la Corte Española, 1554–1838* (Madrid: 1998).

Probert, Alan, 'Bartolomé de Medina: The Patio Process and the Sixteenth-Century Silver Crisis', in Peter Bakewell (ed.), *Mines of Silver and Gold in the Americas*, vol. 19 of *An Expanding World: The European Impact on World History* (Aldershot: 1997), 96–130, originally published in *Journal of the West*, 8:1 (1969), 90–124.

Quérillacq, René, 'Los moriscos de Cervantes', *Anales Cervantinos*, 30 (1992), 77–98.

Ramírez de Arellano, Rafael, *Ensayo de un catálogo biográfico de escritores de la provincia y diócesis de Córdoba . . .*, 2 vols (Madrid: 1922–3).

Ramírez-Araujo, Alejandro, 'El morisco Ricote y la libertad de conciencia', *Hispanic Review*, 24:4 (1956), 278–89.

Ramón Carande, *Carlos V y sus banqueros*, ed. Antonio-Miguel Bernal (Barcelona: 2000 [1943]).

Ramos, Demetrio, *Ximénez de Quesada en su relación con los cronistas y el Epítome de Conquista del Nuevo Reino de Granada* (Seville: 1972).

Randall, Dale B. J., and Jackson C. Boswell, *Cervantes in Seventeeth-Century England: The Tapestry Turned* (Oxford: 2009).

Redworth, Glyn, *The Prince and the Infanta: The Cultural Politics of the Spanish Match* (New Haven and London: 2003).

Rennert, Hugo A., and Américo Castro, *Vida de Lope de Vega (1562–1635)* (Madrid: 1919).

Rey, Eusebio, 'San Ignacio Loyola y el problema de los "Cristianos Nuevos"', *Razón y Fé*, 153 (1956), 117–204.

Rivera Blanco, José Javier, *Juan Bautista de Toledo y Felipe II: La implantación del clasicismo en España* (Valladolid: 1984).

Rodríguez Jurado, Adolfo, *Discursos leídos en la Real Academia Sevillana de Buenas Letras, Proceso seguido a instancias de Tomás Gutiérrez . . .* (Seville: 1914).

Rodríguez López-Vázquez, Alfredo, 'Don Pedro y Don Juan', in Francisco Ruíz Ramón and César Oliva (eds), *El mito en el teatro clásico español: Ponencias y debates de las VII jornadas de teatro clásico español (Almagro, 25 al 27 de septiembre, 1984)* (Madrid: 1988), 192–5.

Rodríguez Sánchez, Angel, *Población y Comportamiento Demográficos en el Siglo XVI* (Cáceres: 1977).

Rodríguez Villa, Antonio, *Ambrosio Spínola: primer Marqués de los Balbases* (Madrid: 1904).

—, 'El Emperador Carles V y su Corte', *Boletín de la Academia de la Historia*, 42–4 (1903–5).

Rodríguez-Salgado, M. J., 'Charles V and the Dynasty', in Soly (ed.), *Charles V and his Time*, 26–111.

—, 'The Court of Philip II of Spain', in Ronald G. Asch and Adolf M. Birke (eds), *Princes, Patronage and the Nobility: The Court at the Beginning of the Modern Age, c.1450–1650* (New York: 1991), 205–44.

—, 'Philip II and the "Great Armada" of 1588', in *Armada, 1588–1988*, exhibition catalogue, 12–38.

Rogers, Peter, *The Mystery Play in Madame Bovary: Moeurs de Province* (Amsterdam: 2009).

Rosales, Luis, *Pasión y muerte del conde de Villamediana* (Madrid: 1969).

Rosenblat, Angel, *La población indígena y el mestizaje en América, 1492–1950*, 2 vols (Buenos Aires: 1954).

Rosenthal, Earl E., *The Palace of Charles V in Granada* (Princeton: 1985).

Rossi, R., *Escuchar a Cervantes: Un ensayo biográfico* (Valladolid: 1988).

Ruíz Martín, Felipe, 'Las finanzas de la monarquía hispánica y la Liga Santa Cuadro', in Benzoni (ed.), *Il Mediterraneo*, 325–70.

Salaman, Radcliffe, *The History and Social Influence of the Potato* (Cambridge and New York: 2000).

Salas, Xavier de, *El Bosco en la literatura española: discurso leído el día 30 de mayo de 1943 en la recepción pública de Don Savier de Salas en la Real Academia de Buenas Letras de Barcelona* (Barcelona: 1943).

San Román y Fernández, Francisco de Borja de, *El Greco en Toledo o nuevas investigaciones acerca de la vida y obras de Dominico Theotocópuli* (Madrid: 1910).

—, 'Garcilaso, desterrado de Toledo', *Boletín de la Real Academia de Bellas Artes y Ciencias Históricas de Toledo*, 2:5 (1919), 193–5.

Sánchez, José, *Academias literarias del Siglo de Oro español* (Madrid: 1961).

Sánchez Jiménez, Antonio, 'Lope de Vega y la Armada Invencible de 1588. Biografía y poses del autor', at http://uva.academia.edu/AntonioSanchezJimenez/Papers/857038/Lope_de_Vega_y_la_Armada_Invencible_de_1588.

Sánchez-Blanco, R. Bénitez, 'La odisea del manchego Diego Díaz', in *Los olvidados de la historia: Herejes*, ed. R. García Cárcel (Barcelona: 2004), 214–36.

Schevill, Rudolph, 'Lope de Vega and the Year 1588', *Hispanic Review*, 9:1 (1941), 65–78.

Scott, James Brown, *The Spanish Origin of International Law: Francisco de Vitoria and his Law of Nations* (Oxford: 1934).

Sebastián Lozano, Jorge, 'Choices and Consequences: The Construction of Isabel de Portugal's Image', in Theresa Earenfight (ed.), *Queenship and Political Power in Medieval and Early Modern Spain* (Aldershot: 2005), 145–62.

Simpson, Leonard Francis (ed. and trans.), *The Autobiography of the Emperor Charles V. Recently discovered in the Portuguese language by Baron Kervyn de Lettenhove* (London: 1863).

Sliwa, Krzysztof, 'Andrea Cervantes, nieta más querida de la abuela paterna, Leonor Fernández de Torreblanca, y Constanza de Ovando y Figueroa, la simpática sobrina de Miguel de Cervantes Saavedra', *RILCE*, 20:1 (2004), 241–54.

—, *El licenciado Juan de Cervantes: Efemérides del licenciado Juan de Cervantes, documentos y datos para una biografía del abuelo paterno del autor del Quijote* (Kassel: 2001).

Smith, Paul Julian, 'Garcilaso's Homographesis', in *Estudios de literatura española del Siglo de Oro dedicados a Elias L. Rivers* (Madrid: 1992), 243–52.

Smith, Paul Julian, 'Homographesis in Salicio's Song', in Marina S. Brownlee and Hans Ulrich Gumbrecht (eds), *Cultural Authority in Golden Age Spain* (Baltimore: 1995), 131–42.

Sola, Emilio, and José F. de la Peña, *Cervantes y la Berbería: Cervantes, mundo turco-berberisco y servicios secretos en la epoca de Felipe II* (Madrid and Mexico City: 1995).

Soler i Terol, Lluís, *Perot Roca Guinarda: Història d'aquest bandoler* (Manrèsa: 1909).

Soly, Hugh (ed.), *Charles V and his Time, 1500–1558* (Antwerp: 1999).

Starkey, David, *The Queens of Henry VIII* (London: 2003).

— 'Representation through Intimacy: A Study in the Symbolism of Monarchy and Court Office in Early-Modern England', in Ioan Lewis (ed.), *Symbols and Sentiments: Cross-cultural Studies in Symbolism* (London: 1977), 187–224.

Stein, Stanley J., and Barbara H. Stein, *Silver, Trade, and War: Spain and America in the Making of Early Modern Europe* (Baltimore and London: 2000).

Stirling, William, *The Cloister Life of the Emperor Charles the Fifth* (London: 1853).

Stradling, R. A., *Philip IV and the Government of Spain, 1621–1665* (Cambridge: 1988).

—, *Spain's Struggle for Europe, 1598–1668* (London and Rio Grande: 1994).

Stratton, Suzanne L., *The Immaculate Conception in Spanish Art* (New York: 1994).

Surtz, Ronald E., *Writing Women in Late Medieval and Early Modern Spain: The Mothers of Saint Teresa of Avila* (Philadelphia: 1995).

Tapia Sánchez, Serafín de, 'La alfabetización de la población urbana castellana en el Siglo de Oro', *Historia de la Educación*, 12–13 (1993–4), 274–307.

Tate Lanning, John, 'Cortes and his First Official Remission of Treasure to Charles V', *Revista de Historia de América*, 2 (1938), 5–9.

Taylor, René, 'Architecture and Magic: Considerations on the Idea of the Escorial', in *Essays in the History of Architecture Presented to Rudolf Wittkower* (London: 1967), 81–107.

Tellechea Idigoras, J. J., *Fray Bartolomé de Carranza. Mis treinta años de investigaciones Carrancianas*, 6 vols (Salamanca: 1962–81), 5:71–2.

Terry, Arthur, *Seventeenth-Century Spanish Poetry: The Power of Artifice* (Cambridge: 1993).

Thacker, Jonathan, *A Companion to Golden-Age Drama* (London: 2007).

Thomas, Hugh, *The Conquest of Mexico* (London: 1993).

—, *The Golden Age: The Spanish Empire of Charles V* (London: 2011).

Thomas, Werner, *Los protestantes y la Inquisición en España en tiempos de Reforma y Contrarreforma* (Leuven: 2001).

—, *La represión del protestantismo en España, 1517–1648* (Leuven: 2001).

Thompson, Colin, *The Strife of Tongues: Fray Luis de León and the Golden Age of Spain* (Cambridge: 1988).

Torre, José de la, 'Documentos gongorinos', *Boletín de la Real Academia de Ciencias, Bellas Letras y Nobles Artes de Córdoba*, 18 (1927), 65–218.

Trevor-Roper, P., *The World through Blunted Sight: An Inquiry into the Influence of Defective Vision on Art and Character* (London: 1970).

Trueman, R. W., 'The Rev. John Bowle's Quixotic Woes Further Explored', *Cervantes: Bulletin of the Cervantes Society of America*, 23:2 (2003), 9–43.

Turner, Raymond, 'Oviedo's *Claribalte*: The First American Novel', *Romance Notes*, 6 (1964), 65–8.

Tytler, Patrick Frazer, *England under the reigns of Edward VI, and Mary, with a contemporary history of Europe*, 2 vols (London: 1839).

Úbeda de los Cobos, Andrés, 'The History of Rome Cycle', in Úbeda de los Cobos (ed.), *Paintings for the Planet King*, 169–89.

Úbeda de los Cobos, Andrés (ed.), *Paintings for the Planet King: Philip IV and the Buen Retiro Palace* (Madrid and London: 2005).

Unamuno, Miguel de, *Andanzas y visiones españolas* (Madrid: 1922).

Valdivieso, E., and J. M. Serrera, *El Hospital de la Caridad de Sevilla* (Seville: 1980).

Vaquero Serrano, Carmen, *Garcilaso: Poeta del amor, caballero de la guerra* (Madrid: 2002).

Varner, John Grier, *El Inca: The Life and Times of Garcilaso de la Vega* (Austin and London: 1968).

Vergara, Alexander, *Rubens and his Spanish Patrons* (Cambridge: 1999).

Vicens Vives, Jaime, *Los Austrias: imperio español en América*, vol. 3 of *Historia social y economica de España y America* (Barcelona: 1982).

Vila Vilar, Enriqueta, 'Las ferias de Portobelo: apariencia y realidad del comercio con Indias', *Anuario de Estudios Americanos*, 39 (1982), 275–340.

—, 'El poder del Consulado Sevillano y los hombres del comercio en el siglo XVII: una aproximación', in Enriqueta Vila Vilar and Allan J. Kuethe (eds), *Relaciones de poder y comercio colonial: nuevas perspectivas* (Seville: 1999), 3–34.

Vilar, Juan Bautista, 'La expulsión de los moriscos del Reino de Murcia. Sus efectos demográficos y económicos sobre la región de origen', in *L'expulsió dels moriscos: conseqüències en el món ilsàmic i el món cristià* (Barcelona: 1994), 86–95.

Vilches, Elvira, *New World Gold: Cultural Anxiety and Monetary Disorder in Early Modern Spain* (Chicago and London: 2010).

Villanueva, Jaime, *Viage literario a las iglesias de España*, 22 vols (Valencia: 1821).

Vitoria, Francisco de, *Political Writings*, ed. Anthony Pagden and Jeremy Lawrance (Cambridge: 1991).

Volk, Mary C., 'Rubens in Madrid and the Decoration of the King's Summer Apartments', *Burlington Magazine*, 123:942 (1981), 513–29.

Wagner, Henry R., 'Translation of a Letter from the Archbishop of Cosenza to Petrus de Acosta', *Hispanic American Historical Review*, 9:3 (1929), 361–3.

Wardropper, Bruce W., *Siglos de Oro: Barroco*, vol. 3 of *Historia y crítica de la literatura española*, ed. Francisco Rico, 8 vols (Barcelona: 1983).

Webster, Susan Verdi, *Art and Ritual in Golden-Age Spain: Sevillian Confraternities and the Processional Sculpture of Holy Week* (Princeton: 1998).

—, 'Art, Ritual, and Confraternities in Sixteenth-Century New Spain', *Anales del Instituto de Investigaciones Estéticas*, 70 (1997), 5–43.

Wethy, Harold E., *El Greco and his School*, 2 vols (Princeton: 1962).

Whitlock, Keith, *The Renaissance in Europe* (New Haven and London: 2000).

Wiffin, J. H. (ed. and trans.), *The Works of Garcilasso de la Vega Surnamed the Prince of Castilian Poets* (London: 1823).

Wilkinson Catherine, 'The Escorial and the Invention of the Imperial Staircase', *Art Bulletin*, 57:1 (1975), 65–90.

Woodall, Joanna, 'An Exemplary Consort: Antonis Mor's Portrait of Mary Tudor', *Art History*, 14:2 (1991), 81–103.

Yarza Luaces, Joaquín, 'Aspectos incográficos de la pintura de Juan Fernández Navarrete, "el Mudo" y relaciones con la contrareforma', *Boletín del Seminario de Estudios de Arte y Arqueología de la Universidad de Valladolid*, 36 (1970), 43–68.

Yates, Frances, 'The Art of Ramon Lull: An Approach to It through Lull's Theory of the Elements', *Journal of the Warburg and Courtauld Institutes*, 17:1–2 (1954), 115–73.

Zamora, Margarita, *Language, Authority, and Indigenous History in the* Comentarios reales de los incas (Cambridge: 1988).

Zamora Vicente, Alonso, 'El cautiverio en la obra cervantina', in Francisco Sánchez-Castañer (ed.), *Homenaje a Cervantes*, 2 vols (Valencia: 1950), 2:237–56.

Zunino Garrido, María de la Cinta, 'Boscán and Garcilaso as Rhetorical Models in the English Renaissance: The Case of Abraham Fraunce's *The Arcadian Rhetorike*', *Atlantis*, 27:2 (2005), 119–34.

Acknowledgements

Michael Jacobs recommended Charlie Viney as an agent and suggested that Bill Swainson would be an ideal editor; he unflaggingly inspired, encouraged, enthused, and fulminated and laughed, but mostly he was a friend.

Charlie and Bill have been a pleasure to work with, and George Gibson has been a gracious host; a big thank-you to all at Bloomsbury who have worked so hard to publish the book, especially Peter James and Anna Simpson. The book would not have been possible without the work of hundreds of specialist scholars, but I have had especially important personal encouragement from David Starkey, who first pointed me in the direction of Barry Ife, whose teaching inspired me to write about the Golden Age; thanks also to Trudi Darby, David Castillejo and Antonio Fernández Puertas for all their valuable support and teaching over the years. Al Samson, Xavier Bray, Richard Kagan, Trevor Dadson, Harald Braun, Aurelio Espinosa, Helen Nader, David Davies, Charles Hope, Ian Michael and Sir John Elliott have all been incredibly kind and generous with their time. University College London has loyally kept me on as an Honorary Research Associate, allowing me easy access to a range of remarkable research facilities. I have especially enjoyed long periods working at the Warburg Institute, where I have found the staff and students warm, welcoming and helpfully intelligent in their conversation and comments. I have been helped by staff at the British Library, the Biblioteca Nacional in Madrid, the Archivo Provincial de Toledo, the Archivo General de Indias, the Biblioteca Colombina and the University Library in Seville, the Hispanic Society of America and a host of other institutions. I must say special thanks to Jim Anaya and Rob Williams at the University of Arizona, who have so often welcomed me to Tucson with open arms; and, of course, Jana, Andrea, Emilio and Joy. Likewise, Jennifer Snead and Chad Covey have been wonderful hosts in New Mexico and Texas, as has Gaby Derbyshire in New York.

In Spain, there is a long list of friends: Alicia Rios has always been amazingly generous and introduced me to Michael Jacobs in the first place. In Seville, Javier and Manuel Rodríguez-Piñero have shown astonishing professional patience in designing and creating hispano-file.com as well as frequently making insightful observations about Spanish art and culture in general, as has Luis Méndez and was Manolo Perales. Ana María Rengel, Cristina, Ana, Javi, Bea, Manu, Juan, Chutney and Jaime have provided me with a family in Seville, as always, as have Pedro, Isa, Marina, Concha, Loly, Jesús, Gloria, Lupe, Anchy, Cuqui and Jesús. Equally, life would not be the same without the support and encouragement of Berta (*madre y hija*), Rocío, Pilar, Carmen, Teresa, Pepe, Los Luíses, Falique, Eladio and Vicente, while Javier Gómez has kept me healthy; all those friendships began with Esperanza Flores, of course. In Granada, I have been friends with Juan Antonio, Matilde, Mamen and Javier for longer than I can remember; Chris and I have wept with laughter on the Cidian Way and he and Ana have been wonderful hosts, as have Manolo and Merce in Frailes; while Jackie Rae has been a constant support. *Un abrazo muy fuerte a todos.*

Finally, I would like to thank Clare Adams, who read long sections of the manuscript and commented on them and has encouraged me all along.

Index

A Note on the Author

Dr Robert T. C. Goodwin was born and educated in London and was awarded his PhD by the University of London for his thesis on Golden Age Spain. His first major book, *Crossing the Continent 1527–1540: The Story of the First African-American Explorer of the American South*, was published in 2008. He is currently a full-time writer and historian and is a Research Associate at University College. He divides his time between London and Seville.

A Note on the Type

The text of this book is set in Linotype Stempel Garamond, a version of Garamond adapted and first used by the Stempel foundry in 1924. It is one of several versions of Garamond based on the designs of Claude Garamond. It is thought that Garamond based his font on Bembo, cut in 1495 by Francesco Griffo in collaboration with the Italian printer Aldus Manutius. Garamond types were first used in books printed in Paris around 1532. Many of the present-day versions of this type are based on the *Typi Academiae* of Jean Jannon cut in Sedan in 1615.

Claude Garamond was born in Paris in 1480. He learned how to cut type from his father and by the age of fifteen he was able to fashion steel punches the size of a pica with great precision. At the age of sixty he was commissioned by King Francis I to design a Greek alphabet, and for this he was given the honourable title of royal type founder. He died in 1561.